THE OXFORD BOOK OF AMERICAN
DETECTIVE STORIES

THE OXFORD BOOK OF

American Detective Stories

EDITED BY

Tony Hillerman
Rosemary Herbert

OXFORD UNIVERSITY PRESS
New York   Oxford

Oxford University Press

Oxford   New York
Athens   Auckland   Bangkok   Bogotá   Bombay   Buenos Aires
Calcutta   Cape Town   Dar es Salaam   Delhi   Florence
Hong Kong   Istanbul   Karachi   Kuala Lumpur   Madras   Madrid
Melbourne   Mexico City   Nairobi   Paris   Singapore   Taipei
Tokyo   Toronto

and associated companies in
Berlin   Ibadan

First published by Oxford University Press, Inc., 1996

First issued as an Oxford University Press paperback, 1997

Oxford is a registered trademark of Oxford University Press

Library of Congress Cataloging-in-Publication Data
The Oxford book of American detective stories /
edited by Tony Hillerman, Rosemary Herbert.
p.   cm.   Includes index.
ISBN 0-19-508581-7
ISBN 0-19-511792-1 (Pbk.)
1. Detective and mystery stories, American.
I. Hillerman, Tony.   II. Herbert, Rosemary.
PS3648.D4098   1996
813'.087208—dc20   95-4504

9 8 7 6 5 4 3 2 1
Printed in the United States of America

For
Eliza, Daisy, and Juliet
with love

ACKNOWLEDGMENTS

||||||||||||||||||||||||||||||||||||||||||||||||| ■ |||||||||||||||||||||||||||||||||||||||||||||||||

The editors would like to thank the following individuals, who provided library assistance, practical support, or editorial advice: Jean C. Behnke, Dana Bisbee, Henri J. Bourneuf, Jon L. Breen, Brenda Briggs, J. Randolph Cox, Eddie Doctoroff, Roberta Farina, Jeremiah Healy, Alea Henle, Barbara Herbert, Robert D. Herbert, Margaret Herrick, Edward D. Hoch, Perry Knowlton, J. Dayne Lamb, Jane Langton, Kate Mattes, John McAleer, Charles J. Montalbano, Stephen Moody, Susan K. Moody, Linda Halvorson Morse, Susan Oleksiw, Diana O'Neill, Daisy Partington, Irene Pavitt, Barbara Peters, Dan Posnansky, Enid Schantz, Marion Schoon, Gardner N. Stratton, Ken Taylor, Joyce Williams, and Scott Williamson.

Invaluable to our research were the Harry Elkins Widener Memorial Library at Harvard University and the Boston Atheneum.

CONTENTS

Introduction		3
Edgar Allan Poe	The Murders in the Rue Morgue	10
Bret Harte	The Stolen Cigar Case	40
Jacques Futrelle	The Problem of Cell 13	49
Melville Davisson Post	The Doomdorf Mystery	81
Anna Katharine Green	Missing: Page Thirteen	93
Arthur B. Reeve	The Beauty Mask	124
Susan Glaspell	A Jury of Her Peers	142
Carroll John Daly	The False Burton Combs	162
Clinton H. Stagg	The Keyboard of Silence	184
Richard Sale	A Nose for News	217
Mignon G. Eberhart	Spider	239
Erle Stanley Gardner	Leg Man	261
Raymond Chandler	I'll Be Waiting	295
John Dickson Carr	The Footprint in the Sky	310
Cornell Woolrich	Rear Window	326
Mary Roberts Rinehart	The Lipstick	356
Robert Leslie Bellem	Homicide Highball	375
William Faulkner	An Error in Chemistry	414
Clayton Rawson	From Another World	431
T. S. Stribling	A Daylight Adventure	456
William Campbell Gault	See No Evil	471
Anthony Boucher	Crime Must Have a Stop	480
Ed McBain	Small Homicide	499

Ross Macdonald	Guilt-Edged Blonde	512
Rex Stout	Christmas Party	526
Dorothy Salisbury Davis	A Matter of Public Notice	570
Ellery Queen	The Adventure of Abraham Lincoln's Clue	587
Bill Pronzini	Words Do Not a Book Make	602
Edward D. Hoch	Christmas Is for Cops	608
Linda Barnes	Lucky Penny	621
Sue Grafton	The Parker Shotgun	639
Tony Hillerman	Chee's Witch	655
Marcia Muller	Benny's Space	665
Credits		683
Index		685

THE OXFORD BOOK OF AMERICAN DETECTIVE STORIES

INTRODUCTION

||||||||||||||||||||||||||||||||||||||||||||| ■ |||||||||||||||||||||||||||||||||||||||||||||

Twenty-five years ago, when I was a first novelist on a visit to my editor, I had the occasion to read the galley proofs of *A Catalog of Crime*, now a bible of the detective-fiction genre. My editor, who was also editing the *Catalog*, was called away to deal with another problem. The author of the *Catalog* was due to pick up his proofs, I was told. Why didn't I take a look to see if my book had made it into the volume?

I found it on page 247. The author had recommended "less routine plots" and said that "unbelievable feats of survival and retaliation by people badly wounded and hemorrhaging make the reader impatient." I checked the title page to find the author of this affront. Jacques Barzun! I knew the name: a giant of the humanities, former dean and provost of Columbia University, and author of *House of the Intellect* and other weighty books. Until then, I had no idea that he was also an eminent critic of detective fiction. In fact, I knew almost nothing about the field.

My ignorance was quickly dented. Barzun arrived to collect his galleys and sensed from my sullen expression that he hadn't approved my work. In the ensuing conversation, I first learned that the game I had been playing had rules, many of which I had violated.

The point of the anecdote is the purpose of this anthology. While the detective story is founded on rules that remain important today, the distinctly American "take" on these rules has vastly enriched the genre. When Rosemary Herbert and I determined to select stories that would trace the evolution of the American detective short story, we discovered that I was far from the first American author to break or bend the rules. My American predecessors had been early pioneers in playing the detective game on their own terms.

But nobody can deny that assumptions, traditions, and rules of the genre remain important. Just what are they?

Early detective fiction was categorized as a tale rather than as serious fiction. As Barzun tells us, Edgar Allan Poe is not only the founding father and "the complete authority" on the form but also the one who "first made the point that the regular novel and the legitimate mystery will not combine."

Why not? Because in the tradition originated by the genius of Poe, the detective story emerged as a competition between writer and reader.

3

It was a game intended to challenge the intellect. Although Poe himself, in "The Murders in the Rue Morgue," did arouse awe and horror, the major preoccupation—and innovation—in this story is the introduction of the puzzle. The reader is challenged to attempt to solve it with the clues provided. In the final pages, the reader will learn if his or her solution matches that of the detective.

Given such a purpose, the reader and writer had to be playing by the same rules. Even though the rules are rather self-evident, they were formalized by Monsignor Ronald Knox in his introduction to *The Best Detective Stories of 1928*. His rendition of the rules came to be known as the "Detective Decalogue." Perhaps because Father Knox was known as a theologian and translator of the Bible as well as a crime writer, the rules were also referred to as the "Ten Commandments of Detective Writing."

The rules are technical. The writer must introduce the criminal early, produce all clues found for immediate inspection by the reader, use no more than one secret room or passageway, and eschew acts of God, unknown poisons, unaccountable intuitions, helpful accidents, and so forth. Identical twins and doubles are prohibited unless the reader is prepared for them, and having the detective himself commit the crime is specifically barred. Some rules are whimsical at best or sadly indicative of the prejudices of Knox's day. Rule V, for example, provides that "no Chinaman must figure in the story." In all, the rules confirm the fact that detective stories are a game.

It is worth noting that all but one of those "best" detective stories in the 1928 anthology were written by British authors. It was the golden age of the classic form, and though the American Poe was considered the inventor of the form, England was where the traditional side of the genre flourished. Sir Arthur Conan Doyle, with Sherlock Holmes as his detective and Dr. John H. Watson as his narrator straight man, had earlier brought the detective short story to its finest flowering. And Agatha Christie polished the puzzle form, particularly in her novels, to perfection. But this volume shows that even then, things were changing in America.

As our selections show, American writers had been injecting new elements into and otherwise tinkering with Poe's classic form since the nineteenth century. Then came the "Era of Disillusion," which followed World War I; the cultural revolt of the "Roaring Twenties"; the rise of organized crime and of political and police corruption, which accompanied national Prohibition; and the ensuing Great Depression. All contributed to changing the nature of American literature—with detective fiction leading the way in its recording of a distinctive American voice and its depiction of the social scene. In fact, I believe that Raymond Chandler was a greater influence on later generations of American writers—in and out of the detective genre—than was that darling of the literary establishment, F. Scott Fitzgerald.

Barzun told us that the classic detective story is written by and for the educated upper-middle classes. Particularly in the British manifestation, it was typically set in upper-crust milieus. But we've chosen Susan Glaspell to demonstrate that in an American writer's hands, the story can also succeed in a remote, rural farmhouse literally in the middle of America. Glaspell's story "A Jury of Her Peers" also proves that social concerns like wife battering can be used to evoke an emotional reaction on the part of the reader, even while the puzzle element remains central.

While in Britain readers were puzzling over whodunit in stories sold at railway stations, in the United States the newspaper stands and drugstore magazine racks held detective fiction of a different sort—published in pulp magazines with garish covers and cheap prices. One of these was *Black Mask*, and one who wrote for it was a former Pinkerton private detective named Dashiell Hammett.*

Like many of his fellow American producers of detective fiction, Hammett was definitely not an effete product of the upper or even solidly middle class. Neither were the settings of his stories nor the characters who populated them. He and other American crime writers during the Depression years were taking crime out of the drawing rooms of country houses and putting it back on the "mean streets" where it was actually happening.

This is not to say that the classic form was dead or even ailing. Early examples in this volume are the work of Bret Harte and Jacques Futrelle. Harte, known for his depictions of American life in Gold Rush territory, could turn his hand to writing the quintessential Sherlockian pastiche: "The Stolen Cigar Case." And Jacques Futrelle's "The Problem of Cell 13" obeys all the rules of the locked-room mystery with a character locked into a high-security "death cell" in an American prison.

Meanwhile, on the novel scene, until the end of the 1930s the best-selling American author of detective fiction was S. S. Van Dine, whose super-sleuth Philo Vance is among the most thoroughgoing snobs ever to appear in fiction. Van Dine's intricate plots follow the rules of Knox's "Decalogue" and are played out in aristocratic settings into which the reality of corrupt cops, soup lines, and American hard times never in-

---

*With great regret, we are unable to include a Hammett story in this volume, since permission to reprint his shorter works is not available.

trudes. The purpose is the puzzle. Even today, literally millions of American readers buy detective fiction principally for the classical game.

In one way or another, the puzzle remains essential to the form, as demonstrated in the variety of mutations the detective story has been generating through the twentieth century. To consider the variations, one must start at the base, with "The Murders in the Rue Morgue." In this story, Poe gives us the model for the classic detective tale, which is still alive and thriving in various modifications. Chevalier Auguste Dupin, his sleuth, not only is, in my opinion, the first detective of detective fiction, but is white, male, of an "excellent—indeed illustrious family," financially independent, and an amateur. The police are inept. The crime was the model for thousands of locked-room murders, done in a setting from which it seems impossible for the killer to escape, and the solution is based on close observation of physical evidence to which the superior "ratiocination" of Dupin is applied. And, true to Poe's disdain for the notion of democracy and the uncouth laboring class, the principal characters (except the killer) are well-bred folks. In "The Purloined Letter," Poe produced an even purer model, moving crime into the marble halls of the artistocracy.

A century later, with the traditional form enjoying its golden age, many writers still followed Poe's pattern. Locked-room crimes continued to flourish; the murder was done in a world of manor houses, formal gardens, faithful butlers, haughty house guests, and stupid police. The blood on the Persian carpet was usually blue, and everything was divorced from reality. Into this quiet haven, the skillful writer allowed no realism to intrude. It would distract the reader from the intricate puzzle the writer was unfolding.

Properly done, such stories are perfect escape literature. Book dealers labeled them "cozies," and Julian Symons, British crime writer and longtime literary critic for the *Times* of London, called them "humdrums." Fans bought them by the millions, and still do.

In his introduction to *A Catalog of Crime*, Barzun explained what the detective story should give those readers and what it should avoid. First, he stressed that the detective story is a tale, not a novel. "The tale does not pretend to social significance nor does it probe the depth of the soul," he wrote. "The characters it presents are not persons but types, as in the Gospels: the servant, the rich man, the camel driver (now a chauffeur)." Properly done, detective fiction is a high-brow form, according to Barzun. It is escape literature for the intellectual. It should deal with the workings of human reason, not with human emotion. "To put our creed positively," said Barzun (speaking for co-author

Wendell Hertig Taylor as well), "we hold with the best philosophers that a detective story should be mainly occupied with detection, and not (say) with the forgivable nervousness of a man planning to murder his wife."

That great essay was published in 1971. But three years earlier, Raymond Chandler's *The Simple Art of Murder* had been republished, including the famous introductory essay, which served as a sort of writer's declaration of independence from the strictures of the classic form. I suspect that Barzun's essay was intended, at least in part, as a counterattack against the case that Chandler made for the detective story as novel and for the myriad modifications the genre had been undergoing, particularly in America.

Fortunately for me, and for hundreds of other mystery writers attracted into the genre for the other creative possibilities it offers, an increasing number of readers came to care less about whodunit and more about character development, social problems, settings, mood, culture, and all those aspects that involve emotion and not just the intellect. With the so-called mainstream of American literature polluted by the notions of the minimalists, and literary criticism entangled in the various fads of the mid-century, writers who thought they had something to say or a story to tell discovered detective fiction as Hammett and Chandler had been writing it. The mainstream novel, lying moribund under mid-century faddism, was being crowded off the best-seller lists by crime novels and mysteries.

Many of detective fiction's new practitioners leaped into the game, as did I, happily ignorant of Knox's "Ten Commandments" or the genre's purpose as escapism for the intellectual. Instead of turning on whodunit, the focus shifted elsewhere. Sometimes, as in Ed McBain's story "Small Homicide," the writers were chiefly interested in why the crime had been committed, or perhaps they merely used the sleuthing to draw the reader into a world they wanted to explore.

As the stories in this volume illustrate, Americans who wrote in the detective form had been branching out in all directions. The tale had been moved out of the isolation of the privileged class and into work-a-day America, and was often drawn with an excellent eye for regional settings and a keen ear for local voices. A bit of social purpose and realism had seeped in. In the United States, the sleuthing game had never been the exclusive domain of well-bred male amateurs; more and more of the popular writers—and their sleuths—were women. An early female detective found in these pages is Violet Strange, in Anna Katharine Green's "Missing: Page Thirteen." But until the work of Hammett

7

in the 1930s and Raymond Chandler in the 1940s began to have its effect, the puzzle generally remained at the heart of the work. Certainly in the minds of the publishing fraternity, that was what the public wanted.

But even Chandler encountered editing that sought to trim his appeal to readers' emotions. In a letter to a friend written in 1947, Chandler noted that when he was writing short stories for the pulp-magazine market, editors cut out the language he used to establish mood and emotion on the grounds that their readers wanted action, not description: "My theory was that the readers just thought they cared about nothing but the action, that really, although they didn't know it, the thing they cared about, was the creation of emotion through dialogue and description."* As our selection "I'll Be Waiting" shows, Chandler was not interested in producing the classic form as outlined by Knox's rules. He was interested in using crime as the center around which he could spin a novel that illuminates social decadence and the human condition.

In this volume, Rosemary Herbert and I have assembled thirty-three stories that represent the evolution of the American detective story. Because the wealth of talent over the past century and a half was so great, we found ourselves in a position reminiscent of that of professional football coaches facing the deadline for cutting their teams down to the legal limit with too many outstanding players to chose among. Just as coaches sometimes keep a player because he can serve in more than one position, we chose our stories to illustrate more than one development in the field. Rex Stout's "Christmas Party," for example, shows Nero Wolfe unusually active for an "armchair detective"—but it beautifully illuminates how the "Holmes and Watson" relationship had been modified. In making another selection, we evaluated several journalist sleuths, including George Harmon Coxe's photojournalist Flashgun Casey, but we picked Joe "Daffy" Dill for this volume because we found Richard Sale's story "A Nose for News" irresistibly entertaining.

Our goal was to illustrate as many aspects of the American detective short story as we could. Thus we present examples of sleuth types, including amateurs like Poe's Dupin, "scientific sleuths" like Futrelle's Professor S. F. X. Van Dusen and Arthur B. Reeve's Professor Craig Kennedy, hard-boiled dicks like Robert Leslie Bellem's Dan Turner, and police characters like Ed McBain's Eighty-seventh Precinct cop Dave Levine and my own Jim Chee and Joe Leaphorn. We also feature "acci-

---

*Dorothy Gardiner and Katharine Walker, eds., *Raymond Chandler Speaking* (Boston: Houghton Mifflin, 1977), p. 219.

dental sleuths"—characters who happen upon a crime and manage to discover the truth—as do the characters in Glaspell's "A Jury of Her Peers" and Mary Roberts Rinehart's "The Lipstick." And Mignon G. Eberhart's Susan Dare, Sue Grafton's Kinsey Millhone, and Linda Barnes's Carlotta Carlyle join Green's Violet Strange as female private investigators. Melville Davisson Post's Uncle Abner and William Faulkner's Uncle Gavin Stevens are sermonizing sleuths who grind moral axes until they shine, while Clayton Rawson's The Great Merlini adds sparkle to his sleuthing by means of his practical expertise in magic.

Stories that succeed in presenting examples of sleuth types also demonstrate regionalism, for which American detective fiction has become known. The works of Glaspell, Post, Bellem, and Faulkner portray distinctly American scenes, as does my own short story "Chee's Witch," which illustrates the move into the use of ethnic detectives.

Although our table of contents includes the names of a good number of famous authors, we were more concerned to find the best story to represent a trend in the genre. Some of our selections are classics; some represent little-known writers whom we consider "good finds" for readers. For example, we considered Clinton H. Stagg's "The Keyboard of Silence" delightful and included it as a gem that deserves to be better known, and not only because Stagg's blind sleuth demonstrates how disabled detectives can function efficiently.

While we represent as many decades as possible, and male and female sleuths and authors, we also chose our selections to show emotional range. We cover humor with Harte and Barnes, pathos with Glaspell and McBain. And we are sure that readers will have fun with Reeve's "The Beauty Mask," in which the scientific jiggery-pokery is so dated that readers will find themselves chuckling even while being taken in by the earnestness with which it was written.

I join with Rosemary Herbert in the belief that we have fairly represented the evolution of the detective story in America. But our mission was to entertain as well as to educate. We trust that you will find this volume just plain fun to read.

Tony Hillerman, with Rosemary Herbert

EDGAR ALLAN POE

(1809–1849)

||||||||||||||||||||||||||||||||||||||||||||||| ■ |||||||||||||||||||||||||||||||||||||||||||||||

Although his life was short and tragic, Edgar Allan Poe is considered by a few to be the founder of American letters, by many to be the inventor of horror stories and fantasy novels, and by one and all to be the father of detective fiction. He was the child of two actors, orphaned as a tot, expelled from West Point, and rejected by his fiancée. He married his cousin and, after she died of tuberculosis, wed the original fiancée. Through much of his forty years, his health was poor.

Despite—or perhaps inspired by—his circumstances, Poe became a published poet at age twenty, and he served as editor of the *Southern Literary Messenger* until he was fired at age twenty-eight for drunkenness. By the time Poe wrote "The Murders in the Rue Morgue," when he was thirty-two, he was already well established with his literary criticism, magazine articles, short stories, and poetry.

"The Murders in the Rue Morgue" is considered to be the single most important piece in the literary history of detective fiction. While some elements that are now common to the genre, like the locked-room scenario, had been used previous to the publication of Poe's masterpiece, Poe was the first to play with what were to become conventions of the genre. These include the introduction of an eccentric detective who relies on ratiocination to solve crimes and the use of a narrator who, while awestruck at the sleuth's powers, nonetheless lays out a clearly described problem and details the steps toward its solution.

The purpose of literature, Poe said, "is to amuse by arousing thought." He also said that "tales of ratiocination" should stick to the puzzle and not wander off into novelistic digressions of mood and character. Thus he not only invented the detective form but also provided its credo.

Despite its atmosphere of horror, "The Murders in the Rue Morgue" shows Poe practicing what he preached. The focus remains on the puzzle and the process of solving it. His sleuth, Chevalier Auguste Dupin, is a private person, a "thinking machine," with his ratiocination narrated by a faceless friend. The police are depicted as inept and looked on with disdain; clues are presented fairly, and the reader is invited to interpret them.

Readers of this anthology will notice that the form Poe created in the 1840s has been followed, with modifications, throughout the literary history of the genre. Variations on the form continue to challenge writers and excite readers today.

1841

The Murders in the Rue Morgue

■

What song the Syrens sang, or what name Achilles assumed when he hid himself among women, although puzzling questions, are not beyond all conjecture.

SIR THOMAS BROWNE

The mental features discoursed of as the analytical are, in themselves, but little susceptible of analysis. We appreciate them only in their effects. We know of them, among other things, that they are always to their possessor, when inordinately possessed, a source of the liveliest enjoyment. As the strong man exults in his physical ability, delighting in such exercises as call his muscles into action, so glories the analyst in that moral activity which *disentangles.* He derives pleasure from even the most trivial occupations bringing his talent into play. He is fond of enigmas, of conundrums, of hieroglyphics; exhibiting in his solutions of each a degree of *acumen* which appears to the ordinary apprehension præternatural. His results, brought about by the very soul and essence of method, have, in truth, the whole air of intuition.

The faculty of re-solution is possibly much invigorated by mathematical study, and especially by that highest branch of it which, unjustly, and merely on account of its retrograde operations, has been called, as if *par excellence*, analysis. Yet to calculate is not in itself to analyse. A chess-player, for example, does the one without effort at the other. It follows that the game of chess, in its effects upon mental character, is greatly misunderstood. I am not now writing a treatise, but simply prefacing a somewhat peculiar narrative by observations very much at random; I will, therefore, take occasion to assert that the higher powers of the reflective intellect are more decidedly and more usefully tasked by the unostentatious game of draughts than by all the elaborate frivolity of chess. In this latter, where the pieces have different and *bizarre* motions, with various and variable values, what is only complex is mistaken (a not unusual error) for what is profound. The *attention* is here called powerfully into play. If it flag for an instant, an oversight is committed, resulting in injury or defeat. The possible moves being not only manifold but involute, the chances of such oversights are multiplied; and in nine cases out of ten it is the more concentrative rather than the more acute player who conquers. In draughts, on the contrary, where the moves are *unique* and have but little variation, the probabilities of inadvertence are diminished, and the mere attention being left comparatively unemployed, what advantages are obtained by either party are obtained by superior *acumen*. To be less abstract—Let us suppose a game of draughts where the pieces are reduced to four kings, and where, of course, no oversight is to be expected. It is obvious that here the victory can be decided (the players being at all equal) only by some *recherché* movement, the result of some strong exertion of the intellect. Deprived of ordinary resources, the analyst throws himself into the spirit of his opponent, identifies himself therewith, and not unfrequently sees thus, at a glance, the sole methods (sometimes indeed absurdly simple ones) by which he may seduce into error or hurry into miscalculation.

Whist has long been noted for its influence upon what is termed the calculating power; and men of the highest order of intellect have been known to take an apparently unaccountable delight in it, while eschewing chess as frivolous. Beyond doubt there is nothing of a similar nature so greatly tasking the faculty of analysis. The best chess-player in Christendom *may* be little more than the best player of chess; but proficiency in whist implies capacity for success in all those more important undertakings where mind struggles with mind. When I say proficiency, I mean that perfection in the game which includes a comprehension of *all* the sources whence legitimate advantage may be derived. These are not only manifold but multiform, and lie frequently among recesses of thought altogether inaccessible to the ordinary understanding. To observe attentively is to remember distinctly; and, so far, the concentrative chess-player will do very well at whist; while the rules of Hoyle (themselves based upon the mere mechanism of the game) are sufficiently and generally comprehensible. Thus to have a retentive memory, and to proceed by "the book," are points commonly regarded as the sum total of good playing. But it is in matters beyond the limits of mere rule that the skill of the analyst is evinced. He makes, in silence, a host of observations and inferences. So, perhaps, do his companions; and the difference in the extent of the information obtained lies not so much in the validity of the inference as in the quality of the observation. The necessary knowledge is that of *what* to observe. Our player confines himself not at all; nor, because the game is the object, does he reject deductions from things external to the game. He examines the countenance of his partner, comparing it carefully with that of each of his opponents. He considers the mode of assorting the cards in each hand; often counting trump by trump, and honor by honor, through the glances bestowed by their holders upon each. He notes every variation of face as the play progresses, gathering a fund of thought from the differences in the expression of certainty, of surprise, of triumph, or of chagrin. From the manner of gathering up a trick he judges whether the person taking it can make another in the suit. He recognises what is played through feint, by the air with which it is thrown upon the table. A casual or inadvertent word; the accidental dropping or turning of a card, with the accompanying anxiety or carelessness in regard to its concealment; the counting of the tricks, with the order of their arrangement; embarrassment, hesitation, eagerness or trepidation—all afford, to his apparently intuitive perception, indications of the true state of affairs. The first two or three rounds having been played, he is in full possession of the contents of each hand, and thenceforward puts down his cards with as absolute a precision of purpose as if the rest of the party had turned outward the faces of their own.

The analytical power should not be confounded with simple ingenuity; for while the analyst is necessarily ingenious, the ingenious man is often remarkably incapable of analysis. The constructive or combining power, by which ingenuity is usually manifested, and to which the phrenologists (I believe erroneously) have assigned a separate organ, supposing it a primitive faculty, has been so frequently seen in those whose intellect bordered otherwise upon idiocy, as to have attracted general observation among writers on morals. Between ingenuity and the analytic ability there exists a difference far greater, indeed, than that between the fancy and the imagination, but of a character very strictly analogous. It will be found, in fact, that the ingenious are always fanciful, and the *truly* imaginative never otherwise then analytic.

The narrative which follows will appear to the reader somewhat in the light of a commentary upon the propositions just advanced.

Residing in Paris during the spring and part of the summer of 18—, I there became acquainted with a Monsieur C. Auguste Dupin. This young gentleman was of an excellent—indeed of an illustrious family, but, by a variety of untoward events, had been reduced to such poverty that the energy of his character succumbed beneath it, and he ceased to bestir himself in the world, or to care for the retrieval of his fortunes. By courtesy of his creditors, there still remained in his possession a small remnant of his patrimony; and, upon the income arising from this, he managed, by means of a rigorous economy, to procure the necessaries of life, without troubling himself about its superfluities. Books, indeed, were his sole luxuries, and in Paris these are easily obtained.

Our first meeting was at an obscure library in the Rue Montmartre, where the accident of our both being in search of the same very rare and very remarkable volume brought us into closer communion. We saw each other again and again. I was deeply interested in the little family history which he detailed to me with all that candor which a

Frenchman indulges whenever mere self is his theme. I was astonished, too, at the vast extent of his reading; and, above all, I felt my soul enkindled within me by the wild fervor, and the vivid freshness of his imagination. Seeking in Paris the objects I then sought, I felt that the society of such a man would be to me a treasure beyond price; and this feeling I frankly confided to him. It was at length arranged that we should live together during my stay in the city; and as my worldly circumstances were somewhat less embarrassed than his own, I was permitted to be at the expense of renting, and furnishing in a style which suited the rather fantastic gloom of our common temper, a time-eaten and grotesque mansion, long deserted through superstitions into which we did not inquire, and tottering to its fall in a retired and desolate portion of the Faubourg St. Germain.

Had the routine of our life at this place been known to the world, we should have been regarded as madmen—although, perhaps, as madmen of a harmless nature. Our seclusion was perfect. We admitted no visitors. Indeed the locality of our retirement had been carefully kept a secret from my own former associates; and it had been many years since Dupin had ceased to know or be known in Paris. We existed within ourselves alone.

It was a freak of fancy in my friend (for what else shall I call it?) to be enamored of the Night for her own sake; and into this *bizarrerie*, as into all his others, I quietly fell; giving myself up to his wild whims with a perfect *abandon*. The sable divinity would not herself dwell with us always; but we could counterfeit her presence. At the first dawn of the morning we closed all the massy shutters of our old building, lighting a couple of tapers which, strongly perfumed, threw out only the ghastliest and feeblest of rays. By the aid of these we then busied our souls in dreams—reading, writing, or conversing, until warned by the clock of the advent of the true Darkness. Then we sallied forth into the streets, arm in arm, continuing the topics of the day, or roaming far and wide until a late hour, seeking, amid the wild lights and shadows of the populous city, that infinity of mental excitement which quiet observation can afford.

At such times I could not help remarking and admiring (although from his rich ideality I had been prepared to expect it) a peculiar analytic ability in Dupin. He seemed, too, to take an eager delight in its exercise—if not exactly in its display—and did not hesitate to confess the pleasure thus derived. He boasted to me, with a low chuckling laugh, that most men, in respect to himself, wore windows in their bosoms, and was wont to follow up such assertions by direct and very startling proofs of his intimate knowledge of my own. His manner at these moments was frigid and abstract; his eyes were vacant in expression; while his voice, usually a rich tenor, rose into a treble which would have sounded petulantly but for the deliberateness and entire distinctness of the enunciation. Observing him in these moods, I often dwelt meditatively upon the old philosophy of the Bi-Part Soul, and amused myself with the fancy of a double Dupin—the creative and the resolvent.

Let it not be supposed, from what I have just said, that I am detailing any mystery, or penning any romance. What I have described in the Frenchman was merely the result of an excited, or perhaps of a diseased intelligence. But of the character of his remarks at the periods in question an example will best convey the idea.

We were strolling one night down a long dirty street, in the vicinity of the Palais Royal. Being both, apparently, occupied with thought, neither of us had spoken a syllable for fifteen minutes at least. All at once Dupin broke forth with these words:

"He is a very little fellow, that's true, and would do better for the *Théâtre des Variétés*."

"There can be no doubt of that," I replied unwittingly, and not at first observing (so much had I been absorbed in reflection) the extraordinary manner in which the speaker had chimed in with my meditations. In an instant afterward I recollected myself, and my astonishment was profound.

"Dupin," said I, gravely, "this is beyond my comprehension. I do not hesitate to say that I am amazed, and can scarcely credit my senses. How was it possible you should know I was thinking of ——?" Here I paused, to ascertain beyond a doubt whether he really knew of whom I thought.

"—— of Chantilly," said he, "why do you pause? You were remarking to yourself that his diminutive figure unfitted him for tragedy."

This was precisely what had formed the subject of my reflections. Chantilly was a *quondam* cobbler of the Rue St. Denis, who, becoming stage-mad, had attempted the *rôle* of Xerxes, in Crébillon's tragedy so called, and been notoriously Pasquinaded for his pains.

"Tell me, for Heaven's sake," I exclaimed, "the method—if method there is—by which you have been enabled to fathom my soul in this matter." In fact I was even more startled than I would have been willing to express.

"It was the fruiterer," replied my friend, "who brought you to the conclusion that the mender of soles was not of sufficient height for Xerxes *et id genus omne*."

"The fruiterer!—you astonish me—I know no fruiterer whomsoever."

15

"The man who ran up against you as we entered the street—it may have been fifteen minutes ago."

I now remembered that, in fact, a fruiterer, carrying upon his head a large basket of apples, had nearly thrown me down, by accident, as we passed from the Rue C—— into the thoroughfare where we stood; but what this had to do with Chantilly I could not possibly understand.

There was not a particle of *charlatanerie* about Dupin. "I will explain," he said, "and that you may comprehend all clearly, we will first retrace the course of your meditations, from the moment in which I spoke to you until that of the *rencontre* with the fruiterer in question. The larger links of the chain run thus—Chantilly, Orion, Dr. Nichol, Epicurus, Stereotomy, the street stones, the fruiterer."

There are few persons who have not, at some period of their lives, amused themselves in retracing the steps by which particular conclusions of their own minds have been attained. The occupation is often full of interest; and he who attempts it for the first time is astonished by the apparently illimitable distance and incoherence between the starting-point and the goal. What, then, must have been my amazement when I heard the Frenchman speak what he had just spoken, and when I could not help acknowledging that he had spoken the truth. He continued:

"We had been talking of horses, if I remember aright, just before leaving the Rue C——. This was the last subject we discussed. As we crossed into this street, a fruiterer, with a large basket upon his head, brushing quickly past us, thrust you upon a pile of paving-stones collected at a spot where the causeway is undergoing repair. You stepped upon one of the loose fragments, slipped, slightly strained your ankle, appeared vexed or sulky, muttered a few words, turned to look at the pile, and then proceeded in silence. I was not particularly attentive to what you did; but observation has become with me, of late, a species of necessity.

"You kept your eyes upon the ground—glancing, with a petulant expression, at the holes and ruts in the pavement, (so that I saw you were still thinking of the stones,) until we reached the little alley called Lamartine, which has been paved, by way of experiment, with the overlapping and riveted blocks. Here your countenance brightened up, and, perceiving your lips move, I could not doubt that you murmured the word 'stereotomy,' a term very affectedly applied to this species of pavement. I knew that you could not say to yourself 'stereotomy' without being brought to think of atomies, and thus of the theories of Epicurus; and since, when we discussed this subject not very long ago, I mentioned to you how singularly, yet with how little notice, the vague guesses of that noble Greek had met with confirmation in the late nebular cosmogony, I felt that you could not avoid casting your eyes upward to the great *nebula* in Orion, and I certainly expected that you would do so. You did look up; and I was now assured that I had correctly followed your steps. But in that bitter *tirade* upon Chantilly, which appeared in yesterday's 'Musée,' the satirist, making some disgraceful allusions to the cobbler's change of name upon assuming the buskin, quoted a Latin line about which we have often conversed. I mean the line

Perdidit antiquum litera prima sonum

I had told you that this was in reference to Orion, formerly written Urion; and, from certain pungencies connected with this explanation, I was aware that you could not have forgotten it. It was clear, therefore, that you would not fail to combine the two ideas of Orion and Chantilly. That you did combine them I saw by the character of the smile which passed over your lips. You thought of the poor cobbler's immolation. So far, you had been stooping in your gait; but now I saw you draw yourself up to your full height. I was then sure that you reflected upon the diminutive figure of Chantilly. At this point I interrupted your meditations to remark that as, in fact, he *was* a very little fellow—that Chantilly—he would do better at the *Théâtre des Variétés*."

Not long after this, we were looking over an evening edition of the "Gazette des Tribunaux," when the following paragraphs arrested our attention.

"Extraordinary Murders.—This morning, about three o'clock, the inhabitants of the Quartier St. Roch were aroused from sleep by a succession of terrific shrieks, issuing, apparently, from the fourth story of a house in the Rue Morgue, known to be in the sole occupancy of one Madame L'Espanaye, and her daughter Mademoiselle Camille L'Espanaye. After some delay, occasioned by a fruitless attempt to procure admission in the usual manner, the gateway was broken in with a crowbar, and eight or ten of the neighbors entered, accompanied by two *gendarmes*. By this time the cries had ceased; but, as the party rushed up the first flight of stairs, two or more rough voices, in angry contention, were distinguished, and seemed to proceed from the upper part of the house. As the second landing was reached, these sounds, also, had ceased, and everything remained perfectly quiet. The party spread themselves, and hurried from room to room. Upon arriving at a large back chamber in the fourth story, (the door of which, being found locked, with the key inside, was forced open,) a spectacle presented itself which struck every one present not less with horror than with astonishment.

"The apartment was in the wildest disorder—the furniture broken and thrown about in all directions. There was only one bedstead; and from this the bed had been removed, and thrown into the middle of the floor. On a chair lay a razor, besmeared with blood. On the hearth were two or three long and thick tresses of grey human hair, also dabbled in blood, and seeming to have been pulled out by the roots. On the floor were found four Napoleons, an ear-ring of topaz, three large silver spoons, three smaller of *métal d'Alger*, and two bags, containing nearly four thousand francs in gold. The drawers of a *bureau*, which stood in one corner, were open, and had been, apparently, rifled, although many articles still remained in them. A small iron safe was discovered under the *bed* (not under the bedstead). It was open, with the key still in the door. It had no contents beyond a few old letters, and other papers of little consequence.

"Of Madame L'Espanaye no traces were here seen; but an unusual quantity of soot being observed in the fire-place, a search was made in the chimney, and (horrible to relate!) the corpse of the daughter, head downward, was dragged therefrom; it having been thus forced up the narrow aperture for a considerable distance. The body was quite warm. Upon examining it, many excoriations were perceived, no doubt occasioned by the violence with which it had been thrust up and disengaged. Upon the face were many severe scratches, and, upon the throat, dark bruises, and deep indentations of finger nails, as if the deceased had been throttled to death.

"After a thorough investigation of every portion of the house, without farther discovery, the party made its way into a small paved yard in the rear of the building, where lay the corpse of the old lady, with her throat so entirely cut that, upon an attempt to raise her, the head fell off. The body, as well as the head, was fearfully mutilated—the former so much so as scarcely to retain any semblance of humanity.

"To this horrible mystery there is not as yet, we believe, the slightest clew."

The next day's paper had these additional particulars.

"The Tragedy in the Rue Morgue. Many individuals have been examined in relation to this most extraordinary and frightful affair." [The word *'affaire'* has not yet, in France, that levity of import which it conveys with us,] "but nothing whatever has transpired to throw light upon it. We give below all the material testimony elicited.

"*Pauline Dubourg*, laundress, deposes that she has known both the deceased for three years, having washed for them during that period. The old lady and her daughter seemed on good terms—very affectionate towards each other. They were excellent pay. Could not speak in regard to their mode or means of living. Believed that Madame L. told fortunes for a living. Was reputed to have money put by. Never met any persons in the house when she called for the clothes or took them home. Was sure that they had no servant in employ. There appeared to be no furniture in any part of the building except in the fourth story.

"*Pierre Moreau*, tobacconist, deposes that he has been in the habit of selling small quantities of tobacco and snuff to Madame L'Espanaye for nearly four years. Was born in the neighborhood, and has always resided there. The deceased and her daughter had occupied the house in which the corpses were found, for more than six years. It was formerly occupied by a jeweller, who under-let the upper rooms to various persons. The house was the property of Madame L. She became dissatisfied with the abuse of the premises by her tenant, and moved into them herself, refusing to let any portion. The old lady was childish. Witness had seen the daughter some five or six times during the six years. The two lived an exceedingly retired life—were reputed to have money. Had heard it said among the neighbors that Madame L. told fortunes—did not believe it. Had never seen any person enter the door except the old lady and her daughter, a porter once or twice, and a physician some eight or ten times.

"Many other persons, neighbors, gave evidence to the same effect. No one was spoken of as frequenting the house. It was not known whether there were any living connexions of Madame L. and her daughter. The shutters of the windows were seldom opened. Those in the rear were always closed, with the exception of the large back room, fourth story. The house was a good house—not very old.

"*Isidore Musèt*, gendarme, deposes that he was called to the house about three o'clock in the morning, and found some twenty or thirty persons at the gateway, endeavoring to gain admittance. Forced it open, at length, with a bayonet—not with a crowbar. Had but little difficulty in getting it open, on account of its being a double or folding gate, and bolted neither at bottom nor top. The shrieks were continued until the gate was forced—and then suddenly ceased. They seemed to be screams of some person (or persons) in great agony—were loud and drawn out, not short and quick. Witness led the way up stairs. Upon reaching the first landing, heard two voices in loud and angry contention—the one a gruff voice, the other much shriller—a very strange

19

voice. Could distinguish some words of the former, which was that of a Frenchman. Was positive that it was not a woman's voice. Could distinguish the words *'sacré'* and *'diable.'* The shrill voice was that of a foreigner. Could not be sure whether it was the voice of a man or of a woman. Could not make out what was said, but believed the language to be Spanish. The state of the room and of the bodies was described by this witness as we described them yesterday.

"*Henri Duval*, a neighbor, and by trade a silver-smith, deposes that he was one of the party who first entered the house. Corroborates the testimony of Musèt in general. As soon as they forced an entrance, they reclosed the door, to keep out the crowd, which collected very fast, notwithstanding the lateness of the hour. The shrill voice, this witness thinks, was that of an Italian. Was certain it was not French. Could not be sure that it was a man's voice. It might have been a woman's. Was not acquainted with the Italian language. Could not distinguish the words, but was convinced by the intonation that the speaker was an Italian. Knew Madame L. and her daughter. Had conversed with both frequently. Was sure that the shrill voice was not that of either of the deceased.

"—— *Odenheimer, restaurateur*. This witness volunteered his testimony. Not speaking French, was examined through an interpreter. Is a native of Amsterdam. Was passing the house at the time of the shrieks. They lasted for several minutes—probably ten. They were long and loud—very awful and distressing. Was one of those who entered the building. Corroborated the previous evidence in every respect but one. Was sure that the shrill voice was that of a man—of a Frenchman. Could not distinguish the words uttered. They were loud and quick—unequal—spoken apparently in fear as well as in anger. The voice was harsh—not so much shrill as harsh. Could not call it a shrill voice. The gruff voice said repeatedly *'sacré,' 'diable,'* and once *'mon Dieu.'*

"*Jules Mignaud*, banker, of the firm of Mignaud et Fils, Rue Deloraine. Is the elder Mignaud. Madame L'Espanaye had some property. Had opened an account with his banking house in the spring of the year —— (eight years previously). Made frequent deposits in small sums. Had checked for nothing until the third day before her death, when she took out in person the sum of 4000 francs. This sum was paid in gold, and a clerk sent home with the money.

"*Adolphe Le Bon*, clerk to Mignaud et Fils, deposes that on the day in question, about noon, he accompanied Madame L'Espanaye to her residence with the 4000 francs, put up in two bags. Upon the door being opened, Mademoiselle L. appeared and took from his hands one of the bags, while the old lady relieved him of the other. He then bowed and departed. Did not see any person in the street at the time. It is a bye-street—very lonely.

"*William Bird*, tailor, deposes that he was one of the party who entered the house. Is an Englishman. Has lived in Paris two years. Was one of the first to ascend the stairs. Heard the voices in contention. The gruff voice was that of a Frenchman. Could make out several words, but cannot now remember all. Heard distinctly '*sacré*' and '*mon Dieu.*' There was a sound at the moment as if of several persons struggling— a scraping and scuffling sound. The shrill voice was very loud—louder than the gruff one. Is sure that it was not the voice of an Englishman. Appeared to be that of a German. Might have been a woman's voice. Does not understand German.

"Four of the above-named witnesses, being recalled, deposed that the door of the chamber in which was found the body of Mademoiselle L. was locked on the inside when the party reached it. Every thing was perfectly silent—no groans or noises of any kind. Upon forcing the door no person was seen. The windows, both of the back and front room, were down and firmly fastened from within. A door between the two rooms was closed, but not locked. The door leading from the front room into the passage was locked, with the key on the inside. A small room in the front of the house, on the fourth story, at the head of the passage, was open, the door being ajar. This room was crowded with old beds, boxes, and so forth. These were carefully removed and searched. There was not an inch of any portion of the house which was not carefully searched. Sweeps were sent up and down the chimneys. The house was a four story one, with garrets (*mansardes*). A trap-door on the roof was nailed down very securely—did not appear to have been opened for years. The time elapsing between the hearing of the voices in contention and the breaking open of the room door, was variously stated by the witnesses. Some made it as short as three minutes—some as long as five. The door was opened with difficulty.

"*Alfonzo Garcio*, undertaker, deposes that he resides in the Rue Morgue. Is a native of Spain. Was one of the party who entered the house. Did not proceed up stairs. Is nervous, and was apprehensive of the consequences of agitation. Heard the voices in contention. The gruff voice was that of a Frenchman. Could not distinguish what was said. The shrill voice was that of an Englishman—is sure of this. Does not understand the English language, but judges by the intonation.

"*Alberto Montani*, confectioner, deposes that he was among the first to ascend the stairs. Heard the voices in question. The gruff voice was that of a Frenchman. Distinguished several words. The speaker appeared to be expostulating. Could not make out the words of the shrill voice. Spoke quick and unevenly. Thinks it the voice of a Russian. Corroborates the general testimony. Is an Italian. Never conversed with a native of Russia.

"Several witnesses, recalled, here testified that the chimneys of all the rooms on the fourth story were too narrow to admit the passage of a human being. By 'sweeps' were meant cylindrical sweeping-brushes, such as are employed by those who clean chimneys. These brushes were passed up and down every flue in the house. There is no back passage by which any one could have descended while the party proceeded up stairs. The body of Mademoiselle L'Espanaye was so firmly wedged in the chimney that it could not be got down until four or five of the party united their strength.

"*Paul Dumas*, physician, deposes that he was called to view the bodies about day-break. They were both then lying on the sacking of the bedstead in the chamber where Mademoiselle L. was found. The corpse of the young lady was much bruised and excoriated. The fact that it had been thrust up the chimney would sufficiently account for these appearances. The throat was greatly chafed. There were several deep scratches just below the chin, together with a series of livid spots which were evidently the impression of fingers. The face was fearfully discolored, and the eye-balls protruded. The tongue had been partially bitten through. A large bruise was discovered upon the pit of the stomach, produced, apparently, by the pressure of a knee. In the opinion of M. Dumas, Mademoiselle L'Espanaye had been throttled to death by some person or persons unknown. The corpse of the mother was horribly mutilated. All the bones of the right leg and arm were more or less shattered. The left *tibia* much splintered, as well as all the ribs of the left side. Whole body dreadfully bruised and discolored. It was not possible to say how the injuries had been inflicted. A heavy club of wood, or a broad bar of iron—a chair—any large, heavy, and obtuse weapon would have produced such results, if wielded by the hands of a very powerful man. No woman could have inflicted the blows with any weapon. The head of the deceased, when seen by witness, was entirely separated from the body, and was also greatly shattered. The throat had evidently been cut with some very sharp instrument—probably with a razor.

"*Alexandre Etienne*, surgeon, was called with M. Dumas to view the bodies. Corroborated the testimony, and the opinions of M. Dumas.

"Nothing farther of importance was elicited, although several other persons were examined. A murder so mysterious, and so perplexing in all its particulars, was never before committed in Paris—if indeed a murder has been committed at all. The police are entirely at fault—an unusual occurrence in affairs of this nature. There is not, however, the shadow of a clew apparent."

The evening edition of the paper stated that the greatest excitement still continued in the Quartier St. Roch—that the premises in question had been carefully re-searched, and fresh examinations of witnesses instituted, but all to no purpose. A postscript, however, mentioned that Adolphe Le Bon had been arrested and imprisoned—although nothing appeared to criminate him, beyond the facts already detailed.

Dupin seemed singularly interested in the progress of this affair—at least so I judged from his manner, for he made no comments. It was only after the announcement that Le Bon had been imprisoned, that he asked me my opinion respecting the murders.

I could merely agree with all Paris in considering them an insoluble mystery. I saw no means by which it would be possible to trace the murderer.

"We must not judge of the means," said Dupin, "by this shell of an examination. The Parisian police, so much extolled for *acumen*, are cunning, but no more. There is no method in their proceedings, beyond the method of the moment. They make a vast parade of measures; but, not unfrequently, these are so ill adapted to the objects proposed, as to put us in mind of Monsieur Jourdain's calling for his *robe-de-chambre— pour mieux entendre la musique.* The results attained by them are not unfrequently surprising, but, for the most part, are brought about by simple diligence and activity. When these qualities are unavailing, their schemes fail. Vidocq, for example, was a good guesser, and a persevering man. But, without educated thought, he erred continually by the very intensity of his investigations. He impaired his vision by holding the object too close. He might see, perhaps, one or two points with unusual clearness, but in so doing he, necessarily, lost sight of the matter as a whole. Thus there is such a thing as being too profound. Truth is not always in a well. In fact, as regards the more important knowledge, I do believe that she is invariably superficial. The depth lies in the valleys where we seek her, and not upon the mountain-tops where she is found. The modes and sources of this kind of error are well typified in the contemplation of the heavenly bodies. To look at a star by glances—to view it in a side-long way, by turning toward it the exterior portions of the *retina* (more susceptible of feeble impressions of light than the interior), is to behold the star distinctly—is to have the best appreciation of its lustre—a lustre which grows dim just in proportion as we turn our vision *fully* upon it. A greater number of rays actually fall upon the eye in the latter case, but, in the former, there is the more refined capacity for comprehension. By undue profundity we perplex and enfeeble thought; and it is possible to make even Venus herself vanish from the firmament by a scrutiny too sustained, too concentrated, or too direct.

"As for these murders, let us enter into some examinations for ourselves, before we make up an opinion respecting them. An inquiry will afford us amusement," [I thought this an odd term, so applied, but said nothing] "and, besides, Le Bon once rendered me a service for which I am not ungrateful. We will go and see the premises with our own eyes. I know G——, the Prefect of Police, and shall have no difficulty in obtaining the necessary permission."

The permission was obtained, and we proceeded at once to the Rue Morgue. This is one of those miserable thoroughfares which intervene between the Rue Richelieu and the Rue St. Roch. It was late in the afternoon when we reached it; as this quarter is at a great distance from that in which we resided. The house was readily found; for there were still many persons gazing up at the closed shutters, with an objectless curiosity, from the opposite side of the way. It was an ordinary Parisian house, with a gateway, on one side of which was a glazed watch-box, with a sliding panel in the window, indicating a *loge de concierge*. Before going in we walked up the street, turned down an alley, and then, again turning, passed in the rear of the building—Dupin, meanwhile, examining the whole neighborhood, as well as the house, with a minuteness of attention for which I could see no possible object.

Retracing our steps, we came again to the front of the dwelling, rang, and, having shown our credentials, were admitted by the agents in charge. We went up stairs—into the chamber where the body of Mademoiselle L'Espanaye had been found, and where both the deceased still lay. The disorders of the room had, as usual, been suffered to exist. I saw nothing beyond what had been stated in the "Gazette des Tribunaux." Dupin scrutinized every thing—not excepting the bodies of the victims. We then went into the other rooms, and into the yard; a *gendarme* accompanying us throughout. The examination occupied us until dark, when we took our departure. On our way home my companion stepped in for a moment at the office of one of the daily papers.

I have said that the whims of my friend were manifold, and that *Je les ménageais:*—for this phrase there is no English equivalent. It was his humor, now, to decline all conversation on the subject of the murder, until about noon the next day. He then asked me, suddenly, if I had observed any thing *peculiar* at the scene of the atrocity.

There was something in his manner of emphasizing the word "peculiar," which caused me to shudder, without knowing why.

"No, nothing *peculiar*," I said; "nothing more, at least, than we both saw stated in the paper."

"The 'Gazette,'" he replied, "has not entered, I fear, into the unusual horror of the thing. But dismiss the idle opinions of this print. It appears to me that this mystery is considered insoluble, for the very reason which should cause it to be regarded as easy of solution—I mean for the *outré* character of its features. The police are confounded by the seeming absence of motive—not for the murder itself—but for the atrocity of the murder. They are puzzled, too, by the seeming impossibility of reconciling the voices heard in contention, with the facts that no one was discovered up stairs but the assassinated Mademoiselle L'Espanaye, and that there were no means of egress without the notice of the party ascending. The wild disorder of the room; the corpse thrust, with the head downward, up the chimney; the frightful mutilation of the body of the old lady; these considerations, with those just mentioned, and others which I need not mention, have sufficed to paralyze the powers, by putting completely at fault the boasted *acumen*, of the government agents. They have fallen into the gross but common error of confounding the unusual with the abstruse. But it is by these deviations from the plane of the ordinary, that reason feels its way, if at all, in its search for the true. In investigations such as we are now pursuing, it should not be so much asked 'what has occurred,' as 'what has occurred that has never occurred before.' In fact, the facility with which I shall arrive, or have arrived, at the solution of this mystery, is in the direct ratio of its apparent insolubility in the eyes of the police."

I stared at the speaker in mute astonishment.

"I am now awaiting," continued he, looking toward the door of our apartment—"I am now awaiting a person who, although perhaps not the perpetrator of these butcheries, must have been in some measure implicated in their perpetration. Of the worst portion of the crimes committed, it is probable that he is innocent. I hope that I am right in this supposition; for upon it I build my expectation of reading the entire riddle. I look for the man here—in this room—every moment. It is true that he may not arrive; but the probability is that he will. Should he come, it will be necessary to detain him. Here are pistols; and we both know how to use them when occasion demands their use."

I took the pistols, scarcely knowing what I did, or believing what I heard, while Dupin went on, very much as if in a soliloquy. I have already spoken of his abstract manner at such times. His discourse was addressed to myself; but his voice, although by no means loud, had that intonation which is commonly employed in speaking to some one at a great distance. His eyes, vacant in expression, regarded only the wall.

"That the voices heard in contention," he said, "by the party upon the stairs, were not the voices of the women themselves, was fully proved by the evidence. This relieves us of all doubt upon the question whether the old lady could have first destroyed the daughter, and afterward have committed suicide. I speak of this point chiefly for the sake of method; for the strength of Madame L'Espanaye would have been utterly unequal to the task of thrusting her daughter's corpse up the chimney as it was found; and the nature of the wounds upon her own person entirely preclude the idea of self-destruction. Murder, then, has been committed by some third party; and the voices of this third party were those heard in contention. Let me now advert—not to the whole testimony respecting these voices—but to what was *peculiar* in that testimony. Did you observe any thing peculiar about it?"

I remarked that, while all the witnesses agreed in supposing the gruff voice to be that of a Frenchman, there was much disagreement in regard to the shrill, or, as one individual termed it, the harsh voice.

"That was the evidence itself," said Dupin, "but it was not the peculiarity of the evidence. You have observed nothing distinctive. Yet there *was* something to be observed. The witnesses, as you remark, agreed about the gruff voice; they were here unanimous. But in regard to the shrill voice, the peculiarity is—not that they disagreed—but that, while an Italian, an Englishman, a Spaniard, a Hollander, and a Frenchman attempted to describe it, each one spoke of it as that *of a foreigner*. Each is sure that it was not the voice of one of his own countrymen. Each likens it—not to the voice of an individual of any nation with whose language he is conversant—but the converse. The Frenchman supposes it the voice of a Spaniard, and 'might have distinguished some words *had he been acquainted with the Spanish.*' The Dutchman maintains it to have been that of a Frenchman; but we find it stated that '*not understanding French this witness was examined through an interpreter.*' The Englishman thinks it the voice of a German, and '*does not understand German.*' The Spaniard 'is sure' that it was that of an Englishman, but 'judges by the intonation' altogether, '*as he has no knowledge of the English.*' The Italian believes it the voice of a Russian, but '*has never conversed with a native of Russia.*' A second Frenchman differs, moreover, with the first, and is positive that the voice was that of an Italian; but, *not being cognizant of that tongue*, is, like the Spaniard, 'convinced by the intonation.' Now, how strangely unusual must that voice have really been, about which such testimony as this *could* have been elicited!—in whose *tones*, even, denizens of the five great divisions of Europe could

26

recognise nothing familiar! You will say that it might have been the voice of an Asiatic—of an African. Neither Asiatics nor Africans abound in Paris; but, without denying the inference, I will now merely call your attention to three points. The voice is termed by one witness 'harsh rather than shrill.' It is represented by two others to have been 'quick and *unequal.*' No words—no sounds resembling words—were by any witness mentioned as distinguishable.

"I know not," continued Dupin, "what impression I may have made, so far, upon your own understanding; but I do not hesitate to say that legitimate deductions even from this portion of the testimony—the portion respecting the gruff and shrill voices—are in themselves sufficient to engender a suspicion which should give direction to all farther progress in the investigation of the mystery. I said 'legitimate deductions;' but my meaning is not thus fully expressed. I designed to imply that the deductions are the *sole* proper ones, and that the suspicion arises *inevitably* from them as the single result. What the suspicion is, however, I will not say just yet. I merely wish you to bear in mind that, with myself, it was sufficiently forcible to give a definite form—a certain tendency—to my inquiries in the chamber.

"Let us now transport ourselves, in fancy, to this chamber. What shall we first seek here? The means of egress employed by the murderers. It is not too much to say that neither of us believe in præternatural events. Madame and Mademoiselle L'Espanaye were not destroyed by spirits. The doers of the deed were material, and escaped materially. Then how? Fortunately, there is but one mode of reasoning upon the point, and that mode *must* lead us to a definite decision.—Let us examine, each by each, the possible means of egress. It is clear that the assassins were in the room where Mademoiselle L'Espanaye was found, or at least in the room adjoining, when the party ascended the stairs. It is then only from these two apartments that we have to seek issues. The police have laid bare the floors, the ceilings, and the masonry of the walls, in every direction. No *secret* issues could have escaped their vigilance. But, not trusting to *their* eyes, I examined with my own. There were, then, *no* secret issues. Both doors leading from the rooms into the passage were securely locked, with the keys inside. Let us turn to the chimneys. These, although of ordinary width for some eight or ten feet above the hearths, will not admit, throughout their extent, the body of a large cat. The impossibility of egress, by means already stated, being thus absolute, we are reduced to the windows. Through those of the front room no one could have escaped without notice from the crowd in the street. The murderers *must* have passed, then, through those of the back room. Now, brought to this conclusion in so unequivocal a manner as we are, it is not our part, as reasoners, to reject it on account of apparent impossibilities. It is only left for us to prove that these apparent 'impossibilities' are, in reality, not such.

"There are two windows in the chamber. One of them is unobstructed by furniture, and is wholly visible. The lower portion of the other is hidden from view by the head of the unwieldy bedstead which is thrust close up against it. The former was found securely fastened from within. It resisted the utmost force of those who endeavored to raise it. A large gimlet-hole had been pierced in its frame to the left, and a very stout nail was found fitted therein, nearly to the head. Upon examining the other window, a similar nail was seen similarly fitted in it; and a vigorous attempt to raise this sash failed also. The police were now entirely satisfied that egress had not been in these directions. And, *therefore*, it was thought a matter of supererogation to withdraw the nails and open the windows.

"My own examination was somewhat more particular, and was so for the reason I have just given—because here it was, I knew, that all apparent impossibilities *must* be proved to be not such in reality.

"I proceeded to think thus—*à posteriori*. The murderers *did* escape from one of these windows. This being so, they could not have refastened the sashes from the inside, as they were found fastened;—the consideration which put a stop, through its obviousness, to the scrutiny of the police in this quarter. Yet the sashes *were* fastened. They *must*, then, have the power of fastening themselves. There was no escape from this conclusion. I stepped to the unobstructed casement, withdrew the nail with some difficulty, and attempted to raise the sash. It resisted all my efforts, as I had anticipated. A concealed spring must, I now knew, exist; and this corroboration of my idea convinced me that my premises, at least, were correct, however mysterious still appeared the circumstances attending the nails. A careful search soon brought to light the hidden spring. I pressed it, and, satisfied with the discovery, forbore to upraise the sash.

"I now replaced the nail and regarded it attentively. A person passing out through this window might have reclosed it, and the spring would have caught—but the nail could not have been replaced. The conclusion was plain, and again narrowed in the field of my investigations. The assassins *must* have escaped through the other window. Supposing, then, the springs upon each sash to be the same, as was probable, there *must* be found a difference between the nails, or at least between the modes of their fixture. Getting upon the sacking of the bedstead, I looked over the head-board minutely at the second casement. Passing my hand down behind the board, I readily discovered and pressed the spring, which was, as I had supposed, identical in character with its neighbor. I now looked at the nail. It was as stout as the other, and apparently fitted in in the same manner—driven in nearly up to the head.

"You will say that I was puzzled; but, if you think so, you must have misunderstood the nature of the inductions. To use a sporting phrase, I had not been once 'at fault.' The scent had never for an instant been lost. There was no flaw in any link of the chain. I had traced the secret to its ultimate result,—and that result was *the nail*. It had, I say, in every respect, the appearance of its fellow in the other window; but this fact was an absolute nullity (conclusive as it might seem to be) when compared with the consideration that here, at this point, terminated the clew. 'There *must* be something wrong,' I said, 'about the nail.' I touched it; and the head, with about a quarter of an inch of the shank, came off in my fingers. The rest of the shank was in the gimlet-hole, where it had been broken off. The fracture was an old one (for its edges were encrusted with rust), and had apparently been accomplished by the blow of a hammer, which had partially imbedded, in the top of the bottom sash, the head portion of the nail. I now carefully replaced this head portion in the indentation whence I had taken it, and the resemblance to a perfect nail was complete—the fissure was invisible. Pressing the spring, I gently raised the sash for a few inches; the head went up with it, remaining firm in its bed. I closed the window, and the semblance of the whole nail was again perfect.

"The riddle, so far, was now unriddled. The assassin had escaped through the window which looked upon the bed. Dropping of its own accord upon his exit (or perhaps purposely closed), it had become fastened by the spring; and it was the retention of this spring which had been mistaken by the police for that of the nail,—farther inquiry being thus considered unnecessary.

"The next question is that of the mode of descent. Upon this point I had been satisfied in my walk with you around the building. About five feet and a half from the casement in question there runs a lightning-rod. From this rod it would have been impossible for any one to reach the window itself, to say nothing of entering it. I observed, however, that the shutters of the fourth story were of the peculiar kind called by Parisian carpenters *ferrades*—a kind rarely employed at the present day, but frequently seen upon very old mansions at Lyons and Bourdeaux. They are in the form of an ordinary door, (a single, not a folding door) except that the upper half is latticed or worked in open trellis—thus affording an excellent hold for the hands. In the present instance these shutters are fully three feet and a half broad. When we saw them from the rear of the house, they were both about half open—that is to say, they stood off at right angles from the wall. It is probable that the police, as well as myself, examined the back of the tenement; but, if so, in looking at these *ferrades* in the line of their breadth (as they must have done), they did not perceive this great breadth itself, or, at all events, failed to take it into due consideration. In fact, having once satisfied themselves that no egress could have been made in this quarter, they would naturally bestow here a very cursory examination. It was clear to me, however, that the shutter belonging to the window at the head of the bed, would, if swung fully back to the wall, reach to within two feet of the lightning-rod. It was also evident that, by exertion of a very unusual degree of activity and courage, an entrance into the window, from the rod, might have been thus effected.—By reaching to the distance of two feet and a half (we now suppose the shutter open to its whole extent) a robber might have taken a firm grasp upon the trellis-work. Letting go, then, his hold upon the rod, placing his feet securely against the wall, and springing boldly from it, he might have swung the shutter so as to close it, and, if we imagine the window open at the time, might even have swung himself into the room.

"I wish you to bear especially in mind that I have spoken of a *very* unusual degree of activity as requisite to success in so hazardous and so difficult a feat. It is my design to show you, first, that the thing might possibly have been accomplished:—but, secondly and *chiefly*, I wish to impress upon your understanding the *very extraordinary*—the almost præternatural character of that agility which could have accomplished it.

"You will say, no doubt, using the language of the law, that 'to make out my case,' I should rather undervalue, than insist upon a full estimation of the activity required in this matter. This may be the practice in law, but it is not the usage of reason. My ultimate object is only the truth. My immediate purpose is to lead you to place in juxtaposition, that *very unusual* activity of which I have just spoken, with that *very peculiar* shrill (or harsh) and *unequal* voice, about whose nationality no two persons could be found to agree, and in whose utterance no syllabification could be detected."

At these words a vague and half-formed conception of the meaning of Dupin flitted over my mind. I seemed to be upon the verge of comprehension, without power to comprehend—as men, at times, find themselves upon the brink of remembrance, without being able, in the end, to remember. My friend went on with his discourse.

"You will see," he said, "that I have shifted the question from the mode of egress to that of ingress. It was my design to suggest the idea that both were effected in the same manner, at the same point. Let us now revert to the interior of the room. Let us survey the appearances here. The drawers of the bureau, it is said, had been rifled, although many articles of apparel still remained within them. The conclusion here is absurd. It is a mere guess—a very silly one—and no more. How are we to know that the articles found in the drawers were not all these drawers had originally contained? Madame L'Espanaye and her daughter lived an exceedingly retired life—saw no company—seldom went out—had little use for numerous changes of habiliment. Those found were at least of as good quality as any likely to be possessed by these ladies. If a thief had taken any, why did he not take the best—why did he not take all? In a word, why did he abandon four thousand francs in gold to encumber himself with a bundle of linen? The gold *was* abandoned. Nearly the whole sum mentioned by Monsieur Mignaud, the banker, was discovered, in bags, upon the floor. I wish you, therefore, to discard from your thoughts the blundering idea of *motive*, engendered in the brains of the police by that portion of the evidence which speaks of money delivered at the door of the house. Coincidences ten times as remarkable as this (the delivery of the money, and murder committed within three days upon the party receiving it), happen to all of us every hour of our lives, without attracting even momentary notice. Coincidences, in general, are great stumbling-blocks in the way of that class of thinkers who have been educated to know nothing of the theory of probabilities—that theory to which the most glorious objects of human research are indebted for the most glorious of illustration. In the present instance, had the gold been gone, the fact of its delivery three days before would have formed something more than a coincidence. It would have been corroborative of this idea of motive. But, under the real circumstances of the case, if we are to suppose gold the motive of this outrage, we must also imagine the perpetrator so vacillating an idiot as to have abandoned his gold and his motive together.

"Keeping now steadily in mind the points to which I have drawn your attention—that peculiar voice, that unusual agility, and that startling absence of motive in a murder so singularly atrocious as this—let us glance at the butchery itself. Here is a woman strangled to death by manual strength, and thrust up a chimney, head downward. Ordinary assassins employ no such modes of murder as this. Least of all, do they thus dispose of the murdered. In the manner of thrusting the corpse up the chimney, you will admit that there was something *excessively outré*—something altogether irreconcilable with our common notions of human action, even when we suppose the actors the most depraved of men. Think, too, how great must have been that strength which could have thrust the body *up* such an aperture so forcibly that the united vigor of several persons was found barely sufficient to drag it *down!*

"Turn, now, to other indications of the employment of a vigor most marvellous. On the hearth were thick tresses—very thick tresses—of grey human hair. These had been torn out by the roots. You are aware of the great force necessary in tearing thus from the head even twenty or thirty hairs together. You saw the locks in question as well as myself. Their roots (a hideous sight!) were clotted with fragments of the flesh of the scalp—sure token of the prodigious power which had been exerted in uprooting perhaps half a million of hairs at a time. The throat of the old lady was not merely cut, but the head absolutely severed from the body: the instrument was a mere razor. I wish you also to look at the *brutal* ferocity of these deeds. Of the bruises upon the body of Madame L'Espanaye I do not speak. Monsieur Dumas, and his worthy coadjutor Monsieur Etienne, have pronounced that they were inflicted by some obtuse instrument; and so far these gentlemen are very correct. The obtuse instrument was clearly the stone pavement in the yard, upon which the victim had fallen from the window which looked in upon the bed. This idea, however simple it may now seem, escaped the police for the same reason that the breadth of the shutters escaped them—because, by the affair of the nails, their perceptions had been hermetically sealed against the possibility of the windows having ever been opened at all.

"If now, in addition to all these things, you have properly reflected upon the odd disorder of the chamber, we have gone so far as to combine the ideas of an agility astounding, a strength superhuman, a ferocity brutal, a butchery without motive, a *grotesquerie* in horror absolutely alien from humanity, and a voice foreign in tone to the ears of men of many nations, and devoid of all distinct or intelligible syllabification. What result, then, has ensued? What impression have I made upon your fancy?"

I felt a creeping of the flesh as Dupin asked me the question. "A madman," I said, "has done this deed—some raving maniac, escaped from a neighboring *Maison de Santé.*"

"In some respects," he replied, "your idea is not irrelevant. But the voices of madmen, even in their wildest paroxysms, are never found to tally with that peculiar voice heard upon the stairs. Madmen are of some nation, and their language, however incoherent in its words, has always the coherence of syllabification. Besides, the hair of a madman is not such as I now hold in my hand. I disentangled this little tuft from the rigidly clutched fingers of Madame L'Espanaye. Tell me what you can make of it."

"Dupin!" I said, completely unnerved; "this hair is most unusual—this is no *human* hair."

"I have not asserted that it is," said he; "but, before we decide this point, I wish you to glance at the little sketch I have here traced upon this paper. It is a *fac-simile* drawing of what has been described in one portion of the testimony as 'dark bruises, and deep indentations of finger nails,' upon the throat of Mademoiselle L'Espanaye, and in another, (by Messrs. Dumas and Etienne,) as a 'series of livid spots, evidently the impression of fingers.'

"You will perceive," continued my friend, spreading out the paper upon the table before us, "that this drawing gives the idea of a firm and fixed hold. There is no *slipping* apparent. Each finger has retained—possibly until the death of the victim—the fearful grasp by which it originally imbedded itself. Attempt, now, to place all your fingers, at the same time, in the respective impressions as you see them."

I made the attempt in vain.

"We are possibly not giving this matter a fair trial," he said. "The paper is spread out upon a plane surface; but the human throat is cylindrical. Here is a billet of wood, the circumference of which is about that of the throat. Wrap the drawing around it, and try the experiment again."

I did so; but the difficulty was even more obvious than before. "This," I said, "is the mark of no human hand."

"Read now, replied Dupin, "this passage from Cuvier."

It was a minute anatomical and generally descriptive account of the large fulvous Ourang-Outang of the East Indian Islands. The gigantic stature, the prodigious strength and activity, the wild ferocity, and the imitative propensities of these mammalia are sufficiently well known to all. I understood the full horrors of the murder at once.

"The description of the digits," said I, as I made an end of reading, "is in exact accordance with this drawing. I see that no animal but an Ourang-Outang, of the species here mentioned, could have impressed the indentations as you have traced them. This tuft of tawny hair, too, is identical in character with that of the beast of Cuvier. But I cannot possibly comprehend the particulars of this frightful mystery. Besides, there were *two* voices heard in contention, and one of them was unquestionably the voice of a Frenchman."

"True; and you will remember an expression attributed almost unanimously, by the evidence, to this voice,—the expression 'mon Dieu!' This, under the circumstances, has been justly characterized by one of the witnesses (Montani, the confectioner,) as an expression of remonstrance or expostulation. Upon these two words, therefore, I have mainly built my hopes of a full solution of the riddle. A Frenchman was cognizant of the murder. It is possible—indeed it is far more than probable—that he was innocent of all participation in the bloody transactions which took place. The Ourang-Outang may have escaped from him. He may have traced it to the chamber; but, under the agitating circumstances which ensued, he could never have re-captured it. It is still at large. I will not pursue these guesses—for I have no right to call them more—since the shades of reflection upon which they are based are scarcely of sufficient depth to be appreciable by my own intellect, and since I could not pretend to make them intelligible to the understanding of another. We will call them guesses then, and speak of them as such. If the Frenchman in question is indeed, as I suppose, innocent of this atrocity, this advertisement, which I left last night, upon our return home, at the office of 'Le Monde,' (a paper devoted to the shipping interest, and much sought by sailors,) will bring him to our residence."

He handed me a paper, and I read thus:

CAUGHT—In the Bois de Boulogne, early in the morning of the —— inst., (the morning of the murder,) a very large, tawny Ourang-Outang of the Bornese species. The owner, (who is ascertained to be a sailor, belonging to a Maltese vessel,) may have the animal again, upon identifying it satisfactorily, and paying a few charges arising from its capture and keeping. Call at No. ——, Rue ——, Faubourg St. Germain—au troisième.

"How was it possible," I asked, "that you should know the man to be a sailor, and belonging to a Maltese vessel?"

"I do *not* know it," said Dupin. "I am not *sure* of it. Here, however, is a small piece of ribbon, which from its form and from its greasy appearance, has evidently been used in tying the hair in one of those long *queues* of which sailors are so fond. Moreover, this knot is one which few besides sailors can tie, and is peculiar to the Maltese. I picked the ribbon up at the foot of the lightning-rod. It could not have belonged to either of the deceased. Now if, after all, I am wrong in my induction from this ribbon, that the Frenchman was a sailor belonging to a Maltese vessel, still I can have done no harm in saying what I did in the advertisement. If I am in error, he will merely suppose that I have been misled by some circumstance into which he will not take the trouble to inquire. But if I am right, a great point is gained. Cognizant although innocent of the murder, the Frenchman will naturally hesitate about replying to the advertisement—about demanding the Ourang-Outang. He will reason thus: 'I am innocent; I am poor; my Ourang-Outang is of great value—to one in my circumstances a fortune of itself—why should I lose it through idle apprehensions of danger? Here it is, within my grasp. It was found in the Bois de Boulogne—at a vast distance from the scene of that butchery. How can it ever be suspected that a brute beast should have done the deed? The police are at fault—they have failed to procure the slightest clew. Should they even trace the animal, it would be impossible to prove me cognizant of the murder, or to implicate me in guilt on account of that cognizance. Above all, *I am known*. The advertiser designates me as the possessor of the beast. I am not sure to what limit his knowledge may extend. Should I avoid claiming a property of so great value, which it is known that I possess, I will render the animal at least, liable to suspicion. It is not my policy to attract attention either to myself or to the beast. I will answer the advertisement, get the Ourang-Outang, and keep it close until this matter has blown over.'"

At this moment we heard a step upon the stairs.

"Be ready," said Dupin, "with your pistols, but neither use them nor show them until at a signal from myself."

The front door of the house had been left open, and the visiter had entered, without ringing, and advanced several steps upon the staircase. Now, however, he seemed to hesitate. Presently we heard him descending. Dupin was moving quickly to the door, when we again heard him coming up. He did not turn back a second time, but stepped up with decision, and rapped at the door of our chamber.

"Come in," said Dupin, in a cheerful and hearty tone.

A man entered. He was a sailor, evidently,—a tall, stout, and muscular-looking person, with a certain dare-devil expression of countenance, not altogether unprepossessing. His face, greatly sunburnt, was more than half hidden by whisker and *mustachio*. He had with him a huge oaken cudgel, but appeared to be otherwise unarmed. He bowed awkwardly, and bade us "good evening," in French accents, which, although somewhat Neufchatel-ish, were still sufficiently indicative of a Parisian origin.

"Sit down, my friend," said Dupin. "I suppose you have called about the Ourang-Outang. Upon my word, I almost envy you the possession of him; a remarkably fine, and no doubt a very valuable animal. How old do you suppose him to be?"

The sailor drew a long breath, with the air of a man relieved of some intolerable burden, and then replied, in an assured tone:

"I have no way of telling—but he can't be more than four or five years old. Have you got him here?"

"Oh no; we had no conveniences for keeping him here. He is at a livery stable in the Rue Dubourg, just by. You can get him in the morning. Of course you are prepared to identify the property?"

"To be sure I am, sir."

"I shall be sorry to part with him," said Dupin.

"I don't mean that you should be at all this trouble for nothing, sir," said the man. "Couldn't expect it. Am very willing to pay a reward for the finding of the animal—that is to say, any thing in reason."

"Well," replied my friend, "that is all very fair, to be sure. Let me think!—what should I have? Oh! I will tell you. My reward shall be this. You shall give me all the information in your power about these murders in the Rue Morgue."

Dupin said the last words in a very low tone, and very quietly. Just as quietly, too, he walked toward the door, locked it, and put the key in his pocket. He then drew a pistol from his bosom and placed it, without the least flurry, upon the table.

The sailor's face flushed up as if he were struggling with suffocation. He started to his feet and grasped his cudgel; but the next moment he fell back into his seat, trembling violently, and with the countenance of death itself. He spoke not a word. I pitied him from the bottom of my heart.

"My friend," said Dupin, in a kind tone, "you are alarming yourself unnecessarily—you are indeed. We mean you no harm whatever. I pledge you the honor of a gentleman, and of a Frenchman, that we intend you no injury. I perfectly well know that you are innocent of the atrocities in the Rue Morgue. It will not do, however, to deny that you are in some measure implicated in them. From what I have already said, you must know that I have had means of information about this matter—means of which you could never have dreamed. Now the thing stands thus. You have done nothing which you could have avoided—nothing, certainly, which renders you culpable. You were not even guilty of robbery, when you might have robbed with impunity. You have nothing to conceal. You have no reason for concealment. On the other hand, you are bound by every principle of honor to confess all you know. An innocent man is now imprisoned, charged with that crime of which you can point out the perpetrator."

The sailor had recovered his presence of mind, in a great measure, while Dupin uttered these words; but his original boldness of bearing was all gone.

"So help me God," said he, after a brief pause, "I *will* tell you all I know about this affair;—but I do not expect you to believe one half I say—I would be a fool indeed if I did. Still, I *am* innocent, and I will make a clean breast if I die for it."

What he stated was, in substance, this. He had lately made a voyage to the Indian Archipelago. A party, of which he formed one, landed at Borneo, and passed into the interior on an excursion of pleasure. Himself and a companion had captured the Ourang-Outang. This companion dying, the animal fell into his own exclusive possession. After great trouble, occasioned by the intractable ferocity of his captive during the home voyage, he at length succeeded in lodging it safely at his own residence in Paris, where, not to attract toward himself the unpleasant curiosity of his neighbors, he kept it carefully secluded, until such time as it should recover from a wound in the foot, received from a splinter on board ship. His ultimate design was to sell it.

Returning home from some sailors' frolic on the night, or rather in the morning of the murder, he found the beast occupying his own bedroom, into which it had broken from a closet adjoining, where it had been, as was thought, securely confined. Razor in hand, and fully lathered, it was sitting before a looking-glass, attempting the operation of shaving, in which it had no doubt previously watched its master through the key-hole of the closet. Terrified at the sight of so dangerous a weapon in the possession of an animal so ferocious, and so well able to use it, the man, for some moments, was at a loss what to do. He had been accustomed, however, to quiet the creature, even in its fiercest moods, by the use of a whip, and to this he now resorted. Upon sight of it, the Ourang-Outang sprang at once through the door of the chamber, down the stairs, and thence, through a window, unfortunately open, into the street.

The Frenchman followed in despair; the ape, razor still in hand, occasionally stopping to look back and gesticulate at its pursuer, until the latter had nearly come up with it. It then again made off. In this manner the chase continued for a long time. The streets were profoundly quiet, as it was nearly three o'clock in the morning. In passing down an alley in the rear of the Rue Morgue, the fugitive's attention was arrested by a light gleaming from the open window of Madame L'Espanaye's chamber, in the fourth story of her house. Rushing to the building, it perceived the lightning-rod, clambered up with inconceivable agility, grasped the shutter, which was thrown fully back against the wall, and, by its means, swung itself directly upon the headboard of the bed. The whole feat did not occupy a minute. The shutter was kicked open again by the Ourang-Outang as it entered the room.

The sailor, in the meantime, was both rejoiced and perplexed. He had strong hopes of now recapturing the brute, as it could scarcely escape from the trap into which it had ventured, except by the rod, where it might be intercepted as it came down. On the other hand, there was cause for anxiety as to what it might do in the house. This latter reflection urged the man still to follow the fugitive. A lightning-rod is ascended without difficulty, especially by a sailor; but, when he had arrived as high as the window, which lay far to his left, his career was stopped; the most that he could accomplish was to reach over so as to obtain a glimpse of the interior of the room. At this glimpse he nearly fell from his hold through excess of horror. Now it was that those hideous shrieks arose upon the night, which had startled from slumber the inmates of the Rue Morgue. Madame L'Espanaye and her daughter, habited in their night clothes, had apparently been occupied in arranging some papers in the iron chest already mentioned, which had been wheeled into the middle of the room. It was open, and its contents lay beside it on the floor. The victims must have been sitting with their backs toward the window; and, from the time elapsing between the ingress of the beast and the screams, it seems probable that it was not immediately perceived. The flapping-to of the shutter would naturally have been attributed to the wind.

As the sailor looked in, the gigantic animal had seized Madame L'Espanaye by the hair, (which was loose, as she had been combing it,) and was flourishing the razor about her face, in imitation of the motions of a barber. The daughter lay prostrate and motionless; she had swooned. The screams and struggles of the old lady (during which the hair was torn from her head) had the effect of changing the probably pacific purposes of the Ourang-Outang into those of wrath. With one determined sweep of its muscular arm it nearly severed her head from her body. The sight of blood inflamed its anger into phrenzy. Gnashing its teeth, and flashing fire from its eyes, it flew upon the body of the girl, and imbedded its fearful talons in her throat, retaining its grasp until she expired. Its wandering and wild glances fell at this moment upon the head of the bed, over which the face of its master, rigid with horror, was just discernible. The fury of the beast, who no doubt bore still in mind the dreaded whip, was instantly converted into fear. Conscious of having deserved punishment, it seemed desirous of concealing its bloody deeds, and skipped about the chamber in an agony of nervous agitation; throwing down and breaking the furniture as it moved, and dragging the bed from the bedstead. In conclusion, it seized first the corpse of the daughter, and thrust it up the chimney, as it was found; then that of the old lady, which it immediately hurled through the window headlong.

As the ape approached the casement with its mutilated burden, the sailor shrank aghast to the rod, and, rather gliding than clambering down it, hurried at once home—dreading the consequences of the butchery, and gladly abandoning, in his terror, all solicitude about the fate of the Ourang-Outang. The words heard by the party upon the staircase were the Frenchman's exclamations of horror and affright, commingled with the fiendish jabberings of the brute.

I have scarcely anything to add. The Ourang-Outang must have escaped from the chamber, by the rod, just before the breaking of the door. It must have closed the window as it passed through it. It was subsequently caught by the owner himself, who obtained for it a very large sum at the *Jardin des Plantes*. Le Bon was instantly released, upon our narration of the circumstances (with some comments from Dupin) at the *bureau* of the Prefect of Police. This functionary, however well disposed to my friend, could not altogether conceal his chagrin at the turn which affairs had taken, and was fain to indulge in a sarcasm or two, about the propriety of every person minding his own business.

"Let him talk," said Dupin, who had not thought it necessary to reply. "Let him discourse; it will ease his conscience. I am satisfied with having defeated him in his own castle. Nevertheless, that he failed in the solution of this mystery, is by no means that matter for wonder which he supposes it; for, in truth, our friend the Prefect is somewhat too cunning to be profound. In his wisdom is no *stamen*. It is all head and no body, like the pictures of the Goddess Laverna,—or, at best, all head and shoulders, like a codfish. But he is a good creature after all. I like him especially for one master stroke of cant, by which he has attained his reputation for ingenuity. I mean the way he has *'de nier ce qui est, et d'expliquer ce qui n'est pas.'"*

*Rousseau, *Nouvelle Heloise*.

BRET HARTE

(1836–1902)

‖‖‖ ■ ‖‖‖

It may at first seem surprising that the writer best known for putting the California of Gold Rush days on the literary map also produced "The Stolen Cigar Case," a story widely regarded as the quintessential Sherlockian parody. But Bret Harte, who also did a great deal to establish the formula used in Westerns to this day, was a master of generic conventions and a skilled editor and literary critic. This story, and others collected in two volumes of *Condensed Novels*, were written to indulge Harte's passion for critiquing the very conventions that were the mainstays of his and other writers' popular success.

Born Francis Bret Harte in Albany, New York, in 1836, he was a precocious child who at the age of five burlesqued his school primers. He was raised in the eastern United States, where he moved from school to school according to his father's varying ability to pay tuition. His father changed the family name to Harte a year before he died. Soon afterward, the teenage Harte began to support himself, establishing a lifelong pattern of moving from job to job while pursuing his writing.

At the age of eighteen, Harte joined his remarried mother in California, where he was to spend the next sixteen years of his life. His first six years out west were not successful in terms of either literary or ordinary employment. But in drifting from job to job and dabbling in experiences like riding shotgun on a stagecoach and tutoring ranchers' children, he gathered a wealth of material that he would mine for years as he put "Bret Harte Country" on the literary map.

Harte's connections with literary journals and newspapers ranged from writing for them to physically printing them. He simultaneously lost his job and made a name for himself when, in February 1860, he strongly editorialized about a massacre of Indians perpetrated by whites. Left in charge of the *Northern Californian* while the editor was away, he printed such bold statements about a rival paper and the local sheriff that he was fired within the month.

In his nonfiction and lectures, Harte revealed that he despised the corruption and lawlessness of the very world in which he chose to set his fiction. In his literary criticism, he disdained the use of formula and stock characters while unabashedly using both to his advantage in his highly popular fiction.

If "The Stolen Cigar Case" is one of Harte's most lasting gems, it may be because in it he could dissect and use to his advantage both formula and someone else's stock characters. And at the same time he could indulge a bad boy's sense of play.

1900

The Stolen Cigar Case

■

I found Hemlock Jones in the old Brook Street lodgings, musing before the fire. With the freedom of an old friend I at once threw myself in my usual familiar attitude at his feet, and gently caressed his boot. I was induced to do this for two reasons: one, that it enabled me to get a good look at his bent, concentrated face, and the other, that it seemed to indicate my reverence for his superhuman insight. So absorbed was he even then, in tracking some mysterious clue, that he did not seem to notice me. But therein I was wrong—as I always was in my attempt to understand that powerful intellect.

"It is raining," he said, without lifting his head.

"You have been out, then?" I said quickly.

"No. But I see that your umbrella is wet, and that your overcoat has drops of water on it."

I sat aghast at his penetration. After a pause he said carelessly, as if dismissing the subject: "Besides, I hear the rain on the window. Listen."

I listened. I could scarcely credit my ears, but there was the soft pattering of drops on the panes. It was evident there was no deceiving this man!

"Have you been busy lately?" I asked, changing the subject. "What new problem—given up by Scotland Yard as inscrutable—has occupied that gigantic intellect?"

He drew back his foot slightly, and seemed to hesitate ere he returned it to its original position. Then he answered wearily: "Mere trifles—nothing to speak of. The Prince Kupoli has been here to get my advice regarding the disappearance of certain rubies from the Kremlin; the Rajah of Pootibad, after vainly beheading his entire bodyguard, has been obliged to seek my assistance to recover a jeweled sword. The Grand Duchess of Pretzel-Brauntswig is desirous of discovering where her husband was on the night of February 14; and last night"—he lowered his voice slightly—"a lodger in this very house, meeting me on the stairs, wanted to know why they didn't answer his bell."

I could not help smiling—until I saw a frown gathering on his inscrutable forehead.

"Pray remember," he said coldly, "that it was through such an apparently trivial question that I found out Why Paul Ferroll Killed His Wife, and What Happened to Jones!"

I became dumb at once. He paused for a moment, and then sud-

41

denly changing back to his usual pitiless, analytical style, he said: "When I say these are trifles, they are so in comparison to an affair that is now before me. A crime has been committed,—and, singularly enough, against myself. You start," he said. "You wonder who would have dared to attempt it. So did I; nevertheless, it has been done. *I* have been *robbed!*"

"*You* robbed! You, Hemlock Jones, the Terror of Peculators!" I gasped in amazement, arising and gripping the table as I faced him.

"Yes! Listen. I would confess it to no other. But *you* who have followed my career, who know my methods; you, for whom I have partly lifted the veil that conceals my plans from ordinary humanity,—you, who have for years rapturously accepted my confidences, passionately admired my inductions and inferences, placed yourself at my beck and call, become my slave, groveled at my feet, given up your practice except those few unremunerative and rapidly decreasing patients to whom, in moments of abstraction over *my* problems, you have administered strychnine for quinine and arsenic for Epsom salts; you, who have sacrificed anything and everybody to me,—*you* I make my confidant!"

I arose and embraced him warmly, yet he was already so engrossed in thought that at the same moment he mechanically placed his hand upon his watch chain as if to consult the time. "Sit down," he said. "Have a cigar?"

"I have given up cigar smoking," I said.

"Why?" he asked.

I hesitated, and perhaps colored. I had really given it up because, with my diminished practice, it was too expensive. I could afford only a pipe. "I prefer a pipe," I said laughingly. "But tell me of this robbery. What have you lost?"

He arose, and planting himself before the fire with his hands under his coattails, looked down upon me reflectively for a moment. "Do you remember the cigar case presented to me by the Turkish Ambassador for discovering the missing favorite of the Grand Vizier in the fifth chorus girl at the Hilarity Theatre? It was that one. I mean the cigar case. It was incrusted with diamonds."

"And the largest one had been supplanted by paste," I said.

"Ah," he said, with a reflective smile, "you know that?"

"You told me yourself. I remember considering it a proof of your extraordinary perception. But, by Jove, you don't mean to say you have lost it?"

He was silent for a moment. "No; it has been stolen, it is true, but I shall still find it. And by myself alone! In your profession, my dear fellow, when a member is seriously ill, he does not prescribe for himself, but calls in a brother doctor. Therein we differ. I shall take this matter in my own hands."

"And where could you find better?" I said enthusiastically. "I should say the cigar case is as good as recovered already."

"I shall remind you of that again," he said lightly. "And now, to show you my confidence in your judgment, in spite of my determination to pursue this alone, I am willing to listen to any suggestions from you."

He drew a memorandum book from his pocket and, with a grave smile, took up his pencil.

I could scarcely believe my senses. He, the great Hemlock Jones, accepting suggestions from a humble individual like myself! I kissed his hand reverently, and began in a joyous tone:

"First, I should advertise, offering a reward; I should give the same intimation in hand-bills, distributed at the 'pubs' and the pastry-cooks'. I should next visit the different pawnbrokers; I should give notice at the police station. I should examine the servants. I should thoroughly search the house and my own pockets. I speak relatively," I added, with a laugh. "Of course I mean *your* own."

He gravely made an entry of these details.

"Perhaps," I added, "you have already done this?"

"Perhaps," he returned enigmatically.

"Now, my dear friend," he continued, putting the note-book in his pocket and rising, "would you excuse me for a few moments? Make yourself perfectly at home until I return; there may be some things," he added with a sweep of his hand toward his heterogeneously filled shelves, "that may interest you and while away the time. There are pipes and tobacco in that corner."

Then nodding to me with the same inscrutable face he left the room. I was too well accustomed to his methods to think much of his unceremonious withdrawal, and made no doubt he was off to investigate some clue which had suddenly occurred to his active intelligence.

Left to myself I cast a cursory glance over his shelves. There were a number of small glass jars containing earthy substances, labeled "Pavement and Road Sweepings," from the principal thoroughfares and suburbs of London, with the sub-directions "for identifying foot-tracks." There were several other jars, labeled "Fluff from Omnibus and Road Car Seats," "Cocoanut Fibre and Rope Strands from Mattings in Public Places," "Cigarette Stumps and Match Ends from Floor of Palace Theatre, Row A, 1 to 50." Everywhere were evidences of this wonderful man's system and perspicacity.

I was thus engaged when I heard the slight creaking of a door, and

I looked up as a stranger entered. He was a rough-looking man, with a shabby overcoat and a still more disreputable muffler around his throat and the lower part of his face. Considerably annoyed at his intrusion, I turned upon him rather sharply, when, with a mumbled, growling apology for mistaking the room, he shuffled out again and closed the door. I followed him quickly to the landing and saw that he disappeared down the stairs. With my mind full of the robbery, the incident made a singular impression upon me. I knew my friend's habit of hasty absences from his room in his moments of deep inspiration; it was only too probable that, with his powerful intellect and magnificent perceptive genius concentrated on one subject, he should be careless of his own belongings, and no doubt even forget to take the ordinary precaution of locking up his drawers. I tried one or two and found that I was right, although for some reason I was unable to open one to its fullest extent. The handles were sticky, as if some one had opened them with dirty fingers. Knowing Hemlock's fastidious cleanliness, I resolved to inform him of this circumstance, but I forgot it, alas! until—but I am anticipating my story.

His absence was strangely prolonged. I at last seated myself by the fire, and lulled by warmth and the patter of the rain on the window, I fell asleep. I may have dreamt, for during my sleep I had a vague semi-consciousness as of hands being softly pressed on my pockets—no doubt induced by the story of the robbery. When I came fully to my senses, I found Hemlock Jones sitting on the other side of the hearth, his deeply concentrated gaze fixed on the fire.

"I found you so comfortably asleep that I could not bear to awaken you," he said, with a smile.

I rubbed my eyes. "And what news?" I asked. "How have you succeeded?"

"Better than I expected," he said, "and I think," he added, tapping his note-book, "I owe much to *you*."

Deeply gratified, I awaited more. But in vain. I ought to have remembered that in his moods Hemlock Jones was reticence itself. I told him simply of the strange intrusion, but he only laughed.

Later, when I arose to go, he looked at me playfully. "If you were a married man," he said, "I would advise you not to go home until you had brushed your sleeve. There are a few short brown sealskin hairs on the inner side of your forearm, just where they would have adhered if your arm had encircled a sealskin coat with some pressure!"

"For once you are at fault," I said triumphantly; "the hair is my own, as you will perceive; I have just had it cut at the hairdresser's, and no doubt this arm projected beyond the apron."

He frowned slightly, yet, nevertheless, on my turning to go he embraced me warmly—a rare exhibition in that man of ice. He even helped me on with my overcoat and pulled out and smoothed down the flaps of my pockets. He was particular, too, in fitting my arm in my overcoat sleeve, shaking the sleeve down from the armhole to the cuff with his deft fingers. "Come again soon!" he said, clapping me on the back.

"At any and all times," I said enthusiastically; "I only ask ten minutes twice a day to eat a crust at my office, and four hours' sleep at night, and the rest of my time is devoted to you always, as you know."

"It is indeed," he said, with his impenetrable smile.

Nevertheless, I did not find him at home when I next called. One afternoon, when nearing my own home, I met him in one of his favorite disguises,—a long blue swallow-tailed coat, striped cotton trousers, large turn-over collar, blacked face, and white hat, carrying a tambourine. Of course to others the disguise was perfect, although it was known to myself, and I passed him—according to an old understanding between us—without the slightest recognition, trusting to a later explanation. At another time, as I was making a professional visit to the wife of a publican at the East End, I saw him, in the disguise of a broken-down artisan, looking into the window of an adjacent pawnshop. I was delighted to see that he was evidently following my suggestions, and in my joy I ventured to tip him a wink; it was abstractedly returned.

Two days later I received a note appointing a meeting at his lodgings that night. That meeting, alas! was the one memorable occurrence of my life, and the last meeting I ever had with Hemlock Jones! I will try to set it down calmly, though my pulses still throb with the recollection of it.

I found him standing before the fire, with that look upon his face which I had seen only once or twice in our acquaintance—a look which I may call an absolute concatenation of inductive and deductive ratiocination—from which all that was human, tender, or sympathetic was absolutely discharged. He was simply an icy algebraic symbol! Indeed, his whole being was concentrated to that extent that his clothes fitted loosely, and his head was absolutely so much reduced in size by his mental compression that his hat tipped back from his forehead and literally hung on his massive ears.

After I had entered he locked the doors, fastened the windows, and even placed a chair before the chimney. As I watched these significant precautions with absorbing interest, he suddenly drew a revolver and, presenting it to my temple, said in low, icy tones:

"Hand over that cigar case!"

Even in my bewilderment my reply was truthful, spontaneous, and involuntary.

"I haven't got it," I said.

He smiled bitterly, and threw down his revolver. "I expected that reply! Then let me now confront you with something more awful, more deadly, more relentless and convincing than that mere lethal weapon,— the damning inductive and deductive proofs of your guilt!" He drew from his pocket a roll of paper and a note-book.

"But surely," I gasped, "you are joking! You could not for a moment believe—"

"Silence! Sit down!" I obeyed.

"You have condemned yourself," he went on pitilessly. "Condemned yourself on my processes,—processes familiar to you, applauded by you, accepted by you for years! We will go back to the time when you first saw the cigar case. Your expressions," he said in cold, deliberate tones, consulting his paper, were, 'How beautiful! I wish it were mine.' This was your first step in crime—and my first indication. From 'I *wish* it were mine' to 'I *will* have it mine,' and the mere detail, '*How can* I make it mine?' the advance was obvious. Silence! But as in my methods it was necessary that there should be an overwhelming inducement to the crime, that unholy admiration of yours for the mere trinket itself was not enough. You are a smoker of cigars."

"But," I burst out passionately, "I told you I had given up smoking cigars."

"Fool!" he said coldly, "that is the *second* time you have committed yourself. Of course you told me! What more natural than for you to blazon forth that prepared and unsolicited statement to *prevent* accusation. Yet, as I said before, even that wretched attempt to cover up your tracks was not enough. I still had to find that overwhelming, impelling motive necessary to affect a man like you. That motive I found in the strongest of all impulses—Love, I suppose you would call it," he added bitterly, "that night you called! You had brought the most conclusive proofs of it on your sleeve."

"But—" I almost screamed.

"Silence!" he thundered. "I know what you would say. You would say that even if you had embraced some Young Person in a sealskin coat, what had that to do with the robbery? Let me tell you, then, that that sealskin coat represented the quality and character of your fatal entanglement! You bartered your honor for it—that stolen cigar case was the purchaser of the sealskin coat!

"Silence! Having thoroughly established your motive, I now proceed to the commission of the crime itself. Ordinary people would have begun with that—with an attempt to discover the whereabouts of the missing object. These are not *my* methods."

So overpowering was his penetration that, although I knew myself innocent, I licked my lips with avidity to hear the further details of this lucid exposition of my crime.

"You committed that theft the night I showed you the cigar case, and after I had carelessly thrown it in that drawer. You were sitting in that chair, and I had arisen to take something from that shelf. In that instant you secured your booty without rising. Silence! Do you remember when I helped you on with your overcoat the other night? I was particular about fitting your arm in. While doing so I measured your arm with a spring tape measure, from the shoulder to the cuff. A later visit to your tailor confirmed that measurement. It proved to be *the exact distance between your chair and that drawer!*"

I sat stunned.

"The rest are mere corroborative details! You were again tampering with the drawer when I discovered you doing so! Do not start! The stranger that blundered into the room with a muffler on—was myself! More, I had placed a little soap on the drawer handles when I purposely left you alone. The soap was on your hand when I shook it at parting. I softly felt your pockets, when you were asleep, for further developments. I embraced you when you left—that I might feel if you had the cigar case or any other articles hidden on your body. This confirmed me in the belief that you had already disposed of it in the manner and for the purpose I have shown you. As I still believed you capable of remorse and confession, I twice allowed you to see I was on your track: once in the garb of an itinerant negro minstrel, and the second time as a workman looking in the window of the pawnshop where you pledged your booty."

"But," I burst out, "if you had asked the pawnbroker, you would have seen how unjust—"

"Fool!" he hissed, "that was one of *your* suggestions—to search the pawnshops! Do you suppose I followed any of your suggestions, the suggestions of the thief? On the contrary, they told me what to avoid."

"And I suppose," I said bitterly, "you have not even searched your drawer?"

"No," he said calmly.

I was for the first time really vexed. I went to the nearest drawer and pulled it out sharply. It stuck as it had before, leaving a part of the drawer unopened. By working it, however, I discovered that it was impeded by some obstacle that had slipped to the upper part of the drawer, and held it firmly fast. Inserting my hand, I pulled out the impeding object. It was the missing cigar case! I turned to him with a cry of joy.

But I was appalled at his expression. A look of contempt was now added to his acute, penetrating gaze. "I have been mistaken," he said slowly; "I had not allowed for your weakness and cowardice! I thought too highly of you even in your guilt! But I see now why you tampered with that drawer the other night. By some inexplicable means—possibly another theft—you took the cigar case out of pawn and, like a whipped hound, restored it to me in this feeble, clumsy fashion. You thought to deceive me, Hemlock Jones! More, you thought to destroy my infallibility. Go! I give you your liberty. I shall not summon the three policemen who wait in the adjoining room—but out of my sight forever!"

As I stood once more dazed and petrified, he took me firmly by the ear and led me into the hall, closing the door behind him. This reopened presently, wide enough to permit him to thrust out my hat, overcoat, umbrella, and overshoes, and then closed against me forever!

I never saw him again. I am bound to say, however, that thereafter my business increased, I recovered much of my old practice, and a few of my patients recovered also. I became rich. I had a brougham and a house in the West End. But I often wondered, pondering on that wonderful man's penetration and insight, if, in some lapse of consciousness, I had not really stolen his cigar case!

JACQUES FUTRELLE

(1875–1912)

||||||||||||||||||||||||||||||||||||||||||||||| ■ |||||||||||||||||||||||||||||||||||||||||||||

Critics agree that when Boston journalist Jacques Futrelle went down with the *Titanic* at the age of thirty-seven, the world lost an innovative master of the short story. The Georgia-born author also penned novels that have not stood the test of time. But his short stories gave us his great achievement: the American proto-type of the scientific sleuth.

There is no doubt that Futrelle was building on the creations of Eugène Fran-çois Vidocq, Edgar Allan Poe, and Sir Arthur Conan Doyle, when he invented Professor S. F. X. Van Dusen, Ph.D., LL.D., F.R.S., and M.D. However, no reader is likely to mistake Van Dusen for Sherlock Holmes, despite their cerebral similarities. With his outsize cranium, his mane of yellow hair, his petite body, and his arrogant freakishness, Van Dusen can't be imagined as welcome among the upper-crust British. And Van Dusen's character fits the American mold. His superlative reasoning powers are accompanied by a "can-do" attitude that leads him to declare, "Nothing is impossible."

"How about an airship?" his friend challenges him.

"That's not impossible at all," Van Dusen asserts. "It will be invented some-time. I'd do it myself, but I'm busy."

Dubbed "The Thinking Machine" by the press after "a remarkable exhibition at chess," the professor is aided by newspaper reporter Hutchinson Hatch, who runs the research and rescue operations while Van Dusen does the thinking. Setting the stage for sidekicks like Archie Goodwin in Rex Stout's later Nero Wolfe stories and Paul Drake in Erle Stanley Gardner's Perry Mason mysteries, Hatch is the more physically active partner.

Futrelle was on the editorial staff of the *Boston American* when "The Problem of Cell 13" made him famous. Like most of his Thinking Machine stories, it was first published in that newspaper (the predecessor of the present-day *Boston Herald*), with a challenge to the reader to furnish a solution. The story demon-strates the author's forte in the locked-room branch of detective fiction, with The Thinking Machine taking up a challenge to escape from a maximum-security prison cell with nothing but "shoes, stockings, trousers and shirt"—and, of course, his power to think.

1905

The Problem of Cell 13

∎

I

Practically all those letters remaining in the alphabet after Augustus S. F. X. Van Dusen was named were afterward acquired by that gentleman in the course of a brilliant scientific career, and, being honorably acquired, were tacked on to the other end. His name, therefore, taken with all that belonged to it, was a wonderfully imposing structure. He was a Ph.D., an LL.D., an F.R.S., an M.D., and an M.D.S. He was also some other things—just what he himself couldn't say—through recognition of his ability by various foreign educational and scientific institutions.

In appearance he was no less striking than in nomenclature. He was slender with the droop of the student in his thin shoulders and the pallor of a close, sedentary life on his clean-shaven face. His eyes wore a perpetual, forbidding squint—of a man who studies little things—and when they could be seen at all through his thick spectacles, were mere slits of watery blue. But above his eyes was his most striking feature. This was a tall, broad brow, almost abnormal in height and width, crowned by a heavy shock of bushy, yellow hair. All these things conspired to give him a peculiar, almost grotesque, personality.

Professor Van Dusen was remotely German. For generations his ancestors had been noted in the sciences; he was the logical result, the master mind. First and above all he was a logician. At least thirty-five years of the half-century or so of his existence had been devoted exclusively to proving that two and two always equal four, except in unusual cases, where they equal three or five, as the case may be. He stood broadly on the general proposition that all things that start must go somewhere, and was able to bring the concentrated mental force of his forefathers to bear on a given problem. Incidentally it may be remarked that Professor Van Dusen wore a No. 8 hat.

The world at large had heard vaguely of Professor Van Dusen as The Thinking Machine. It was a newspaper catch-phrase applied to him at the time of a remarkable exhibition at chess; he had demonstrated then that a stranger to the game might, by the force of inevitable logic, defeat a champion who had devoted a lifetime to its study. The Thinking Machine! Perhaps that more nearly described him than all his honorary initials, for he spent week after week, month after month, in the seclusion of his small laboratory from which had gone forth thoughts that staggered scientific associates and deeply stirred the world at large.

It was only occasionally that The Thinking Machine had visitors, and these were usually men who, themselves high in the sciences, dropped in to argue a point and perhaps convince themselves. Two of these men, Dr. Charles Ransome and Alfred Fielding, called one evening to discuss some theory which is not of consequence here.

"Such a thing is impossible," declared Dr. Ransome emphatically, in the course of the conversation.

"Nothing is impossible," declared The Thinking Machine with equal emphasis. He always spoke petulantly. "The mind is master of all things. When science fully recognizes that fact a great advance will have been made."

"How about the airship?" asked Dr. Ransome.

"That's not impossible at all," asserted The Thinking Machine. "It will be invented some time. I'd do it myself, but I'm busy."

Dr. Ransome laughed tolerantly.

"I've heard you say such things before," he said. "But they mean nothing. Mind may be master of matter, but it hasn't yet found a way to apply itself. There are some things that can't be *thought* out of existence, or rather which would not yield to any amount of thinking."

"What, for instance?" demanded The Thinking Machine.

Dr. Ransome was thoughtful for a moment as he smoked. "Well, say prison walls," he replied. "No man can *think* himself out of a cell. If he could, there would be no prisoners."

"A man can so apply his brain and ingenuity that he can leave a cell, which is the same thing," snapped The Thinking Machine.

Dr. Ransome was slightly amused.

"Let's suppose a case," he said, after a moment. "Take a cell where prisoners under sentence of death are confined—men who are desperate and, maddened by fear, would take any chance to escape—suppose you were locked in such a cell. Could you escape?"

"Certainly," declared The Thinking Machine.

"Of course," said Mr. Fielding, who entered the conversation for the first time, "you might wreck the cell with an explosive—but inside, a prisoner, you couldn't have that."

"There would be nothing of that kind," said The Thinking Machine. "You might treat me precisely as you treated prisoners under sentence of death, and I would leave the cell."

"Not unless you entered it with tools prepared to get out," said Dr. Ransome.

The Thinking Machine was visibly annoyed and his blue eyes snapped.

"Lock me in any cell in any prison anywhere at any time, wearing only what is necessary, and I'll escape in a week," he declared, sharply.

Dr. Ransome sat up straight in the chair, interested. Mr. Fielding lighted a new cigar.

"You mean you could actually *think* yourself out?" asked Dr. Ransome.

"I would get out," was the response.

"Are you serious?"

"Certainly I am serious."

Dr. Ransome and Mr. Fielding were silent for a long time.

"Would you be willing to try it?" asked Mr. Fielding, finally.

"Certainly," said Professor Van Dusen, and there was a trace of irony in his voice. "I have done more asinine things than that to convince other men of less important truths."

The tone was offensive and there was an undercurrent strongly resembling anger on both sides. Of course it was an absurd thing, but Professor Van Dusen reiterated his willingness to undertake the escape and it was decided upon.

"To begin now," added Dr. Ransome.

"I'd prefer that it begin to-morrow," said The Thinking Machine, "because—"

"No, now," said Mr. Fielding, flatly. "You are arrested, figuratively, of course, without any warning locked in a cell with no chance to communicate with friends, and left there with identically the same care and attention that would be given to a man under sentence of death. Are you willing?"

"All right, now, then," said The Thinking Machine, and he arose.

"Say, the death-cell in Chisholm Prison."

"The death-cell in Chisholm Prison."

"And what will you wear?"

"As little as possible," said The Thinking Machine. "Shoes, stockings, trousers and a shirt."

"You will permit yourself to be searched, of course?"

"I am to be treated precisely as all prisoners are treated," said The Thinking Machine. "No more attention and no less."

There were some preliminaries to be arranged in the matter of obtaining permission for the test, but all three were influential men and everything was done satisfactorily by telephone, albeit the prison commissioners, to whom the experiment was explained on purely scientific grounds, were sadly bewildered. Professor Van Dusen would be the most distinguished prisoner they had ever entertained.

When The Thinking Machine had donned those things which he was to wear during his incarceration he called the little old woman who was his housekeeper, cook and maid-servant all in one.

"Martha," he said, "it is now twenty-seven minutes past nine o'clock. I am going away. One week from to-night at half-past nine, these gentlemen and one, possibly two, others will take supper with me here. Remember Dr. Ransome is very fond of artichokes."

The three men were driven to Chisholm Prison, where the warden was awaiting them, having been informed of the matter by telephone. He understood merely that the eminent Professor Van Dusen was to be his prisoner, if he could keep him, for one week; that he had committed no crime, but that he was to be treated as all other prisoners were treated.

"Search him," instructed Dr. Ransome.

The Thinking Machine was searched. Nothing was found on him; the pockets of the trousers were empty; the white, stiff-bosomed shirt had no pocket. The shoes and stockings were removed, examined, then replaced. As he watched all these preliminaries—the rigid search and noted the pitiful, childlike physical weakness of the man, the colorless face, and the thin, white hands—Dr. Ransome almost regretted his part in the affair.

"Are you sure you want to do this?" he asked.

"Would you be convinced if I did not?" inquired The Thinking Machine in turn.

"No."

"All right. I'll do it."

What sympathy Dr. Ransome had was dissipated by the tone. It nettled him, and he resolved to see the experiment to the end; it would be a stinging reproof to egotism.

"It will be impossible for him to communicate with any one outside?" he asked.

"Absolutely impossible," replied the warden. "He will not be permitted writing materials of any sort."

"And your jailers, would they deliver a message from him?"

"Not one word, directly or indirectly," said the warden. "You may rest assured of that. They will report anything he might say or turn over to me anything he might give them."

"That seems entirely satisfactory," said Mr. Fielding, who was frankly interested in the problem.

"Of course, in the event he fails," said Dr. Ransome, "and asks for his liberty, you understand you are to set him free?"

"I understand," replied the warden.

The Thinking Machine stood listening, but had nothing to say until this was all ended, then:

"I should like to make three small requests. You may grant them or not, as you wish."

"No special favors, now," warned Mr. Fielding.

"I am asking none," was the stiff response. "I would like to have some tooth powder—buy it yourself to see that it is tooth powder—and I should like to have one five-dollar and two ten-dollar bills."

Dr. Ransome, Mr. Fielding and the warden exchanged astonished glances. They were not surprised at the request for tooth powder, but were at the request for money.

"Is there any man with whom our friend would come in contact that he could bribe with twenty-five dollars?" asked Dr. Ransome of the warden.

"Not for twenty-five hundred dollars," was the positive reply.

"Well, let him have them," said Mr. Fielding. "I think they are harmless enough."

"And what is the third request?" asked Dr. Ransome.

"I should like to have my shoes polished."

Again the astonished glances were exchanged. This last request was the height of absurdity, so they agreed to it. These things all being attended to, The Thinking Machine was led back into the prison from which he had undertaken to escape.

"Here is Cell 13," said the warden, stopping three doors down the steel corridor. "This is where we keep condemned murderers. No one can leave it without my permission; and no one in it can communicate with the outside. I'll stake my reputation on that. It's only three doors back of my office and I can readily hear any unusual noise."

"Will this cell do, gentlemen?" asked The Thinking Machine. There was a touch of irony in his voice.

"Admirably," was the reply.

The heavy steel door was thrown open, there was a great scurrying and scampering of tiny feet, and The Thinking Machine passed into the gloom of the cell. Then the door was closed and double locked by the warden.

"What is that noise in there?" asked Dr. Ransome, through the bars.

"Rats—dozens of them," replied The Thinking Machine, tersely.

The three men, with final good nights, were turning away when The Thinking Machine called:

"What time is it exactly, warden?"

"Eleven seventeen," replied the warden.

"Thanks. I will join you gentlemen in your office at half-past eight o'clock one week from to-night," said The Thinking Machine.

"And if you do not?"

"There is no 'if' about it."

II

Chisholm Prison was a great, spreading structure of granite, four stories in all, which stood in the center of acres of open space. It was surrounded by a wall of solid masonry eighteen feet high, and so smoothly finished inside and out as to offer no foothold to a climber, no matter how expert. Atop of this fence, as a further precaution, was a five-foot fence of steel rods, each terminating in a keen point. This fence in itself marked an absolute deadline between freedom and imprisonment, for, even if a man escaped from his cell, it would seem impossible for him to pass the wall.

The yard, which on all sides of the prison building was twenty-five feet wide, that being the distance from the building to the wall, was by day an exercise ground for those prisoners to whom was granted the boon of occasional semi-liberty. But that was not for those in Cell 13.

At all times of the day there were armed guards in the yard, four of them, one patrolling each side of the prison building.

By night the yard was almost as brilliantly lighted as by day. On each of the four sides was a great arc light which rose above the prison wall and gave to the guards a clear sight. The lights, too, brightly illuminated the spiked top of the wall. The wires which fed the arc light ran up the side of the prison building on insulators and from the top story led out to the poles supporting the arc lights.

All these things were seen and comprehended by The Thinking Machine, who was only enabled to see out his closely barred cell window by standing on his bed. This was on the morning following his incarceration. He gathered, too, that the river lay over there beyond the wall somewhere, because he heard faintly the pulsation of a motor boat and high up in the air saw a river bird. From that same direction came the shouts of boys at play and the occasional crack of a batted ball. He knew then that between the prison wall and the river was an open space, a playground.

Chisholm Prison was regarded as absolutely safe. No man had ever escaped from it. The Thinking Machine, from his perch on the bed, seeing what he saw, could readily understand why. The walls of the cell, though built he judged twenty years before, were perfectly solid, and the window bars of new iron had not a shadow of rust on them. The window itself, even with the bars out, would be a difficult mode of egress because it was small.

Yet, seeing these things, The Thinking Machine was not discouraged. Instead, he thoughtfully squinted at the great arc light—there was bright sunlight now—and traced with his eyes the wire which led from it to the building. That electric wire, he reasoned, must come down the side of the building not a great distance from his cell. That might be worth knowing.

Cell 13 was on the same floor with the offices of the prison—that is, not in the basement, nor yet upstairs. There were only four steps up to the office floor, therefore the level of the floor must be only three or four feet above the ground. He couldn't see the ground directly beneath his window, but he could see it further out toward the wall. It would be an easy drop from the window. Well and good.

Then The Thinking Machine fell to remembering how he had come to the cell. First, there was the outside guard's booth, a part of the wall. There were two heavily barred gates there, both of steel. At this gate was one man always on guard. He admitted persons to the prison after much clanking of keys and locks, and let them out when ordered to do so. The warden's office was in the prison building, and in order to reach that official from the prison yard one had to pass a gate of solid steel with only a peep-hole in it. Then coming from that inner office to Cell 13, where he was now, one must pass a heavy wooden door and two steel doors into the corridors of the prison; and always there was the double-locked door to Cell 13 to reckon with.

There were then, The Thinking Machine recalled, seven doors to be overcome before one could pass from Cell 13 into the outer world, a free man. But against this was the fact that he was rarely interrupted. A jailer appeared at his cell door at six in the morning with a breakfast of prison fare; he would come again at noon, and again at six in the afternoon. At nine o'clock at night would come the inspection tour. That would be all.

"It's admirably arranged, this prison system," was the mental tribute paid by The Thinking Machine. "I'll have to study it a little when I get out. I had no idea there was such great care exercised in the prisons."

There was nothing, positively nothing, in his cell, except his iron bed, so firmly put together that no man could tear it to pieces save with sledges or a file. He had neither of these. There was not even a chair, or a small table, or a bit of tin or crockery. Nothing! The jailer stood by when he ate, then took away the wooden spoon and bowl which he had used.

One by one these things sank into the brain of The Thinking Machine. When the last possibility had been considered he began an examination of his cell. From the roof, down the walls on all sides, he examined the stones and the cement between them. He stamped over the floor carefully time after time, but it was cement, perfectly solid. After the examination he sat on the edge of the iron bed and was lost in thought for a long time. For Professor Augustus S. F. X. Van Dusen, The Thinking Machine, had something to think about.

He was disturbed by a rat, which ran across his foot, then scampered away into a dark corner of the cell, frightened at its own daring. After a while The Thinking Machine, squinting steadily into the darkness of the corner where the rat had gone, was able to make out in the gloom many little beady eyes staring at him. He counted six pair, and there were perhaps others; he didn't see very well.

Then The Thinking Machine, from his seat on the bed, noticed for the first time the bottom of his cell door. There was an opening there of two inches between the steel bar and the floor. Still looking steadily at this opening, The Thinking Machine backed suddenly into the corner where he had seen the beady eyes. There was a great scampering of tiny feet, several squeaks of frightened rodents, and then silence.

None of the rats had gone out the door, yet there were none in the cell. Therefore there must be another way out of the cell, however small. The Thinking Machine, on hands and knees, started a search for this spot, feeling in the darkness with his long, slender fingers.

At last his search was rewarded. He came upon a small opening in the floor, level with the cement. It was perfectly round and somewhat larger than a silver dollar. This was the way the rats had gone. He put his fingers deep into the opening; it seemed to be a disused drainage pipe and was dry and dusty.

Having satisfied himself on this point, he sat on the bed again for an hour, then made another inspection of his surroundings through the small cell window. One of the outside guards stood directly opposite, beside the wall, and happened to be looking at the window of Cell 13 when the head of The Thinking Machine appeared. But the scientist didn't notice the guard.

Noon came and the jailer appeared with the prison dinner of repulsively plain food. At home The Thinking Machine merely ate to live; here he took what was offered without comment. Occasionally he spoke to the jailer who stood outside the door watching him.

"Any improvements made here in the last few years?" he asked.

"Nothing particularly," replied the jailer. "New wall was built four years ago."

"Anything done to the prison proper?"

"Painted the woodwork outside, and I believe about seven years ago a new system of plumbing was put in."

"Ah!" said the prisoner. "How far is the river over there?"

"About three hundred feet. The boys have a baseball ground between the wall and the river."

The Thinking Machine had nothing further to say just then, but when the jailer was ready to go he asked for some water.

"I get very thirsty here," he explained. "Would it be possible for you to leave a little water in a bowl for me?"

"I'll ask the warden," replied the jailer, and he went away.

Half an hour later he returned with water in a small earthen bowl.

"The warden says you may keep this bowl," he informed the prisoner. "But you must show it to me when I ask for it. If it is broken, it will be the last."

"Thank you," said The Thinking Machine. "I shan't break it."

The jailer went on about his duties. For just the fraction of a second it seemed that The Thinking Machine wanted to ask a question, but he didn't.

Two hours later this same jailer, in passing the door of Cell No. 13, heard a noise inside and stopped. The Thinking Machine was down on his hands and knees in a corner of the cell, and from that same corner came several frightened squeaks. The jailer looked on interestedly.

"Ah, I've got you," he heard the prisoner say.

"Got what?" he asked, sharply.

"One of these rats," was the reply. "See?" And between the scientist's long fingers the jailer saw a small gray rat struggling. The prisoner brought it over to the light and looked at it closely. "It's a water rat," he said.

"Ain't you got anything better to do than to catch rats?" asked the jailer.

"It's disgraceful that they should be here at all," was the irritated reply. "Take this one away and kill it. There are dozens more where it came from."

The jailer took the wriggling, squirmy rodent and flung it down on the floor violently. It gave one squeak and lay still. Later he reported the incident to the warden, who only smiled.

Still later that afternoon the outside armed guard on Cell 13 side of the prison looked up again at the window and saw the prisoner looking out. He saw a hand raised to the barred window and then something white fluttered to the ground, directly under the window of Cell 13. It was a little roll of linen, evidently of white shirting material, and tied around it was a five-dollar bill. The guard looked up at the window again, but the face had disappeared.

With a grim smile he took the little linen roll and the five-dollar bill to the warden's office. There together they deciphered something which was written on it with a queer sort of ink, frequently blurred. On the outside was this:

"Finder of this please deliver to Dr. Charles Ransome."

"Ah," said the warden, with a chuckle. "Plan of escape number one has gone wrong." Then, as an afterthought: "But why did he address it to Dr. Ransome?"

"And where did he get the pen and ink to write with?" asked the guard.

The warden looked at the guard and the guard looked at the warden. There was no apparent solution of that mystery. The warden studied the writing carefully, then shook his head.

"Well, let's see what he was going to say to Dr. Ransome," he said at length, still puzzled, and he unrolled the inner piece of linen.

"Well, if that—what—what do you think of that?" he asked, dazed.

The guard took the bit of linen and read this:

"Epa cseot d'net niiy awe htto n'si sih. T."

III

The warden spent an hour wondering what sort of a cipher it was, and half an hour wondering why his prisoner should attempt to communicate with Dr. Ransome, who was the cause of him being there. After this the warden devoted some thought to the question of where the prisoner got writing materials, and what sort of writing materials he had. With the idea of illuminating this point, he examined the linen again. It was a torn part of a white shirt and had ragged edges.

Now it was possible to account for the linen, but what the prisoner had used to write with was another matter. The warden knew it would have been impossible for him to have either pen or pencil, and, besides, neither pen nor pencil had been used in this writing. What, then? The warden decided to personally investigate. The Thinking Machine was his prisoner; he had orders to hold his prisoners; if this one sought to escape by sending cipher messages to persons outside, he would stop it, as he would have stopped it in the case of any other prisoner.

The warden went back to Cell 13 and found The Thinking Machine on his hands and knees on the floor, engaged in nothing more alarming than catching rats. The prisoner heard the warden's step and turned to him quickly.

"It's disgraceful," he snapped, "these rats. There are scores of them."

"Other men have been able to stand them," said the warden. "Here is another shirt for you—let me have the one you have on."

"Why?" demanded The Thinking Machine, quickly. His tone was hardly natural, his manner suggested actual perturbation.

"You have attempted to communicate with Dr. Ransome," said the warden severely. "As my prisoner, it is my duty to put a stop to it."

The Thinking Machine was silent for a moment.

"All right," he said, finally. "Do your duty."

The warden smiled grimly. The prisoner arose from the floor and removed the white shirt, putting on instead a striped convict shirt the warden had brought. The warden took the white shirt eagerly, and then and there compared the pieces of linen on which was written the cipher with certain torn places in the shirt. The Thinking Machine looked on curiously.

"The guard brought *you* those, then?" he asked.

"He certainly did," replied the warden triumphantly. "And that ends your first attempt to escape."

The Thinking Machine watched the warden as he, by comparison, established to his own satisfaction that only two pieces of linen had been torn from the white shirt.

"What did you write this with?" demanded the warden.

"I should think it a part of your duty to find out," said The Thinking Machine, irritably.

The warden started to say some harsh things, then restrained himself and made a minute search of the cell and of the prisoner instead. He found absolutely nothing; not even a match or toothpick which might have been used for a pen. The same mystery surrounded the fluid with which the cipher had been written. Although the warden left Cell 13 visibly annoyed, he took the torn shirt in triumph.

"Well, writing notes on a shirt won't get him out, that's certain," he told himself with some complacency. He put the linen scraps into his desk to await developments. "If that man escapes from that cell I'll—hang it—I'll resign."

On the third day of his incarceration The Thinking Machine openly attempted to bribe his way out. The jailer had brought his dinner and was leaning against the barred door, waiting, when The Thinking Machine began the conversation.

"The drainage pipes of the prison lead to the river, don't they?" he asked.

"Yes," said the jailer.

"I suppose they are very small?"

"Too small to crawl through, if that's what you're thinking about," was the grinning response.

There was silence until The Thinking Machine finished his meal. Then:

"You know I'm not a criminal, don't you?"

"Yes."

"And that I've a perfect right to be freed if I demand it?"

"Yes."

"Well, I came here believing that I could make my escape," said the prisoner, and his squint eyes studied the face of the jailer. "Would you consider a financial reward for aiding me to escape?"

The jailer, who happened to be an honest man, looked at the slender, weak figure of the prisoner, at the large head with its mass of yellow hair, and was almost sorry.

"I guess prisons like these were not built for the likes of you to get out of," he said, at last.

"But would you consider a proposition to help me get out?" the prisoner insisted, almost beseechingly.

"No," said the jailer, shortly.

"Five hundred dollars," urged The Thinking Machine. "I am not a criminal."

"No," said the jailer.

"A thousand?"

"No," again said the jailer, and he started away hurriedly to escape further temptation. Then he turned back. "If you should give me ten thousand dollars I couldn't get you out. You'd have to pass through seven doors, and I only have the keys to two."

Then he told the warden all about it.

"Plan number two fails," said the warden, smiling grimly. "First a cipher, then bribery."

When the jailer was on his way to Cell 13 at six o'clock, again bearing food to The Thinking Machine, he paused, startled by the unmistakable scrape, scrape of steel against steel. It stopped at the sound of his steps, then craftily the jailer, who was beyond the prisoner's range of vision, resumed his tramping, the sound being apparently that of a man going away from Cell 13. As a matter of fact he was in the same spot.

After a moment there came again the steady scrape, scrape, and the jailer crept cautiously on tiptoes to the door and peered between the bars. The Thinking Machine was standing on the iron bed working at the bars of the little window. He was using a file, judging from the backward and forward swing of his arms.

Cautiously the jailer crept back to the office, summoned the warden in person, and they returned to Cell 13 on tiptoes. The steady scrape was still audible. The warden listened to satisfy himself and then suddenly appeared at the door.

"Well?" he demanded, and there was a smile on his face.

The Thinking Machine glanced back from his perch on the bed and leaped suddenly to the floor, making frantic efforts to hide something. The warden went in, with hand extended.

"Give it up," he said.

"No," said the prisoner, sharply.

"Come, give it up," urged the warden. "I don't want to have to search you again."

"No," repeated the prisoner.

"What was it, a file?" asked the warden.

The Thinking Machine was silent and stood squinting at the warden with something very nearly approaching disappointment on his face—nearly, but not quite. The warden was almost sympathetic.

"Plan number three fails, eh?" he asked, good-naturedly. "Too bad, isn't it?"

The prisoner didn't say.

"Search him," instructed the warden.

The jailer searched the prisoner carefully. At last, artfully concealed in the waistband of the trousers, he found a piece of steel about two inches long, with one side curved like a half moon.

"Ah," said the warden, as he received it from the jailer. "From your shoe heel," and he smiled pleasantly.

The jailer continued his search and on the other side of the trousers waistband found another piece of steel identical with the first. The edges showed where they had been worn against the bars of the window.

"You couldn't saw a way through those bars with these," said the warden.

"I could have," said the The Thinking Machine firmly.

"In six months, perhaps," said the warden, good-naturedly.

The warden shook his head slowly as he gazed into the slightly flushed face of his prisoner.

"Ready to give it up?" he asked.

"I haven't started yet," was the prompt reply.

Then came another exhaustive search of the cell. Carefully the two men went over it, finally turning out the bed and searching that. Nothing. The warden in person climbed upon the bed and examined the bars of the window where the prisoner had been sawing. When he looked he was amused.

"Just made it a little bright by hard rubbing," he said to the prisoner, who stood looking on with a somewhat crestfallen air. The warden grasped the iron bars in his strong hands and tried to shake them. They were immovable, set firmly in the solid granite. He examined each in turn and found them all satisfactory. Finally he climbed down from the bed.

"Give it up, professor," he advised.

The Thinking Machine shook his head and the warden and jailer passed on again. As they disappeared down the corridor The Thinking Machine sat on the edge of the bed with his head in his hands.

"He's crazy to try to get out," said the warden. "But he's clever. I would like to know what he wrote that cipher with."

It was four o'clock next morning when an awful, heart-racking shriek of terror resounded through the great prison. It came from a cell, some-where about the center, and its tone told a tale of horror, agony, terrible fear. The warden heard and with three of his men rushed into the long corridor leading to Cell 13.

IV

As they ran there came again that awful cry. It died away in a sort of wail. The white faces of prisoners appeared at cell doors upstairs and down, staring out wonderingly, frightened.

"It's that fool in Cell 13," grumbled the warden.

He stopped and stared in as one of the jailers flashed a lantern. "That fool in Cell 13" lay comfortably on his cot, flat on his back with his mouth open, snoring. Even as they looked there came again the piercing cry, from somewhere above. The warden's face blanched a little as he started up the stairs. There on the top floor he found a man in Cell 43, directly above Cell 13, but two floors higher, cowering in a corner of his cell.

"What's the matter?" demanded the warden.

"Thank God you've come," exclaimed the prisoner, and he cast him-self against the bars of his cell.

"What is it?" demanded the warden again.

He threw open the door and went in. The prisoner dropped on his knees and clasped the warden about the body. His face was white with terror, his eyes were widely distended, and he was shuddering. His hands, icy cold, clutched at the warden's.

"Take me out of this cell, please take me out," he pleaded.

"What's the matter with you, anyhow?" insisted the warden, impatiently.

"I heard something—something," said the prisoner, and his eyes roved nervously around the cell.

"What did you hear?"

"I—I can't tell you," stammered the prisoner. Then, in a sudden burst of terror: "Take me out of this cell—put me anywhere—but take me out of here."

The warden and three jailers exchanged glances.

"Who is this fellow? What's he accused of?" asked the warden.

"Joseph Ballard," said one of the jailers. "He's accused of throwing acid in a woman's face. She died from it."

"But they can't prove it," gasped the prisoner. "They can't prove it. Please put me in some other cell."

He was still clinging to the warden, and that official threw his arms off roughly. Then for a time he stood looking at the cowering wretch, who seemed possessed of all the wild, unreasoning terror of a child.

"Look here, Ballard," said the warden, finally, "if you heard anything, I want to know what it was. Now tell me."

"I can't, I can't," was the reply. He was sobbing.

"Where did it come from?"

"I don't know. Everywhere—nowhere. I just heard it."

"What was it—a voice?"

"Please don't make me answer," pleaded the prisoner.

"You must answer," said the warden, sharply.

"It was a voice—but—but it wasn't human," was the sobbing reply.

"Voice, but not human?" repeated the warden, puzzled.

"It sounded muffled and—and far away—and ghostly," explained the man.

"Did it come from inside or outside the prison?"

"It didn't seem to come from anywhere—it was just here, here, everywhere. I heard it. I heard it."

For an hour the warden tried to get the story, but Ballard had become suddenly obstinate and would say nothing—only pleaded to be placed in another cell, or to have one of the jailers remain near him until daylight. These requests were gruffly refused.

"And see here," said the warden, in conclusion, "if there's any more of this screaming I'll put you in the padded cell."

Then the warden went his way, a sadly puzzled man. Ballard sat at his cell door until daylight, his face, drawn and white with terror, pressed against the bars, and looked out into the prison with wide, staring eyes.

That day, the fourth since the incarceration of The Thinking Machine, was enlivened considerably by the volunteer prisoner, who spent most of his time at the little window of his cell. He began proceedings by throwing another piece of linen down to the guard, who picked it up dutifully and took it to the warden. On it was written:

"Only three days more."

The warden was in no way surprised at what he read; he understood that The Thinking Machine meant only three days more of his imprisonment, and he regarded the note as a boast. But how was the thing written? Where had The Thinking Machine found this new piece of linen? Where? How? He carefully examined the linen. It was white, of fine texture, shirting material. He took the shirt which he had taken and carefully fitted the two original pieces of the linen to the torn places. This third piece was entirely superfluous; it didn't fit anywhere, and yet it was unmistakably the same goods.

"And where—where does he get anything to write with?" demanded the warden of the world at large.

Still later on the fourth day The Thinking Machine, through the window of his cell, spoke to the armed guard outside.

"What day of the month is it?" he asked.

"The fifteenth," was the answer.

The Thinking Machine made a mental astronomical calculation and satisfied himself that the moon would not rise until after nine o'clock that night. Then he asked another question:

"Who attends to those arc lights?"

"Man from the company."

"You have no electricians in the building?"

"No."

"I should think you could save money if you had your own man."

"None of my business," replied the guard.

The guard noticed The Thinking Machine at the cell window frequently during that day, but always the face seemed listless and there was a certain wistfulness in the squint eyes behind the glasses. After a while he accepted the presence of the leonine head as a matter of course. He had seen other prisoners do the same thing; it was the longing for the outside world.

That afternoon, just before the day guard was relieved, the head appeared at the window again, and The Thinking Machine's hand held something out between the bars. It fluttered to the ground and the guard picked it up. It was a five-dollar bill.

"That's for you," called the prisoner.

As usual, the guard took it to the warden. That gentleman looked at it suspiciously; he looked at everything that came from Cell 13 with suspicion.

"He said it was for me," explained the guard.

"It's sort of a tip, I suppose," said the warden. "I see no particular reason why you shouldn't accept—"

Suddenly he stopped. He had remembered that The Thinking Machine had gone into Cell 13 with one five-dollar bill and two ten-dollar bills; twenty-five dollars in all. Now a five-dollar bill had been tied around the first pieces of linen that came from the cell. The warden still had it, and to convince himself he took it out and looked at it. It was five dollars; yet here was another five dollars, and The Thinking Machine had only had ten-dollar bills.

"Perhaps somebody changed one of the bills for him," he thought at last, with a sigh of relief.

But then and there he made up his mind. He would search Cell 13 as a cell was never before searched in this world. When a man could write at will, and change money, and do other wholly inexplicable things, there was something radically wrong with his prison. He planned to enter the cell at night—three o'clock would be an excellent time. The Thinking Machine must do all the weird things he did some time. Night seemed the most reasonable.

Thus it happened that the warden stealthily descended upon Cell 13 that night at three o'clock. He paused at the door and listened. There was no sound save the steady, regular breathing of the prisoner. The keys unfastened the double locks with scarcely a clank, and the warden entered, locking the door behind him. Suddenly he flashed his dark-lantern in the face of the recumbent figure.

If the warden had planed to startle The Thinking Machine he was mistaken, for that individual merely opened his eyes quietly, reached for his glasses and inquired, in a most matter-of-fact tone:

"Who is it?"

It would be useless to describe the search that the warden made. It was minute. Not one inch of the cell or the bed was overlooked. He found the round hole in the floor, and with a flash of inspiration thrust his thick fingers into it. After a moment of fumbling there he drew up something and looked at it in the light of his lantern.

"Ugh!" he exclaimed.

The thing he had taken out was a rat—a dead rat. His inspiration fled as a mist before the sun. But he continued the search.

The Thinking Machine, without a word, arose and kicked the rat out of the cell into the corridor.

The warden climbed on the bed and tried the steel bars in the tiny window. They were perfectly rigid; every bar of the door was the same. Then the warden searched the prisoner's clothing, beginning at the shoes. Nothing hidden in them! Then the trousers waistband. Still nothing! Then the pockets of the trousers. From one side he drew out some paper money and examined it.

"Five one-dollar bills," he gasped.

"That's right," said the prisoner.

"But the—you had two tens and a five—what the—how do you do it?"

"That's my business," said The Thinking Machine.

"Did any of my men change this money for you—on your word of honor?"

The Thinking Machine paused just a fraction of a second.

"No," he said.

"Well, do you make it?" asked the warden. He was prepared to believe anything.

"That's my business," again said the prisoner.

The warden glared at the eminent scientist fiercely. He felt—he knew—that this man was making a fool of him, yet he didn't know how. If he were a real prisoner he would get the truth—but, then, perhaps, those inexplicable things which had happened would not have been brought before him so sharply. Neither of the men spoke for a long time, then suddenly the warden turned fiercely and left the cell, slamming the door behind him. He didn't care to speak, then.

He glanced at the clock. It was ten minutes to four. He had hardly settled himself in bed when again came that heart-breaking shriek through the prison. With a few muttered words, which, while not elegant, were highly expressive, he relighted his lantern and rushed through the prison again to the cell on the upper floor.

Again Ballard was crushing himself against the steel door, shrieking, shrieking at the top of his voice. He stopped only when the warden flashed his lamp in the cell.

"Take me out, take me out," he screamed. "I did it, I did it, I killed her. Take it away."

"Take what away?" asked the warden.

"I threw the acid in her face—I did it—I confess. Take me out of here."

Ballard's condition was pitiable; it was only an act of mercy to let him out into the corridor. There he crouched in a corner, like an animal at bay, and clasped his hands to his ears. It took half an hour to calm him sufficiently for him to speak. Then he told incoherently what had happened. On the night before at four o'clock he had heard a voice—a sepulchral voice, muffled and wailing in tone.

"What did it say?" asked the warden, curiously.

"Acid—acid—acid!" gasped the prisoner. "It accused me. Acid! I threw the acid, and the woman died. Oh!" It was a long, shuddering wail of terror.

"Acid?" echoed the warden, puzzled. The case was beyond him.

"Acid. That's all I heard—that one word, repeated several times. There were other things, too, but I didn't hear them."

"That was last night, eh?" asked the warden. "What happened to-night—what frightened you just now?"

"It was the same thing," gasped the prisoner. "Acid—acid—acid." He covered his face with his hands and sat shivering. "It was acid I used on her, but I didn't mean to kill her. I just heard the words. It was something accusing me—accusing me." He mumbled, and was silent.

"Did you hear anything else?"

"Yes—but I couldn't understand—only a little bit—just a word or two."

"Well, what was it?"

"I heard 'acid' three times, then I heard a long, moaning sound, then—then—I heard 'No. 8 hat.' I heard that voice."

"No. 8 hat," repeated the warden. "What the devil—No. 8 hat? Accusing voices of conscience have never talked about No. 8 hats, so far as I ever heard."

"He's insane," said one of the jailers, with an air of finality.

"I believe you," said the warden. "He must be. He probably heard something and got frightened. He's trembling now. No. 8 hat! What the—"

V

When the fifth day of The Thinking Machine's imprisonment rolled around the warden was wearing a hunted look. He was anxious for the end of the thing. He could not help but feel that his distinguished prisoner had been amusing himself. And if this were so, The Thinking Machine had lost none of his sense of humor. For on this fifth day he flung down another linen note to the outside guard, bearing the words: "Only two days more." Also he flung down half a dollar.

Now the warden knew—he *knew*—that the man in Cell 13 didn't have any half dollars—he *couldn't* have any half dollars, no more than he could have pen and ink and linen, and yet he did have them. It was a condition, not a theory; that is one reason why the warden was wearing a hunted look.

That ghastly, uncanny thing, too, about "Acid" and "No. 8 hat" clung to him tenaciously. They didn't mean anything, of course, merely the ravings of an insane murderer who had been driven by fear to confess his crime, still there were so many things that "didn't mean anything" happening in the prison now since The Thinking Machine was there.

On the sixth day the warden received a postal stating that Dr. Ransome and Mr. Fielding would be at Chisholm Prison on the following evening, Thursday, and in the event Professor Van Dusen had not yet escaped—and they presumed he had not because they had not heard from him—they would meet him there.

"In the event he had not yet escaped!" The warden smiled grimly. Escaped!

The Thinking Machine enlivened this day for the warden with three notes. They were on the usual linen and bore generally on the appointment at half-past eight o'clock Thursday night, which appointment the scientist had made at the time of his imprisonment.

On the afternoon of the seventh day the warden passed Cell 13 and glanced in. The Thinking Machine was lying on the iron bed, apparently sleeping lightly. The cell appeared precisely as it always did from a casual glance. The warden would swear that no man was going to leave it between that hour—it was then four o'clock—and half-past eight o'clock that evening.

On his way back past the cell the warden heard the steady breathing again, and coming close to the door looked in. He wouldn't have done so if The Thinking Machine had been looking, but now—well, it was different.

A ray of light came through the high window and fell on the face of the sleeping man. It occurred to the warden for the first time that his prisoner appeared haggard and weary. Just then The Thinking Machine stirred slightly and the warden hurried on up the corridor guiltily. That evening after six o'clock he saw the jailer.

"Everything all right in Cell 13?" he asked.

"Yes, sir," replied the jailer. "He didn't eat much, though."

It was with a feeling of having done his duty that the warden received Dr. Ransome and Mr. Fielding shortly after seven o'clock. He intended to show them the linen notes and lay before them the full story of his woes, which was a long one. But before this came to pass the guard from the river side of the prison yard entered the office.

"The arc light in my side of the yard won't light," he informed the warden.

"Confound it, that man's a hoodoo," thundered the official. "Everything has happened since he's been here."

The guard went back to his post in the darkness, and the warden phoned to the electric light company.

"This is Chisholm Prison," he said through the 'phone. "Send three or four men down here quick, to fix an arc light."

The reply was evidently satisfactory, for the warden hung up the receiver and passed out into the yard. While Dr. Ransome and Mr. Fielding sat waiting, the guard at the outer gate came in with a special delivery letter. Dr. Ransome happened to notice the address, and, when the guard went out, looked at the letter more closely.

"By George!" he exclaimed.

"What is it?" asked Mr. Fielding.

Silently the doctor offered the letter. Mr. Fielding examined it closely.

"Coincidence," he said. "It must be."

It was nearly eight o'clock when the warden returned to his office. The electricians had arrived in a wagon, and were now at work. The warden pressed the buzz-button communicating with the man at the outer gate in the wall.

"How many electricians came in?" he asked, over the short 'phone. "Four? Three workmen in jumpers and overalls and the manager? Frock coat and silk hat? All right. Be certain that only four go out. That's all."

He turned to Dr. Ransome and Mr. Fielding. "We have to be careful here—particularly," and there was broad sarcasm in his tone, "since we have scientists locked up."

The warden picked up the special delivery letter carelessly, and then began to open it.

"When I read this I want to tell you gentlemen something about how—Great Cæsar!" he ended, suddenly, as he glanced at the letter. He sat with mouth open, motionless, from astonishment.

"What is it?" asked Mr. Fielding.

"A special delivery letter from Cell 13," gasped the warden. "An invitation to supper."

"What?" and the two others arose, unanimously.

The warden sat dazed, staring at the letter for a moment, then called sharply to a guard outside in the corridor.

"Run down to Cell 13 and see if that man's in there."

The guard went as directed, while Dr. Ransome and Mr. Fielding examined the letter.

"It's Van Dusen's handwriting; there's no question of that," said Dr. Ransome. "I've seen too much of it."

Just then the buzz on the telephone from the outer gate sounded, and the warden, in a semi-trance, picked up the receiver.

"Hello! Two reporters, eh? Let 'em come in." He turned suddenly to the doctor and Mr. Fielding. "Why, the man *can't* be out. He must be in his cell."

Just at that moment the guard returned.

"He's still in his cell, sir," he reported. "I saw him. He's lying down."

"There, I told you so," said the warden, and he breathed freely again. "But how did he mail that letter?"

There was a rap on the steel door which led from the jail yard into the warden's office.

"It's the reporters," said the warden. "Let them in," he instructed the guard; then to the two other gentlemen: "Don't say anything about this before them, because I'd never hear the last of it."

The door opened, and the two men from the front gate entered.

"Good-evening, gentlemen," said one. That was Hutchinson Hatch; the warden knew him well.

"Well?" demanded the other, irritably. "I'm here."

That was The Thinking Machine.

He squinted belligerently at the warden, who sat with mouth agape. For the moment that official had nothing to say. Dr. Ransome and Mr. Fielding were amazed, but they didn't know what the warden knew. They were only amazed; he was paralyzed. Hutchinson Hatch, the reporter, took in the scene with greedy eyes.

"How—how—how did you do it?" gasped the warden, finally.

"Come back to the cell," said The Thinking Machine, in the irritated voice which his scientific associates knew so well.

The warden, still in a condition bordering on trance, led the way.

"Flash your light in there," directed The Thinking Machine.

The warden did so. There was nothing unusual in the appearance of the cell, and there—there on the bed lay the figure of The Thinking Machine. Certainly! There was the yellow hair! Again the warden looked at the man beside him and wondered at the strangeness of his own dreams.

With trembling hands he unlocked the cell door and The Thinking Machine passed inside.

"See here," he said.

He kicked at the steel bars in the bottom of the cell door and three of them were pushed out of place. A fourth broke off and rolled away in the corridor.

"And here, too," directed the erstwhile prisoner as he stood on the bed to reach the small window. He swept his hand across the opening and every bar came out.

"What's this in the bed?" demanded the warden, who was slowly recovering.

"A wig," was the reply. "Turn down the cover."

The warden did so. Beneath it lay a large coil of strong rope, thirty feet or more, a dagger, three files, ten feet of electric wire, a thin, powerful pair of steel pliers, a small tack hammer with its handle, and—and a Derringer pistol.

"How did you do it?" demanded the warden.

"You gentlemen have an engagement to supper with me at half-past nine o'clock," said The Thinking Machine. "Come on, or we shall be late."

"But how did you do it?" insisted the warden.

"Don't ever think you can hold any man who can use his brain," said The Thinking Machine. "Come on; we shall be late."

VI

It was an impatient supper party in the rooms of Professor Van Dusen and a somewhat silent one. The guests were Dr. Ransome, Albert Fielding, the warden, and Hutchinson Hatch, reporter. The meal was served to the minute, in accordance with Professor Van Dusen's instructions of one week before; Dr. Ransome found the artichokes delicious. At last the supper was finished and The Thinking Machine turned full on Dr. Ransome and squinted at him fiercely.

"Do you believe it now?" he demanded.

"I do," replied Dr. Ransome.

"Do you admit that it was a fair test?"

"I do."

With the others, particularly the warden, he was waiting anxiously for the explanation.

"Suppose you tell us how—" began Mr. Fielding.

"Yes, tell us how," said the warden.

The Thinking Machine readjusted his glasses, took a couple of preparatory squints at his audience, and began the story. He told it from the beginning logically; and no man ever talked to more interested listeners.

"My agreement was," he began, "to go into a cell, carrying nothing except what was necessary to wear, and to leave that cell within a week. I had never seen Chisholm Prison. When I went into the cell I asked for tooth powder, two ten and one five-dollar bills, and also to have my shoes blacked. Even if these requests had been refused it would not have mattered seriously. But you agreed to them.

"I knew there would be nothing in the cell which you thought I might use to advantage. So when the warden locked the door on me I was apparently helpless, unless I could turn three seemingly innocent things to use. They were things which would have been permitted any prisoner under sentence of death, were they not, warden?"

"Tooth powder and polished shoes, yes, but not money," replied the warden.

"Anything is dangerous in the hands of a man who knows how to use it," went on The Thinking Machine. "I did nothing that first night but sleep and chase rats." He glared at the warden. "When the matter was broached I knew I could do nothing that night, so suggested next day. You gentlemen thought I wanted time to arrange an escape with outside assistance, but this was not true. I knew I could communicate with whom I pleased, when I pleased."

The warden stared at him a moment, then went on smoking solemnly.

"I was aroused next morning at six o'clock by the jailer with my breakfast," continued the scientist. "He told me dinner was at twelve and supper at six. Between these times, I gathered, I would be pretty much to myself. So immediately after breakfast I examined my outside surroundings from my cell window. One look told me it would be useless to try to scale the wall, even should I decide to leave my cell by the window, for my purpose was to leave not only the cell, but the prison. Of course, I could have gone over the wall, but it would have taken me longer to lay my plans that way. Therefore, for the moment, I dismissed all idea of that.

"From this first observation I knew the river was on that side of the prison, and that there was also a playground there. Subsequently these surmises were verified by a keeper. I knew then one important thing—that any one might approach the prison wall from that side if necessary without attracting any particular attention. That was well to remember. I remembered it.

"But the outside thing which most attracted my attention was the feed wire to the arc light which ran within a few feet—probably three or four—of my cell window. I knew that would be valuable in the event I found it necessary to cut off that arc light."

"Oh, you shut it off to-night, then?" asked the warden.

"Having learned all I could from that window," resumed The Thinking Machine, without heeding the interruption, "I considered the idea of escaping through the prison proper. I recalled just how I had come into the cell, which I knew would be the only way. Seven doors lay between me and the outside. So, also for the time being, I gave up the idea of escaping that way. And I couldn't go through the solid granite walls of the cell."

The Thinking Machine paused for a moment and Dr. Ransome lighted a new cigar. For several minutes there was silence, then the scientific jail-breaker went on:

"While I was thinking about these things a rat ran across my foot. It suggested a new line of thought. There were at least half a dozen rats in the cell—I could see their beady eyes. Yet I had noticed none come under the cell door. I frightened them purposely and watched the cell door to see if they went out that way. They did not, but they were gone. Obviously they went another way Another way meant another opening.

"I searched for this opening and found it. It was an old drain pipe, long unused and partly choked with dirt and dust. But this was the way the rats had come. They came from somewhere. Where? Drain pipes usually lead outside prison grounds. This one probably led to the river, or near it. The rats must therefore come from that direction. If they came a part of the way, I reasoned that they came all the way, because it was extremely unlikely that a solid iron or lead pipe would have any hole in it except at the exit.

"When the jailer came with my luncheon he told me two important things, although he didn't know it. One was that a new system of plumbing had been put in the prison seven years before; another that the river was only three hundred feet away. Then I knew positively that the pipe was a part of an old system; I knew, too, that it slanted generally toward the river. But did the pipe end in the water or on land?

"This was the next question to be decided. I decided it by catching several of the rats in the cell. My jailer was surprised to see me engaged in this work. I examined at least a dozen of them. They were perfectly dry; they had come through the pipe, and, most important of all, they were *not house rats, but field rats*. The other end of the pipe was on land, then, outside the prison walls. So far, so good.

"Then, I knew that if I worked freely from this point I must attract the warden's attention in another direction. You see, by telling the warden that I had come here to escape you made the test more severe, because I had to trick him by false scents."

The warden looked up with a sad expression in his eyes.

"The first thing was to make him think I was trying to communicate with you, Dr. Ransome. So I wrote a note on a piece of linen I tore from my shirt, addressed it to Dr. Ransome, tied a five-dollar bill around it and threw it out the window. I knew the guard would take it to the warden, but I rather hoped the warden would send it as addressed. Have you that first linen note, warden?"

The warden produced the cipher.

"What the deuce does it mean, anyhow?" he asked.

"Read it backward, beginning with the 'T' signature and disregard the division into words" instructed The Thinking Machine.

The warden did so.

"T-h-i-s, this," he spelled, studied it a moment, then read it off, grinning:

"This is not the way I intend to escape."

"Well, now what do you think o' that?" he demanded, still grinning.

"I knew that would attract your attention, just as it did," said The Thinking Machine, "and if you really found out what it was it would be a sort of gentle rebuke."

"What did you write it with?" asked Dr. Ransome, after he had examined the linen and passed it to Mr. Fielding.

"This," said the erstwhile prisoner, and he extended his foot. On it was the shoe he had worn in prison, though the polish was gone—scraped off clean. "The shoe blacking, moistened with water, was my ink; the metal tip of the shoe lace made a fairly good pen."

The warden looked up and suddenly burst into a laugh, half of relief, half of amusement.

"You're a wonder," he said, admiringly. "Go on."

"That precipitated a search of my cell by the warden, as I had intended," continued The Thinking Machine. "I was anxious to get the warden into the habit of searching my cell, so that finally, constantly finding nothing, he would get disgusted and quit. This at last happened, practically."

The warden blushed.

"He then took my white shirt away and gave me a prison shirt. He was satisfied that those two pieces of the shirt were all that was missing. But while he was searching my cell I had another piece of that same shirt, about nine inches square, rolled into a small ball in my mouth."

"Nine inches of that shirt?" demanded the warden. "Where did it come from?"

"The bosoms of all stiff white shirts are of triple thickness," was the explanation. "I tore out the inside thickness, leaving the bosom only two thicknesses. I knew you wouldn't see it. So much for that."

There was a little pause, and the warden looked from one to another of the men with a sheepish grin.

"Having disposed of the warden for the time being by giving him something else to think about, I took my first serious step toward freedom," said Professor Van Dusen. "I knew, within reason, that the pipe led somewhere to the playground outside; I knew a great many boys played there; I knew that rats came into my cell from out there. Could I communicate with some one outside with these things at hand?

"First was necessary, I saw, a long and fairly reliable thread, so— but here," he pulled up his trousers legs and showed that the tops of both stockings, of fine, strong lisle, were gone. "I unraveled those— after I got them started it wasn't difficult—and I had easily a quarter of a mile of thread that I could depend on.

"Then on half of my remaining linen I wrote, laboriously enough, I assure you, a letter explaining my situation to this gentleman here," and he indicated Hutchinson Hatch. "I knew he would assist me—for the value of the newspaper story. I tied firmly to this linen letter a ten-dollar bill—there is no surer way of attracting the eye of any one—and wrote on the linen: 'Finder of this deliver to Hutchinson Hatch, *Daily American*, who will give another ten dollars for the information.'

"The next thing was to get this note outside on the playground where a boy might find it. There were two ways, but I chose the best. I took one of the rats—I became adept in catching them—tied the linen and money firmly to one leg, fastened my lisle thread to another, and turned him loose in the drain pipe. I reasoned that the natural fright of the rodent would make him run until he was outside the pipe and then out on earth he would probably stop to gnaw off the linen and money.

"From the moment the rat disappeared into that dusty pipe I became anxious. I was taking so many chances. The rat might gnaw the string, of which I held one end; other rats might gnaw it; the rat might run out of the pipe and leave the linen and money where they would never be found; a thousand other things might have happened. So began some nervous hours, but the fact that the rat ran on until only a few feet of the string remained in my cell made me think he was outside the pipe. I had carefully instructed Mr. Hatch what to do in case the note reached him. The question was: Would it reach him?

"This done, I could only wait and make other plans in case this one failed. I openly attempted to bribe my jailer, and learned from him that he held the keys to only two of seven doors between me and freedom. Then I did something else to make the warden nervous. I took the steel supports out of the heels of my shoes and made a pretense of sawing the bars of my cell window. The warden raised a pretty row about that. He developed, too, the habit of shaking the bars of my cell window to see if they were solid. They were—then."

Again the warden grinned. He had ceased being astonished.

"With this one plan I had done all I could and could only wait to see what happened," the scientist went on. "I couldn't know whether my note had been delivered or even found, or whether the rat had gnawed it up. And I didn't dare to draw back through the pipe that one slender thread which connected me with the outside.

"When I went to bed that night I didn't sleep, for fear there would come the slight signal twitch at the thread which was to tell me that Mr. Hatch had received the note. At half-past three o'clock, I judge, I felt this twitch, and no prisoner actually under sentence of death ever welcomed a thing more heartily."

The Thinking Machine stopped and turned to the reporter.

"You'd better explain just what you did," he said.

"The linen note was brought to me by a small boy who had been playing baseball," said Mr. Hatch. "I immediately saw a big story in it, so I gave the boy another ten dollars, and got several spools of silk, some twine, and a roll of light, pliable wire. The professor's note suggested that I have the finder of the note show me just where it was picked up, and told me to make my search from there, beginning at two o'clock in the morning. If I found the other end of the thread I was to twitch it gently three times, then a fourth.

"I began to search with a small bulb electric light. It was an hour and twenty minutes before I found the end of the drain pipe, half hidden in weeds. The pipe was very large there, say twelve inches across. Then I found the end of the lisle thread, twitched it as directed and immediately I got an answering twitch.

"Then I fastened the silk to this and Professor Van Dusen began to pull it into his cell. I nearly had heart disease for fear the string would break. To the end of the silk I fastened the twine, and when that had been pulled in I tied on the wire. Then that was drawn into the pipe and we had a substantial line, which the rats couldn't gnaw, from the mouth of the drain into the cell."

The Thinking Machine raised his hand and Hatch stopped.

"All this was done in absolute silence," said the scientist. "But when the wire reached my hand I could have shouted. Then we tried another experiment, which Mr. Hatch was prepared for. I tested the pipe as a speaking tube. Neither of us could hear very clearly, but I dared not speak loud for fear of attracting attention in the prison. At last I made him understand what I wanted immediately. He seemed to have great difficulty in understanding when I asked for nitric acid, and I repeated the word 'acid' several times.

"Then I heard a shriek from a cell above me. I knew instantly that some one had overheard, and when I heard you coming, Mr. Warden, I feigned sleep. If you had entered my cell at that moment that whole plan of escape would have ended there. But you passed on. That was the nearest I ever came to being caught.

"Having established this improvised trolley it is easy to see how I got things in the cell and made them disappear at will. I merely dropped them back into the pipe. You, Mr. Warden, could not have reached the connecting wire with your fingers; they are too large. My fingers, you see, are longer and more slender. In addition I guarded the top of that pipe with a rat—you remember how."

"I remember," said the warden, with a grimace.

"I thought that if any one were tempted to investigate that hole the rat would dampen his ardor. Mr. Hatch could not send me anything useful through the pipe until next night, although he did send me change for ten dollars as a test, so I proceeded with other parts of my plan. Then I evolved the method of escape, which I finally employed.

"In order to carry this out successfully it was necessary for the guard in the yard to get accustomed to seeing me at the cell window. I arranged this by dropping linen notes to him, boastful in tone, to make the warden believe, if possible, one of his assistants was communicating with the outside for me. I would stand at my window for hours gazing out, so the guard could see, and occasionally I spoke to him. In that way I learned that the prison had no electricians of its own, but was dependent upon the lighting company if anything should go wrong.

"That cleared the way to freedom perfectly. Early in the evening of the last day of my imprisonment, when it was dark, I planned to cut the feed wire which was only a few feet from my window, reaching it with an acid-tipped wire I had. That would make that side of the prison perfectly dark while the electricians were searching for the break. That would also bring Mr. Hatch into the prison yard.

"There was only one more thing to do before I actually began the work of setting myself free. This was to arrange final details with Mr. Hatch through our speaking tube. I did this within half an hour after the warden left my cell on the fourth night of my imprisonment. Mr. Hatch again had serious difficulty in understanding me, and I repeated the word 'acid' to him several times, and later the words: 'Number eight hat'—that's my size—and these were the things which made a prisoner upstairs confess to murder, so one of the jailers told me next day. This prisoner heard our voices, confused of course, through the pipe, which also went to his cell. The cell directly over me was not occupied, hence no one else heard.

"Of course the actual work of cutting the steel bars out of the window and door was comparatively easy with nitric acid, which I got through the pipe in thin bottles, but it took time. Hour after hour on the fifth and sixth and seventh days the guard below was looking at me as I worked on the bars of the window with the acid on a piece of wire. I used the tooth powder to prevent the acid spreading. I looked away abstractly as I worked and each minute the acid cut deeper into the metal. I noticed that the jailers always tried the door by shaking the upper part, never the lower bars, therefore I cut the lower bars, leaving them hanging in place by thin strips of metal. But that was a bit of dare-deviltry. I could not have gone that way so easily."

The Thinking Machine sat silent for several minutes.

"I think that makes everything clear," he went on. "Whatever points I have not explained were merely to confuse the warden and jailers. These things in my bed I brought in to please Mr. Hatch, who wanted to improve the story. Of course, the wig was necessary in my plan. The special delivery letter I wrote and directed in my cell with Mr. Hatch's fountain pen, then sent it out to him and he mailed it. That's all, I think."

"But your actually leaving the prison grounds and then coming in through the outer gate to my office?" asked the warden.

"Perfectly simple," said the scientist. "I cut the electric light wire with acid, as I said, when the current was off. Therefore when the current was turned on the arc didn't light. I knew it would take some time to find out what was the matter and make repairs. When the guard went to report to you the yard was dark. I crept out the window—it was a tight fit, too—replaced the bars by standing on a narrow ledge and remained in a shadow until the force of electricians arrived. Mr. Hatch was one of them.

"When I saw him I spoke and he handed me a cap, a jumper and overalls, which I put on within ten feet of you, Mr. Warden, while you were in the yard. Later Mr. Hatch called me, presumably as a workman, and together we went out the gate to get something out of the wagon. The gate guard let us pass out readily as two workmen who had just passed in. We changed our clothing and reappeared, asking to see you. We saw you. That's all."

There was silence for several minutes. Dr. Ransome was first to speak.

"Wonderful!" he exclaimed. "Perfectly amazing."

"How did Mr. Hatch happen to come with the electricians?" asked Mr. Fielding.

"His father is manager of the company," replied The Thinking Machine.

"But what if there had been no Mr. Hatch outside to help?"

"Every prisoner has one friend outside who would help him escape if he could."

"Suppose—just suppose—there had been no old plumbing system there?" asked the warden, curiously.

"There were two other ways out," said The Thinking Machine, enigmatically.

Ten minutes later the telephone bell rang. It was a request for the warden.

"Light all right, eh?" the warden asked, through the 'phone. "Good. Wire cut beside Cell 13? Yes, I know. One electrician too many? What's that? Two came out?"

The warden turned to the others with a puzzled expression.

"He only let in four electricians, he has let out two and says there are three left."

"I was the odd one," said The Thinking Machine.

"Oh," said the warden. "I see." Then through the 'phone: "Let the fifth man go. He's all right."

MELVILLE DAVISSON POST

(1869–1930)

||||||||||||||||||||||||||||||||||||||||||||| ■ |||||||||||||||||||||||||||||||||||||||||||||

Melville Davisson Post's two series characters, who earned their author wide popular acclaim in his day, are a study in contrasts. The antihero in his first book of crime stories and two later anthologies is Randolph Mason, an unscrupulous lawyer who expertly levers his criminal clients through legal loopholes. Mason's opposite is the scrupulous, Bible-quoting moralist Uncle Abner, whose efforts at uncovering crime in the hearts and actions of backwoods Virginians establish not only man's justice but God's.

Both of Post's characters are larger-than-life figures who use their different expertise to amaze their clients and Post's readers alike. Mason's legal expertise comes from his creator's own experience of the law. Post practiced criminal and corporate law for eleven years before becoming involved in Democratic politics. Criticized for allowing Mason to use the law to help criminals, Post wrote, "Nothing but good can come of exposing the law's defects." Some changes in criminal codes were actually made in response to Mason stories.

Abner was Post's answer to the lawlessness of the mountain men whom he knew intimately. Born in Romines Mills, West Virginia, Post was raised in the wild hills that he depicted in the Abner stories. His highly successful regional writing is considered to be an early influence leading to the blossoming of regionalism in American detective fiction.

Even critics who have not been enthusiastic about the literary quality of his work acknowledge Post's skill at plotting. They concede, along with Chris Steinbrunner and Otto Penzler in their *Encyclopedia of Mystery and Detection*, that he did much to speed up the pace of the detective story "by developing the mystery and its solution simultaneously."

A great commercial success as a magazine writer, the versatile and confident Post also dared to create a British sleuth, Sir Henry Marquis, chief of the Criminal Investigation Department of Scotland Yard, whose work takes him to international locales, including Asia and the United States. Another character, Walker of the Secret Service, had robbed trains until he reformed and became a federal agent. Post ventured into Paris with Monsieur Jonquelle, Prefect of Police of Paris, and returned to the Virginia hills with his gentleman lawyer, Colonel Braxton.

Loaded with biblical allusions and quotations, "The Doomdorf Mystery" exemplifies the Abner stories. The final line is an Abner classic.

1914

The Doomdorf Mystery

■

The pioneer was not the only man in the great mountains behind Virginia. Strange aliens drifted in after the Colonial wars. All foreign armies are sprinkled with a cockle of adventurers that take root and remain. They were with Braddock and La Salle, and they rode north out of Mexico after her many empires went to pieces.

I think Doomdorf crossed the seas with Iturbide when that ill-starred adventurer returned to be shot against a wall; but there was no Southern blood in him. He came from some European race remote and barbaric. The evidences were all about him. He was a huge figure of a man, with a black spade beard, broad, thick hands, and square, flat fingers.

He had found a wedge of land between the Crown's grant to Daniel Davisson and a Washington survey. It was an uncovered triangle not worth the running of the lines; and so, no doubt, was left out, a sheer rock standing up out of the river for a base, and a peak of the mountain rising northward behind it for an apex.

Doomdorf squatted on the rock. He must have brought a belt of gold pieces when he took to his horse, for he hired old Robert Steuart's slaves and built a stone house on the rock, and he brought the furnishings overland from a frigate in the Chesapeake; and then in the handfuls of earth, wherever a root would hold, he planted the mountain behind his house with peach trees. The gold gave out; but the devil is fertile in resources. Doomdorf built a log still and turned the first fruits of the garden into a hell-brew. The idle and the vicious came with their stone jugs, and violence and riot flowed out.

The government of Virginia was remote and its arm short and feeble; but the men who held the lands west of the mountains against the savages under grants from George, and after that held them against George himself, were efficient and expeditious. They had long patience, but when that failed they went up from their fields and drove the thing before them out of the land, like a scourge of God.

There came a day, then, when my Uncle Abner and Squire Randolph rode through the gap of the mountains to have the thing out with Doomdorf. The work of this brew, which had the odors of Eden and the impulses of the devil in it, could be borne no longer. The drunken negroes had shot old Duncan's cattle and burned his haystacks, and the land was on its feet.

They rode alone, but they were worth an army of little men. Randolph was vain and pompous and given over to extravagance of words, but he was a gentleman beneath it, and fear was an alien and a stranger to him. And Abner was the right hand of the land.

It was a day in early summer and the sun lay hot. They crossed through the broken spine of the mountains and trailed along the river in the shade of the great chestnut trees. The road was only a path and the horses went one before the other. It left the river when the rock began to rise and, making a detour through the grove of peach trees, reached the house on the mountain side. Randolph and Abner got down, unsaddled their horses and turned them out to graze, for their business with Doomdorf would not be over in an hour. Then they took a steep path that brought them out on the mountain side of the house.

A man sat on a big red-roan horse in the paved court before the door. He was a gaunt old man. He sat bare-headed, the palms of his hands resting on the pommel of his saddle, his chin sunk in his black stock, his face in retrospection, the wind moving gently his great shock of voluminous white hair. Under him the huge red horse stood with his legs spread out like a horse of stone.

There was no sound. The door to the house was closed; insects moved in the sun; a shadow crept out from the motionless figure, and swarms of yellow butterflies maneuvered like an army.

Abner and Randolph stopped. They knew the tragic figure—a circuit rider of the hills who preached the invective of Isaiah as though he were the mouthpiece of a militant and avenging overlord; as though the government of Virginia were the awful theocracy of the Book of Kings. The horse was dripping with sweat and the man bore the dust and the evidences of a journey on him.

"Bronson," said Abner, "where is Doomdorf?"

The old man lifted his head and looked down at Abner over the pommel of the saddle.

"'Surely,'" he said, "''he covereth his feet in his summer chamber.'"

Abner went over and knocked on the closed door, and presently the white, frightened face of a woman looked out at him. She was a little, faded woman, with fair hair, a broad foreign face, but with the delicate evidences of gentle blood.

Abner repeated his question.

"Where is Doomdorf?"

"Oh, sir," she answered with a queer lisping accent, "he went to lie down in his south room after his midday meal, as his custom is; and I went to the orchard to gather any fruit that might be ripened." She hesitated and her voice lisped into a whisper: "He is not come out and I cannot wake him."

The two men followed her through the hall and up the stairway to the door.

"It is always bolted," she said, "when he goes to lie down." And she knocked feebly with the tips of her fingers.

There was no answer and Randolph rattled the doorknob.

"Come out, Doomdorf!" he called in his big, bellowing voice.

There was only silence and the echoes of the words among the rafters. Then Randolph set his shoulder to the door and burst it open.

They went in. The room was flooded with sun from the tall south windows. Doomdorf lay on a couch in a little offset of the room, a great scarlet patch on his bosom and a pool of scarlet on the floor.

The woman stood for a moment staring; then she cried out:

"At last I have killed him!" And she ran like a frightened hare.

The two men closed the door and went over to the couch. Doomdorf had been shot to death. There was a great ragged hole in his waistcoat. They began to look about for the weapon with which the deed had been accomplished, and in a moment found it—a fowling piece lying in two dogwood forks against the wall. The gun had just been fired; there was a freshly exploded paper cap under the hammer.

There was little else in the room—a loom-woven rag carpet on the floor; wooden shutters flung back from the windows; a great oak table, and on it a big, round, glass water bottle, filled to its glass stopper with raw liquor from the still. The stuff was limpid and clear as spring water; and, but for its pungent odor, one would have taken it for God's brew instead of Doomdorf's. The sun lay on it and against the wall where hung the weapon that had ejected the dead man out of life.

"Abner," said Randolph, "this is murder! The woman took that gun down from the wall and shot Doomdorf while he slept."

Abner was standing by the table, his fingers round his chin.

"Randolph," he replied, "what brought Bronson here?"

"The same outrages that brought us," said Randolph. "The mad old circuit rider has been preaching a crusade against Doomdorf far and wide in the hills."

Abner answered, without taking his fingers from about his chin:

"You think this woman killed Doomdorf? Well, let us go and ask Bronson who killed him."

They closed the door, leaving the dead man on his couch, and went down into the court.

The old circuit rider had put away his horse and got an ax. He had taken off his coat and pushed his shirtsleeves up over his long elbows. He was on his way to the still to destroy the barrels of liquor. He stopped when the two men came out, and Abner called to him.

"Bronson," he said, "who killed Doomdorf?"

"I killed him," replied the old man, and went on toward the still.

Randolph swore under his breath. "By the Almighty," he said, "everybody couldn't kill him!"

"Who can tell how many had a hand in it?" replied Abner.

"Two have confessed!" cried Randolph. "Was there perhaps a third? Did you kill him, Abner? And I too? Man, the thing is impossible!"

"The impossible," replied Abner, "looks here like the truth. Come with me, Randolph, and I will show you a thing more impossible than this."

They returned through the house and up the stairs to the room. Abner closed the door behind them.

"Look at this bolt," he said; "it is on the inside and not connected with the lock. How did the one who killed Doomdorf get into this room, since the door was bolted?"

"Through the windows," replied Randolph.

There were but two windows, facing the south, through which the sun entered. Abner led Randolph to them.

"Look!" he said. "The wall of the house is plumb with the sheer face of the rock. It is a hundred feet to the river and the rock is as smooth as a sheet of glass. But that is not all. Look at these window frames; they are cemented into their casement with dust and they are bound along their edges with cobwebs. These windows have not been opened. How did the assassin enter?"

"The answer is evident," said Randolph: "The one who killed Doomdorf hid in the room until he was asleep; then he shot him and went out."

"The explanation is excellent but for one thing," replied Abner: "How did the assassin bolt the door behind him on the inside of this room after he had gone out?"

Randolph flung out his arms with a hopeless gesture.

"Who knows?" he cried. "Maybe Doomdorf killed himself."

Abner laughed.

"And after firing a handful of shot into his heart he got up and put the gun back carefully into the forks against the wall!"

"Well," cried Randolph, "there is one open road out of this mystery. Bronson and this woman say they killed Doomdorf, and if they killed him they surely know how they did it. Let us go down and ask them."

"In the law court," replied Abner, "that procedure would be considered sound sense; but we are in God's court and things are managed there in a somewhat stranger way. Before we go let us find out, if we can, at what hour it was that Doomdorf died."

He went over and took a big silver watch out of the dead man's pocket. It was broken by a shot and the hands lay at one hour after noon. He stood for a moment fingering his chin.

"At one o'clock," he said. "Bronson, I think, was on the road to this place, and the woman was on the mountain among the peach trees."

Randolph threw back his shoulders.

"Why waste time in a speculation about it, Abner?" he said. "We know who did this thing. Let us go and get the story of it out of their own mouths. Doomdorf died by the hands of either Bronson or this woman."

"I could better believe it," replied Abner, "but for the running of a certain awful law."

"What law?" said Randolph. "Is it a statute of Virginia?"

"It is a statute," replied Abner, "of an authority somewhat higher. Mark the language of it: 'He that killeth with the sword must be killed with the sword.'"

He came over and took Randolph by the arm.

"Must! Randolph, did you mark particularly the word 'must'? It is a mandatory law. There is no room in it for the vicissitudes of chance or fortune. There is no way round that word. Thus, we reap what we sow and nothing else; thus, we receive what we give and nothing else. It is the weapon in our own hands that finally destroys us. You are looking at it now." And he turned him about so that the table and the weapon and the dead man were before him. "'He that killeth with the sword must be killed with the sword.' And now," he said, "let us go and try the method of the law courts. Your faith is in the wisdom of their ways."

They found the old circuit rider at work in the still, staving in Doomdorf's liquor casks, splitting the oak heads with his ax.

"Bronson," said Randolph, "how did you kill Doomdorf?"

The old man stopped and stood leaning on his ax.

"I killed him," replied the old man, "as Elijah killed the captains of Ahaziah and their fifties. But not by the hand of any man did I pray the Lord God to destroy Doomdorf, but with fire from heaven to destroy him."

He stood up and extended his arms.

"His hands were full of blood," he said. "With his abomination from these groves of Baal he stirred up the people to contention, to strife and murder. The widow and the orphan cried to heaven against him. 'I will surely hear their cry,' is the promise written in the Book. The land was weary of him; and I prayed the Lord God to destroy him with fire from heaven, as he destroyed the Princes of Gomorrah in their palaces!"

Randolph made a gesture as of one who dismisses the impossible, but Abner's face took on a deep, strange look.

"With fire from heaven!" he repeated slowly to himself. Then he asked a question. "A little while ago," he said, "when we came, I asked you where Doomdorf was, and you answered me in the language of the third chapter of the Book of Judges. Why did you answer me like that, Bronson?—'Surely he covereth his feet in his summer chamber.'"

"The woman told me that he had not come down from the room where he had gone up to sleep," replied the old man, "and that the door was locked. And then I knew that he was dead in his summer chamber like Eglon, King of Moab."

He extended his arm toward the south.

"I came here from the Great Valley," he said, "to cut down these groves of Baal and to empty out this abomination; but I did not know that the Lord had heard my prayer and visited His wrath on Doomdorf until I was come up into these mountains to his door. When the woman spoke I knew it." And he went away to his horse, leaving the ax among the ruined barrels.

Randolph interrupted.

"Come, Abner," he said; "this is wasted time. Bronson did not kill Doomdorf."

Abner answered slowly in his deep, level voice:

"Do you realize, Randolph, how Doomdorf died?"

"Not by fire from heaven, at any rate," said Randolph.

"Randolph," replied Abner, "are you sure?"

"Abner," cried Randolph, "you are pleased to jest, but I am in deadly earnest. A crime has been done here against the state. I am an officer of justice and I propose to discover the assassin if I can."

He walked away toward the house and Abner followed, his hands behind him and his great shoulders thrown loosely forward, with a grim smile about his mouth.

"It is no use to talk with the mad old preacher," Randolph went on. "Let him empty out the liquor and ride away. I won't issue a warrant against him. Prayer may be a handy implement to do a murder with, Abner, but it is not a deadly weapon under the statutes of Virginia. Doomdorf was dead when old Bronson got here with his Scriptural jargon. This woman killed Doomdorf. I shall put her to an inquisition."

"As you like," replied Abner. "Your faith remains in the methods of the law courts."

"Do you know of any better methods?" said Randolph.

"Perhaps," replied Abner, "when you have finished."

Night had entered the valley. The two men went into the house and set about preparing the corpse for burial. They got candles, and made a coffin, and put Doomdorf in it, and straightened out his limbs, and folded his arms across his shot-out heart. Then they set the coffin on benches in the hall.

They kindled a fire in the dining room and sat down before it, with the door open and the red firelight shining through on the dead man's narrow, everlasting house. The woman had put some cold meat, a golden cheese and a loaf on the table. They did not see her, but they heard her moving about the house; and finally, on the gravel court outside, her step and the whinny of a horse. Then she came in, dressed as for a journey. Randolph sprang up.

"Where are you going?" he said.

"To the sea and a ship," replied the woman. Then she indicated the hall with a gesture. "He is dead and I am free."

There was a sudden illumination in her face. Randolph took a step toward her. His voice was big and harsh.

"Who killed Doomdorf?" he cried.

"I killed him," replied the woman. "It was fair!"

"Fair!" echoed the justice. "What do you mean by that?"

The woman shrugged her shoulders and put out her hands with a foreign gesture.

"I remember an old, old man sitting against a sunny wall, and a little girl, and one who came and talked a long time with the old man, while the little girl plucked yellow flowers out of the grass and put them into her hair. Then finally the stranger gave the old man a gold chain and took the little girl away." She flung out her hands. "Oh, it was fair to kill him!" She looked up with a queer, pathetic smile.

"The old man will be gone by now," she said; "but I shall perhaps find the wall there, with the sun on it, and the yellow flowers in the grass. And now, may I go?"

It is a law of the story-teller's art that he does not tell a story. It is the listener who tells it. The story-teller does but provide him with the stimuli.

Randolph got up and walked about the floor. He was a justice of the peace in a day when that office was filled only by the landed gentry, after the English fashion; and the obligations of the law were strong on him. If he should take liberties with the letter of it, how could the weak and the evil be made to hold it in respect? Here was this woman before him a confessed assassin. Could he let her go?

Abner sat unmoving by the hearth, his elbow on the arm of his chair, his palm propping up his jaw, his face clouded in deep lines. Randolph was consumed with vanity and the weakness of ostentation, but he shouldered his duties for himself. Presently he stopped and looked at the woman, wan, faded like some prisoner of legend escaped out of fabled dungeons into the sun.

The firelight flickered past her to the box on the benches in the hall, and the vast, inscrutable justice of heaven entered and overcame him.

"Yes," he said. "Go! There is no jury in Virginia that would hold a woman for shooting a beast like that." And he thrust out his arm, with the fingers extended toward the dead man.

The woman made a little awkward curtsy.

"I thank you, sir." Then she hesitated and lisped, "But I have not shoot him."

"Not shoot him!" cried Randolph. "Why, the man's heart is riddled!"

"Yes, sir," she said simply, like a child. "I kill him, but have not shoot him."

Randolph took two long strides toward the woman.

"Not shoot him!" he repeated. "How then, in the name of heaven, did you kill Doomdorf?" And his big voice filled the empty places of the room.

"I will show you, sir," she said.

She turned and went away into the house. Presently she returned with something folded up in a linen towel. She put it on the table between the loaf of bread and the yellow cheese.

Randolph stood over the table, and the woman's deft fingers undid the towel from round its deadly contents; and presently the thing lay there uncovered.

It was a little crude model of a human figure done in wax with a needle thrust through the bosom.

Randolph stood up with a great intake of the breath.

"Magic! By the eternal!"

"Yes, sir," the woman explained, in her voice and manner of a child. "I have try to kill him many times—oh, very many times!—with witch words which I have remember; but always they fail. Then, at last, I make him in wax, and I put a needle through his heart; and I kill him very quickly."

It was as clear as daylight, even to Randolph, that the woman was innocent. Her little harmless magic was the pathetic effort of a child to kill a dragon. He hesitated a moment before he spoke, and then he decided like the gentleman he was. If it helped the child to believe that her enchanted straw had slain the monster—well, he would let her believe it.

"And now, sir, may I go?"

Randolph looked at the woman in a sort of wonder.

"Are you not afraid," he said, "of the night and the mountains, and the long road?"

"Oh no, sir," she replied simply. "The good God will be everywhere now."

It was an awful commentary on the dead man—that this strange half-child believed that all the evil in the world had gone out with him; that now that he was dead, the sunlight of heaven would fill every nook and corner.

It was not a faith that either of the two men wished to shatter, and they let her go. It would be daylight presently and the road through the mountains to the Chesapeake was open.

Randolph came back to the fireside after he had helped her into the saddle, and sat down. He tapped on the hearth for some time idly with the iron poker; and then finally he spoke.

"This is the strangest thing that ever happened," he said. "Here's a mad old preacher who thinks that he killed Doomdorf with fire from Heaven, like Elijah the Tishbite; and here is a simple child of a woman who thinks she killed him with a piece of magic of the Middle Ages— each as innocent of his death as I am. And yet, by the eternal, the beast is dead!"

He drummed on the hearth with the poker, lifting it up and letting it drop through the hollow of his fingers.

"Somebody shot Doomdorf. But who? And how did he get into and out of that shut-up room? The assassin that killed Doomdorf must have gotten into the room to kill him. Now, how did he get in?" He spoke as to himself; but my uncle sitting across the hearth replied:

"Through the window."

"Through the window!" echoed Randolph. "Why, man, you yourself showed me that the window had not been opened, and the precipice below it a fly could hardly climb. Do you tell me now that the window was opened?"

"No," said Abner, "it was never opened."

Randolph got on his feet.

"Abner," he cried, "are you saying that the one who killed Doomdorf climbed the sheer wall and got in through a closed window, without disturbing the dust or the cobwebs on the window frame?"

My uncle looked Randolph in the face.

"The murderer of Doomdorf did even more," he said. "That assassin not only climbed the face of that precipice and got in through the closed window, but he shot Doomdorf to death and got out again through the closed window without leaving a single track or trace behind, and without disturbing a grain of dust or a thread of a cobweb."

Randolph swore a great oath.

"The thing is impossible!" he cried. "Men are not killed today in Virginia by black art or a curse of God."

"By black art, no," replied Abner; "but by the curse of God, yes. I think they are."

Randolph drove his clenched right hand into the palm of his left.

"By the eternal!" he cried. "I would like to see the assassin who could do a murder like this, whether he be an imp from the pit or an angel out of heaven."

"Very well," replied Abner, undisturbed. "When he comes back tomorrow I will show you the assassin who killed Doomdorf."

When day broke they dug a grave and buried the dead man against the mountain among his peach trees. It was noon when that work was ended. Abner threw down his spade and looked up at the sun.

"Randolph," he said, "let us go and lay an ambush for this assassin. He is on the way here."

And it was a strange ambush that he laid. When they were come again into the chamber where Doomdorf died he bolted the door; then he loaded the fowling piece and put it carefully back on its rack against the wall. After that he did another curious thing: He took the blood-stained coat, which they had stripped off the dead man when they had prepared his body for the earth, put a pillow in it and laid it on the couch precisely where Doomdorf had slept. And while he did these things Randolph stood in wonder and Abner talked:

"Look you, Randolph. . . . We will trick the murderer. . . . We will catch him in the act."

Then he went over and took the puzzled justice by the arm.

"Watch!" he said. "The assassin is coming along the wall!"

But Randolph heard nothing, saw nothing. Only the sun entered. Abner's hand tightened on his arm.

"It is here! Look!" And he pointed to the wall.

Randolph, following the extended finger, saw a tiny brilliant disk of light moving slowly up the wall toward the lock of the fowling piece. Abner's hand became a vise and his voice rang as over metal.

"'He that killeth with the sword must be killed with the sword.' It is the water bottle, full of Doomdorf's liquor, focusing the sun. . . . And look, Randolph, how Bronson's prayer was answered!"

The tiny disk of light traveled on the plate of the lock.

"It is fire from heaven!"

The words rang above the roar of the fowling piece, and Randolph saw the dead man's coat leap up on the couch, riddled by the shot. The gun, in its natural position on the rack, pointed to the couch standing at the end of the chamber, beyond the offset of the wall, and the focused sun had exploded the percussion cap.

Randolph made a great gesture, with his arm extended.

"It is a world," he said, "filled with the mysterious joinder of accident!"

"It is a world," replied Abner, "filled with the mysterious justice of God!"

ANNA KATHARINE GREEN

(1846–1935)

||||||||||||||||||||||||||||||||||||||||||||||| ■ |||||||||||||||||||||||||||||||||||||||||||||

Often referred to as the mother of detective fiction, Anna Katharine Green deserves her distinction. Her accomplishments included the establishment and refining of many of the conventions of the genre that we now take for granted, and—along with depicting a male police detective—the creation of two of the earliest women sleuths in fiction. A contemporary of Sir Arthur Conan Doyle, this New Yorker produced both police procedurals and private-investigator fiction. The heart of Green's literary career, which provided the main support for her family, spanned two decades on each side of the turn of the century.

While Conan Doyle was developing the civilian sleuth, Green wrote one of the first authentic police procedurals, *The Leavenworth Case: A Lawyer's Story*, in 1878. In this hugely successful first novel, she followed the work of New York City police detective Ebenezer Gryce. It might be noted that Gryce's reasoning is sometimes dubious. (For example, he clears a niece of suspicion when he sees lint from a cleaning cloth on the cylinder of the murder weapon. A woman, he declares, would fire a pistol but never clean it.)

The Leavenworth Case is said to be the first detective novel written by a woman under her own name. It is notable not only for the sleuth's reliance on reason to solve the case but also for pointing out the problems inherent in undue reliance on circumstantial evidence. The Yale Law School assigned it as required reading, and it sold a million copies in Green's day.

Gryce appeared in more than a dozen novels, often in the company of other series characters, including the sometimes rivalrous Caleb Sweetwater and the spinster-sleuth Amelia Butterworth. This last, a middle-age, upper-middle-class, middlebrow detective, is a prototype for Agatha Christie's Miss Jane Marple and other female amateur investigators of the golden age of detective fiction.

Violet Strange, who appears in "Missing: Page Thirteen," is less staunch than Butterworth but more determined to make a paying career of the detective business. She pursues her work in order to pay for her widowed sister's voice lessons, an enterprise so frowned upon by their father that he has disowned Strange's sister. In order to avoid a similar fate, Strange keeps her sleuthing secret. An active social life provides her with entrée into households where family wealth walks hand in hand with family secrets, where the atmosphere is Gothic, and where intuition guides her interpretation of evidence acquired through earnest—and sometimes courageous—resourcefulness. As do Green's novels, this tale illuminates social conventions oppressive to women.

1915

Missing: Page Thirteen

■

I

"One more! just one more well paying affair, and I promise to stop; really and truly to stop."

"But, Puss, why one more? You have earned the amount you set for yourself,—or very nearly,—and though my help is not great, in three months I can add enough—"

"No, you cannot, Arthur. You are doing well; I appreciate it; in fact, I am just delighted to have you work for me in the way you do, but you cannot, in your present position, make enough in three months, or in six, to meet the situation as I see it. Enough does not satisfy me. The measure must be full, heaped up, and running over. Possible failure following promise must be provided for. Never must I feel myself called upon to do this kind of thing again. Besides, I have never got over the Zabriskie tragedy. It haunts me continually. Something new may help to put it out of my head. I feel guilty. I was responsible—"

"No, Puss. I will not have it that you were responsible. Some such end was bound to follow a complication like that. Sooner or later he would have been driven to shoot himself—"

"But not her."

"No, not her. But do you think she would have given those few minutes of perfect understanding with her blind husband for a few years more of miserable life?"

Violet made no answer; she was too absorbed in her surprise. Was this Arthur? Had a few weeks' work and a close connection with the really serious things of life made this change in him? Her face beamed at the thought, which seeing, but not understanding what underlay this evidence of joy, he bent and kissed her, saying with some of his old nonchalance:

"Forget it, Violet; only don't let any one or anything lead you to interest yourself in another affair of the kind. If you do, I shall have to consult a certain friend of yours as to the best way of stopping this folly. I mention no names. Oh! you need not look so frightened. Only behave; that's all."

"He's right," she acknowledged to herself, as he sauntered away; "altogether right."

Yet because she wanted the extra money—

The scene invited alarm—that is, for so young a girl as Violet, surveying it from an automobile some time after the stroke of midnight. An unknown house at the end of a heavily shaded walk, in the open doorway of which could be seen the silhouette of a woman's form leaning eagerly forward with arms outstretched in an appeal for help! It vanished while she looked, but the effect remained, holding her to her seat for one startled moment. This seemed strange, for she had anticipated adventure. One is not summoned from a private ball to ride a dozen miles into the country on an errand of investigation, without some expectation of encountering the mysterious and the tragic. But Violet Strange, for all her many experiences, was of a most susceptible nature, and for the instant in which that door stood open, with only the memory of that expectant figure to disturb the faintly lit vista of the hall beyond, she felt that grip upon the throat which comes from an indefinable fear which no words can explain and no plummet sound.

But this soon passed. With the setting of her foot to ground, conditions changed and her emotions took on a more normal character. The figure of a man now stood in the place held by the vanished woman, and it was not only that of one she knew but that of one whom she trusted—a friend whose very presence gave her courage. With this recognition came a better understanding of the situation, and it was with a beaming eye and unclouded features that she tripped up the walk to meet the expectant figure and outstretched hand of Roger Upjohn.

"You here!" she exclaimed, amid smiles and blushes, as he drew her into the hall.

He at once launched forth into explanations mingled with apologies for the presumption he had shown in putting her to this inconvenience. There was trouble in the house—great trouble. Something had occurred for which an explanation must be found before morning, or the happiness and honour of more than one person now under this unhappy roof would be wrecked. He knew it was late—that she had been obliged to take a long and dreary ride alone, but her success with the problem which had once come near wrecking his own life had emboldened him to telephone to the office and— "But you are in ball-dress," he cried in amazement. "Did you think—"

"I came from a ball. Word reached me between the dances. I did not go home. I had been bidden to hurry."

He looked his appreciation, but when he spoke it was to say:

"This is the situation. Miss Digby—"

"The lady who is to be married to-morrow?"

"Who *hopes* to be married to-morrow."

"How, *hopes*?"

"Who *will* be married to-morrow, if a certain article lost in this house to-night can be found before any of the persons who have been dining here leave for their homes."

Violet uttered an exclamation.

"Then, Mr. Cornell," she began—

"Mr. Cornell has our utmost confidence," Roger hastened to interpose. "But the article missing is one which he might reasonably desire to possess and which he alone of all present had the opportunity of securing. You can therefore see why he, with his pride—the pride of a man not rich, engaged to marry a woman who is—should declare that unless his innocence is established before daybreak, the doors of St. Bartholomew will remain shut to-morrow."

"But the article lost—what is it?"

"Miss Digby will give you the particulars. She is waiting to receive you," he added with a gesture towards a half-open door at their right.

Violet glanced that way, then cast her looks up and down the hall in which they stood.

"Do you know that you have not told me in whose house I am? Not hers, I know. She lives in the city."

"And you are twelve miles from Harlem. Miss Strange, you are in the Van Broecklyn mansion, famous enough you will acknowledge. Have you never been here before?"

"I have been by here, but I recognized nothing in the dark. What an exciting place for an investigation!"

"And Mr. Van Broecklyn? Have you never met him?"

"Once, when a child. He frightened me *then.*"

"And may frighten you now; though I doubt it. Time has mellowed him. Besides, I have prepared him for what might otherwise occasion him some astonishment. Naturally he would not look for just the sort of lady investigator I am about to introduce to him."

She smiled. Violet Strange was a very charming young woman, as well as a keen prober of odd mysteries.

The meeting between herself and Miss Digby was a sympathetic one. After the first inevitable shock which the latter felt at sight of the beauty and fashionable appearance of the mysterious little being who was to solve her difficulties, her glance, which, under other circumstances, might have lingered unduly upon the piquant features and exquisite dressing of the fairy-like figure before her, passed at once to Violet's eyes in whose steady depths beamed an intelligence quite at odds with the coquettish dimples which so often misled the casual observer in his estimation of a character singularly subtle and well-poised.

As for the impression she herself made upon Violet, it was the same she made upon everyone. No one could look long at Florence Digby and not recognize the loftiness of her spirit and the generous nature of her impulses. In person she was tall, and as she leaned to take Violet's hand, the difference between them brought out the salient points in each, to the great admiration of the one onlooker.

Meantime, for all her interest in the case in hand, Violet could not help casting a hurried look about her, in gratification of the curiosity incited by her entrance into a house signalized from its foundation by such a series of tragic events. The result was disappointing. The walls were plain, the furniture simple. Nothing suggestive in either, unless it was the fact that nothing was new, nothing modern. As it looked in the days of Burr and Hamilton so it looked to-day, even to the rather startling detail of candles which did duty on every side in place of gas.

As Violet recalled the reason for this, the fascination of the past seized upon her imagination. There was no knowing where this might have carried her, had not the feverish gleam in Miss Digby's eyes warned her that the present held its own excitement. Instantly, she was all attention and listening with undivided mind to that lady's disclosures.

They were brief and to the following effect:

The dinner which had brought some half-dozen people together in this house had been given in celebration of her impending marriage. But it was also in a way meant as a compliment to one of the other guests, a Mr. Spielhagen, who, during the week, had succeeded in demonstrating to a few experts the value of a discovery he had made which would transform a great industry.

In speaking of this discovery, Miss Digby did not go into particulars, the whole matter being far beyond her understanding; but in stating its value she openly acknowledged that it was in the line of Mr. Cornell's own work, and one which involved calculations and a formula which, if prematurely disclosed, would invalidate the contract Mr. Spielhagen hoped to make, and thus destroy his present hopes.

Of this formula but two copies existed. One was locked up in a safe deposit vault in Boston, the other he had brought into the house on his person, and it was the latter which was now missing, it having been abstracted during the evening from a manuscript of sixteen or more sheets, under circumstances which she would now endeavour to relate.

Mr. Van Broecklyn, their host, had in his melancholy life but one interest which could be called at all absorbing. This was for explosives. As a consequence, much of the talk at the dinner-table had been on Mr. Spielhagen's discovery, and the possible changes it might introduce into this especial industry. As these, worked out from a formula kept secret from the trade, could not but affect greatly Mr. Cornell's interests, she found herself listening intently, when Mr. Van Broecklyn, with an apology for his interference, ventured to remark that if Mr. Spielhagen had made a valuable discovery in this line, so had he, and one which he had substantiated by many experiments. It was not a marketable one, such as Mr. Spielhagen's was, but in his work upon the same, and in the tests which he had been led to make, he had discovered certain instances he would gladly name, which demanded exceptional procedure to be successful. If Mr. Spielhagen's method did not allow for these exceptions, nor make suitable provision for them, then Mr. Spielhagen's method would fail more times than it would succeed. Did it so allow and so provide? It would relieve him greatly to learn that it did.

The answer came quickly. Yes, it did. But later and after some further conversation, Mr. Spielhagen's confidence seemed to wane, and before they left the dinner-table, he openly declared his intention of looking over his manuscript again that very night, in order to be sure that the formula therein contained duly covered all the exceptions mentioned by Mr. Van Broecklyn.

If Mr. Cornell's countenance showed any change at this moment, she for one had not noticed it; but the bitterness with which he remarked upon the other's good fortune in having discovered this formula of whose entire success he had no doubt, was apparent to everybody, and naturally gave point to the circumstances which a short time afterward associated him with the disappearance of the same.

The ladies (there were two others besides herself) having withdrawn in a body to the music-room, the gentlemen all proceeded to the library to smoke. Here, conversation, loosed from the one topic which had hitherto engrossed it, was proceeding briskly, when Mr. Spielhagen, with a nervous gesture, impulsively looked about him and said:

"I cannot rest till I have run through my thesis again. Where can I find a quiet spot? I won't be long; I read very rapidly."

It was for Mr. Van Broecklyn to answer, but no word coming from him, every eye turned his way, only to find him sunk in one of those fits of abstraction so well known to his friends, and from which no one who has this strange man's peace of mind at heart ever presumes to rouse him.

What was to be done? These moods of their singular host sometimes lasted half an hour, and Mr. Spielhagen had not the appearance of a man of patience. Indeed he presently gave proof of the great uneasiness he was labouring under, for noticing a door standing ajar on the other side of the room, he remarked to those around him:

"A den! and lighted! Do you see any objection to my shutting myself in there for a few minutes?"

No one venturing to reply, he rose, and giving a slight push to the door, disclosed a small room exquisitely panelled and brightly lighted, but without one article of furniture in it, not even a chair.

"The very place," quoth Mr. Spielhagen, and lifting a light cane-bottomed chair from the many standing about, he carried it inside and shut the door behind him.

Several minutes passed during which the man who had served at table entered with a tray on which were several small glasses evidently containing some choice liqueur. Finding his master fixed in one of his strange moods, he set the tray down and, pointing to one of the glasses, said:

"That is for Mr. Van Broecklyn. It contains his usual quieting powder." And urging the gentlemen to help themselves, he quietly left the room.

Mr. Upjohn lifted the glass nearest him, and Mr. Cornell seemed about to do the same when he suddenly reached forward and catching up one farther off started for the room in which Mr. Spielhagen had so deliberately secluded himself.

Why he did all this—why, above all things, he should reach across the tray for a glass instead of taking the one under his hand, he can no more explain than why he has followed many another unhappy impulse. Nor did he understand the nervous start given by Mr. Spielhagen at his entrance, or the stare with which that gentleman took the glass from his hand and mechanically drank its contents, till he saw how his hand had stretched itself across the sheet of paper he was reading, in an open attempt to hide the lines visible between his fingers. Then indeed the intruder flushed and withdrew in great embarrassment, fully conscious of his indiscretion but not deeply disturbed till Mr. Van Broecklyn, suddenly arousing and glancing down at the tray placed very near his hand, remarked in some surprise: "Dobbs seems to have forgotten me." Then indeed, the unfortunate Mr. Cornell realized what he had done. It was the glass intended for his host which he had caught up and carried into the other room—the glass which he had been told contained a drug. Of what folly he had been guilty, and how tame would be any effort at excuse!

Attempting none, he rose and with a hurried glance at Mr. Upjohn who flushed in sympathy at his distress, he crossed to the door he had so lately closed upon Mr. Spielhagen. But feeling his shoulder touched as his hand pressed the knob, he turned to meet the eye of Mr. Van

Broecklyn fixed upon him with an expression which utterly confounded him.

"Where are you going?" that gentleman asked.

The questioning tone, the severe look, expressive at once of displeasure and astonishment, were most disconcerting, but Mr. Cornell managed to stammer forth:

"Mr. Spielhagen is in here consulting his thesis. When your man brought in the cordial, I was awkward enough to catch up your glass and carry it in to Mr. Spielhagen. He drank it and I—I am anxious to see if it did him any harm."

As he uttered the last word he felt Mr. Van Broecklyn's hand slip from his shoulder, but no word accompanied the action, nor did his host make the least move to follow him into the room.

This was a matter of great regret to him later, as it left him for a moment out of the range of every eye, during which he says he simply stood in a state of shock at seeing Mr. Spielhagen still sitting there, manuscript in hand, but with head fallen forward and eyes closed; dead, asleep or—he hardly knew what; the sight so paralysed him.

Whether or not this was the exact truth and the whole truth, Mr. Cornell certainly looked very unlike himself as he stepped back into Mr. Van Broecklyn's presence; and he was only partially reassured when that gentleman protested that there was no real harm in the drug, and that Mr. Spielhagen would be all right if left to wake naturally and without shock. However, as his present attitude was one of great discomfort, they decided to carry him back and lay him on the library lounge. But before doing this, Mr. Upjohn drew from his flaccid grasp, the precious manuscript, and carrying it into the larger room placed it on a remote table, where it remained undisturbed till Mr. Spielhagen, suddenly coming to himself at the end of some fifteen minutes, missed the sheets from his hand, and bounding up, crossed the room to repossess himself of them.

His face, as he lifted them up and rapidly ran through them with ever-accumulating anxiety, told them what they had to expect.

The page containing the formula was gone!

Violet now saw her problem.

II

There was no doubt about the loss I have mentioned; all could see that page 13 was not there. In vain a second handling of every sheet, the one so numbered was not to be found. Page 14 met the eye on the top of the pile, and page 12 finished it off at the bottom, but no page 13 in between, or anywhere else.

Where had it vanished, and through whose agency had this misadventure occurred? No one could say, or, at least, no one there made any attempt to do so, though everybody started to look for it.

But where look? The adjoining small room offered no facilities for hiding a cigar-end, much less a square of shining white paper. Bare walls, a bare floor, and a single chair for furniture, comprised all that was to be seen in this direction. Nor could the room in which they then stood be thought to hold it, unless it was on the person of some one of them. Could this be the explanation of the mystery? No man looked his doubts; but Mr. Cornell, possibly divining the general feeling, stepped up to Mr. Van Broecklyn and in a cool voice, but with the red burning hotly on either cheek, said, so as to be heard by everyone present:

"I demand to be searched—at once and thoroughly."

A moment's silence, then the common cry:

"We will all be searched."

"Is Mr. Spielhagen sure that the missing page was with the others when he sat down in the adjoining room to read his thesis?" asked their perturbed host.

"Very sure," came the emphatic reply. "Indeed, I was just going through the formula itself when I fell asleep."

"You are ready to assert this?"

"I am ready to swear it."

Mr. Cornell repeated his request.

"I demand that you make a thorough search of my person. I must be cleared, and instantly, of every suspicion," he gravely asserted, "or how can I marry Miss Digby to-morrow."

After that there was no further hesitation. One and all subjected themselves to the ordeal suggested; even Mr. Spielhagen. But this effort was as futile as the rest. The lost page was not found.

What were they to think? What were they to do?

There seemed to be nothing left to do, and yet some further attempt must be made towards the recovery of this important formula. Mr. Cornell's marriage and Mr. Spielhagen's business success both depended upon its being in the latter's hands before six in the morning, when he was engaged to hand it over to a certain manufacturer sailing for Europe on an early steamer.

Five hours!

Had Mr. Van Broecklyn a suggestion to offer? No, he was as much at sea as the rest.

Simultaneously look crossed look. Blankness was on every face.

"Let us call the ladies," suggested one.

It was done, and however great the tension had been before, it was even greater when Miss Digby stepped upon the scene. But she was not a woman to be shaken from her poise even by a crisis of this importance. When the dilemma had been presented to her and the full situation grasped, she looked first at Mr. Cornell and then at Mr. Spielhagen, and quietly said:

"There is but one explanation possible of this matter. Mr. Spielhagen will excuse me, but he is evidently mistaken in thinking that he saw the lost page among the rest. The condition into which he was thrown by the unaccustomed drug he had drank, made him liable to hallucinations. I have not the least doubt he thought he had been studying the formula at the time he dropped off to sleep. I have every confidence in the gentleman's candour. But so have I in that of Mr. Cornell," she supplemented, with a smile.

An exclamation from Mr. Van Broecklyn and a subdued murmur from all but Mr. Spielhagen testified to the effect of this suggestion, and there is no saying what might have been the result if Mr. Cornell had not hurriedly put in this extraordinary and most unexpected protest:

"Miss Digby has my gratitude," said he, "for a confidence which I hope to prove to be deserved. But I must say this for Mr. Spielhagen. He was correct in stating that he was engaged in looking over his formula when I stepped into his presence with the glass of cordial. If you were not in a position to see the hurried way in which his hand instinctively spread itself over the page he was reading, I was; and if that does not seem conclusive to you, then I feel bound to state that in unconsciously following this movement of his, I plainly saw the number written on the top of the page, and that number was—13."

A loud exclamation, this time from Spielhagen himself, announced his gratitude and corresponding change of attitude toward the speaker.

"Wherever that damned page has gone," he protested, advancing towards Cornell with outstretched hand, "you have nothing to do with its disappearance."

Instantly all constraint fled, and every countenance took on a relieved expression. *But the problem remained.*

Suddenly those very words passed some one's lips, and with their utterance Mr. Upjohn remembered how at an extraordinary crisis in his own life, he had been helped and an equally difficult problem settled, by a little lady secretly attached to a private detective agency. If she could only be found and hurried here before morning, all might yet be well. He would make the effort. Such wild schemes sometimes work. He telephoned to the office and—

Was there anything else Miss Strange would like to know?

III

Miss Strange, thus appealed to, asked where the gentlemen were now.

She was told that they were still all together in the library; the ladies had been sent home.

"Then let us go to them," said Violet, hiding under a smile her great fear that here was an affair which might very easily spell for her that dismal word, *failure.*

So great was that fear that under all ordinary circumstances she would have had no thought for anything else in the short interim between this stating of the problem and her speedy entrance among the persons involved. But the circumstances of this case were so far from ordinary, or rather let me put it in this way, the setting of the case was so very extraordinary, that she scarcely thought of the problem before her, in her great interest in the house through whose rambling halls she was being so carefully guided. So much that was tragic and heartrending had occurred here. The Van Broecklyn name, the Van Broecklyn history, above all the Van Broecklyn tradition, which made the house unique in the country's annals (of which more hereafter), all made an appeal to her imagination, and centred her thoughts on what she saw about her. There was a door which no man ever opened—had never opened since Revolutionary times—should she see it? Should she know it if she did see it? Then Mr. Van Broecklyn himself! Just to meet him, under any conditions and in any place, was an event. But to meet him here, under the pall of his own mystery! No wonder she had no words for her companions, or that her thoughts clung to this anticipation in wonder and almost fearsome delight.

His story was a well-known one. A bachelor and a misanthrope, he lived absolutely alone save for a large entourage of servants, all men and elderly ones at that. He never visited. Though he now and then, as on this occasion, entertained certain persons under his roof, he declined every invitation for himself, avoiding even, with equal strictness, all evening amusements of whatever kind, which would detain him in the city after ten at night. Perhaps this was to ensure no break in his rule of life never to sleep out of his own bed. Though he was a man well over fifty he had not spent, according to his own statement, but two nights out of his own bed since his return from Europe in early boyhood, and those were in obedience to a judicial summons which took him to Boston.

This was his main eccentricity, but he had another which is apparent enough from what has already been said. He avoided women. If thrown in with them during his short visits into town, he was invariably polite and at times companionable, but he never sought them out, nor had gossip, contrary to its usual habit, ever linked his name with one of the sex.

Yet he was a man of more than ordinary attraction. His features were fine and his figure impressive. He might have been the cynosure of all eyes had he chosen to enter crowded drawing-rooms, or even to frequent public assemblages, but having turned his back upon everything of the kind in his youth, he had found it impossible to alter his habits with advancing years; nor was he now expected to. The position he had taken was respected. Leonard Van Broecklyn was no longer criticized.

Was there any explanation for this strangely self-centred life? Those who knew him best seemed to think so. In the first place he had sprung from an unfortunate stock. Events of an unusual and tragic nature had marked the family of both parents. Nor had his parents themselves been exempt from this seeming fatality. Antagonistic in tastes and temperament, they had dragged on an unhappy existence in the old home, till both natures rebelled, and a separation ensued which not only disunited their lives but sent them to opposite sides of the globe never to return again. At least, that was the inference drawn from the peculiar circumstances attending the event. On the morning of one never-to-be-forgotten day, John Van Broecklyn, the grandfather of the present representative of the family, found the following note from his son lying on the library table:

> Father:
>   Life in this house, or any house, with *her* is no longer endurable. One of us must go. The mother should not be separated from her child. Therefore it is I whom you will never see again. Forget me, but be considerate of her and the boy.
>
> WILLIAM

Six hours later another note was found, this time from the wife:

> Father:
>   Tied to a rotting corpse what does one do? Lop off one's arm if necessary to rid one of the contact. As all love between your son and myself is dead, I can no longer live within the sound of his voice. As this is his home, he is the one to remain in it. May our child reap the benefit of his mother's loss and his father's affection.
>
> RHODA

Both were gone, and gone forever. Simultaneous in their departure, they preserved each his own silence and sent no word back. If the one went east and the other west, they may have met on the other side of the globe, but never again in the home which sheltered their boy. For him and for his grandfather they had sunk from sight in the great sea of humanity, leaving them stranded on an isolated and mournful shore. The grandfather steeled himself to the double loss, for the child's sake; but the boy of eleven succumbed. Few of the world's great sufferers, of whatever age or condition, have mourned as this child mourned, or shown the effects of his grief so deeply or so long. Not till he had passed his majority did the line, carved in one day in his baby forehead, lose any of its intensity; and there are those who declare that even later than that, the midnight stillness of the house was disturbed from time to time by his muffled shriek of "Mother! Mother!" sending the servants from the house, and adding one more horror to the many which clung about this accursed mansion.

Of this cry Violet had heard, and it was that and the door— But I have already told you about the door which she was still looking for, when her two companions suddenly halted, and she found herself on the threshold of the library, in full view of Mr. Van Broecklyn and his two guests.

Slight and fairy-like in figure, with an air of modest reserve more in keeping with her youth and dainty dimpling beauty than with her errand, her appearance produced an astonishment which none of the gentlemen were able to disguise. This the clever detective, with a genius for social problems and odd elusive cases! This darling of the ball-room in satin and pearls! Mr. Spielhagen glanced at Mr.[1] Carroll, and Mr. Carroll at Mr. Spielhagen, and both at Mr. Upjohn, in very evident distrust. As for Violet, she had eyes only for Mr. Van Broecklyn, who stood before her in a surprise equal to that of the others but with more restraint in its expression.

She was not disappointed in him. She had expected to see a man, reserved almost to the point of austerity. And she found his first look even more awe-compelling than her imagination had pictured; so much so indeed, that her resolution faltered, and she took a quick step backward; which seeing, he smiled and her heart and hopes grew warm again. That he could smile, and smile with absolute sweetness, was her great comfort when later— But I am introducing you too hurriedly to the catastrophe. There is much to be told first.

I pass over the preliminaries, and come at once to the moment when Violet, having listened to a repetition of the full facts, stood with downcast eyes before these gentlemen, complaining in some alarm to herself:

"They expect me to tell them now and without further search or parley just where this missing page is. I shall have to balk that expectation without losing their confidence. But how?"

Summoning up her courage and meeting each inquiring eye with a look which seemed to carry a different message to each, she remarked very quietly:

"This is not a matter to guess at. I must have time and I must look a little deeper into the facts just given me. I presume that the table I see over there is the one upon which Mr. Upjohn laid the manuscript during Mr. Spielhagen's unconsciousness."

All nodded.

"Is it—I mean the table—in the same condition it was then? Has nothing been taken from it except the manuscript?"

"Nothing."

"Then the missing page is not there," she smiled, pointing to its bare top. A pause, during which she stood with her gaze fixed on the floor before her. She was thinking and thinking hard.

Suddenly she came to a decision. Addressing Mr. Upjohn, she asked if he were quite sure that in taking the manuscript from Mr. Spielhagen's hand he had neither disarranged nor dropped one of its pages.

The answer was unequivocal.

"Then," she declared, with quiet assurance and a steady meeting with her own of every eye, "as the thirteenth page was not found among the others when they were taken from this table, nor on the persons of either Mr. Carroll or Mr. Spielhagen, it is still in that inner room."

"Impossible!" came from every lip, each in a different tone. "That room is absolutely empty."

"May I have a look at its emptiness?" she asked, with a naïve glance at Mr. Van Broecklyn.

"There is positively nothing in the room but the chair Mr. Spielhagen sat on," objected that gentleman with a noticeable air of reluctance.

"Still, may I not have a look at it?" she persisted, with that disarming smile she kept for great occasions.

Mr. Van Broecklyn bowed. He could not refuse a request so urged, but his step was slow and his manner next to ungracious as he led the way to the door of the adjoining room and threw it open.

Just what she had been told to expect! Bare walls and floors and an empty chair! Yet she did not instantly withdraw, but stood silently contemplating the panelled wainscoting surrounding her, as though she suspected it of containing some secret hiding-place not apparent to the eye.

Mr. Van Broecklyn, noting this, hastened to say:

"The walls are sound, Miss Strange. They contain no hidden cupboards."

"And that door?" she asked, pointing to a portion of the wainscoting so exactly like the rest that only the most experienced eye could detect the line of deeper colour which marked an opening.

For an instant Mr. Van Broecklyn stood rigid, then the immovable pallor, which was one of his chief characteristics, gave way to a deep flush, as he explained:

"There was a door there once; but it has been permanently closed. With cement," he forced himself to add, his countenance losing its evanescent colour till it shone ghastly again in the strong light.

With difficulty Violet preserved her show of composure. "*The* door!" she murmured to herself. "I have found it. The great historic door!" But her tone was light as she ventured to say:

"Then it can no longer be opened by your hand or any other?"

"It could not be opened with an axe."

Violet sighed in the midst of her triumph. Her curiosity had been satisfied, but the problem she had been set to solve looked inexplicable. But she was not one to yield easily to discouragement. Marking the disappointment approaching to disdain in every eye but Mr. Upjohn's, she drew herself up—(she had not far to draw) and made this final proposal.

"A sheet of paper," she remarked, "of the size of this one cannot be spirited away, or dissolved into thin air. It exists; it is here; and all we want is some happy thought in order to find it. I acknowledge that that happy thought has not come to me yet, but sometimes I get it in what may seem to you a very odd way. Forgetting myself, I try to assume the individuality of the person who has worked the mystery. If I can think with his thoughts, I possibly may follow him in his actions. In this case I should like to make believe for a few moments that I am Mr. Spielhagen" (with what a delicious smile she said this) "I should like to hold his thesis in my hand and be interrupted in my reading by Mr. Cornell offering his glass of cordial; then I should like to nod and slip off mentally into a deep sleep. Possibly in that sleep the dream may come which will clarify the whole situation. Will you humour me so far?"

A ridiculous concession, but finally she had her way; the farce was enacted and they left her as she had requested them to do, alone with her dreams in the small room.

Suddenly they heard her cry out, and in another moment she appeared before them, the picture of excitement.

"Is this chair standing exactly as it did when Mr. Spielhagen occupied it?" she asked.

"No," said Mr. Upjohn, "it faced the other way."

She stepped back and twirled the chair about with her disengaged hand.

"So?"

Mr. Upjohn and Mr. Spielhagen both nodded, so did the others when she glanced at them.

With a sign of ill-concealed satisfaction, she drew their attention to herself; then eagerly cried:

"Gentlemen, look here!"

Seating herself, she allowed her whole body to relax till she presented the picture of one calmly asleep. Then, as they continued to gaze at her with fascinated eyes, not knowing what to expect, they saw something white escape from her lap and slide across the floor till it touched and was stayed by the wainscot. It was the top page of the manuscript she held, and as some inkling of the truth reached their astonished minds, she sprang impetuously to her feet and, pointing to the fallen sheet, cried:

"Do you understand now? Look where it lies, and then look here!"

She had bounded towards the wall and was now on her knees pointing to the bottom of the wainscot, just a few inches to the left of the fallen page.

"A crack!" she cried, "under what was once the door. It's a very thin one, hardly perceptible to the eye. But see!" Here she laid her finger on the fallen paper and drawing it towards her, pushed it carefully against the lower edge of the wainscot. Half of it at once disappeared.

"I could easily slip it all through," she assured them, withdrawing the sheet and leaping to her feet in triumph. "You know now where the missing page lies, Mr. Spielhagen. All that remains is for Mr. Van Broecklyn to get it for you."

IV

The cries of mingled astonishment and relief which greeted this simple elucidation of the mystery were broken by a curiously choked, almost unintelligible, cry. It came from the man thus appealed to, who, unnoticed by them all, had started at her first word and gradually, as action followed action, withdrawn himself till he now stood alone and in an attitude almost of defiance behind the large table in the centre of the library.

"I am sorry," he began, with a brusqueness which gradually toned down into a forced urbanity as he beheld every eye fixed upon him in amazement, "that circumstances forbid my being of assistance to you in this unfortunate matter. If the paper lies where you say, and I see no other explanation of its loss, I am afraid it will have to remain there for this night at least. The cement in which that door is embedded is thick as any wall; it would take men with pickaxes, possibly with dynamite, to make a breach there wide enough for any one to reach in. And we are far from any such help."

In the midst of the consternation caused by these words, the clock on the mantel behind his back rang out the hour. It was but a double stroke, but that meant two hours after midnight and had the effect of a knell in the hearts of those most interested.

"But I am expected to give that formula into the hands of our manager before six o'clock in the morning. The steamer sails at a quarter after."

"Can't you reproduce a copy of it from memory?" some one asked; "and insert it in its proper place among the pages you hold there?"

"The paper would not be the same. That would lead to questions and the truth would come out. As the chief value of the process contained in that formula lies in its secrecy, no explanation I could give would relieve me from the suspicions which an acknowledgment of the existence of a third copy, however well hidden, would entail. I should lose my great opportunity."

Mr. Cornell's state of mind can be imagined. In an access of mingled regret and despair, he cast a glance at Violet, who, with a nod of understanding, left the little room in which they still stood, and approached Mr. Van Broecklyn.

Lifting up her head,—for he was very tall,—and instinctively rising on her toes the nearer to reach his ear, she asked in a cautious whisper: "Is there no other way of reaching that place?"

She acknowledged afterwards, that for one moment her heart stood still from fear, such a change took place in his face, though she says he did not move a muscle. Then, just when she was expecting from him some harsh or forbidding word, he wheeled abruptly away from her and crossing to a window at his side, lifted the shade and looked out. When he returned, he was his usual self so far as she could see.

"There is a way," he now confided to her in a tone as low as her own, "but it can only be taken by a child."

"Not by me?" she asked, smiling down at her own childish proportions.

For an instant he seemed taken aback, then she saw his hand begin to tremble and his lips twitch. Somehow—she knew not why—she began to pity him, and asked herself as she felt rather than saw the struggle in his mind, that here was a trouble which if once understood would greatly dwarf that of the two men in the room behind them.

"I am discreet," she whisperingly declared. "I have heard the history of that door—how it was against the tradition of the family to have it opened. There must have been some dreadful reason. But old superstitions do not affect me, and if you will allow me to take the way you mention, I will follow your bidding exactly, and will not trouble myself about anything but the recovery of this paper, which must lie only a little way inside that blocked-up door."

Was his look one of rebuke at her presumption, or just the constrained expression of a perturbed mind? Probably, the latter, for while she watched him for some understanding of his mood, he reached out his hand and touched one of the satin folds crossing her shoulder.

"You would soil this irretrievably," said he.

"There is stuff in the stores for another," she smiled. Slowly his touch deepened into pressure. Watching him she saw the rust of some old fear or dominant superstition melt under her eyes, and was quite prepared, when he remarked, with what for him was a lightsome air:

"I will buy the stuff, if you will dare the darkness and intricacies of our old cellar. I can give you no light. You will have to feel your way according to my direction."

"I am ready to dare anything."

He left her abruptly.

"I will warn Miss Digby," he called back. "She shall go with you as far as the cellar."

V

Violet in her short career as an investigator of mysteries had been in many a situation calling for more than womanly nerve and courage. But never—or so it seemed to her at the time—had she experienced a greater depression of spirit than when she stood with Miss Digby before a small door at the extreme end of the cellar, and understood that here was her road—a road which once entered, she must take alone.

First, it was such a small door! No child older than eleven could possibly squeeze through it. But she was of the size of a child of eleven and might possibly manage that difficulty.

Secondly: there are always some unforeseen possibilities in every situation, and though she had listened carefully to Mr. Van Broecklyn's directions and was sure that she knew them by heart, she wished she had kissed her father more tenderly in leaving him that night for the ball, and that she had not pouted so undutifully at some harsh stricture he had made. Did this mean fear? She despised the feeling if it did.

Thirdly: she hated darkness. She knew this when she offered herself for this undertaking; but she was in a bright room at the moment and only imagined what she must now face as a reality. But one jet had been lit in the cellar and that near the entrance. Mr. Van Broecklyn seemed not to need light, even in his unfastening of the small door which Violet was sure had been protected by more than one lock.

Doubt, shadow, and a solitary climb between unknown walls, with only a streak of light for her goal, and the clinging pressure of Florence Digby's hand on her own for solace—surely the prospect was one to tax the courage of her young heart to its limit. But she had promised, and she would fulfil. So with a brave smile she stooped to the little door, and in another moment had started on her journey.

For journey the shortest distance may seem when every inch means a heart-throb and one grows old in traversing a foot. At first the way was easy; she had but to crawl up a slight incline with the comforting consciousness that two people were within reach of her voice, almost within sound of her beating heart. But presently she came to a turn, beyond which her fingers failed to reach any wall on her left. Then came a step up which she stumbled, and farther on a short flight, each tread of which she had been told to test before she ventured to climb it, lest the decay of innumerable years should have weakened the wood too much to bear her weight. One, two, three, four, five steps! Then a landing with an open space beyond. Half of her journey was done. Here she felt she could give a minute to drawing her breath naturally, if the air, unchanged in years, would allow her to do so. Besides, here she had been enjoined to do a certain thing and to do it according to instructions. Three matches had been given her and a little night candle. Denied all light up to now, it was at this point she was to light her candle and place it on the floor, so that in returning she should not miss the staircase and get a fall. She had promised to do this, and was only too happy to see a spark of light scintillate into life in the immeasurable darkness.

She was now in a great room long closed to the world, where once officers in Colonial wars had feasted, and more than one council had been held. A room, too, which had seen more than one tragic happening, as its almost unparalleled isolation proclaimed. So much Mr. Van Broecklyn had told her; but she was warned to be careful in traversing it and not upon any pretext to swerve aside from the right-hand wall till she came to a huge mantelpiece. This passed, and a sharp corner turned, she ought to see somewhere in the dim spaces before her a streak of vivid light shining through the crack at the bottom of the blocked-up door. The paper should be somewhere near this streak.

All simple, all easy of accomplishment, if only that streak of light were all she was likely to see or think of. If the horror which was gripping her throat should not take shape! If things would remain shrouded in impenetrable darkness, and not force themselves in shadowy suggestion upon her excited fancy! But the blackness of the passage-way through which she had just struggled, was not to be found here. Whether it was the effect of that small flame flickering at the top of the staircase behind her, or of some change in her own powers of seeing, surely there was a difference in her present outlook. Tall shapes were becoming visible—the air was no longer blank—she could see— Then suddenly she saw why. In the wall high up on her right was a window. It was small and all but invisible, being covered on the outside with vines, and on the inside with the cobwebs of a century. But some small gleams from the starlight night came through, making phantasms out of ordinary things, which unseen were horrible enough, and half seen choked her heart with terror.

"I cannot bear it," she whispered to herself even while creeping forward, her hand upon the wall. "I will close my eyes" was her next thought. "I will make my own darkness," and with a spasmodic forcing of her lids together, she continued to creep on, passing the mantelpiece, where she knocked against something which fell with an awful clatter.

This sound, followed as it was by that of smothered voices from the excited group awaiting the result of her experiment from behind the impenetrable wall she should be nearing now if she had followed her instructions aright, freed her instantly from her fancies; and opening her eyes once more, she cast a look ahead, and to her delight, saw but a few steps away, the thin streak of bright light which marked the end of her journey.

It took her but a moment after that to find the missing page, and picking it up in haste from the dusty floor, she turned herself quickly about and joyfully began to retrace her steps. Why then, was it that in the course of a few minutes more her voice suddenly broke into a wild, unearthly shriek, which ringing with terror burst the bounds of that dungeon-like room, and sank, a barbed shaft, into the breasts of those awaiting the result of her doubtful adventure, at either end of this dread no-thoroughfare.

What had happened?

If they had thought to look out, they would have seen that the moon—held in check by a bank of cloud occupying half the heavens—had suddenly burst its bounds and was sending long bars of revealing light into every uncurtained window.

VI

Florence Digby, in her short and sheltered life, had possibly never known any very great or deep emotion. But she touched the bottom of extreme terror at that moment, as with her ears still thrilling with Violet's piercing cry, she turned to look at Mr. Van Broecklyn, and beheld the instantaneous wreck it had made of this seemingly strong man. Not till he came to lie in his coffin would he show a more ghastly countenance; and trembling herself almost to the point of falling, she caught him by the arm and sought to read in his face what had happened. Something disastrous she was sure; something which he had feared and was partially prepared for, yet which in happening had crushed him. Was it a pitfall into which the poor little lady had fallen? If so— But he is speaking—mumbling low words to himself. Some of them she can hear. He is reproaching himself—repeating over and over that he should never have taken such a chance; that he should have remembered her youth—the weakness of a young girl's nerve. He had been mad, and now—and now—

With the repetition of this word his murmuring ceased. All his energies were now absorbed in listening at the low door separating him from what he was agonizing to know—a door impossible to enter, impossible to enlarge—a barrier to all help—an opening whereby sound might pass but nothing else, save her own small body, now lying—where?

"Is she hurt?" faltered Florence, stooping, herself, to listen. "Can you hear anything—anything?"

For an instant he did not answer; every faculty was absorbed in the one sense; then slowly and in gasps he began to mutter:

"I think—I hear—*something*. Her step—no, no, no step. All is as quiet as death; not a sound,—not a breath—she has fainted. O God! O God! Why this calamity on top of all!"

He had sprung to his feet at the utterance of this invocation, but next moment was down on his knees again, listening—listening.

Never was silence more profound; they were hearkening for murmurs from a tomb. Florence began to sense the full horror of it all, and was swaying helplessly when Mr. Van Broecklyn impulsively lifted his hand in an admonitory Hush! and through the daze of her faculties a small far sound began to make itself heard, growing louder as she waited, then becoming faint again, then altogether ceasing only to renew itself once more, till it resolved into an approaching step, faltering in its course, but coming ever nearer and nearer.

"She's safe! She's not hurt!" sprang from Florence's lips in inexpressible relief; and expecting Mr. Van Broecklyn to show an equal joy, she turned towards him, with the cheerful cry:

"Now if she has been so fortunate as to find that missing page, we shall all be repaid for our fright."

A movement on his part, a shifting of position which brought him finally to his feet, but he gave no other proof of having heard her, nor did his countenance mirror her relief. "It is as if he dreaded, instead of hailed, her return," was Florence's inward comment as she watched him involuntarily recoil at each fresh token of Violet's advance.

Yet because this seemed so very unnatural, she persisted in her efforts to lighten the situation, and when he made no attempt to encourage Violet in her approach, she herself stooped and called out a cheerful welcome which must have rung sweetly in the poor little detective's ears.

A sorry sight was Violet, when, helped by Florence, she finally crawled into view through the narrow opening and stood once again on the cellar floor. Pale, trembling, and soiled with the dust of years, she presented a helpless figure enough, till the joy in Florence's face recalled some of her spirit, and, glancing down at her hand in which a sheet of paper was visible, she asked for Mr. Spielhagen.

"I've got the formula," she said. "If you will bring him, I will hand it over to him here."

Not a word of her adventure; nor so much as one glance at Mr. Van Broecklyn, standing far back in the shadows.

Nor was she more communicative, when, the formula restored and everything made right with Mr. Spielhagen, they all came together again in the library for a final word.

"I was frightened by the silence and the darkness, and so cried out," she explained in answer to their questions. "Any one would have done so who found himself alone in so musty a place," she added, with an attempt at lightsomeness which deepened the pallor on Mr. Van Broecklyn's cheek, already sufficiently noticeable to have been remarked upon by more than one.

"No ghosts?" laughed Mr. Cornell, too happy in the return of his hopes to be fully sensible of the feelings of those about him. "No whispers from impalpable lips or touches from spectre hands? Nothing to explain the mystery of that room so long shut up that even Mr. Van Broecklyn declares himself ignorant of its secret?"

"Nothing," returned Violet, showing her dimples in full force now.

"If Miss Strange had any such experiences—if she has anything to tell worthy of so marked a curiosity, she will tell it now," came from the gentleman just alluded to, in tones so stern and strange that all show of frivolity ceased on the instant. "Have you anything to tell, Miss Strange?"

Greatly startled, she regarded him with widening eyes for a moment, then with a move towards the door, remarked, with a general look about her:

"Mr. Van Broecklyn knows his own house, and doubtless can relate its histories if he will. I am a busy little body who having finished my work am now ready to return home, there to wait for the next problem which an indulgent fate may offer me."

She was near the threshold—she was about to take her leave, when suddenly she felt two hands fall on her shoulder, and turning, met the eyes of Mr. Van Broecklyn burning into her own.

"*You saw!*" dropped in an almost inaudible whisper from his lips.

The shiver which shook her answered him better than any word.

With an exclamation of despair, he withdrew his hands, and facing the others now standing together in a startled group, he said, as soon as he could recover some of his self-possession:

"I must ask for another hour of your company. I can no longer keep my sorrow to myself. A dividing line has just been drawn across my life, and I must have the sympathy of someone who knows my past, or I shall go mad in my self-imposed solitude. Come back, Miss Strange. You of all others have the prior right to hear."

VII

"I shall have to begin," said he, when they were all seated and ready to listen, "by giving you some idea, not so much of the family tradition, as of the effect of this tradition upon all who bore the name of Van Broecklyn. This is not the only house, even in America, which contains a room shut away from intrusion. In England there are many. But there is this difference between most of them and ours. No bars or locks forcibly held shut the door we were forbidden to open. The command was enough; that and the superstitious fear which such a command, attended by a long and unquestioning obedience, was likely to engender.

"I know no more than you do why some early ancestor laid his ban upon this room. But from my earliest years I was given to understand that there was one latch in the house which was never to be lifted; that any fault would be forgiven sooner than that; that the honour of the whole family stood in the way of disobedience, and that I was to preserve that honour to my dying day. You will say that all this is fantastic, and wonder that sane people in these modern times should subject themselves to such a ridiculous restriction, especially when no good reason was alleged, and the very source of the tradition from which it sprung forgotten. You are right; but if you look long into human nature, you will see that the bonds which hold the firmest are not material ones—that an idea will make a man and mould a character—that it lies at the source of all heroisms and is to be courted or feared as the case may be.

"For me it possessed a power proportionate to my loneliness. I don't think there was ever a more lonely child. My father and mother were so unhappy in each other's companionship that one or other of them was almost always away. But I saw little of either even when they were at home. The constraint in their attitude towards each other affected their conduct towards me. I have asked myself more than once if either of them had any real affection for me. To my father I spoke of her; to her of him; and never pleasurably. This I am forced to say, or you cannot understand my story. Would to God I could tell another tale! Would to God I had such memories as other men have of a father's clasp, a mother's kiss—but no! my grief, already profound, might have become abysmal. Perhaps it is best as it is; only, I might have been a different child, and made for myself a different fate—who knows.

"As it was, I was thrown almost entirely upon my own resources for any amusement. This led me to a discovery I made one day. In a far part of the cellar behind some heavy casks, I found a little door. It was so low—so exactly fitted to my small body, that I had the greatest desire to enter it. But I could not get around the casks. At last an expedient occurred to me. We had an old servant who came nearer loving me than any one else. One day when I chanced to be alone in the cellar, I took out my ball and began throwing it about. Finally it landed behind the casks, and I ran with a beseeching cry to Michael, to move them.

"It was a task requiring no little strength and address, but he managed, after a few herculean efforts, to shift them aside and I saw with delight my way opened to that mysterious little door. But I did not approach it then; some instinct deterred me. But when the opportunity came for me to venture there alone, I did so, in the most adventurous spirit, and began my operations by sliding behind the casks and testing the handle of the little door. It turned, and after a pull or two the door yielded. With my heart in my mouth, I stooped and peered in. I could see nothing—a black hole and nothing more. This caused me a moment's hesitation. I was afraid of the dark—had always been. But curiosity and the spirit of adventure triumphed. Saying to myself that I was

Robinson Crusoe exploring the cave, I crawled in, only to find that I had gained nothing. It was as dark inside as it had looked to be from without.

"There is no fun in this, so I crawled back, and when I tried the experiment again, it was with a bit of candle in my hand, and a surreptitious match or two. What I saw, when with a very trembling little hand I had lighted one of the matches, would have been disappointing to most boys, but not to me. The litter and old boards I saw in odd corners about me were full of possibilities, while in the dimness beyond I seemed to perceive a sort of staircase which might lead—I do not think I made any attempt to answer that question even in my own mind, but when, after some hesitation and a sense of great daring, I finally crept up those steps, I remember very well my sensation at finding myself in front of a narrow closed door. It suggested too vividly the one in Grandfather's little room—the door in the wainscot which we were never to open. I had my first real trembling fit here, and at once fascinated and repelled by this obstruction I stumbled and lost my candle, which, going out in the fall, left me in total darkness and a very frightened state of mind. For my imagination which had been greatly stirred by my own vague thoughts of the forbidden room, immediately began to people the space about me with ghoulish figures. How should I escape them, how ever reach my own little room again undetected and in safety?

"But these terrors, deep as they were, were nothing to the real fright which seized me when, the darkness finally braved, and the way found back into the bright, wide-open halls of the house, I became conscious of having dropped something besides the candle. My match-box was gone—not *my* match-box, but my grandfather's which I had found lying on his table and carried off on this adventure, in all the confidence of irresponsible youth. To make use of it for a little while, trusting to his not missing it in the confusion I had noticed about the house that morning, was one thing; to lose it was another. It was no common box. Made of gold and cherished for some special reason well known to himself, I had often heard him say that some day I would appreciate its value and be glad to own it. And I had left it in that hole and at any minute he might miss it—possibly ask for it! The day was one of torment. My mother was away or shut up in her room. My father—I don't know just what thoughts I had about him. He was not to be seen either, and the servants cast strange looks at me when I spoke his name. But I little realized the blow which had just fallen upon the house in his definite departure, and only thought of my own trouble, and of how I should meet my grandfather's eye when the hour came for him to draw me to his knee for his usual good-night.

"That I was spared this ordeal for the first time this very night first comforted me, then added to my distress. He had discovered his loss and was angry. On the morrow he would ask me for the box and I would have to lie, for never could I find the courage to tell him where I had been. Such an act of presumption he would never forgive, or so I thought as I lay and shivered in my little bed. That his coldness, his neglect, sprang from the discovery just made that my mother as well as my father had just fled the house forever was as little known to me as the morning calamity. I had been given my usual tendance and was tucked safely into bed; but the gloom, the silence which presently settled upon the house had a very different explanation in my mind from the real one. My sin (for such it loomed large in my mind by this time) coloured the whole situation and accounted for every event.

"At what hour I slipped from my bed on to the cold floor, I shall never know. To me it seemed to be in the dead of night; but I doubt if it were more than ten. So slowly creep away the moments to a wakeful child. I had made a great resolve. Awful as the prospect seemed to me,—frightened as I was by the very thought,—I had determined in my small mind to go down into the cellar, and into that midnight hole again, in search of the lost box. I would take a candle and matches, this time from my own mantel-shelf, and if everyone was asleep, as appeared from the deathly quiet of the house, I would be able to go and come without anybody ever being the wiser.

"Dressing in the dark, I found my matches and my candle and, putting them in one of my pockets, softly opened my door and looked out. Nobody was stirring; every light was out except a solitary one in the lower hall. That this still burned conveyed no meaning to my mind. How could I know that the house was so still and the rooms so dark because everyone was out searching for some clue to my mother's flight? If I had looked at the clock—but I did not; I was too intent upon my errand, too filled with the fever of my desperate undertaking, to be affected by anything not bearing directly upon it.

"Of the terror caused by my own shadow on the wall as I made the turn in the hall below, I have as keen a recollection to-day as though it happened yesterday. But that did not deter me; nothing deterred me, till safe in the cellar I crouched down behind the casks to get my breath again before entering the hole beyond.

"I had made some noise in feeling my way around these casks, and I trembled lest these sounds had been heard upstairs! But this fear soon gave place to one far greater. Other sounds were making themselves heard. A din of small skurrying feet above, below, on every side of me! Rats! rats in the wall! rats on the cellar bottom! How I ever stirred from the spot I do not know, but when I did stir, it was to go forward, and enter the uncanny hole.

"I had intended to light my candle when I got inside; but for some reason I went stumbling along in the dark, following the wall till I got to the steps where I had dropped the box. Here a light was necessary, but my hand did not go to my pocket. I thought it better to climb the steps first, and softly one foot found the tread and then another. I had only three more to climb and then my right hand, now feeling its way along the wall, would be free to strike a match. I climbed the three steps and was steadying myself against the door for a final plunge, when something happened—something so strange, so unexpected, and so incredible that I wonder I did not shriek aloud in my terror. The door was moving under my hand. It was slowly opening inward. I could feel the chill made by the widening crack. Moment by moment this chill increased; the gap was growing—a presence was there—a presence before which I sank in a small heap upon the landing. Would it advance? Had it feet—hands? Was it a presence which could be felt?

"Whatever it was, it made no attempt to pass, and presently I lifted my head only to quake anew at the sound of a voice—a human voice— my mother's voice—so near me that by putting out my arms I might have touched her.

"She was speaking to my father. I knew it from the tone. She was saying words which, little understood as they were, made such a havoc in my youthful mind that I have never forgotten them.

"'I have come!' she said. 'They think I have fled the house and are looking far and wide for me. We shall not be disturbed. Who would think of looking here for either you or me.'

"*Here!* The word sank like a plummet in my breast. I had known for some few minutes that I was on the threshold of the forbidden room; but they were *in* it. I can scarcely make you understand the tumult which this awoke in my brain. Somehow, I had never thought that any such braving of the house's law would be possible.

"I heard my father's answer, but it conveyed no meaning to me. I also realized that he spoke from a distance,—that he was at one end of the room while we were at the other. I was presently to have this idea confirmed, for while I was striving with all my might and main to subdue my very heart-throbs so that she would not hear me or suspect my presence, the darkness—I should rather say the blackness of the place yielded to a flash of lightning—heat lightning, all glare and no sound— and I caught an instantaneous vision of my father's figure standing with gleaming things about him, which affected me at the moment as supernatural, but which, in later years, I decided to have been weapons hanging on a wall.

"She saw him too, for she gave a quick laugh and said they would not need any candles; and then, there was another flash and I saw something in his hand and something in hers, and though I did not yet understand, I felt myself turning deathly sick and gave a choking gasp which was lost in the rush she made into the centre of the room, and the keenness of her swift low cry.

"'Garde-toi! for only one of us will ever leave this room alive!'

"A duel! a duel to the death between this husband and wife—this father and mother—in this hole of dead tragedies and within the sight and hearing of their child! Has Satan ever devised a scheme more hideous for ruining the life of an eleven-year-old boy!

"Not that I took it all in at once. I was too innocent and much too dazed to comprehend such hatred, much less the passions which engendered it. I only knew that something horrible—something beyond the conception of my childish mind—was going to take place in the darkness before me; and the terror of it made me speechless; would to God it had made me deaf and blind and dead!

"She had dashed from her corner and he had slid away from his, as the next fantastic gleam which lit up the room showed me. It also showed the weapons in their hands, and for a moment I felt reassured when I saw that these were swords, for I had seen them before with foils in their hands practising for exercise, as they said, in the great garret. But the swords had buttons on them, and this time the tips were sharp and shone in the keen light.

"An exclamation from her and a growl of rage from him were followed by movements I could scarcely hear, but which were terrifying from their very quiet. Then the sound of a clash. The swords had crossed.

"Had the lightning flashed forth then, the end of one of them might have occurred. But the darkness remained undisturbed, and when the glare relit the great room again, they were already far apart. This called out a word from him; the one sentence he spoke—I can never forget it:

"'Rhoda, there is blood on your sleeve; I have wounded you. Shall we call it off and fly, as the poor creatures in there think we have, to the opposite ends of the earth?'

"I almost spoke; I almost added my childish plea to his for them to stop—to remember me and stop. But not a muscle in my throat responded to my agonized effort. Her cold, clear 'No!' fell before my tongue was loosed or my heart freed from the ponderous weight crushing it.

" 'I have vowed and *I* keep my promises,' she went on in a tone quite strange to me. 'What would either's life be worth with the other alive and happy in this world.'

"He made no answer; and those subtle movements—shadows of movements I might almost call them—recommenced. Then there came a sudden cry, shrill and poignant—had Grandfather been in his room he would surely have heard it—and the flash coming almost simultaneously with its utterance, I saw what has haunted my sleep from that day to this, my father pinned against the wall, sword still in hand, and before him my mother, fiercely triumphant, her staring eyes fixed on his and—

"Nature could bear no more; the band loosened from my throat; the oppression lifted from my breast long enough for me to give one wild wail and she turned, saw (heaven sent its flashes quickly at this moment) and recognizing my childish form, all the horror of her deed (or so I have fondly hoped) rose within her, and she gave a start and fell full upon the point upturned to receive her.

"A groan; then a gasping sigh from him, and silence settled upon the room and upon my heart, and so far as I knew upon the whole created world.

"That is my story, friends. Do you wonder that I have never been or lived like other men?"

After a few moments of sympathetic silence, Mr. Van Broecklyn went on to say:

"I don't think I ever had a moment's doubt that my parents both lay dead on the floor of that great room. When I came to myself—which may have been soon, and may not have been for a long while—the lightning had ceased to flash, leaving the darkness stretching like a blank pall between me and that spot in which were concentrated all the terrors of which my imagination was capable. I dared not enter it. I dared not take one step that way. My instinct was to fly and hide my trembling body again in my own bed; and associated with this, in fact dominating it and making me old before my time, was another—never to tell; never to let any one, least of all my grandfather—know what that forbidden room now contained. I felt in an irresistible sort of way that my father's and mother's honour was at stake. Besides, terror held me back; I felt that I should die if I spoke. Childhood has such terrors and such heroisms. Silence often covers in such, abysses of thought and feeling which astonish us in later years. There is no suffering like a child's, terrified by a secret which it dare not for some reason disclose.

"Events aided me. When, in desperation to see once more the light and all the things which linked me to life—my little bed, the toys on the window-sill, my squirrel in its cage—I forced myself to retraverse the empty house, expecting at every turn to hear my father's voice or come upon the image of my mother—yes, such was the confusion of my mind, though I knew well enough even then that they were dead and that I should never hear the one or see the other. I was so benumbed with the cold in my half-dressed condition, that I woke in a fever next morning after a terrible dream which forced from my lips the cry of 'Mother! Mother!'—only that.

"I was cautious even in delirium. This delirium and my flushed cheeks and shining eyes led them to be very careful of me. I was told that my mother was away from home; and when after two days of search they were quite sure that all efforts to find either her or my father were likely to prove fruitless, that she had gone to Europe where we would follow her as soon as I was well. This promise, offering as it did, a prospect of immediate release from the terrors which were consuming me, had an extraordinary effect upon me. I got up out of my bed saying that I was well now and ready to start on the instant. The doctor, finding my pulse equable, and my whole condition wonderfully improved, and attributing it, as was natural, to my hope of soon joining my mother, advised my whim to be humoured and this hope kept active till travel and intercourse with children should give me strength and prepare me for the bitter truth ultimately awaiting me. They listened to him and in twenty-four hours our preparations were made. We saw the house closed—with what emotions surging in one small breast, I leave you to imagine—and then started on our long tour. For five years we wandered over the continent of Europe, my grandfather finding distraction, as well as myself, in foreign scenes and associations.

"But return was inevitable. What I suffered on re-entering this house, God and my sleepless pillow alone know. Had any discovery been made in our absence; or would it be made now that renovation and repairs of all kinds were necessary? Time finally answered me. My secret was safe and likely to continue so, and this fact once settled, life became endurable, if not cheerful. Since then I have spent only two nights out of this house, and they were unavoidable. When my grandfather died I had the wainscot door cemented in. It was done from this side and the cement painted to match the wood. No one opened the door nor have I ever crossed its threshold. Sometimes I think I have been foolish; and sometimes I know that I have been very wise. My reason has stood firm; how do I know that it would have done so if I had subjected myself to the possible discovery that one or both of them might have been saved if I had disclosed instead of concealed my adventure."

A pause during which white horror had shone on every face; then with a final glance at Violet, he said:

"What sequel do you see to this story, Miss Strange? I can tell the past, I leave you to picture the future."

Rising, she let her eye travel from face to face till it rested on the one awaiting it, when she answered dreamily:

"If some morning in the news column there should appear an account of the ancient and historic home of the Van Broecklyns having burned to the ground in the night, the whole country would mourn, and the city feel defrauded of one of its treasures. But there are five persons who would see in it the sequel which you ask for."

When this happened, as it did happen, some few weeks later, the astonishing discovery was made that no insurance had been put upon this house. Why was it that after such a loss Mr. Van Broecklyn seemed to renew his youth? It was a constant source of comment among his friends.

---

[1]The name change for this character, earlier referred to as "Mr. Cornell" is retained from an earlier printing of this story. Later, this character is referred to as "Mr. Cornell" again.

ARTHUR B. REEVE

(1880–1936)

||||||||||||||||||||||||||||||||||||||||||||| ■ |||||||||||||||||||||||||||||||||||||||||

It is sometimes said that Thomas Edison invented the twentieth century. It could be said with equal justification that the public's fascination with science and inventions produced before World War I made possible the widespread success of Arthur B. Reeve's scientific sleuth, Craig Kennedy.

Reeve graduated from Princeton University with a Phi Beta Kappa key. He then studied law, but opted to practice journalism instead. He worked as an editor of *Public Opinion*, began writing science articles for magazines, and created detective stories in which scientific gadgets are the focus of the plot and the means of its solution.

Chemistry professor Craig Kennedy is Reeve's sleuth. A newspaper reporter named Walter Jameson is the tag-along narrator who, in the Watson tradition, asks the questions that provoke the scientific-sounding explanations that made Reeve's books best-sellers in the United States and Europe. Read today, some of the professor's science seems doubtful at best; but in Reeve's day, the pseudo-science sounded authentic enough to wow readers.

Without the science, Reeve's plots would be mundane. Certainly, his characters are cut out of cardboard. Kennedy is a Sherlock Holmes imitation, an omniscient sleuth whose ratiocinative powers are enhanced by his specialized knowledge. Whereas Holmes is an expert on gentlemanly clues like varieties of cigar ash, Kennedy is a wiz regarding whatever is new in the world of science. Years before the Federal Bureau of Investigation and its famous crime laboratory were created, Professor Kennedy was bringing criminals to justice by identifying typewriter keys, analyzing blood stains, detecting drugs through chemistry, using X-rays, and applying modern psychological principles. The War Department was so impressed by Professor Kennedy that it asked Reeve to establish a scientific crime laboratory to help in the detection of the kaiser's spies during World War I.

"The Beauty Mask" is typical of Reeve's work. While readers today may chuckle delightedly at the no longer impressive "scientific" explanations that Kennedy offers, his earnestness only adds to the period charm of the piece. And it is easy to imagine that the application of futuristic nuclear science to the unraveling of a crime was very exciting stuff in more innocent times.

1917

The Beauty Mask

∎

"Oh, Mr. Jameson, if they could only wake her up—find out what is the matter—do something! This suspense is killing both mother and myself."

Scenting a good feature story, my city editor had sent me out on an assignment, my sole equipment being a clipping of two paragraphs from the morning *Star*.

GIRL IN COMA SIX DAYS—SHOWS NO SIGN OF REVIVAL

Virginia Blakeley, the nineteen-year-old daughter of Mrs. Stuart Blakeley, of Riverside Drive, who has been in a state of coma for six days, still shows no sign of returning consciousness.

   Ever since Monday some member of her family has been constantly beside her. Her mother and sister have both vainly tried to coax her back to consciousness, but their efforts have not met with the slightest response. Dr. Calvert Haynes, the family physician, and several specialists who have been called in consultation, are completely baffled by the strange malady.

Often I had read of cases of morbid sleep lasting for days and even for weeks. But this was the first case I had ever actually encountered and I was glad to take the assignment.

The Blakeleys, as every one knew, had inherited from Stuart Blakeley a very considerable fortune in real estate in one of the most rapidly developing sections of upper New York, and on the death of their mother the two girls, Virginia and Cynthia, would be numbered among the wealthiest heiresses of the city.

They lived in a big sandstone mansion fronting the Hudson and it was with some misgiving that I sent up my card. Both Mrs. Blakeley and her other daughter, however, met me in the reception-room, thinking, perhaps, from what I had written on the card, that I might have some assistance to offer.

Mrs. Blakeley was a well-preserved lady, past middle-age, and very nervous.

"Mercy, Cynthia!" she exclaimed, as I explained my mission, "it's another one of those reporters. No, I cannot say anything—not a word. I don't know anything. See Doctor Haynes. I—"

"But, mother," interposed Cynthia, more calmly, "the thing is in the papers. It may be that some one who reads of it may know of something that can be done. Who can tell?"

"Well, I won't say anything," persisted the elder woman. "I don't like all this publicity. Did the newspapers ever do anything but harm to your poor dear father? No, I won't talk. It won't do us a bit of good. And you, Cynthia, had better be careful."

Mrs. Blakeley backed out of the door, but Cynthia, who was a few years older than her sister, had evidently acquired independence. At least she felt capable of coping with an ordinary reporter who looked no more formidable than myself.

"It is quite possible that some one who knows about such cases may learn of this," I urged.

She hesitated as her mother disappeared, and looked at me a moment, then, her feelings getting the better of her, burst forth with the strange appeal I have already quoted.

It was as though I had come at just an opportune moment when she must talk to some outsider to relieve her pent-up feelings.

By an adroit question here and there, as we stood in the reception-hall, I succeeded in getting the story, which seemed to be more of human interest than of news. I even managed to secure a photograph of Virginia as she was before the strange sleep fell on her.

Briefly, as her sister told it, Virginia was engaged to Hampton Haynes, a young medical student at the college where his father was a professor of diseases of the heart. The Hayneses were of a fine Southern family which had never recovered from the war and had finally come to New York. The father, Dr. Calvert Haynes, in addition to being a well-known physician, was the family physician of the Blakeleys, as I already knew.

"Twice the date of the marriage has been set, only to be postponed," added Cynthia Blakeley. "We don't know what to do. And Hampton is frantic."

"Then this is really the second attack of the morbid sleep?" I queried.

"Yes—in a few weeks. Only the other wasn't so long—not more than a day."

She said it in a hesitating manner which I could not account for. Either she thought there might be something more back of it or she recalled her mother's aversion to reporters and did not know whether she was saying too much or not.

"Do you really fear that there is something wrong?" I asked, significantly, hastily choosing the former explanation.

Cynthia Blakeley looked quickly at the door through which her mother had retreated.

"I—I don't know," she replied, tremulously. "I don't know why I am talking to you. I'm so afraid, too, that the newspapers may say something that isn't true."

"You would like to get at the truth, if I promise to hold the story back?" I persisted, catching her eye.

"Yes," she answered, in a low tone, "but—" then stopped.

"I will ask my friend, Professor Kennedy, at the university, to come here," I urged.

"You know him?" she asked, eagerly. "He will come?"

"Without a doubt," I reassured, waiting for her to say no more, but picking up the telephone receiver on a stand in the hall.

Fortunately I found Craig at his laboratory and a few hasty words were all that was necessary to catch his interest.

"I must tell mother," Cynthia cried, excitedly, as I hung up the receiver. "Surely she cannot object to that. Will you wait here?"

As I waited for Craig, I tried to puzzle the case out for myself. Though I knew nothing about it as yet, I felt sure that I had not made a mistake and that there was some mystery here.

Suddenly I became aware that the two women were talking in the next room, though too low for me to catch what they were saying. It was evident, however, that Cynthia was having some difficulty in persuading her mother that everything was all right.

"Well, Cynthia," I heard her mother say, finally, as she left the room for one farther back, "I hope it will be all right—that is all I can say."

What was it that Mrs. Blakeley so feared? Was it merely the unpleasant notoriety? One could not help the feeling that there was something more that she suspected, perhaps knew, but would not tell. Yet, apparently, it was aside from her desire to have her daughter restored to normal. She was at sea, herself, I felt.

"Poor dear mother!" murmured Cynthia, rejoining me in a few moments. "She hardly knows just what it is she does want—except that we want Virginia well again."

We had not long to wait for Craig. What I had told him over the telephone had been quite enough to arouse his curiosity.

Both Mrs. Blakeley and Cynthia met him, at first a little fearfully, but quickly reassured by his manner, as well as my promise to see that nothing appeared in the *Star* which would be distasteful.

"Oh, if some one could only bring back our little girl!" cried Mrs. Blakeley, with suppressed emotion, leading the way with her daughter up-stairs.

It was only for a moment that I could see Craig alone to explain the impressions I had received, but it was enough.

"I'm glad you called me," he whispered. "There is something queer."

We followed them up to the dainty bedroom in flowered enamel where Virginia Blakeley lay, and it was then for the first time that we saw her. Kennedy drew a chair up beside the little white bed and went to work almost as though he had been a physician himself.

Partly from what I observed myself and partly from what he told me afterward, I shall try to describe the peculiar condition in which she was.

She lay there lethargic, scarcely breathing. Once she had been a tall, slender, fair girl, with a sort of wild grace. Now she seemed to be completely altered. I could not help thinking of the contrast between her looks now and the photograph in my pocket.

Not only was her respiration slow, but her pulse was almost imperceptible, less than forty a minute. Her temperature was far below normal, and her blood pressure low. Once she had seemed fully a woman, with all the strength and promise of precocious maturity. But now there was something strange about her looks. It is difficult to describe. It was not that she was no longer a young woman, but there seemed to be something almost sexless about her. It was as though her secondary sex characteristics were no longer feminine, but—for want of a better word—neuter.

Yet, strange to say, in spite of the lethargy which necessitated at least some artificial feeding, she was not falling away. She seemed, if anything, plump. To all appearances there was really a retardation of metabolism connected with the trance-like sleep. She was actually gaining in weight!

As he noted one of these things after another, Kennedy looked at her long and carefully. I followed the direction of his eyes. Over her nose, just a trifle above the line of her eyebrows, was a peculiar red mark, a sore, which was very disfiguring, as though it were hard to heal.

"What is that?" he asked Mrs. Blakeley, finally.

"I don't know," she replied, slowly. "We've all noticed it. It came just after the sleep began."

"You have no idea what could have caused it?"

"Both Virginia and Cynthia have been going to a face specialist," she admitted, "to have their skins treated for freckles. After the treatment they wore masks which were supposed to have some effect on the skin. I don't know. Could it be that?"

Kennedy looked sharply at Cynthia's face. There was no red mark over her nose. But there were certainly no freckles on either of the girls' faces now, either.

"Oh, mother," remonstrated Cynthia, "it couldn't be anything Doctor Chapelle did."

"Doctor Chapelle?" repeated Kennedy.

"Yes, Dr. Carl Chapelle," replied Mrs. Blakeley. "Perhaps you have heard of him. He is quite well known, has a beauty-parlor on Fifth Avenue. He—"

"It's ridiculous," cut in Cynthia, sharply. "Why, my face was worse than Virgie's. Car— He said it would take longer."

I had been watching Cynthia, but it needed only to have heard her to see that Doctor Chapelle was something more than a beauty specialist to her.

Kennedy glanced thoughtfully from the clear skin of Cynthia to the red mark on Virginia. Though he said nothing, I could see that his mind was on it. I had heard of the beauty doctors who promise to give one a skin as soft and clear as a baby's—and often, by their inexpert use of lotions and chemicals, succeed in ruining the skin and disfiguring the patient for life. Could this be a case of that sort? Yet how explain the apparent success with Cynthia?

The elder sister, however, was plainly vexed at the mention of the beauty doctor's name at all, and she showed it. Kennedy made a mental note of the matter, but refrained from saying any more about it.

"I suppose there is no objection to my seeing Doctor Haynes?" asked Kennedy, rising and changing the subject.

"None whatever," returned Mrs. Blakeley. "If there's anything you or he can do to bring Virginia out of this—anything safe—I want it done," she emphasized.

Cynthia was silent as we left. Evidently she had not expected Doctor Chapelle's name to be brought into the case.

We were lucky in finding Doctor Haynes at home, although it was not the regular time for his office hours. Kennedy introduced himself as a friend of the Blakeleys who had been asked to see that I made no blunders in writing the story for the *Star*. Doctor Haynes did not question the explanation.

He was a man well on toward the sixties, with that magnetic quality that inspires the confidence so necessary for a doctor. Far from wealthy, he had attained a high place in the profession.

As Kennedy finished his version of our mission, Doctor Haynes shook his head with a deep sigh.

"You can understand how I feel toward the Blakeleys," he remarked, at length. "I should consider it unethical to give an interview under any circumstances—much more so under the present."

"Still," I put in, taking Kennedy's cue, "just a word to set me straight can't do any harm. I won't quote you directly."

He seemed to realize that it might be better to talk carefully than to leave all to my imagination.

"Well," he began, slowly, "I have considered all the usual causes assigned for such morbid sleep. It is not auto-suggestion or trance, I am positive. Nor is there any trace of epilepsy. I cannot see how it could be due to poisoning, can you?"

I admitted readily that I could not.

"No," he resumed, "it is just a case of what we call narcolepsy— pathological somnolence—a sudden, uncontrollable inclination to sleep, occurring sometimes repeatedly or at varying intervals. I don't think it hysterical, epileptic, or toxemic. The plain fact of the matter, gentlemen, is that neither myself nor any of my colleagues whom I have consulted have the faintest idea what it is—yet."

The door of the office opened, for it was not the hour for consulting patients, and a tall, athletic young fellow, with a keen and restless face, though very boyish, entered.

"My son," the doctor introduced, "soon to be the sixth Doctor Haynes in direct line in the family."

We shook hands. It was evident that Cynthia had not by any means exaggerated when she said that he was frantic over what had happened to his *fiancée*.

Accordingly, there was no difficulty in reverting to the subject of our visit. Gradually I let Kennedy take the lead in the conversation so that our position might not seem to be false.

It was not long before Craig managed to inject a remark about the red spot over Virginia's nose. It seemed to excite young Hampton.

"Naturally I look on it more as a doctor than a lover," remarked his father, smiling indulgently at the young man, whom it was evident he regarded above everything else in the world. "I have not been able to account for it, either. Really the case is one of the most remarkable I have ever heard of."

"You have heard of a Dr. Carl Chapelle?" inquired Craig, tentatively.

"A beauty doctor," interrupted the young man, turning toward his father. "You've met him. He's the fellow I think is really engaged to Cynthia."

Hampton seemed much excited. There was unconcealed animosity in the manner of his remark, and I wondered why it was. Could there be some latent jealousy?

"I see," calmed Doctor Haynes. "You mean to infer that this—er—this Doctor Chapelle—" He paused, waiting for Kennedy to take the initiative.

"I suppose you've noticed over Miss Blakeley's nose a red sore?" hazarded Kennedy.

"Yes," replied Doctor Haynes, "rather refractory, too. I—"

"Say," interrupted Hampton, who by this time had reached a high pitch of excitement, "say, do you think it could be any of his confounded nostrums back of this thing?"

"Careful, Hampton," cautioned the elder man.

"I'd like to see him," pursued Craig to the younger. "You know him?"

"Know him? I should say I do. Good-looking, good practice, and all that, but—why, he must have hypnotized that girl! Cynthia thinks he's wonderful."

"I'd like to see him," suggested Craig.

"Very well," agreed Hampton, taking him at his word. "Much as I dislike the fellow, I have no objection to going down to his beauty-parlor with you."

"Thank you," returned Craig, as we excused ourselves and left the elder Doctor Haynes.

Several times on our journey down Hampton could not resist some reference to Chapelle for commercializing the profession, remarks which sounded strangely old on his lips.

Chapelle's office, we found, was in a large building on Fifth Avenue in the new shopping district, where hundreds of thousands of women passed almost daily. He called the place a Dermatological Institute, but, as Hampton put it, he practised "decorative surgery."

As we entered one door, we saw that patients left by another. Evidently, as Craig whispered, when sixty sought to look like sixteen the seekers did not like to come in contact with one another.

We waited some time in a little private room. At last Doctor Chapelle himself appeared, a rather handsome man with the manner that one instinctively feels appeals to the ladies.

He shook hands with young Haynes, and I could detect no hostility on Chapelle's part, but rather a friendly interest in a younger member of the medical profession.

Again I was thrown forward as a buffer. I was their excuse for being there. However, a newspaper experience gives you one thing, if no other—assurance.

"I believe you have a patient, a Miss Virginia Blakeley?" I ventured.

"Miss Blakeley? Oh yes, and her sister, also."

The mention of the names was enough. I was no longer needed as a buffer.

"Chapelle," blurted out Hampton, "you must have done something to her when you treated her face. There's a little red spot over her nose that hasn't healed yet."

Kennedy frowned at the impetuous interruption. Yet it was perhaps the best thing that could have happened.

"So," returned Chapelle, drawing back and placing his head on one side as he nodded it with each word, "you think I've spoiled her looks? Aren't the freckles gone?"

"Yes," retorted Hampton, bitterly, "but on her face is this new disfigurement."

"That?" shrugged Chapelle. "I know nothing of that—nor of the trance. I have only my specialty."

Calm though he appeared outwardly, one could see that Chapelle was plainly worried. Under the circumstances, might not his professional reputation be at stake? What if a hint like this got abroad among his rich clientele?

I looked about his shop and wondered just how much of a faker he was. Once or twice I had heard of surgeons who had gone legitimately into this sort of thing. But the common story was that of the swindler—or worse. I had heard of scores of cases of good looks permanently ruined, seldom of any benefit. Had Chapelle ignorantly done something that would leave its scar forever? Or was he one of the few who were honest and careful?

Whatever the case, Kennedy had accomplished his purpose. He had seen Chapelle. If he were really guilty of anything the chances were all in favor of his betraying it by trying to cover it up. Deftly suppressing Hampton, we managed to beat a retreat without showing our hands any further.

"Humph!" snorted Hampton, as we rode down in the elevator and hopped on a 'bus to go up-town. "Gave up legitimate medicine and took up this beauty doctoring—it's unprofessional, I tell you. Why, he even advertises!"

We left Hampton and returned to the laboratory, though Craig had no present intention of staying there. His visit was merely for the purpose of gathering some apparatus, which included a Crookes tube, carefully packed, a rheostat, and some other paraphernalia which we divided. A few moments later we were on our way again to the Blakeley mansion.

No change had taken place in the condition of the patient, and Mrs.

Blakeley met us anxiously. Nor was the anxiety wholly over her daughter's condition, for there seemed to be an air of relief when Kennedy told her that we had little to report.

Up-stairs in the sick-room, Craig set silently to work, attaching his apparatus to an electric-light socket from which he had unscrewed the bulb. As he proceeded I saw that it was, as I had surmised, his new X-ray photographing machine which he had brought. Carefully, from several angles, he took photographs of Virginia's head, then, without saying a word, packed up his kit and started away.

We were passing down the hall, after leaving Mrs. Blakeley, when a figure stepped out from behind a portière. It was Cynthia, who had been waiting to see us alone.

"You—don't think Doctor Chapelle had anything to do with it?" she asked, in a hoarse whisper.

"Then Hampton Haynes has been here?" avoided Kennedy.

"Yes," she admitted, as though the question had been quite logical. "He told me of your visit to Carl."

There was no concealment, now, of her anxiety. Indeed, I saw no reason why there should be. It was quite natural that the girl should worry over her lover, if she thought there was even a haze of suspicion in Kennedy's mind.

"Really I have found out nothing yet," was the only answer Craig gave, from which I readily deduced that he was well satisfied to play the game by pitting each against all, in the hope of gathering here and there a bit of the truth. "As soon as I find out anything I shall let you and your mother know. And you must tell me everything, too."

He paused to emphasize the last words, then slowly turned again toward the door. From the corner of my eye I saw Cynthia take a step after him, pause, then take another.

"Oh, Professor Kennedy," she called.

Craig turned.

"There's something I forgot," she continued. "There's something wrong with mother!" She paused, then resumed: "Even before Virginia was taken down with this—illness I saw a change. She is worried. Oh, Professor Kennedy, what is it? We have all been so happy. And now— Virgie, mother—all I have in the world. What shall I do?"

"Just what do you mean?" asked Kennedy, gently.

"I don't know. Mother has been so different lately. And now, every night, she goes out."

"Where?" encouraged Kennedy, realizing that his plan was working.

"I don't know. If she would only come back looking happier." She was sobbing, convulsively, over she knew not what.

"Miss Blakeley," said Kennedy, taking her hand between both of his, "only trust me. If it is in my power I shall bring you all out of this uncertainty that haunts you."

She could only murmur her thanks as we left.

"It is strange," ruminated Kennedy, as we sped across the city again to the laboratory. "We must watch Mrs. Blakeley."

That was all that was said. Although I had no inkling of what was back of it all, I felt quite satisfied at having recognized the mystery even on stumbling on it as I had.

In the laboratory, as soon as he could develop the skiagraphs he had taken, Kennedy began a minute study of them. It was not long before he looked over at me with the expression I had come to recognize when he found something important. I went over and looked at the radiograph which he was studying. To me it was nothing but successive gradations of shadows. But to one who had studied roentgenography as Kennedy had each minute gradation of light and shade had its meaning.

"You see," pointed out Kennedy, tracing along one of the shadows with a fine-pointed pencil, and then along a corresponding position on another standard skiagraph which he already had, "there is a marked diminution in size of the *sella turcica*, as it is called. Yet there is no evidence of a tumor." For several moments he pondered deeply over the photographs. "And it is impossible to conceive of any mechanical pressure sufficient to cause such a change," he added.

Unable to help him on the problem, whatever it might be, I watched him pacing up and down the laboratory.

"I shall have to take that picture over again—under different circumstances," he remarked, finally, pausing and looking at his watch. "Tonight we must follow this clue which Cynthia has given us. Call a cab, Walter."

We took a stand down the block from the Blakeley mansion, near a large apartment, where the presence of a cab would not attract attention. If there is any job I despise it is shadowing. One must keep his eyes riveted on a house, for, once let the attention relax and it is incredible how quickly any one may get out and disappear.

Our vigil was finally rewarded when we saw Mrs. Blakeley emerge and hurry down the street. To follow her was easy, for she did not suspect that she was being watched, and went afoot. On she walked, turning off the Drive and proceeding rapidly toward the region of cheap tenements. She paused before one, and as our cab cruised leisurely past we saw her press a button, the last on the right-hand side, enter the door, and start up the stairs.

Instantly Kennedy signaled our driver to stop and together we hopped out and walked back, cautiously entering the vestibule. The name in the letter box was "Mrs. Reba Rinehart." What could it mean?

Just then another cab stopped up the street, and as we turned to leave the vestibule Kennedy drew back. It was too late, however, not to be seen. A man had just alighted and, in turn, had started back, also realizing that it was too late. It was Chapelle! There was nothing to do but to make the best of it.

"Shadowing the shadowers?" queried Kennedy, keenly watching the play of his features under the arc-light of the street.

"Miss Cynthia asked me to follow her mother the other night," he answered, quite frankly. "And I have been doing so ever since."

It was a glib answer, at any rate, I thought.

"Then, perhaps you know something of Reba Rinehart, too," bluffed Kennedy.

Chapelle eyed us a moment, in doubt how much we knew. Kennedy played a pair of deuces as if they had been four aces instead.

"Not much," replied Chapelle, dubiously. "I know that Mrs. Blakeley has been paying money to the old woman, who seems to be ill. Once I managed to get in to see her. It's a bad case of pernicious anemia, I should say. A neighbor told me she had been to the college hospital, had been one of Doctor Haynes's cases, but that he had turned her over to his son. I've seen Hampton Haynes here, too."

There was an air of sincerity about Chapelle's words. But, then, I reflected that there had also been a similar ring to what we had heard Hampton say. Were they playing a game against each other? Perhaps—but what was the game? What did it all mean and why should Mrs. Blakeley pay money to an old woman, a charity patient?

There was no solution. Both Kennedy and Chapelle, by a sort of tacit consent, dismissed their cabs, and we strolled on over toward Broadway, watching one another, furtively. We parted finally, and Craig and I went up to our apartment, where he sat for hours in a brown study. There was plenty to think about even so far in the affair. He may have sat up all night. At any rate, he roused me early in the morning.

"Come over to the laboratory," he said. "I want to take that X-ray machine up there again to Blakeley's. Confound it! I hope it's not too late."

I lost no time in joining him and we were at the house long before any reasonable hour for visitors.

Kennedy asked for Mrs. Blakeley and hurriedly set up the X-ray apparatus. "I wish you would place that face mask which she was wearing exactly as it was before she became ill," he asked.

Her mother did as Kennedy directed, replacing the rubber mask as Virginia had worn it.

"I want you to preserve that mask," directed Kennedy, as he finished taking his pictures. "Say nothing about it to any one. In fact, I should advise putting it in your family safe for the present."

Hastily we drove back to the laboratory and Kennedy set to work again developing the second set of skiagraphs. I had not long to wait, this time, for him to study them. His first glance brought me over to him as he exclaimed loudly.

At the point just opposite the sore which he had observed on Virginia's forehead, and overlying the *sella turcica*, there was a peculiar spot on the radiograph.

"Something in that mask has affected the photographic plate," he explained, his face now animated.

Before I could ask him what it was he had opened a cabinet where he kept many new things which he studied in his leisure moments. From it I saw him take several glass ampules which he glanced at hastily and shoved into his pocket as we heard a footstep out in the hall. It was Chapelle, very much worried. Could it be that he knew his society clientele was at stake, I wondered. Or was it more than that?

"She's dead!" he cried. "The old lady died last night!"

Without a word Kennedy hustled us out of the laboratory, stuffing the X-ray pictures into his pocket, also, as we went.

As we hurried down-town Chapelle told us how he had tried to keep a watch by bribing one of the neighbors, who had just informed him of the tragedy.

"It was her heart," said one of the neighbors, as we entered the poor apartment. "The doctor said so."

"Anemia," insisted Chapelle, looking carefully at the body.

Kennedy bent over, also, and examined the poor, worn frame. As he did so he caught sight of a heavy linen envelope tucked under her pillow. He pulled it out gently and opened it. Inside were several time-worn documents and letters. He glanced over them hastily, unfolding first a letter.

"Walter," he whispered, furtively, looking at the neighbors in the room and making sure that none of them had seen the envelope already. "Read these. That's her story."

One glance was sufficient. The first was a letter from old Stuart Blakeley. Reba Rinehart had been secretly married to him—and never divorced. One paper after another unfolded her story.

I thought quickly. Then she had had a right in the Blakeley millions. More than that, the Blakeleys themselves had none, at least only what came to them by Blakeley's will.

I read on, to see what, if any, contest she had intended to make. And as I read I could picture old Stuart Blakeley to myself—strong, direct, unscrupulous, a man who knew what he wanted and got it, dominant, close-mouthed, mysterious. He had understood and estimated the future of New York. On that he had founded his fortune.

According to the old lady's story, the marriage was a complete secret. She had demanded marriage when he had demanded her. He had pointed out the difficulties. The original property had come to him and would remain in his hands only on condition that he married one of his own faith. She was not of the faith and declined to become so. There had been other family reasons, also. They had been married, with the idea of keeping it secret until he could arrange his affairs so that he could safely acknowledge her.

It was, according to her story, a ruse. When she demanded recognition he replied that the marriage was invalid, that the minister had been unfrocked before the ceremony. She was not in law his wife and had no claim, he asserted. But he agreed to compromise, in spite of it all. If she would go West and not return or intrude, he would make a cash settlement. Disillusioned, she took the offer and went to California. Somehow, he understood that she was dead. Years later he married again.

Meanwhile she had invested her settlement, had prospered, had even married herself, thinking the first marriage void. Then her second husband died and evil times came. Blakeley was dead, but she came East. Since then she had been fighting to establish the validity of the first marriage and hence her claim to dower rights. It was a moving story.

As we finished reading, Kennedy gathered the papers together and took charge of them. Taking Chapelle, who by this time was in a high state of excitement over both the death and the discovery, Kennedy hurried to the Blakeley mansion, stopping only long enough to telephone to Doctor Haynes and his son.

Evidently the news had spread. Cynthia Blakeley met us in the hall, half frightened, yet much relieved.

"Oh, Professor Kennedy," she cried, "I don't know what it is, but mother seems so different. What is it all about?"

As Kennedy said nothing, she turned to Chapelle, whom I was watching narrowly. "What is it, Carl?" she whispered.

"I—I can't tell," he whispered back, guardedly. Then, with an anxious glance at the rest of us, "Is your sister any better?"

Cynthia's face clouded. Relieved though she was about her mother, there was still that horror for Virginia.

"Come," I interrupted, not wishing to let Chapelle get out of my sight, yet wishing to follow Kennedy, who had dashed up-stairs.

I found Craig already at the bedside of Virginia. He had broken one of the ampules and was injecting some of the extract in it into the sleeping girl's arm. Mrs. Blakeley bent over eagerly as he did so. Even in her manner she was changed. There was anxiety for Virginia yet, but one could feel that a great weight seemed to be lifted from her.

So engrossed was I in watching Kennedy that I did not hear Doctor Haynes and Hampton enter. Chapelle heard, however, and turned.

For a moment he gazed at Hampton. Then with a slight curl of the lip he said, in a low tone, "Is it strictly ethical to treat a patient for disease of the heart when she is suffering from anemia—if you have an interest in the life and death of the patient?"

I watched Hampton's face closely. There was indignation in every line of it. But before he could reply Doctor Haynes stepped forward.

"My son was right in the diagnosis," he almost shouted, shaking a menacing finger at Chapelle. "To come to the point, sir, explain that mark on Miss Virginia's forehead!"

"Yes," demanded Hampton, also taking a step toward the beauty doctor, "explain it—if you dare."

Cynthia suppressed a little cry of fear. For a moment I thought that the two young men would forget everything in the heat of their feelings.

"Just a second," interposed Kennedy, quickly stepping between them. "Let me do the talking." There was something commanding about his tone as he looked from one to the other of us.

"The trouble with Miss Virginia," he added, deliberately, "seems to lie in one of what the scientists have lately designated the 'endocrine glands'—in this case the pituitary. My X-ray pictures show that conclusively.

"Let me explain for the benefit of the rest. The pituitary is an oval glandular body composed of two lobes and a connecting area, which rest in the *sella turcica*, enveloped by a layer of tissue, about under this point." He indicated the red spot on her forehead as he spoke. "It is, as the early French surgeons called it, *l'organe énigmatique*. The ancients thought it discharged the pituita, or mucus, into the nose. Most scientists of the past century asserted that it was a vestigial relic of prehistoric usefulness. To-day we know better.

"One by one the functions of the internal secretions are being discovered. Our variously acquired bits of information concerning the ductless glands lie before us like the fragments of a modern picture puzzle. And so, I may tell you, in connection with recent experimental studies in the rôle of the pituitary, Doctor Cushing and other collaborators at Johns Hopkins have noticed a marked tendency to pass into a profoundly lethargic state when the secretion of the pituitary is totally or nearly so removed."

Kennedy now had every eye riveted on him as he deftly led the subject straight to the case of the poor girl before us.

"This," he added, with a wave of his hand toward her, "is much like what is called the Fröhlich syndrome—the lethargy, the subnormal temperature, slow pulse, and respiration, lowered blood pressure, and insensitivity, the growth of fat and the loss of sex characteristics. It has a name—dystrophia adiposogenitalis."

He nodded to Doctor Haynes, but did not pause. "This case bears a striking resemblance to the pronounced natural somnolence of hibernation. And induced hypopituitarism—under activity of the gland—produces a result just like natural hibernation. Hibernation has nothing to do with winter, or with food, primarily; it is connected in some way with this little gland under the forehead.

"As the pituitary secretion is lessened, the blocking action of the fatigue products in the body becomes greater and morbid somnolence sets in. There is a high tolerance of carbohydrates which are promptly stored as fat. I am surprised, Doctor Haynes, that you did not recognize the symptoms."

A murmur from Mrs. Blakeley cut short Doctor Haynes's reply. I thought I noticed a movement of the still face on the white bed.

"Virgie! Virgie!" called Mrs. Blakeley, dropping on her knee beside her daughter.

"I'm here—mother!"

Virginia's eyes opened ever so slightly. Her face turned just an inch or two. She seemed to be making a great effort, but it lasted only a moment. Then she slipped back into the strange condition that had baffled skilled physicians and surgeons for nearly a week.

"The sleep is being dispelled," said Kennedy, quietly placing his hand on Mrs. Blakeley's shoulder. "It is a sort of semi-consciousness now and the improvement should soon be great."

"And that?" I asked, touching the empty ampule from which he had injected the contents into her.

"Pituitrin—the extract of the anterior lobe of the pituitary body. Some one who had an object in removing her temporarily probably counted on restoring her to her former blooming womanhood by pituitrin—and by removing the cause of the trouble."

Kennedy reached into his pocket and drew forth the second X-ray photograph he had taken. "Mrs. Blakeley, may I trouble you to get that beauty mask which your daughter wore?"

Mechanically Mrs. Blakeley obeyed. I expected Chapelle to object, but not a word broke the deathlike stillness.

"The narcolepsy," continued Kennedy, taking the mask, "was due, I find, to something that affected the pituitary gland. I have here a photograph of her taken when she was wearing the mask." He ran his finger lightly over the part just above the eyes. "Feel that little lump, Walter," he directed.

I did so. It was almost imperceptible, but there was something. "What is it?" I asked.

"Located in one of the best protected and most inaccessible parts of the body," Kennedy considered, slowly, "how could the pituitary be reached? If you will study my skiagraph, you will see how I got my first clue. There was something over that spot which caused the refractory sore. What was it? Radium—carefully placed in the mask with guards of lead foil in such a way as to protect the eyes, but direct the emission full at the gland which was to be affected, and the secretions stopped."

Chapelle gave a gasp. He was pale and agitated.

"Some of you have already heard of Reba Rinehart," shot out Kennedy, suddenly changing the subject.

Mrs. Blakeley could not have been more astounded if a bomb had dropped before her. Still kneeling before Virginia's bed, she turned her startled face at Kennedy, clasping her hands in appeal.

"It was for my girls that I tried to buy her off—for their good name—their fortune—their future," she cried, imploringly.

Kennedy bent down, "I know that is all," he reassured, then, facing us, went on: "Behind that old woman was a secret of romantic interest. She was contemplating filing suit in the courts to recover a widow's interest in the land on which now stand the homes of millionaires, hotel palaces, luxurious apartments, and popular theaters—millions of dollars' worth of property."

Cynthia moved over and drew her arms about the convulsed figure of her mother.

"Some one else knew of this old marriage of Stuart Blakeley," proceeded Kennedy, "knew of Reba Rinehart, knew that she might die at any moment. But until she died none of the Blakeleys could be entirely sure of their fortune."

It flashed over me that Chapelle might have conceived the whole scheme, seeking to gain the entire fortune for Cynthia.

"Who was interested enough to plot this postponement of the wedding until the danger to the fortune was finally removed?" I caught sight of Hampton Haynes, his eyes riveted on the face on the bed before us.

Virginia stirred again. This time her eyes opened wider. As if in a dream she caught sight of the face of her lover and smiled wanly.

Could it have been Hampton? It seemed incredible.

"The old lady is dead," pursued Kennedy, tensely. "Her dower right died with her. Nothing can be gained by bringing her case back again—except to trouble the Blakeleys in what is rightfully theirs."

Gathering up the beauty mask, the X-ray photographs, and the papers of Mrs. Rinehart, Kennedy emphasized with them the words as he whipped them out suddenly.

"Postponing the marriage, at the possible expense of Chapelle, until Reba Rinehart was dead, and trusting to a wrong diagnosis and Hampton's inexperience as the surest way of bringing that result about quickly, it was your inordinate ambition for your son, Doctor Haynes, that led you on. I shall hold these proofs until Virginia Blakeley is restored completely to health and beauty."

SUSAN GLASPELL

(1882–1948)

||||||||||||||||||||||||||||||||||||||||||| ■ |||||||||||||||||||||||||||||||||||||||||||

Susan Glaspell was not only a Pulitzer Prize–winning playwright but a novelist and writer of short stories that established her as an important writer of local-color fiction. Born in Davenport, Iowa, she relied on her midwestern roots to nurture a writing career that took her to Provincetown, Massachusetts (where she founded the Provincetown Players with Eugene O'Neill), to New York City's Greenwich Village, and to Greece.

Always a woman ahead of her time, Glaspell graduated from Davenport public schools and Drake University in Des Moines, Iowa. She served for two years as a court and legislative reporter for the *Des Moines Daily News* before turning to writing for women's magazines full-time in 1901. Her short stories for such publications as *Good Housekeeping* and *Women's Home Companion* were set in the fictional town of Freeport, Iowa, which she based on her home town of Davenport. Her work treated romantic problems in a formula that incorporated setting the problem, flashbacks, obstacles overcome, and a happy ending. She also set out consciously to record the unique qualities of her region, including the strengths and failings of people who came of pioneer stock but possessed a small-town mentality.

After Glaspell met and married George Cram Cook, a well-to-do rebel against Davenport's small-town pretensions, her work began to incorporate politically idealist overtones, including pacifist and socialist views. She moved away from the local-color tradition's emphasis on sentimentality and began to employ realism to discuss more contemporary themes.

From 1913 to 1922, Glaspell wrote seven one-act and four full-length plays, including the one-act play *Trifles*, which she rewrote as the short story "A Jury of Her Peers." The plot is based on an actual case that Glaspell covered as a reporter in Des Moines involving an abusive husband. "A Jury of Her Peers" is a strong example of writing that transcends local-color conventions to become a classic of realism. Here Glaspell demonstrates how the straightforward delivery of dialogue in ordinary voices can make a poignant and powerful point. The carefully drawn setting is one of the earliest examples of regional writing in a genre that now thrives on the enrichment of formula with descriptions of distinctly American environments.

1917
_____

A Jury of Her Peers

∎

When Martha Hale opened the storm-door and got a cut of the north wind, she ran back for her big woolen scarf. As she hurriedly wound that round her head her eye made a scandalized sweep of her kitchen. It was no ordinary thing that called her away—it was probably farther from ordinary than anything that had ever happened in Dickson County. But what her eye took in was that her kitchen was in no shape for leaving: her bread all ready for mixing, half the flour sifted and half unsifted.

She hated to see things half done; but she had been at that when the team from town stopped to get Mr. Hale, and then the sheriff came running in to say his wife wished Mrs. Hale would come too—adding, with a grin, that he guessed she was getting scarey and wanted another woman along. So she had dropped everything right where it was.

"Martha!" now came her husband's impatient voice. "Don't keep folks waiting out here in the cold."

She again opened the storm-door, and this time joined the three men and the one woman waiting for her in the big two-seated buggy.

After she had the robes tucked around her she took another look at the woman who sat beside her on the back seat. She had met Mrs. Peters the year before at the county fair, and the thing she remembered about her was that she didn't seem like a sheriff's wife. She was small and thin and didn't have a strong voice. Mrs. Gorman, sheriff's wife before Gorman went out and Peters came in, had a voice that somehow seemed to be backing up the law with every word. But if Mrs. Peters didn't look like a sheriff's wife, Peters made it up in looking like a sheriff. He was to a dot the kind of man who could get himself elected sheriff—a heavy man with a big voice, who was particularly genial with the law-abiding, as if to make it plain that he knew the difference between criminals and non-criminals. And right there it came into Mrs. Hale's mind, with a stab, that this man who was so pleasant and lively with all of them was going to the Wrights' now as a sheriff.

"The country's not very pleasant this time of year," Mrs. Peters at last ventured, as if she felt they ought to be talking as well as the men.

Mrs. Hale scarcely finished her reply, for they had gone up a little hill and could see the Wright place now, and seeing it did not make her feel like talking. It looked very lonesome this cold March morning. It had always been a lonesome-looking place. It was down in a hollow, and the poplar trees around it were lonesome-looking trees. The men were looking at it and talking about what had happened. The county attorney was bending to one side of the buggy, and kept looking steadily at the place as they drew up to it.

"I'm glad you came with me," Mrs. Peters said nervously, as the two women were about to follow the men in through the kitchen door.

Even after she had her foot on the door-step, her hand on the knob, Martha Hale had a moment of feeling she could not cross the threshold. And the reason it seemed she couldn't cross it now was simply because she hadn't crossed it before. Time and time again it had been in her mind, "I ought to go over and see Minnie Foster"—she still thought of her as Minnie Foster, though for twenty years she had been Mrs. Wright. And then there was always something to do and Minnie Foster would go from her mind. But *now* she could come.

The men went over to the stove. The women stood close together by the door. Young Henderson, the county attorney, turned around and said, "Come up to the fire, ladies."

Mrs. Peters took a step forward, then stopped. "I'm not—cold," she said.

And so the two women stood by the door, at first not even so much as looking around the kitchen.

The men talked for a minute about what a good thing it was the sheriff had sent his deputy out that morning to make a fire for them, and then Sheriff Peters stepped back from the stove, unbuttoned his outer coat, and leaned his hands on the kitchen table in a way that seemed to mark the beginning of official business. "Now, Mr. Hale," he said in a sort of semi-official voice, "before we move things about, you tell Mr. Henderson just what it was you saw when you came here yesterday morning."

The county attorney was looking around the kitchen.

"By the way," he said, "has anything been moved?" He turned to the sheriff. "Are things just as you left them yesterday?"

Peters looked from cupboard to sink; from that to a small worn rocker a little to one side of the kitchen table.

"It's just the same."

"Somebody should have been left here yesterday," said the county attorney.

"Oh—yesterday," returned the sheriff, with a little gesture as of yesterday having been more than he could bear to think of. "When I had to send Frank to Morris Center for that man who went crazy—let me tell you, I had my hands full *yesterday*. I knew you could get back from

Omaha by to-day, George, and as long as I went over everything here myself—"

"Well, Mr. Hale," said the county attorney, in a way of letting what was past and gone go, "tell just what happened when you came here yesterday morning."

Mrs. Hale, still leaning against the door, had that sinking feeling of the mother whose child is about to speak a piece. Lewis often wandered along and got things mixed up in a story. She hoped he would tell this straight and plain, and not say unnecessary things that would just make things harder for Minnie Foster. He didn't begin at once, and she noticed that he looked queer—as if standing in that kitchen and having to tell what he had seen there yesterday morning made him almost sick.

"Yes, Mr. Hale?" the county attorney reminded.

"Harry and I had started to town with a load of potatoes," Mrs. Hale's husband began.

Harry was Mrs. Hale's oldest boy. He wasn't with them now, for the very good reason that those potatoes never got to town yesterday and he was taking them this morning, so he hadn't been home when the sheriff stopped to say he wanted Mr. Hale to come over to the Wright place and tell the county attorney his story there, where he could point it all out. With all Mrs. Hale's other emotions came the fear that maybe Harry wasn't dressed warm enough—they hadn't any of them realized how that north wind did bite.

"We come along this road," Hale was going on, with a motion of his hand to the road over which they had just come, "and as we got in sight of the house I says to Harry, 'I'm goin' to see if I can't get John Wright to take a telephone.' You see," he explained to Henderson, "unless I can get somebody to go in with me they won't come out this branch road except for a price I can't pay. I'd spoke to Wright about it once before; but he put me off, saying folks talked too much anyway, and all he asked was peace and quiet—guess you know about how much he talked himself. But I thought maybe if I went to the house and talked about it before his wife, and said all the women-folks liked the telephones, and that in this lonesome stretch of road it would be a good thing—well, I said to Harry that that was what I was going to say— though I said at the same time that I didn't know as what his wife wanted made much difference to John—"

Now, there he was!—saying things he didn't need to say. Mrs. Hale tried to catch her husband's eye, but fortunately the county attorney interrupted with:

"Let's talk about that a little later, Mr. Hale. I do want to talk about that, but I'm anxious now to get along to just what happened when you got here."

When he began this time, it was very deliberately and carefully:

"I didn't see or hear anything. I knocked at the door. And still it was all quiet inside. I knew they must be up—it was past eight o'clock. So I knocked again, louder, and I thought I heard somebody say 'Come in.' I wasn't sure—I'm not sure yet. But I opened the door—this door," jerking a hand toward the door by which the two women stood, "and there, in that rocker"—pointing to it—"sat Mrs. Wright."

Every one in the kitchen looked at the rocker. It came into Mrs. Hale's mind that that rocker didn't look in the least like Minnie Foster—the Minnie Foster of twenty years before. It was a dingy red, with wooden rungs up the back, and the middle rung was gone, and the chair sagged to one side.

"How did she—look?" the county attorney was inquiring.

"Well," said Hale, "she looked—queer."

"How do you mean—queer?"

As he asked it he took out a note-book and pencil. Mrs. Hale did not like the sight of that pencil. She kept her eye fixed on her husband, as if to keep him from saying unnecessary things that would go into that note-book and make trouble.

Hale did speak guardedly, as if the pencil had affected him too.

"Well, as if she didn't know what she was going to do next. And kind of—done up."

"How did she seem to feel about your coming?"

"Why, I don't think she minded—one way or other. She didn't pay much attention. I said, 'Ho' do, Mrs. Wright? It's cold, ain't it?' And she said, 'Is it?'—and went on pleatin' at her apron.

"Well, I was surprised. She didn't ask me to come up to the stove, or to sit down, but just set there, not even lookin' at me. And so I said: 'I want to see John.'

"And then she—laughed. I guess you would call it a laugh.

"I thought of Harry and the team outside, so I said, a little sharp, 'Can I see John?' 'No,' says she—kind of dull like. 'Ain't he home?' says I. Then she looked at me. 'Yes,' says she, 'he's home.' 'Then why can't I see him?' I asked her, out of patience with her now. ' 'Cause he's dead.' says she, just as quiet and dull—and fell to pleatin' her apron. 'Dead?' says I, like you do when you can't take in what you've heard.

"She just nodded her head, not getting a bit excited, but rockin' back and forth.

" 'Why—where is he?' says I, not knowing *what* to say.

"She just pointed upstairs—like this"—pointing to the room above.

"I got up, with the idea of going up there myself. By this time I—didn't know what to do. I walked from there to here; then I says: 'Why, what did he die of?'

"'He died of a rope around his neck,' says she; and just went on pleatin' at her apron."

Hale stopped speaking, and stood staring at the rocker, as if he were still seeing the woman who had sat there the morning before. Nobody spoke; it was as if every one were seeing the woman who had sat there the morning before.

"And what did you do then?" the county attorney at last broke the silence.

"I went out and called Harry. I thought I might—need help. I got Harry in, and we went upstairs." His voice fell almost to a whisper. "There he was—lying over the—"

"I think I'd rather have you go into that upstairs," the county attorney interrupted, "where you can point it all out. Just go on now with the rest of the story."

"Well, my first thought was to get that rope off. It looked—"

He stopped, his face twitching.

"But Harry, he went up to him, and he said, 'No, he's dead all right, and we'd better not touch anything.' So we went downstairs.

"She was still sitting that same way. 'Has anybody been notified?' I asked. 'No,' says she, unconcerned.

"'Who did this, Mrs. Wright?' said Harry. He said it businesslike, and she stopped pleatin' at her apron. 'I don't know,' she says. 'You don't *know*?' says Harry. 'Weren't you sleepin' in the bed with him?' 'Yes,' says she, 'but I was on the inside.' 'Somebody slipped a rope round his neck and strangled him, and you didn't wake up?' says Harry. 'I didn't wake up,' she said after him.

"We may have looked as if we didn't see how that could be, for after a minute she said, 'I sleep sound.'

"Harry was going to ask her more questions, but I said maybe that weren't our business; maybe we ought to let her tell her story first to the coroner or the sheriff. So Harry went fast as he could over to High Road—the Rivers' place, where there's a telephone."

"And what did she do when she knew you had gone for the coroner?" The attorney got his pencil in his hand all ready for writing.

"She moved from that chair to this one over here"—Hale pointed to a small chair in the corner—"and just sat there with her hands held together and looking down. I got a feeling that I ought to make some conversation, so I said I had come in to see if John wanted to put in a telephone; and at that she started to laugh, and then she stopped and looked at me—scared."

At the sound of a moving pencil the man who was telling the story looked up.

"I dunno—maybe it wasn't scared," he hastened; "I wouldn't like to say it was. Soon Harry got back, and then Dr. Lloyd came, and you, Mr. Peters, and so I guess that's all I know that you don't."

He said that last with relief, and moved a little, as if relaxing. Every one moved a little. The county attorney walked toward the stair door.

"I guess we'll go upstairs first—then out to the barn and around there."

He paused and looked around the kitchen.

"You're convinced there was nothing important here?" he asked the sheriff. "Nothing that would—point to any motive?"

The sheriff too looked all around, as if to re-convince himself.

"Nothing here but kitchen things," he said, with a little laugh for the insignificance of kitchen things.

The county attorney was looking at the cupboard—a peculiar, ungainly structure, half closet and half cupboard, the upper part of it being built in the wall, and the lower part just the old-fashioned kitchen cupboard. As if its queerness attracted him, he got a chair and opened the upper part and looked in. After a moment he drew his hand away sticky.

"Here's a nice mess," he said resentfully.

The two women had drawn nearer, and now the sheriff's wife spoke.

"Oh—her fruit," she said, looking to Mrs. Hale for sympathetic understanding. She turned back to the county attorney and explained: "She worried about that when it turned so cold last night. She said the fire would go out and her jars might burst."

Mrs. Peters's husband broke into a laugh.

"Well, can you beat the women! Held for murder, and worrying about her preserves!"

The young attorney set his lips.

"I guess before we're through with her she may have something more serious than preserves to worry about."

"Oh, well," said Mrs. Hale's husband, with good-natured superiority, "women are used to worrying over trifles."

The two women moved a little closer together. Neither of them spoke. The county attorney seemed suddenly to remember his manners—and think of his future.

"And yet," said he, with the gallantry of a young politician, "for all their worries, what would we do without the ladies?"

The women did not speak, did not unbend. He went to the sink and began washing his hands. He turned to wipe them on the roller towel— whirled it for a cleaner place.

"Dirty towels! Not much of a housekeeper, would you say, ladies?" He kicked his foot against some dirty pans under the sink.

"There's a great deal of work to be done on a farm," said Mrs. Hale stiffly.

"To be sure. And yet"—with a little bow to her—"I know there are some Dickson County farm-houses that do not have such roller towels." He gave it a pull to expose its full length again.

"Those towels get dirty awful quick. Men's hands aren't always as clean as they might be."

"Ah, loyal to your sex, I see," he laughed. He stopped and gave her a keen look. "But you and Mrs. Wright were neighbors. I suppose you were friends, too."

Martha Hale shook her head.

"I've seen little enough of her of late years. I've not been in this house—it's more than a year."

"And why was that? You didn't like her?"

"I liked her well enough," she replied with spirit. "Farmers' wives have their hands full, Mr. Henderson. And then"—She looked around the kitchen.

"Yes?" he encouraged.

"It never seemed a very cheerful place," said she, more to herself than to him.

"No," he agreed; "I don't think any one could call it cheerful. I shouldn't say she had the home-making instinct."

"Well, I don't know as Wright had, either," she muttered.

"You mean they didn't get on very well?" he was quick to ask.

"No; I don't mean anything," she answered, with decision. As she turned a little away from him, she added: "But I don't think a place would be any the cheerfuler for John Wright's bein' in it."

"I'd like to talk to you about that a little later, Mrs. Hale," he said. "I'm anxious to get the lay of things upstairs now."

He moved toward the stair door, followed by the two men.

"I suppose anything Mrs. Peters does'll be all right?" the sheriff inquired. "She was to take in some clothes for her, you know—and a few little things. We left in such a hurry yesterday."

The county attorney looked at the two women whom they were leaving alone there among the kitchen things.

"Yes—Mrs. Peters," he said, his glance resting on the woman who was not Mrs. Peters, the big farmer woman who stood behind the sheriff's wife. "Of course Mrs. Peters is one of us," he said, in a manner of entrusting responsibility. "And keep your eye out, Mrs. Peters, for anything that might be of use. No telling; you women might come upon a clue to the motive—and that's the thing we need."

Mr. Hale rubbed his face after the fashion of a show man getting ready for a pleasantry.

"But would the women know a clue if they did come upon it?" he said; and, having delivered himself of this, he followed the others through the stair door.

The women stood motionless and silent, listening to the footsteps, first upon the stairs, then in the room above them.

Then, as if releasing herself from something strange, Mrs. Hale began to arrange the dirty pans under the sink, which the county attorney's disdainful push of the foot had deranged.

"I'd hate to have men comin' into my kitchen," she said testily— "snoopin' around and criticizin'."

"Of course it's no more than their duty," said the sheriff's wife, in her manner of timid acquiescence.

"Duty's all right," replied Mrs. Hale bluffly; "but I guess that deputy sheriff that come out to make the fire might have got a little of this on." She gave the roller towel a pull. "Wish I'd thought of that sooner! Seems mean to talk about her for not having things slicked up when she had to come áway in such a hurry."

She looked around the kitchen. Certainly it was not "slicked up." Her eye was held by a bucket of sugar on a low shelf. The cover was off the wooden bucket, and beside it was a paper bag—half full.

Mrs. Hale moved toward it.

"She was putting this in here," she said to herself—slowly.

She thought of the flour in her kitchen at home—half sifted, half not sifted. She had been interrupted, and had left things half done. What had interrupted Minnie Foster? Why had that work been left half done? She made a move as if to finish it,—unfinished things always bothered her,—and then she glanced around and saw that Mrs. Peters was watching her—and she didn't want Mrs. Peters to get that feeling she had got of work begun and then—for some reason—not finished.

"It's a shame about her fruit," she said, and walked toward the cupboard that the county attorney had opened, and got on the chair, murmuring: "I wonder if it's all gone."

It was a sorry enough looking sight, but "Here's one that's all right," she said at last. She held it toward the light. "This is cherries, too." She looked again. "I declare I believe that's the only one."

With a sigh, she got down from the chair, went to the sink, and wiped off the bottle.

"She'll feel awful bad, after all her hard work in the hot weather. I remember the afternoon I put up my cherries last summer."

She set the bottle on the table, and, with another sigh, started to sit down in the rocker. But she did not sit down. Something kept her from sitting down in that chair. She straightened—stepped back, and, half turned away, stood looking at it, seeing the woman who sat there "pleatin' at her apron."

The thin voice of the sheriff's wife broke in upon her: "I must be getting those things from the front room closet." She opened the door into the other room, started in, stepped back. "You coming with me, Mrs. Hale?" she asked nervously. "You—you could help me get them."

They were soon back—the stark coldness of that shut-up room was not a thing to linger in.

"My!" said Mrs. Peters, dropping the things on the table and hurrying to the stove.

Mrs. Hale stood examining the clothes the woman who was being detained in town had said she wanted.

"Wright was close!" she exclaimed, holding up a shabby black skirt that bore the marks of much making over. "I think maybe that's why she kept so much to herself. I s'pose she felt she couldn't do her part; and then, you don't enjoy things when you feel shabby. She used to wear pretty clothes and be lively—when she was Minnie Foster, one of the town girls, singing in the choir. But that—oh, that was twenty years ago."

With a carefulness in which there was something tender, she folded the shabby clothes and piled them at one corner of the table. She looked at Mrs. Peters, and there was something in the other woman's look that irritated her.

"She don't care," she said to herself. "Much difference it makes to her whether Minnie Foster had pretty clothes when she was a girl."

Then she looked again, and she wasn't so sure; in fact, she hadn't at any time been perfectly sure about Mrs. Peters. She had that shrinking manner, and yet her eyes looked as if they could see a long way into things.

"This all you was to take in?" asked Mrs. Hale.

"No," said the sheriff's wife; "she said she wanted an apron. Funny thing to want," she ventured in her nervous little way, "for there's not much to get you dirty in jail, goodness knows. But I suppose just to make her feel more natural. If you're used to wearing an apron—. She said they were in the bottom drawer of this cupboard. Yes—here they are. And then her little shawl that always hung on the stair door."

She took the small gray shawl from behind the door leading upstairs, and stood a minute looking at it.

Suddenly Mrs. Hale took a quick step toward the other woman.

"Mrs. Peters!"

"Yes, Mrs. Hale?"

"Do you think she—did it?"

A frightened look blurred the other things in Mrs. Peters's eyes.

"Oh, I don't know," she said, in a voice that seemed to shrink away from the subject.

"Well, I don't think she did," affirmed Mrs. Hale stoutly. "Asking for an apron, and her little shawl. Worryin' about her fruit."

"Mr. Peters says—" Footsteps were heard in the room above; she stopped, looked up, then went on in a lowered voice: "Mr. Peters says—it looks bad for her. Mr. Henderson is awful sarcastic in a speech, and he's going to make fun of her saying she didn't—wake up."

For a moment Mrs. Hale had no answer. Then, "Well, I guess John Wright didn't wake up—when they was slippin' that rope under his neck," she muttered.

"No, it's *strange*," breathed Mrs. Peters. "They think it was such a—funny way to kill a man."

She began to laugh; at the sound of the laugh, abruptly stopped.

"That's just what Mr. Hale said," said Mrs. Hale, in a resolutely natural voice. "There was a gun in the house. He says that's what he can't understand."

"Mr. Henderson said, coming out, that what was needed for the case was a motive. Something to show anger—or sudden feeling."

"Well, I don't see any signs of anger around here," said Mrs. Hale. "I don't—"

She stopped. It was as if her mind tripped on something. Her eye was caught by a dish-towel in the middle of the kitchen table. Slowly she moved toward the table. One half of it was wiped clean, the other half messy. Her eyes made a slow, almost unwilling turn to the bucket of sugar and the half empty bag beside it. Things begun—and not finished.

After a moment she stepped back, and said, in that manner of releasing herself:

"Wonder how they're finding things upstairs? I hope she had it a little more red up up there. You know,"—she paused, and feeling gathered,—"it seems kind of *sneaking;* locking her up in town and coming out here to get her own house to turn against her!"

"But, Mrs. Hale," said the sheriff's wife, "the law is the law."

"I s'pose 'tis," answered Mrs. Hale shortly.

She turned to the stove, saying something about that fire not being much to brag of. She worked with it a minute, and when she straightened up she said aggressively:

"The law is the law—and a bad stove is a bad stove. How'd you like to cook on this?"—pointing with the poker to the broken lining. She opened the oven door and started to express her opinion of the oven; but she was swept into her own thoughts, thinking of what it would mean, year after year, to have that stove to wrestle with. The thought of Minnie Foster trying to bake in that oven—and the thought of her never going over to see Minnie Foster—

She was startled by hearing Mrs. Peters say: "A person gets discouraged—and loses heart."

The sheriff's wife had looked from the stove to the sink—to the pail of water which had been carried in from outside. The two women stood there silent, above them the footsteps of the men who were looking for evidence against the woman who had worked in that kitchen. That look of seeing into things, of seeing through a thing to something else, was in the eyes of the sheriff's wife now. When Mrs. Hale next spoke to her, it was gently:

"Better loosen up your things, Mrs. Peters. We'll not feel them when we go out."

Mrs. Peters went to the back of the room to hang up the fur tippet she was wearing. A moment later she exclaimed, "Why, she was piecing a quilt," and held up a large sewing basket piled high with quilt pieces.

Mrs. Hale spread some of the blocks on the table.

"It's log-cabin pattern," she said, putting several of them together. "Pretty, isn't it?"

They were so engaged with the quilt that they did not hear the footsteps on the stairs. Just as the stair door opened Mrs. Hale was saying:

"Do you suppose she was going to quilt it or just knot it?"

The sheriff threw up his hands.

"They wonder whether she was going to quilt it or just knot it!"

There was a laugh for the ways of women, a warming of hands over the stove, and then the county attorney said briskly:

"Well, let's go right out to the barn and get that cleared up."

"I don't see as there's anything so strange," Mrs. Hale said resentfully, after the outside door had closed on the three men—"our taking up our time with little things while we're waiting for them to get the evidence. I don't see as it's anything to laugh about."

"Of course they've got awful important things on their minds," said the sheriff's wife apologetically.

They returned to an inspection of the blocks for the quilt. Mrs. Hale was looking at the fine, even sewing, and preoccupied with thoughts of the woman who had done that sewing, when she heard the sheriff's wife say, in a queer tone:

"Why, look at this one."

She turned to take the block held out to her.

"The sewing," said Mrs. Peters, in a troubled way. "All the rest of them have been so nice and even—but—this one. Why, it looks as if she didn't know what she was about!"

Their eyes met—something flashed to life, passed between them; then, as if with an effort, they seemed to pull away from each other. A moment Mrs. Hale sat there, her hands folded over that sewing which was so unlike all the rest of the sewing. Then she had pulled a knot and drawn the threads.

"Oh, what are you doing, Mrs. Hale?" asked the sheriff's wife, startled.

"Just pulling out a stitch or two that's not sewed very good," said Mrs. Hale mildly.

"I don't think we ought to touch things," Mrs. Peters said, a little helplessly.

"I'll just finish up this end," answered Mrs. Hale, still in that mild, matter-of-fact fashion.

She threaded a needle and started to replace bad sewing with good. For a little while she sewed in silence. Then, in that thin, timid voice, she heard:

"Mrs. Hale!"

"Yes, Mrs. Peters?"

"What do you suppose she was so—nervous about?"

"Oh, I don't know," said Mrs. Hale, as if dismissing a thing not important enough to spend much time on. "I don't know as she was— nervous. I sew awful queer sometimes when I'm just tired."

She cut a thread, and out of the corner of her eye looked up at Mrs. Peters. The small, lean face of the sheriff's wife seemed to have tightened up. Her eyes had that look of peering into something. But the next moment she moved, and said in her thin, indecisive way:

"Well, I must get those clothes wrapped. They may be through sooner than we think. I wonder where I could find a piece of paper— and string."

"In that cupboard, maybe," suggested Mrs. Hale, after a glance around.

One piece of the crazy sewing remained unripped. Mrs. Peters's back turned, Martha Hale now scrutinized that piece, compared it with the dainty, accurate sewing of the other blocks. The difference was startling. Holding this block made her feel queer, as if the distracted thoughts of the woman who had perhaps turned to it to try and quiet herself were communicating themselves to her.

Mrs. Peters's voice roused her.

"Here's a bird-cage," she said. "Did she have a bird, Mrs. Hale?"

"Why, I don't know whether she did or not." She turned to look at the cage Mrs. Peters was holding up. "I've not been here in so long." She sighed. "There was a man round last year selling canaries cheap—but I don't know as she took one. Maybe she did. She used to sing real pretty herself."

Mrs. Peters looked around the kitchen.

"Seems kind of funny to think of a bird here." She half laughed—an attempt to put up a barrier. "But she must have had one—or why would she have a cage? I wonder what happened to it."

"I suppose maybe the cat got it," suggested Mrs. Hale, resuming her sewing.

"No, she didn't have a cat. She's got that feeling some people have about cats—being afraid of them. When they brought her to our house yesterday, my cat got in the room, and she was real upset and asked me to take it out."

"My sister Bessie was like that," laughed Mrs. Hale.

The sheriff's wife did not reply. The silence made Mrs. Hale turn around. Mrs. Peters was examining the bird-cage.

"Look at this door," she said slowly. "It's broke. One hinge has been pulled apart."

Mrs. Hale came nearer.

"Looks as if some one must have been—rough with it."

Again their eyes met—startled, questioning, apprehensive. For a moment neither spoke nor stirred. Then Mrs. Hale, turning away, said brusquely:

"If they're going to find any evidence, I wish they'd be about it. I don't like this place."

"But I'm awful glad you came with me, Mrs. Hale." Mrs. Peters put the bird-cage on the table and sat down. "It would be lonesome for me—sitting here alone."

"Yes, it would, wouldn't it?" agreed Mrs. Hale, a certain determined naturalness in her voice. She picked up the sewing, but now it dropped in her lap, and she murmured in a different voice: "But I tell you what I *do* wish, Mrs. Peters. I wish I had come over sometimes when she was here. I wish—I had."

"But of course you were awful busy, Mrs. Hale. Your house—and your children."

"I could've come," retorted Mrs. Hale shortly. "I stayed away because it weren't cheerful—and that's why I ought to have come. I"—she looked around—"I've never liked this place. Maybe because it's down in a hollow and you don't see the road. I don't know what it is, but it's a lonesome place, and always was. I wish I had come over to see Minnie Foster sometimes. I can see now—" She did not put it into words.

"Well, you mustn't reproach yourself," counseled Mrs. Peters. "Somehow, we just don't see how it is with other folks till—something comes up."

"Not having children makes less work," mused Mrs. Hale, after a silence, "but it makes a quiet house—and Wright out to work all day— and no company when he did come in. Did you know John Wright, Mrs. Peters?"

"Not to know him. I've seen him in town. They say he was a good man."

"Yes—good," conceded John Wright's neighbor grimly. "He didn't drink, and kept his word as well as most, I guess, and paid his debts. But he was a hard man, Mrs. Peters. Just to pass the time of day with him—" She stopped, shivered a little. "Like a raw wind that gets to the bone." Her eye fell upon the cage on the table before her, and she added, almost bitterly: "I should think she would've wanted a bird!"

Suddenly she leaned forward, looking intently at the cage. "But what do you s'pose went wrong with it?"

"I don't know," returned Mrs. Peters; "unless it got sick and died."

But after she said it she reached over and swung the broken door. Both women watched it as if somehow held by it.

"You didn't know—her?" Mrs. Hale asked, a gentler note in her voice.

"Not till they brought her yesterday," said the sheriff's wife.

"She—come to think of it, she was kind of like a bird herself. Real sweet and pretty, but kind of timid and—fluttery. How—she—did— change."

That held her for a long time. Finally, as if struck with a happy thought and relieved to get back to everyday things, she exclaimed:

"Tell you what, Mrs. Peters, why don't you take the quilt in with you? It might take up her mind."

"Why, I think that's a real nice idea, Mrs. Hale," agreed the sheriff's wife, as if she too were glad to come into the atmosphere of a simple kindness. "There couldn't possibly be any objection to that, could there? Now, just what will I take? I wonder if her patches are in here—and her things."

They turned to the sewing basket.

"Here's some red," said Mrs. Hale, bringing out a roll of cloth. Underneath that was a box. "Here, maybe her scissors are in here—and her things." She held it up. "What a pretty box! I'll warrant that was something she had a long time ago—when she was a girl."

She held it in her hand a moment; then, with a little sigh, opened it. Instantly her hand went to her nose.

"Why—!"

Mrs. Peters drew nearer—then turned away.

"There's something wrapped up in this piece of silk," faltered Mrs. Hale.

"This isn't her scissors," said Mrs. Peters in a shrinking voice.

Her hand not steady, Mrs. Hale raised the piece of silk. "Oh, Mrs. Peters!" she cried. "It's—"

Mrs. Peters bent closer.

"It's the bird," she whispered.

"But, Mrs. Peters!" cried Mrs. Hale. "*Look* at it! Its neck—look at its neck! It's all—other side *to.*"

She held the box away from her.

The sheriff's wife again bent closer.

"Somebody wrung its neck," said she, in a voice that was slow and deep.

And then again the eyes of the two women met—this time clung together in a look of dawning comprehension, of growing horror. Mrs. Peters looked from the dead bird to the broken door of the cage. Again their eyes met. And just then there was a sound at the outside door.

Mrs. Hale slipped the box under the quilt pieces in the basket, and sank into the chair before it. Mrs. Peters stood holding to the table. The county attorney and the sheriff came in from outside.

"Well, ladies," said the county attorney, as one turning from serious things to little pleasantries, "have you decided whether she was going to quilt it or knot it?"

"We think," began the sheriff's wife in a flurried voice, "that she was going to —knot it."

He was too preoccupied to notice the change that came in her voice on that last.

"Well, that's very interesting, I'm sure," he said tolerantly. he caught sight of the bird-cage. "Has the bird flown?"

"We think the cat got it," said Mrs. Hale in a voice curiously even.

He was walking up and down, as if thinking something out.

"Is there a cat?" he asked absently.

Mrs. Hale shot a look up at the sheriff's wife.

"Well, not *now*," said Mrs. Peters. "They're superstitious, you know; they leave."

She sank into her chair.

The county attorney did not heed her. "No sign at all of any one having come in from the outside," he said to Peters, in the manner of continuing an interrupted conversation. "Their own rope. Now let's go upstairs again and go over it, piece by piece. It would have to have been some one who knew just the—"

The stair door closed behind them and their voices were lost.

The two women sat motionless, not looking at each other, but as if peering into something and at the same time holding back. When they spoke now it was as if they were afraid of what they were saying, but as if they could not help saying it.

"She liked the bird," said Martha Hale, low and slowly. "She was going to bury it in that pretty box."

"When I was a girl," said Mrs. Peters, under her breath, "my kitten—there was a boy took a hatchet, and before my eyes—before I could get there—" She covered her face an instant. "If they hadn't held me back I would have"—she caught herself, looked upstairs where footsteps were heard, and finished weakly—"hurt him."

Then they sat without speaking or moving.

"I wonder how it would seem," Mrs. Hale at last began, as if feeling her way over strange ground—"never to have had any children around?" Her eyes made a slow sweep of the kitchen, as if seeing what that kitchen had meant through all the years. "No, Wright wouldn't like the bird," she said after that—"a thing that sang. She used to sing. He killed that too." Her voice tightened.

Mrs. Peters moved uneasily.

"Of course we don't know who killed the bird."

"I knew John Wright," was Mrs. Hale's answer.

"It was an awful thing was done in this house that night, Mrs. Hale," said the sheriff's wife. "Killing a man while he slept—slipping a thing round his neck that choked the life out of him."

Mrs. Hale's hand went out to the bird-cage.

"His neck. Choked the life out of him."

"We don't *know* who killed him," whispered Mrs. Peters wildly. "We don't *know*."

Mrs. Hale had not moved. "If there had been years and years of—nothing, then a bird to sing to you, it would be awful—still—after the bird was still."

It was as if something within her not herself had spoken, and it found in Mrs. Peters something she did not know as herself.

"I know what stillness is," she said, in a queer, monotonous voice. "When we homesteaded in Dakota, and my first baby died—after he was two years old—and me with no other then—"

Mrs. Hale stirred.

"How soon do you suppose they'll be through looking for evidence?"

"I know what stillness is," repeated Mrs. Peters, in just that same way. Then she too pulled back. "The law has got to punish crime, Mrs. Hale," she said in her tight little way.

"I wish you'd seen Minnie Foster," was the answer, "when she wore a white dress with blue ribbons, and stood up there in the choir and sang."

The picture of that girl, the fact that she had lived neighbor to that girl for twenty years, and had let her die for lack of life, was suddenly more than she could bear.

"Oh, I *wish* I'd come over here once in a while!" she cried. "That was a crime! That was a crime! Who's going to punish that?"

"We mustn't take on," said Mrs. Peters, with a frightened look toward the stairs.

"I might 'a' *known* she needed help! I tell you, it's *queer*, Mrs. Peters. We live close together, and we live far apart. We all go through the same things—it's all just a different kind of the same thing! If it weren't—why do you and I *understand?* Why do we *know*—what we know this minute?"

She dashed her hand across her eyes. Then, seeing the jar of fruit on the table, she reached for it and choked out:

"If I was you I wouldn't *tell* her her fruit was gone! Tell her it *ain't*. Tell her it's all right—all of it. Here—take this in to prove it to her! She—she may never know whether it was broke or not."

She turned away.

Mrs. Peters reached out for the bottle of fruit as if she were glad to take it—as if touching a familiar thing, having something to do, could keep her from something else. She got up, looked about for something to wrap the fruit in, took a petticoat from the pile of clothes she had brought from the front room, and nervously started winding that round the bottle.

"My!" she began, in a high, false voice, "it's a good thing the men couldn't hear us! Getting all stirred up over a little thing like a—dead canary." She hurried over that. "As if that could have anything to do with—with—My, wouldn't they *laugh?*"

Footsteps were heard on the stairs.

"Maybe they would," muttered Mrs. Hale—"maybe they wouldn't."

"No, Peters," said the county attorney incisively; "it's all perfectly clear, except the reason for doing it. But you know juries when it comes to women. If there was some definite thing—something to show. Something to make a story about. A thing that would connect up with this clumsy way of doing it."

In a covert way Mrs. Hale looked at Mrs. Peters. Mrs. Peters was looking at her. Quickly they looked away from each other. The outer door opened and Mr. Hale came in.

"I've got the team round now," he said. "Pretty cold out there."

"I'm going to stay here awhile by myself," the county attorney suddenly announced. "You can send Frank out for me, can't you?" he asked the sheriff. "I want to go over everything. I'm not satisfied we can't do better."

Again, for one brief moment, the two women's eyes found one another.

The sheriff came up to the table.

"Did you want to see what Mrs. Peters was going to take in?"

The county attorney picked up the apron. He laughed.

"Oh, I guess they're not very dangerous things the ladies have picked out."

Mrs. Hale's hand was on the sewing basket in which the box was concealed. She felt that she ought to take her hand off the basket. She did not seem able to. He picked up one of the quilt blocks which she had piled on to cover the box. Her eyes felt like fire. She had a feeling that if he took up the basket she would snatch it from him.

But he did not take it up. With another little laugh, he turned away, saying:

"No; Mrs. Peters doesn't need supervising. For that matter, a sheriff's wife is married to the law. Ever think of it that way, Mrs. Peters?"

Mrs. Peters was standing beside the table. Mrs. Hale shot a look up at her; but she could not see her face. Mrs. Peters had turned away. When she spoke, her voice was muffled.

"Not—just that way," she said.

"Married to the law!" chuckled Mrs. Peters's husband. He moved toward the door into the front room, and said to the county attorney:

"I just want you to come in here a minute, George. We ought to take a look at these windows."

"Oh—windows," said the county attorney scoffingly.

"We'll be right out, Mr. Hale," said the sheriff to the farmer, who was still waiting by the door.

Hale went to look after the horses. The sheriff followed the county attorney into the other room. Again—for one moment—the two women were alone in that kitchen.

Martha Hale sprang up, her hands tight together, looking at that other woman, with whom it rested. At first she could not see her eyes, for the sheriff's wife had not turned back since she turned away at that suggestion of being married to the law. But now Mrs. Hale made her turn back. Her eyes made her turn back. Slowly, unwillingly, Mrs. Peters turned her head until her eyes met the eyes of the other woman. There was a moment when they held each other in a steady, burning look in which there was no evasion nor flinching. Then Martha Hale's eyes pointed the way to the basket in which was hidden the thing that would make certain the conviction of the other woman—that woman who was not there and yet who had been there with them all through the hour.

For a moment Mrs. Peters did not move. And then she did it. With a rush forward, she threw back the quilt pieces, got the box, tried to put in in her handbag. It was too big. Desperately she opened it, started to take the bird out. But there she broke—she could not touch the bird. She stood helpless, foolish.

There was a sound of a knob turning in the inner door. Martha Hale snatched the box from the sheriff's wife, and got it in the pocket of her big coat just as the sheriff and the county attorney came back into the kitchen.

"Well, Henry," said the county attorney facetiously, "at least we found out that she was not going to quilt it. She was going to—what is it you call it, ladies?"

Mrs. Hale's hand was against the pocket of her coat.

"We call it—knot it, Mr. Henderson."

CARROLL JOHN DALY

(1889–1958)

||||||||||||||||||||||||||||||||||||||||||| ■ |||||||||||||||||||||||||||||||||||||||||||

Carroll John Daly, identified as the "pioneer of the private eye," is credited with creating the hard-boiled detective. Daly demonstrates why he deserves that title in "The False Burton Combs," which is considered to be the genesis of the private eye. In it, Daly defines the credo and personality not only of the unnamed protagonist in the story but also of his soon-to-be-created hero Race Williams, the tough-talking hard-boiled private eye of his own most successful series, and a thousand who would follow the pattern. The hero says, "I ain't a crook; just a gentleman adventurer and make my living working against the law breakers. Not that I work with the police—no, not me." He adds, "I'm no knight errant, either," anticipating how the hard-boiled hero would be used by Dashiell Hammett and, especially, Raymond Chandler.

Daly, born in Yonkers, New York, and a graduate of the American Academy of Dramatic Arts, had given up on an acting career, become a movie projectionist, and moved from that into ownership of a chain of movie theaters. He didn't begin his writing career until the Roaring Twenties was in its third year, and the tone of his tales exactly fits the American hedonism of the period.

In a sense, Daly took the moralistic, "white knight" hero of the pulp Westerns and converted him to fit the mood of a country turned cynical by World War I and by the official corruption that accompanied Prohibition. Race Williams declares that he makes his own ethics, and his solutions are more likely to be accomplished with a pistol shot or a punch than with the sharp reasoning of the courtly sleuths who had preceded him. His adventures are told in the first person, allowing the reader at once to experience the physical sensations and inner thoughts of the hero. Two other hard-boiled detectives created by Daly, Vee Brown and Satan Hall, followed in the same formula.

In disclaiming any moral intentions and describing himself as a soldier of fortune, the protagonist of "The False Burton Combs" sets the Race Williams pattern. He also anticipates Williams's attitude toward the establishment: "There ain't nothing in government unless you're a politician. And, as I said before, I ain't a crook."

The hero also states that he "never took women seriously. My game and women don't go well together." That attitude was often reflected in detective fiction of the 1920s. But while Daly's male heroes disdain women, the author is able to create the occasional exemplar of a woman who is clearly heroic. Strong female characters like the "pretty game little kid" Marion St. James, whose courage is essential to the hero's well-being, were as unusual in Daly's era as is the resolution of this remarkable story.

1922

The False Burton Combs

■

I had an outside stateroom on the upper deck of the Fall River boat and ten minutes after I parked my bag there I knew that I was being watched. The boat had already cleared and was slowly making its way toward the Battery.

I didn't take the shadowing too seriously. There was nothing to be nervous about—my little trip was purely a pleasure one this time. But then a dick getting your smoke is not pleasant under the best of circumstances. And yet I was sure I had come aboard unobserved.

This chap was a new one on me and I thought he must have just picked me up on suspicion—trailed along in the hope of getting something. But I checked up my past offences and there was really nothing they could hold me on.

I ain't a crook; just a gentleman adventurer and make my living working against the law breakers. Not that I work with the police—no, not me. I'm no knight errant, either. It just came to me that the simplest people in the world are crooks. They are so set on their own plans to fleece others that they never imagine that they are the simplest sort to do. Why, the best safe cracker in the country—the dread of the police of seven States—will drop all his hard-earned money in three weeks on the race track and many a well-thought-of stick-up man will turn out his wad in one evening's crap game. Get the game? I guess I'm just one of the few that see how soft the lay is.

There's a lot of little stunts to tell about if I wanted to give away professional secrets but the game's too good to spread broadcast. It's enough to say that I've been in card games with four sharpers and did the quartet. At that I don't know a thing about cards and couldn't stack a deck if I was given half the night.

But as I say, I'm an adventurer. Not the kind the name generally means; those that sit around waiting for a sucker or spend their time helping governments out of trouble. Not that I ain't willing to help governments at a certain price but none have asked me. Those kind of chaps are found between the pages of a book, I guess. I know. I tried the game just once and nearly starved to death. There ain't nothing in governments unless you're a politician. And as I said before, I ain't a crook.

I've done a lot of business in blackmail cases. I find out a lad that's being blackmailed and then I visit him. He pays me for my services and like as not we do the blackmailers every time. You see I'm a kind of a fellow in the center—not a crook and not a policeman. Both of them look on me with suspicion, though the crooks don't often know I'm out after their hides. And the police—well, they run me pretty close at times but I got to take the chances.

But it ain't a nice feeling to be trailed when you're out for pleasure so I trot about the deck a few times whistling just to be sure there wasn't any mistake. And that bird come a-tramping after me as innocent as if it was his first job.

Then I had dinner and he sits at the next table and eyes me with a wistful longing like he hadn't made a pinch in a long time and is just dying to lock somebody up. But I study him, too, and he strikes me queer. He ain't got none of the earmarks of a dick. He acts like a lad with money and orders without even looking at the prices and it comes to me that I may have him wrong and that he might be one of these fellows that wanted to sell me oil stock. I always fall hard for the oil stock game. There ain't much in it but it passes the time and lets you eat well without paying for it.

Along about nine o'clock I am leaning over the rail just thinking and figuring how far the swim to shore is if a fellow had to do it. Not that I had any thought of taking to the water—no, not me—but I always like to figure what the chances are. You never can tell.

Well, that bird with the longing eyes cuddles right up and leans over the rail alongside of me.

"It's a nice night," he says.

"A first rate night for a swim."

I looked him over carefully out of the corner of my eyes.

He sort of straightens up and looks out toward the flickering shore lights.

"It *is* a long swim," he says, just like he had the idea in mind.

Then he asks me to have a cigar and it's a quarter one and I take it.

"I wonder would you do me a favor," he says, after a bit.

This was about what I expected. Con men are full of that kind of gush.

"Hmmm," is all I get off. My game is a waiting one.

"I came aboard a bit late," he goes right on. "I couldn't get a room—now I wonder would you let me take the upper berth in yours. I have been kind of watching you and saw that you were all alone."

Kind of watching me was right. And now he wanted to share my room. Well, that don't exactly appeal to me, for I'm banking on a good night's sleep. Besides, I know that the story is fishy, for I bought my room aboard and got an outsider. But I don't tell him that right off. I think I'll work him out a bit first.

"I'm a friend of the purser," I tell him. "I'll get you a room."

And I make to pass him.

"No—don't do that," he takes me by the arm. "It isn't that."

"Isn't what?"

I look him straight in the eyes and there's a look there that I have seen before and comes in my line of business. As he half turned and I caught the reflection of his eyes under the tiny deck light I read fear in his face—a real fear—almost a terror.

Then I give it to him straight.

"Out with what you want," I says. "Maybe I can help you but let me tell you first that there are plenty of rooms aboard the boat. Now, you don't look like a crook—you don't look sharp enough. What's the big idea of wanting to bunk with me?"

He thought a moment and then leaned far over the rail and started to talk, keeping his eyes on the water.

"I'm in some kind of trouble. I don't know if I have been followed aboard this boat or not. I don't think so but I can't chance it. I haven't had any sleep in two nights and while I don't expect to sleep tonight I'm afraid I may drop off. I don't want to be alone and—and you struck me as an easy-going fellow who might—might—"

"Like to take a chance on getting bumped off," I cut in.

He kind of drew away when I said this but I let him see right away that perhaps he didn't have me wrong. "And you would like me to sit up and protect you, eh?"

"I didn't exactly mean that but I—I don't want to be alone. Now, if you were a man I could offer money to—"

He paused and waited. I give him credit for putting the thing delicately and leaving the next move to me.

I didn't want to scare him off by putting him wise that he had come within my line of business. It might look suspicious to him. And I didn't want him to get the impression that I was a novice. There might be some future money in a job like this and it wouldn't do to be underrated.

"I'll tell you what I'll do," I says. "I've been all over the world and done some odd jobs for different South American governments"—that always has its appeal—"and I'll sit up and keep an eye on you for a hundred bucks."

Crude?—maybe—but then I know my game and you don't.

"And I can sleep?" he chirps, and his eyes sort of brighten up.

"Like a baby," I tells him.

"Good," he says, and "Come to my cabin."

So I take the number of his cabin and tell him that I'll meet him there as soon as I get my bag. Then I leave him and fetch my bag and put what money I have in the purser's office, for, although I can size up a game right away, a fellow can't afford to take chances. I have run across queerer ducks than this in my time.

Twenty minutes later he's in bed and we've turned the sign about smoking to the wall and are puffing away on a couple of good cigars. All content—he's paid me the hundred like a man; two nice new fifties.

He just lay there and smoked and didn't talk much and didn't seem as sleepy as I had thought he was. But I guess he was too tired to sleep, which is a queer thing but I've had it lots of times myself.

He seemed to be thinking, too. Like he was planning something and I was concerned in it. But I didn't bother him none. I saw what was on his chest and he didn't seem in a condition to keep things to himself. I thought he'd out with some proposition for me. But I didn't know. I wasn't anxious to travel about and be a nurse to him. That's more of a job for a private detective but they ain't used over much because they want to know all about your business and then you're worse off than you were before.

At last he opens up.

"What's your business?" he says.

And seeing I got his hundred there ain't no reason to dodge the question. I up and tells him.

"I'm a soldier of fortune."

He kind of blinks at this and then asks.

"That means a chap who takes chances for—for a consideration."

"Certain kind of chances." I qualify his statement.

"Like this for instance?"

"Sometimes; but I don't reckon to travel around as a body guard if that's what you're thinking."

He laughs like he was more at ease. But I often see them laugh when they are getting ready to send me into the danger that they fear. It's not downright meanness like I used to think when I was younger. It's relief, I guess.

"I think I can use you," he said slowly. "And pay you well and you won't need to see me again."

"Oh, I ain't got any particular dislike to you," I tell him. "It's only that I like to work alone. Let me hear what you have to offer and then— well, you can get some sleep tonight anyways."

He thought a moment.

"How much do I have to tell you?" he asked.

"As much or as little as you like. The less the better—but all I ought to know to make things go right for you."

"Well, then, there isn't much to tell. In the first place I want you to impersonate me for the summer or a greater part of it."

"That's not so easy." I shook my head.

"It's easy enough," he went on eagerly. "I am supposed to go to my father's hotel on Nantucket Island—"

Then he leaned out of the bed and talked quickly. He spoke very low and was very much in earnest. They could not possibly know me there. His father was abroad and he had not been to Nantucket since he was ten.

"How old are you?" he asked me suddenly.

"Thirty," I told him.

"You don't look more than I do. We are much alike—about the same size—the same features. And you won't meet anyone I know. If things should go wrong I'll be in touch with you."

"And your trouble?" I questioned. "What should I know about that?"

"That my life is threatened. I have been mixed up with some people whom I am not proud of."

"And they threaten to kill you."

I stroked my chin. Not that I minded taking the chances but somewheres I had learned that a laborer is worthy of his hire. It looked like he was hiring me to get bumped off in his place. Which was all right if I was paid enough. I had taken such chances before and nothing had come of it. That is nothing to me.

"Yes, they threaten my life—but I think it's all bluff."

I nodded. I could plainly see it was that, so I handed out a little talk.

"And that's why you paid me a hundred to sit up with you all night. Mind you, I don't mind the risk, but I must be paid accordingly."

When he saw that it was only a question of money he opens up considerable. He didn't exactly give me the facts in the case but he tells me enough and I learned that he had never seen the parties.

The end of it was that he draws up a paper which asks me to impersonate him and lets me out of all trouble. Of course, the paper wouldn't be much good in a bad jam but it would help if his old man should return suddenly from Europe. But I don't aim to produce that paper. I play the game fair and the figure he names was a good one—not what I would have liked perhaps but all he could afford to pay without bringing his old man into the case, which could not be done.

Somehow, when we finished talking, I got the idea that he had been mixed up in a shady deal—bootlegging or something—and a couple of friends had gone to jail on his evidence. There were three others from Canada who were coming on to get him—the three he had never seen. But it didn't matter much to me. I was just to show them that he wasn't afraid and then when they called things off or got me all was over.

Personally I did think that there was a lot of bluff in the whole business but he didn't and it wasn't my game to wise him up.

It was a big hotel I was going to for the summer and if things got melodramatic, why, I guess I could shoot as good as any bootlegger that ever robbed a church. They're hard guys, yes, but then I ain't exactly a cake-eater myself.

An hour or more talk in which I learn all about his family and the hotel and Burton Combs drops off for his first real sleep in months.

The next morning we part company in his stateroom and I taxied over to New Bedford. He thinks that's better than taking the train because there is a change of cars in the open country and he don't want me to drop too soon.

There are only about ten staterooms on the little tub that makes the trip from New Bedford to Nantucket and I have one of them which is already reserved in Burton Combs's name. After taking a walk about the ship I figure that there ain't no Desperate Desmonds aboard, and having earned my hundred the night before I just curl up in that little cabin and hit the hay.

Five hours and not a dream disturbed me and when I come on deck there's Nantucket right under our nose and we are rounding the little lighthouse that stands on the point leading into the bay.

There's a pile of people on the dock and they sure did look innocent enough and I take a stretch and feel mighty good. From some of the outfits I see I know that I'm going to travel in class and I hope that Burton Combs's clothes fit me for I didn't come away prepared for any social gayety. But it's early in the season yet and I'll get a chance to look around before the big rush begins.

There is a bus at the dock which is labeled "Sea Breeze Inn" and that's my meat. I climb in with about five others and we are off. Up one shady street and down another; up a bit of a hill and a short straightaway and we are at the hotel. It's a peach, too, with a view of the ocean that would knock your eye out.

The manager spots me at once and says that he'd know me among a thousand as a Combs. Which was real sweet of him seeing that he was expecting me, and the others in the bus were an old man, three old women and a young girl about nineteen. But it wasn't my part to enlighten him and tell him that I was on to his flattery. Besides he was an old bird and probably believed what he said.

He was right glad to see me and tried to look like he meant it and wondered why I hadn't come up there again in all these years but guessed it was because it was kind of slow with my father having a hotel at Atlantic City and at Ostend. And he wanted to know if I was going to study the business. Said my father wrote him that he would like to see me interested in the hotel line.

I didn't say much. There wasn't no need. Mr. Rowlands, the manager, was one of those fussy old parties and he talked all the way up in the elevator and right into the room.

There were about fifty people there all told on the first of July but they kept coming in all the time and after I was there about two weeks the place was fairly well crowded. But I didn't make any effort to learn the business, thinking it might hurt young Combs who didn't strike me as a chap who would like any kind of work.

There was one young girl there—the one that came up in the bus with me—Marion St. James, and we had quite some times together. She was young and full of life and wanted to be up and doing all the time and we did a great deal of golf together.

Then there was another who took an interest in me. She was a widow and a fine looker and it was her first season there. I thought that she was more used to playing Atlantic City for she didn't look like the usual run of staunch New England dames. Sort of out of place and she looked to me to trot her around.

But I didn't have the time; there was Marion to be taken about. She was what you'd call a flapper and talked of the moonlight and such rot but she was real and had a big heart and after all a sensible little head on her shoulders. And she couldn't see the widow a mile and looked upon me as her own special property and blew the widow up every chance she got.

But the widow, I guess, was bent on making a match and she was finding the Island pretty dead though the son of John B. Combs, the hotel magnate, looked like a big catch. So you see my time was fairly well taken up and I grabbed many a good laugh. I never took women seriously. My game and women don't go well together.

Yet that widow was persistent and curious and wanted to know every place Marion and me went and used to keep asking me where we drove to nights. For the kid and me did a pile of motoring. Yes, I had a car. A nice little touring car came with the Burton Combs moniker.

Marion was different. She was just a slip of a kid stuck up in a place like that and it was up to me to show her a good time. I kind of felt sorry for her and then she was pretty and a fellow felt proud to be seen with her.

All the time I kept an eye peeled for the bad men. I wondered if they'd come at all and if they did I thought that they would come in the busy season when they wouldn't be noticed much. But that they'd come at all I very much doubted.

And then they came—the three of them. I knew them the very second they entered the door. They were dolled right up to the height of fashion—just what the others were wearing. But I knew them. They just didn't belong. Maybe the others didn't spot them as outsiders but I did.

They were no bluff, either. I have met all kinds of men in my day; bad and worse and these three were the real thing. It came to me that if these gents were bent on murder I had better be up and doing.

And that Island boasted that it had never had a real murder. Yes, it sure did look like all records were going to be broken.

One of them was a tall skinny fellow and he looked more like a real summer visitor than the others. But his mouth gave him away. When he thought he was alone with the others he'd talk through the side of it, a trick which is only found in the underworld or on the track.

One of the others was fat and looked like an ex-bartender and the third I should say was just a common jailbird that could cut a man's throat with a smile.

The tall skinny one was the leader and he was booked as Mr. James Farrow. He made friends with me right off the bat. Didn't overdo it, you know; just gave me the usual amount of attention that most of the guests showed toward the owner's son. He must-a read a book about the Island for he tried to tell me things about the different points of interest like he'd been there before. But he had a bad memory like on dates and things. Marion gave me the dope on that. She knew that Island like a book.

I didn't have much doubt as to who they were but I checked them up, liking to make sure. I didn't know just what their game was and I didn't see the big idea of wanting to bump me off. If they wanted money I could catch their point but they seemed well supplied with the ready. Yes, sir, I looked this Farrow over and he's a tough bird and no mistake. But then I've seen them just as tough before and pulled through it. Besides, I hold a few tricks myself. They don't know I'm on and they don't know that I'm mighty quick with the artillery myself.

And that gun is always with me. It ain't like I only carry it when I think there's trouble coming. I always have it. You see, a chap in my line of work makes a lot of bad friends and he can't tell when one of them is going to bob up and demand an explanation. But they all find out that I ain't a bird to fool with and am just as likely to start the fireworks as they are.

Nearly every night after dinner I'd take the car and Marion and me would go for a little spin about the Island. I don't know when I ever enjoyed anything so much and sometimes I'd forget the game I was playing and think that things were different. I've met a pile of women in my time but none like Marion nor near like her. Not since the days when I went to school—and that's a memory only.

Well, we'd just drive about and talk and she'd ask me about the different places I had been to. And I could hold my own there, for I've been all over the world.

Then one night—about ten days after the troupe arrived—I get a real scare. We've been over 'Sconset way and are driving home along about nine-thirty when—*zip*—there's a whiz in the air and a hole in the windshield. Then there's another *zip* and I see Marion jump.

It's nothing new to me. I knew that sound right away. It's a noiseless gun and someone has taken a couple of plugs at us from the distance. Well, it ain't my cue to stop, so I speed up and it's pretty near town before I slow down beneath a lamp and turn to Marion.

There is a little trickle of blood running down her cheek and she's pretty white. But she ain't hurt any. It's just a scratch and I stop in the drug store and get some stuff and bathe it off.

She is a mighty game little kid and don't shake a bit and act nervous. But I'm unsteady for the first time in my life and my hand shook. I wouldn't of been much good on a quick draw then. But later I would, for I was mad—bad mad—if you know what that is. I see that all the danger ain't mine. Not that I think they meant to get Marion. But I had brought that Kid into something, and all because she kind of liked me a bit and I took her around.

On the way back to the hotel I buck up and tell her that it must have been some of the natives hunting the hares and not to say anything about it but that I would speak to the authorities in the morning.

She just looked at me funny and I knew that she did not believe me but she let it go at that.

"If that's all you want to tell me, Burt—why—all right—I shan't say a word to anyone. You can trust me."

That was all. Neither of us spoke again until we reached the hotel and I had parked the car under the shed at the side and we were standing at the bottom of the steps by the little side entrance. Then she turned and put her two tiny hands up on my shoulders and the paleness had gone from her face but just across her cheek where the bullet had passed was the smallest streak of vivid red.

"You can trust me, Burt," she said again and there seemed to be a question in her voice.

"Of course I trust you, Marion," I answered and my voice was husky and seemed to come from a distance.

It all happened very suddenly after that. Her head was very close. I know, for her soft hair brushed my cheek. I think that she leaned forward but I know that she looked up into my eyes and that the next moment I had leaned down and kissed and held her so a moment. So we stood and she did not draw away and I made no movement to release her. We were alone there, very much alone.

Then there was the sudden chug of a motor, a second's flash of light and I had opened my arms and Marion was gone and I stood alone in the blackness.

So the spell of Marion's presence was broken and I stood silently in the shadow as Farrow and his two companions passed and entered the hotel lobby.

Had they seen us? Yes—I knew that they had. For they smiled as they passed. Smiled and never knew that they had passed close to death. For at that moment it was only the press of a trigger that lay between them and eternity.

The curtain had been rung up on the first act and the show was on. Before, I could sleep easy at night for the danger was mine and I had thought little of it. But now I felt that it was another's—and—well, I resolved to bring things to a head that night.

Ten minutes later I went to my room but not to bed. I put my light out and sat in the room until about twelve o'clock. At that time the hotel was as quiet as death.

Then I stepped out of my window and climbed down the fire escape which led to the little terrace which overlooked the ocean. I knew just where Farrow's room was and I walked along the terrace until I was under it and then swung myself up the fire escape and climbed to the third story. His window was open and thirty seconds later I had dropped into the room and was seated on the end of Farrow's bed.

Then I switched on the light and waited till he woke up. Guess he didn't have much fear of me for he slept right on for another five minutes and then he kind of turned over and blinked and—opened his eyes. He was awake fast enough then for he was looking in the mean end of my automatic.

He was quick witted, too, for he rubbed his eyes with one hand while he let the other slip under his pillow. Then I laughed and he drew it out empty and sat bolt upright in bed and faced the gun.

"Farrow," I says. "You were mighty near to going out tonight. And if I hadn't already lifted that gun of yours I'd a popped you then."

And I half wished that I had let his gun stay there for then there would have been an excuse to let him have it. A poor excuse but still an excuse. It's hard to shoot a man when he ain't armed and prepared but it's another thing to shoot when he's reaching for a gun and it's your life or his. Then you can let him have it with your mind easy.

He was a game bird, was Farrow, for he must have had plenty to think about at that moment. You see he couldn't tell just what was coming to him and from his point of view it must have looked mighty bad but he started right in to talk. Told me the chances I was taking and that I couldn't possibly get away with it. He didn't waste any time in bluffing and pretending surprise at seeing me sitting there with the gun. I give him credit—now—for understanding the situation.

But I stopped his wind.

"Shut up," I says.

And he caught the anger in my eyes and in my voice and he shut— which was good for him, for a chap can't tell for sure what he's going to do when he's seeing red and has the drop on a lad that he figures needs killing.

Then I did a bit of talking. I told him what had taken place that night and I knew it was his doing. And he nodded and never tried to deny it.

"You killed my brother," he says, "for he died in trying to break jail a few months ago—the jail where you sent him."

"So—I killed your brother, eh? Well, every man is entitled to his own opinion. Now, I don't know about the killing of your brother but I'll tell you this, my friend, I come mighty near to killing you and I don't miss either and I don't crack windshields and I don't go for to hit innocent parties."

I could see that he was kind of surprised at the way I talked for I wasn't specially careful about my language like I had been about the hotel and like what he would expect from the real Burton Combs. But I could see that he kind of smacked his lips at the mention of the girl and he knew that he had a hold on me there. But I didn't care what was on his chest. I knew that the morning would see the end of the thing one way or the other.

"I am going to give you until the six-thirty boat tomorrow morning to leave the Island," I told him.

And I was not bluffing, either. After a man has had his warning it's good ethics to shoot him down—at least I see it that way. That is, if he needs it bad and you happen to have my code of morals. Also if you want to live to a ripe old age.

"What then?" he sort of sneers.

Seeing as how he wasn't going over the hurdles right away he thinks I'm a bit soft. In the same position his own doubt about shooting me would be the chances of a getaway. And the chances were not good on that Island unless you had made plans in advance. Perhaps he had— I didn't know then for I hadn't seen any boat hanging about the harbor.

"What then?" he sneers again.

"Then—" I says very slowly and thinking of Marion. "Then I'll cop you off at breakfast tomorrow morning. Yes—as soon as that boat leaves the dock I'll be gunning for you, Mr. James Farrow. And as sure as you're not a better shot than you were tonight out on the moors you'll go join your brother."

With that I turned from the bed and, unlocking his door, walked out of his room. The temptation to shoot was too great.

But I didn't go to bed that night. I just put out my light and sat smoking in my room—smoking and thinking. So I spent the second night that summer awake. I knew that the three would meet and talk it over and no doubt—get. But I just sat there; half facing the door and half facing the window with my gun on my knees waiting.

How nice would it be if they would only come by the window? It would be sweet then—and what a lot of credit I'd get as Burton Combs protecting his father's property. They meant real business all right for I see now that there was sentiment behind the whole thing—sentiment and honor. That peculiar honor of the underworld which goes and gets a squealer. Combs had evidently squealed and Farrow's brother had paid the price. And Combs went free. Position and evidence and politics had done the trick, I guess.

I heard the clock strike two and then two-thirty and then there was a footstep in the hall and I turned and faced the door and then there come a light tap on the door. This sure was a surprise.

I didn't turn on the electric light but just went to the door and swung it open suddenly and stepped back. But no one came in.

Then I heard a kind of a gasp—a woman's voice. The first thing I thought of was Marion and then I see the widow in the dim hall light. Her hair was all down and she had thrown a light robe about her and she was excited and her eyes were wide open and she looked frightened.

"It's Marion—little Miss St. James," she sobbed, "and she's in my room now—and it was terrible and I think—I think she fainted."

Then she stopped and kind of choked a bit.

Right away it came to me that this gang had done something to her and I wished that I had settled the whole thing earlier in the evening when I had the chance but—

"Come," I said to the widow and took her by the arm and led her down the hall to her room. The door was open and gun in hand I rushed into the room ahead of her.

"There on the bed," she gasped behind me.

I turned to the bed—and it was empty and then I knew. But it was too late, for I was trapped. There was a muzzle of a gun shoved into the middle of my back and a hard laugh. Then Farrow spoke.

"Throw that gun on the bed and throw it quick."

And—and I threw it and threw it quick. I was done. I should have suspected the widow from the first day I laid eyes on her, for she didn't belong. Yes, she was this gang's come on. And me, who had never fallen for women, was now caught by women. A good one and a bad one. One whom I wanted to protect and one who knew it. Now you see how the game is played. Neither a good nor a bad woman can help you in my sort of life. And yet I would take any chance for that little Marion who used to stand out on the moor at the—but Farrow was talking.

"And now, Mr. Combs, we meet again—and you're the one to do the listening. We are going to take you for a little motor ride—that is, you are going out with me to meet my friends. We don't intend to kill you. That is, if you have proved yourself a man and come along quietly. There is some information I want from you. And thanks for the return of my gun," he finished as he picked the gun off the bed.

Yes, it was his gun and mine was still in my pocket and I'd-a shot him then only I saw that the widow was covering me.

"Come."

Farrow turned and, poking the gun close to my ribs, he induced me to leave the room with him.

"If you make a noise you go," he told me as we walked down the long narrow hall to the servants' stairs. But I didn't intend to cry out. If he would just move that gun of his the least little bit I could draw and shoot. I almost laughed, the thing was so easy.

"The *Elsie* is lying right off the point," he went on, as we approached the little shed where my car was kept. "You remember the *Elsie*—it used to be your boat. The government remembers it, too. But they don't know it now nor would you. But enough of that. Climb into your car—we'll use that for our little jaunt."

We had reached the little shed now and I climbed into the car, always waiting for a chance to use my gun, but he watched me like a hawk. Then he laughed—a queer, weird laugh which had the ring of death in it.

I drove as he said and we turned from the hotel and out onto the moors—that long stretch of desolate road that leads across the Island. And then he made me stop the car and stand up.

"I'll take your gun," he said and he lifted it from my hip. "We won't need more than one gun between us tonight. For if it comes to shooting I'll take care of that end of it."

He threw the gun into the back of the car where I heard it strike the cushion of the rear seat and bounce to the floor.

We drove on in silence. He never said a word but I felt as clearly as if he had told me so that he was driving me to my death. The gun, he had let me carry until we were safe away. Perhaps he had thought that without it I might have cried out in the hotel but this I shall never know. That he knew all along I had it I have no doubt.

More than once I was on the edge of telling him that I was not the man he thought I was, for it looked as though the game was up. But he would not have believed me and besides my little agreement with Combs was back in my hotel room.

Not a soul did we pass as we sped over the deserted road. No light but the dulled rays of the moon broke the darkness all around us. Half hour or more and then suddenly I see a car in the road as the moon pops out from behind the clouds.

Then Farrow spoke and there was the snarl of an animal in his voice.

"Here's where you stop," he growled, "and here's where you get yours. They'll find you out here in the morning and they can think what they want; we'll be gone. And the killing of a rat like you is the only business I've got on the moors this night."

I had pulled up short in the center of the road now for a big touring car which I recognized as Farrow's was stretched across our path blocking the passage. In it I clearly saw his two friends.

It was death now sure but I made up my mind to go out as gracefully as possible and when he ordered me to open the door I leaned over and placed my hand upon the seat. And it fell on the cool muzzle of a revolver. Yes, my fingers closed over a gun and I knew that that gun was mine.

Thrills in life—yes—there are many but I guess that that moment was my biggest. I didn't stop to think how that gun got there. I didn't care. I just tightened on it and felt the blood of life pass quickly through my body—if you know what I mean.

I couldn't turn and shoot him for he had his pistol pressed close against my side. What he feared I don't know but I guess he was just one of these overcareful fellows who didn't take any chances.

"Open that door and get out," he ordered again as he gave me a dig in the ribs.

I leaned over again and placed my hand upon the handle of the door and then I got a happy thought.

"I can't open it," I said and I let my voice tremble and my hand shake. But in my left hand I now held my gun and thanked my lucky stars that I was lefthanded, for I knew if I got the one chance that I hoped for it would have to be a perfect shot.

"White livered after all," he muttered and he stooped over and placed his left hand upon the handle of the door.

His right hand still held the gun close to my side and his eyes were watching my every movement. I never seen a man so careful before. I couldn't pull the gun up and shoot for he would get me at the very first movement—and although I was tempted I waited. The other two sat in the car ahead and were smoking and laughing. Of course I knew that if I once stepped out in the moonlight with the gun in my hand that it was all up but I waited and then—

The door really stuck a bit, for the nights are mighty damp on that island and it was that dampness which saved my life. For just the fraction of a second he took his eyes off me—just a glance down at the door with a curse on his lips.

And with that curse on his lips he died.

For as he turned the handle I give it to him right through the heart. I don't miss at that range—no—not me. The door flew open and he tumbled out on the road—dead.

I don't offer no apologies, for it was his life or mine and—as I said— he tumbled out on the road—dead.

Another fellow writing might say that things weren't clear after that. But they were clear enough to me because I never lose my head. That's why I have lived to be thirty and expect to die in bed. Yes, things are always clear when clearness means a little matter of life or death.

Those other chaps were so surprised at the turn things had taken that I had jumped to the road and winged one of them before they knew what had happened. But the other fellow was quick and had started shooting and I felt a sharp pain in my right shoulder. But one shot was all that he fired and then I had him—one good shot was all I needed and—he went out. I don't go for to miss.

I didn't take the time to examine them to see if they were dead. I'm not an undertaker and it wasn't my business. I guessed they were but if they wasn't I didn't intend to finish the job. I'm not a murderer, either. Then there were a couple of houses not so far off and I could see lights—lights that weren't there before—in both of them. Even on a quiet island like that you can't start a gun party without disturbing some of the people.

I just turned my car around and started back to the hotel. Twenty minutes later I had parked it in the shed and gone to my room. As far as I knew no one could know what had taken place on the lonely moor that night. I played doctor to my shoulder. It wasn't so very bad, either, though it pained a lot, but the bullet had gone through the flesh and passed out. I guess a little home treatment was as good as any doctor could do.

Then the morning came and my arm was not so good but I dressed and went down to breakfast and saw the manager and he told me that the widow had gone on the early boat. I don't think that she was a real widow but that she was the wife of one of those chaps. Farrow, I guess. But that didn't bother me none. She was a widow now all right.

And then about nine o'clock news of the three dead men being found away off on the road came in. And I know I got all three of them.

There was a lot of talk and newspaper men from the city came over and detectives and one thing and another. The morning papers of the following day had it all in and wild guesses as to how it happened. The three were recognized by the police as notorious characters and then it got about that a rum-runner had been seen off the east shore that very morning. The general opinion seemed to be that there had been a fight among the pirates and that these three men got theirs—which suited me to a T.

I would-a beat it only that would have looked mighty queer and honestly I didn't see where they had a thing on me. I thought the best thing to do was to sit tight and for nearly a week I sat.

And then the unexpected—unexpected by me at least—happened.

The widow sent a telegram to the Boston police and they came down and nailed me. You see the writing on the wall? Keep clear of the women.

A dick from Boston dropped in one morning and I knew him the minute he stepped foot in the hotel. And I also knew that he was after me though at the time I didn't wise up as to how he was on. But he wasn't sure of himself and he had the manager introduce him to me. Then he talked about everything but the killing and of course he was the only one at the hotel that left that topic out of his conversation. And that was his idea of hiding his identity!

But he was sharp enough at that and hadn't gone about the Island more than a couple of days before he stuck this and that together and had enough on me to make the charge. But he was a decent sort of chap and came up to my room late at night with the manager and put the whole thing straight up to me and told me about the widow's telegram and that I was under arrest and that I had better get a hold of the best lawyer that money could buy for I was in for a tough time.

He was right and I knew that I was in a mighty bad hole. But I also knew that there would be plenty of money behind me when the whole thing came out and money is a mighty good thing to get out of a hole with.

So I played the game and never let on that I wasn't the real Burton Combs. They locked me up and notified my adopted father and the next morning the news was shouted all over the world, for John B. Combs cut a big figure and his son's arrest made some music.

And then the Combs lawyer, Harvey Benton, came up to see me and the minute he set eyes on me the cat was out of the bag and I up and tells him the whole story though I didn't give him the reason for Combs being frightened but just said that he was threatened by these three rum-runners. I felt that my playing the game fair would give me a better standing with the Combses and help loosen up the old purse strings.

Young Combs wasn't such a bad fellow either, for the next day he was down to see me and ready to tell the whole story and stand up for me.

The we moved over to the mainland and I couldn't get out on bail and the prosecuting attorney started to have my record looked up and I can tell you that after that things didn't look so rosy. It all goes to prove that a clean sheet helps a man though mine wasn't nothing to be ashamed of. But I will admit that it looked pretty sick on the front pages of the newspapers.

Then John B. Combs himself arrives and comes up to see me. He listens to my story at first with a hard, cold face but when I come to the part where I have to shoot quick or die his eyes kind of fill and I see he's thinking of his son and the chances he would of had in the same place—and how if I hadn't got them they would-a got Burton.

Then he stretches forth his hand and grasps mine and I see it would have been better if Burton had taken his father into his confidence in the first place.

Yes, the old boy was a good scout and he told me that he loved his son and that I had saved his son's life and he didn't care what my past had been. And he would see me through this thing that his son had gotten me into if it cost a fortune.

It was a funny thing all around. Here was me, the sufferer, comforting the old boy and telling him that it was nothing. Just like the chair looking me in the face was an everyday affair. But I didn't much like the idea of his being so sad, for it gives me the impression that my chances are not so good and that I am going to pay the price for his son. Which ain't nothing to sing about. But it was my word against the word of the gang, and they being dead wouldn't have much to say.

Yes, I was indicted all right and held for the grand jury—first degree murder was the charge. Then come a wait with my lawyers trying to get a hold of some farmer who might of seen something of the shooting and would corroborate my story.

Then comes the trial and you would-a thought that the District Attorney had a personal grudge against me all his life and that all the politicians and one-horse newspapers were after his job. He paints up those three crooks like they were innocent young country girls that had been trapped by a couple of designing men. And he tells how Burton Combs done them in a shady deal and when he feared they was going to tell the authorities he up and hires a professional murderer to kill them.

I tell you it made a mighty good story and he told it well. One could almost see those three cherubs going forth in child-like innocence to be slaughtered by the butcher—which is me.

And he punched holes in my story. Especially that part about how I put down my hand and found the gun on the seat. And he said that I took them out on some pretense and shot them down in cold blood—quick shooting being my business and shady deals my living.

When he got through with my story it was as full of holes as a sieve and I had a funny feeling around the chest because I thought anyone could see what a rotten gang this was and what a clean-living young fellow I was. For my lawyer painted me up as a young gentleman what went around the world trying to help others.

Just when I think that things are all up and the jury are eyeing me with hard, stern faces comes the surprise. You see, I had never told a soul about Marion being in the car with me when that gang first started the gun play out on the 'Sconset road. You see, I didn't see the need of it and—and—well, somehow I just couldn't drag her into it. Weakness, I'll admit, for a fellow facing death should fight with every weapon he can grab. And there's that thing about women cropping up again.

But somehow there in that stuffy courtroom her innocent face and those soft, child-like eyes come up before me and I see she might of helped me a lot with the simple truth about the bullet that crossed her cheek. And while I was thinking about Marion and telling myself that my goose was cooked comes that big surprise.

My lawyer calls a witness, and it's Marion St. James. Gad! my heart just stops beating for the moment.

She was very quiet and very calm but her voice was low and the jury had to lean forward to catch what she said. She told about the ride that night and how the bullet broke the windshield and scratched her cheek.

And then came the shock. I was just dreaming there and thinking of the trouble I had caused her when I heard what she was saying and I woke up—quick.

"—after I left Mr. Combs—I called him Burton," and she pointed down at me. "I went upstairs but I couldn't sleep. I was thinking about what had happened out on the moor that night. Of course, I didn't believe what Burton had told me—about the hares. And then I remembered the look on his face as he bathed off my cheek—and it was terrible to see and—"

Then she paused a moment and wiped her eyes and went on.

"After a bit I looked out the window and I could see the little shed, where Burt kept his car, and I just caught the glimpse of a man going into it. I thought it was Burt and that he was going to drive out on the moor and—Oh, I don't know what I thought, but I was frightened and didn't want him to go and I just rushed out of my room and down the back stairs and out toward the shed.

"I was just in time to see a big touring car pull out and two men were in it. And then I waited a minute and went and looked into the shed and Burt's car was still there. I don't know why but I was frightened and I climbed into the little touring car and sat down in the back and kind of rested.

"Then I heard someone coming and I hid down in the back of the car and pulled some rugs up over me and waited."

"And why did you wait?" my lawyer asked her kindly.

"I just thought that I would be able to help Mr.—Burt—and I wanted to help him."

"Was there any other reason?"

"Yes—I thought that he was going into trouble for me and—and—" she paused a moment.

"Yes," the lawyer encouraged.

"And I wanted to help him."

She said the words so low that you could hardly catch them. But the lawyer didn't ask her to repeat them. I guess he thought it went over better that way and it sure did—at least with me. For I knew what she meant.

Then she went on.

"Pretty soon Mr. Combs came along" (for she kept calling me Burton Combs) "and that big man was with him. The one they called Mr. Farrow. I looked carefully up over the door, for it was very dark where I was, and I saw that Mr. Farrow had a gun in his hand and that he held it close up against Mr. Combs's back. And he talked rough but too low to understand and then they both climbed into the front of the machine. I did not know just what I could do, but I thought—oh—I don't know what I thought, but I did so want to help him and I was just too scared to cry out.

"And then they started off and after they were a little way out in the country Mr. Farrow made Burton stop the car and stand up while he searched him. And he found his revolver and took it from him and threw it into the back of the car. It landed on the seat and bounced off and I stretched out my hand and took hold of it and held it there under the rugs. I didn't know what to do with it at first for I had never fired a gun.

"Then I heard Mr. Farrow say that he was going to kill Mr. Combs and I was terribly frightened but I leaned up and stretched my hand over the seat and tried to give the pistol to Mr. Combs. But Mr. Farrow turned suddenly and I became frightened and dropped the pistol. Then I dropped back in the car again but I was half out of the covers and afraid to pull them over me for the car had stopped again and I had a feeling that someone was looking down at me. Then I heard them moving in front of the car and I looked up and I saw that Mr. Farrow had his gun pressed close against Mr. Combs's side and that Mr. Combs was trying to open the door.

"Then came the sudden report and I think that I cried out, for I thought that Burt was shot. Then came several more shots, one right after another, and I looked out and saw Mr. Combs standing in the moonlight and a man beside another big car firing at him—and then the man fell and—"

She broke off suddenly and started to cry.

"And after that?" my lawyer smiled at her.

"I climbed back under the robes and—Mr. Combs drove me back to the hotel—but he never knew I was there."

Well, that just about settled it, I guess. The room was in more or less of an uproar. And you ought to have heard my lawyer! Now I know why good lawyers get so much money. He started in and he sure did paint that gang up mighty black, and now I was the innocent boy led into danger by these hardened criminals. And he showed how the gun was held close to my side when I fired.

"And if that isn't self-defense and good American pluck I'd like to ask you what in heaven's name is?"

And that's the whole show. One hour later I was a free man. Everybody was shaking hands with me, and from a desperate criminal I had suddenly become a hero. And I guess that Marion had done it.

Then Old Combs came up to me and shook me by the hand and told me how glad he was that I was free and what a plucky little thing Marion was, and how I owed my life twice over to her.

Then he offered me a job. Imagine! Another job for the Combs family. But this was different.

"There is too much good in you to lead the life you have been leading. You may think that it is all right, but there will be others that won't. I can offer you something that will be mighty good."

But I shook my head.

"I guess I'll stick to my trade," I said. "I've had good offers before, and in my line—this little notoriety won't hurt none."

"It's a good position," he says, not paying much attention to what I was getting off. "The right people will be glad to know you—and there will be enough money in it to get married."

I started to shake my head again when he handed me a note.

"Read this note and then let me know. Not another word until you have read it."

He smiles.

I took the little blue envelope and tore it open, and it was from Marion:

I would like to see you again when you take that position of Mr. Combs.

I guess I read that simple sentence over a couple of dozen times before I again turned to Mr. Combs.

"I guess I'll take that job—if it pays enough to get married on," was all that I said.

There ain't no explanation unless—unless I wanted to see Marion again myself.

That's all, unless to warn you that it would be kind of foolish to take too seriously anything I said about keeping clear of the women.

CLINTON H. STAGG

(1890–1916)

||||||||||||||||||||||||||||||||||||||||||| ■ |||||||||||||||||||||||||||||||||||||||||||

Little is known about the short-lived Clinton H. Stagg, creator of Thornley Colton, Blind Detective. Readers must turn to the fiction itself for clues about the character of its author.

In inventing an early example of a sleuth who uses a physical handicap to advantage, Stagg repeatedly proved that apparent limitations can be overcome with intelligence. At a time when people with disabilities were commonly viewed as figures of pity, Stagg made his blind sleuth a figure of admiration.

Stagg worked in the Sherlock Holmes tradition, endowing his sleuth with superb mental powers enhanced by extraordinary abilities in interpreting clues. Whereas Holmes may have known how to identify numerous varieties of cigar ash, Colton uses supersensitive powers of hearing and touch to provide a unique outlook on clues that the sighted police cannot see. Like Holmes, Colton is teamed with a Watson figure, Sydney Thames, whom Colton picked up on the banks of that London river; he accompanies Colton and receives his explanations with awe. When, for instance, in a crowded New York hotel dining room the blind sleuth remarks that a woman is too heavily rouged, Thames is predictably amazed. "Good heavens, Thorn!" he exclaims in Watsonesque wonder. "Sometimes I wonder if you *are* blind!" His mentor explains that his fingers tell him much. "In the lights of a Broadway restaurant the keyboard of silence gives me the secrets of living hearts," Colton intones. Such heightened sensitivity as compensation for blindness was used earlier by the British author Ernest Bramah, who created the blind detective Max Carrados, and later by the American writer Baynard Kendrick, whose sightless sleuth was Captain Duncan Maclain.

Colton's leg man, Shrimp, is another sad case whom the hero has rescued. This freckle-faced lad with a penchant for imitating his dime-novel hero, Nick Carter, is also known as "The Fee," because he was the only payment Colton received for a case in which the murder of Shrimp's mother by his father left him orphaned.

"The Keyboard of Silence" is collected in a volume of eight problems solved by the supersensitive sleuth. It demonstrates Stagg's extraordinary eye for detail and shows the characters—hero and criminal alike—as spokesmen for their creator, who has eluded literary historians. Like the major players in his story, Stagg was a "detailist" who plotted his mysteries and planned their solutions with consummate care. Along the way, a profound insight into character guides the blind detective toward the truth. Readers may agree that they cannot see the solution to this problem "until a blind man has shown them."

1923

The Keyboard of Silence

■

I

Not often did mere man attract attention in the famous dining-room of the "Regal," but men and women alike, who were seated near the East Archway, raised their eyes to stare at the man who stood in the doorway, calmly surveying them. The smoke-glass, tortoise-shell library spectacles, which made of his eyes two great circles of dull brown, brought out the whiteness of the face strikingly. The nose, with its delicately sensitive nostrils, was thin and straight; the lips, now curved in a smile, somehow gave one the impression that, released by the mind, they would suddenly spring back to their accustomed thin, straight line. For a smile seemed out of place on that pale, masterful face, with its lean, cleft chin. The snow-white hair of silky fineness that curled away from the part to show the pink scalp underneath contrasted sharply with the sober black of the faultless dinner-coat that fell in just the proper folds from the broad shoulders and deep chest.

The eyes of the girl at the sixth table seemed to be held, fascinated. The elder woman, who was with her, toyed with her salad and conformed to convention by stealing covert glances at the man in the archway, and the square-chinned, clean-looking young man who made the third of the party stared openly, unashamed; but his eyes held not the other diners' rude questioning, nor yet the girl's frank fascination.

"You are staring, Rhoda," rebuked the elder woman mildly.

The girl turned her eyes with a little sigh.

"What wonderful character there is in his face!" she murmured.

"He *is* a wonderful character," asserted the man, his face lighting up boyishly, his tone one of admiration.

"You know him?" Both asked it in a breath, eyes eager.

"Yes. He is Thornley Colton, man about town, club member, musician, whose recreation is the solving of problems that baffle other men. It was he who found the murderer of President Parkins of the up-town National, and, when the crash came, secured me my position in the Berkley Trust."

"A detective?" The elder woman asked it; the girl's eyes were again on Colton.

"No." The man shook his head. "He jokingly calls himself a problemist, and accepts only those cases that he thinks will prove interesting, for the solving of them is merely his recreation. He takes no fees. The man with him is his secretary, Sydney Thames, whose name is pronounced like that of the river. He, too, is a remarkably handsome man, but he is never noticed when with Thornley Colton, except as his coal-black hair and eyes, and red cheeks, form a striking contrast to Colton."

"I had not even noticed him," confessed the elder woman, as she glanced for the first time at the slim young man of twenty-five or six, who stood at Colton's side, eyes apparently taking in every detail of the big dining-room. Then she remembered her duty as mentor. "You *must* not stare so rudely, Rhoda!" she chided.

"I don't think Mr. Colton minds the stare," the man said quietly. "He has been totally blind since birth, though many people refuse to believe it."

"Blind!" They both breathed it, in their voices the tender sympathy all women feel for the misfortunes of others.

"He is coming," warned the elder woman unnecessarily.

They had seen the head-waiter apparently apologize to Colton, and step aside. The secretary had whispered a few words, and Thornley Colton, his slim stick held lightly and idly in his fingers, started down the aisle between the rows of tables, shoulders swung back, chin up, followed by Sydney Thames. The woman and the girl watched his approach with parted lips, in their eyes mother fear for his safety as he hurried toward them, stepping aside at exactly the proper moment to avoid a hurrying waiter, walking around the very much overdressed, stout woman whose chair projected a foot over the unmarked aisle line. As he neared their table, they saw the thin lips frame a smile of friendly greeting.

"How do you do, Mr. Norris?" His voice, rich, of wonderful musical timbre, seemed to thrill the girl with its kindliness and strength, as he stepped around her chair to shake hands with her escort. "Sydney saw you while we were waiting for our table."

"Will you meet Miss Richmond?" asked Norris, when he had answered the greeting in kind. Colton turned instantly to face the girl, his slim white hand, with its long, tapering fingers, outstretched.

"It is a concession we of the darkness ask of every one," he apologized.

Their hands met, the girl felt the warm grip, and her sensitive wrist seemed to feel a touch, light as the touch of wind-blown thistle-down, but it was gone instantly, and she knew it was but the telepathic thrill of the meeting palms. She murmured a commonplace, and bit her lips in vexation, because it was a commonplace. The man before her seemed to call for more.

"Your singing is wonderful, Miss Richmond," he declared enthusiastically. "Sydney and I have had orchestra seats three nights this week. You know, to me music must give the combined pleasures of painting, sculpture, architecture, and other beautiful things the average person doesn't even appreciate."

Her eyes expressed their pity, but her lips said only: "My mother, Mr. Colton." They shook hands across the table, Mrs. Richmond with a heartiness that was not part of the artificial code New York has fixed, he with a few words that brought a flush of pleasure to her faded cheeks.

"Why didn't Mr. Thames stay?" asked Norris curiously. "He hurried on as though he thought we were plague victims."

"He usually does," smiled Colton. "He has a very curious fear. I'll tell you about it some time."

"Why don't you drop into the bank and see me some day? You haven't been in my tomb-like office for months. Miss Richmond and her mother saw me at work for a few minutes this afternoon. It compares very favourably with the dressing-rooms given to opera-singers, they say."

"I should say so!" laughed the girl. "If you can compare Persian rugs and mahogany with our cracked walls, and box-propped dressing-tables, and plugged gas-jets!"

"Men always do take the best," conceded Colton smilingly. Then he addressed Norris directly. "How is Simpson attending to business nowadays?"

"He has been away for a week. He came in this afternoon to amaze us with the news that he had just been married. He didn't have much to say about his wife, however, except that he was going to turn over a new leaf."

"That's news!" whistled Colton. "He never struck me as the marrying kind."

"Nor any one else," laughed Norris, with a tender, significant glance at the girl across the table.

"I'll have to look him up and congratulate him. Till we meet again, then." And with a pleasant nod of parting to each of them, a touch of a chair leg with his slim stick, Colton hurried down the aisle to the small table in the far corner, where Sydney Thames was giving his order to the waiter. The serving-man responded to a friendly nod from Colton, closed his order tablet, and hurried away. Thornley took a cigarette from his case, scratched a match on the bronze box, and learned comfortably back in his chair.

"Some time, Sydney, your terrible fear of beautiful women is going to get me into a very embarrassing position." He said it half seriously, half smilingly. "Instead of seventeen steps, it was but sixteen and a short half. If it hadn't been for Norris's habit of nervously tapping his glass with his finger-tips, my outstretched hand would have gone back of his neck."

"I thought I had figured it exactly!" There was earnest contrition in the tone; the sombre, black eyes showed the pain of the mistake.

"It is forgotten," dismissed Colton. Then: "But you should have stopped, Sydney. Miss Richmond's personality is as remarkable as her singing, and her mother is so proud and happy she forgets to be embarrassed at the difference between Keokuk and the Regal. Norris is lucky, for she loves him, and he—" The smiling lips needed no finishing words.

"But she is already commanding two hundred dollars a week at the very beginning of her career, and Norris cannot be earning more than five thousand a year," protested Thames.

"You poor boy!" smiled Colton. "You'll never know women; that susceptible heart of yours, which drives you away like a scared sheep whenever a beautiful woman approaches, will never be good for anything but pumping blood."

"Thorn, don't I know my weakness!" The tone was indescribably bitter. "I must keep away, though I'm starving for the society of good women. To meet one would be to fall in love, hopelessly, helplessly. I'd forget that I was a thing of shame, a brat picked up on the banks of the river that gave me the only name I know."

Colton was instantly serious. "Starvation seems a peculiar cure for hunger," he mused. "But we have argued that so many times—" Again the thin, expressive lips finished the sentence.

Then came the waiter with a club sandwich for Thames and Colton's invariable after-theatre supper that was always ready when he came, and which he never needed to order; two slices of graham bread covered with rich, red beef-blood gravy, and a bottle of mineral water. Colton's slim cane, hollow, and light as a feather, the slightest touch of which sent its warning to his supersensitive finger-tips, rested between his knees as he ate.

Sydney Thames nibbled his sandwich absent-mindedly, eyes roving around the dining-room, now stopping at a gaudily-dressed dowager, now at an overpainted lady who smiled her fixed smile at the bull-necked man at her table, now at the circle-eyed girl who stabbed the cherry from her empty cocktail glass with a curved tine of her oyster fork; but always coming back to the fresh, wholesomely beautiful face of Rhoda Richmond. Then the sombre eyes would light up; for a beautiful face, to Sydney Thames, was more intoxicating than wine, and, to his highly sensitive nature, more dangerous.

Colton pushed his plate aside as the other's eyes once more started their round of the dining-room.

"The gods give gaudiness in recompense for the eye-sparkle they have taken, and the wrinkles they have given," Thornley Colton murmured quietly. "One must come to a New York restaurant to realize the true pathos of beauty." Colton's mood had been curiously serious since those few words at Norris's table.

Thames did not answer, for no answer was needed. His wandering eyes had rested on a table to the left.

"One often wonders," continued Colton, in that same musing, low-pitched voice, "why a stout woman, like that one two tables to our left, for instance, will suffer the tortures of her hereafter for the sake of drinking high balls in a tight, purple gown."

Sydney had turned his eyes to stare at Colton, as he always did when the man who had picked him up as a bundle of baby-clothes on the banks of the Thames, twenty-five years before, made an observation of this kind. Many such had he heard, but never did they fail to startle him.

"How, in Heaven's name, did you know what I was doing, or that she was dressed in purple?" he demanded.

"You should keep both feet flat on the floor if you want to keep your staring a secret," laughed Colton quietly. "You forget that crossed knees make your suspended foot tell my cane each time you turn your head ever so slightly. See that my fingers are not on my stick when you covertly watch the women you fear to meet."

"But the purple gown?" demanded Sydney, repressing the inclination to uncross his knees, and flushing at the amused smile the involuntary first motion of the foot had brought to the lips of Colton.

"All stout women who breathe asthmatically wear purple," declared Colton emphatically. "It is the only unfailing rule of femininity. And to one who has practised the locating of sounds that come to doubly sharp ears the breathing part was easy. There is no one at the next table on the left, you'll observe. Now you can resume your overt watching of Miss Richmond; see"—he laid both hands on the white table-cloth before him—"I won't look."

The head-waiter stopped at the table.

"Mr. Simpson would like to have you come to his table, Mr. Colton. He wants you to meet his wife."

"His wife?" put in Thames quickly.

"She is, sir." It was said with a positiveness there was no gain-saying."

"Where is Mr. Simpson?" asked Colton. "We had not seen him."

"In the east wing, sir, where the palms are."

"We will go to him immediately."

"I'll tell him, sir." His beckoning finger brought the waiter who had served them with the check.

Sydney Thames spoke. "Some one of his cheap actress friends has roped him at last," he said scornfully. "He's a pretty specimen of man to be first vice-president of the conservative Berkley Trust Company."

"I'll wager you're wrong," declared Colton quietly, as he handed the waiter a two-dollar bill from his fold. "If it were one of the women for whom he has been buying wine suppers for the past two years, she wouldn't be 'where the palms are,' nor would the waiter be so positive of the marriage relation."

"I'm not going," protested Thames quickly.

"Surely, Sydney, you are not afraid a married woman will kidnap you?" smiled Colton, as he took the stick between his fingers and prepared to rise. "How many?"

Sydney, who had turned half around in his chair to gaze toward the entrance to the east wing, faced him. "I'll go," he said shortly; another hasty glance, and he rose with Colton. "Thirty-seven straight, eighteen left, nine right. We will stop at the door of the east wing. I can't see it."

"There are no pretty women to disturb the distance judgment you have been so many years acquiring?" queried Colton mildly.

Without answering, Thames turned on his heel, and made his way rapidly between the tables toward the east wing. Colton laughed silently, picked up his change, and hurried after, his perfectly trained brain counting the steps automatically, his thoughts busy elsewhere. He was thinking of Simpson, who had gained such an unenviable reputation as a spender along the gay White Way during the past two years.

Simpson had always interested him, student of human nature that he was, as the one man who had never lived up to the impression Colton's unerring instinct had told him was the right one the first time they had met. The problemist had expected things of Simpson, and Simpson had done nothing but idle as much time as possible in the position as first vice-president of one of the most conservative banks in the city, and spend money on women.

Colton stopped for an instant beside Thames in the archway, apparently gazing idly at the crowd of men and women at the palm-shaded tables.

"Two left, nineteen straight, half in," directed Thames, stepping aside to follow.

The heavy-lidded, thickset man, with the faint lines of blue vein traceries in his cheeks, rose to meet them.

"This is a pleasure, Mr. Colton," he exclaimed, in heavy-voiced heartiness. "You are the one man I wanted to see; though I hardly believed it would be my luck to catch you this night of all nights. You knew the pace I was going, and I want you to meet the little girl I went back to the old town to marry. We've been friends since we were tots. Thank God, I waked up in time to know what a good woman means! When next you see us it will be in our own home. One moment, please"—his voice sank to an almost reverent whisper—"my wife is deaf and dumb, Mr. Colton."

Thames had heard; had seen, with curiously mixed feelings, the little woman with the small, boyish face around which the tendrils of brown hair curled from under the close-fitting toque, and had appraised the slim, quietly dressed figure, the half smile as she stared inquiringly at them. The girl seemed but a child, but he saw that her face was heavily daubed with powder and rouge, as though its application had neither been taught nor practised. Until those last explaining words he had stood back with a half-pitying light in his eyes, for he knew Simpson's reputation with women. But at the quietly spoken sentence he had undergone an instant change of feeling, such as only highly-strung, hypersensitive men like him are capable of, toward the man who had gone away from his women of wine to marry a simple country girl who could neither speak nor hear.

Simpson's fingers had been moving rapidly; he bowed toward Thornley Colton. The girl smiled, and put out her small hand, the movement throwing back from her wrist the filmy lace of the long sleeve. For a moment they clasped hands; then the girl's fingers worked again.

Simpson laughed. "She does not believe you are blind, Mr. Colton; she says you have eyes like every one else."

Thornley Colton smiled. "If you tell her that I've got to wear these large-lensed, smoked glasses to prevent the light giving me a headache you will probably never convince her," he observed, as he refused the chair the waiter had drawn up.

Sydney Thames acknowledged his introduction with a bow and the usual meaningless words, but his eyes were soft and tender as a woman's as they met those of the girl in the instant's glance she gave him before the lashes were lowered. A woman's face never failed to stir him.

"Won't you sit down?" pleaded Simpson. "It will probably be the last time you will ever find me in one of these glided palaces. A man who has been my kind of a fool *can* appreciate his own fireside, and Gertie, who was all aflutter to visit one of the famous Broadway restaurants, recognized in ten minutes the crass artificiality it took me years to discover." He was holding her hand openly and unashamed as he said it.

Thornley Colton shook his head. "It is past my time for going home, and you know my habits. A glass of Célestin's at one-fifteen, the beauties of the Moonlight Sonata on my piano for fifteen minutes, and then to bed. If I may visit you at your home, Mrs. Simpson?" his outstretched hand met that of the girl. "Ah, you read the lips? A wonderful accomplishment to us who have never had eyes." His lips framed a smile of pleasure; he turned to Thames. "The same, Sydney?" he asked.

The secretary's eyes travelled up the aisle. "The man nine steps up is gesticulating quite freely."

"Lots of room." Colton's slim stick touched a chair-leg, he bowed, and hurried away, the hearty good-night of Simpson following. Thornley Colton never needed any direction for going back over the same route, for his mind, trained to the figures of steps, neither hesitated nor made mistakes in following them backward. He stepped aside to avoid the swinging arm of the loud-voiced man who was punctuating his liquor-born blatancy with violent gestures, and paused at the archway of the main dining-room for Thames.

"Is Norris still at his table?" he asked.

"It is empty."

"Um!" Colton's high forehead wrinkled a frown, his slim stick tapped his leg. "Time enough to-morrow," he announced finally, and started through the maze of tables towards the entrance.

They received their hats and overcoats and left the big hotel to enter the long, black car that awaited them at the north entrance at one o'clock each morning. They were well on their way to the big, old-fashioned brownstone house where Thornley Colton had been born, before the silence was broken. Then Sydney Thames spoke:

"There must be a lot of latent goodness in a man who could take a woman like that to love, and cherish, and protect," he said slowly.

"You mean Miss Richmond?" The darkness concealed the whimsical smile on Colton's lips.

"No!" The negative was short. "Norris will marry Miss Richmond just because she is beautiful and accomplished; because his man's vanity will be tickled to exhibit her before men as his possession. I mean

Simpson, who took a simple country girl whom God had handicapped, just because he loved her. That means something."

"But, Sydney"—Colton's thin fingers rested lightly on the other's sleeve; there was just the faintest trace of laughter in the words—"don't you think she was a bit too heavily rouged?"

He felt the highly-strung man jump under his hand.

"Good heavens, Thorn!" Sydney burst out. "Sometimes I wonder if you *are* blind!"

"God gives fingers to the sightless, Sydney," Colton's voice was quietly serious. "In the darkness the keyboard of my piano gives me the soul secrets of dead men gone to dust. In the lights of a Broadway restaurant the keyboard of silence gives me the secrets of living hearts. And they cannot lie."

"What do you mean? What have I missed?" Thames asked the questions eagerly, tensely, for he knew the moods of this man who had been the only father he had ever known; he understood that something of grave portent had given its significance to the man who could not see, while he with five perfect senses, had seen nothing, suspected nothing.

Colton pulled his crystalless watch from his pocket, and touched it with a finger-tip. "One-thirty; we are fifteen minutes late." He put his hand on the door catch as the big machine slowed up before his home. And it was not until they were ascending the broad brownstone steps that he answered the question.

"You have missed the first act of what promises to be a very remarkable crime, Sydney," he said quietly.

II

Colton scowled when the red jack failed to turn up, but the mouth corners smiled when the ace of diamonds slid between the sensitive fingers to take its place in the top row of Mr. Canfield's famous game. The deuce followed, the red jack immediately after; then the problemist looked up toward the doorway of the library.

"Well, Shrimp?" he smiled.

"They's the theatrical papers yuh wanted." The red-headed, freckle-faced boy with the slightly-twisted nose came forward with an armful of big magazines and newspapers, the front pages of which were adorned with full-length portraits of stage celebrities. Before he quite reached the table he stopped short, eyes crackling their excitement. "Snakes! You're gettin' it, Mr. Colton! They's the four of hearts and the five of spades. Don't stop now."

Colton laughed. "All right, Shrimp. Do you want to do a little detective work for me?"

"Do I?" The eyes danced with eagerness. "Ain't I been studyin'? Nineteen steps from the kitchen t' the first chair in the dinin'-room. Six—"

"I know," assured Colton hastily. "But you take those papers to your room and write down the names of all the vaudeville actors—men, you know—who have quit the stage within the last two months; where they have gone, and why, if possible."

"Snakes!" The boy's face showed his disappointment. "Nick Carter never had t' do that."

"He never had to count steps for a blind man, either," smiled Thornley Colton. "You do that and there'll probably be some real detective work—shadowing, disguises, and the rest of it."

There was no answer. The boy had taken a firmer grip on the papers, and was already out of the room.

The four of hearts and the five of spades had been placed when Sydney, face broad in a smile, entered.

"What's the matter with 'The Fee'?" he demanded. "He ran past me as though he were on his way to a fire." Thames always referred to Shrimp as The Fee, because the red-headed, freckle-faced boy had become part of the Colton household after a particularly baffling case, at the conclusion of which the joy of capturing the murderer had been overshadowed by the blind man's sorrow for the broken-nosed boy who had jumped between him and a vicious blackjack. And Shrimp had been his fee for the case. As the boy's mother was the murdered one, and his father the murderer, there had been no one to object.

Before Colton had a chance to voice his laughing explanation, the tinkling telephone-bell on the desk demanded attention. At the first words the thin lips tautened to a straight line, the voice became pistol-like in its crispness, the muscles under the pale skin of the face became tense.

The problemist had a problem.

"When? Last night. All right. Still that two-wire burglar connection on the safe? Never mind further details. We'll be right down."

As his hand dropped the receiver on the hook a finger pressed the garage bell button that would bring his machine instantly at any hour of the day or night.

"Get your hat and coat, Sydney," he ordered curtly. "We're going to the Berkley Trust Company. Somebody's gotten away with half a million in negotiable bonds!"

"Half a million?" gasped Thames.

"So they said. Didn't wait for details." Colton grabbed his private phone-book of often-needed numbers, and ran his fingers down the backs of the thin pages on which the names and numbers had been heavily written with a hard pencil. As Sydney hurried out he heard the curt voice give a number over the phone. And it was fully five minutes before Colton took his place in the car.

In the smooth-running machine, with the wooden-faced Irish chauffeur at the wheel, Sydney Thames voiced the question:

"Last night, you said?"

"Yes, the second act came sooner than I expected," broke in Thornley Colton. "I underrated the man." And the expression on the pale face augured ill for some one.

The funereal atmosphere of the Berkley Trust Company could be *felt* as they entered. In the office of the third secretary, the white-haired president of the institution stopped his nervous pacing to mumble a greeting in tremulous accents. First Vice-President Simpson's grave face broke into a smile of welcome. Norris raised his bowed head from his hands, and came forward joyfully, pleadingly. The red-faced man who had been standing over him kept a step away, but always near enough to touch him with an outstretched hand.

"My God, Mr. Colton! They think I'm guilty!" There was agony unutterable in Norris's voice.

"Ridiculous!" snapped Simpson, his heavy-lidded eyes half closed. "Mr. Colton will soon put this detective right."

The problemist nodded a grim acquiescence, and took the outstretched hand of Norris. "I know better," he said kindly. The red-faced man gave voice to a grunt, and Colton instantly swung around to face him. "So you've cleaned it up already, Jamison?" he asked mildly.

"Nobody said he was guilty," growled the red-faced central-office man significantly. "I just been questionin' him, that's all."

"And accusing him with every question!" snapped Colton. "Like the rest of your kind, you haven't the intelligence to suit your methods to the crime. Every crime must be worked according to the old Mulberry Street formula. That didn't change with the modern Centre Street building."

"But we know enough not to make any cracks till we get all the information," sneered Jamison. "We don't hand out that know-it-all stuff till we know *something!*"

"True," smiled the problemist with his lips, but there was no smile in his tone. Two hectic spots glowed in his cheeks, the muscles worked under the pale skin. "What do you think, President Montrose?" The white-haired president halted his pacing once more, and stroked his Vandyke.

"The first stain on the unsullied escutcheon of the Berkley Trust Company," he groaned. "In all of the half century—"

"I know all that!" broke in Colton impatiently. "What happened? Why are the police here instead of the protective-agency men?"

"I was excited," moaned the president. "It was the first thing that occurred to me. In all the half century of—"

"I guess we were all excited," interjected Simpson, his lips twisted in a wry smile. "I know I was up in the air. I came down here, happier than I ever was before in my life, to arrange for a short vacation to take a wedding trip. Now this comes up. When I came to my senses I telephoned for you, because I want the robbery solved as soon as possible. The little girl has banked so much on our little time."

"Too bad," murmured Colton. "Tell me the story, Norris." Before he could get an answer he turned to Thames, who always stayed discreetly in the background when Colton was on a case. "See that no one goes near that safe, Sydney; I may want to examine it."

"Kind of dropped that bluff of bein' blind, ain't you?" sneered Jamison, who was one of the hundreds of persons in New York who would not believe that Thornley Colton was really sightless. And the problemist did not deign to explain that once he had been in a room and touched its objects with his cane his trained brain held the correct mental picture for ever.

"The bonds were fifty in number, ten thousand each, government fours, negotiable anywhere," began Norris, licking his dry lips to make the words come easier. "They were the bulk of the Stillson estate, on which I was working. We are settling it up. As third secretary my work is with trusts and estates. It was necessary to have everything finished by to-night. I worked late yesterday, so late that the bonds and other papers could not go into the time-locked vaults, and I had to be at work on them this morning before the clock-release time."

"Is it customary to keep valuable bonds in the small safe in this office?" interrupted Colton.

"It is not unusual. The safe is practically as strong as the big vaults, and only lacks the clocks. This office is really part of the vault itself, the walls are windowless, and of four-foot concrete reinforced by interlocked steel rails. The sheet-steel door, the only entrance to the room, opens into a small cage that is occupied during the day by Thompson, head of the trust and estate routine clerks, and at night by one of our two watchmen. The watchmen never leave it, because it often happens that valuable papers and bonds are left out of the big vaults so that we can work on them before nine o'clock, the hour set on the vault's clocks. To get to the steel door of this office one would have to enter the outer and inner steel cages, the steel-barred door of the small ante-room, besides setting off burglar-alarms on all, disturbing the watchman, and ringing the bells in the burglar-alarm department of the Bankers' Protective Association, of which we are a member. And there was no sign of a break, the safe was opened with the combination that only Mr. Montrose and Mr. Simpson and myself know."

"The watchman could get to this door without any trouble?"

"Both have been in the employ of the bank for forty years. They are absolutely above suspicion. Both are illiterate. Even though they could enter the office, they could not open the safe, and even if they did that they would not know enough to steal all the notes I had made regarding the estate, or the bonds that have so utterly vanished. They have been sent for, however, and should be here any minute."

"Were the notes you made stolen, too?"

"All of them."

"Any of the other employees of the bank know the bonds were in this safe?"

"Several, probably."

"All have access to this room, at any time?"

"Only Thomas, the head of the T. and E. clerks."

"Trustworthy?"

"He grew up with the bank."

"You require other clerical assistance at times?"

"Thomas takes the papers from this office, and the clerks get them from him outside. All must be returned to me before closing time. I carefully checked over every one last night before any of them went away."

"Any one in here yesterday while you were at work on the papers; any one who could have seen the bonds?"

For a moment there was no answer; then it came, almost in a whisper: "Miss Richmond and her mother were in for a few moments—"

"And I was, too, by Jove!" The interruption came from Simpson. "And I remember asking you how you were getting on with the Stillson estate. I just finished my part when I went away. I guess I really held them up longer than I should."

"Has Miss Richmond been sent for?" Colton paid absolutely no heed to the first vice-president.

A grunting laugh from the detective. "She sure has, bo. After I found out this guy's stage lady had been in here with a tailor's suit-box after closin' time, my partner went right up to her hotel."

"By Heaven! You—" Norris rose to his feet, face black with fury. Colton's hand on his shoulder forced him back into the chair. Sydney Thames, to whom all women were angels, clenched his fists.

"Is that true?" There was a new tone to Colton's voice.

Norris seemed to recognize the menace. "She isn't guilty, I tell you! She can't be. She's—Listen, man! She's my wife!"

"Your wife!" They all echoed it. The detective with laughing triumph; President Montrose with horror; Sydney Thames in dazed surprise; Simpson with a half-suppressed, significant gasp.

"We were married two days ago; but it was to be a secret until the end of her season."

"How long ago was she sent for?"

The detective answered: "My side kick ought to be back now. We was on the job there, all right, all right."

Voices outside came to their ears—the harsh, commanding voice of a man, the half-subdued sobbing of a woman. The door was thrown open, and Rhoda Richmond, opera-singer, and wife of Norris, was half pushed, half carried into the small room.

"Good work, Jim!" grinned Jamison. "Did she put up a howl at the hotel?"

"Hotel?" growled the other scornfully. "No hotel for her. I had a lot of luck or I'd never've got her. She was boardin' a boat fer South America that sails in an hour."

"It's a lie!" Norris screamed the words as he leaped toward the man whose rough hand was clenched around the slim arm of the girl. Sydney Thames, obeying Colton's silent signal, forced him back, his own hands trembling. The problemist without a word untwisted the central-office man's fingers, and gently seated the girl in a chair at the long table.

"Who the—" The blustering detective was cut off suddenly.

"We've had enough of your strong-arm methods!" Colton's voice was hard as flint. "We'll get some facts now." The hardness vanished; in its place came gentle sympathy. "When did you get the message, Miss Richmond?" he asked.

The voice seemed to have the reassuring effect of a pat on the head of a hurt child. With an effort the girl controlled her sobs, and answered as though it had been the most natural question in the world: "An hour ago—over the telephone—I thought I recognized How—Mr. Norris's voice. He wanted me to meet him at the Buenos Aires dock. He had to go to South America secretly, he said, and I must tell no one. I hurried to the dock without even telling mother. I waited for an hour, but he did not come; then I decided to go aboard and see if he had missed me and gone to his state room. This man—said Howard had—robbed—I thought—" She broke down again.

"I guess that's bad!" grinned Jamison gloatingly. "In another hour there'd of been a clean get-away."

"The whereabouts of the bonds doesn't seem to worry you!" snapped Colton sarcastically.

"The stuff ain't never far away from the guy that took it," growled Jamison. "When you get through your know-it-all talk we'll sweat that out, all right."

"Did you have a tailor's suit-box with you yesterday?" asked Colton abruptly of the girl.

"Yes. I called to see if my new walking-suit was finished. It was all ready to be sent to my home, but when I saw the poor, tired little boy who would have to carry it I took it myself. The tailor is just around the corner, on the avenue; that is why mother and I dropped in here."

"Of course," nodded Colton, his teeth snapping together as he seemed to sense the derisive grins on the faces of the detectives. "Did you recognize the bonds among the papers on which Mr. Norris was working?"

"Oh, he showed them to me, and we laughingly spoke of what we could do with half a million dollars. Then, when he took mother out to show her around the bank—I was too tired—I picked one up and read it."

"Rhoda!" cried Norris. He could realize the present significance of yesterday's innocent words.

"That'll be about all from you!" scowled Jamison. "If this guy wants to third-degree her, and cinch it for us, let him."

"An' if he don't cinch it this will." The other detective pulled a paper from his pocket. "Here's the *Buenos Aires's* passenger list, and here's Mr. and Mrs. Frank Morris, who booked yesterday, added in pencil. Morris for Norris! Slick enough to be almost good."

Every one in the room but Colton seemed to be shocked into a state of stupefied rigidity.

"Now—" Jamison said that word in the tone one uses to introduce some especially clever thing, and accompanied it with a sarcastic glance toward the blind man, who tapped his trouser leg with his cane in thoughtful silence. "If *you* ain't got no objection we'll take these two to head-quarters, and get a line on where they got the stuff cached." He paused suggestively, mockingly.

The permission came, with a deprecatory wave of the cane, and a smile that was menacing in its very suaveness. "Go as far as you like, Jamison. Don't be too gentle with them."

"My God, Mr. Colton! You don't think—" The words choked in Norris's throat.

"I think you had better go." The problemist's tone was peculiarly quiet. "Jamison and his partner have the reputation of being the two wealthiest detectives in the department. No one knows how they got it, but they've enough to give you and your wife a twenty-thousand-dollar nest egg each on a false-arrest suit. Isn't that worth a few hours' discomfort? I can prove your innocence when they have gone. They worry me here."

Simpson whistled, and turned it into a jerky laugh. "Gad, that was clever!" he exclaimed.

"Oh, is that so!" The detectives chorused it, in their voices sarcasm—and just a tinge of something else, too. Colton knew the one thing that would make them stop and think.

"Are you going?" snapped Colton.

"We'll see them two watchmen first," growled Jamison.

"Good!" The problemist laughed at the sudden change. "I think you'll have quite a crowd to take down to head-quarters if you hang around long enough. Before I started I telephoned to the burglar-alarm telegraph department of the protective agency to get hold of the men who answered the alarm that rang in from this office early this morning."

"What burglar-alarm?" snarled Jamison. He whirled on the white-haired president. "Why didn't you tell us there was an alarm rung in?"

"Really"—the Vandyke received several severe yanks—"I didn't know it. We do not receive the clock reports and emergency alarm sheets until about noon. Er—Mr. Colton, might I ask where you got this information?"

"I telephoned for it," answered Colton curtly. "If these policemen hadn't been so anxious to make arrests, and the robbery hadn't been too obvious for their thick heads, they might have investigated. But they are just head-quarters men; the obvious arrest is the one they always make. Feet make good central-office men, not heads. Ah, here are the men, all together."

They came in slowly, two old men first; one with straggly, white whiskers that concealed the weak chin and grew up around the faded, watery eyes; the other's parchment-like face a network of wrinkles. Honesty shone from every part of them; the weak, helpless honesty of their kind.

As Colton took each man's hand with a murmured greeting he felt it tremble in his. The aged watchmen knew that something had happened; something that concerned them and the bank they had guarded so long. The two men from the burglar-alarm company nodded to the two detectives, and their eyes narrowed as they shook the hand of the problemist. Both knew him, and both knew this had been no common summons. Thornley Colton never bothered with common things. Sydney Thames had pulled two chairs up to the table, and the old men sat down. Colton lighted a cigarette thoughtfully, then he spoke:

"This morning, gentlemen, that small safe was robbed of five hundred thousand dollars' worth of government bonds." His slim cane, apparently held idly between his fingers, touching the chair of the man nearest him, felt the watchman's involuntary jump. The others saw the old jaws drop, saw the watchmen glance helplessly at each other, their trembling fingers picking at worn trouser-knees. Colton heard the gasp of the two protective-agency men.

"I knowed it!" quavered the white-whiskered watchman. "I knowed something'd happen when Mary took sick."

"Who's Mary?" queried Colton interestedly. The others crowded forward.

"She's Mary, my wife. She's been scrubbin' the bank floors fer thirty years, an' nobody ever said a word against her." He glanced at them all with pathetic belligerence. "She even picked up the pins she found on the floor, and put 'em in a box on the cashier's desk."

"That's true," laughed Simpson. "It's the joke of the bank."

"And she was taken sick last night?" Thornley asked gently.

"A week ago." The other watchman answered, while the first brushed his dry lips with his work-gnarled hand. "Mrs. Bowden, she's got the consumption, and lives across the hall from us and—"

"Where do you live?" interrupted Colton.

"Sixteen hundred Third Avenue. I been boardin' with him an' his wife fer thirty years. Mrs. Bowden's been doing' Mary's work. We didn't say nothin' about Mary bein' sick, 'cause she might get laid off. An' Mrs. Bowden's awful poor." His voice was a childish, quavering treble.

"Last night, after Mrs. Bowden had gained your confidence, you allowed her to scrub Mr. Norris's office?" encouraged Colton.

Norris started. "I'd forgotten that!" he ejaculated. A motion from Colton commanded silence.

"Yes," trembled Mary's husband. "John opened the door, an' started to punch his clocks, an' I stayed in the ante-room, like I allus do, to watch Mrs. Bowden. Then somehow the door got closed. An' Mrs.

Bowden got scared there in the dark. She screamed an' cried till it was real sad. But John had the key, an' he had to punch his clocks on the minute, er Mr. Montrose'd be mad when he got the records next day. An' I couldn't leave my place in the ante-room. So I encouraged her, sayin' that John'ld be back in half an hour an' let her out. She quieted after a while, an' didn't scream so loud, but I could hear her stumblin' around. Then John had to run to the front door to see who was knockin', an' he let these gentlemen in. The burglar-alarm on the safe had rung, they said, an'—"

"Never mind that part," halted Colton. "One of these men will tell me that part."

"We was called at seven-eighteen," began the taller of the two Bankers' Protective Agency men, "by the safe bell. The safe is connected with one wire, and under the carpet, running all around the safe, is a thin steel plate connected with the other. A man standing near enough to touch the safe forms a connection that rings our gong. In the daytime, of course, we pull the switch. We got here, and found the door locked, an' we could hear moaning. This guy"—he indicated the one with the straggly beard—"unlocked the door, and behind it was a woman, her skirt pinned up around her, laying on the floor, frightened to death. When she seen us she jumped to her feet with a little screech, and muttered something about thanking God."

"You were satisfied that she was frightened?"

"Sure! But we didn't let it go at that. We snapped on every light, and examined the room. Nothing had been touched. We frisked the woman, gentle, of course, but enough to know that she hadn't a thing on her. We finally got it out of her that she'd fell against the safe trying to find the door in the dark. She didn't know enough to snap on a light."

"She couldn't have had fifty ten-thousand-dollar bonds on her person?"

Both men laughed. "Gee, Mr. Colton," laughed the short one. "She was so frail you could almost see through her. She couldn't hardly have hid a cigarette paper without making a hump."

"What happened then?"

"She picked up the pail she had—it was full of dirty scrub water, and the yellow bar of soap was bobbing around in it—and John, here, took her into the cashier's cage. We hung around, talking, an' watching her scrub and weep into the pail until it was time fer her to go home. She was so all in I put her on a car."

"Um!" Colton puffed his cigarette in silence; then he turned to Jamison and his partner. "Looks mighty suspicious, doesn't it, Jamison? I'd advise you to arrest these four men and get the woman. Five hundred thousand is likely to make any honest man a crook."

"Some kidder, ain't you?" sneered Jamison. "I know Pete, there, an' if he says it was all right, it was. We got the guilty parties first off, an' we'll get the stuff, too!"

The smile went from Colton's lips instantly. "You arrest them, and we'll start false-arrest proceedings in an hour!" he warned. "You leave Norris and Miss Richmond here! Any one but a fool detective would know they weren't guilty."

As he said the last word he jumped toward the safe, ran his highly sensitive fingers over the steel surface, knelt down, brushed the heavy carpet lightly with his finger-tips. The two hectic spots on his cheeks glowed redder; the nostrils quivered like those of a hound on the scent, even the eyes, behind the great, round, smoked glass lenses seemed to shine. Silently they watched him. He lowered his face almost to the floor, the cane was laid down, and his hand gave the carpet a resounding slap. They crowded closer. One hand went to his hip-pocket, a handkerchief brushed the hard-wood floor under the safe, between the edge of the rug and the wall. He rose, touched the burning end of his cigarette ever so lightly to the linen handkerchief that was now covered with a fine yellow powder.

"See it! See it!" he snapped. "You couldn't before because it was the same colour as the hard-wood floor."

"It's wood-polish powder, used for cleaning the varnished wood," sneered Jamison, stepping forward. "We don't want—"

"Smell it, then!" The blind man thrust the handkerchief under the central-office man's nose. "Do you recognize it now? It's sulphur. Ordinary powdered sulphur. The thing that would tell any man how the bonds were taken out of the office. Go to a drug store and find out what sulphur is used for."

He thrust the handkerchief into his coat-pocket, brushed off the knees of his trousers, and picked up his stick.

"Come, Sydney," he said quietly. "We've finished."

Before the astonished men could make move or protest he hurried from the office, automatically counting the steps. He jumped into the waiting machine, Sydney Thames followed, and as Simpson and Jamison ran to the door, he snapped: "Home, John!" to the Irish chauffeur, and the machine sped away.

Around the first corner he leaned forward.

"Sixteen hundred Third Avenue—quick!" he ordered.

"You don't think those two old watchmen guilty?" asked Thames, in surprise.

"No!" The tone was almost brusque. "Merely an unimportant detail I want to clear up."

"You certainly left that crowd in the office at sixes and sevens." Thames laughed at the recollection.

"I intended to. That's why I went into all those details. I wanted to leave every one up in the air, especially the two detectives. They'll begin to think now. And they won't let any one get away before we have made this call. I want to think, now."

Sydney Thames knew the moods of the blind man; knew he could expect no explanations, or even replies, until Colton was ready to give them; so they sped in silence to the upper East Side.

Soon they were on upper Third Avenue. Overhead the clanking "L" trains pounded their din into the two men's ears. The streets were crowded with their heterogeneous mass of men, women, and children. The rusty fire-escapes staggered drunkenly across the dirty, red tenement-fronts.

The look of tense concentration left Colton's face.

"A far cry from the luxurious, staidly conservative Berkley Trust, eh, Sydney?" He smiled, leaning back in the cushions, puffing his cigarette as though untroubled by a serious thought; his eyes, behind the smoked library glasses, seemingly fixed on the narrow strip of blue sky overhead.

The car came to a stop.

"Is this it, John?"

"Th' saloon on th' corner is fifteen-ninety-four, sorr."

"Lead the way, Sydney." Again the twin red spots glowed in Colton's white cheeks, he jumped to the sidewalk, his slim stick tapping his trouser-leg eagerly.

Thames stepped along beside him, close enough for his coat-sleeve to touch that of Thornley Colton. And with that slight touch to guide him the problemist followed; for Thornley Colton was a trifle sensitive over his blindness, and nothing made him angrier than an attempt to lead him. Sydney found the entrance, between a second-hand-clothing store and a pawnbroker's shop. As he stopped to make sure of the weather-dimmed, painted number the clothing-store proprietor popped out, rubbing his dirty palms together, and coughing apologetically.

"On which floor does Mrs. Bowden live?" asked Colton sharply.

"Der fourt', front. You maybe like some clo'es?"

"Is her husband watchman at the Berkley Trust Company?"

"He's dead. You means Mrs. Schneider, across the hall. Her man watches. Dere boarder also. You like a elegant skirt for der poor vimens. Such a—"

Thames opened the door, and they left the clothing man in the middle of his sentence. In the dark hall Sydney made his way cautiously. Colton, cane lightly touching the heels of the man ahead, followed unhesitatingly. The journey up the rickety steps was torture to Colton. To his doubly acute ears and sense of smell the odours, the squalling of half-starved babies were terrible, but his brain automatically counted the steps so that he would have not the slightest difficulty in finding his way back to the automobile.

"Schneider first," whispered Colton, as Thames stopped in the fourth-floor hall.

In the dim light Thames saw that they were standing between two doors.

"I don't know which it is, but I'll take a chance." He knocked on the one at his left.

The one behind immediately popped open.

"Mrs. Bowden's gone away," shrilly proclaimed a tottery old woman, bobbing her head.

"Could you give us her address?" asked Colton, doffing his hat and bowing politely.

"Laws!" The woman's fluttering hand set her spectacles farther askew, in a hurried effort to straighten them. "She's gone to spend the day with her sister in Brooklyn. Them boys of mine pestered her till she's near sick. And she bein' so delicat' an' out late last night washin' dishes at the church sociable."

"Are you Mrs. Schneider?"

The darkness hid the smile the reference to the "boys" had caused.

"I'm her. Be you the Associated Charities? Mis' Bowden said she'd asked fer help. She came here two weeks ago, after losin' her job in the department store on account of her weak lungs. She had to take in odd day's work. Asthma, *she* calls it, but I ain't fooled on consumption. Two of my—"

"And you helped her by pretending you were ill?" interrupted Colton.

"I was sick fer two days." The woman hastened to set him right. "But she was so powerful glad to earn a few cents fer her asthma snuff, not that it is asthma. My sister's brother—"

"Of course she left the key with you until her return?" Colton left the sister's brother in mid-air.

"Yes; but—" There was just a shade of suspicion in the voice.

"As agents of the Associated Charities we must make an examination of the room, to prove that she is really in need of financial help," assured Colton gravely. "We can wait until she returns, of course, but this is the last application day for this month."

"Laws! I'll get it right away." She darted back into the room with surprising agility, and returned a moment later with an iron key tied to a broken-tined fork.

"There's no need of bothering you, Mrs. Schneider," declared Colton earnestly, as Thames took the key.

"Laws! Soon's I get these pataters on I'll be right with you. My boys had to go down to their bank—" The rest of the sentence was lost, for as she turned to the stove Colton had jerked Thames from the door.

"Quick!" he whispered. In an instant the key was in the lock, and the door was open. Colton pushed his way in, his cane touching the scarred, tumbled bed and the one broken chair. "Where's the trunk?" he queried, cane feeling around.

"No sign of one, nor a case."

"Damn!" snapped Colton. "The bureau drawers! See what your eyes find."

Thames had the top drawer open almost before he had finished. He whistled in amazement. "Nothing but an empty pill-box, with no druggist's label, three quills with the feathers cut off, and a tuft of cotton. What the—"

"Those are what I want! Put them in your pocket!" The tenseness went out of his voice; it became politely ingratiating, for his keen ears had heard the woman coming. "There is no doubt that Mrs. Bowden is in need of our assistance, Mrs. Schneider," he said smoothly. "Er—is that some of her asthma snuff in the top bureau-drawer?"

She ran past him, and bobbed her head over the open drawer. "Yes, sir; there is a little sprinkled over the bottom. You got mighty powerful eyes, mister." She nodded vigorously at the blind man. He had not been within five feet of the bureau. "She's dead set on it bein' asthma, but my sister's brother was—"

"Do you know anything against Mrs. Bowden's character?" Again the sister's brother was left dangling.

"Laws, no. She's that frightened she's afraid of her own shadow. I'm the on'y one in the house she took to, an' even me she kept at a distance." Another vigorous nod. "An' so modest! Laws, she wouldn't ha' come into the halls half dressed, like some of the other women does. An' clean! Laws! She lugged all her clo'es over to her sister's in Brooklyn to-day, to be washed in their Thirtieth Century Washer; not that I—"

"Ah, thank you, but we have four other calls to make." And, bowing gravely, Colton backed from the room, and hurried toward the head of the stairs, followed by Thames and the shrill-voiced encomiums of the woman.

They took their places in the car silently, and it was not until they had left the noise of the avenue for the quiet of the side-streets that Colton spoke.

"What do you think of it, Sydney?" asked the problemist gravely.

"I'm completely at sea," confessed Thames, with a shake of his head. "It looked awfully bad for Norris when we arrived at the bank. Then that South American boat business. How did you know she had received a message?" he asked suddenly.

"Didn't. But I knew Miss Richmond, or rather Mrs. Norris. Common sense would have told any one that could be the only reason for her presence at the dock. Jamison and his kind don't use common sense. They use the old policeman's formula; arrest the logical suspect and then convict him. With persons like Norris and his wife, each half doubting, half suspecting, either would have confessed to save the other. It was an ideal arrest, from the police view-point."

"Then you seemed to involve the two watchmen and the two men from the protective agency. Jamison will have a whole waggon-load."

"He'll take no one," answered Colton. "I know him. He'll spend the rest of the day trying to find out what I was talking about. Then he'll telephone to head-quarters, and they'll send men to find out who sent the message to Miss Richmond, and to locate Mrs. Bowden."

"There's the woman, Thorn!" Thames spoke nervously, excitedly. "She took a dress-suit case, presumably full of clothes, to her 'sister' in Brooklyn. The bonds—"

"You forget that the agency men saw her come out of the room empty-handed; they even searched her, and one put her on the trolley." Colton smiled curiously. "This was wholly a man's job, Sydney. The work of the rarest kind of criminal; a detailist. This crime, while perfectly simple, is, I think, unique in its attention to details. That's why it interests me."

"Simple!" ejaculated Thames. "Simple? You speak as though you knew the guilty man."

"I do. Perfectly. I knew last night."

"Last night? The—"

"The robbery was committed early to-day. Exactly."

"Why—why—" Helpless amazement was in Sydney Thames's voice. "Why don't you arrest him? Why all this—"

"Simply because I would be laughed at. I haven't the proof—yet. The usual criminal stumbles on his opportunity, and seizes it in a haphazard fashion. The rare criminal, the detailist, attends to every detail; works his problem out with the shrewdness and forethought of a captain of finance, plans a coup months ahead. Then he creates the opportunity. You must understand, Sydney, that half a million is worth a few months' work."

"But suspicion points only to Miss Richmond, Norris, and this Mrs. Bowden."

"Suspicion points to every one," corrected the problemist. "Doesn't it seem suspicious that President Montrose should call in the police when he would naturally take all steps in his power to avoid publicity? Doesn't the very eagerness of the central-office men to arrest Norris and his wife seem queer? Isn't there a bit of suspicion in Simpson's confession that he delayed the Stillson estate until Norris was compelled to work after hours on them? Doesn't Miss Richmond's story that she was carrying her suit home to save work for a delivery boy seem highly improbable and unwomanlike? How about Norris telling his wife of the bonds? An unbusinesslike proceeding in the case of half a million's worth of negotiable bonds, truly. Didn't the two men who answered the early-morning alarm seem a bit too sure that nothing was wrong? Weren't the two watchmen in the conspiracy to pretend that Mrs. Schneider was ill, so that a woman whom they had known but two weeks could gain access to the bank? Doesn't the finding of an unlabelled pill-box, three featherless quills, and surgeon's cotton in the otherwise empty room of a woman dying with tuberculosis strike you as strange? As a further detail in this crime of details, doesn't my confession that I knew the criminal before the crime was committed seem a trifle like guilty knowledge?" He smiled broadly.

"Great Scott, Thorn!" Sydney Thames's voice trailed off in a whistle of pure bewilderment. "You've involved every one."

"Oh, no." Colton snapped his cigarette into the street. "Not every one. An unfortunate vaudeville actor will appear on the scene as soon as I get the list on which I left Shrimp busily at work."

III

In the absolute darkness of the shade-drawn library Thornley Colton softly whistled a syncopated version of Mendelssohn's "Spring Song" as his deft fingers filled an empty goose-quill with a fine white powder from an improvised paper funnel. He plugged the open end with a small wad of cotton; then his wonderfully sharp ears caught the rustle of the double portières.

"Oh, Sydney," he called, "have you heard anything from the bank this morning?"

Thames entered the darkness unhesitatingly, for his constant practice of judging distance and figuring steps for Colton had made him almost as much at home in the darkness as the blind man himself.

"No," he answered shortly. Then, with the frank criticism of long friendship: "It's a crime, Thorn, for you to be idle while that girl is being dogged, and harassed, and—"

"I thought she sang remarkably well last night for a person under such a strain," interrupted Colton musingly.

"It was wonderful, wonderful!" Sydney Thames spoke with the breathless enthusiasm a beautiful girl always aroused in his woman-hungry heart.

"Here, here!" protested the problemist laughingly. "Remember that she is another man's wife!"

"Great heavens, Thorn! How can you laugh?" cried Thames resentfully. "Think of those two dogs of detectives, questioning, bulldozing, shadowing! Why, they didn't let Miss Richmond get away from the bank until late in the afternoon, then Jamison insisted on going with her. His partner hung around the bank till it closed—"

"Trying to discover the use of powdered sulphur," smiled Colton. "I thought he would. Any one but a central-office man would have gone to a drug store, as I suggested."

"Two other head-quarters men hauled that frail old Mrs. Schneider and the two watchmen to police head-quarters, and put them through the third degree."

"And a half-dozen more were on the trail of Mrs. Bowden, while we were enjoying the opera and an alleged cabaret show afterward, for which this dark room is the penalty. Too much light yesterday gave me a frightful headache."

The sudden ringing of the telephone in the darkness made Thames jump, and Colton's cane, which was never away from him, felt the movement.

"Answer it, Sydney," he requested.

The secretary's hands had not the sureness of his feet, and he had to fumble a moment. When he had given the customary salutation and had listened a moment he gasped.:

"It's Simpson, Thorn. His wife is missing! He wants you." He extended the phone in the darkness, but Thornley Colton made no move to take it.

"Tell him I'll be down to the bank in an hour or so. I'll see him then." Colton spoke idly.

Sydney repeated the message. Followed a silence. "He's frantic, Thorn!" Thames's voice shook with excitement. "When he got home last night she was gone. The doorman at his apartment house said that she had gone out in the morning, for a short walk, he supposed. Simpson was so excited about the robbery he did not telephone her during the day, as he had promised. He spent half the night searching, and tried a dozen times to get you. She is deaf and dumb, Thorn. Think of it! Deaf and dumb, and lost!" It only needed a woman in trouble to shatter Sydney Thames's nerves.

"Tell him that I'm trying to figure out that robbery. Tell him also that I never let one case interfere with another. I'm not a detective. There's nothing interesting about a missing woman. Hundreds of 'em every day. I find my pleasure in interesting problems, not in police work." Colton's voice was sharp, curt, utterly devoid of sympathy.

Sydney knew that tone, as he knew the man who used it. He repeated part of the message, added gentle-voiced apologies, and hung up the receiver with a sigh.

"That was heartless, Thorn! Think of that woman, deaf and dumb, lost in this—"

"Sometimes, Sydney, that susceptible heart of yours becomes wearisome." Colton spoke a bit sharply. "A moment ago you were protesting because I was here instead of running around after the man who stole the half-million in bonds from the Berkley Trust Company."

"But Mrs. Norris is not helpless—" And for fifteen minutes he argued, while Colton smiled imperturbably in the darkness, and filled two other quills with the white powder, and plugged the ends with tufts of cotton.

Suddenly Thames stopped, for Colton had picked up the telephone and was giving a number.

"Hello, Shrimp!" he called, when the connection had been made. "Everything all right? Fine business. Three hours, eh? Good! Be on time, and obey orders. Good-bye!"

"Where's The Fee?" demanded Sydney. "I haven't seen him since yesterday."

"Emulating the example of his worthy hero, Nick Carter. Shrimp is a real detective now." Colton returned the crystalless watch to his pocket, picked up the three quills, and arose. "Come on, Sydney. We'll walk over to the bank."

"Walk?" ejaculated Thames, for he knew the blind man's aversion to walking when he could ride. "Where's the machine?"

"John and the machine are helping Shrimp in his detective work," explained Colton. And in the twenty minutes' walk to the Berkley Trust Company he absolutely refused to answer questions, but kept up a continuous conversation on trivial topics, that was maddening to the nervous secretary.

The effect of the previous day's badgering, questioning, and threats of the central-office men could be seen as one entered the bank. The aged cashier's hands trembled as he tried to count a sheaf of new bills. Book-keepers in the rear wrote figures and erased them. Thompson, head of the trust and estate clerks, in his little ante-room cage, was in a pitiable state of nerves. The typewriter's chair by President Montrose's desk was vacant, because the lady stenographer was at home under the care of a doctor. The fifty years of staid, conservative calm that had characterized the Berkley Trust Company during its long and useful life had been hit by a five-hundred-thousand-dollar storm.

The group in the vaultlike office of Third Secretary Norris was little better. President Montrose could hardly control his trembling hand to stroke his Vandyke; Norris's eyes showed the sleeplessness of the night before; Miss Richmond was calm with the calmness that means coming nervous collapse; her mother was crying softly; Simpson seemed positively haggard, and Sydney Thames murmured words of sympathy for the man who had two troubles. Jamison and the other central-office man could not make their sneers wholly sceptical. The protective-agency men were plainly puzzled.

"I see you are all on hand." There was no smile in Colton's voice now, or on his lips; he was deadly calm, coldly earnest. "You didn't think it necessary to send for the two watchmen?"

"We got men watchin' them," put in the surly Jamison.

"Thanks!" came curtly from Colton. "Sit down at this table, all of you. I want to tell you a story."

"We didn't come to hear—"

Simpson interrupted the detective: "For God's sake, make it short, Mr. Colton! My wife—"

"I'll look into that later." Colton's cane assured him that the chairs were around the long table, and his finger-tips felt the face of his watch in his pocket.

"Will you?" Simpson's voice was almost sarcastically eager, his heavy-lidded eyes narrowed. Thames could not blame the man's natural resentment for Colton's offhandedness.

Silently they took seats. Colton sat facing the closed door; across the table was Simpson and Norris. Miss Richmond and her mother were at the end. The four detectives were on either side of the problemist.

"This is a story of a criminal who was born a criminal; who couldn't be honest if he tried," began Colton, in his quietly expressive voice.

One hand lay idly on the table before him, the other on his knees, fingers holding the slim, hollow cane. "He wasn't just born crooked. He started petty thieving before he was out of short trousers. He was the rare criminal that works years as an honest man to pave the way for criminality. He had brains. He could have been a wonderful success as an honest man. But he couldn't be straight. The criminal instinct was there. He was waiting for the proper time. But the coarser side of his nature refused to be held in leash. He needed money. And with the inherent craft of his kind he began to plan the robbery of the Berkley Trust Company. It wasn't so hard, because, being an old, conservative institution, in which men had grown gray, the personal side entered as it cannot in the modern, up-to-date institutions where men come and go. Instead of elaborate safeguards the simple protection of proven honesty entered largely into the protection of the bank's valuables. And where there is simple honesty there is always vulnerability.

"This criminal had found the vulnerable spot years before the robbery was actually planned; when the time came for its consummation luck came to his aid, as it often does." He paused. On the outside door came a knock, so faint that only his wonderfully sharp ears heard it. "There was no possibility of suspicion attaching itself to him, for he had planned an elaborate program to foist suspicion on others. And this robbery was but one of a series, for the method his shrewd brain had devised was capable of endless combinations. In a few years the Berkley Trust losses would have mounted to millions!"

His fist crashed down on the heavy table. The door opened. Between the sober-faced Shrimp and the expressionless Irish chauffeur was a sunken-eyed, tottering creature, unshaven—

"*There's your wife, Simpson!*" In the silence Colton's voice came like the crack of a pistol.

"My God, Thorn, it's a *man!*" In Sydney Thames's tone was agony that the sensitive blind man whom he loved could have made such a mistake.

"Yes, a man! *Sit still, Simpson!*" With a movement as quick as light itself Colton's fingers had dropped the slim cane that had given its warning, and held a blue-steel automatic. "Or rather what was once a man." His tone rang with deadly menace. "Charlie De Roque, vaudeville actor, the youngest and best female impersonator on the stage; Mrs. Bowden, the consumptive who played so well on the sympathies of the three simple-minded souls at sixteen hundred Third Avenue; Mrs. Simpson, the deaf-and-dumb little girl who was going to make Simpson lead a better life."

"You lie!" The shambling shadow of a man screamed it as he tried to jerk away from the chauffeur. "They told me they were going to take me to a sanatorium. I don't know what you're talking about. They've kept me—" His whole body racked with sobs.

"Would you tell the truth for these?" The automatic did not waver a fraction of an inch as Colton's unoccupied hand threw down on the table three cotton-plugged quills.

"Merciful God! *Yes!*" With insane strength he broke away from the big Irishman and darted to the table. His twitching fingers snatched a quill, pulled the cotton from the end, threw his head back—

"Enough of these damn' theatrics!" Simpson snarled it viciously, but he did not move. "By Heaven, Colton, you can't railroad me to save Norris and his wife with the fool ravings of a cocaine snuffler!" His face was purple, the veins in his forehead seemed ready to burst. "Mrs. Bowden!" He scoffed. "How did she get the bonds? Where are they? Find 'em!" he laughed triumphantly at Colton across the table, and the two central-office men who now stood over him.

"Here yuh are, Mr. Colton." It was Shrimp, staggering under the weight of a big bucket of dirty water. He set it down beside the problemist's chair.

"The bonds are here, Simpson!" Colton's hand plunged into the water, and came up with a dripping, shiny black object. "There's the first package, in an all-rubber ice bag!"

"You devil!" Simpson's rage made his voice a scream.

"Take your prisoner, policemen." Colton could not refrain from adding that last scornful word to the two detectives who had not seen until a blind man had shown them.

IV

"Of course, De Roque, who was merely the drug-crazed tool of the real criminal, would have told where the bonds were," declared Thornley Colton, when they were once more in the shade-drawn library of the big, old-fashioned house. "But Simpson would have had time to be on his guard. The finding of the bonds, as I did, before he had time to recover his nerve, drew from him those last betraying words. The police can establish his connection with the telephone message to Miss Richmond, the booking of the two passages under the name of Morris, and the place where he and De Roque met while the fake Mrs. Bowden was supposed to be out at day's work. Those details were not even worth bothering with, for me, because the keyboard of silence told me the guilty persons before the robbery was committed."

"I am as much at sea as ever," confessed Sydney Thames.

"In the Regal we saw the first act. Simpson, with the dare-

213

devilishness that characterizes the type, introduced me to the accomplice. It was not wholly dare-devilishness, however, for it was to prepare the get-away. He wanted, before the time came for her to disappear, to arouse your sympathy and my interest in the deaf-and-dumb woman, whom he had married to accomplish his reformation. After a fruitless search he would need a long vacation in Europe, with the bonds, of course, to recover from the shock. There could be no suspicion attached to him. No sane man would look for a deaf-and-dumb wife in the person of a vaudeville actor dying of tuberculosis and cocaine who had drug dreams of money coming his way. Once Simpson had gotten out of the country, De Roque could have raved and stormed, even confessed, and his confession would have been accepted as nothing but cocaine dementia. Simpson never intended to play fair; it isn't his nature. From the first time I ever shook his hand I have known him to be a born criminal, for I can read hands as the physiognomist reads faces. And I have the advantage, because men like Simpson, with the aid of their strong wills, can mask their emotions behind eyes and faces so that no man can read their minds. But they have never given a thought to their hands."

"Do you mean to say you could tell what Simpson was planning by shaking his hands there in the Regal?" demanded Thames incredulously.

"Not quite," protested Colton laughingly. "But you know how I shake hands. My long index finger always rests lightly on the keyboard of silence—the wrist. With a touch like mine, so light that I can read handwriting by feeling the ridges left on the blank side of the paper, not one person in a million could feel it. I think Miss Richmond did, when I shook hands with her, because I felt a responsive thrill. In the case of Simpson his heart was working like a steam-engine, though his face and eyes were a mask that neither you nor any man with eyes could read; my finger-tip on his pulse told me that he was labouring under some strong excitement. When I shook hands with his 'wife,' I discovered why."

"Why?" echoed Thames blankly.

"Because the wife was a man, and a drug-fiend."

"Your hand told you that, and my eyes were deceived!"

"My knowledge of anatomy told me the man part. Don't you know that over the muscles of a woman is a layer of fat that gives the beautiful feminine curves? The man's muscles play directly under the skin, and the curves of female impersonators are due to flabby muscles, and not the feminine fat layer. Besides the cocaine pulse of the 'wife,' my fingertip immediately felt the play of the muscles as the hand gripped mine. Knowing Simpson, the impersonation could mean nothing else but a contemplated crime. I further proved it by getting her to put out her hand before she could have had any knowledge, by signs, of my intention to say good-bye. Remember my reference to lip-reading? Simpson was taking no chance of letting her talk. The cocaine gave her the brightness of eye, and the heavily-daubed rouge I knew would have to be there to convince you that she was really a country girl who didn't know the use of cosmetics, and also to cover any trace of man's beard and cocaine pastiness of skin. It would have deceived any one who had eyes, where an artistic make-up would immediately have aroused suspicion. Simpson was a wonderful detailist.

"Common sense told me that Simpson could not risk working with an amateur. Therefore I set Shrimp to looking up actors who had been forced to leave the stage on account of ill health within the last two months. The whole thing must have been rehearsed many times, for the detailist would overlook no detail. In Shrimp's list was De Roque. A few telephone inquiries proved that he was really a cocaine fiend of the worst kind, also that he had returned, yesterday morning, from a sanatorium, no better, to his old boarding-house. It was Simpson's scheme to let him do that, for it eliminated him. As soon as I found out that Simpson would not risk visiting him, Shrimp and John got him on the pretense that they were from Simpson. Cocaine snufflers as far gone as he need the drug every hour. For three hours before the time arranged for Shrimp to bring him to the bank De Roque hadn't had a pinch; he was insane with craving. The visit to Third Avenue, and the finding of the quills which cocaine snufflers use to hide the stuff on their bodies and conceal it in their palms so that no one can see them snuff it gave me the things I needed to make him talk. You saw how they worked."

"But the detectives who helped him out of the room? How did you ever figure the possibility of the bonds being in the scrub water?"

"The protective-agency men told me. Their eyes saw what my lack of eyes understood. The yellow bar of soap bobbing on top of the water, I think one of them expressed it. An instant's intelligent thought would tell any one that the yellow soap used for scrubbing floors never floats. The finding of the powdered sulphur showed me the clever ice-bag trick, for powdered sulphur is always used by druggists to keep the thin rubber from sticking together when the bags are in the boxes. Of course, De Roque carried it with him every night waiting for his opportunity, and in pulling it out the powder scattered on the carpet. The natural thing was to brush it under the safe, where my handkerchief found it after my slapping hand had raised the scattered grains he had missed.

"The ringing of the burglar-alarm was a master-stroke. It was the link necessary to establish the innocence of Mrs. Bowden. Simpson, of course, knew of the connection. De Roque probably removed his shoes and stood on the rubber ice-bag while he opened the safe and took out the bonds and papers Simpson had so accurately described. Then, when they had all been packed and the safe closed, a natural stumbling against the safe would bring the protective-agency men to swear that nothing could have been taken from the room. When the time came to leave the building, the pail, still full of water, was carefully put in a far, dark corner of the cellar closet, where the scrub pails and mops are kept. It would have been safe until Simpson was ready to take the bonds away. That was why I worked to keep Jamison and his partner around the bank; I didn't want Simpson to have any opportunity to get the loot out.

"Of course, it was he who suggested the calling of the regular police to the flustered President Montrose. Because, while he was sure that he could deceive me, he wasn't taking any foolish risks. He wanted the central-office men to muddle the thing as much as possible, and he was shrewd enough not to overdo the casting of suspicion on Norris and his wife; the way he put in a word here and there, and looks, of course, was quite in keeping with the other details. This morning, I think, he had begun to realize what I was doing, but there was nothing he could do but count on a bluff. I took him off his guard."

For several minutes the two men smoked in silence.

"But why didn't you warn some one instead of letting the robbery go on?" Sydney asked finally.

Colton's expressive lips framed a wry smile. "You will insist on showing the fly in the ointment, Sydney. The truth is, I was caught napping. But I guess it's just as well I didn't. Jails are built for the protection of society, and Simpson is the one man in a thousand against whom society needs protection."

RICHARD SALE

(1911–1993)

||||||||||||||||||||||||||||||||||||||||||||||| ■ |||||||||||||||||||||||||||||||||||||||||||||

With his profession providing a passport into many spheres of life, the news-paperman is a stock character in pulp detective fiction. Sometimes referred to as "surrogate sleuths," journalists use their skills to search out the truth and solve crimes, even though they are neither police professionals nor amateur detectives. One of the best-known reporter heroes is Joe "Daffy" Dill, the creation of Richard Sale, who drew on his own early experience as a New York reporter to craft his crime stories.

Sale soon left the world of journalism for a career in popular writing that mirrored the development of the various media. He got his start in the pulp magazines of the 1930s, including *Detective Fiction Weekly*, *Argosy*, *Double Detective*, and *Baffling Detective*, turning out some forty-six short stories featuring Dill. In the 1940s, he began to write for the burgeoning "slicks": his series character Lieutenant Alec Mason solved cases set in type on the glossy pages of the *Saturday Evening Post*, *Esquire*, and *Blue Book*. During the 1940s, too, he turned out the bulk of his longer fiction, including six novels and a collection of novelettes. Another novelette collection followed in 1950, another mystery novel appeared in 1971, and he published a mainstream novel in 1975.

In the interim, Sale had turned his talents to screenwriting and directing. His screenplays demonstrated versatility and allowed him to indulge his passion for writing snappy dialogue. He wrote several screenplays with Mary Loos and others, ranging from Westerns to sports sagas to suspense yarns. His directing career blossomed during the 1950s, and then he began to write for television series, including *Yancy Derringer* and *The FBI*.

Typical of the time and the medium, Sale's pulp fiction is chiefly composed of dialogue. Animated exchanges are enlivened with exclamations. The repartee is quick, spiced with wisecracks, and leavened with humor. The characters "snap" at one another. And the delivery of information is expressed in a vernacular that could only be American: "Listen, my little rattlesnake . . . I just put the bite on Rigo."

Sale's hero is no stranger to violence. Despite his lighthearted nickname, Daffy Dill's adventures prove that when it comes to securing a scoop, the fist is mightier than the pencil.

1934

_____

A Nose for News

■

The telephone on my desk rang, so I stopped banging out the lead of the double suicide story I had just covered and answered it. It was Dinah Mason, who is decidely bad for my heart. She was the reception girl for the *Chronicle*, and she had buzzed me from the outer office.

"Hello, Garbo," I said.

"Listen, Daffy," she said in a low voice, "a lunatic just went by here yelling your name. He looks angry. I couldn't stop him."

"Thanks for the warning, gel," I said. "But I'm not on the spot for anything—as far as I can recall."

"O.K." She sounded funereal. "He sure looks mad."

She hung up as did I, and no sooner had I shoved the telephone back where it belonged than the door to the city room burst open and the maniac stalked in.

He was a little guy, well dressed, with a black derby perched on the top of his skull. He was waving a home edition of the *Chronicle* in his right hand like a red flag. He kept saying: "Which one of you is Joe Dill? Which one of you pencil-pushers is Joe Dill?"

I kept my mouth shut, waiting for him to reach me before identifying myself, and hoping that by that time some of the hot blood would have cooled off.

The rest of the staff, in the tradition, kept their pans a perfect blank. If I wanted to make myself known, that was my business alone.

But just then Harry Lyons, the rat of our sheet, who had been sore at me since I got his job, gave me a dirty look and pointed at me. His biggest aspiration, you see, was to find me flat on my face with a knife between my shoulder blades. He said: "Here he is, mister. Meet Daffy Dill, the world's worst newspaper man."

I snapped: "Button your lip, Lyons!"

But he saw trouble for me. He smirked broadly, got up, and took the maniac by the arm. He pulled the guy right over to my desk and put a chair there for him.

"Here," he said, motioning at me, "is the Cyrano de Bergerac of the newspaper racket. All nose—no news! Ha-ha!"

"Ha-ha!" I said sadly, surveying Lyons' face for the exact spot where I was going to hang a haymaker very shortly. I picked his eye. That was the most ignominious spot.

"Are you Joe Dill?" the maniac asked loudly.

"I am," I said, "Joe Dill. Sit down, my fran. What's wrong?"

"What's *wrong?*" he bellowed with new fervor, slapping his copy of the home edition on my desk and hurling the chair aside. "He asks me what's wrong. *Du lieber Gott!*"

I got more and more puzzled.

"Mr. Dill," he said sibilantly, "do you know who I am, *hein?*"

I said: "You've got me there, mister."

"I am Adolph," he went on. "Adolph, America's premier chef! Do you know what you have done?"

"Adolph?" I echoed. "Well, I'll be damned! Adolph, the chef of the Grenada Hotel? Well, what in hell are you sore about? Didn't you see that swell feature I wrote about you in the second section today?"

"Swell feature," Adolph moaned. "Mr. Dill, you should be arrested! *Verdamnt*—you should never be allowed to write again. You have libeled me! You have been malicious! I will sue this damn paper to heaven!"

He turned stoically to Lyons and asked with dignity: "Where is the editor?"

"Right this way," Lyons said, smiling sweetly at me. "I'll take you right in. Don't blame you a bit. Newspaper men shouldn't libel their readers. You're absolutely right. This way."

When he had gone in the vague direction of the Old Man's office I grabbed a stray copy of the *Chronicle* and hurriedly thumbed through it to my story, which had made a big enough hit with the Old Man to net me a by-line. I read it through carefully. Near the end I groaned. It went like this:

"Adolph was famous long before he entered the cuisine of the Grenada Hotel. For ten years before the war, he was the most famous of all the crooks of Vienna."

Libel? It was dynamite, fuse lighted and all! I had meant to say that he was the most famous *cook* in all Vienna. But somehow my typewriter must have slipped in that wandering *r* while I was pounding the keys. I groaned. I locked my desk, got up, and found my hat and coat. I knew right then that I had joined the legion of the unemployed, but somehow that word *crook* still rankled me. I was damn positive that I hadn't written *crook* for *cook*. And if I had—why hadn't the copyreader picked it up and fixed it? Suspicion grew, and in five short minutes I realized that Harry Lyons, C. T. (Cut-Throat), had pulled a sandy on me. So I waited for him.

In a little while, Adolph came out of the Old Man's office with a happy expression on his face—as though he had just seen my corpse. He sneered a sneer at me and left the city room. No sooner had he gone out than Lyons came to my desk.

"Why, hello, Daffy," he said. "The Old Man wants to see you right away."

"You don't say," I said. "And some one wants to see you right away too."

"Who is it?" he asked.

"Your favorite doctor," I said.

With that I let him have a short sweet haymaker right under his eye, which spot I had chosen previously. There was a pleasant crunch. His teeth clicked together neatly. His eyes closed with a snap you could hear on West Street. He went down and—out.

McGuire, the sports editor, looked up from the story he was writing about Lou Gehrig and yawned: "Nice punch, Daffy. Better see the Old Man anyway. He may have mercy on your soul."

"Thanks, Mac," I said. "I'll see him."

I went to the Old Man's office and knocked. Then I opened the door and stuck my head in, weaving in case he started to throw things.

"Come in here, Daffy," the Old Man ordered. "Sit down a second."

"On the level?"

"Why, Daffy, did I ever—"

"O.K.," I growled. "Ixnay on the pathos. Let's get it over."

He nodded and I sat down.

"In the first place," he said, "you are fired."

"I knew that," I said.

"Listen, Daffy," the Old Man said suddenly. "I hate like hell to do it, but I've got a boss too, the guy who publishes this sheet. I couldn't let you stay."

"I know, I know."

"I had to settle with that frocked cook for one grand. He wouldn't take a cent less for release of that libel." The Old Man shrugged. "I have to fire you. Can't do anything else. But I wanted to speak to you about those gambling exposé articles you've been writing, the ones you left with me for safety."

"They're mine," I said. "I did them on my own time."

"I know it," he said. "But I want them. They'll blow Cantrey's graft organization wide open when I break them.

"Now I'll tell you what I'll do. I'll keep 'em here. You go out and run into the prize scoopy of the year. It'll have to be an exclusive. Then I'll just be forced to hire you again, over the publisher's head, to get your yarn. And all will be serene once more."

"You mean," I said, "that I've got to scoop the A. P., the U. P., the

Metropolitan News Service and every other rag in this city to get my job back?"

"Yeah."

I sighed. "The day of miracles is past, my fran."

The Old Man shrugged. "You'll have to do it. I can't take you back otherwise. I've got to protect myself. I want you. You're a good newspaper man, Daffy. And I want that gambling exposé too. Make a try anyhow. You've got thirty bucks due on salary. How about it?"

"Slave-driver," I said, "I will try. I'll do my damnedest, even if I have to steal or murder myself. So long. When you see this intelligent phiz again it will hold in its mind the greatest circulation yarn in days."

I went out. I felt enthusiastic and fine. The Old Man was a prince. He liked me—or my gambling story. When I reached the street, I went limp. Where in hell could you get a scoop in a modern newspaper day like this? I began to feel down. So I took the subway up to Times Square, which is my happy hunting ground. And then I went to the Hot Spot Club to drown my sorrows for awhile.

TWO

The Hot Spot is on West Forty-third, and it is owned by Mike Cantrey, alias the Brain. Cantrey headed just about every racket on the main stem. No murder, beering or bootlegging. Not crude stuff like that. He just took suckers. He ran machines, gambling houses, spots like this one, which were blinds for his crooked wheels in the rear. And it was Cantrey I had written my exposé about.

I went in and took a seat by myself in one of the oaken stalls. A waiter came over and looked questioningly at me. I said: "An Old Fashioned, garsong, as ever."

While I was waiting for him I lighted a cigaret. A shadow fell across my table. I looked up. A girl was standing in front of my stall. She had corn-hair, a smooth-looker, and was dressed like the Queen of Sheba.

"I know you," she said, pointing.

She was a little bit tight and she was holding a rye highball. I thought I'd seen her before somewhere, but I played safe. I said: "You've got the better of me, Garbo."

"You're Daffy Dill," she said.

"Right the first time," I said.

"You're a reporter on the *Chronicle*."

"Wrong there," I said sadly. "I was a reporter on the *Chronicle*. I just lost my job. That's why my tears are staining my best shirt. Sit down and put up your hair and have a good cry with me. Who are you?"

"Tough," she said—about the job, and then added: "I'm Clare Gor-

221

don." I didn't look bright. "You know—Pemberton Gordon's daughter. You interviewed him at the house last week on the N.R.A. He's in the cloak and suit end as administrator."

"Hell, yes!" I said, shaking hands with the gel. "But I didn't see you there or I would have stayed longer." I surveyed her. "You make pretty good copy yourself. Been in any more scrapes lately? I haven't seen a yarn about you since you forced down the police plane when it tried to get you for stunting over the city."

She made a face. "That was a jam. They cracked up in landing. I've reformed. Dad played hell with me on that one."

The waiter brought my Old Fashioned.

"Have one?" I asked.

"Sure," she said. "Thanks."

"Another," I told the waiter. He left.

"How'd you lose your job?"

I said: "I happened to have a guy in the office who hates my nerve. He had my job but he couldn't deliver. They promoted me to his forty fish a week and he's been sore at me ever since. He fixed me into a libelous story. Changed one word and got the paper in a jam. It looked as though I'd written it—and so I am fired."

"Tsk, tsk," she said, shaking her head. "Bad, bad. Daffy, am I a pal?"

"My fran," I said, "I have known you for years."

"You help me out," Clare said, "and I'll get you back your job."

"Why not?" I said. "Consider yourself helped."

She handed me a slip of paper. It had a list of figures on it which added up to five grand. "Know what that is?"

"I.O.U.'s, probably," I said. "Been playing the wheel?"

"Not me," she said. "I'm not that dumb. But my brother has and he's in a real spot. Dad's cracked down on him lately. Won't give him money. Dick was playing the wheel here at Cantrey's. He lost. He gave them an I.O.U. each time. Now they want to collect. They're going to go to dad and I know it'll get Dick disowned or something. I told him I'd fix it up. I saw the Brain. He said no."

"Five grand," I mused. "O.K., girlie. You sit here and devour your drink. I'll be right back."

I got up and went to the back door. Rigo, the Brain's right-hand man, peered out at me through the barred door.

"Oh, it's you," he said, and opened up. I went in.

The tables were all getting a good play, even for daytime. Suckers were plunking down the coppers and having them swept away without a bit of return, but they kept right at it. I asked Rigo: "Where's the Brain?"

"In his office," Rigo said. He was a little guy with black hair, black mustachio, and squinty eyes. "Want to see him?"

"Yeah."

He took me in. The Brain was sitting behind his desk, smoking a cigar. Luke Terk was sitting with him. Luke was the Brain's muscle man when customers were broken-armed about paying up. Rigo closed the door behind us.

"Hello, Daffy," said the Brain. "How's tricks?"

"Fair," I said. "I want to ask a favor."

"Anything for a pal," said the Brain, smiling, and I shivered because I knew damn well he would have liked to have had my throat slit. "What is it?"

"There's a guy named Richard Gordon," I said. "A good pal of mine. He owes you five grand."

"That's right."

"Tear up his I.O.U.," I said. "He's a personal friend, you see. He didn't know your wheels were crooked."

Luke Terk jumped around and stared at me. "Listen, birdie, button your lip or—"

"Why, Luke!" the Brain said. "Don't speak like that. Daffy's my best friend, aren't you, Daffy?"

"How about it?" I asked.

"Afraid the answer's no," the Brain said. "Five grand is five grand."

"I see," I said. "Mind if I use your phone?"

"Go ahead."

I called the Old Man at the *Chronicle*. The three buzzards watched me carefully. The Old Man said irascibly: "Yeah."

"Chief," I said, "this is Daffy Dill. I'm at the Hot Spot seeing Mike Cantrey. He just refused to do a favor for me. Don't you think it was about time the *Chronicle* ran that series of articles exposing his crooked gambling joints all over the city?"

"Hell, no!" the Old Man said. "You haven't finished them up yet."

"Fine," I said. "I'll tell him he can read all about it in tomorrow's editions then."

"Wait a second," the Brain said.

"I get you," said the Old Man. "You're baiting him. Keep talking if you want. I'll play along from this end."

"Nice going, chief," I said. "But wait a second." I put my hand over the mouthpiece and asked: "What is it?"

The Brain studied me. "Is that on the level?"

"You bet your sweet life it is!"

"It can't hurt me. I've got the political boys greased."

"Yeah," I said, "but you haven't got the public greased. You take their money and they'll be sore when they read about it. They'll put the blame for any time they've ever been gypped on you. Maybe there'll be a Federal inquiry. And in two months there's an election coming up. The people won't elect your political boys unless they clean you out."

Luke Terk snapped: "This is one guy we oughta cook, Brain."

"Let me do it!" Rigo growled.

"Boys, boys!" I said. "Don't be silly. You don't kill a reporter who has just written an exposé of you. That adds murder to the other crimes."

The Brain said: "He's right, you lugs. Call off your dogs, Daffy. It's a deal. I'll give you the I.O.U."

"Chief," I said into the phone, "it's all off. You'll have to hold those articles for another favor. So long."

I hung up. The Brain opened his desk, took out a note, handed it to me.

"I'm on the short end," he said. "You've still got those articles for publication. How much for them?"

"I'm not blackmailing," I said.

"You mean you'll run them sometime anyhow?"

"Yeah," I said. "But you'll have time to get your affairs together and start a new racket, Brain. Gambling's dead from now on."

Luke Terk growled: "Get outta here, you rat, before I forget myself and blast you."

I got out.

THREE

Clare Gordon had finished her Old Fashioned when I went back to the stall. She was a little tighter. She laughed at me and asked: "How'd you make out?"

I handed her the I.O.U. "Is this your brother's signature?"

She nodded. "That's it."

"Then you're all set." I took out a match and burned the note. "Tell him he's in the clear. Also tell him to lay off crooked joints. Now, how about my job?"

"That's right," she said. "I told you I'd get it back. I've got a swell plan. I'm going to be kidnaped."

"What?" I cried.

"Sure. I'm going to be kidnaped tomorrow night at eight o'clock. By airplane."

Rigo went by the stall at that moment.

"Shh," I said. "Not so loud. Now, what in hell is this?"

"I just figured it out," she said, "sitting here. You write my folks a threatening letter, saying I've been kidnaped and that the ransom—"

I sighed. "Did you ever hear of the Lindbergh Law?"

"Sure, but what's the difference? All right then. I'll write my own letter. I'll say that I've been kidnaped and the ransom is two hundred thousand. I'll name you as go-between. Then I'll take off from home in my plane tomorrow at 8:00 P.M. and fly up to Binneybunk, Maine, where dad has a cabin. It'll be deserted there now. After a week or two, while you bask in the publicity of go-between and your paper cries for your services, I'll come back and tell a wild story."

"You're hopped," I said. "You're staggering. Forget it. I wouldn't go in on a plan like that for money."

"But I want to help you!"

"Help me? You want me to become a lifer in a Federal jug!"

Clare wrinkled her nose. "All right. But you can't stop *me* from doing it. And I'll write the ransom note and still name you as go-between."

"I'll blow up the story."

"And they'll pinch you for conspiracy or something. I'm telling you, Daffy. Tomorrow at 8:00 P.M. I hop off for Maine and kidnap myself. Them's the kind words that gets back your job."

Well, she meant what she said. I was sitting in my apartment the next night around eight thirty, bemoaning the lack of scoops in this dazzling world. I had had a hard day trying to find a story which would yank back my job, but no luck. My nose simply wasn't in the news. I was washed up. Then my telephone rang.

I answered it with: "Your nickel!"

It was my heart, Dinah Mason. She thrust aside the usual sentimental amenities and said: "Daffy, hell's broken loose!"

"Somebody bomb the office?" I asked cheerfully.

"It's Clare Gordon," Dinah said. "She's been kidnaped. Half an hour ago. She was taking off from her father's estate out near Huntington, Long Island. Three men jumped her. At least that's what the chauffeur says. The snatchers piled into the plane and they all took off for points unknown."

I chuckled. "Damn the gel! Any other fine points?"

"There was a ransom note left behind. It names *you* as go-between! The bulls have been here for you. They're on their way up there now! The Old Man is frantic, trying to find you. The last place we looked was home. You're seldom there."

"Listen, Dinah," I said, "don't get excited. The Gordon skirt framed this whole thing. I'll tell the Old Man when I see him. It was put-up."

"Are you sure, Daffy? It doesn't look like a frame."

"It's a frame, my chickadee," I said. "Forget it. Who's covering for the paper?"

"Harry Lyons."

"Oh me, oh my," I gloated. "What glorious fun! Abyssinia, my hour-glass. Look me up in Atlanta."

I hung up, threw on my hat and coat and took a powder before the police reached my place. I wasn't any too soon either. They roared up the street to the door, sirens going, just as I went down the block. I caught a cab, said: "Headquarters, Mac," and settled back on the cushions to enjoy the ride, which cost me seventy-five cents when I finally paid off in front of the Centre Street building at the other end.

I went up to see Captain George Shane, who, I figured, would be in charge of the case, even if it had taken place on Long Island. They centralize things like kidnapings, because one man has to stand in with the Federal authorities when they come searching. Inspector Calloran and Sergeant Bill Hanley of the Homicide Squad were both on the out in this snatch.

I was right. Captain Shane was my man. Every newshound in the city was outside his door, pounding on it, trying to get in and get hold of some facts. A cop—I recognized him as Curly Newton—was pushing them aside. In the midst of the holocaust I saw Harry Lyons. He had a bad eye where I had brushed him off. I said: "Gentlemen of the Press!"

There was sudden silence. They stopped pushing and turned around. Lyons yelled: "Daffy Dill!" and that started it. I forgot for a moment that I had been named go-between in Clare Gordon's screwy ransom note. I was a public figure in the case. They mobbed me for a statement while Curly Newton tore into Captain Shane's office. In a second or two, before I could say a word, Newton came out again and dragged me through the mob into Shane's office. He closed the door and I liked the quiet for a change.

Captain Shane was pacing the floor in front of Pemberton Gordon, Clare's father. He recognized me easily since I had interviewed him for the paper only the week before, as Clare had said.

There were two other men in the room too. They were Federal operatives. I could see it as plain as day.

"Daffy," said Captain Shane. "You heard what's happened?"

I nodded.

"You heard you've been named go-between?"

I nodded again, looking at Pemberton Gordon's face. He was scared to death. His hands were trembling. I could see a vein in his temple throbbing like hell. I felt sorry for him.

"Listen, Captain," I said, "I just heard about it and I came right down to blow it up. It's a fake."

"A *what?*"

"A fake, a pushover, sandy. It's a frame. The kid did it on purpose to help me get my job back."

Captain Shane stared at me. "Daffy, are you on the level?"

"You know me, Captain," I said. "I don't lie to you."

"Then start talking," he snapped. "Let's hear this one."

I talked and told him all that had happened, how I'd done the gel a favor (I didn't say what it was because her old man was there) and how she wanted to do something for me. I told how she said she'd kidnap herself, name me as the go-between so's I'd get the job back. Shane listened without saying anything, just nodding now and then, but I saw that Pemberton Gordon was regarding me with the kind of a look he'd give Frankenstein's monster. And the Federal dicks were giving me the kind of eye which meant a rubber hose. I prayed.

When I had finished, Captain Shane shook his head.

"Daffy," he said, "it sounds fishy. I've known you a long time and all that, but it sounds fishy. I don't like to say it—but it does. Now come clean."

"Chief," I said shortly, "that's clean. I wouldn't fool you."

"He's one of the gang!" Gordon exclaimed. "I know he's one of the gang. That's why he was named as go-between. He knows where Clare is! I want him arrested!"

One of the Feds said: "Don't worry about that none."

"Wait a second," I said. "Take it easy, boys. I'm telling the God's honest truth." I was sweating like a soda glass. "The girl is up at her father's cabin at Binneybunk, Maine. Why don't you check on that and see if I'm right."

Shane nodded. "That's sound."

"We'll do that little thing," one of the Feds snapped.

"Meanwhile," said the other, "you're being detained as a material witness or suspicious character or anything you'd like. Put him in the can, Captain."

"That's what I'll have to do, Daffy," said Shane. "Sorry."

"O.K., chief," I said. "Just so we clear the thing up. I told that scatterbrained frill I wasn't in on it. She said that wouldn't stop her."

227

"We'll wire the Binneybunk sheriff," said Captain Shane. "Sit tight in the jug. You'll know in an hour."

FOUR

They put me in a cell. The minutes took a hell of a long time to pass. I smoked. I got to smoking so much I used a whole half-pack of cigarets and my tongue felt like the Russian army had walked across it with bayonets fixed. I kept sweating and my hands were trembling. I don't know why, but I felt damned uneasy.

At ten o'clock Captain Shane came to see me.

"Did they find her?" I asked.

"Daffy," he said slowly, "I hate like hell to do this. But Pemberton Gordon just swore out a warrant for your arrest. You're charged with aiding in the kidnaping of one Clare Gordon, and anything you say from now on can be used against you. They're setting your bail at twenty-five grand."

"Twenty-five grand!" I yelled. "Arrest? Chief, for God's sake, listen. The girl—"

"She wasn't there," Captain Shane said. "The cabin hadn't been opened since Gordon was up at Binneybunk last summer."

I wilted. "Oh," I said. "Oh, thanks." I was croaking, not talking. "Thanks, chief. I—I guess I'm in a jam. Do me a favor, will you?"

"Sure," he said.

"Get me some cigs, please?"

"Sure. Anything else?"

"Telephone—telephone the Old Man. Tell him I want to see him."

Captain Shane shook his head. "No need of that, Daffy. The Old Man's here. He wants to see you."

"Can he?"

Captain Shane shrugged. "O.K., I guess. But only for five minutes."

"Thanks," I nodded. I felt better somehow. The sweating stopped. The suspense was killed. I knew where I stood. He went away. In a few seconds the Old Man puffed up to my cell and stared at me.

"Daffy, you old jailbird," he said, "when I told you to go scoopy, I didn't say get a life sentence doing it. Is it a story?"

"It's a story," I said. "But I'm the fall guy."

He looked me straight in the eye.

"Tell me one thing," he said. "One thing, Daffy. You're clean on this thing?"

I said: "I'm clean, chief."

"Good." He chuckled. "Then spill it."

I spilled it, the whole damn thing, and he listened, taking in every news angle it had. When I finished he remarked: "It's a lulu, all right. It'll make us dust off the type we used for the Armistice. But can you write it? If I get a machine up here, can you write that yarn? Can you—" He stopped and glanced warily at me. "Wait a second. If you—hell's bells! The girl wasn't at the Maine cabin. That means she's really been snatched!"

I nodded.

"Daffy," he said, watching my face, "do you know who did it?"

"I've got a good idea," I said.

The Old Man got pale. He paced back and forth a few minutes. Then he called: "Be right back," and left. I felt for a cigaret, but I didn't have any. Captain Shane came along and slipped me a pack. I paid him for them; they hadn't taken my belongings yet. "Thanks," I said. The Old Man showed up just at that instant.

"You're free, Daffy," he said. "I called up Kennril. He said that with the yarn behind it the *Chronicle* was going to post bond for your bail. That's legal. All O.K., Captain?"

"Hell, yes," Shane said. "The *Chronicle* is good for twenty-five grand. Have you signed the papers?"

"No, but I will now. Let the boy out."

"Not till the bond is posted."

They went off and fixed that business up while I jiggled on pins and needles. Every minute was precious. After an awfully long wait the turnkey came and let me out. The Old Man and Shane were waiting for me in Shane's office. Shane gave me a card, in case other bulls tried to put the bite on me.

"Judas," I said to the Old Man, "thanks! Thanks for everything! I'll never—"

"Wait a second," he said. "You've got to earn that bond. Go out and after them, Daffy. And try to break it right for the noon edition."

"Say," asked Shane suspiciously, "does he know the snatchers?"

"I don't know a thing," I said. "See my lawyer. O.K. I'm on my way." I shook hands with the Old Man. "I mean it, chief. Thanks."

"Get to hell out of here," the Old Man snapped.

I had a gun permit for a .32 Colt, but I never carried the rod. I figured I needed it tonight, so I took a cab uptown to my place. There was a cop out front. I didn't want trouble. I went in the back way and upstairs. I found the rod all right, primed and ready to go. I slipped it in my coat pocket and went out the back way. Then I headed for the main stem, crossed it, and went into the Hot Spot. I called a waiter. "Is the Brain in?"

"No." The reply was surly.

"Rigo? Luke Terk?"

"Naw, they're all out."

"O.K.," I said. I went out and turned into the back alley. I knew if any one of the three came they'd go into the Brain's office the back way. I took up a spot in the shadows and waited with my right hand wrapped fondly around my gun.

I waited about fifteen minutes. It was ten after eleven by the Paramount clock. I heard footsteps come along the street. I ducked back farther into the shadows. A man turned into the alley. He was all alone. I recognized him. Rigo, with his short-stepped gait. I let the Colt go. I reached in my pocket and took out my penknife and snapped open the blade.

Rigo was careful. He took a good look around himself, but it was damn dark where I stood. He missed me. He aimed for the side door of the Hot Spot, and for one second he turned his back to me.

I jumped out of the shadows, threw my left arm around his neck and jabbed the knife into his back, just enough for him to feel the cold steel.

"Hello, Rigo," I said. "Nice seeing you again."

He was breathing hard. He gasped: "Who is it?"

"Daffy Dill," I said. "An old friend." I sneaked my left hand into his shoulder holster and put his gun in my pocket. "Don't move, you rat," I snapped, "or I'll give you the length of this blade." He didn't move. He asked:

"What're you after, Dill?"

"Clare Gordon," I answered, "and the boys who snatched her."

He shuddered. I could feel it. He said: "Wrong alley. I don't know nothing about it."

"Listen, you crumby little bun," I snapped, "come clean. I'm not kidding now. The Brain engineered this. You overheard the gel say she was going to stage a fake. You were taking it out on her because I got that I.O.U. of her brother's back. That and the fact that I wrote those gambling exposé articles which will blow your business to hell. You needed a new racket, and the Brain chose this one."

"You're crazy!" he said.

"Rigo," I said coldly, "where is she?"

"I tell you I don't know."

I took the knife and cut him deep across the back of the neck. The blood started running down over his shirt.

"Rigo," I said, "you're going to tell me or I'll cut your head off. Come clean. Where is she?"

"I tell you I don't—know!" His voice was shrill and he was breathing hard from the pain. That pup was scared to death.

"Want another cut?" I asked.

"Leave me alone! For God's sake, leave me alone. I don't know anything about it. I told you—"

I cut him again on the back of the neck, deeper this time. He winced and began to half sob from the pain. "For God's sake, Dill, are you crazy? Leave me alone!"

"Where is she?"

"I don't—"

I put the edge of the blade across the front of his throat. I tightened it there.

"Rigo," I said, "I'm going to tell you a little secret. I'm out on bail. I'm charged with Clare Gordon's snatch. If I don't find out from you where she is I'm due for either a death sentence or a lifer term."

"I don't know where she is!"

"I haven't got much to lose, Rigo," I said coldly. I pressed the knife harder. "Your jugular vein is right there. If you don't spill her location in ten seconds I'm going to slice your throat wide open and let you bleed to death."

"That's murder, Dill!"

"Sure," I said. "But what have I got to lose. Your ten seconds are up. Here goes. So long, Rigo."

I cut him slightly. He half screamed and tried to break away from me. I listened to his shrill words as he got hysterical with terror. "She's at the Brain's place! She's at the Brain's place!"

"Take it easy," I said, easing up on the blade. "What do you mean?"

"The Brain's place!" he babbled. "Uptown. Ritz Towers! The Brain's penthouse!"

It's funny how fear will make a guy squeal on his own mother. I kept the knife on him but just enough for him to feel it. "How'd she get there?" I asked. "You snatched her when she was taking off in her plane from Huntington, Long Island!"

"The Brain and Luke Terk engineered the snatch over there! I waited up at Yonkers with a speedboat!"

"Who piloted?"

"Cantrey! The Brain!" He was gasping.

"What then?"

"Cantrey set the crate down in the Hudson. He had flares."

"Was it an amphibian?"

"Yeah. Land and water. We broke the pontoons and let the crate sink. Then we came down the river in the speedboat. I had left the

Brain's Lincoln by the Fifty-seventh Street pier. We tied up the boat and got in the car. We took the Gordon doll up to the Brain's place. I came back here to make things look right."

"Thanks," I said, "for the interesting lecture."

FIVE

I took out his rod and cracked him on the skull with it. He went out like a light and sagged to the alley floor. I figured him cold for at least an hour. I ran down the street to a cigar store, stuck a nickel in a telephone and called Dinah Mason.

"Hello?" she said.

"It's Daffy," I said.

"Darling," she said, "what's happened to you? The Old Man got word that you were being held in connection—"

"Listen, my little rattlesnake," I said. "I just put the bite on Rigo. You know Rigo—the Brain's right or left hand. I forget which. Anyway, he opened up and squealed beautifully. Now get this, because I'm on my way. Clare Gordon is being held captive at Mike Cantrey's penthouse apartment at the Ritz Towers. In case they should bury me before you see me again, tell some one else that pertinent information and write the story along with my obit."

"Check," she said. "Be careful, you lunatic. Don't get killed just when I've got you that way about me."

"I'm not going to try," I said, "but you never can tell."

I hung up and hooked a cab for uptown. We made the Ritz Towers in nothing flat. I paid off the driver—four bits, it was—and I went in. I found out how the Brain got Clare up there without suspicion. He had a private elevator to his place. I said I wanted to see him. They made a call upstairs.

"The answer," said the desk clerk, "is no. Mr. Cantrey is seeing no one tonight."

"Tell him," I said, "it's about some gambling articles a fellow once wrote."

"He'll see you," the desk clerk said after relaying the kind words. "Take that elevator."

I took it. It was a non-stop at that time of night and we went up so fast I felt as though I'd left my stomach on the first floor. I got out. I didn't have any plan. I was just planning on inspiration. There were only two of them. I knew that. The Brain didn't go in for mobs.

I rang the bell. Luke Terk opened the door.

"Hello, rat," he said.

I went in. He had a gun in his right hand. With the other, as I passed him, he frisked me. He found my Colt and made me take it out. "Drop it on the floor." I dropped it. I felt sort of empty. I had counted on that gun for a jam. "O.K.," Luke Terk said then. "Go on in. One funny move and I give it to you."

His voice was cold and low. He meant it.

The Brain was sitting in the living room. It was a swanky spot, all furnished modernistic, the way the furniture looks when you wake up with the jitters and a bad hangover. He smiled at me in a self-satisfied way. I had a feeling I was in for it.

"Come to the point," he said. "Never mind the gambling stories stall."

"All right," I said. "You snatched Clare Gordon. The gel's here. I want her."

"You want the moon," said the Brain softly.

"Maybe so," I said. "But I want her."

"She ain't here."

I laughed nervously. "You're stalling now, Cantrey. I hopped Rigo in an alley. He squealed."

"I know," the Brain said. "You cut him with your knife. Sorta nasty trick, wasn't it, Daffy?"

I felt icy. "So he came to and called you?"

"Yeah. He's got a tough skull. Sorta nasty, wasn't it?"

"Not for a rat like Rigo," I said. "He had it coming. I don't like snatchers, Brain."

"My, my!" Luke Terk exclaimed. "He don't like snatchers." His voice went taut. "Well, I don't like guys with knives, Dill!"

"He had it coming."

"And so have you," said the Brain. "Ever had your teeth burned with matches? Ever had needles stuck through your skin? We do that with welchers, Daffy. I think we'll stretch a point. Maybe you ain't a welcher. But you was pretty rough on Rigo. And Rigo is a pal of mine, see?"

"You're running a sandy," I said. "You can't scare me now. Go ahead, torture me. Then bump me off. The Feds are still after Clare Gordon. They don't miss out on their cases, Brain."

"She ain't here."

"Sure," I said, "she's flew away with a little birdie. Don't kid me. She's in the Ritz Towers somewhere. Rigo squealed once. He'll squeal again."

"The Feds don't carve guys' throats," snapped Luke Terk.

"Rigo's O.K.," said the Brain. "But you're not, Daffy. You're washed out. You've poked that big nose of yours into trouble this time."

"Into news," I said. "A nose for news."

"You stuck it into a coffin," said Luke Terk. "Only this time the lid's on it and you can't pull out."

I waited for a second and didn't say anything. They had the drop on me coming and going and there wasn't a thing I could do except bluff and stall a little.

"I want Clare Gordon," I said.

"Nuts," Luke Terk growled. "O.K., chief?"

The Brain nodded. "O.K., Luke. Give it to him. And make it hurt."

Luke Terk jabbed his gun in my ribs. "Get over to that sofa," he said. "And lie down."

I started for the sofa. Simultaneously, there was a hell of a racket in the streets below. We were up some sixteen floors, but we could hear the police sirens as plain as day. They were screaming and I could hear the cars grinding up to the curb.

The gun in my ribs loosened. Luke Terk tensed and turned.

"Chief," he snapped. "Bulls! This lug must've tipped them off!"

"Take it easy," the Brain said. "Maybe they're not for us."

"They're for you," I said. "I tipped them."

Luke Terk cried: "Chief—what'll we do with him?"

"Take him along!" the Brain said. "You take him down where the doll is. I'll stay here and parley with the cops. You—"

Now was the time for all good men to come to the aid of their party. I spun around, swinging with my right. It was a good swing, but I hit without a target, since Luke Terk and his rod were behind me. I heard the Brain yell. I missed Terk's chin and hit him on the left shoulder.

SIX

The punch hurt my fist. It hit solidly. Luke Terk went down, but I had fired the arm so hard I fell right on top of him. I hit him again as we sprawled. This time I caught him on the beak. It spouted blood. He tried to bring his gun hand up.

The Brain yelled again. Then there was a shot. The bullet went over my back with an angry whine. If you don't think slugs make noise, you want to get that close to one of them. I shot out my foot and smashed it down on Luke Terk's hand. Terk yelled with pain and his fingers shot open. The gun dropped to the rug.

Another shot from the Brain. The rug in front of Terk's head jumped as the slug dug into the floor.

"For God's sake, chief!" Terk screamed. "Go easy!"

I dove for the gun Terk had dropped, keeping low and not giving a damn whether the Brain hit me or not. I got into the spirit of the thing. I reached the gun, picked it up. I wheeled on my belly, firing twice. The slugs never went near the Brain, but they scared him. He let go another wild shot at me that missed by feet and then tore out of the room into the hall. I could hear the front door slam.

Luke Terk was struggling to his feet. On my knees, I covered him with the gun. He was reaching into his coat pocket.

"Cut it!" I snapped.

He must have figured that I was bluffing. He kept right on into his pocket. I saw his hand come out. He had the .32 pistol in it, the rod he had taken from me in the entrance hall when he frisked me.

"Cut it," I snapped again.

He raised it for a shot. I yanked the trigger of his own gun. It jumped in my hand. It made an awful racket. He fell over backwards as though I had hit him with a sledge-hammer. The .32 flew up into the air and smacked a picture on the wall, knocking the glass pane to bits.

I got to my feet and looked at him. There was a hole in his right lung. His chest was bleeding. He was conscious, his eyes were open and his lips kept moving as though he were trying to say something. Nothing came out. He'd live. Sawbones can fix up wounds like that one.

I stepped over him and started for the entrance hall. At the same time the front door burst open. I turned around and ran for the bedroom, the gun still in my hand. The window there was open. I shut the window after me and started down the fire escape. I knew if the police caught me there with Luke Terk wounded and no Clare Gordon to show for it I would be in a worse jam than ever. I had to get the Brain and the gel.

I went down two floors on the fire escape when I heard the window of the Brain's bedroom open. I hugged the wall of the building and stopped moving. Then I heard him say: "No one down there," and he closed the window again. It was Captain Shane.

I took a breather and wondered what in hell to do. I was marooned on the fire escape. The only chance I had of getting off it and trailing the Brain was by going through a window, into an apartment, and then out into the hall and down, dodging cops all the way. It was a small chance, but the only one. And it wouldn't do to have Luke's gun on me.

Glancing down into the street, I saw it was pretty deserted. This was the side of the hotel, not the front where the cops were. I heaved the gun out and away. I could hear it hit, just dully.

I tried the window in front of me. It was locked. Swearing softly, I went down another flight of the fire escape and tried the next one. It was unlocked. I opened it softly. The shade was down. It was dark green. I pushed it aside and stepped into the room. The lights were out. It was dark as hell. I stood there for a few seconds, trying to adjust my eyes. There wasn't a sound in the room. But in the one adjoining I could hear some one walking around. I started across the room. A floor board creaked. I stopped, stiffened.

Suddenly I gasped. The bed in the room was squealing loudly as some one moved on the springs.

"Take it easy," I whispered. "I'm a friend. I won't hurt you." I felt like a fool, but what else was there to say under circumstances like that?

The bed squeaked more and more. Some one was bouncing up and down on it. I had a hunch. I walked over to it and struck a match.

Just like I thought. There lay Clare Gordon . . .

She was bound with thick adhesive tape both on her ankles and her arms. Her hands were spread out flat against each other and taped. There was a wad of tape across her mouth. Two ropes stretched across her body and under the bed prevented her from rolling off.

She looked at me pleadingly. The match went out. I lighted another and went to work on the tape over her mouth, motioning her to keep quiet when she could speak. I pulled off the tape. They had stuck a lemon in her mouth. I took it out. The first thing she said was: "Judas Priest! I'm nearly dead!"

"Shh," I said.

I took off the rest of the tape and she sat up. She had to rub her legs to bring back the circulation. I said: "Well, you sure did it."

"Thank you, my fran," she said, grinning. She had what it takes. You couldn't keep her down. "They jumped me. They must have overheard me at the Hot Spot yesterday. Just when I was taking off they jumped me and flew off with me in the plane. Landed the plane in some river. Then a speedboat. Finally a car. Then here."

"Were you upstairs first?" I asked.

"Uh-huh. But somebody named Rigo telephoned and that oyster, Luke Terk, took me down here for safety. Thanks for saving me. It was good fun while it lasted, but I was getting stiff. How's your job? Get it back yet?"

"Listen, hare-brain," I said, "you're not saved yet. In the next room there's a mug with a gun and he's just aching to kill me."

"What are you going to do then?" she asked.

I shrugged ruefully. "I don't know. I haven't a rod. Damn it!" I sat down on the bed a second. "Guess we'd better go up by the fire escape. The cops are up there."

"That's safe and sound," she said. "Only you sound disappointed."

"I am. I'd like to get the Brain myself. It'd make a better news story for the *Chronicle*."

"Then get him. Pick up a chair or something. Get behind the door. I'll yell help or something. He'll come in."

"Wahoo," I said, "that's an idea." Picking up a brass candlestick from the mantel, I went over behind the door. "Let go in your best soprano," I said, "but make it muffled, like your gag has worked off."

"Help! Help! Save me!" she half moaned.

Next door there was a strident curse. Heavy footsteps pounded across the floor. The door flew open.

"Shut your mouth, damn you," the Brain greeted, "or I'll cook you right now!"

Clare had nerve. She repeated, "Help! Help!"

He came in. There was a gun in his hand. The light from the other room fell square on his head. It was all I needed. I brought the candlestick down with a swish. He half turned, firing his gun just once. Then he flopped over cold and pieces of plaster from the ceiling caromed onto my hat. I snapped on the lights.

"My hero," Clare grinned.

"My God!" I sighed, sitting down. "What a night . . ." I paused, a brilliant thought pervading my struggling mind. "Listen, heiress," I said, "your old man had me arrested. Now I saved your brother five grand, didn't I?"

"You did."

"Do you think, then, your old man would have any objections to a five grand pay-off out of court?"

"Out of court?"

"Sure, instead of defending himself against my suit for false arrest."

"Daffy Dill!" she exclaimed, laughing, "it's a lulu. It'll do my heart good to see him sign your check!"

The door was being knocked down. I let them knock it. I was too tired, and cops have nervous trigger fingers anyway. In a few seconds Captain Shane, the two Feds, and half the police force came in.

"There's your package," I said. "And here's the wrapper-upper."

Captain Shane grinned. "That cleans you, Daffy. Thanks. Your better-half called me up after your tip-off."

"Did you hear the shot in here?"

"Yeah. That's what brought us in."

I sighed. "Where's a telephone?"

"Wait a second," said Shane. "What in hell happened? Spill it."

"Uh-uh," I said, shaking my head. "See the patient."

"How about it, Miss Gordon?" Shane asked.

"You can read the exclusive story," Clare said, "in tomorrow's edition of the *Chronicle*."

"Listen—" Captain Shane roared.

"Hello, Dinah?" I said in the telephone.

"Howdy, my cherub," Dinah said. "All serene and sound?"

"Not serene," I replied, listening to Shane, "but quite sound."

"Good," said Dinah. "So what?"

"Get out the cold cuts," I said, "and the beer and potato salad. Daffy's on his way up to see you."

MIGNON G. EBERHART

(b. 1899)

|||||||||||||||||||||||||||||||||||||||||||||| ■ |||||||||||||||||||||||||||||||||||||||||||||

Mignon G(ood) Eberhart turned to plotting fictional murders in order to break the boredom induced by following her husband to the civil-engineering projects that took them to odd corners of the world. But what this Mystery Writers of America Grand Master had added to detective fiction by the time she'd published her fifty-ninth novel and reached her eighty-ninth year had more to do with her instincts as a storyteller.

Eberhart was born in Nebraska, studied at Nebraska Wesleyan College, married A. C. Eberhart in 1923 (and again in 1948 after a divorce), started her writing career with short stories, and published her first novel in 1929. Her first five books were in the Mary Roberts Rinehart pattern. They featured a middle-aged nurse, Sarah Keate, and her young policeman friend, Lance O'Leary. About the only thing new about these early books was a series character who grew younger as time passed and Hollywood began filming the novels.

Eberhart then created two amateur detectives. The mystery writer–sleuth Susan Dare anticipates many imitators. And the banker-sleuth James Wickwire is also a good example of a character who brings his professional expertise to bear on his amateur detections.

When Eberhart decided to give up the quest for a series character, she—as critics love to say—found her own voice and blazed a new trail. If we can credit Rinehart with developing the "Had I But Known" form, Eberhart was best known for adapting the Gothic "dark and stormy night" and elements of romance into mysterious crime. She is credited with an unusual ability to make those stormy nights, and particularly the places where those tempests raged, highly realistic. This is because, as she put it, "a good many of these places, I've lived in myself." She used the places she had visited during travels with her husband to provide her exotic settings, thereby anchoring her scenes with specific details that lend reality to inherently suspenseful and physically strange or threatening situations.

Eberhart was also keen on romance. She frequently featured a female protagonist and a love affair—described without the coyness usual for the period and also without the explicit sex that writers of her later years would be describing.

"Spider" features Susan Dare and illustrates the author's use of devices from Gothic romance to heighten tension. While today's feminists might find reason enough to fault her characterization of the female, it was a long step ahead of what other writers were doing in the early 1930s.

1934

_____

Spider

■

"But it is fantastic," said Susan Dare, clutching the telephone. "You can't just be afraid. You've got to be afraid of something." She waited, but there was no reply.

"You mean," she said presently, in a hushed voice, "that I'm to go to this perfectly strange house, to be the guest of a perfectly strange woman—"

"To you," said Jim Byrne. "Not, I tell you, to me."

"But you said you had never seen her—"

"Don't maunder," said Jim Byrne sharply. "Of course I've never seen her. Now, Susan, do try to get this straight. This woman is Caroline Wray. One of the Wrays."

"Perfectly clear," said Susan. "Therefore I'm to go to her house and see why she's got an attack of nerves. Take a bag and prepare to spend the next few days as her guest. I'm sorry, Jim, but I'm busy. I've got to do a murder story this week and—"

"Sue," said Jim, "I'm serious."

Susan paused abruptly. He _was_ serious.

"It's—I don't know how to explain it, Susan," he said. "It's just— well, I'm Irish, you know. And I'm—fey. Don't laugh."

"I'm not laughing," said Susan. "Tell me exactly what you want me to do."

"Just—watch things. There ought not to be any danger—don't see how there could be. To you."

Susan realized that she was going. "How many Wrays are there, and what do you think is going to happen?"

"There are four Wrays. But I don't know what is going on that has got Caroline so terrified. It was that—the terror in her voice—that made me call you."

"What's the number of the house?" said Susan.

He told her. "It's away north," he said. "One of those old houses— narrow, tall, hasn't changed, I suppose, since old Ephineas Wray died. He was a close friend, you know, of my father's. Don't know why Caroline called me: I suppose some vague notion that a man on a newspaper would know what to do. Now let me see—there's Caroline. She's the daughter of Ephineas Wray. David is his grandson and Caroline's nephew and the only man—except the houseman—in the place. He's young—in his twenties, I believe. His father and mother died when he was a child."

"You mean there are three women?"

"Naturally. There's Marie—she is old Wray's adopted daughter—not born a Wray, but more like him than the rest of them. And Jessica— she's Caroline's cousin; but she's always lived with the Wrays because her father died young. People always assume that the three women are sisters. Actually, of course, they are not. But old Ephineas Wray left his fortune divided equally among them."

"And they all live there together?"

"Yes. David's not married."

"Is that," said Susan, at the note of finality in his voice, "all you know about them?"

"Absolutely everything. Not much for you to go on, is it? It was just," said Jim Byrne soberly, with the effect of a complete explanation, "that she was so—so horribly scared. Old Caroline, I mean."

Susan retraced the address slowly before she said again: "What was she afraid of?"

"I don't know," said Jim Byrne. "And—it's queer—but I don't think she knew either."

It was approaching five o'clock, with a dark fog rolling up from the lake and blending itself with the early winter twilight, when Susan Dare pressed the bell beside the wide old door—pressed it and waited. Lights were on in the street, but the house before her was dark, its windows curtained. The door was heavy and secretive.

But they were expecting her—or at least Caroline Wray was; it had all been arranged by telephone. Susan wondered what Caroline had told them; what Jim Byrne had told Caroline to say to explain her presence; and, suddenly, what Caroline was like.

> Little Johnny hung his sister.
> She was dead before they missed her.
> Johnny's always up to tricks,
> Ain't he cute, and only six—

The jingle had been haunting her with the persistency of a popular dance tune, and it gave accent to the impatient little beat of her brown Oxford upon the stone step. Then a light flashed on above the door. Susan took a deep breath of the moist cold air and felt a sudden tightening of her nerves. The door was going to open.

It swung wider, and a warm current of air struck Susan's cheeks.

Beyond was a dimly lit hall and a woman's figure—a tall, corseted figure with full sweeping skirts.

"Yes?" said a voice harshly out of the dimness.

"I am Susan Dare," said Susan.

"Oh—oh, yes." The figure moved aside and the door opened wider. "Come in, Miss Dare. We were expecting you."

Afterward Susan remembered her own hesitation on the dark threshold as the door closed with finality behind her, and the woman turned.

"I am Miss Jessica Wray," she said.

Jessica. This was the cousin, then.

She was a tall woman, large-boned, with a heavy, dark face, thick, iron-gray hair done high and full on her head, and long, strong hands. She was dressed after a much earlier fashion; one which, indeed, Susan was unable to date.

"We were expecting you," she said. "Caroline, however, was obliged to go out." She paused just under the light and beside a long mirror.

Susan had a confused impression of the house in that moment; an impression of old, crowded elegance. The mirror was wavery and framed in wide gilt; there were ferns in great marble urns; there were marble figures.

"We'll go up to your room," said Jessica. "Caroline said you would be in Chicago for several days. This way. You can leave your bag here. James will take it up later; he is out just now."

Susan put down her small suitcase, and followed Jessica. The newel post and stair rail were heavy and carved. The steps were carpeted and thickly padded. And the house was utterly, completely still. As they ascended the quiet stairs it grew increasingly hot and airless.

At the top of the stairs Jessica turned with a rigid motion of her strong body.

"Will you wait here a moment?" she said. "I'm not sure which room—"

Susan made some assenting gesture, and Jessica turned along the passage which ran toward the rear of the house.

So terrifically hot the house was. So crowded with old and almost sentient furniture. So very silent.

Susan moved a bit restively. It was not a pleasant house. But Caroline had to be afraid of something—not just silence and heat and brooding, secretive old walls. She glanced down the length of hall, moved again to put her hand upon the tall newel post of the stair rail beside her. The carved top of it seemed to shift and move slightly under the pressure of her hand and confirmed in the strangest way her feeling that the house itself had a singular kind of life.

Then she was staring straight ahead of her through an open, lighted doorway. Beyond it was a large room, half bedroom and half sitting room. A lamp on a table cast a circle of light, and beside the table, silhouetted against the light, sat a woman with a book in her lap.

It must be Marie Wray—the older sister; the adopted Wray who was more like old Ephineas Wray than any of them.

Her face was in shadow with the light beyond it, so Susan could see only a blunt, fleshy white profile and a tight knot of shining black hair above a massive black-silk bosom. She did not, apparently, know of Susan's presence, for she did not turn. There was a kind of patience about that massive, relaxed figure; a waiting. An enormous black female spider waiting in a web of shadows. But waiting for what?

The suggestion was not one calculated to relieve the growing tension of Susan's nerves. The heat was making her dizzy; fanciful. Calling a harmless old woman a black spider merely because she was wearing a shiny black-silk dress! Marie Wray still, so far as Susan could see, did not look at her, but there was suddenly the flicker of a motion on the table.

Susan looked and caught her breath in an incredulous little gasp.

There was actually a small gray creature on that table, directly under the lamplight. A small gray creature with a long tail. It sat down nonchalantly, pulled the lid off a box and dug its tiny hands into the box.

"It's a monkey," thought Susan with something like a clutch of hysteria. "It's a monkey—a spider monkey, is it?—with that tiny face."

It was turning its face jerkily about the room, peering with bright, anxious eyes here and there, and busily, furiously eating candy. It failed somehow to see Susan; or perhaps she was too far away to interest it. There was suddenly something curiously unreal about the scene. That, thought Susan, or the heat in this fantastic house, and turned at the approaching rustle of skirts down the passage. It was Jessica, and she looked at Susan and then through the open doorway and smiled coldly.

"Marie is deaf," she said. "I suppose she didn't realize you were here."

"No," said Susan.

"I'll tell her—" She made a stiff gesture with her long hand and turned to enter the room beyond the open door. As her gray silk rustled through the door the little monkey jerked around, gave her one piercing black glance and was gone from the table in a swift gray streak. He fled across the room, darted under an old sofa.

243

But Jessica did not reprove him. "Marie," she said loudly and distinctly.

There was a pause. Jessica's flowing gray-silk skirts were now silhouetted against the table lamp, and the monkey absently began to lick its paw.

"Yes, Jessica." The voice was that of a person long deaf—entirely without tone.

"Susan Dare is here—you know—the daughter of Caroline's friend. Do you want to see her?"

"See her? No. No, not now. Later."

"Very well. Do you want anything?"

"No."

"Your cushions?"

Jessica's rigid back bent over Marie as she arranged a cushion. Then she turned and walked again toward Susan. Susan felt queerly fascinated and somehow oddly shocked to note that, as Jessica turned her rigid back to the room, the monkey darted out from under the sofa and was suddenly skittering across the room again in the direction of the table and the candy.

He would be, thought Susan, one very sick monkey. The house was too hot, and yet Susan shivered a bit. Why did people keep monkeys?

"This way," said Jessica firmly, and Susan preceded her down the hall and into exactly the kind of bedroom she might have expected it to be.

But Jessica did not intend to leave her alone to explore its Victorian fastnesses. Under her somewhat unnerving dark gaze, Susan removed her cockeyed little hat, smoothed back her light hair and put her coat across a chair, only to have it placed immediately by Jessica in the enormous gloomy wardrobe. The servants, said Jessica, were out; the second girl and James because it was their half day out, the cook to do an errand.

"You are younger than I should have expected," she said abruptly to Susan. "Shall we go down now?"

As they passed down the stairs to the drawing room, a clock somewhere struck slowly, with long trembling variations.

"Five," said Jessica. "Caroline ought to return very soon. And David. He usually reaches home shortly after five. That is, if it isn't rainy. Traffic sometimes delays him. But it isn't rainy tonight!"

"Foggy," said Susan and obeyed the motion of Jessica's long gray hand toward a chair. It was not, however, a comfortable chair. And neither were the moments that followed comfortable, for Jessica sat sternly erect in a chair opposite Susan, folded her hands firmly in her silk lap and said exactly nothing. Susan started to speak a time or two, thought better of it, and herself sat in rather rigid silence. And was suddenly aware that she was acutely receptive to sight and sound and feeling.

It was not a pleasant sensation.

For she felt queerly as if the lives that were living themselves out in that narrow old house were pressing in upon her—as if long-spoken words and long-stifled whispers were living yet in the heated air.

She stirred restively and tried not to think of Marie Wray. Queer how difficult it was, once having seen Marie and heard her speak, not to think of that brooding figure—sitting in its web of shadows, waiting.

Three old women living in an old house. What were their relations to one another? Two of them she had seen and had heard speak, and knew no more of them than she had known. What about Caroline—the one who was afraid? She stirred again and knew Jessica was watching her.

They heard the bell, although it rang in some back part of the house. Jessica looked satisfied and rose.

It's David," she said. At the door into the hall she added in a different tone: "And I suppose Caroline, too."

Susan knew she was tense. Yet there was nothing in that house for her—Susan Dare—to fear. It was Caroline who was afraid.

Then another woman stood in the doorway. Caroline, no doubt. A tall slender woman, a blonde who had faded into tremulous, wispy uncertainty. She did not speak. Her eyes were large and blue and feverish, and two bright pink spots fluttered in her thin cheeks, and her bare thin hands moved. Susan rose and went to her and took the two hands.

"But you're so young," said Caroline. Disappointment throbbed in her voice.

"I'm not really," said Susan.

"And so little—" breathed Caroline.

"But that doesn't matter at all," said Susan, speaking slowly, as one does to a nervous child. There were voices in the hall, but she was mainly aware of Caroline.

"No, I suppose not," said Caroline, finally looking into Susan's eyes. Terrified, Jim had said. Curious how right Jim managed to be.

Caroline's eyes sought into Susan's, and she was about to speak when there was a rustle in the doorway. Caroline's uncertain lips closed in a kind of gasp, and Jessica swept into the room.

"But I must know what she's afraid of," thought Susan. "I must get her alone—away from Jessica."

"Take off your coat, Caroline," said Jessica. "Don't stand there. I see you've spoken to Susan Dare. Put away your hat and coat and then come down again."

"Yes, Jessica," said Caroline. Her hands were moving again, and she looked away.

"Go on," said Jessica. Her voice was not sharp, it was merely undefeatable.

"Yes, Jessica," said Caroline.

"Marie is reading," said Jessica. "You needn't speak to her now unless you wish to do so. You may take Susan Dare in to see her later."

"Yes, Jessica."

Caroline disappeared and in her place stood a man, and Susan was murmuring words of acknowledgment to Jessica's economical introduction.

David, too, was blond, and his eyes were darkly blue. He was slender and fairly tall; his mouth was fine and sensitive, and there was a look about his temples and around his eyes that was—Susan sought for the word and found it—wistful. He was young and strong and vibrant—the only young thing in the house—but he was not happy. Susan knew that at once. He said:

"How do you do, Miss Dare?"

"Don't go upstairs yet, David," said Jessica. Her voice was less harsh, she watched him avidly. "You ought to rest."

"Not now, Aunt Jessica. I'll see you again, Miss Dare."

He walked away. "Aunt Marie all right?" he called from the stairway.

"Perfectly," said Jessica. Her voice was harsh again. "She's reading . . ."

Afterward Susan tried to remember whether she could actually hear David's steps upon the padded stairs or whether she was only half consciously calculating the time it took to climb the stairs—the time it took, or might have taken to walk along the hall, to enter a room. She was sure that Jessica did not speak. She merely sat there.

Why did Jessica become rigid and harsh again when David spoke of Marie? Why did—

A loud, dreadful crash of sound forever shattered the silence in the house. It fell upon Susan and immersed her and shook the whole house and then receded in waves. Waves that left destruction and intolerable confusion.

Susan realized dimly that she was on her feet and trying to move toward the stairway, and that Jessica's mouth was gray, and that Jessica's hands were clutching her.

"Oh, my God—David—" said Jessica intelligibly, and Susan pushed the woman away from her.

She reached the stairway, Jessica beside her, and at the top of the stairs two figures were locked together and struggling in the upper hall.

"Caroline," screamed Jessica. "What are you doing? Where's Marie—where—"

"Let me go, Caroline!" David was pulling Caroline's thin clutching arms from around him. "Let me go, I tell you. Something terrible has happened. You must—"

Jessica brushed past them and then was at the door of Marie's room. "*It's Marie!*" she cried harshly. "*Who shot her?*"

Susan was vaguely conscious of Caroline's sobbing breaths and of David's shoulder pressing against her own. Somehow they had all got to that open doorway and were crowding there together.

It *was* Marie.

She sat in the same chair in which she'd been sitting when Susan saw her so short a time ago. But her head had fallen forward, her whole body crumpled grotesquely into black-silk folds.

Jessica was the first to enter the room. Then David. Susan, feeling sick and shaken, followed. Only Caroline remained in the doorway, clinging to the casing with thin hands, her face like chalk and her lips blue.

"She's been shot," said Jessica. "Straight through the heart." Then she looked at David. "Did Caroline kill her, David?"

"*Caroline* kill Marie! Why, Caroline couldn't kill anything!" he cried.

"Then who killed her?" said Jessica. "You realize, don't you, that she's dead?"

Her dark gaze probed deeper and she said in a grating whisper: "Did you kill her, David?"

"No!" cried David. "*No!*"

"She's dead," said Jessica.

Susan said as crisply as she could: "Why don't you call a doctor?"

Jessica's silk rustled, and she turned to give Susan a long cold look. "There's no need to call a doctor. Obviously she's dead."

"The police, then," said Susan softly. "Obviously, too—she's been murdered."

"The police," cried Jessica scornfully. "Turn over my own cousin—my own nephew—to the police. Never."

"I'll call them," Susan said crisply, and whirled and left them with their dead.

On the silent stairway her knees began to shake again. So this was what the house had been waiting for. Murder! And this was why Caroline had been afraid. What, then, had she known? Where was the revolver that had shot Marie? There was nothing of the kind to be seen in the room.

The air was hot—the house terribly still—and she, Susan Dare, was hunting for a telephone—calling a number—talking quite sensibly on the whole—and all the time it was entirely automatic action on her part. It was automatic, even, when she called and found Jim Byrne.

"I'm here," she said. "At the Wrays'. Marie has been murdered—"

"My God!" said Jim and slammed up the receiver.

The house was so hot. Susan sat down weakly on the bottom step and huddled against the newel post and felt extremely ill. If she were really a detective, of course, she would go straight upstairs and wring admissions out of them while they were shaken and confused and before they'd had time to arrange their several defenses. But she wasn't a detective, and she had no wish to be, and all she wanted just then was to escape. Something moved in the shadows under the stairs—moved. Susan flung her hands to her throat to choke back a scream, and the little monkey whirled out, peered at her worriedly, then darted up the window curtain and sat nonchalantly on the heavy wooden rod.

Her coat and hat were upstairs. She couldn't go out into the cold and fog without them—and Jim Byrne was on the way. If she could hold out till he got there—

David was coming down the stairs.

"She says it's all right to call the police," he said in a tight voice.

"I've called them."

He looked down at her and suddenly sat on the bottom step beside her.

"It's been hell," he said quite simply. "But I didn't think of—murder." He stared at nothing, and Susan could not bear the look of horror on his young face.

"I understand," she said, wishing she did understand.

"I didn't," he said. "Until—just lately. I knew—oh, since I was a child I've known I must—"

"Must what?" said Susan gravely.

He flushed quickly and was white again.

"Oh, it's a beastly thing to say. I was the only—child, you know. And I grew up knowing that I dared have no—no favorite—you see? If there'd been more of us—or if the aunts had married and had their own children—but I didn't understand how—how violent—" the word stopped in his throat, and he coughed and went on—"how strongly they felt—"

"Who?"

"Why, Aunt Jessica, of course. And Aunt Marie. And Aunt Caroline."

"Too many aunts," said Susan dryly. "What was it they were violent about?"

"The house. And each other. And—and other things. Oh, I've always known, but it was all—hidden, you know. The surface was—all right."

Susan groped through the fog. The surface was all right, he'd said. But the fog parted for a rather sickening instant and gave her an ugly glimpse of an abyss below.

"Why was Caroline afraid?" said Susan.

"*Caroline?*" he said, staring at her. "*Afraid!*" His blue eyes were brilliant with anxiety and excitement. "See here," he said, "if you think it was Caroline who killed Marie, it wasn't. She couldn't. She'd never have dared. I m-mean—" he was stammering in his excitement— "I mean, Caroline wouldn't hurt a fly. And Caroline wouldn't have opposed Marie about anything. Marie—you don't know what Marie was like."

"Exactly what happened in the upstairs hall?"

"You mean—when the shot—"

"Yes."

"Why, I—I was in my room—no, not quite—I was nearly at the door. And I heard the shot. And it's queer, but I believe—I believe I knew right away that it was a revolver shot. It was as if I had expected—" He checked himself. "But I *hadn't* expected—I—" He stopped; dug his fists desperately into his pockets and was suddenly firm and controlled— "But I hadn't actually expected it, you understand."

"Then when you heard the shot you turned, I suppose, and looked."

"Yes. Yes, I think so. Anyway, there was Caroline in the hall, too. I think she was screaming. We were both running. I thought of Marie—I don't know why. But Caroline clutched at me and held me. She didn't want me to go into Marie's room. She was terrified. And then I think you were there and Jessica. Were you?"

"Yes. And there was no one else in the hall? No one came from Marie's room?"

His face was perplexed, terribly puzzled.

"Nobody."

"Except—Caroline?"

"But I tell you it couldn't have been Caroline."

The doorbell began to ring—shrill sharp peals that stabbed the shadows and the thickness of the house.

"It's the police," thought Susan, catching her breath sharply. The boy beside her had straightened and was staring at the wide old door that must be opened.

Behind them on the padded stairway something rustled. "It's the police," said Jessica harshly. "Let them in."

Susan had not realized that there would be so many of them. Or that they would do so much. Or that an inquiry could last so long. She had not realized either how amazingly thorough they were with their photographs and their fingerprinting and their practiced and rapid and incredibly searching investigation. She was a little shocked and more than a little awed, sheerly from witnessing at first hand and with her own eyes what police actually did when there was murder.

Yet her own interview with Lieutenant Mohrn was not difficult. He was brisk, youthful, kind, and Jim Byrne was there to explain her presence. She had been very thankful to see Jim Byrne, who arrived on the heels of the police.

"Tell the police everything you know," he had said.

"But I don't know anything."

And it was Lieutenant Mohrn who, oddly enough, brought Susan into the very center and hub of the whole affair.

But that was later—much later. After endless inquiry, endless search, endless repetitions, endless conferences. Endless waiting in the gloomy dining room with portraits of dead and vanished Wrays staring fixedly down upon policemen. Upon Susan. Upon servants whose alibis had, Jim had informed her, been immediately and completely established.

It was close to one o'clock when Jim came to her again.

"See here," he said. "You look like a ghost. Have you had anything to eat?"

"No," said Susan.

A moment later she was in the kitchen, accepting provender that Jim Byrne brought from the icebox.

"You do manage to get things done," she said. "I thought newspapermen wouldn't even be permitted in the house."

"Oh, the police are all right—they'll give a statement to all of us—treat us right, you know. More cake? And don't forget I'm in on this case. Have you found out yet what Caroline was afraid of?"

"No. I've not had a chance to talk to her. Jim, who did it?"

He smiled mirthlessly.

"You're asking me! They've established, mainly, three things: the servants are clear; there was no one in the house besides Jessica and David and Caroline."

"And me," said Susan with a small shudder. "And—Marie."

"And you," agreed Jim imperturbably. "And Marie. Third, they can't find the gun. Jessica and you alibi each other. That leaves David and Caroline. Well—which of them did it? And why?"

"I don't know," she said. "But, Jim, I'm frightened."

"Frightened! With the house full of police? Why?"

"I don't know," said Susan again. "It's nothing I can explain. It's just—a queer kind of menace. Somewhere—somehow—in this house. It's like Marie—only Marie is dead and this is alive. Horribly alive." Susan knew she was incoherent and that Jim was staring at her worriedly, and suddenly the swinging door behind her opened, and Susan's heart leaped to her throat before the policeman spoke.

"The lieutenant wants you both, please," he said.

As they passed through the hall, the clock struck a single note that vibrated long afterward. It had been, then, eight hours and more since she had entered that wide door and been met by Jessica.

Lights were on everywhere now, and there were policemen, and the old-fashioned sliding doors between the hall and the drawing room had been closed, and they shut in the sound of voices.

"In there," said the policeman and drew back one of the doors.

It was entirely silent in the heavily furnished room. Lights were on in the chandelier above and it was eerily, dreadfully bright. The streaks showed in the faded brown-velvet curtains at the windows, and the wavery lines in the mantelpiece mirror, and the worn spots in the old Turkish rug. And every gray shadow on Jessica's face was darker, and the fine, sharp lines around Caroline's mouth and her haunted eyes showed terribly clear, and there were two bright-scarlet spots in David's cheeks. Lieutenant Mohrn had lost his look of youth and freshness and looked the weary, graying forty that he was. A detective in plain clothes was sitting on the small of his back in one of the slippery plush chairs.

The door slid together again behind them, and still no one spoke, although Jessica turned to look at them. And, oddly, Susan had a feeling that everything in that household had changed. Yet Jessica had not actually changed; her eyes met Susan's with exactly the same cold, remote command. Then what was it that was different?

Caroline—Susan's eyes went to the thin bent figure, hunched tragically on the edge of her chair. Her fine hair was in wisps about her face; her mouth tremulous.

Why, of course! It was not a change. It was merely that both Jessica and Caroline had become somehow intensified. They were both etched more sharply. The shadows were deeper, the lines blacker.

Lieutenant Mohrn turned to Caroline. "This is the young woman you refer to, isn't it, Miss Caroline?"

Caroline's eyes fluttered to Susan, avoided Jessica, and returned fascinated to Lieutenant Mohrn. "Yes—yes."

David whirled from the window and crossed to stand directly above Caroline.

"Look here, Aunt Caroline, you realize that whatever you tell Miss Dare she'll be bound to tell the police? It's just the same thing—you know that, don't you?"

"Oh, yes, David. That's what—*he*—said."

Lieutenant Mohrn cleared his throat abruptly and a bit uncomfortably.

"She understands that, Wray. I don't know why she won't tell me. But she won't. And she says she will talk to Miss Dare."

"Caroline," said Jessica, "is a fool." She moved rigidly to look at Caroline, who refused to meet her eyes, and said: "You'll find Caroline's got nothing to tell."

Caroline's eyes went wildly to the floor, to the curtains, to David, and both her hands fluttered to her trembling mouth.

"I'd rather talk to her," she said.

"Caroline," said Jessica, "you are behaving irrationally. You have been like this for days. You brought this—this Susan Dare into the house. You lied to me about her—told me it was a daughter of a school friend. I might have known you had no such intimate friend!" She shot a dark look at Susan and swept back to Caroline. "Now you've told the police that you were afraid and that you telephoned to a perfect stranger—"

"Jim Byrne," fluttered Caroline. "His father and my father—"

"That means nothing," said Jessica harshly. "Don't interrupt me. And then this young woman comes into our house. Why? Answer me, Caroline. Why?"

"I—was afraid—"

"Of what?"

"I—I—" Caroline stood, motioning frantically with her hands— "I'll tell. I'll tell Miss Dare. She'll know what to do."

"This is the situation, Miss Dare," said Lieutenant Mohrn patiently. "Miss Caroline has admitted that she was alarmed about something and why you are here. She has also admitted that there was an urgent and pressing problem that was causing dissension in the household. But she's—very tired, as you see—a little nervous, perhaps. And she says she is willing to tell, but that she prefers talking to you." He smiled wearily. "At any rate—it's asking a great deal of you, but will you hear what she has to tell? It's—a whim, of course." There was something friendly and kind in the look he gave Caroline. "But we'll humor her. And she understands—"

"I understand," said Caroline with a flash of decision. "But I don't want—anyone but Susan Dare."

"Nonsense, Caroline," said Jessica, "I have a right to hear. So has David."

Caroline's eyes, glancing this way and that to avoid Jessica, actually met Jessica's gaze, and she succumbed at once.

"Yes, Jessica," she said obediently.

"All right, then. Now, we are going outside, Miss Caroline. You can say anything you want to say. And remember we are here only to help." Lieutenant Mohrn paused at the sliding door, and Susan saw a look flash between him and Jim Byrne. She also saw Jim Byrne's hand go to his pocket and the brief little nod he gave the lieutenant.

"Do you mind if I stay in the room but out of earshot, Miss Jessica?" Jim asked.

"No," Jessica agreed grudgingly.

"We'll be just outside," said Lieutenant Mohrn, speaking to Jim. Something in his voice added: "Ready for any kind of trouble." She saw, too, the look in Jim's eyes as he glanced at her and then back to the lieutenant, and all at once she understood the meaning of that look and the meaning of his gesture toward his pocket. He had a revolver there, then. And the lieutenant was promising protection. But that meant that they were going to leave her alone with the Wrays. Alone with three people one of whom was a murderer.

But she was not entirely alone. Jim Byrne was there, in the far corner, his eyes wary and alert and his smile unperturbed.

"Very well now, Caroline," said Jessica. "Let's hear your precious story."

"It's about the house," began Caroline, looking at Susan as if she dared not permit her glance to swerve. "The police dragged it out of me—"

Jessica laughed harshly and interrupted.

"So that's your important evidence. I can tell it with less foolishness. It is simply that we have had an offer of a considerable sum of money for the purchase of this house. We happen to hold this house—all four of us—with equal interest. Thus it is necessary for us to agree before we can sell or otherwise dispose of the property. That's really all there is to it. Caroline and David wanted to sell. I didn't care."

"But Marie didn't want to sell," cried Caroline. "And Marie was stronger than any of us."

"Miss Caroline," said Susan softly. "Why were you afraid?"

For a dreadful second or two there was utter silence.

Then, as dreadfully, Caroline collapsed into her chair again and put her hands over her mouth and moaned.

But Jessica was ready to speak.

"She had nothing to be afraid of. She's merely nervous—very nervous. I know, Caroline, what you have been doing with every cent of money you could get your silly hands upon. But I intended to do nothing about it."

Caroline had given up her effort to avoid Jessica. She was staring at her like a terrified, panting bird.

"You—know" she gasped in a thin, high voice.

"Of course, I know. You are completely transparent, Caroline. I know that you were gambling away your inheritance—or at least what you could touch—"

"Gambling!" cried David. "What do you mean?"

"Stocks," said Jessica harshly. "Speculative stocks. It got her like a fever. Caroline has always been susceptible. So you have no money at all left, Caroline? Is that why you were so anxious to sell the house? You surely haven't been fool enough to buy on margin."

Caroline's distraught hands confessed what her trembling lips could not speak.

David was suddenly standing beside her, his hand on her thin shoulder.

"Don't worry, Aunt Carrie," he said. "It'll be all right. You've got enough in trust to take care of you."

Over Caroline's head he looked at Jessica. The look or the tenderness in his voice when he spoke to Caroline seemed to infuriate Jessica, and she arose amid a rustling of silk and stood there tall and rigid, facing him.

"Why don't you offer to take care of her yourself, David?" she said gratingly.

David was white, and his eyes brilliant with pain, but he replied steadily: "You know why, Aunt Jessica. And you know why she gambled, too. We were both trying to make enough money to get away. To get away from this house. To get away from—" He stopped.

"From what, David?" said Jessica.

"From Marie," said David desperately. "And from you."

Jessica did not move. Her face did not change. There was only a queer luminous flash in her eyes. After a horribly long moment she said:

"I loved you far better than Marie loved you, David. You feared her.

254

I intended to give you money when you came to me. You *had* to come to me. You would have begged me for help—me, Jessica! Why did you or Caroline kill Marie? Was it because she refused to sell the house? I know why she refused. She pretended that it was sentiment; that she, the adopted daughter, was more a Wray than any of us. But it wasn't that, really. She hated us. And we wanted to sell. That is, you and Caroline wanted to sell for your own selfish interests. I—it made no difference to me."

Caroline sobbed and cried jerkily:

"But you did care, Jessica. You wanted the money. You—you love money." There was a strangely incredulous wail in her thin voice. "*Money—money!* Not the things it will buy. Not the freedom it might give you. But money—bonds, mortgages, gold. You love money first, Jessica, and you—"

"*Caroline,*" said Jessica in a terrible voice. Caroline babbled and sobbed into silence. "Caroline, you are not responsible. You forget that there are strangers here. That Marie has been murdered. Try to collect yourself. At once. You are making a disgusting exhibition."

All three looked at Susan.

And as suddenly as they had been diverted from each other they were, for a moment, united in their feeling against Susan. She was the intruder, the instrument of the police, placed there by the law for the purpose of discovering evidence.

Their eyes were not pleasant.

Susan smoothed back her hair, and she was acutely aware of the small telegram of warning that ran along her nerves. One of them had murdered. She turned to Caroline.

"Then were you afraid that Marie would discover what you had been doing with your money?" she asked gently.

Caroline blinked and was immediately ready to reply, her momentary feeling against Susan disseminated by the small touch of kindness in Susan's manner.

"No," she said in a confidential way. "That wasn't what I was afraid of."

"Then was there something unusual about the house? Something that troubled you?"

"Oh, yes, yes," said Caroline.

"What was it?" asked Susan, scarcely daring to breathe. If only Jessica would remain silent for another moment.

But Caroline was fluttering again.

"I don't know. I don't know. You see, it was all so queer, Marie holding out against us all, and we all—except Jessica sometimes—

obeyed Marie. We've always obeyed Marie. Everything in the house has done that. Even Spider—the—the monkey, you know."

Susan permitted her eyes to flicker toward Jessica. She stood immovable, watching David. Susan could not interpret that dark look, and she did not try. Instead she leaned over to Caroline, took her fluttering, ineffectual hands, and said, still gently: "Tell me exactly why you telephoned to Jim Byrne. What was it that happened in the morning—or maybe the night before—that made you afraid?"

"How did you know?" said Caroline. "It happened that night."

"What was it?" said Susan so softly that it was scarcely more than a whisper.

But Caroline quite suddenly swerved.

"I wasn't afraid of Marie," she said. "But everyone obeyed Marie. Even the house always seemed more Marie's house than—than Jessica's. But I didn't kill Marie."

"Tell me," repeated Susan. "What happened last night that was—queer?"

"Caroline," said Jessica harshly, dragging herself back from some deep brooding gulf, "you've said enough."

Susan ignored her and held Caroline's feverishly bright eyes with her own. "Tell me—"

"It was—Marie—" gasped Caroline.

"Marie—what did she do?" said Susan.

"She didn't do anything," said Caroline. "It was what she said. No, it wasn't that exactly. It was—"

"If you insist upon talking, Caroline, you might at least try to be intelligible," said Jessica coldly.

Could she get Jessica out of the room? thought Susan; probably not. And it was all too obvious that she was standing by, permitting Caroline to talk only so long as Caroline said nothing that she, Jessica, did not want her to say. Susan said quietly: "Did you hear Marie speak?"

"Yes, that was just it," cried Caroline eagerly. "And it was so very queer. That is, of course we—that is, I—have often thought that Marie must be about the house much more than she pretended to be, in order to know all the things she knew. That is, she always knew everything that happened in the house. It—sometimes it was queer, you know, because it was like—like magic or something. It was quite," said Caroline with an unexpected burst of imagery, "as if she had one of those astral-body things, and it walked all around the house while Marie just sat there in her room."

"Astral—body—things," said Jessica deliberately. Caroline crimsoned and Jessica's hands gestured outward as much as to say: "You see for yourself what a state she's in."

The old room was silent again. Susan's heart was pounding, and again those small tocsins of warning were sounding in some subconscious realm. All those forces were silently, invisibly combating—struggling against each other. And somewhere amid them was the truth—quite tangible—altogether real.

"But the astral body," said Caroline suddenly into the silence, "couldn't have talked. And I heard Marie speak. She was in Jessica's room, and the door was closed, and I heard her talking to Jessica. And then—that's what's queer—I went straight on past the door and into Marie's room, and there was Marie sitting there. Isn't it queer?"

"Why were you frightened?"

"Because—because—" Caroline's hands twisted together. "I don't know why. Except that I had a—a feeling."

"Nonsense," Jessica laughed. There was again the luminous flash in her shadowed eyes, and she spoke more rapidly than usual. "You see, Susan Dare, how nonsensical all this is. How utterly fantastic!"

"There was Marie," said Caroline. "She was talking to you."

Jessica's silks rustled, and she walked rigidly and quickly to Caroline and leaned over so that she could grip Caroline's shoulder and force Caroline to meet her eyes. David tried to intervene, and she brushed him away and said hoarsely:

"Caroline, you poor little fool. You thought you'd get this young woman here and try to establish your innocence of the crime. All this talk is sheer nonsense. You are cunning after the way of fools such as you. Tell me this, Caroline—" She paused long enough to take a great gasp of breath. She was more powerful, more invincible than Susan had seen her. "Tell me. Where was David when the revolver was fired?"

Caroline was shrinking backward. David said quickly: "She'll say anything to protect me. She'll say anything, and you—"

"Be quiet, David. Caroline, answer me."

"He was at the door of his room," said Caroline.

For a long moment Jessica waited. Then with terrible deliberation she relaxed her grip and straightened and looked slowly from one to the other.

"You've as good as confessed, Carrie," she said. "There was no one else. You admit that it was not David. Why did you kill her, Carrie?"

"She didn't kill her!" David was between the two women, his face white and his eyes blazing. "It was you, Jessica. You—"

"*David! Stop!*" The two sharp exclamations were like lashes. "I was here in this room when the shot was fired. I didn't kill Marie. I couldn't have killed her. You know that. Come, Caroline."

She put her gray hand upon Caroline's shoulder. Caroline, as if mesmerized by that touch, arose, and Jessica turned to the doorway. No one moved as the two women crossed the room. Jim Byrne glanced at Susan unrevealingly and then, at Jessica's imperious gesture, opened the door. Susan was vaguely aware that there were men in the hall outside, but she was held as if enchanted by the extraordinary scene she was witnessing.

No one moved, and there was no sound save the rustle of Jessica's silks while she led Caroline to the stairway. At the bottom step Jessica turned, and there was suddenly something less harsh in her face; it was for an instant almost kind, and there was a queer sort of tenderness in the pressure of her hand upon Caroline's shrinking shoulder.

But that hand was nevertheless compelling.

"Go upstairs," she said to Caroline, in a voice loud enough so that they all heard. "Go upstairs and do what is necessary. There's enough veronal on my dresser. We'll give you time."

She turned as if to barricade the stairway with her own rigid body and looked slowly and defiantly around her. "I'll *make them* give you time, Carrie. *Go on.*"

There was the complete and utter silence of sheer horror. And in that silence something small and gray and quick flashed down from the curtain and up the stairs.

"Holy Mother," cried someone. "What was that?"

And David sprang forward.

"You can't do that—you can't do that! Caroline, don't move—" Susan knew that he was thrusting himself between Jessica and Caroline, that there was sudden confusion. But she was mainly aware of something that had clicked in her own mind.

Somehow she got through the confusion in the hall to Lieutenant Mohrn, and Jim Byrne was at her side. Both of them listened to the brief words she said; Lieutenant Mohrn ran rapidly upstairs, and Jim disappeared toward the dining room.

Jim was back first. He pulled Susan to one side.

"You are right," he said. "The cook and the houseman both say that Marie was very strict about the monkey and that the monkey always obeyed her. But what do you mean?"

"I'm not sure, Jim. But I've just told Lieutenant Mohrn that I think there should be a bullet hole somewhere upstairs. It was made by the second bullet. It is in the ceiling, perhaps—or wall. I think it's in Jessica's room."

Lieutenant Mohrn was coming down the stairway. He reached the bottom of the stairs and looked wearily and a bit sadly at the group there. At Caroline crumpled against the wall. At David white and taut. At Jessica, a rigid figure of hatred. Then he sighed and looked at the policeman nearest him and nodded.

"Will you go into the drawing room, please?" he asked Susan. "And you, Jim."

The doors slid together and, still wearily, Lieutenant Mohrn pulled out from his pocket a revolver, a long cord, a piece of cotton, and a small alarm clock.

"They were all there hidden in the newel post at the top of the stairway. The carved top was loose as you remembered it, Miss Dare. And there's two shots gone from the revolver, and there's a bullet hole in the wall of Jessica's bedroom. How did you know it was Jessica, Miss Dare?"

"It was the monkey," said Susan. Her voice sounded unnatural in her own ears, terribly tired, terribly sad. "It was the monkey all the time. You see, he was sitting there, stealing candy *right beside Marie's chair.* He would have been afraid to do that if he had not known she was dead. And when Jessica entered the room he fled. When I thought of that, the whole thing fell together: the hot house, obviously to keep Marie's body warm and confuse the time of death; everyone out of the house to permit Jessica to do murder; then this thing you've found—"

"It's simple, of course," said Lieutenant Mohrn. "The cord fastened tight between the alarm lever and the trigger—the bit of cotton to pad the alarm. The clock is set for ten minutes after five. When did she hide it in the newel post?"

"When I went down to telephone the police, I suppose, and David and Caroline were in Marie's room—I want to go home," said Susan wearily.

"Look here," said Jim Byrne. "This sounds all right, Susan, but remember, Marie couldn't have been dead then. You heard her talk."

"I had never heard her speak before. And I heard the flat, dead tone of a person who has been deaf a long time. It was Caroline who actually solved the thing. And Jessica knew it. She knew it and at once tried to fasten the blame upon Caroline—to compel her to commit suicide."

"What did Caroline say?" Lieutenant Mohrn was very patient.

"She said that she'd heard Marie speaking with Jessica in Jessica's room behind a closed door. And that she'd gone straight on past that door to Marie's room and found Marie sitting there. Caroline was confused, frightened, talked of astral bodies. Naturally, we knew that Jessica was—rehearsing—her imitation of Marie's way of speaking."

"Premeditated," said Jim. "Planned to the last detail. And your coming merely gave her the opportunity. You were to provide the alibi, Susan."

Susan shivered.

"That was the trouble. She was sitting directly opposite me when the shot was fired upstairs. Yet she was the only person who hated Marie sufficiently to—murder her. It wasn't money. It was hatred. Growing for years in this horrible house, nourished by jealousy over David, brought to a climax that was inevitable." Susan smoothed her hair. "Please may I go?"

"Then Marie was dead when you entered the house?"

"Yes. Propped up by pillows. I—I saw the whole thing, you know. Saw Jessica approach her and talk, heard the reply—and how was I to know it was Jessica speaking and not Marie? Then Jessica bent and did something to her cushions, pulled them away, I suppose, so the body was ro longer erect. And she turned at once and was between me and Marie all the way to the door so I could not see Marie, then, at all. (I couldn't see Marie very well at any time, because she was in the shadow.) And when David and Caroline came upstairs, Jessica warned both of them that Marie was reading. I suppose she knew that they were only too glad to be relieved of the necessity to speak to Marie." Susan shivered again and smoothed back her hair and felt dreadfully that she might cry. "It's a t-terrible house," she said indecisively, and Jim Byrne said hurriedly:

"She can go now, can't she? I've got a car out here. She doesn't have to see them again."

The air was cold and fresh and the sky very black before dawn, and the pavements glistened.

They swerved onto the Drive and stopped for a red light, and Jim turned to her as they waited. Through the dusk in the car she could feel his scrutiny.

"I didn't expect anything like this," he said gravely. "Will you forgive me?"

"Next time," said Susan in a small clear voice, "I'll not get scared."

"Next time!" said Jim derisively. "There won't be a next time! I was the one that was scared. I had my finger on the trigger of a revolver all the time you were talking to them. No, indeedy, there won't be a next time—not if I can help it!"

ERLE STANLEY GARDNER

(1889–1970)

||||||||||||||||||||||||||||||||||||||||||||||| ■ |||||||||||||||||||||||||||||||||||||||||||||||

Although Erle Stanley Gardner didn't turn to writing until he reached the relatively ripe age of thirty-four, when he died at age eighty-one on his California ranch, 141 of his books were in print and 5 more were awaiting publication. By 1986, a staggering 319 million copies of his books had been sold in thirty-seven languages, making him one of the most popular writers of fiction ever. The Mystery Writers of America made it official by declaring him a Grand Master in 1962.

Gardner was born in Malden, Massachusetts, the son of an engineer whose work moved him to Oregon and then California—a state that the boy loved and the man used as the base of his fiction. As a youth, he boxed professionally and promoted boxing bouts and, reputedly, was expelled from college for slugging a professor. He educated himself by reading law books and helping an attorney, passed the bar exam at twenty-one, and established a reputation as a canny defense attorney. He learned the writing trade in the same way—reading and studying the work of others in the field.

Gardner had been writing prolifically for ten years before he published the first of the Perry Mason series. His huge output for the pulps introduced numerous characters, including Speed Dash, a detective who can scale the sides of buildings in the event that a door is locked, and the armchair detective Lester Leith, whose specialty is solving jewel thefts by means of reading newspaper accounts.

Mason is introduced in *The Case of the Velvet Claws*. In this novel, Mason deduces that dampness around an umbrella stand means that a witness was at the murder scene when he said he was. He thereby saves an obnoxious character and makes the point that justice and law are more important than personal considerations. Gardner's knowledge of and respect for criminal law form a thread that runs through all the Mason books.

Gardner created other series characters with legal connections. Middle-aged sleuth Bertha Cool teams up with Donald Lam, a disbarred attorney whose legal advice helps to solve cases. Gardner used district attorney Doug Selby to illustrate his appreciation of the prosecution's outlook on crime.

"Leg Man" also features a character from the world of law. The story is unusual in that it puts the legal assistant at center stage as protagonist. It is typical of Gardner's work in its use of canny tricks and an eye for detail to solve the mystery.

1938

_____

Leg Man

■

Mae Devers came into my office with the mail. She stood by my chair for a moment putting envelopes on the desk, pausing to make little adjustments of the inkwell and paper weights, tidying things up a bit.

There was a patent-leather belt around her waist, and below that belt I could see the play of muscles as her supple figure moved from side to side. I slid my arm around the belt and started to draw her close to me.

"Don't get fresh!" she said, trying to pull my hand away, but not trying too hard.

"Listen, I have work to do," she said. "Let me loose, Pete."

"Holding you for ransom, smile-eyes," I told her.

She suddenly bent down. Her lips formed a hot circle against mine—and Cedric L. Boniface had to choose that moment to come busting into my office without knocking.

Mae heard the preliminary rattle of the door-knob, and scooped up a bunch of papers from the desk. I ran fingers through my hair, and Boniface cleared his throat in his best professional manner.

I couldn't be certain whether I had any lipstick on my mouth, so I put my elbow on my desk, covered my mouth with the fingers of my hand and stared intently at an open law book.

Mae Devers said, "Very well, Mr. Wennick, I'll see that it gets in the mail," and started for the door. As she passed Boniface, she turned and gave me a roguish glance, as much as to say, "Now, smartie, see what you've got yourself into."

Boniface stared at me, hard. His yellowish eyes, with the bluish-white eyeballs, reminded me of hard-boiled eggs which had been peeled and cut in two lengthwise. He was in a vile humor.

"What was all the commotion about?" he asked.

"Commotion?" I inquired raising my eyes, but keeping my hand to my mouth. "Where?"

"In here," he said.

Mae Devers was just closing the door. "Did you hear anything, Miss Devers?" I asked in my most dignified manner.

"No, sir," she said demurely, and slipped out into the corridor.

I frowned down at the open law book on the desk. "I can't seem to make any sense out of the distinction between a bailment of the first class and a bailment of the second class."

That mollified Boniface somewhat. He loved to discourse on the academic legal points which no one else ever gave a damn about.

"The distinction," he said, "is relatively simple, if you can keep from becoming confused by the terminology. Primarily, the matter of consideration is the determining factor in the classification of all bailments."

"Yes, sir," I said, my voice muffled behind my hand.

Boniface stared at me. "Wennick," he said, "there's something queer about your connection with this firm. You're supposed to be studying law. You're supposed to make investigations. You're a cross between a sublimated law clerk and a detective. It just happens, however, that in checking over our income tax, I find that the emoluments which have been paid you during the past three months would fix your salary at something over fifteen thousand dollars a year."

There was nothing I could say to that, so I kept quiet.

Mae Devers opened the door and said, "Mr. Jonathan wants to see you at once, Mr. Wennick."

I got out of the chair as though it had been filled with tacks and said, "I'm coming at once. Excuse me, Mr. Boniface."

Mae Devers stood in the doorway which led to the general offices and laughed at me as I jerked out a handkerchief and wiped lipstick from my mouth. "That," she told me, "is what you get for playing around."

I didn't have time to say anything. When old E. B. Jonathan sent word that he wanted to see me at once, it meant that he wanted to see me at once. Cedric L. Boniface followed me to the door of my office and stared meditatively down the corridor as though debating with himself whether or not to invade the sanctity of E. B.'s office to pursue the subject further. I popped into E. B.'s private office like a rabbit making its burrow two jumps ahead of a fox.

Old E. B. looked worse than ever this morning. His face was the color of skimmed milk. There were pouches underneath his tired eyes as big as my fist. His face was puckered up into the acrimonious expression of one who has just bit into a sour lemon.

"Lock the door, Wennick," he said.

I locked the door.

"Take a seat."

I sat down.

"Wennick," he said, "we're in a devil of a mess."

I sat there, waiting for him to go on.

"There was some question over certain deductions in my income tax statement," he said. "Without thinking, I told Mr. Boniface to brief the point. That made it necessary for him to consult the income tax return, and he saw how much you'd been paid for the last three months."

"So he was just telling me," I said.

"Well," E. B. said, "it's embarrassing. I need Boniface in this business. He can spout more academic law than a college professor, and he's so damn dumb he doesn't know that I'm using him for a stuffed shirt. No one would ever suspect him of being implicated in the—er, more spectacular methods which you use to clean up the cases on which he's working."

"Yes," I conceded, "the man's a veritable talking encyclopedia of law."

E. B. said, "We'll have to handle it some way. If he asks you any questions, tell him it's a matter you'd prefer to have him discuss with me. Wennick! Is that lipstick on the corner of your mouth?"

Mechanically, I jerked a handkerchief out of my pocket to the corner of my mouth. "No, sir," I said, "just a bit of red crayon I was using to mark up that brief and . . ."

I stopped as I saw E. B.'s eyes on the handkerchief. It was a red smear. There was no use lying to the old buzzard now. I stuck the handkerchief back in my pocket and said, "Hell, yes, it's lipstick."

"Miss Devers, I presume," he said dryly.

I didn't say anything.

"I'm afraid," he said, "it's going to be necessary to dispense with her services. At the time I hired her, I thought she was just a bit too— er, voluptuous. However, she was so highly recommended by the employment agency that—"

"It's all right," I said. "Go ahead and fire her."

"You won't mind?"

"Certainly not," I told him. "I can get a job some other place and get one for her at the same time."

"Now, wait a minute, Wennick," he said, "don't misunderstand me. I'm very well satisfied with your services, if you could only learn to leave women alone."

I decided I might as well give him both barrels. "Listen," I said, "you think women are poison. I think they're damned interesting. The only reason I'm not going to ask you whether the rumor is true that you're paying simultaneous alimony to two wives is that I don't think I have any business inquiring into your private life, and the only reason I'm not going to sit here and talk about my love life is that I know damned well you haven't any business prying into mine."

His long, bony fingers twisted restlessly, one over the other, as he wrapped his fists together. Then he started cracking his knuckles, one at a time.

"Wennick," he said at length, "I have great hopes for your future. I hate to see you throw yourself away on the fleeting urge of a biological whim."

"All right," I told him, "I won't."

He finished his ten-knuckle salute and shook his head lugubriously. "They'll get you in the long run, Wennick," he said.

"I'm not interested in long runs," I told him. "I like the sprints."

He sighed, unlaced his fingers and got down to business. "The reason I'm particularly concerned about this, Wennick, is that the case I'm going to send you out on involves a woman, a very attractive woman. Unless I'm sadly mistaken, she is a very vital woman, very much alive, very—er, amorous."

"Who is she?" I asked.

"Her name is Pemberton, Mrs. Olive Pemberton. Her husband's Harvey C. Pemberton, of the firm of Bass & Pemberton, Brokers, in Culverton."

"What does she want?" I asked.

"Her husband's being taken for a ride."

"What sort of a ride?"

He let his cold eyes regard me in a solemn warning. "A joy ride, Pete."

"Who's the woman?"

Old E. B. consulted a memo. "Her name is Diane Locke—and she's redheaded."

"What do I do?"

"You find some way to spike her guns. Apparently she has an iron-clad case against Pemberton. I'll start Boniface working on it. He'll puzzle out some legal technicality on which he'll hang a defense. But you beat him to it by spiking her guns."

"Has the redhead filed suit?" I asked.

"Not yet," E. B. said. "At present it's in the milk-and-honey stage. She's getting ready to tighten the screws, and Mrs. Pemberton has employed us to see that this other woman doesn't drain her husband's pocketbook with this threatened suit. Incidentally, you're to stay at the Pemberton house, and remember, Mr. Pemberton doesn't know his wife is wise to all this and is trying to stop it."

"Just how," I asked, "do I account for my presence to Mr. Harvey C. Pemberton?"

"You're to be Mrs. Pemberton's brother."

"How do you figure that?"

"Mrs. Pemberton has a brother living in the West. Her husband has never seen him. Fortunately, his name also is Peter, so you won't have any difficulty over names."

"Suppose," I asked, "the real brother shows up while I'm there at the house?"

"He won't," E. B. said. "All you have to do is to go to the door at seven-thirty this evening. She'll be waiting for your ring. She'll come to the door and put on all the act that's necessary. You'll wear a red carnation in your left coat lapel so there'll be no mistake. Her maiden name, by the way, was Crowe. You'll be Peter Crow, sort of a wandering ne'er-do-well brother. The husband knows all about you by reputation."

"And hasn't seen any pictures or anything?" I asked.

"Apparently not," E. B. said.

"It sounds like a plant to me," I told him dubiously.

"I'm quite certain it's all right," he said. "I have collected a substantial retainer."

"O.K.," I told him, "I'm on my way."

"Pete," he called, as I placed my hand on the door.

"What is it?"

"You'll be discreet," he warned.

I turned to give him a parting shot. "I certainly hope I'll be able to," I said, "but I doubt it," and pulled the door shut behind me.

I looked at my wrist watch, saw I had three minutes to go, and put the red carnation in the left lapel of my coat. I'd already spotted the house. It was a big, rambling affair which oozed an atmosphere of suburban prosperity. I took it that Bass & Pemberton, Brokers, had an income which ran into the upper brackets.

I jerked down my vest, adjusted the knot in my tie, smoothed the point of my collar, and marched up the front steps promptly at seven-thirty. I jabbed the bell. I heard slow, dignified masculine steps in the corridor. That wasn't what E. B. had led me to expect. I wondered for a moment if there'd been a hitch in plans and I was going to have to face the husband. The door opened. I took one look at the sour puss on the guy standing in the doorway and knew he was the butler. He was looking at me as a judge looks at a murderer when I heard a feminine squeal and caught a flying glimpse of a woman with jet-black hair, dusky olive complexion and a figure that would get by anywhere. She gave a squeal of delight and flung her arms around my neck.

"Pete!" she screamed. "Oh, Pete, you darling. You dear! I knew you'd look me up if you ever came near here."

The butler stepped back and coughed. The woman hugged me, jumped up and down in an ecstasy of glee, then said, "Let me look at you." She stepped back, her hands on my shoulders, her eyes studying me.

Up to that point, it had been rehearsed, but the rest of it wasn't. I saw approval in her eyes, a certain trump-this-ace expression, and she tilted her head to offer me her lips.

I don't know just what E. B. referred to as being discreet. I heard the butler cough more violently. I guess he didn't know she had a brother. I let her lead. She led with an ace. I came up for air, to see a short-coupled chap with a tight vest regarding me from brown, mildly surprised eyes. Back of him was a tall guy fifteen years older, with fringes of what had once been red hair around his ears. The rest of his dome was bald. He had a horse face, and the march of time had done things to it. It was a face which showed character.

Mrs. Pemberton said, "Pete, you've never met my husband."

The chunky chap stepped forward and I shoved out my hand. "Well, well, well," I said, "so this is Harvey. How are you, Harvey?"

"And Mr. Bass, my husband's partner," she said.

I shook hands with the tall guy "Pete Crowe, my rolling-stone brother," Mrs. Pemberton observed. "Where's your baggage, Pete?"

"I left it down at the station," I told her.

She laughed nervously and said, "It's just like you to come without sending a wire. We'll drive down and pick up your baggage."

"Got room for me?" I asked.

"Have we!" she exclaimed. "I've just been dying to see you. Harvey is so busy with his mergers and his horrid old business that I don't ever get a chance to see him any more. You're a God-send."

Harvey put his arm around his wife's waist. "There, there, little girl," he said, "it won't be much longer, and then we'll take a vacation. We can go for a cruise somewhere. How about the South Seas?"

"Is that a promise?" she asked.

"That's a promise," he told her so solemnly I felt certain he was lying.

"You've made promises before," she pouted, "but something new always came up in the business."

"Well, it won't come up this time. I'll even sell the business before I get in another spell of work like this."

I caught him glancing significantly at his partner.

"We've just finished dinner," Mrs. Pemberton explained to me, "and Mr. Bass and my husband are going back to their stuffy old office. How about going down and picking up your baggage now?"

"Anything you say," I told her, leaving it up to her to take the lead.

"Come on then," she invited. "Harvey's car is out front. Mine's in the garage. We'll go get it out. Oh, you darling! I'm so glad to see you!" And she went into another clinch.

Harvey Pemberton regarded me with a patronizing smile. "Olive's told me a lot about you, Pete," he said. "I'm looking forward to a chance to talk with you."

Bass took a cigar from his pocket. "Is Pete the one who did all the big game hunting down in Mexico?" he asked.

"That's the one," Mrs. Pemberton told him.

Bass said, "You and I must have a good long chat some time, young man. I used to be a forest ranger when I was just out of school. I was located up in the Upper Sespe, and the Pine Mountain country. I suppose you know the section."

"I've hunted all over it," I said.

He nodded. "I was ranger there for three years. Well, come on, Harvey, let's go down and go over those figures."

"We go out the back way," Olive Pemberton told me, grabbing my hand and hurrying me out a side door. She skipped on ahead toward the garage. "Hurry," she said. "They have a conference on at their office and I want to hear what it's about."

She jerked open the garage door. I helped her into the car and she smiled her thanks as she adjusted herself in the seat. "I like my feet free when I'm driving," she said, pulling her skirt up to her knees.

She had pretty legs.

I climbed in beside her and she started the motor. We went out of there like a fire wagon charging down the main stem of a hick town. Her husband and Bass were just getting into their car as we hit the incline to the street. The car flattened down on its springs, then shot up in the air. I hung on. I heard rubber scream as she spun the wheel, waved her hand to her husband, and went streaking down the street.

"You always drive like that?" I asked.

"Most of the time," she said. "Sometimes I go faster."

"No wonder you want your feet free," I told her.

She glanced down at her legs, then her eyes were back on the road. "I want to beat them there," she explained. "I've bribed the janitor and I have an office next to theirs." She stepped harder on the gas, angrily.

"Hope I didn't scare you with my greeting," she said, with a sidelong glance. "I had to act cordial, you know."

"I like cordiality," I told her. "It becomes you."

She gave attention to her driving. It was the sort of driving which needed lots of attention. She reached the business section of town, hogged the traffic, crowded the signals at the intersections, and whipped the car into a parking lot. She said, "Come on, Pete," and led the way toward a seven-story building which apparently was the town's best in the way of office buildings.

"It's fortunate your name's really Pete," she commented as we entered the building.

I nodded and let it go at that. I was sizing her up out of the corner of my eye. She was one of these supple women who seem to be just about half panther. She must have been around thirty-two or three, but her figure and walk were what you'd expect to find on a woman in the early twenties. There was a peculiar husky note to her voice, and her eyes were just a little bit more than provocative.

The night elevators were on. The janitor came up in response to her ring. His face lit up like a Christmas tree when he saw her. He looked over at me and looked dubious.

"It's all right, Olaf," she said. "This man's helping me. Hurry up because my husband's coming."

We got in the cage. Olaf slammed the door and sent us rattling upward, his eyes feasting on Olive's profile. I've seen dogs look at people with exactly that same expression—inarticulate love and a dumb, blind loyalty.

He let us out at the sixth floor. "This way," she said, and walked on ahead of me down the corridor.

I noticed the swing of her hips as she walked. I think she wanted me to—not that she gave a particular damn about me, she was simply one of those women who like to tease the animals—or was she making a play for me?

"No chance of the janitor selling you out?" I asked as she fitted a key in the lock.

"No," she said.

"You seem to have a lot of faith in human nature," I told her, as she clicked back the lock and snapped on lights in the office.

"I have," she told me, "in masculine nature. Men always play fair with me. It's women who double-cross me. I hate women."

The office was bare of furnishings, save for a battered stenographer's desk, a couple of straightback chairs, an ash-tray and waste basket. Wires ran down from a hole in the plaster, to terminate in an electrical gadget. She opened a drawer in the desk, took out two head pieces and handed me one. "When you hear my husband come in the next office," she said, "plug that in, and remember what you hear. I think things are coming to a show-down tonight."

I sat across from her and nursed the last of my cigarette. "Anything in particular I'm supposed to do about it?" I asked.

"Of course," she said.

"What?" I asked.

"That's up to you."

"Want me to bust things up with a club?" I asked.

She studied me with her dark, seductive eyes. "I may as well be frank with you," she said in that rich, throaty voice. "I don't care a thing in the world about my husband. I don't think he cares any more about me. A separation is inevitable. When it happens I want my share of the property."

"What's the property?" I asked her.

"Mostly a partnership interest," she said. "He's a free spender and he's been stepping around high, wide and handsome. After a man gets to be forty-three and starts stepping around, it takes money.

"So far, he's been just a mild sugar daddy. I haven't cared particularly just so there was plenty for me to spend. But now he's put his neck in a noose. This Diane Locke is shrewd. She's too damn shrewd, or maybe somebody with brains is back of her. I think it must be a lawyer somewhere. Anyway, they have Harvey over a barrel. He needs money, lots of money. The only way he can get it is to sell his partnership interest. You heard that crack he made about selling out so he could take me on a cruise."

I nodded.

"Well," she said, "if that's what's in the wind, I'm going to throw a lot of monkey wrenches in that machinery."

I did a little thinking. "The redhead," I said, "might open her bag, take out a nice, pearl-handled gun, and go rat-a-tat-tat. They have been known to do that, you know."

It was just a feeler. I wanted to see what she'd say. She said it. "That's all right, too. There's a big life insurance policy in my favor. But what I don't want is to have him stripped. He—Here they come now."

I heard the elevator door clang. There were steps in the corridor, then I heard keys rattling and the door in the adjoining office creaked back and I heard the click of the light switch. Mrs. Pemberton nodded to me, and I plugged in the jack and put the ear pieces over my head. She snapped a switch, and I could hear faint humming noises in the ear pieces. Then I heard a voice that I recognized as Bass' saying, "But, Harvey, why the devil do you want to sell out?"

"I want to play a little bit," Harvey Pemberton said. "I want to have a real honeymoon with my wife before I'm too old to enjoy it. We've never traveled. I married her four years ago, when we were putting through that big hotel deal. And I've had my nose pushed against the grindstone ever since. We never had a honeymoon."

"What are you going to do after you get back?"

"I don't know."

"You could arrange things so you could take a honeymoon without selling out," Bass said. "I hate to lose you as a partner, Harvey."

"No, I wouldn't leave a business behind in which I had all my money tied up," Pemberton said. "I'd worry about it so I'd be a rotten companion. I want to step out footloose and fancy-free."

"One of the reasons I don't want you to do it right now," Bass said, is that I'm rather short of money myself. I couldn't offer you anywhere near what your interest in the business is worth."

"What could you offer?" Pemberton said, an edge to his voice.

"I don't know," I heard Bass say.

"Oh, come," Pemberton told him impatiently. "You can't pull that stuff with me, Arthur. I told you this afternoon that I wanted to figure on some sort of a deal. You've had all afternoon to think it over."

There was silence for several seconds, and I gathered that Bass was, perhaps, making figures on paper. I heard Harvey Pemberton say, "I'm going to have an accountant work up a statement showing the status of the business and—"

"That doesn't have anything to do with it," Bass said. "It's not a question of what the business is worth, it's a question of what I can afford to pay without jeopardizing my working capital. I'll tell you frankly, Harvey, that I don't want you to sell. I don't want to lose you as a partner and you can't get anything like a fair value for your holdings at the present time. There's no one else you can sell them to. Under our articles of partnership, one partner has to give the other six months' notice before—"

"I understand all that," Pemberton said impatiently. "What's the price?"

"Ten thousand," Bass said.

"Ten thousand!" Pemberton shouted. "My God, you're crazy! The business is worth fifty thousand. I'm going to have an audit made in order to determine a fair figure. But I know my share's worth twenty-five. I'll take twenty for it, and that's the lowest price I'll even consider."

There was relief in Bass' voice. "That settles it then and I'm glad to hear it! You know, Pemberton, I was afraid you were in a jam over money matters and might have considered ten thousand dollars. It would be an awful mistake. I don't want you to sell."

Pemberton started to swear. Bass said, "Well, I'm glad we have an understanding on that, Harvey. Of course, I wouldn't try to exert any pressure to hold you here. In some ways it would be a good business deal for me to buy you out now. But I don't want to do it, either for my sake or yours. I'd have paid you every cent I could have scraped up, but—well, I'm glad you're staying. The business needs you, and I need you, and you need the business. Well, I'll be going. See you later. Good night."

Over the electrical gadget came the sound of a slamming door. Pemberton yelled, "Come back here, Arthur! I want to talk with you," but there was no other sound. I exchanged glances with our client.

"You see," she said, "he's trying to sell the business. That vamp would get most of the money. He'd probably run away with her. I want you to stop that."

"What's the program now?" I asked.

"I think he has an appointment with her," she said. "The janitor told me that he'd left instructions to pass a young woman to his office."

Pretty soon I heard the clang of the elevator door, and light, quick steps in the corridor past our door, then a gentle tapping on the panels of the adjoining office. I put the head phones back on, and heard the sound of a door opening and closing.

"Did you bring the letters?" Harvey Pemberton asked.

A woman's voice said, "Don't be such an old granny. Kiss me, and quit worrying about the letters. They're in a safe place."

"You said you could put your hand on them any time," Pemberton charged, "and were going to bring them here to show me just what I'd written."

"I brought you copies instead," she said. "My lawyer wouldn't let me take the originals."

"Why not?"

"I don't know. I guess he doesn't trust me. Harvey, I don't want you to think that I'm utterly mercenary, but you broke my heart. It isn't money I'm after, dear, I want you. But you hurt me, and I went to that horrid lawyer, and he had me sign some papers, and now it seems I have to go through with it, unless you go away with me. That's what I want."

"*My* lawyer tells me you can't sue a married man for breach of promise," Pemberton interrupted. "I think your lawyer is a shyster who's trying to stir up trouble and turn you into a blackmailer."

"No, he isn't, Harvey. There's some wrinkle in the law. If a girl doesn't know a man's married and he conceals that fact from her, why then he can be sued for breach of promise, just the same as though he hadn't been married. Oh, Harvey, I don't want to deal with all these lawyers! I want you. Can't you divorce that woman and come with me?"

"Apparently not," Harvey Pemberton said. "Since you've been such a little fool and signed your life away to this lawyer, he isn't going to let me get free. There's enough stuff in those letters to keep me from getting a divorce from my wife, and she won't get a divorce from me unless I turn over everything in the world to her. She wants to strip me clean. You want to do almost that."

For a moment there was silence, then the sound of a woman sobbing.

Pemberton started speaking again. His voice rose and fell at regular intervals, and I gathered he was walking the floor and talking as he walked. "Go ahead and sob," he said. "Sit there and bawl into your handkerchief! And if you want to know it, it looks fishy as hell to me. When I first met you on that steamboat, you didn't have any of this bawling complex. You wanted to play around."

"You w-w-wanted to m-m-marry me!" she wailed.

"All right," he told her, "I was on the up-and-up on that, too. I thought my wife was going to get a divorce. Hell's fire, I didn't *have* to use marriage for bait. You know that. That came afterward. Then, when I break a date with you because of a business deal, you rush up to see this lawyer."

"I went to him as a friend," she said in a wailing, helpless voice. "I'd known him for years. He told me you'd been t-t-trifling with me and I should get r-revenge. After all, all I want is just enough to get me b-b-back on my feet once more."

Pemberton said, "Add that to what your lawyer wants, and see where that leaves me. Why the hell don't you ditch the lawyer?"

"I c-can't. He made me sign papers."

Once more there was silence, then Pemberton said, "How the hell do I know you're on the level? You could have engineered this whole business."

"You know me better than that," she sobbed.

"I'm not so certain I do," Pemberton told her. "You were a push-over for me and now—"

Her voice came in good and strong then. "All right, then," she said, "if you don't want the pill sugar-coated we'll make it bitter. I'm getting tired of putting on this sob-sister act for you. I never saw a sucker who was so damn dumb in my life. You seem to think a middle-aged old gander is going to get a sweet, innocent girl to fall for just your own sweet self. Bunk! If you'd been a good spender, taken what you wanted and left me with a few knick-knacks, I'd have thought you were swell.

273

But you thought I was an innocent little kid who'd fall for this Model T line of yours. All right, get a load of this: You're being stood up. And what're you going to do about it? I have your letters. They show the kind of game you were trying to play. So quite stalling."

"So that's it, is it?" he said. "You've been a dirty double-crosser all along."

"Oh, I'm a double-crosser, am I? Just a minute, Mr. Harvey Pemberton, and I'll read from one of your letters. Figure how it will sound to the jury.

"'Remember, sweetheart, that except for the silly conventions of civilization, we are already man and wife. There is, of course, a ceremony to be performed, but I'll attend to that just as soon as I can arrange certain business details. It would hurt certain business plans which are rapidly coming to maturity if I should announce I was going to marry you right now. I ask you to have confidence in me, sweetheart, and to know that I cherish you. I could no more harm you than I could crush a beautiful rose. I love you, my sweetheart—'" She broke off and said, "God knows how much more of that drivel there is."

"You dirty, double-crossing tramp," he said.

Her voice sounded less loud. I gathered she'd moved over toward the door. "Now then," she said, "quit stalling. You have twenty-four hours. Either put up or shut up."

I heard the door slam, then the click of heels in the hall, and, after a moment, the clang of an elevator door.

All was silent in the other office.

I slipped the head pieces off my head.

"Well," Mrs. Pemberton said, "there it is in a nutshell. I suppose he'll sell out to Bass for about half what his interest is worth and that little redhead will get it all."

"How do you know she's redheaded?" I asked.

"I've seen her and I've had detectives on her tail turning up her past and trying to get something on her. I can't uncover a thing on her, though. She dressed the window for this play."

"All right," I told her, "let your husband go ahead and fight. Even if he can't prove anything, a jury isn't going to give her so much in the line of damages."

"It isn't that alone," she said, "it's a question of the letters. He writes foolish letters. Whenever he loses his head, he goes all the way. He can't learn to keep his fountain pen in his pocket. Remember that Bass & Pemberton have some rather influential clients. They can't carry out business unless those clients believe in the business acumen of the members of the partnership."

"Those things blow over," I told her. "Your husband could take a trip to Europe."

"You don't understand," she said. "He made a fool of himself once before. That's why Bass had a clause in the partnership contract. Each of them put in two thousand dollars when they started the partnership. The articles of partnership provide that neither can sell his interest without first giving six months' notice to his partner. And then there's some provision in the contract by which Bass can buy Harvey out by returning the original two thousand dollars to him if Harvey gets in any more trouble with women. I don't know the exact provision. Now then, I want you to nip this thing in the bud. Harvey's desperate. Something's got to be done within twenty-four hours."

"All right," I told her, "I'll see what I can do. What's the girl's address?"

"Diane Locke, apartment 3A, forty-two fifteen Center Street. And it won't do you any good to try and frame her, because she's wise to all the tricks. I think she's a professional; but try and prove it."

"One thing more," I told her. "I want the name of the lawyer."

"You mean Diane Locke's lawyer?"

"Yes."

"I can't give it to you."

"Why not?"

"I don't know it," she said. "He's keeping very much in the background. He's some friend of the girl's. Probably he's afraid, he might be disbarred for participating in a blackmail action."

"How long has this thing been going on?" I asked.

"You mean the affair with that redhead? It started—"

"No," I said, "I mean this," indicating the office with a sweep of my hand.

"Since I couldn't get anywhere with the detective agency," she said. "Olaf, the janitor, is an electrician. He helped me rig things up. He got some old parts—"

"Think you can trust him?"

"With my life," she said.

I lit a cigarette and said, "How about the wash-room? Is it open?"

"I'll have to give you my key," she told me, opening her handbag. Then she hesitated a second and said, "I think it's in another purse. But the lock's mostly ornamental. Any key will work it. Or you can use the tip of a penknife."

275

I looked down into her handbag. "What's the idea of the gun?"

"For protection," she said, closing the bag.

"All right," I told her, "pass it over. I'm your protection now. You'll get in trouble with that gun."

She hesitated a moment while I held my hand out, then reluctantly took the gun from her purse and hesitated with it in her hand.

"But suppose you're not with me, and something should happen? Suppose he should find the wires and follow them in here and catch me?"

"Keep with me all the time," I told her.

The business end of the gun waved around in a half-circle. "Want me to go with you now?" she asked.

"Don't be a sap," I told her. "I'm going to the wash-room. I'll be right back."

"And if my husband comes in while you're gone, I suppose I'm to tell him it's no fair, that you're seeing a man about a dog, and he mustn't choke me until you get back."

I strode over to the door. "Keep your plaything until I come back," I said. "When we go out, you either get rid of the gun, or get rid of me. You're the one who's paying the money, so you can take your choice."

I crossed the office to the door, opened it, and pushed the catch so I could open the door from the outside. I wondered what would happen if Harvey Pemberton should make up his mind to go to the wash-room while I was in there, or should meet me in the corridor. I'd kill that chance by going to the floor below. I saw stairs to the right of the elevator, and went down.

The men's room was at the far end of the corridor. The first key on my ring did the trick.

Five minutes later, when I got back to Mrs. Pemberton, I saw that she was nervous and upset.

"What's the matter?" I asked. "Did something happen?"

She said in a nervous, strained voice, "I was just thinking of what would happen if my husband ran into you in the corridor."

I said, "Well, he didn't."

"You shouldn't take chances like that," she told me.

I grinned. "I didn't. I ran down the stairs for a couple of flights and used the room on the fourth floor."

Her face showed relief. "All right," I told her, "let's go. We'll pick up my baggage and then I'm going to take you home. Then, if you don't mind, I'll borrow your car. I have work to do."

"Have you any plan?" she asked.

"I'm an opportunist."

"All right," she said, "let's go. We'd better run down the stairs and ring the elevator from the lower floor."

We started for the door. She clicked out the light.

"Just a minute," I told her. "You're forgetting something."

"What?"

"The gun."

"It's all right. I thought it over. I decided you were right about it, so I ditched the gun."

"Where?"

"In the desk drawer."

I switched the lights back on and went over to look.

"The upper right-hand drawer," she said, her voice showing amusement.

I opened the drawer. The gun was there. I picked it up, started to put it in my pocket, then changed my mind and dropped it back in the drawer. "Come on," I told her, closing the drawer and switching off the lights.

We sneaked across the hall and down the flight of stairs to the lower floor. I rang for the elevator. Olaf brought the cage up and I took another look at him. He was a big raw-boned Swede with a bony nose, a drooping blond mustache, and dog eyes. His eyes never left Mrs. Pemberton all the way down to the ground floor.

Mrs. Pemberton kept her head turned away from him, toward the side of the elevator shaft, watching the doors creep by. When we got to the ground floor, she turned and looked at him. It was some look. His eyes glowed back at her like a couple of coals. Olaf opened the door, I took Mrs. Pemberton's arm and we crossed over to the parking station.

"I'll drive," I told her. "I want to get accustomed to the car."

I drove down to the station, got my baggage and drove Mrs. Pemberton back out to the house. The butler carried my things up and showed me my room.

After he left, I opened my suit-case. There were two guns in it. I selected one with a shiny leather shoulder holster. I put it on under my coat and knocked on the door of Mrs. Pemberton's room.

She opened the door and stood in the doorway. The light was behind her, throwing shadows of seductive curves through billowy, gossamer silk. I resolutely kept my eyes on her face. "I'm going out," I told her. "Will you hear me when I come in?"

"Yes," she said. "I'll wait up."

"If I cough when I pass your door, it means I have good news for you. If I don't cough, it means things aren't going so well."

She nodded, stepped toward me so that her lithe body was very close to mine. She put her hand on my arm and said in that peculiar, throaty voice of hers, "Please be careful."

I nodded and turned away. My eyes hadn't strayed once. Walking down the corridor and tiptoeing down the stairs, I reflected that I never had known a woman with that peculiar husky note in her voice who didn't like to tease the animals.

Forty-two fifteen Center Street was a three-story frame apartment house, the lower floor given over to stores. A doorway from the street opened on a flight of stairs. I tried the door, and it was unlocked.

I went back to sit in the car and think. It was queer the lawyer had never appeared in the picture except as a shadowy figure. No one knew his name. He was quoted freely, but he left it up to his client to do all the negotiating. Therefore, if the racket turned out to be successful, the client would be the one to collect the money. Then it would be up to her to pay the lawyer. That didn't sound right to me. It was like adding two and two and getting two as the answer.

I looked the block over. There was a little jewelry store in the first floor of the apartment house. It was closed up now, with a night light in the window, showing a few cheap wrist watches and some costume jewelry.

I drove around the corner and parked the car. A catch-all drugstore was open. I went in, bought some adhesive tape, a small bottle of benzine, a package of cotton, a writing pad and a police whistle. "Got any cheap imitation pearls?" I asked the clerk.

He had some strings at forty-nine cents. I took one of those. Then I went out to the car, cut the string of pearls and threw all but four of them away. I pulled a wad of cotton out of the box, put the four pearls in the cotton and stuffed the wad in my pocket. I popped the pasteboard off the back of the writing pad, cut two eyeholes in it and a place for my nose. I reinforced it with adhesive tape and left ends of adhesive tape on it so I could put it on at a moment's notice. Then I climbed the stairs of the apartment house and located apartment 3A.

There was a light inside the apartment. I could hear the sound of a radio, and gathered the door wasn't very thick. I took a small multiple-tool holder from my pocket and fitted a gimlet into the handle. I put a little grease on the point of the gimlet, bent over and went to work.

The best place to bore a hole in a paneled door is in the upper right- or left-hand corner of the lower panel. The wood is almost paper-thin there and doesn't take much of a hole to give a complete view of a room. Detectives have used it from time immemorial, but it's still a good trick. After the hole is bored, a little chewing gum keeps light from coming through the inside of the door and attracting the attention of a casual passer-by.

Making certain the corridor was deserted, I dropped to one knee and peeked through the hole I'd made. The girl was redheaded, all right. She was listening to the radio and reading a newspaper.

Watching through one hole to make certain that she didn't move in case my gimlet made any noise, I bored two more holes. That gave me a chance to see all of the apartment there was. I put a thin coating of chewing gum over each of the holes, went downstairs and waited for a moment when the sidewalk was deserted and there were no cars in sight on the street. Then I took the police whistle from my pocket and blew three shrill blasts. By the time the windows in the apartments commenced to come up, I'd ducked into the doorway and started up the stairs.

I held my pasteboard mask in my left hand. All I had to do was to raise it to my face, and the adhesive tape would clamp it into position. I backed up against the door of apartment 3A and knocked with my knuckles. When I heard steps coming toward the door, I slapped my left hand up to my face, putting the mask in position, and jerked the gun out of my shoulder holster. The redhead opened the door and I backed in, the gun menacing the corridor. Once inside of the door, I made a quick whirl, kicked the door shut and covered her with the gun.

"Not a peep out of you," I said.

She'd put on a negligée and was holding it tightly about her throat. Her face was white.

"All right, sister," I told her, "get a load of this. If any copper comes wandering down the hallway, you go to the door to see what he wants. If he asks you if anyone's in here or if you've seen anyone in the corridor, tell him no. The reason you'll tell him no, is that I'm going to be standing just behind the door with this gun. They're never going to take me alive. I'd just as soon go out fighting as to be led up thirteen steps and dropped through a hole in the floor. Get it?"

She was white to the lips, but she nodded, her eyes large, round and dilated with fright.

"I stuck up that jewelry store downstairs," I told her, "and I've got some swag that's worth money. Now, I want some wrapping paper and some string. I'm going to drop that swag in the first mailbox I come to and let Uncle Sam take the responsibility of the delivery. Get me?"

She swallowed a couple of times and said, "Y-yes."

"And I'll tell you something else: Don't hold that filmy stuff so tight around you. I'm not going to bite you, but if a cop comes to the door and sees you all bundled up that way, he'll figure out what's happened.

If there's a knock, I want you to open the door a crack and have that thing pretty well open in front, when you do. Then you can pull it shut when you see there's a man at the door and give a little squeal and say, 'Oh, I thought it was Mamie!' Do you get that?"

"You're asking a lot of me," she said.

I made motions with the business end of the gun. "You've got a nice figure," I said. "It would be a shame to blow it in two. These are soft-nosed bullets. You'd have splinters from your spinal cord all mixed into your hip bone if I pulled this trigger. The cop in the doorway would get the next shot. Then I'd take a chance on the fire-escape."

She didn't say anything and I jabbed at her with the gun. "Come on, how about the wrapping paper?"

She opened a door into a little kitchenette, pulled out a drawer. There was brown paper and string in there. I said, "Get over there away from the window; stand over there in the corner."

I crossed over to the little card table. There was an ash-tray there with four or five cigarette ends in it and some burnt matches. I noticed that a couple of the matches had been broken in two. I pushed the tray to one side, spread the paper out, and took the cotton from my pocket.

When I opened the cotton, she saw the four big pearls nested in it and gave a little gasp. Standing eight or ten feet away as she was and seeing those pearls on the cotton, she felt she was looking at ready money.

"That all you took?" she asked in a voice that had a can't-we-be-friends note in it.

"Is that all I took?" I asked, and laughed, a nasty, sarcastic laugh. "That jeweler," I told her, "has been trying to get those four pearls for a client for more than two years. They're perfectly matched pearls that came in from the South Seas, and, in case you want to know it, they didn't pay any duty. I know what I'm after before I heist a joint."

I put the cotton around the pearls again, wrapped them in the paper, tied the paper with string and ostentatiously set my gun on the corner of the table while I took a fountain pen from my pocket to write an address on the package. I printed the first name which popped into my head, and a Los Angeles address. Then I reached in my pocket, took out my wallet and from it extracted a strip of postage stamps.

"What—what are they worth?" she asked.

"Singly," I told her, "they aren't worth over five thousand apiece, but the four of them taken together, with that perfect matching and luster, are worth forty grand in any man's dough." I shot her a look to see if she thought there was anything phony about my appraisal. She didn't. Her eyes were commencing to narrow now as ideas raced through her head.

"I suppose," she told me, "you'll peddle them to a fence and only get about a tenth of what they're worth."

"Well, a tenth of forty grand buys a lot of hamburgers," I told her.

She moved over toward a small table, slid one hip up on that, and let the negligée slide carelessly open, apparently too much interested in the pearls to remember that she wasn't clothed for the street. She had plenty to look at, that girl.

"You make a working girl dizzy," she said wistfully. "Think how hard I'd have to work to make four thousand dollars."

"Not with that shape."

Indignantly she pulled the robe around her. Then she leaned forward, let the silk slip from her fingers and slide right back along the smooth line of her leg.

"I suppose it's wicked of me," she said, "but I can't help thinking what an awful shame it is to sell anything as valuable as that for a fraction of what it's worth. I should think you'd get yourself some good-looking female accomplice, someone who could really wear clothes. You could doll her up with some glad rags and show up in Santa Barbara or Hollywood, or perhaps in New Orleans. She could stay at a swell hotel, make friends, and finally confide to one of her gentlemen friends that she was temporarily embarrassed and wanted to leave some security with him and get a really good loan. Gosh, you know, there are lots of ways of playing a game like that."

I frowned contemplatively. "You've got something there, baby," I told her. "But it would take a girl who could wear clothes; it'd take a baby who'd be able to knock 'em dead and keep her head while she was doing it; it'd take a fast thinker, and it would take someone who'd be one hundred per cent loyal. Where are you going to find a moll like that?"

She got up off the table, gave a little shrug with her shoulders, and the negligée slipped down to the floor. She turned slowly around as though she'd been modeling the peach-colored underwear. "I can wear clothes," she said.

I let my eyes show suspicion. "Yeah," I told her. "You sure got what it takes on that end, but how do I know you wouldn't cross me to the bulls if anybody came along and offered a reward?"

Her eyes were starry now. She came toward me. "I don't double-cross people I like," she said. "I liked you from the minute I saw you— something in your voice, something in the way you look. I don't know what it is. When I fall, I fall fast and I fall hard. And I play the game all the way. You and I could go places together. I could put you up right here until the excitement's over. Then we could go places and—"

I said suspiciously, "You aren't handing me a line?"

"Handing you a line!" she said scornfully. "Do I look like the sort of girl who'd have to hand anyone a line? I'm not so dumb. I know I have a figure. But you don't see me living in a swell apartment with some guy footing the bills, do you? I'm just a working girl, plugging along and trying to be on the up-and-up. I'm not saying that I like it. I'm not even saying that I'm not sick of it. But I am telling you that you and I could go places together. You could use me and I'd stick."

"Now, wait a minute, baby," I temporized. "Let me get this package stamped and think this thing over a minute. You sure have got me going. Cripes! I've been in stir where I didn't see a frail for months on end, and now you come along and dazzle me with a shape like that. Listen, baby, I—"

I raised the stamps to my tongue, licked them and started to put them on the package. The wet mucilage touched my thumb and the stamps stuck. I tried to shake my thumb loose and the stamps fell to the floor, windmilling around as they dropped. I swooped after the stamps, and sensed motion over on the other side of the table.

I straightened, to find myself staring into the business end of my gun, which she'd snatched up from the table.

"Now then, sucker," she said, "start reaching."

I stood, muscles tensed, hands slowly coming up. "Now, take it easy, baby. You wouldn't shoot me."

"Don't think I wouldn't," she told me. "I'd shoot you in a minute. I'd tell the cops you'd busted in here after your stick-up and I distracted your attention long enough to grab your gun; that you made a grab for me and I acted in self-defense."

"Now listen, baby," I told her, keeping my hands up, "let's be reasonable about this thing. I thought you and I were going away together. I'd show you London and Paris and—"

She laughed scornfully and said, "What a sap I'd be to start traveling with a boob like you. A pair of pretty legs, and you forget all about your gun and leave it on the table while you chase postage stamps to the floor."

"You going to call the cops?" I asked.

She laughed. "Do I look dumb? I'm going to give you a chance to escape."

"Why?"

"Because," she said, "I haven't got the heart to see a nice-looking young man like you go to jail. I'm going to call the cops and tell them I saw you in the corridor. I'll give you ten seconds start. That ten seconds will keep you from hanging around here, and calling the cops will put me in the clear in case anybody sees you."

"Oh, I see," I said sarcastically. "You mean you're going to grab off the gravy."

"Ideas don't circulate through that dome of yours very fast, do they?" she asked.

I made a lunge toward the paper parcel I'd wrapped up, but the gun snapped up to a level with my chest. Her eyes glittered. "Don't crowd me, you fool!" she said. "Of all the dumbhead plays you've made, that's the worst. I'll do it, and don't think I don't know how to shoot a gun, because I do."

I backed slowly away.

"There's the door," she said. "Get going." She started toward the telephone and said, "I'm going to call the cops. You have ten seconds."

I spilled a lot of cuss words, to make the act look good, unlocked the door, jerked it open and jumped out into the corridor. I made pounding noises with my feet in the direction of the fire-escape and then tiptoed back. I heard a metallic click as she shot the bolt home in the door.

After waiting a couple of minutes, I dropped to one knee and peeked through the hole in the door. She was over at the table, ripping the wrappings from the parcel. I straightened, and pounded with my knuckles on the door.

"Police call," I said in a deep gruff voice. "Open up."

Her voice sounded thick with sleep. "What is it?"

"Police," I said, and dropped again, to put an eye to the peep hole in the door.

She ran to a corner of the carpet, raised it, did something to the floor and then snatched up a kimona.

I pounded with my knuckles again.

"Coming," she said drowsily.

She twisted back the bolt, opened the door about the width of a newspaper and asked, "What do you want?"

I stood aside so she couldn't see me.

"We're looking for a man who robbed the jewelry store downstairs," I growled in my throat. "We think he came up here."

"Well, he didn't."

"Would you mind letting me in?"

She hesitated a moment, then said, "Oh, very well, if you have to come in, I guess you have to. Just a minute. I'll put something on. . . . All right."

She pulled the door back. I pushed my way into the room and kicked the door shut. She looked at me with wide, terror-stricken eyes, then jumped back and said, "Listen, you can't pull this. I'll have the police here! I'll—"

I walked directly to the corner of the carpet. She flung herself at me. I pushed her off. I pulled back the corner of the carpet and saw nothing except floor. But I knew it was there and kept looking, pressing with my fingers. Suddenly I found it—a little cunningly joined section in the hardwood floor. I opened it. My package had been shoved in there, and down below it was a package of letters.

Bending down so that my body concealed just what I was doing, I pulled out pearls and letters and stuffed them in my inside coat pocket.

When I straightened, I found myself facing the gun.

"I told you you couldn't get away with this," she warned. "I'll claim you held up the jewelry store and then crashed the gate here. What're you going to do about that?"

"Nothing," I told her, smiling. "I have everything I came for."

"I can kill you," she said, "and the police would give me a vote of thanks."

"You could," I told her, "but nice girls don't go around killing men."

I saw her face contort in a spasm of emotion. "The hell they don't!" she said, and pulled the trigger.

The hammer clicked on an empty cylinder. She reinforced the index finger of her right hand with the index finger of her left. Her eyes were blazing. She clicked the empty cylinder six times and then threw the gun at me. I caught it by the barrel and side-stepped her rush. She tripped over a chair and fell on the couch.

"Take it easy," I told her.

She raised her voice then and started to call me names. At the end of the first twenty seconds, I came to the conclusion I didn't know any words she didn't. I started for the door. She made a dash for the telephone and was yelling: "Police headquarters!" into the transmitter as I closed the door and drifted noiselessly down the corridor.

In the hallway I pulled off the pasteboard mask, moistened a piece of cotton in the benzine and scrubbed off the bits of adhesive which had stuck to my face and forehead. I wadded the mask into a ball, walked around to my car and drove away.

I heard the siren of a police radio car when I was three blocks away. The machine roared by me, doing a good sixty miles an hour.

Walking down the corridor of the Pemberton home, I coughed as I passed Mrs. Pemberton's door. I walked into my bedroom and waited. Nothing happened. I took out the letters and looked at them. They were plenty torrid. Some men like to put themselves on paper. Harvey Pemberton had indulged himself to the limit.

I heard a scratching noise on my door, then it slowly opened. Mrs. Pemberton, walking as though she'd carefully rehearsed her entrance, came into the light of the room and pulled lacy things around her. "My husband hasn't come in yet," she said. "But he may come in any minute."

I looked her over. "Even supposing that I'm your brother," I said, "don't you think he'd like it a lot better if you had on something a little more tangible?"

She said, "I wear what I want. After all, you're my brother."

"Well, go put on a bathrobe over that," I told her, "so I won't be so apt to forget it."

She moved a step or two toward the door, then paused. "You don't need to be so conventional," she said.

"That's what you think."

"I want to know what you've found out."

"You're out in the clear," I told her. "All we need now is to—" I broke off as I heard the sound of an automobile outside. There was a business-like snarl to the motor which I didn't like, and somebody wore off a lot of rubber as the car was slammed to a stop.

"That's Harvey now," she said.

"Harvey wouldn't park his car at the curb in front, would he?" I asked.

"No," she admitted.

"Get back to your room," I told her.

"But I don't see what you're so—"

"Get started!" I said.

"Very well, Sir Galahad," she told me.

She started down the corridor toward her room. I heard the pound of feet as someone ran around the house toward the back door. Then I heard feet on the stairs, crossing the porch, and the doorbell rang four or five times, long, insistent rings.

I slipped some shells into the empty chambers of my gun, switched off the lights, opened my door, picked up my bag and waited.

I heard Mrs. Pemberton go to the head of the stairs, stand there, listening. After a moment I heard the rustle of her clothes as she started down. I stepped out to the hallway and stood still.

I heard her say, "Who is it?" and a voice boom an answer through the closed door. "Police," it said. "Open up."

"But I—I don't understand."

"Open up!"

She unlocked the door. I heard men coming into the corridor, then a man's voice say, "I'm Lieutenant Sylvester. I want to talk with you. You're Mrs. Pemberton?"

"Yes, but I can't understand what could bring you here at this hour. After all, Lieutenant, I'm—"

"I'm sorry," the lieutenant interrupted, "this is about your husband. When did you see him last?"

"Why, just this evening."

"What time this evening?"

"Why, I don't know exactly."

"Where did you see him last?"

"Will you please tell me the reason for these questions?"

"Where," he repeated, "did you see your husband last?"

"Well, if you insist on knowing, he was here for dinner and then left for the office about seven-thirty."

"And you haven't seen him since?"

"No."

The officer said, "I'm sorry, Mrs. Pemberton, but your husband's body was found on the floor of his office by the janitor about half an hour ago."

"My husband's body!" she screamed.

"Yes, ma'am," the lieutenant said. "He'd been killed by two bullets fired from a thirty-two caliber automatic. The ejected shells were on the floor of his office. In an adjoining office, furnished with a dilapidated desk and a couple of chairs, we found a home-rigged microphone arrangement which would work as a dictograph. In the drawer of that desk we found the gun with which the murder had been committed. Now, Mrs. Pemberton, what do you know about it?"

There was silence for a second or two, then she said in a thin, frightened voice, "Why, I don't know anything about it."

"What do you know about that office next to your husband's?"

"Nothing."

"You've never been in there?"

This time she didn't hesitate. "No," she said, "never. I don't know what makes you think I would be spying on my husband. Perhaps someone has hired detectives. I wouldn't know."

I tiptoed back to my room, picked up my bag and started silently down the corridor toward the back stairs. I could hear the rumble of a man's voice from the front room, and, at intervals, the thin, shrill sound of Mrs. Pemberton's half-hysterical answers.

I felt my way down the back stairs. There was a glass window in the back door, with a shade drawn over it. I raised a corner of the shade and peered through the glass. I could see the bulky figure of a man silhouetted against the lights which filtered in from the back yard. He was holding a sawed-off police riot gun in his hands.

I took a flash-light from my pocket and started exploring the kitchen. I found the door to the cellar, and went down. From the floor above came the scrape of chairs, then the noise of feet moving about the house.

There was a little window in the cellar. I scraped cobwebs away and shook off a couple of spiders I could feel crawling on my hand. I worked the catch on the sash and pulled it open. It dropped down on hinges and hung down on the inside. I pushed my bag out, breathed a prayer to Lady Luck, and gave a jump. My elbows caught on the cement. I wiggled and twisted, pulling myself up, and fighting to keep the side of the window from catching on my knees and coming up with me. I scrambled out to the lawn.

No one was watching this side of the house. I picked up my bag, tiptoed across the lawn and pushed my way through a hedge. In the next yard a dog commenced to bark. I turned back to the sidewalk and started walking fast. I looked back over my shoulder and saw lights coming on in the second story of the Pemberton house.

I walked faster.

From a pay station, I put in a long distance call for old E. B. Jonathan. E. B. didn't appreciate being called out of his slumber, but I didn't give him a chance to do any crabbing.

"Your client down here," I told him, "is having trouble."

"Well," he said, "it can keep until morning."

"No," I told him, "I don't think it can."

"Why can't it?"

"She's going to jail."

"What's she going to jail for?"

"Taking a couple of pot shots at her husband with a thirty-two automatic."

"Did she hit him?"

"Dead center."

"Where does that leave you?" Jonathan asked.

"As a fugitive from justice, talking from a pay station," I told him. "The janitor will testify that I was with her when she went up to the place, where the shooting occurred. The janitor is her dog. He lies down and rolls over when she snaps her fingers. She thinks it'd be nice to make me the goat."

"You mean by blaming the shooting on you?"

"Exactly."

"What makes you think so?"

"I'd trust some women a hell of a lot more than you do, and some women a hell of a lot less. This one I trust a lot less."

"She's a client," E. B. said testily. "She wouldn't do that."

"I know she's a client," I told him. "That may put whitewash all over her as far as you're concerned, but it doesn't as far as I'm concerned. I made her ditch the gun out of her handbag so she wouldn't be tempted to use it. I got my finger-prints on the gun doing it. When the going gets rough, she'll think of that, and the janitor in the building will swear to anything she suggests."

He made clucking noises with his tongue against the roof of his mouth. "I'll have Boniface drive down there right away," he said. "Where can Boniface find you?"

"Nowhere," I said and hung up.

There was an all-night hamburger stand down by the depot. I ordered six hamburgers with plenty of onions and had them put in a bag to take out. I'd noticed there was a rooming-house across from the apartment where Diane Locke lived. I went there.

The landlady grumbled about the lateness of the hour, but I paid two days' rent in advance and she showed me a front room.

I said to her "I work nights, and will be sleeping daytimes. Please don't let anyone disturb me."

I told her I was Peter J. Gibbens from Seattle. She digested this sleepily and ambled away. I found a "Do not Disturb" sign in the room which I hung on the door. I locked the door and went to bed.

About three o'clock in the afternoon, I sneaked out in the hallway for a reconnaissance. There were newspapers on the desk. I picked up one, left a nickel, and went back to the room.

My own picture stared at me from the front page. "Peter Wennick, connected with prominent law firm in the metropolis, being sought for questioning by local police in connection with Pemberton murder." This was in bold, black type.

It was quite an account: Mrs. Pemberton had "told all." She had consulted the law firm in connection with some blackmail letters. The law firm had said I was a "leg man and detective." I had been sent down to investigate the situation and report on the evidence. She had taken me to the office, where, with a friendly janitor, she had rigged up a dictaphone. I had listened to a conversation between her husband and "the woman in the case."

On the pretext of leaving for the wash-room, I had thrown the night latch on the door of the office so I could return at any time. She had forgotten to put the night latch back on when we left. Therefore, I had left myself an opportunity to return and gain access to the room.

The janitor remembered when we had left. Something like an hour later, he had heard muffled sounds which could have been the two shots which were fired. He thought they had been the sounds of back-fire from a truck. He'd been in the basement, reading. The sounds had apparently come from the alley, but might have been shots echoed back from the walls of an adjoining building. The medical authorities fixed the time of death as being probably half an hour to an hour and a half after we'd left the building.

Mrs. Pemberton had insisted she'd gone home, and that I had immediately gone out. She didn't know where. I had returned, to tell her that I had good news for her, but before I could report, police had come to the house to question her in connection with her husband's death. I had made my escape through a cellar window while police were searching the house.

Arthur H. Bass, Pemberton's partner, had stated that Pemberton had been very much worried for the past few days, that he had announced it was necessary for him to raise immediate funds and had offered to sell his interest in the partnership business for much less than its value. Bass had reluctantly made a nominal offer, but had advised Pemberton not to accept it, and when Pemberton had refused to consider such a nominal amount, Bass had been jubilant because he didn't want to lose Pemberton as a partner. He had met Pemberton at Pemberton's request, to discuss the matter.

The district attorney announced that he had interviewed "the woman in the case." Inasmuch as she seemed to have been "wronged" by Pemberton, and, inasmuch as a Peeping Tom who had tried to crash the gate of her apartment had caused her to place a call for the police at approximately the time Pemberton must have been killed, the police absolved her of all responsibility.

It seemed that this Peeping Tom, evidently trying to make a mash, had knocked at her door and advised her he had held up the jewelry store downstairs. She had promptly reported to the police, who had visited her apartment, to find her very much undressed, very much excited and shaken, and apparently sincere. Police records of the call showed that the police were actually in her apartment at the time the janitor had heard the sounds of what were undoubtedly the shots which took Pemberton's life.

Mrs. Pemberton, the news account went on to say, could give no evidence in support of her alibi, but police were inclined to absolve her of blame, concentrating for the moment on a search for Pete Wennick, the leg man for the law firm.

Cedric L. Boniface, a member of the law firm, very much shocked at developments, had made a rush trip to the city and was staying at the Palace Hotel. So far, authorities had not let him talk to Mrs. Pemberton, but they would probably do so at an early hour in the afternoon. Mr. Boniface said he "hoped Mr. Wennick would be able to absolve himself."

That was that.

Just for the fun of the thing, I turned to the Personals. It's a habit with me. I always read them in any paper. Under the heading: "Too late to classify," I came on one which interested me. It read simply: "P. W. Can I help? Call on me for anything. M. D."

Now there was a girl! Old E. B. Jonathan, with his warped, distorted, jaundiced idea of the sex, suspected all women except clients. Clients to him were sacred. I took women as I found them. Mae Devers would stick through thick and thin.

Mrs. Pemberton had paraded around in revealing silks and had called me Sir Galahad when I'd told her to go put on a bathrobe. The minute the going got rough, she'd tossed me to the wolves. The question was whether she either killed her husband while I was in the washroom or had gone back and killed him afterwards and deliberately imported me as the fall guy for the police. If she had, she'd made a damn good job of it.

Supper consisted of a couple of cold hamburgers. About five o'clock, I drew up a chair in front of the window and started watching. The redhead had accused me of being a Peeping Tom and now I was going to be one.

I didn't see Diane Locke come in or go out, and I didn't see anyone else I knew. After it got dark, a light came on in Diane's apartment. I sat there and waited. About nine o'clock I had another hamburger. I got tired of waiting and decided I'd force the play. I looked up the telephone number of Bass & Pemberton's office and memorized it. It was Temple 491. I shaved, combed my hair, put on a suit none of my new playmates had seen me wear, crossed the street, climbed the stairs of the apartment house and knocked on the door of apartment 3A.

Nothing happened at once. I dropped to one knee, scooped dried chewing gum out of the hole in the door and looked through. She was coming toward the door. And she had her clothes on.

I straightened as she came to the door, opened it, and asked, "What is it?"

"I'm from the police," I said in a thin, high, nasal voice this time. "I'm trying to check up on that call you put through to police headquarters last night."

"Yes?" she asked. She'd never seen me without a mask. "What is it you wanted to know?"

"I'm trying to check your call," I told her. "If you don't mind, I'll come in." I came in before she had a chance to mind. I walked over to the chair and sat down. She sat down in the other chair.

The chair I was sitting in was warm. "Pardon me," I said, "was this your chair?"

"No. I was sitting in this one," she told me.

She looked at me and said, "I've seen you before. There's something vaguely familiar about your face. And I think I've heard your voice somewhere."

I grinned across at her and said, "I never contradict a lady, but if I'd ever met you, I'd remember it until I was a hundred and ten."

She smiled at that and crossed her knees. I looked over at the ashtray. There were two cigarette stubs on it. Both were smoldering. There was only one match in the tray. It was broken in two.

She followed the direction of my eyes, laughed, and pinched out the stubs. "I'm always leaving cigarette stubs burning," she said. "What was it you wanted?"

I slid my hand under the lapel of my coat and loosened the gun. "Miss Locke," I said, "you understand that the time element here is important. It's a question of when you placed that call to the police, as well as when the police got here. We want to check carefully on all those times. Now, in order to do that, I've been checking your calls with the telephone company. It seems that you put through a call to Temple 491 very shortly after you called the police. Can you tell me about that call?"

She studied her tinted fingernails for a minute, then raised her eyes and said, "Yes, frankly, I can. I called Mr. Pemberton."

"Why did you call him?"

She said, "I think you'll understand that I felt very close to Mr.

Pemberton in many ways. He had—well, he'd tricked me and betrayed me, but, nevertheless. . . . Oh, I just hated to make trouble for him. I called him to tell him I was sorry."

"Did you talk with him?" My throat was getting irritated from straining my voice high.

Once more she hesitated, then said, "No, he didn't answer the telephone."

"The telephone company has you on a limited call basis," I said. "They report that the call was completed."

Once more she studied her fingernails.

"Someone answered the phone," she said, "but said he was the janitor cleaning up the offices. So I hung up on him."

That gave me all I wanted to know. I said, and I spoke in my own voice now, "You know, it was a dirty trick they played on you, Diane. I don't think Bass cared whether you got anything out of it or not. He wanted Pemberton's interest in the partnership. In fact he had to have it because he'd been juggling funds. He was the mythical 'lawyer' behind you. You're his woman and he put you up to playing Pemberton for a sucker, hoping Pemberton would be involved enough so he could put into effect that trick clause in the partnership agreement and buy him out for two thousand dollars. When Pemberton said he was going to have an auditor make a complete analysis of the books for the purpose of finding out what a half interest was worth, Bass went into a panic."

She went white to her lips, but said nothing.

I went on: "As soon as your 'burglar' left and you found you'd lost the letters, you called Bass up and told him what had happened. He was in his private office, waiting for a call, waiting also for Pemberton to come back and accept his offer as a final last resort.

"But Bass was pretty smooth. He probably knew I wasn't Olive Pemberton's brother. He guessed I was a detective. That meant Olive was wise to the Diane business, and he was shrewd enough to figure there might be a dictograph running into Pemberton's office. He did a little exploring. The door to the adjoining office was unlocked, and he stepped in, looked the plant over, and found the gun. Obviously either Olive or I had left the gun there. It could be traced to one of us. It looked like a set-up. Bass took the gun with him, did the job and returned it.

"Killing Pemberton was his only out. Without the letters, his little blackmail scheme had fallen through. There'd be no money coming in to cover the shortage the audit would turn up. That meant he'd go to prison. Well, he'll go anyway, and he'll stay just long enough to be made ready for a pine box."

By this time the redhead had recognized me, of course. "You and your pearls," she sneered, but the sneer was only a camouflage for the growing fright in her eyes.

"Now," I went on, "you're in Bass' way. Bass can't have the police knowing he was behind the blackmail business, and you can show he was. He'll have to try to get rid of both of us."

"Arthur would never do anything like that," she cried.

The closet door was in front of me. The bathroom door was behind me. But a mirror in the closet door enabled me to see the bathroom one. I kept my eyes on these doors.

"He will, though," I told her, "and you know it. He's already killed once. Otherwise why did he come here tonight to tell you that under no circumstances were you to admit you'd talked with him over the telephone?"

She moistened her lips with her tongue. "How do you know all these things?" she asked.

"I know them," I told her, "because I know that persons who have ever worked as forest rangers in the dry country make it an invariable habit to break their matches in two before they throw them away. I know that he was here the other night because there were broken matches in your ash-tray. He'd sent you up to put the screws on Harvey Pemberton. I know that he's here tonight. I know he was in the office last night. Just before you came in he'd been talking with Harvey Pemberton. I didn't hear him take the elevator, so I know he went in to his private office after he'd finished that talk. He was still there when I left. I'm Wennick."

"But he wouldn't have done anything like that," she said. "Arthur couldn't."

"But you did telephone right after those letters had been stolen, and told him about it, didn't you?"

"Yes," she said, "I—"

The door behind me opened a half inch. I saw the muzzle of the gun slowly creep out, but it wasn't until I had my fingers on the butt of my own gun that I realized the barrel wasn't pointing at me, but at her.

"Duck!" I yelled.

I think it was the sudden yell which frightened her half out of her wits. She didn't duck, but she recoiled from me as though I'd thrown a brick at her instead of my voice. The gun went off. The bullet whizzed through the air right where her head had been, and buried itself in the plaster. I whirled and shot, through the door. I saw the gun barrel waver. I shot again, and then an arm came into sight, drooping toward the floor. The gun fell from nerveless fingers, and Arthur Bass crashed full length into the room.

Old E. B. glowered at me with little, malevolent eyes which glittered from above the bluish-white pouches which puffed out from under his eyeballs. "Wennick," he said, "you look like the devil!"

"I'm sorry," I told him.

"You look dissipated."

"I haven't shaved yet."

"From all reports," he said, "you cleaned up this Pemberton murder case and were released by the police at Culverton with a vote of thanks, some time before ten o'clock yesterday evening. Cedric Boniface was in the law library, briefing the question of premeditation in connection with murder. He didn't know what had happened until after the police had obtained Bass' dying statement and you had left."

I nodded.

"Now then," E. B. said, "why the hell is it that you didn't report to me?"

"I'm sorry," I told him, "but, after all, I have social engagements."

"Social engagements!" he stormed. "You were out with some woman!"

I nodded. "I was out with a young lady," I admitted, "celebrating her birthday."

He started cracking his knuckles. "Out with a young lady!" he snorted. "I had your apartment watched so I could be notified the minute you got in. You didn't get in until six o'clock this morning."

I listened to the dull cracking of his knuckles, then grinned at him. "The young lady," I said, "happens to have been born at five o'clock in the morning, so I had to wait until then to help her celebrate her birthday. If you doubt me, you might ask Mae Devers."

RAYMOND CHANDLER

(1888–1959)

||||||||||||||||||||||||||||||||||||||||||||||| ■ |||||||||||||||||||||||||||||||||||||||||||||

Raymond Chandler, the writer who proved that private-eye fiction can be high art, was born in Chicago but educated in England, where his mother moved after his father faded from the scene. He worked in the English civil service, wrote newspaper articles and poetry, and moved to California in 1912. With the outbreak of World War I, he enlisted in the Canadian army, fought in France, was injured, and returned to California. By 1919, he had become a vice president of an oil company. He didn't begin publishing hard-boiled private-eye short stories in the pulps until 1933—the year after the oil company fired him for drunkenness.

Chandler wrote slowly and struggled with plots. He disdained the puzzle-oriented detective story in the British tradition, referring to it as "an exhausting concatenation of insignificant clues." In his landmark essay, "The Simple Art of Murder," he stated his belief that it is better to "give characters their heads and let them make their own mystery."

In the same essay, Chandler articulated the grace that takes fiction to the level of art and molds the raw stuff of an ordinary protagonist into a hero. "In everything that can be called art there is a quality of redemption," Chandler wrote. "It may be pure tragedy, if it is high tragedy, and it may be pity and irony, and it may be the raucous laughter of the strong man. But down these mean streets a man must go who is not himself mean, who is neither tarnished nor afraid. The detective in this kind of story must be such a man. He is the hero; he is everything."

Chandler's work gained the immense admiration of readers the world over. More significantly, his work is admired by other writers. It has been said that Chandler's work has done more to influence American writers who followed him than did the *oeuvre* of an author like F. Scott Fitzgerald, who was a darling of the literary and academic establishment. And his influence is not confined to those writing genre fiction.

The private eye in Chandler's novels is Philip Marlowe, a self-declared romantic who thinks of himself, with a trace of self-contempt, as a sort of knight in a corrupt, decadent society where chivalry is an aberration. Chandler admired Dashiell Hammett's work, and Marlowe can be described as Sam Spade with morals and introspection added.

While "I'll Be Waiting" doesn't include Marlowe, it does display Chandler's genius in choosing the telling detail to establish mood and create a scene that lingers in the mind, and in using the genre for powerful social commentary. It also reveals his ambivalence toward his women characters and his tendency to leave things not quite resolved. In a sense, "I'll Be Waiting" is as much a love story as it is a crime tale.

1939

I'll Be Waiting

■

At one o'clock in the morning, Carl, the night porter, turned down the last of three table lamps in the main lobby of the Windermere Hotel. The blue carpet darkened a shade or two and the walls drew back into remoteness. The chairs filled with shadowy loungers. In the corners were memories like cobwebs.

Tony Reseck yawned. He put his head on one side and listened to the frail, twittery music from the radio room beyond a dim arch at the far side of the lobby. He frowned. That should be his radio room after one A.M. Nobody should be in it. That red-haired girl was spoiling his nights.

The frown passed and a miniature of a smile quirked at the corners of his lips. He sat relaxed, a short, pale, paunchy, middle-aged man with long, delicate fingers clasped on the elk's tooth on his watch chain; the long delicate fingers of a sleight-of-hand artist, fingers with shiny, molded nails and tapering first joints, fingers a little spatulate at the ends. Handsome fingers. Tony Reseck rubbed them gently together and there was peace in his quiet sea-gray eyes.

The frown came back on his face. The music annoyed him. He got up with a curious litheness, all in one piece, without moving his clasped hands from the watch chain. At one moment he was leaning back relaxed, and the next he was standing balanced on his feet, perfectly still, so that the movement of rising seemed to be a thing perfectly perceived, an error of vision. . . .

He walked with small, polished shoes delicately across the blue carpet and under the arch. The music was louder. It contained the hot, acid blare, the frenetic, jittering runs of a jam session. It was too loud. The red-haired girl sat there and stared silently at the fretted part of the big radio cabinet as though she could see the band with its fixed professional grin and the sweat running down its back. She was curled up with her feet under her on a davenport which seemed to contain most of the cushions in the room. She was tucked among them carefully, like a corsage in the florist's tissue paper.

She didn't turn her head. She leaned there, one hand in a small fist on her peach-colored knee. She was wearing lounging pajamas of heavy ribbed silk embroidered with black lotus buds.

"You like Goodman, Miss Cressy?" Tony Reseck asked.

The girl moved her eyes slowly. The light in there was dim, but the violet of her eyes almost hurt. They were large, deep eyes without a trace of thought in them. Her face was classical and without expression.

She said nothing.

Tony smiled and moved his fingers at his sides, one by one, feeling them move. "You like Goodman, Miss Cressy?" he repeated gently.

"Not to cry over," the girl said tonelessly.

Tony rocked back on his heels and looked at her eyes. Large, deep, empty eyes. Or were they? He reached down and muted the radio.

"Don't get me wrong," the girl said. "Goodman makes money, and a lad that makes legitimate money these days is a lad you have to respect. But this jitterbug music gives me the backdrop of a beer flat. I like something with roses in it."

"Maybe you like Mozart," Tony said.

"Go on, kid me," the girl said.

"I wasn't kidding you, Miss Cressy. I think Mozart was the greatest man that ever lived—and Toscanini is his prophet."

"I thought you were the house dick." She put her head back on a pillow and stared at him through her lashes.

"Make me some of that Mozart," she added.

"It's too late," Tony sighed. "You can't get it now."

She gave him another long lucid glance. "Got the eye on me, haven't you, flatfoot?" She laughed a little, almost under her breath. "What did I do wrong?"

Tony smiled his toy smile. "Nothing, Miss Cressy. Nothing at all. But you need some fresh air. You've been five days in this hotel and you haven't been outdoors. And you have a tower room."

She laughed again. "Make me a story about it. I'm bored."

"There was a girl here once had your suite. She stayed in the hotel a whole week, like you. Without going out at all, I mean. She didn't speak to anybody hardly. What do you think she did then?"

The girl eyed him gravely. "She jumped her bill."

He put his long delicate hand out and turned it slowly, fluttering the fingers, with an effect almost like a lazy wave breaking. "Unh-uh. She sent down for her bill and paid it. Then she told the hop to be back in half an hour for her suitcases. Then she went out on her balcony."

The girl leaned forward a little, her eyes still grave, one hand capping her peach-colored knee. "What did you say your name was?"

"Tony Reseck."

"Sounds like a hunky."

"Yeah," Tony said. "Polish."

"Go on, Tony."

"All the tower suites have private balconies, Miss Cressy. The walls of them are too low for fourteen stories above the street. It was a dark night, that night, high clouds." He dropped his hand with a final gesture, a farewell gesture. "Nobody saw her jump. But when she hit, it was like a big gun going off."

"You're making it up, Tony." Her voice was a clean dry whisper of sound.

He smiled his toy smile. His quiet sea-gray eyes seemed almost to be smoothing the long waves of her hair. "Eve Cressy," he said musingly. "A name waiting for lights to be in."

"Waiting for a tall dark guy that's no good, Tony. You wouldn't care why. I was married to him once. I might be married to him again. You can make a lot of mistakes in just one lifetime." The hand on her knee opened slowly until the fingers were strained back as far as they would go. Then they closed quickly and tightly, and even in that dim light the knuckles shone like the little polished bones. "I played him a low trick once. I put him in a bad place—without meaning to. You wouldn't care about that either. It's just that I owe him something."

He leaned over softly and turned the knob on the radio. A waltz formed itself dimly on the warm air. A tinsel waltz, but a waltz. He turned the volume up. The music gushed from the loudspeaker in a swirl of shadowed melody. Since Vienna died, all waltzes are shadowed.

The girl put her hand on one side and hummed three or four bars and stopped with a sudden tightening of her mouth.

"Eve Cressy," she said. "It was in lights once. At a bum night club. A dive. They raided it and the lights went out."

He smiled at her almost mockingly. "It was no dive while you were there, Miss Cressy . . . That's the waltz the orchestra always played when the old porter walked up and down in front of the hotel entrance, all swelled up with his medals on his chest. *The Last Laugh*. Emil Jannings. You wouldn't remember that one, Miss Cressy."

"'Spring, Beautiful Spring,'" she said. "No, I never saw it."

He walked three steps away from her and turned. "I have to go upstairs and palm doorknobs. I hope I didn't bother you. You ought to go to bed now. It's pretty late."

The tinsel waltz stopped and a voice began to talk. The girl spoke through the voice. "You really thought something like that—about the balcony?"

He nodded. "I might have," he said softly. "I don't any more."

"No chance, Tony." Her smile was a dim lost leaf. "Come and talk to me some more. Redheads don't jump, Tony. They hang on—and wither."

He looked at her gravely for a moment and then moved away over the carpet. The porter was standing in the archway that led to the main lobby. Tony hadn't looked that way yet, but he knew somebody was there. He always knew if anybody was close to him. He could hear the grass grow, like the donkey in *The Blue Bird*.

The porter jerked his chin at him urgently. His broad face above the uniform collar looked sweaty and excited. Tony stepped up close to him and they went together through the arch and out to the middle of the dim lobby.

"Trouble?" Tony asked wearily.

"There's a guy outside to see you, Tony. He won't come in. I'm doing a wipe-off on the plate glass of the doors and he comes up beside me, a tall guy. 'Get Tony,' he says, out of the side of his mouth."

Tony said: "Uh-huh," and looked at the porter's pale blue eyes. "Who was it?"

"Al, he said to say he was."

Tony's face became as expressionless as dough. "Okey." He started to move off.

The porter caught his sleeve. "Listen, Tony. You got any enemies?"

Tony laughed politely, his face still like dough.

"Listen, Tony." The porter held his sleeve tightly. "There's a big black car down the block, the other way from the hacks. There's a guy standing beside it with his foot on the running board. This guy that spoke to me, he wears a dark-colored, wrap-around overcoat with a high collar turned up against his ears. His hat's way low. You can't hardly see his face. He says, 'Get Tony,' out of the side of his mouth. You ain't got any enemies, have you, Tony?"

"Only the finance company," Tony said. "Beat it."

He walked slowly and a little stiffly across the blue carpet, up the three shallow steps to the entrance lobby with the three elevators on one side and the desk on the other. Only one elevator was working. Beside the open doors, his arms folded, the night operator stood silent in a neat blue uniform with silver facings. A lean, dark Mexican named Gomez. A new boy, breaking in on the night shift.

The other side was the desk, rose marble, with the night clerk leaning on it delicately. A small neat man with a wispy reddish mustache and cheeks so rosy they looked rouged. He stared at Tony and poked a nail at his mustache.

Tony pointed a stiff index finger at him, folded the other three fingers tight to his palm, and flicked his thumb up and down on the stiff finger. The clerk touched the other side of his mustache and looked bored.

Tony went on past the closed and darkened newsstand and the side entrance to the drugstore, out to the brassbound plate-glass doors. He stopped just inside them and took a deep, hard breath. He squared his shoulders, pushed the doors open and stepped out into the cold damp night air.

The street was dark, silent. The rumble of traffic on Wilshire, two blocks away, had no body, no meaning. To the left were two taxis. Their drivers leaned against a fender, side by side, smoking. Tony walked the other way. The big dark car was a third of a block from the hotel entrance. Its lights were dimmed and it was only when he was almost up to it that he heard the gentle sound of its engine turning over.

A tall figure detached itself from the body of the car and strolled toward him, both hands in the pockets of the dark overcoat with the high collar. From the man's mouth a cigarette tip glowed faintly, a rusty pearl.

They stopped two feet from each other.

The tall man said, "Hi, Tony. Long time no see."

"Hello, Al. How's it going?"

"Can't complain." The tall man started to take his right hand out of his overcoat pocket, then stopped and laughed quietly. "I forgot. Guess you don't want to shake hands."

"That don't mean anything," Tony said. "Shaking hands. Monkeys can shake hands. What's on your mind, Al?"

"Still the funny little fat guy, eh, Tony?"

"I guess." Tony winked his eyes tight. His throat felt tight.

"You like your job back there?"

"It's a job."

Al laughed his quiet laugh again. "You take it slow, Tony. I'll take it fast. So it's a job and you want to hold it. Okey. There's a girl named Eve Cressy flopping in your quiet hotel. Get her out. Fast and right now."

"What's the trouble?"

The tall man looked up and down the street. A man behind in the car coughed lightly. "She's hooked with a wrong number. Nothing against her personal, but she'll lead trouble to you. Get her out, Tony. You got maybe an hour."

"Sure," Tony said aimlessly, without meaning.

Al took his hand out of his pocket and stretched it against Tony's chest. He gave him a light lazy push. "I wouldn't be telling you just for the hell of it, little fat brother. Get her out of there."

"Okey," Tony said, without any tone in his voice.

The tall man took back his hand and reached for the car door. He opened it and started to slip in like a lean black shadow.

Then he stopped and said something to the men in the car and got out again. He came back to where Tony stood silent, his pale eyes catching a little dim light from the street.

"Listen, Tony. You always kept your nose clean. You're a good brother, Tony."

Tony didn't speak.

Al leaned toward him, a long urgent shadow, the high collar almost touching his ears. "It's trouble business, Tony. The boys won't like it, but I'm telling you just the same. This Cressy was married to a lad named Johnny Ralls. Ralls is out of Quentin two, three days, or a week. He did a three-spot for manslaughter. The girl put him there. He ran down an old man one night when he was drunk, and she was with him. He wouldn't stop. She told him to go in and tell it, or else. He didn't go in. So the Johns come for him."

Tony said, "That's too bad."

"It's kosher, kid. It's my business to know. This Ralls flapped his mouth in stir about how the girl would be waiting for him when he got out, all set to forgive and forget, and he was going straight to her."

Tony said, "What's he to you?" His voice had a dry, stiff crackle, like thick paper.

Al laughed. "The trouble boys want to see him. He ran a table at a spot on the Strip and figured out a scheme. He and another guy took the house for fifty grand. The other lad coughed up, but we still need Johnny's twenty-five. The trouble boys don't get paid to forget."

Tony looked up and down the dark street. One of the taxi drivers flicked a cigarette stub in a long arc over the top of one of the cabs. Tony watched it fall and spark on the pavement. He listened to the quiet sound of the big car's motor.

"I don't want any part of it," he said. "I'll get her out."

Al backed away from him, nodding. "Wise kid. How's mom these days?"

"Okey," Tony said.

"Tell her I was asking for her."

"Asking for her isn't anything," Tony said.

Al turned quickly and got into the car. The car curved lazily in the middle of the block and drifted back toward the corner. Its lights went up and sprayed on a wall. It turned a corner and was gone. The lingering smell of its exhaust drifted past Tony's nose. He turned and walked back to the hotel and into it. He went along to the radio room.

The radio still muttered, but the girl was gone from the davenport in front of it. The pressed cushions were hollowed out by her body. Tony reached down and touched them. He thought they were still warm. He turned the radio off and stood there, turning a thumb slowly in front of his body, his hand flat against his stomach. Then he went back through the lobby toward the elevator bank and stood beside a majolica jar of white sand. The clerk fussed behind a pebbled-glass screen at one end of the desk. The air was dead.

The elevator bank was dark. Tony looked at the indicator of the middle car and saw that it was at 14.

"Gone to bed," he said under his breath.

The door of the porter's room beside the elevators opened and the little Mexican night operator came out in street clothes. He looked at Tony with a quiet sidewise look out of eyes the color of dried-out chestnuts.

"Good night, boss."

"Yeah," Tony said absently.

He took a thin dappled cigar out of his vest pocket and smelled it. He examined it slowly, turning it around in his neat fingers. There was a small tear along the side. He frowned at that and put the cigar away.

There was a distant sound and the hand on the indicator began to steal around the bronze dial. Light glittered up in the shaft and the straight line of the car floor dissolved the darkness below. The car stopped and the doors opened, and Carl came out of it.

His eyes caught Tony's with a kind of jump and he walked over to him, his head on one side, a thin shine along his pink upper lip.

"Listen, Tony."

Tony took his arm in a hard swift hand and turned him. He pushed him quickly, yet somehow casually, down the steps to the dim main lobby and steered him into a corner. He let go of the arm. His throat tightened again, for no reason he could think of.

"Well?" he said darkly. "Listen to what?"

The porter reached into a pocket and hauled out a dollar bill. "He gimme this," he said loosely. His glittering eyes looked past Tony's shoulder at nothing. They winked rapidly. "Ice and ginger ale."

"Don't stall," Tony growled.

"Guy in Fourteen-B," the porter said.

"Lemme smell your breath."

The porter leaned toward him obediently.

"Liquor," Tony said harshly.

"He gimme a drink."

Tony looked down at the dollar bill. "Nobody's in Fourteen-B. Not on my list," he said.

"Yeah. There is." The porter licked his lips and his eyes opened and shut several times. "Tall dark guy."

"All right," Tony said crossly. "All right. There's a tall dark guy in Fourteen-B and he gave you a buck and a drink. Then what?"

"Gat under his arm," Carl said, and blinked.

Tony smiled, but his eyes had taken on the lifeless glitter of thick ice. "You take Miss Cressy up to her room?"

Carl shook his head. "Gomez. I saw her go up."

"Get away from me," Tony said between his teeth. "And don't accept any more drinks from the guests."

He didn't move until Carl had gone back into his cubbyhole by the elevators and shut the door. Then he moved silently up the three steps and stood in front of the desk, looking at the veined rose marble, the onyx pen set, the fresh registration card in its leather frame. He lifted a hand and smacked it down hard on the marble. The clerk popped out from behind the glass screen like a chipmunk coming out of its hole.

Tony took a flimsy out of his breast pocket and spread it on the desk. "No Fourteen-B on this," he said in a bitter voice.

The clerk wisped politely at his mustache. "So sorry. You must have been out to supper when he checked in."

"Who?"

"Registered as James Watterson, San Diego." The clerk yawned.

"Ask for anybody?"

The clerk stopped in the middle of the yawn and looked at the top of Tony's head. "Why yes. He asked for a swing band. Why?"

"Smart, fast and funny," Tony said. "If you like 'em that way." He wrote on his flimsy and stuffed it back into his pocket. "I'm going upstairs and palm doorknobs. There's four tower rooms you ain't rented yet. Get up on your toes, son. You're slipping."

"I made out," the clerk drawled, and completed his yawn. "Hurry back, pop. I don't know how I'll get through the time."

"You could shave that pink fuzz off your lip," Tony said, and went across to the elevators.

He opened up a dark one and lit the dome light and shot the car up to fourteen. He darkened it again, stepped out and closed the doors. This lobby was smaller than any other, except the one immediately below it. It had a single blue-paneled door in each of the walls other than the elevator wall. On each door was a gold number and letter with a gold wreath around it. Tony walked over to 14A and put his ear to the panel. He heard nothing. Eve Cressy might be in bed asleep, or in the bathroom, or out on the balcony. Or she might be sitting there in the room, a few feet from the door, looking at the wall. Well, he wouldn't expect to be able to hear her sit and look at the wall. He went over to 14B and put his ear to that panel. This was different. There was a sound in there. A man coughed. It sounded somehow like a solitary cough. There were no voices. Tony pressed the small nacre button beside the door.

Steps came without hurry. A thickened voice spoke through the panel. Tony made no answer, no sound. The thickened voice repeated the question. Lightly, maliciously, Tony pressed the bell again.

Mr. James Watterson, of San Diego, should now open the door and give forth noise. He didn't. A silence fell beyond that door that was like the silence of a glacier. Once more Tony put his ear to the wood. Silence utterly.

He got out a master key on a chain and pushed it delicately into the lock of the door. He turned it, pushed the door inward three inches and withdrew the key. Then he waited.

"All right," the voice said harshly. "Come in and get it."

Tony pushed the door wide and stood there, framed against the light from the lobby. The man was tall, black-haired, angular and white-faced. He held a gun. He held it as though he knew about guns.

"Step right in," he drawled.

Tony went in through the door and pushed it shut with his shoulder. He kept his hands a little out from his sides, the clever fingers curled and slack. He smiled his quiet little smile.

"Mr. Watterson?"

"And after that what?"

"I'm the house detective here."

"It slays me."

The tall, white-faced, somehow handsome and somehow not handsome man backed slowly into the room. It was a large room with a low balcony around two sides of it. French doors opened out on the little private open-air balcony that each of the tower rooms had. There was a grate set for a log fire behind a paneled screen in front of a cheerful davenport. A tall misted glass stood on a hotel tray beside a deep, cozy chair. The man backed toward this and stood in front of it. The large, glistening gun drooped and pointed at the floor.

"It slays me," he said. "I'm in the dump an hour and the house copper gives me the bus. Okey, sweetheart, look in the closet and bathroom. But she just left."

"You didn't see her yet," Tony said.

The man's bleached face filled with unexpected lines. His thickened voice edged toward a snarl. "Yeah? Who didn't I see yet?"

"A girl named Eve Cressy."

The man swallowed. He put his gun down on the table beside the tray. He let himself down into the chair backwards, stiffly, like a man with a touch of lumbago. Then he leaned forward and put his hands on his kneecaps and smiled brightly between his teeth. "So she got here, huh? I didn't ask about her yet. I'm a careful guy. I didn't ask yet."

"She's been here five days," Tony said. "Waiting for you. She hasn't left the hotel a minute."

The man's mouth worked a little. His smile had a knowing tilt to it. "I got delayed a little up north," he said smoothly. "You know how it is. Visiting old friends. You seem to know a lot about my business, copper."

"That's right, Mr. Ralls."

The man lunged to his feet and his hand snapped at the gun. He stood leaning over, holding it on the table, staring. "Dames talk too much," he said with a muffled sound in his voice as though he held something soft between his teeth and talked through it.

"Not dames, Mr. Ralls."

"Huh?" The gun slithered on the hard wood of the table. "Talk it up, copper. My mind reader just quit."

"Not dames, guys. Guys with guns."

The glacier silence fell between them again. The man straightened his body out slowly. His face was washed clean of expression, but his eyes were haunted. Tony leaned in front of him, a shortish plump man with a quiet, pale, friendly face and eyes as simple as forest water.

"They never run out of gas—those boys," Johnny Ralls said, and licked at his lip. "Early and late, they work. The old firm never sleeps."

"You know who they are?" Tony said softly.

"I could maybe give nine guesses. And twelve of them would be right."

"The trouble boys," Tony said, and smiled a brittle smile.

"Where is she?" Johnny Ralls asked harshly.

"Right next door to you."

The man walked to the wall and left his gun lying on the table. He stood in front of the wall, studying it. He reached up and gripped the grillwork of the balcony railing. When he dropped his hand and turned, his face had lost some of its lines. His eyes had a quieter glint. He moved back to Tony and stood over him.

"I've got a stake," he said. "Eve sent me some dough and I built it up with a touch I made up north. Case dough, what I mean. The trouble boys talk about twenty-five grand." He smiled crookedly. "Five C's I can count. I'd have a lot of fun making them believe that, I would."

"What did you do with it?" Tony asked indifferently.

"I never had it, copper. Leave that lay. I'm the only guy in the world that believes it. It was a little deal that I got suckered on."

"I'll believe it," Tony said.

"They don't kill often. But they can be awful tough."

"Mugs," Tony said with a sudden bitter contempt. "Guys with guns. Just mugs."

Johnny Ralls reached for his glass and drained it empty. The ice cubes tinkled softly as he put it down. He picked his gun up, danced it on his palm, then tucked it, nose down, into an inner breast pocket. He stared at the carpet.

"How come you're telling me this, copper?"

"I thought maybe you'd give her a break."

"And if I wouldn't?"

"I kind of think you will," Tony said.

Johnny Ralls nodded quietly. "Can I get out of here?"

"You could take the service elevator to the garage. You could rent a car. I can give you a card to the garage man."

"You're a funny little guy," Johnny Ralls said.

Tony took out a worn ostrich-skin billfold and scribbled on a printed card. Johnny Ralls read it, and stood holding it, tapping it against a thumbnail.

"I could take her with me," he said, his eyes narrow.

"You could take a ride in a basket too," Tony said. "She's been here five days, I told you. She's been spotted. A guy I know called me up and told me to get her out of here. Told me what it was all about. So I'm getting you out instead."

"They'll love that," Johnny Ralls said. "They'll send you violets."

"I'll weep about it on my day off."

Johnny Ralls turned his hand over and stared at the palm. "I could see her, anyway. Before I blow. Next door to here, you said?"

Tony turned on his heel and started for the door. He said over his shoulder, "Don't waste a lot of time, handsome. I might change my mind."

The man said, almost gently: "You might be spotting me right now, for all I know."

Tony didn't turn his head. "That's a chance you have to take."

He went on to the door and passed out of the room. He shut it carefully, silently, looked once at the door of 14A and got into his dark elevator. He rode it down to the linen-room floor and got out to remove the basket that held the service elevator open at that floor. The door slid quietly shut. He held it so that it made no noise. Down the corridor, light came from the open door of the housekeeper's office. Tony got back into his elevator and went on down to the lobby.

The little clerk was out of sight behind his pebbled-glass screen, auditing accounts. Tony went through the main lobby and turned into the radio room. The radio was on again, soft. She was there, curled on the davenport again. The speaker hummed to her, a vague sound so low that what it said was as wordless as the murmur of trees. She turned her head slowly and smiled at him.

"Finished palming doorknobs? I couldn't sleep worth a nickel. So I came down again. Okey?"

He smiled and nodded. He sat down in a green chair and patted the plump brocade arms of it. "Sure, Miss Cressy."

"Waiting is the hardest kind of work, isn't it? I wish you'd talk to that radio. It sounds like a pretzel being bent."

Tony fiddled with it, got nothing he liked, set it back where it had been.

"Beer-parlor drunks are all the customers now."

She smiled at him again.

"I don't bother you being here, Miss Cressy?"

"I like it. You're a sweet little guy, Tony."

He looked stiffly at the floor and a ripple touched his spine. He waited for it to go away. It went slowly. Then he sat back, relaxed again, his neat fingers clasped on his elk's tooth. He listened. Not to the radio—to far-off, uncertain things, menacing things. And perhaps to just the safe whir of wheels going away into a strange night.

"Nobody's all bad," he said out loud.

The girl looked at him lazily. "I've met two or three I was wrong on, then."

He nodded. "Yeah," he admitted judiciously. "I guess there's some that are."

The girl yawned and her deep violet eyes half closed. She nestled back into the cushions. "Sit there for a while, Tony. Maybe I could nap."

"Sure. Not a thing for me to do. Don't know why they pay me."

She slept quickly and with complete stillness, like a child. Tony hardly breathed for ten minutes. He just watched her, his mouth a little open. There was a quiet fascination in his limpid eyes, as if he was looking at an altar.

Then he stood up with infinite care and padded away under the arch to the entrance lobby and the desk. He stood at the desk listening for a little while. He heard a pen rustling out of sight. He went around the corner to the row of house phones in little glass cubbyholes. He lifted one and asked the night operator for the garage.

It rang three or four times and then a boyish voice answered: "Windermere Hotel. Garage speaking."

"This is Tony Reseck. That guy Watterson I gave a card to. He leave?"

"Sure, Tony. Half an hour almost. Is it your charge?"

"Yeah," Tony said. "My party. Thanks. Be seein' you."

He hung up and scratched his neck. He went back to the desk and slapped a hand on it. The clerk wafted himself around the screen with his greeter's smile in place. It dropped when he saw Tony.

"Can't a guy catch up on his work?" he grumbled.

"What's the professional rate on Fourteen-B?"

The clerk stared morosely. "There's no professional rate in the tower."

"Make one. The fellow left already. Was there only an hour."

"Well, well," the clerk said airily. "So the personality didn't click tonight. We get a skip-out."

"Will five bucks satisfy you?

"Friend of yours?"

"No. Just a drunk with delusions of grandeur and no dough."

"Guess we'll have to let it ride, Tony. How did he get out?"

"I took him down the service elevator. You was asleep. Will five bucks satisfy you?"

"Why?"

The worn ostrich-skin wallet came out and a weedy five slipped across the marble. "All I could shake him for," Tony said loosely.

The clerk took the five and looked puzzled. "You're the boss," he said, and shrugged. The phone shrilled on the desk and he reached for it. He listened and then pushed it toward Tony. "For you."

Tony took the phone and cuddled it close to his chest. He put his mouth close to the transmitter. The voice was strange to him. It had a metallic sound. Its syllables were meticulously anonymous.

"Tony? Tony Reseck?"

"Talking."

"A message from Al. Shoot?"

Tony looked at the clerk. "Be a pal," he said over the mouthpiece. The clerk flicked a narrow smile at him and went away. "Shoot," Tony said into the phone.

"We had a little business with a guy in your place. Picked him up scramming. Al had a hunch you'd run him out. Tailed him and took him to the curb. Not so good. Backfire."

Tony held the phone very tight and his temples chilled with the evaporation of moisture. "Go on," he said. "I guess there's more."

"A little. The guy stopped the big one. Cold. Al—Al said to tell you goodbye."

Tony leaned hard against the desk. His mouth made a sound that was not speech.

"Get it?" The metallic voice sounded impatient, a little bored. "This guy had him a rod. He used it. Al won't be phoning anybody any more."

Tony lurched at the phone, and the base of it shook on the rose marble. His mouth was a hard dry knot.

The voice said: "That's as far as we go, bub. G'night." The phone clicked dryly, like a pebble hitting a wall.

Tony put the phone down in its cradle very carefully, so as not to make any sound. He looked at the clenched palm of his left hand. He took a handkerchief out and rubbed the palm softly and straightened the fingers out with his other hand. Then he wiped his forehead. The clerk came around the screen again and looked at him with glinting eyes.

"I'm off Friday. How about lending me that phone number?"

Tony nodded at the clerk and smiled a minute frail smile. He put his handkerchief away and patted the pocket he had put it in. He turned and walked away from the desk, across the entrance lobby, down the three shallow steps, along the shadowy reaches of the main lobby, and so in through the arch to the radio room once more. He walked softly, like a man moving in a room where somebody is very sick. He reached the chair he had sat in before and lowered himself into it inch by inch. The girl slept on, motionless, in that curled-up looseness achieved by some women and all cats. Her breath made no slightest sound against the vague murmur of the radio.

Tony Reseck leaned back in the chair and clasped his hands on his elk's tooth and quietly closed his eyes.

JOHN DICKSON CARR
(1906–1977)

||||||||||||||||||||||||||||||||||||||||||||||||| ■ |||||||||||||||||||||||||||||||||||||||||||||||||

It seems fitting that the author most memorable as the creator of locked-room puzzles set largely in upper-crust and often British milieus should also be a political conservative. Since John Dickson Carr spent his writing life being more English than the English, it is not surprising that many readers are surprised to learn that Carr was American.

If one can call an American a Tory, John Dickson Carr deserves the title. Born into a prominent Pennsylvania family (his father was a United States congressman), he attended prep school and exclusive Haverford College before completing his education in Paris. After marrying an Englishwoman in 1932, he lived in Great Britain, writing an average of four novels a year plus radio dramas for the British Broadcasting Corporation. His draft board called him back to the United States in 1942, but he was sent back to London to continue writing propaganda for the BBC. After the war, he moved back to the United States whenever the Labour Party held power in Britain.

Carr produced seventy novels, most of them falling within three series. His major series characters include Henri Bencolin, an elegant Parisian *juge d'instruction* whose adventures are narrated by Jeff Marle, a young American in Paris. Another of Carr's series sleuths is Dr. Gideon Fell, an obese and omniscient sleuth who works on English shores, sometimes along parallel lines of investigation with Chief Inspector David Hadley of Scotland Yard. Using the pseudonym Carter Dickson, he created Sir Henry Merrivale, another highly intelligent character whose legal and medical expertise is put to good use in investigating seemingly impossible crimes. Inspector Humphrey Masters often investigates alongside Merrivale.

Among Carr's historical mysteries is *The Hungry Goblin*, featuring Wilkie Collins as a sleuth. And he wrote an authorized biography, *Life of Sir Arthur Conan Doyle*. He also collaborated with Adrian Conan Doyle on a pastiche, *The Exploits of Sherlock Holmes*.

An examination of Carr's fiction proves that he possessed a great sense of play within a form that requires considerable structure and adherence to rules of fair play and careful clueing. Many of Carr's locked-room mysteries deliver comedy, atmosphere, and bizarre twists that are rarely surpassed in the genre. In 1963, he was named Grand Master by the Mystery Writers of America.

Written under the Carter Dickson name, "The Footprint in the Sky" is a prime example of straightforward narration and a neatly tied ending, in sharp contrast with the nearly unbelievable events and unlikely clues that the sleuth must interpret. Colonel March of "The Department of Queer Complaints" is called in to provide a surprising solution to what appears to be an open-and-shut case. March appears in nine stories written under the Carter Dickson pen name, originally collected in *The Department of Queer Complaints.*

1940

The Footprint in the Sky

∎

She awoke out of confused dreams; awoke with a start, and lay staring at the white ceiling of her bedroom for a minute or two before she could convince herself it was anything but a dream.

But it was a dream.

The cold, brittle sunlight poured in at the open window. The cold, brittle air, blowing the curtains, stirred a light coating of snow on the window-sill. It stirred briskly in that little, bare room; it should have set the blood racing, and Dorothy Brant breathed it deeply.

Everything was all right. She was at the country cottage, where she and Dad and Harry had come down for the skating on the frozen lake; possibly even a little mild ski-ing, if the snow came on according to the weather forecast. And the snow had fallen. She should have been glad of that, though for some reason the sight of it on the window-sill struck her with a kind of terror.

Shivering in the warm bed, the clothes pulled up about her chin, she looked at the little clock on her bedside. Twenty minutes past nine. She had overslept; Dad and Harry would be wanting their breakfast. Again she told herself that everything was all right: though now, fully awake, she knew it was not. The unpleasantness of yesterday returned. Mrs. Topham next door—that old shrew and thief as well . . .

It was the only thing which could have marred this week-end. They had looked forward to the skating: the crisp blades thudding and ringing on the ice, the flight, the long scratching drag as you turned, the elm-trees black against a clear cold sky. But there was Mrs. Topham with her stolen watch and her malicious good manners, huddled up in the cottage next door and spoiling everything.

Put it out of your mind! No good brooding over it: put it out of your mind!

Dorothy Brant braced herself and got out of bed, reaching for her dressing-gown and slippers. But it was not her dressing-gown she found draped across the chair; it was her heavy fur coat. And there were a pair of soft-leather slippers. They were a pair of soft-leather moccasins, ornamented with bead-work, which Harry had brought her back from the States; but now the undersides were cold, damp, and stiff, almost frozen. That was when a subconscious fear struck at her, took possession, and would not leave.

Closing the window, she padded out to the bathroom. The small cottage, with its crisp white curtains and smell of old wood, was so quiet that she could hear voices talking downstairs. It was a mumble in which no words were distinguishable: Harry's quick tenor, her father's slower and heavier voice, and another she could not identify, but which was slowest and heaviest of all.

What was wrong? She hurried through her bath and through her dressing. Not only were they up but they must be getting their own breakfast, for she could smell coffee boiling. And she was very slow; in spite of nine hours' sleep she felt as edgy and washed-out as though she had been up all night.

Giving a last jerk of the comb through her brown bobbed hair, putting on no powder or lipstick, she ran downstairs. At the door of the living-room she stopped abruptly. Inside were her father, her cousin Harry, and the local Superintendent of Police.

"Good morning, miss," said the Superintendent.

She never forgot the look of that little room or the look on the faces of those in it. Sunlight poured into it, touching the bright-coloured rough-woven rugs, the rough stone fireplace. Through side windows she could see out across the snow-covered lawn to where—twenty yards away and separated from them only by a tall laurel hedge, with a gateway—was Mrs. Topham's white weather-boarded cottage.

But what struck her with a shock of alarm as she came into the room was the sense of a conversation suddenly cut off; the look she surprised on their faces when they glanced round, quick and sallow, as a camera might have surprised it.

"Good morning, miss," repeated Superintendent Mason, saluting.

Harry Ventnor intervened, in a kind of agony. His naturally high colour was higher still; even his large feet and bulky shoulders, his small sinewy hands, looked agitated.

"Don't say anything, Dolly!" he urged. "Don't say anything! They can't make you say anything. Wait until—"

"I certainly think—" began her father slowly. He looked down his nose, and then along the side of his pipe, everywhere except at Dorothy. "I certainly think," he went on, clearing his throat, "that it would be as well not to speak hastily until—"

"*If* you please, sir," said Superintendent Mason, clearing his throat. "Now, miss, I'm afraid I must ask you some questions. But it is my duty to tell you that you need not answer my questions until you have seen your solicitor."

"Solicitor? But I don't want a solicitor. What on earth should I want with a solicitor?"

Superintendent Mason looked meaningly at her father and Harry Ventnor, as though bidding them to mark that.

"It's about Mrs. Topham, miss."

"Oh!"

"Why do you say 'Oh'?"

"Go on, please. What is it?"

"I understand, miss, that you and Mrs. Topham had 'words' yesterday? A bit of a dust-up, like?"

"Yes, you could certainly call it that."

"May I ask what about?"

"I'm sorry," said Dorothy; "I can't tell you that. It would only give the old cat an opportunity to say I had been slandering her. So that's it! What has she been telling you?"

"Why, miss," said Superintendent Mason, taking out a pencil and scratching the side of his jaw with it, "I'm afraid she's not exactly in a condition to tell us anything. She's in a nursing-home at Guildford, rather badly smashed up round the head. Just between ourselves, it's touch and go whether she'll recover."

First Dorothy could not feel her heart beating at all, and then it seemed to pound with enormous rhythm. The Superintendent was looking at her steadily. She forced herself to say:

"You mean she's had an accident?"

"Not exactly, miss. The doctor says she was hit three or four times with that big glass paper-weight you may have seen on the table at her cottage. Eh?"

"You don't mean—you don't mean somebody *did* it? Deliberately? But who did it?"

"Well, miss," said Superintendent Mason, looking at her still harder until he became a huge Puritan face with a small mole beside his nose. "I'm bound to tell you that by everything we can see so far, it looks as though you did it."

This wasn't happening. It couldn't be. She afterwards remembered, in a detached kind of way, studying all of them: the little lines round Harry's eyes in the sunlight, the hastily brushed light hair, the loose leather wind-jacket whose zip fastener was half undone. She remembered thinking that despite his athletic prowess he looked ineffectual and a little foolish. But then her own father was not of much use now.

313

She heard her own voice.

"But that's absurd!"

"I hope so, miss. I honestly hope so. Now tell me: were you out of this house last night?"

"When?"

"At any time."

"Yes. No. I don't know. Yes, I think I was."

"For God's sake, Dolly," said her father, "don't say anything more until we've got a lawyer here. I've telephoned to town; I didn't want to alarm you; I didn't even wake you: there's some explanation of this. There must be!"

It was not her own emotion; it was the wretchedness of his face which held her. Bulky, semi-bald, worried about business, worried about everything else in this world, that was John Brant. His crippled left arm and black glove were pressed against his side. He stood in the bright pool of sunlight, a face of misery.

"I've—seen her," he explained. "It wasn't pretty, that wasn't. Not that I haven't seen worse. In the war." He touched his arm. "But you're a little girl, Dolly; you're only a little girl. You couldn't have done that."

His plaintive tone asked for confirmation.

"Just one moment, sir," interposed Superintendent Mason. "Now, miss! You tell me you *were* outside the house last night?"

"Yes."

"In the snow?"

"Yes, yes, yes!"

"Do you remember the time?"

"No, I don't think so."

"Tell me, miss: what size shoes do you wear?"

"Four."

"That's a rather small size, isn't it?" When she nodded dumbly, Superintendent Mason shut up his notebook. "Now, if you'll just come with me?"

The cottage had a side door. Without putting his fingers on the knob, Mason twisted the spindle round and opened it. The overhang of the eaves had kept clear the two steps leading down; but beyond a thin coating of snow lay like a plaster over the world between here and the shuttered cottage across the way.

There were two strings of footprints in that snow. Dorothy knew whose they were. Hardened and sharp-printed, one set of prints moved out snakily from the steps, passed under the arch of the powdered laurel-hedge, and stopped at the steps to the side door of Mrs. Topham's house. Another set of the same tracks—a little blurred, spaced at longer intervals where the person had evidently been running desperately—came back from the cottage to these steps.

That mute sign of panic stirred Dorothy's memory. It wasn't a dream. She had done it. Subconsciously she had known it all the time. She could remember other things: the fur coat clasped round her pyjamas, the sting of the snow to wet slippers, the blind rush in the dark.

"Yours, miss?" inquired Superintendent Mason.

"Yes. Oh, yes, they're mine."

"Easy, miss," muttered the Superintendent. "You're looking a bit white round the gills. Come in here and sit down; I won't hurt you." Then his own tone grew petulant. Or perhaps something in the heavy simplicity of the girl's manner penetrated his official bearing. "But why did you do it, miss? Lord, why did you do it? That's to say, breaking open that desk of hers to get a handful of trinkets not worth ten quid for the lot? And then not even taking the trouble to mess up your footprints afterwards!" He coughed, checking himself abruptly.

John Brant's voice was acid. "Good, my friend. Very good. The first sign of intelligence so far. I presume you don't suggest my daughter is insane?"

"No, sir. But they were her mother's trinkets, I hear."

"Where did you hear that? You, I suppose, Harry?"

Harry Ventnor pulled up the zip fastener of his wind-jacket as though girding himself. He seemed to suggest that he was the good fellow whom everybody was persecuting; that he wanted to be friends with the world, if they would only let him. Yet such sincerity blazed in his small features that it was difficult to doubt his good intentions.

"Now look here, Dad, old boy. I *had* to tell them, didn't I? It's no good trying to hide things like that. I know that, just from reading those stories—"

"Stories!"

"All right: say what you like. They always find out, and then they make it worse than it really was." He let this sink in. "I tell you, you're going about it in the wrong way. Suppose Dolly did have a row with the Topham about that jewellery? Suppose she *did* go over there last night? Suppose those are her footprints? Does that prove she bashed the Topham? Not that a public service wasn't done; but why couldn't it have been a burglar just as well?"

Superintendent Mason shook his head.

"Because it couldn't, sir."

"But why? I'm asking you, why?"

"There's no harm in telling you that, sir, if you'll just listen. You probably remember that it began to snow last night at a little past eleven o'clock."

"No, I don't. We were all in bed by then."

"Well, you can take my word for it," Mason told him patiently. "I was up half the night at the police station; and it did. It stopped snowing about midnight. You'll have to take my word for that too, but we can easily prove it. You see, sir, Mrs. Topham was alive and in very good health at well after midnight. I know that too, because she rang up the police station and said she was awake and nervous and thought there were burglars in the neighbourhood. Since the lady does that same thing," he explained with a certain grimness, "on the average of about three times a month, I don't stress *that*. What I am telling you is that her call came in at 12.10, at least ten minutes after the snow had stopped."

Harry hesitated, and the Superintendent went on with the same patient air:

"Don't you see it, sir? Mrs. Topham wasn't attacked until after the snow stopped. Round her cottage now there's twenty yards of clean, clear, unmarked snow in every direction. The only marks in that snow, the only marks of any kind at all, are the footprints Miss Brant admits she made herself."

Then he rose at them in exasperation.

"'Tisn't as though anybody else could have made the tracks. Even if Miss Brant didn't admit it herself, I'm absolutely certain nobody else did. You, Mr. Ventnor, wear size ten shoes. Mr. Brant wears size nine. Walk in size four tracks? Ayagh! And yet somebody did get into the cottage with a key, bashed the old lady pretty murderously, robbed her desk, and got away again. If there are no other tracks or marks of any kind in the snow, who did it? Who must have done it?"

Dorothy could consider it, now, in almost a detached way. She remembered the paper-weight with which Mrs. Topham had been struck. It lay on the table in Mrs. Topham's stuffy parlour, a heavy glass globe with a tiny landscape inside. When you shook the glass globe, a miniature snowstorm rose within—which seemed to make the attack more horrible.

She wondered if she had left any fingerprints on it. But over everything rose Renée Topham's face, Renée Topham, her mother's bosom friend.

"I hated her," said Dorothy; and, unexpectedly, she began to cry.

Dennis Jameson, of the law-firm of Morris, Farnsworth & Jameson, Lincoln's Inn Fields, shut up his brief-case with a snap. He was putting on his hat and coat when Billy Farnsworth looked into the office.

"Hullo!" said Farnsworth. "You off to Surrey over that Brant business?"

"Yes."

"H'm. Believe in miracles, do you?"

"No."

"That girl's guilty, my lad. You ought to know that."

"It's our business," said Jameson, "to do what we can for our clients."

Farnsworth looked at him shrewdly. "I see it in your ruddy cheek. Quixotry is alive again. Young idealist storms to relief of good-looker in distress, swearing to—"

"I've met her twice," said Jameson. "I like her, yes. But, merely using a small amount of intelligence on this, I can't see that they've got such a thundering good case against her."

"Oh, my lad!"

"Well, look at it. What do they say the girl did? This Mrs. Topham was struck several times with a glass paper-weight. There are no fingerprints on the paper-weight, which shows signs of having been wiped. But, after having the forethought to wipe her fingerprints carefully off the paper-weight, Dorothy Brant then walks back to her cottage and leaves behind two sets of footprints which could be seen by aerial observation a mile up. Is that reasonable?"

Farnsworth looked thoughtful.

"Maybe they would say she isn't reasonable," he pointed out. "Never mind the psychology. What you've got to get round are the physical facts. Here is the mysterious widow Topham entirely alone in the house; the only servant comes in by day. Here are one person's footprints. Only that girl could have made the tracks; and, in fact, admits she did. It's a physical impossibility for anybody else to have entered or left the house. How do you propose to get round that?"

"I don't know," said Jameson rather hopelessly. "But I want to hear her side of it first. The only thing nobody seems to have heard, or even to be curious about, is what she thinks herself."

Yet, when he met her at the cottage late that afternoon, she cut the ground from under his feet.

Twilight was coming down when he turned in at the gate, a bluish twilight in which the snow looked grey. Jameson stopped a moment at the gate, and stared across at the thin laurel-hedge dividing this property from Mrs. Topham's. There was nothing remarkable about this hedge, which was some six feet high and cut through by a gateway like a Gothic arch. But in front of the arch, peering up at the snow-coated side of the hedge just above it, stood a large figure in cap and water-

317

proof. Somehow he looked familiar. At his elbow another man, evidently the local Superintendent of Police, was holding up a camera; and a flash-bulb glared against the sky. Though he was too far away to hear anything, Jameson had a queer impression that the large man was laughing uproariously.

Harry Ventnor, whom he knew slightly, met Jameson at the door.

"She's in there," Harry explained, nodding towards the front room. "Er—don't upset her, will you? Here, what the devil are they doing with that hedge?"

He stared across the lawn.

"Upset her?" said Jameson with some asperity. "I'm here, if possible, to help her. Won't you or Mr. Brant give some assistance? Do you honestly think that Miss Brant in her rational senses could have done what they say she did?"

"In her rational senses?" repeated Harry. After looking at Jameson in a curious way, he said no more; he turned abruptly and hurried off across the lawn.

Yet Dorothy, when Jameson met her, gave no impression of being out of her rational senses. It was her straightforwardness he had always liked, the straightforwardness which warmed him now. They sat in the homely, firelit room, by the fireplace over which were the silver cups to denote Harry's athletic and gymnastic prowess, and the trophies of John Brant's earlier days at St. Moritz. Dorothy herself was an outdoor girl.

"To advise, me?" she said. "You mean, to advise me what to say when they arrest me?"

"Well, they haven't arrested you yet, Miss Brant."

She smiled at him. "And yet I'll bet that surprises you, doesn't it? Oh, I know how deeply I'm in! I suppose they're only poking about to get more evidence. And then there's a new man here, a man named March, from Scotland Yard. I feel almost flattered."

Jameson sat up. He knew now why that immense figure by the hedge had seemed familiar.

"Not Colonel March?"

"Yes. Rather a nice person, really," answered Dorothy, shading her eyes with her hand. Under her light tone he felt that her nerves were raw. "Then again, they've been all through my room. And they can't find the watch and the brooch and the rings I'm supposed to have stolen from Aunt Renée Topham. Aunt Renée!"

"So I've heard. But that's the point: what are they getting at? A watch and a brooch and a couple of rings! Why should you steal that from anybody, let alone her?"

"Because they weren't hers," said Dorothy, suddenly looking up with a white face, and speaking very fast. "They belonged to my mother."

"Steady."

"My mother is dead," said Dorothy. "I suppose it wasn't just the watch and the rings, really. That was the excuse, the breaking-point, the thing that brought it on. My mother was a great friend of Mrs. Topham. It was 'Aunt Renée' this and 'Aunt Renée' that, while my mother was alive to pamper her. But my mother wanted me to have those trinkets, such as they were. And Aunt Renée Topham coolly appropriated them, as she appropriates everything else she can. I never knew what had happened to them until yesterday.

"Do you know that kind of woman? Mrs. Topham is really charming, aristocratic and charming, with the cool charm that takes all it can get and expects to go on getting it. I know for a fact that she's really got a lot of money, though what she does with it I can't imagine: and the real reason why she buries herself in the country is that she's too mean to risk spending it in town. I never could endure her. Then, when my mother died and I didn't go on pampering Aunt Renée as she thought I should, it was a very different thing. How that woman loves to talk about us! Harry's debts, and my father's shaky business. And *me*."

She checked herself again, smiling at him. "I'm sorry to inflict all this on you."

"You're not inflicting anything on me."

"But it's rather ridiculous, isn't it?"

"'Ridiculous,'" said Jameson grimly, "is not the word I should apply to it. So you had a row with her?"

"Oh, a glorious row. A beautiful row. The grandmother of all rows."

"When?"

"Yesterday. When I saw her wearing my mother's watch."

She looked at the fire, over which the silver cups glimmered.

"Maybe I said more than I should have," she went on. "But I got no support from my father or Harry. I don't blame Dad: he's so worried about business, and that bad arm of his troubles him so much sometimes, that all he wants is peace and quiet. As for Harry, *he* doesn't really like her; but she took rather a fancy to him, and that flatters him. He's a kind of male counterpart of Aunt Renée. Out of a job?—well, depend on somebody else. And I'm in the middle of all this. It's 'Dolly, do this,' and 'Dolly, do that,' and 'Good old Dolly; she won't mind.' But I do mind. When I saw that woman standing there wearing my mother's watch, and saying commiserating things about the fact that we couldn't afford a servant, I felt that something ought to be done about it. So I suppose I must have done something about it."

Jameson reached out and took her hands. "All right," he said. "Did you do it?"

"I don't know! That's just the trouble."

"But surely—"

"No. That was one of the things Mrs. Topham always had such sport with. You don't know much about anything when you walk in your sleep.

"Ridiculous, isn't it?" she went on, after another pause. "Utterly ludicrous. But not to me! Not a bit. Ever since I was a child, when I've been over-tired or nervously exhausted, it's happened. Once I came downstairs and built and lit a fire in the dining-room, and set the table for a meal. I admit it doesn't happen often, and never before with results like this." She tried to laugh. "But why do you think my father and Harry looked at me like that? That's the worst of it. I really don't know whether I'm a near-murderer or not."

This was bad.

Jameson admitted that to himself, even as his reason argued against it. He got up to prowl round the room, and her brown eyes never left him. He could not look away; he saw the tensity of her face in every corner.

"Look here," he said quietly; "this is nonsense."

"Oh, please. Don't you say that. It's not very original."

"But do you seriously think you went for that woman and still don't know anything about it now?"

"Would it be more difficult than building a fire?"

"I don't ask you that. *Do* you think you did it?"

"No," said Dorothy.

That question did it. She trusted him now. There was understanding and sympathy between them, a mental force and communication that could be felt as palpably as the body gives out heat.

"Deep down inside me, no, I don't believe it. I think I should have waked up. And there was no—well, no blood on me, you know. But how are you going to get round the evidence?"

(The evidence. Always the evidence.)

"I did go across there. I can't deny that. I remember half waking up as I was coming back. I was standing in the middle of the lawn in the snow. I had on my fur coat over my pyjamas; I remember feeling snow on my face and my wet slippers under me. I was shivering. And I remember running back. That's all. If I didn't do it, how could anybody else have done it?"

"I beg your pardon," interposed a new voice. "Do you mind if, both figuratively and literally, I turn on the light?"

Dennis Jameson knew the owner of that voice. There was the noise of someone fumbling after an electric switch; then, in homely light, Colonel March beamed and basked. Colonel March's seventeen stone was swathed round in a water-proof as big as a tent. He wore a large tweed cap. Under this his speckled face glowed in the cold; and he was smoking, with gurgling relish, the large-bowled pipe which threatened to singe his sandy moustache.

"Ah, Jameson!" he said. He took the pipe out of his mouth and made a gesture with it. "So it *was* you. I thought I saw you come in. I don't want to intrude; but I think there are at least two things that Miss Brant ought to know."

Dorothy turned round quickly.

"First," pursued Colonel March, "that Mrs. Topham is out of danger. She is at least able, like an after-dinner speaker, to say a few words; though with about as much coherence. Second, that out on your lawn there is one of the queerest objects I ever saw in my life."

Jameson whistled.

"You've met this fellow?" he said to Dorothy. "He is the head of the Queer Complaints Department. When they come across something outlandish, which may be a hoax or a joke but, on the other hand, may be a serious crime, they shout for him. His mind is so obvious that he hits it every time. To my certain knowledge he has investigated a disappearing room, chased a walking corpse, and found an invisible piece of furniture. If he goes so far as to admit that a thing is a bit unusual, you can look out for squalls."

Colonel March nodded quite seriously.

"Yes." he said. "That is why I am here, you see. They thought we might be interested in that footprint."

"That footprint?" cried Dorothy. "You mean—?"

"No, no; not your footprint, Miss Brant. Another one. Let me explain. I want you, both of you, to look out of that window; I want you to take a look at the laurel-hedge between this cottage and the other. The light is almost gone, but study it."

Jameson went to the window and peered out.

"Well?" he demanded. "What about it? It's a hedge."

"As you so shrewdly note, it is a hedge. Now let me ask you a question. Do you think a person could walk along the top of that hedge?"

"Good lord, no!"

"No? Why not?"

"I don't see the joke," said Jameson, "but I'll make the proper replies. Because the hedge is only an inch or two thick. It wouldn't support a cat. If you tried to stand on it, you'd come through like a ton of bricks."

"Quite true. Then what would you say if I told you that someone weighing at least twelve stone must have climbed up the side of it?"

Nobody answered him; the thing was so obviously unreasonable that nobody could answer. Dorothy Brant and Dennis Jameson looked at each other.

"For," said Colonel March, "it would seem that somebody at least climbed up there. Look at the hedge again. You see the arch cut in it for a gate? Just above that, in the snow along the side of the hedge, there are traces of a footprint. It is a large footprint. I think it can be identified by the heel, though most of it is blurred and sketchy."

Walking quickly and heavily, Dorothy's father came into the room. He started to speak, but seemed to change his mind at the sight of Colonel March. He went over to Dorothy, who took his arm.

"Then," insisted Jameson, "somebody did climb up on the hedge?"

"I doubt it," said Colonel March. "How could he?"

Jameson pulled himself together.

"Look here, sir," he said quietly. " 'How could he?' is correct. I never knew you to go on like this without good reason. I know it must have some bearing on the case. But I don't care if somebody climbed up on the hedge. I don't care if he danced the Big Apple on it. The hedge leads nowhere. It doesn't lead to Mrs. Topham's; it only divides the two properties. The point is, how did somebody manage to get from here to that other cottage—across sixty feet of unbroken snow—without leaving a trace on it? I ask you that because I'm certain you don't think Miss Brant is guilty."

Colonel March looked apologetic.

"I know she isn't," he answered.

In Dorothy Brant's mind was again that vision of the heavy globed paper-weight inside which, as you shook it, a miniature snowstorm arose. She felt that her own wits were being shaken and clouded in the same way.

"I knew Dolly didn't do it," said John Brant, suddenly putting his arm round his daughter's shoulder. "I knew that. I told them so. But—"

Colonel March silenced him.

"The real thief, Miss Brant, did not want your mother's watch and brooch and chain and rings. It may interest you to know what he did want. He wanted about fifteen hundred pounds of notes and gold sovereigns, tucked away in that same shabby desk. You seem to have wondered what Mrs. Topham did with her money. That is what she did with it. Mrs. Topham, by the first words she could get out in semiconsciousness, was merely a common or garden variety of miser. That dull-looking desk in her parlour was the last place any burglar would look for a hoard. Any burglar, that is, except one."

"Except one?" repeated John Brant, and his eyes seemed to turn inwards.

A sudden ugly suspicion came to Jameson.

"Except one who knew, yes. You, Miss Brant, had the blame deliberately put on you. There was no malice in it. It was simply the easiest way to avoid pain and trouble to the gentleman who did it.

"Now hear what you really did," said Colonel March, his face darkening. "You did go out into the snow last night. But you did not go over to Mrs. Topham's; and you did not make those two artistic sets of footprints in the snow. When you tell us in your own story that you felt snow sting on your face as well as underfoot, it requires no vast concentration, surely, to realize that the snow was still falling. You went out into it, like many sleep-walkers; you were shocked into semiconsciousness by the snow and the cold air; and you returned long before the end of the snowfall, which covered any real prints you may have made.

"The real thief—who was very much awake—heard you come back and tumble into bed. He saw a heaven-sent opportunity to blame you for a crime you might even think you had committed. He slipped in and took the slippers out of your room. And, when the snow had stopped, he went across to Mrs. Topham's. He did not mean to attack her. But she was awake and surprised him; and so, of course, Harry Ventnor struck her down."

"Harry—"

The word, which Dorothy had said almost at a scream, was checked. She looked round quickly at her father; she stared straight ahead; and then she began to laugh.

"Of course," said Colonel March. "As usual, he was letting his (what is it?) his 'good old Dolly' take the blame."

A great cloud seemed to have left John Brant; but the fussed and worried look had not left him. He blinked at Colonel March.

"Sir," he said, "I would give my good arm to prove what you say. That boy has caused me half the trouble I ever had. But are you raving mad?"

"No."

"I tell you he couldn't have done it! He's Emily's son, my sister's son. He may be a bad lot; but he's not a magician."

"You are forgetting," said Colonel March, "a certain large size-ten footprint. You are forgetting that interesting sight, a smeared and blurred size-ten footprint on the side of a hedge which would not have held up a cat. A remarkable footprint. A disembodied footprint."

"But that's the whole trouble," roared the other. "The two lines of tracks in the snow were made by a size four shoe. Harry couldn't have made them, any more than I could. It's a physical impossibility. Harry wears size ten. You don't say he could get his feet into flat leather moccasins which would fit my daughter?"

"No," said Colonel March. "But he could get his hands into them."

There was a silence. The Colonel wore a dreamy look; almost a pleased look.

"And in this unusual but highly practical pair of gloves," he went on, "Harry Ventnor simply walked across to the other cottage on his hands. No more than that. For a trained gymnast (as those silver cups will indicate) it was nothing. For a rattle-brained gentleman who needed money it was ideal. He crossed in a thin coating of snow, which would show no difference in weight. Doorsteps, cleared of snow by the overhanging roof, protected him at either end when he stood upright. He had endless opportunities to get a key to the side door. Unfortunately, there was that rather low archway in the hedge. Carrying himself on his hands, his feet were curved up and back over the arch of his body to balance him; he blundered, and smeared that disembodied footprint on the side of the hedge. To be quite frank, I am delighted with the device. It was crime upside down; it is leaving a footprint in the sky; it is—"

"A fair cop, sir," concluded Superintendent Mason, sticking his head in at the door. "They got him on the other side of Guildford. He must have smelled something wrong when he saw us taking photographs. But he had the stuff on him."

Dorothy Brant stood looking for a long time at the large, untidy blimp-like man who was still chuckling with pleasure. Then she joined in.

"I trust," observed Dennis Jameson politely, "that everybody is having a good time. For myself, I've had a couple of unpleasant shocks today; and just for a moment I was afraid I should have another one. For a moment I honestly thought you were going to pitch on Mr. Brant."

"So did I," agreed Dorothy, and beamed at her father. "That's why it's so funny now."

John Brant looked startled. But not half so startled as Colonel March.

"Now there," the Colonel said, "I honestly do not understand you. I am the Department of Queer Complaints. If you have a ghost in your attic or a footprint on top of your hedge, ring me up. But a certain success has blessed us because, as Mr. Jameson says, I look for the obvious. And Lord love us!—if you have decided that a crime was committed by a gentleman who could walk on his hands, I would hold under torture that you are not likely to succeed by suspecting the one person in the house who has a crippled arm."

CORNELL WOOLRICH

(1903–1968)

|||||||||||||||||||||||||||||||||||||||||||||||| ◼ ||||||||||||||||||||||||||||||||||||||||||||||||

Cornell Woolrich would have served well as a character in one of his own somber, enigmatic, and somehow slightly bent stories, which he wrote under the pseudonym William Irish. Born Cornell George Hopley-Woolrich, this son of a civil-engineer father and socialite mother spent part of his boyhood in Latin America, obtaining a collection of cartridges that Mexican revolutionaries had fired at one another and watching his parents' marriage fall apart. He studied literature and creative writing at Columbia University, wrote two romantic novels, went to Hollywood as a scriptwriter, and married a film producer's daughter.

His new wife left him in a matter of weeks, fueling speculation that Woolrich was homosexual. The central woman in his life seems to have been his mother. He remained devoted to her until she died in 1957. After that, he wrote relatively little, drank more, rarely emerged from his hotel suite, and ignored the rapid decline of his health (including gangrene, until amputation of a leg was needed). Despite the fame his work had brought him, only a handful of mourners attended his funeral.

The fame was well deserved. Woolrich imbued detective fiction with a dark and ironic fatalism. He used psychology and the strangeness of the human subconscious in new ways, filling his pages with the often self-induced travails of desperate people. He possessed a remarkable ability to take an ordinary character into an uneasy and threatening situation, and to sustain a dark atmosphere of suspense even in situations where the action is slow and deliberate, or observed from a distance.

He also demonstrated a proclivity for unusual plots. If the plot of "Rear Window" no longer seems unusual, it was highly inventive in Woolrich's day. "Rear Window" was made into an immensely successful movie starring Jimmy Stewart, after which the plot was used and abused by numerous imitators. The immobility of the narrator and his sense of foreboding are not uncommon in the author's work. Woolrich's manipulation of these elements makes this story a prime example of the author's ability to build a threatening air of tension for both the character and the reader.

1942

Rear Window

∎

I didn't know their names. I'd never heard their voices. I didn't even know them by sight, strictly speaking, for their faces were too small to fill in with identifiable features at that distance. Yet I could have constructed a timetable of their comings and goings, their daily habits and activities. They were the rear-window dwellers around me.

Sure, I suppose it *was* a little bit like prying, could even have been mistaken for the fevered concentration of a Peeping Tom. That wasn't my fault, that wasn't the idea. The idea was, my movements were strictly limited just around this time. I could get from the window to the bed, and from the bed to the window, and that was all. The bay window was about the best feature my rear bedroom had in the warm weather. It was unscreened, so I had to sit with the light out or I would have had every insect in the vicinity in on me. I couldn't sleep, because I was used to getting plenty of exercise. I'd never acquired the habit of reading books to ward off boredom, so I hadn't that to turn to. Well, what should I do, sit there with my eyes tightly shuttered?

Just to pick a few at random: Straight over, and the windows square, there was a young jitter-couple, kids in their teens, only just married. It would have killed them to stay home one night. They were always in such a hurry to go, wherever it was they went, they never remembered to turn out the lights. I don't think it missed once in all the time I was watching. But they never forgot altogether, either. I was to learn to call this delayed action, as you will see. He'd always come skittering madly back in about five minutes, probably from all the way down in the street, and rush around killing the switches. Then fall over something in the dark on his way out. They gave me an inward chuckle, those two.

The next house down, the windows already narrowed a little with perspective. There was a certain light in that one that always went out each night too. Something about it, it used to make me a little sad. There was a woman living there with her child, a young widow I suppose. I'd see her put the child to bed, and then bend over and kiss her in a wistful sort of way. She'd shade the light off her and sit there painting her eyes and mouth. Then she'd go out. She'd never come back till the night was nearly spent. Once I was still up, and I looked and she was sitting there motionless with her head buried in her arms. Something about it, it used to make me a little sad.

The third one down no longer offered any insight, the windows were just slits like in a medieval battlement, due to foreshortening. That brings us around to the one on the end. In that one, frontal vision came back full-depth again, since it stood at right angles to the rest, my own included, sealing up the inner hollow all these houses backed on. I could see into it, from the rounded projection of my bay window, as freely as into a doll house with its rear wall sliced away. And scaled down to about the same size.

It was a flat building. Unlike all the rest it had been constructed originally as such, not just cut up into furnished rooms. It topped them by two stories and had rear fire escapes, to show for this distinction. But it was old, evidently hadn't shown a profit. It was in the process of being modernized. Instead of clearing the entire building while the work was going on, they were doing it a flat at a time, in order to lose as little rental income as possible. Of the six rearward flats it offered to view, the topmost one had already been completed, but not yet rented. They were working on the fifth-floor one now, disturbing the peace of everyone all up and down the "inside" of the block with their hammering and sawing.

I felt sorry for the couple in the flat below. I used to wonder how they stood it with that bedlam going on above their heads. To make it worse the wife was in chronic poor health, too; I could tell that even at a distance by the listless way she moved about over there, and remained in her bathrobe without dressing. Sometimes I'd see her sitting by the window, holding her head. I used to wonder why he didn't have a doctor in to look her over, but maybe they couldn't afford it. He seemed to be out of work. Often their bedroom light was on late at night behind the drawn shade, as though she were unwell and he was sitting up with her. And one night in particular he must have had to sit up with her all night, it remained on until nearly daybreak. Not that I sat watching all that time. But the light was still burning at three in the morning, when I finally transferred from chair to bed to see if I could get a little sleep myself. And when I failed to, and hopscotched back again around dawn, it was still peering wanly out behind the tan shade.

Moments later, with the first brightening of day, it suddenly dimmed around the edges of the shade, and then shortly afterward, not that one, but a shade in one of the other rooms—for all of them alike had been down—went up, and I saw him standing there looking out.

He was holding a cigarette in his hand. I couldn't see it, but I could tell it was that by the quick, nervous little jerks with which he kept putting his hand to his mouth, and the haze I saw rising around his head. Worried about her, I guess. I didn't blame him for that. Any husband would have been. She must have only just dropped off to sleep, after night-long suffering. And then in another hour or so, at the most, that sawing of wood and clattering of buckets was going to start in over them again. Well, it wasn't any of my business, I said to myself, but he really ought to get her out of there. If I had an ill wife on my hands. . . .

He was leaning slightly out, maybe an inch past the window frame, carefully scanning the back faces of all the houses abutting on the hollow square that lay before him. You can tell, even at a distance, when a person is looking fixedly. There's something about the way the head is held. And yet his scrutiny wasn't held fixedly to any one point, it was a slow, sweeping one, moving along the houses on the opposite side from me first. When it got to the end of them, I knew it would cross over to my side and come back along there. Before it did, I withdrew several yards inside my room, to let it go safely by. I didn't want him to think I was sitting there prying into his affairs. There was still enough blue night-shade in my room to keep my slight withdrawal from catching his eye.

When I returned to my original position a moment or two later, he was gone. He had raised two more of the shades. The bedroom one was still down. I wondered vaguely why he had given that peculiar, comprehensive, semicircular stare at all the rear windows around him. There wasn't anyone at any of them, at such an hour. It wasn't important, of course. It was just a little oddity, it failed to blend in with his being worried or disturbed about his wife. When you're worried or disturbed, that's an internal preoccupation, you stare vacantly at nothing at all. When you stare around you in a great sweeping arc at windows, that betrays external preoccupation, outward interest. One doesn't quite jibe with the other. To call such a discrepancy trifling is to add to its importance. Only someone like me, stewing in a vacuum of total idleness, would have noticed it at all.

The flat remained lifeless after that, as far as could be judged by its windows. He must have either gone out or gone to bed himself. Three of the shades remained at normal height, the one masking the bedroom remained down. Sam, my day houseman, came in not long after with my eggs and morning paper, and I had that to kill time with for awhile. I stopped thinking about other people's windows and staring at them.

The sun slanted down on one side of the hollow oblong all morning long, then it shifted over to the other side for the afternoon. Then it started to slip off both alike, and it was evening again—another day gone.

The lights started to come on around the quadrangle. Here and there a wall played back, like a sounding board, a snatch of radio program that was coming in too loud. If you listened carefully you could hear an occasional clink of dishes mixed in, faint, far off. The chain of little habits that were their lives unreeled themselves. They were all bound in them tighter than the tightest straitjacket any jailer ever devised, though they all thought themselves free. The jitterbugs made their nightly dash for the great open spaces, forgot their lights, he came careening back, thumbed them out, and their place was dark until the early morning hours. The woman put her child to bed, leaned mournfully over its cot, then sat down with heavy despair to redden her mouth.

In the fourth-floor flat at right angles to the long, interior "street" the three shades had remained up, and the fourth shade had remained at full length, all day long. I hadn't been conscious of that because I hadn't particularly been looking at it, or thinking of it, until now. My eyes may have rested on those windows at times, during the day, but my thoughts had been elsewhere. It was only when a light suddenly went up in the end room behind one of the raised shades, which was their kitchen, that I realized that the shades had been untouched like that all day. That also brought something else to my mind that hadn't been in it until now: I hadn't seen the woman all day. I hadn't seen any sign of life within those windows until now.

He'd come in from outside. The entrance was at the opposite side of their kitchen, away from the window. He'd left his hat on, so I knew he'd just come in from the outside.

He didn't remove his hat. As though there was no one there to remove it for any more. Instead, he pushed it farther to the back of his head by pronging a hand to the roots of his hair. That gesture didn't denote removal of perspiration, I knew. To do that a person makes a sidewise sweep—this was up over his forehead. It indicated some sort of harassment or uncertainty. Besides, if he'd been suffering from excess warmth, the first thing he would have done would be to take off his hat altogether.

She didn't come out to greet him. The first link, of the so-strong chain of habit, of custom, that binds us all, had snapped wide open.

She must be so ill she had remained in bed, in the room behind the lowered shade, all day. I watched. He remained where he was, two rooms away from there. Expectancy became surprise, surprise incomprehension. Funny, I thought, that he doesn't go in to her. Or at least go as far as the doorway, look in to see how she is.

Maybe she was asleep, and he didn't want to disturb her. Then immediately: but how can he know for sure that she's asleep, without at least looking in at her? He just came in himself.

He came forward and stood there by the window, as he had at dawn. Sam had carried out my tray quite some time before, and my lights were out. I held my ground, I knew he couldn't see me within the darkness of the bay window. He stood there motionless for several minutes. And now his attitude was the proper one for inner preoccupation. He stood there looking downward at nothing, lost in thought.

He's worried about her, I said to myself, as any man would be. It's the most natural thing in the world. Funny, though, he should leave her in the dark like that, without going near her. If he's worried, then why didn't he at least look in on her on returning? Here was another of those trivial discrepancies, between inward motivation and outward indication. And just as I was thinking that, the original one, that I had noted at daybreak, repeated itself. His head went up with renewed alertness, and I could see it start to give that slow circular sweep of interrogation around the panorama of rearward windows again. True, the light was behind him this time, but there was enough of it falling on him to show me the microscopic but continuous shift of direction his head made in the process. I remained carefully immobile until the distant glance had passed me safely by. Motion attracts.

Why is he so interested in other people's windows, I wondered detachedly. And of course an effective brake to dwelling on that thought too lingeringly clamped down almost at once: Look who's talking. What about you yourself?

An important difference escaped me. I wasn't worried about anything. He, presumably, was.

Down came the shades again. The lights stayed on behind their beige opaqueness. But behind the one that had remained down all along, the room remained dark.

Time went by. Hard to say how much—a quarter of an hour, twenty minutes. A cricket chirped in one of the back yards. Sam came in to see if I wanted anything before he went home for the night. I told him no, I didn't—it was all right, run along. He stood there for a minute, head down. Then I saw him shake it slightly, as if at something he didn't like. "What's the matter?" I asked.

"You know what that means? My old mammy told it to me, and she never told me a lie in her life. I never once seen it to miss, either."

"What, the cricket?"

"Any time you hear one of them things, that's a sign of death— someplace close around."

I swept the back of my hand at him. "Well, it isn't in here, so don't let it worry you."

He went out, muttering stubbornly: "It's somewhere close by, though. Somewhere not very far off. Got to be."

The door closed after him, and I stayed there alone in the dark.

It was a stifling night, much closer than the one before. I could hardly get a breath of air even by the open window at which I sat. I wondered how he—that unknown over there—could stand it behind those drawn shades.

Then suddenly, just as idle speculation about this whole matter was about to alight on some fixed point in my mind, crystallize into something like suspicion, up came the shades again, and off it flitted, as formless as ever and without having had a chance to come to rest on anything.

He was in the middle windows, the living room. He'd taken off his coat and shirt, was bare-armed in his undershirt. He hadn't been able to stand it himself, I guess—the sultriness.

I couldn't make out what he was doing at first. He seemed to be busy in a perpendicular, up-and-down way rather than lengthwise. He remained in one place, but he kept dipping down out of sight and then straightening up into view again, at irregular intervals. It was almost like some sort of calisthenic exercise, except that the dips and rises weren't evenly timed enough for that. Sometimes he'd stay down a long time, sometimes he'd bob right up again, sometimes he'd go down two or three times in rapid succession. There was some sort of a widespread black V railing him off from the window. Whatever it was, there was just a sliver of it showing above the upward inclination to which the window sill deflected my line of vision. All it did was strike off the bottom of his undershirt, to the extent of a sixteenth of an inch maybe. But I hadn't seen it there at other times, and I couldn't tell what it was.

Suddenly he left it for the first time since the shades had gone up, came out around it to the outside, stooped down into another part of the room, and straightened again with an armful of what looked like varicolored pennants at the distance at which I was. He went back behind the V and allowed them to fall across the top of it for a moment, and stay that way. He made one of his dips down out of sight and stayed that way a good while.

The "pennants" slung across the V kept changing color right in front of my eyes. I have very good sight. One moment they were white, the next red, the next blue.

Then I got it. They were a woman's dresses, and he was pulling them down to him one by one, taking the topmost one each time. Suddenly they were all gone, the V was black and bare again, and his torso had reappeared. I knew what it was now, and what he was doing. The dresses had told me. He confirmed it for me. He spread his arms to the ends of the V, I could see him heave and hitch, as if exerting pressure, and suddenly the V had folded up, become a cubed wedge. Then he made rolling motions with his whole upper body, and the wedge disappeared off to one side.

He'd been packing a trunk, packing his wife's things into a large upright trunk.

He reappeared at the kitchen window presently, stood still for a moment. I saw him draw his arm across his forehead, not once but several times, and then whip the end of it off into space. Sure, it was hot work for such a night. Then he reached up along the wall and took something down. Since it was the kitchen he was in, my imagination had to supply a cabinet and a bottle.

I could see the two or three quick passes his hand made to his mouth after that. I said to myself tolerantly: That's what nine men out of ten would do after packing a trunk—take a good stiff drink. And if the tenth didn't, it would only be because he didn't have any liquor at hand.

Then he came closer to the window again, and standing edgewise to the side of it, so that only a thin paring of his head and shoulder showed, peered watchfully out into the dark quadrilateral, along the line of windows, most of them unlighted by now, once more. He always started on the left-hand side, the side opposite mine, and made his circuit of inspection from there on around.

That was the second time in one evening I'd seen him do that. And once at daybreak, made three times altogether. I smiled mentally. You'd almost think he felt guilty about something. It was probably nothing, just an odd little habit, a quirk, that he didn't know he had himself. I had them myself, everyone does.

He withdrew into the room again, and it blacked out. His figure passed into the one that was still lighted next to it, the living room. That blacked next. It didn't surprise me that the third room, the bedroom with the drawn shade, didn't light up on his entering there. He wouldn't want to disturb her, of course—particularly if she was going away tomorrow for her health, as his packing of her trunk showed. She needed all the rest she could get, before making the trip. Simple enough for him to slip into bed in the dark.

It did surprise me, though, when a match-flare winked some time later, to have it still come from the darkened living room. He must be lying down in there, trying to sleep on a sofa or something for the night. He hadn't gone near the bedroom at all, was staying out of it altogether. That puzzled me, frankly. That was carrying solicitude almost too far.

Ten minutes or so later, there was another match-wink, still from that same living room window. He couldn't sleep.

The night brooded down on both of us alike, the curiosity-monger in the bay window, the chain-smoker in the fourth-floor flat, without giving any answer. The only sound was that interminable cricket.

I was back at the window again with the first sun of morning. Not because of him. My mattress was like a bed of hot coals. Sam found me there when he came in to get things ready for me. "You're going to be a wreck, Mr. Jeff," was all he said.

First, for awhile, there was no sign of life over there. Then suddenly I saw his head bob up from somewhere down out of sight in the living room, so I knew I'd been right; he'd spent the night on a sofa or easy chair in there. Now, of course, he'd look in at her, to see how she was, find out if she felt any better. That was only common ordinary humanity. He hadn't been near her, so far as I could make out, since two nights before.

He didn't. He dressed, and he went in the opposite direction, into the kitchen, and wolfed something in there, standing up and using both hands. Then he suddenly turned and moved off side, in the direction in which I knew the flat-entrance to be, as if he had just heard some summons, like the doorbell.

Sure enough, in a moment he came back, and there were two men with him in leather aprons. Expressmen. I saw him standing by while they laboriously maneuvered that cubed black wedge out between them, in the direction they'd just come from. He did more than just stand by. He practically hovered over them, kept shifting from side to side, he was so anxious to see that it was done right.

Then he came back alone, and I saw him swipe his arm across his head, as though it was he, not they, who was all heated up from the effort.

So he was forwarding her trunk, to wherever it was she was going. That was all.

He reached up along the wall again and took something down. He was taking another drink. Two. Three. I said to myself, a little at a loss: Yes, but he hasn't just packed a trunk this time. That trunk has been standing packed and ready since last night. Where does the hard work come in? The sweat and the need for a bracer?

Now, at last, after all those hours, he finally did go in to her. I saw his form pass through the living room and go beyond, into the bedroom. Up went the shade, that had been down all this time. Then he turned his head and looked around behind him. In a certain way, a way that was unmistakable, even from where I was. Not in one certain direction, as one looks at a person. But from side to side, and up and down, and all around, as one looks at—*an empty room.*

He stepped back, bent a little, gave a fling of his arms, and an unoccupied mattress and bedding upended over the foot of a bed, stayed that way, emptily curved. A second one followed a moment later.

She wasn't in there.

They use the expression "delayed action." I found out then what it meant. For two days a sort of formless uneasiness, a disembodied suspicion, I don't know what to call it, had been flitting and volplaning around in my mind, like an insect looking for a landing place. More than once, just as it had been ready to settle, some slight thing, some slight reassuring thing, such as the raising of the shades after they had been down unnaturally long, had been enough to keep it winging aimlessly, prevent it from staying still long enough for me to recognize it. The point of contact had been there all along, waiting to receive it. Now, for some reason, within a split second after he tossed over the empty mattresses, it landed—*zoom!* And the point of contact expanded—or exploded, whatever you care to call it—into a certainty of murder.

In other words, the rational part of my mind was far behind the instinctive, subconscious part. Delayed action. Now the one had caught up to the other. The thought-message that sparked from the synchronization was: He's done something to her!

I looked down and my hand was bunching the goods over my kneecap, it was knotted so tight. I forced it to open. I said to myself, steadyingly: Now wait a minute, be careful, go slow. You've seen nothing. You know nothing. You only have the negative proof that you don't see her any more.

Sam was standing there looking over at me from the pantry way. He said accusingly: "You ain't touched a thing. And your face looks like a sheet."

It felt like one. It had that needling feeling, when the blood has left it involuntarily. It was more to get him out of the way and give myself some elbow room for undisturbed thinking, than anything else, that I said: "Sam, what's the street address of that building down there? Don't stick your head too far out and gape at it."

"Somep'n or other Benedict Avenue." He scratched his neck helpfully.

"I know that. Chase around the corner a minute and get me the exact number on it, will you?"

"Why you want to know that for?" he asked as he turned to go.

"None of your business," I said with the good-natured firmness that was all that was necessary to take care of that once and for all. I called after him just as he was closing the door: "And while you're about it, step into the entrance and see if you can tell from the mailboxes who has the fourth-floor rear. Don't get me the wrong one now. And try not to let anyone catch you at it."

He went out mumbling something that sounded like, "When a man ain't got nothing to do but just sit all day, he sure can think up the blamest things—" The door closed and I settled down to some good constructive thinking.

I said to myself: What are you really building up this monstrous supposition on? Let's see what you've got. Only that there were several little things wrong with the mechanism, the chain-belt, of their recurrent daily habits over there. 1. The lights were on all night the first night. 2. He came in later than usual the second night. 3. He left his hat on. 4. She didn't come out to greet him—she hasn't appeared since the evening before the lights were on all night. 5. He took a drink after he finished packing her truck. But he took three stiff drinks the next morning, immediately after her trunk went out. 6. He was inwardly disturbed and worried, yet superimposed upon this was an unnatural external concern about the surrounding windows that was off-key. 7. He slept in the living room, didn't go near the bedroom, during the night before the departure of the trunk.

Very well. If she had been ill that first night, and he had sent her away for her health, that automatically canceled out points 1, 2, 3, 4. It left points 5 and 6 totally unimportant and unincriminating. But when it came up against 7, it hit a stumbling block.

If she went away immediately after being ill that first night, why didn't he want to sleep in their bedroom *last night?* Sentiment? Hardly. Two perfectly good beds in one room, only a sofa or uncomfortable easy chair in the other. Why should he stay out of there if she was already gone? Just because he missed her, was lonely? A grown man doesn't act that way. All right, then she was still in there.

Sam came back parenthetically at this point and said: "That house is Number 525 Benedict Avenue. The fourth-floor rear, it got the name of Mr. and Mrs. Lars Thorwald up."

"Sh-h," I silenced, and motioned him backhand out of my ken.

"First he want it, then he don't," he grumbled philosophically, and retired to his duties.

I went ahead digging at it. But if she was still in there, in that bedroom last night, then she couldn't have gone away to the country, because I never saw her leave today. She could have left without my seeing her in the early hours of yesterday morning. I'd missed a few hours, been asleep. But this morning I had been up before he was himself, I only saw his head rear up from that sofa after I'd been at the window for some time.

To go at all she would have had to go yesterday morning. Then why had he left the bedroom shade down, left the mattresses undisturbed, until today? Above all, why had he stayed out of that room last night? That was evidence that she hadn't gone, was still in there. Then today, immediately after the trunk had been dispatched, he went in, pulled up the shade, tossed over the mattresses, and showed that she hadn't been in there. The thing was like a crazy spiral.

No, it wasn't either. *Immediately after the trunk had been dispatched—*
The trunk.
That did it.

I looked around to make sure the door was safely closed between Sam and me. My hand hovered uncertainly over the telephone dial a minute. Boyne, he'd be the one to tell about it. He was on Homicide. He had been, anyway, when I'd last seen him. I didn't want to get a flock of strange dicks and cops into my hair. I didn't want to be involved any more than I had to. Or at all, if possible.

They switched my call to the right place after a couple of wrong tries, and I got him finally.

"Look, Boyne? This is Hal Jeffries—"

"Well, where've you been the last sixty-two years?" he started to enthuse.

"We can take that up later. What I want you to do now is take down a name and address. Ready? Lars Thorwald. Five twenty-five Benedict Avenue. Fourth-floor rear. Got it?"

"Fourth-floor rear. Got it. What's it for?"

"Investigation. I've got a firm belief you'll uncover a murder there if you start digging at it. Don't call on me for anything more than that— just a conviction. There's been a man and wife living there until now. Now there's just the man. Her trunk went out early this morning. If you can find someone who saw *her* leave herself—"

Marshaled aloud like that and conveyed to somebody else, a lieutenant of detectives above all, it did sound flimsy, even to me. He said hesitantly, "Well, but—" Then he accepted it as was. Because I was the source. I even left my window out of it completely. I could do that with him and get away with it because he'd known me years, he didn't question my reliability. I didn't want my room all cluttered up with dicks and cops taking turns nosing out of the window in this hot weather. Let them tackle it from the front.

"Well, we'll see what we see," he said. "I'll keep you posted."

I hung up and sat back to watch and wait events. I had a grandstand seat. Or rather a grandstand seat in reverse. I could only see from behind the scenes, but not from the front. I couldn't watch Boyne go to work. I could only see the results, when and if there were any.

Nothing happened for the next few hours. The police work that I knew must be going on was as invisible as police work should be. The figure in the fourth-floor windows over there remained in sight, alone and undisturbed. He didn't go out. He was restless, roamed from room to room without staying in one place very long, but he stayed in. Once I saw him eating again—sitting down this time—and once he shaved, and once he even tried to read the paper, but he didn't stay with it long.

Little unseen wheels were in motion around him. Small and harmless as yet, preliminaries. If he knew, I wondered to myself, would he remain there quiescent like that, or would he try to bolt out and flee? That mightn't depend so much upon his guilt as upon his sense of immunity, his feeling that he could outwit them. Of his guilt I myself was already convinced, or I wouldn't have taken the step I had.

At three my phone rang. Boyne calling back. "Jeffries? Well, I don't know. Can't you give me a little more than just a bald statement like that?"

"Why?" I fenced. "Why do I have to?"

"I've had a man over there making inquiries. I've just had his report. The building superintendent and several of the neighbors all agree she left for the country, to try and regain her health, early yesterday morning."

"Wait a minute. Did any of them *see* her leave, according to your man?"

"No."

"Then all you've gotten is a second-hand version of an unsupported statement by him. Not an eyewitness account."

"He was met returning from the depot, after he'd bought her ticket and seen her off on the train."

"That's still an unsupported statement, once removed."

"I've sent a man down there to the station to try and check with the ticket agent if possible. After all, he should have been fairly conspicuous at that early hour. And we're keeping him under observation, of course, in the meantime, watching all his movements. The first chance we get we're going to jump in and search the place."

I had a feeling that they wouldn't find anything, even if they did.

"Don't expect anything more from me. I've dropped it in your lap. I've given you all I have to give. A name, an address, and an opinion."

"Yes, and I've always valued your opinion highly before now, Jeff—"

"But now you don't, that it?"

"Not at all. The thing is, we haven't turned up anything that seems to bear out your impression so far."

"You haven't gotten very far along, so far."

He went back to his previous cliché. "Well, we'll see what we see. Let you know later."

Another hour or so went by, and sunset came on. I saw him start to get ready to go out, over there. He put on his hat, put his hand in his pocket and stood still looking at it for a minute. Counting change, I guess. It gave me a peculiar sense of suppressed excitement, knowing they were going to come in the minute he left. I thought grimly, as I saw him take a last look around: If you've got anything to hide, brother, now's the time to hide it.

He left. A breath-holding interval of misleading emptiness descended on the flat. A three-alarm fire couldn't have pulled my eyes off those windows. Suddenly the door by which he had just left parted slightly and two men insinuated themselves, one behind the other. There they were now. They closed it behind them, separated at once, and got busy. One took the bedroom, one the kitchen, and they started to work their way toward one another again from those extremes of the flat. They were thorough. I could see them going over everything from top to bottom. They took the living room together. One cased one side, the other man the other.

They'd already finished before the warning caught them. I could tell that by the way they straightened up and stood facing one another frustratedly for a minute. Then both their heads turned sharply, as at a tip-off by doorbell that he was coming back. They got out fast.

I wasn't unduly disheartened, I'd expected that. My own feeling all along had been that they wouldn't find anything incriminating around. The trunk had gone.

He came in with a mountainous brown-paper bag sitting in the curve of one arm. I watched him closely to see if he'd discover that someone had been there in his absence. Apparently he didn't. They'd been adroit about it.

He stayed in the rest of the night. Sat tight, safe and sound. He did some desultory drinking, I could see him sitting there by the window and his hand would hoist every once in a while, but not to excess. Apparently everything was under control, the tension had eased, now that—the trunk was out.

Watching him across the night, I speculated: Why doesn't he get out? If I'm right about him, and I am, why does he stick around—after it? That brought its own answer: Because he doesn't know anyone's on to him yet. He doesn't think there's any hurry. To go too soon, right after she has, would be more dangerous than to stay awhile.

The night wore on. I sat there waiting for Boyne's call. It came later than I thought it would. I picked the phone up in the dark. He was getting ready to go to bed, over there, now. He'd risen from where he'd been sitting drinking in the kitchen, and put the light out. He went into the living room, lit that. He started to pull his shirt-tail up out of his belt. Boyne's voice was in my ear as my eyes were on him, over there. Three-cornered arrangement.

"Hello, Jeff? Listen, absolutely nothing. We searched the place while he was out—"

I nearly said, "I know you did, I saw it," but checked myself in time.

"—and didn't turn up a thing. But—" He stopped as though this was going to be important. I waited impatiently for him to go ahead.

"Downstairs in his letter box we found a post card waiting for him. We fished it up out of the slot with bent pins—"

"And?"

"And it was from his wife, written only yesterday from some farm up-country. Here's the message we copied: 'Arrived O.K. Already feeling a little better. Love, Anna.'"

I said, faintly but stubbornly: "You say, written only yesterday. Have you proof of that? What was the postmark-date on it?"

He made a disgusted sound down in his tonsils. At me, not it. "The postmark was blurred. A corner of it got wet, and the ink smudged."

"All of it blurred?"

"The year-date," he admitted. "The hour and the month came out O.K. August. And seven thirty P.M., it was mailed at."

This time I made the disgusted sound, in my larynx." August, seven thirty P.M.—1937 or 1939 or 1942. You have no proof how it got into that mail box, whether it came from a letter carrier's pouch or from the back of some bureau drawer!"

"Give up, Jeff," he said. "There's such a thing as going too far."

I don't know what I would have said. That is, if I hadn't happened to have my eyes on the Thorwald flat living room windows just then. Probably very little. The post card *had* shaken me, whether I admitted it or not. But I was looking over there. The light had gone out as soon as he'd taken his shirt off. But the bedroom didn't light up. A match-flare winked from the living room, low down, as from an easy chair or sofa. With two unused beds in the bedroom, he was *still staying out of there.*

"Boyne," I said in a glassy voice, "I don't care what post cards from the other world you've turned up, I say that man has done away with his wife! Trace that trunk he shipped out. Open it up when you've located it—and I think you'll find her!"

And I hung up without waiting to hear what he was going to do about it. He didn't ring back, so I suspected he was going to give my suggestion a spin after all, in spite of his loudly proclaimed skepticism.

I stayed there by the window all night, keeping a sort of death-watch. There were two more match-flares after the first, at about half-hour intervals. Nothing more than that. So possibly he was asleep over there. Possibly not. I had to sleep some time myself, and I finally succumbed in the flaming light of the early sun. Anything that he was going to do, he would have done under cover of darkness and not waited for broad daylight. There wouldn't be anything much to watch, for a while now. And what was there that he needed to do any more, anyway? Nothing, just sit tight and let a little disarming time slip by.

It seemed like five minutes later that Sam came over and touched me, but it was already high noon. I said irritably: "Didn't you lamp that note I pinned up, for you to let me sleep?"

He said: "Yeah, but it's your old friend Inspector Boyne. I figured you'd sure want to—"

It was a personal visit this time. Boyne came into the room behind him without waiting, and without much cordiality.

I said to get rid of Sam: "Go inside and smack a couple of eggs together."

Boyne began in a galvanized-iron voice: "Jeff, what do you mean by doing anything like this to me? I've made a fool out of myself, thanks to you. Sending my men out right and left on wild-goose chases. Thank God, I didn't put my foot in it any worse than I did, and have this guy picked up and brought in for questioning."

"Oh, then you don't think that's necessary?" I suggested, drily.

The look he gave me took care of that. "I'm not alone in the department, you know. There are men over me I'm accountable to for my actions. That looks great, don't it, sending one of my fellows one-half-a-day's train ride up into the sticks to some God-forsaken whistle-stop or other at departmental expense—"

"Then you located the trunk?"

"We traced it through the express agency," he said flintily.

"And you opened it?"

"We did better than that. We got in touch with the various farm-houses in the immediate locality, and Mrs. Thorwald came down to the junction in a produce-truck from one of them and opened it for him herself, with her own keys!"

Very few men have ever gotten a look from an old friend such as I got from him. At the door he said, stiff as a rifle barrel: "Just let's forget all about it, shall we? That's about the kindest thing either one of us can do for the other. You're not yourself, and I'm out a little of my own pocket money, time and temper. Let's let it go at that. If you want to telephone me in future I'll be glad to give you my home number."

The door went *whopp!* behind him.

For about ten minutes after he stormed out my numbed mind was in a sort of straitjacket. Then it started to wriggle its way free. The hell with the police. I can't prove it to them, maybe, but I can prove it to myself, one way or the other, once and for all. Either I'm wrong or I'm right. He's got his armor on against them. But his back is naked and unprotected against me.

I called Sam in. "Whatever became of that spyglass we used to have, when we were bumming around on that cabin-cruiser that season?"

He found it some place downstairs and came in with it, blowing on it and rubbing it along his sleeve. I let it lie idle in my lap first. I took a piece of paper and a pencil and wrote six words on it: *What have you done with her?*

I sealed it in an envelope and left the envelope blank. I said to Sam: "Now here's what I want you to do, and I want you to be slick about it. You take this, go in that building 525, climb the stairs to the fourth-floor rear, and ease it under the door. You're fast, at least you used to be. Let's see if you're fast enough to keep from being caught at it. Then when you get safely down again, give the outside doorbell a little poke, to attract attention."

His mouth started to open.

"And don't ask me any questions, you understand? I'm not fooling."

He went, and I got the spyglass ready.

I got him in the right focus after a minute or two. A face leaped up, and I was really seeing him for the first time. Dark-haired, but unmistakable Scandinavian ancestry. Looked like a sinewy customer, although he didn't run to much bulk.

About five minutes went by. His head turned sharply, profilewards. That was the bell-poke, right there. The note must be in already.

He gave me the back of his head as he went back toward the flat-door. The lens could follow him all the way to the rear, where my unaided eyes hadn't been able to before.

He opened the door first, missed seeing it, looked out on a level. He closed it. Then he dipped, straightened up. He had it. I could see him turning it this way and that.

He shifted in, away from the door, nearer the window. He thought danger lay near the door, safety away from it. He didn't know it was the other way around, the deeper into his own rooms he retreated the greater the danger.

He'd torn it open, he was reading it. God, how I watched his expression. My eyes clung to it like leeches. There was a sudden widening, a pulling—the whole skin of his face seemed to stretch back behind the ears, narrowing his eyes to Mongoloids. Shock. Panic. His hand pushed out and found the wall, and he braced himself with it. Then he went back toward the door again slowly. I could see him creeping up on it, stalking it as though it were something alive. He opened it so slenderly you couldn't see it at all, peered fearfully through the crack. Then he closed it, and he came back, zigzag, off balance from sheer reflex dismay. He toppled into a chair and snatched up a drink. Out of the bottle neck itself this time. And even while he was holding it to his lips, his head was turned looking over his shoulder at the door that had suddenly thrown his secret in his face.

I put the glass down.

Guilty! Guilty as all hell, and the police be damned!

My hand started toward the phone, came back again. What was the use? They wouldn't listen now any more than they had before. "You should have seen his face, etc." And I could hear Boyne's answer: "Anyone gets a jolt from an anonymous letter, true or false. You would yourself." They had a real live Mrs. Thorwald to show me—or thought they had. I'd have to show them the dead one, to prove that they both weren't one and the same. I, from my window, had to show them a body.

Well, he'd have to show me first.

It took hours before I got it. I kept pegging away at it, pegging away at it, while the afternoon wore away. Meanwhile he was pacing back and forth there like a caged panther. Two minds with but one thought, turned inside-out in my case. How to keep it hidden, how to see that it wasn't kept hidden.

I was afraid he might try to light out, but if he intended doing that he was going to wait until after dark, apparently, so I had a little time yet. Possibly he didn't want to himself, unless he was driven to it—still felt that it was more dangerous than to stay.

The customary sights and sounds around me went on unnoticed, while the main stream of my thoughts pounded like a torrent against that one obstacle stubbornly damming them up: how to get him to give the location away to me, so that I could give it away in turn to the police.

I was dimly conscious, I remember, of the landlord or somebody bringing in a prospective tenant to look at the sixth-floor apartment, the one that had already been finished. This was two over Thorwald's; they were still at work on the in-between one. At one point an odd little bit of synchronization, completely accidental of course, cropped up. Landlord and tenant both happened to be near the living room windows on the sixth at the same moment that Thorwald was near those on the fourth. Both parties moved onward simultaneously into the kitchen from there, and, passing the blind spot of the wall, appeared next at the kitchen windows. It was uncanny, they were almost like precision-strollers or puppets manipulated on one and the same string. It probably wouldn't have happened again just like that in another fifty years. Immediately afterwards they digressed, never to repeat themselves like that again.

The thing was, something about it had disturbed me. There had been some slight flaw or hitch to mar its smoothness. I tried for a moment or two to figure out what it had been, and couldn't. The landlord and tenant had gone now, and only Thorwald was in sight. My unaided memory wasn't enough to recapture it for me. My eyesight might have if it had been repeated, but it wasn't.

It sank into my subconscious, to ferment there like yeast, while I went back to the main problem at hand.

I got it finally. It was well after dark, but I finally hit on a way. It mightn't work, it was cumbersome and roundabout, but it was the only way I could think of. An alarmed turn of the head, a quick precautionary step in one certain direction, was all I needed. And to get this brief, flickering, transitory give-away, I needed two phone calls and an absence of about half an hour on his part between them.

I leafed a directory by matchlight until I'd found what I wanted: *Thorwald, Lars. 525 Bndct. . . . SWansea 5-2114.*

I blew out the match, picked up the phone in the dark. It was like television. I could see to the other end of my call, only not along the wire but by a direct channel of vision from window to window.

He said "Hullo?" gruffly.

I thought: How strange this is. I've been accusing him of murder for three days straight, and only now I'm hearing his voice for the first time.

I didn't try to disguise my own voice. After all, he'd never see me and I'd never see him. I said: "You got my note?"

He said guardedly: "Who is this?"

"Just somebody who happens to know."

He said craftily: "Know what?"

"Know what you know. You and I, we're the only ones."

He controlled himself well. I didn't hear a sound. But he didn't know he was open another way too. I had the glass balanced there at proper height on two large books on the sill. Through the window I saw him pull open the collar of his shirt as though its stricture was intolerable. Then he backed his hand over his eyes like you do when there's a light blinding you.

His voice came back firmly. "I don't know what you're talking about."

"Business, that's what I'm talking about. It should be worth something to me, shouldn't it? To keep it from going any further." I wanted to keep him from catching on that it was the windows. I still needed them, I needed them now more than ever. "You weren't very careful about your door the other night. Or maybe the draft swung it open a little."

That hit him where he lived. Even the stomach-heave reached me over the wire. "You didn't see anything. There wasn't anything to see."

"That's up to you. Why should I go to the police?" I coughed a little. "If it would pay me not to."

"Oh," he said. And there was relief of a sort in it. "D'you want to— see me? Is that it?"

"That would be the best way, wouldn't it? How much can you bring with you for now?"

"I've only got about seventy dollars around here."

"All right, then we can arrange the rest for later. Do you know where Lakeside Park is? I'm near there now. Suppose we make it there." That was about thirty minutes away. Fifteen there and fifteen back. "There's a little pavilion as you go in."

"How many of you are there?" he asked cautiously.

"Just me. It pays to keep things to yourself. That way you don't have to divvy up."

He seemed to like that too. "I'll take a run out," he said, "just to see what it's all about."

I watched him more closely than ever, after he'd hung up. He flitted straight through to the end room, the bedroom, that he didn't go near any more. He disappeared into a clothes-closet in there, stayed a minute, came out again. He must have taken something out of a hidden cranny or niche in there that even the dicks had missed. I could tell by the piston-like motion of his hand, just before it disappeared inside his coat, what it was. A gun.

It's a good thing, I thought, I'm not out there in Lakeside Park waiting for my seventy dollars.

The place blacked and he was on his way.

I called Sam in. "I want you to do something for me that's a little risky. In fact, damn risky. You might break a leg, or you might get shot, or you might even get pinched. We've been together ten years, and I wouldn't ask you anything like that if I could do it myself. But I can't, and it's got to be done." Then I told him. "Go out the back way, cross the back yard fences, and see if you can get into that fourth-floor flat up the fire escape. He's left one of the windows down a little from the top."

"What do you want me to look for?"

"Nothing." The police had been there already, so what was the good of that? "There are three rooms over there. I want you to disturb everything just a little bit, in all three, to show someone's been in there. Turn up the edge of each rug a little, shift every chair and table around a little, leave the closet doors standing out. Don't pass up a thing. Here, keep your eyes on this." I took off my own wrist watch, strapped it on him. "You've got twenty-five minutes, starting from now. If you stay within those twenty-five minutes, nothing will happen to you. When you see they're up, don't wait any longer, get out and get out fast."

"Climb back down?"

"No." He wouldn't remember, in his excitement, if he'd left the windows up or not. And I didn't want him to connect danger with the back of his place, but with the front. I wanted to keep my own window out of it. "Latch the window down tight, let yourself out the door, and beat it out of the building the front way, for your life!"

"I'm just an easy mark for you," he said ruefully, but he went.

He came out through our own basement door below me, and scrambled over the fences. If anyone had challenged him from one of the surrounding windows, I was going to backstop for him, explain I'd sent him down to look for something. But no one did. He made it pretty good for anyone his age. He isn't so young any more. Even the fire escape backing the flat, which was drawn up short, he managed to contact by standing up on something. He got in, lit the light, looked over at me. I motioned him to go ahead, not weaken.

I watched him at it. There wasn't any way I could protect him, now that he was in there. Even Thorwald would be within his rights in shooting him down—this was break and entry. I had to stay in back behind the scenes, like I had been all along. I couldn't get out in front of him as a lookout and shield him. Even the dicks had had a lookout posted.

He must have been tense, doing it. I was twice as tense, watching him do it. The twenty-five minutes took fifty to go by. Finally he came over to the window, latched it fast. The lights went, and he was out. He'd made it. I blew out a bellyful of breath that was twenty-five minutes old.

I heard him keying the street door, and when he came up I said warningly: "Leave the light out in here. Go and build yourself a great big two-story whisky punch; you're as close to white as you'll ever be."

Thorwald came back twenty-nine minutes after he'd left for Lakeside Park. A pretty slim margin to hang a man's life on. So now for the finale of the long-winded business, and here was hoping. I got my second phone call in before he had time to notice anything amiss. It was tricky timing but I'd been sitting there with the receiver ready in my hand, dialing the number over and over, then killing it each time. He came in on the 2 of 5-2114, and I saved that much time. The ring started before his hand came away from the light switch.

This was the one that was going to tell the story.

"You were supposed to bring money, not a gun; that's why I didn't show up." I saw the jolt that threw into him. The window still had to stay out of it. "I saw you tap the inside of your coat, where you had it, as you came out on the street." Maybe he hadn't, but he wouldn't remember by now whether he had or not. You usually do when you're packing a gun and aren't an habitual carrier.

"Too bad you had your trip out and back for nothing. I didn't waste my time while you were gone, though. I know more now than I knew before." This was the important part. I had the glass up and I was practically fluoroscoping him. "I've found out where—it is. You know what I mean. I know now where you've got—it. I was there while you were out."

Not a word. Just quick breathing.

"Don't you believe me? Look around. Put the receiver down and take a look for yourself. I found it."

He put it down, moved as far as the living room entrance, and touched off the lights. He just looked around him once, in a sweeping, all-embracing stare, that didn't come to a head on any one fixed point, didn't center at all.

He was smiling grimly when he came back to the phone. All he said, softly and with malignant satisfaction, was: "You're a liar."

Then I saw him lay the receiver down and take his hand off it. I hung up at my end.

The test had failed. And yet it hadn't. He hadn't given the location away as I'd hoped he would. And yet that "You're a liar" was a tacit admission that it was there to be found, somewhere around him, somewhere on those premises. In such a good place that he didn't have to worry about it, didn't even have to look to make sure.

So there was a kind of sterile victory in my defeat. But it wasn't worth a damn to me.

He was standing there with his back to me, and I couldn't see what he was doing. I knew the phone was somewhere in front of him, but I thought he was just standing there pensive behind it. His head was slightly lowered, that was all. I'd hung up at my end. I didn't even see his elbow move. And if his index finger did, I couldn't see it.

He stood like that a moment or two, then finally he moved aside. The lights went out over there; I lost him. He was careful not even to strike matches, like he sometimes did in the dark.

My mind no longer distracted by having him to look at, I turned to trying to recapture something else—that troublesome little hitch in synchronization that had occurred this afternoon, when the renting agent and he both moved simultaneously from one window to the next. The closest I could get was this: it was like when you're looking at someone through a pane of imperfect glass, and a flaw in the glass distorts the symmetry of the reflected image for a second, until it has gone on past that point. Yet that wouldn't do, that was not it. The windows had been open and there had been no glass between. And I hadn't been using the lens at the time.

My phone rang. Boyne, I supposed. It wouldn't be anyone else at this hour. Maybe, after reflecting on the way he'd jumped all over me— I said "Hello" unguardedly, in my own normal voice.

There wasn't any answer.

I said: "Hello? Hello? Hello?" I kept giving away samples of my voice.

There wasn't a sound from first to last.

I hung up finally. It was still dark over there, I noticed.

Sam looked in to check out. He was a bit thick-tongued from his restorative drink. He said something about "Awri' if I go now?" I half heard him. I was trying to figure out another way of trapping *him* over there into giving away the right spot. I motioned my consent absently.

He went a little unsteadily down the stairs to the ground floor and after a delaying moment or two I heard the street door close after him. Poor Sam, he wasn't much used to liquor.

I was left alone in the house, one chair the limit of my freedom of movement.

Suddenly a light went on over there again, just momentarily, to go right out again afterwards. He must have needed it for something, to locate something that he had already been looking for and found he wasn't able to put his hands on readily without it. He found it, whatever it was, almost immediately, and moved back at once to put the lights out again. As he turned to do so, I saw him give a glance out the window. He didn't come to the window to do it, he just shot it out in passing.

Something about it struck me as different from any of the others I'd seen him give in all the time I'd been watching him. If you can qualify such an elusive thing as a glance, I would have termed it a glance with a purpose. It was certainly anything but vacant or random, it had a bright spark of fixity in it. It wasn't one of those precautionary sweeps I'd seen him give, either. It hadn't started over on the other side and worked its way around to my side, the right. It had hit dead-center at my bay window, for just a split second while it lasted, and then was gone again. And the lights were gone, and he was gone.

Sometimes your senses take things in without your mind translating them into their proper meaning. My eyes saw that look. My mind refused to smelter it properly. "It was meaningless," I thought. "An unintentional bull's-eye, that just happened to hit square over here, as he went toward the lights on his way out."

Delayed action. A wordless ring of the phone. To test a voice? A period of bated darkness following that, in which two could have played at the same game—stalking one another's window-squares, unseen. A last-moment flicker of the lights, that was bad strategy but unavoidable. A parting glance, radioactive with malignant intention. All these things sank in without fusing. My eyes did their job, it was my mind that didn't—or at least took its time about it.

Seconds went by in packages of sixty. It was very still around the familiar quadrangle formed by the back of the houses. Sort of a breathless stillness. And then a sound came into it, starting up from nowhere, nothing. The unmistakable, spaced clicking a cricket makes in the silence of the night. I thought of Sam's superstition about them, that he claimed had never failed to fulfill itself yet. If that was the case, it looked bad for somebody in one of these slumbering houses around here—

Sam had been gone only about ten minutes. And now he was back again, he must have forgotten something. That drink was responsible. Maybe his hat, or maybe even the key to his own quarters uptown. He knew I couldn't come down and let him in, and he was trying to be quiet about it, thinking perhaps I'd dozed off. All I could hear was this faint jiggling down at the lock of the front door. It was one of those old-fashioned stoop houses, with an outer pair of storm doors that were allowed to swing free all night, and then a small vestibule, and then the inner door, worked by a simple iron key. The liquor had made his hand a little unreliable, although he'd had this difficulty once or twice before, even without it. A match would have helped him find the keyhole quicker, but then, Sam doesn't smoke. I knew he wasn't likely to have one on him.

The sound had stopped now. He must have given up, gone away again, decided to let whatever it was go until tomorrow. He hadn't gotten in, because I knew his noisy way of letting doors coast shut by themselves too well, and there hadn't been any sound of that sort, that loose slap he always made.

Then suddenly it exploded. Why at this particular moment, I don't know. That was some mystery of the inner workings of my own mind. It flashed like waiting gunpowder which a spark has finally reached along a slow train. Drove all thoughts of Sam, and the front door, and this and that completely out of my head. It had been waiting there since midafternoon today, and only now— More of that delayed action. Damn that delayed action.

The renting agent and Thorwald had both started even from the living room window. An intervening gap of blind wall, and both had reappeared at the kitchen window, still one above the other. But some sort of a hitch or flaw or jump had taken place, right there, that bothered me. The eye is a reliable surveyor. There wasn't anything the matter with their timing, it was with their parallel-ness, or whatever the word is. The hitch had been vertical, not horizontal. There had been an upward "jump."

Now I had it, now I knew. And it couldn't wait. It was too good. They wanted a body? Now I had one for them.

Sore or not, Boyne would *have* to listen to me now. I didn't waste any time, I dialed his precinct-house then and there in the dark, working the slots in my lap by memory alone. They didn't make much noise going around, just a light click. Not even as distinct as that cricket out there—

"He went home long ago," the desk sergeant said.

This couldn't wait. "All right, give me his home phone number."

He took a minute, came back again. "Trafalgar," he said. Then nothing more.

"Well? Trafalgar what?" Not a sound.

"Hello? Hello?" I tapped it. "Operator, I've been cut off. Give me that party again." I couldn't get her either.

I hadn't been cut off. My wire had been cut. That had been too sudden, right in the middle of— And to be cut like that it would have to be done somewhere right here inside the house with me. Outside it went underground.

Delayed action. This time final, fatal, altogether too late. A voiceless ring of the phone. A direction-finder of a look from over there. "Sam" seemingly trying to get back in a while ago.

Surely, death was somewhere inside the house here with me. And I couldn't move, I couldn't get up out of this chair. Even if I had gotten through to Boyne just now, that would have been too late. There wasn't time enough now for one of those camera-finishes in this. I could have shouted out the window to that gallery of sleeping rear-window neighbors around me, I supposed. It would have brought them to the windows. It couldn't have brought them over here in time. By the time they had even figured which particular house it was coming from, it would stop again, be over with. I didn't open my mouth. Not because I was brave, but because it was so obviously useless.

He'd be up in a minute. He must be on the stairs now, although I couldn't hear him. Not even a creak. A creak would have been a relief, would have placed him. This was like being shut up in the dark with the silence of a gliding, coiling cobra somewhere around you.

There wasn't a weapon in the place with me. There were books there on the wall, in the dark, within reach. Me, who never read. The former owner's books. There was a bust of Rousseau or Montesquieu, I'd never been able to decide which, one of those gents with flowing manes, topping them. It was a monstrosity, bisque clay, but it too dated from before my occupancy.

I arched my middle upward from the chair seat and clawed desperately up at it. Twice my fingertips slipped off it, then at the third raking I got it to teeter, and the fourth brought it down into my lap, pushing me down into the chair. There was a steamer rug under me. I didn't need it around me in this weather, I'd been using it to soften the seat of the chair. I tugged it out from under and mantled it around me like an Indian brave's blanket. Then I squirmed far down in the chair, let my head and one shoulder dangle out over the arm, on the side next to the wall. I hoisted the bust to my other, upward shoulder, balanced it there precariously for a second head, blanket tucked around its ears. From the back, in the dark, it would look—I hoped—

I proceeded to breathe adenoidally, like someone in heavy upright sleep. It wasn't hard. My own breath was coming nearly that labored anyway, from tension.

He was good with knobs and hinges and things. I never heard the door open, and this one, unlike the one downstairs, was right behind me. A little eddy of air puffed through the dark at me. I could feel it because my scalp, the real one, was all wet at the roots of the hair right then.

If it was going to be a knife or head-blow, the dodge might give me a second chance, that was the most I could hope for, I knew. My arms and shoulders are hefty. I'd bring him down on me in a bear-hug after the first slash or drive, and break his neck or collarbone against me. If it was going to be a gun, he'd get me anyway in the end. A difference of a few seconds. He had a gun, I knew, that he was going to use on me in the open, over at Lakeside Park. I was hoping that here, indoors, in order to make his own escape more practicable—

Time was up.

The flash of the shot lit up the room for a second, it was so dark. Or at least the corners of it, like flickering, weak lightning. The bust bounced on my shoulder and disintegrated into chunks.

I thought he was jumping up and down on the floor for a minute with frustrated rage. Then when I saw him dart by me and lean over the window sill to look for a way out, the sound transferred itself rearwards and downwards, became a pummeling with hoof and hip at the street door. The camera-finish after all. But he still could have killed me five times.

I flung my body down into the narrow crevice between chair arm and wall, but my legs were still up, and so was my head and that one shoulder.

He whirled, fired at me so close that it was like looking a sunrise in the face. I didn't feel it, so—it hadn't hit.

"You—" I heard him grunt to himself. I think it was the last thing he said. The rest of his life was all action, not verbal.

He flung over the sill on one arm and dropped into the yard. Two-story drop. He made it because he missed the cement, landed on the sod-strip in the middle. I jacked myself up over the chair arm and flung myself bodily forward at the window, nearly hitting it chin first.

He went all right. When life depends on it, you go. He took the first fence, rolled over that bellywards. He went over the second like a cat, hands and feet pointed together in a spring. Then he was back in the rear yard of his own building. He got up on something, just about like Sam had— The rest was all footwork, with quick little corkscrew twists at each landing stage. Sam had latched his windows down when he was over there, but he'd reopened one of them for ventilation on his return. His whole life depended now on that casual, unthinking little act—

Second, third. He was up to his own windows. He'd made it. Something went wrong. He veered out away from them in another pretzel-twist, flashed up toward the fifth, the one above. Something sparked in the darkness of one of his own windows where he'd been just now, and a shot thudded heavily out around the quadrangle-enclosure like a big bass drum.

He passed the fifth, the sixth, got up to the roof. He'd made it a second time. Gee, he loved life! The guys in his own windows couldn't get him, he was over them in a straight line and there was too much fire escape interlacing in the way.

I was too busy watching him to watch what was going on around me. Suddenly Boyne was next to me, sighting. I heard him mutter: "I almost hate to do this, he's got to fall so far."

He was balanced on the roof parapet up there, with a star right over his head. An unlucky star. He stayed a minute too long, trying to kill before he was killed. Or maybe he was killed, and knew it.

A shot cracked, high up against the sky, the window pane flew apart all over the two of us, and one of the books snapped right behind me.

Boyne didn't say anything more about hating to do it. My face was pressing outward against his arm. The recoil of his elbow jarred my teeth. I blew a clearing through the smoke to watch him go.

It was pretty horrible. He took a minute to show anything, standing up there on the parapet. Then he let his gun go, as if to say: "I won't need this any more." Then he went after it. He missed the fire escape entirely, came all the way down on the outside. He landed so far out he hit one of the projecting planks, down there out of sight. It bounced his body up, like a springboard. Then it landed again—for good. And that was all.

I said to Boyne: "I got it. I got it finally. The fifth-floor flat, the one over his, that they're still working on. The cement kitchen floor, raised above the level of the other rooms. They wanted to comply with the fire laws and also obtain a dropped living room effect, as cheaply as possible. Dig it up—"

He went right over then and there, down through the basement and over the fences, to save time. The electricity wasn't turned on yet in that one, they had to use their torches. It didn't take them long at that, once they'd got started. In about half an hour he came to the window and wigwagged over for my benefit. It meant yes.

He didn't come over until nearly eight in the morning; after they'd tidied up and taken them away. Both away, the hot dead and the cold dead. He said: "Jeff, I take it all back. That damn fool that I sent up there about the trunk—well, it wasn't his fault, in a way. I'm to blame. He didn't have orders to check on the woman's description, only on the contents of the trunk. He came back and touched on it in a general way. I go home and I'm in bed already, and suddenly pop! into my brain— one of the tenants I questioned two whole days ago had given us a few details and they didn't tally with his on several important points. Talk about being slow to catch on!"

"I've had that all the way through this damn thing," I admitted ruefully. "I call it delayed action. It nearly killed me."

"I'm a police officer and you're not."

"That how you happened to shine at the right time?"

"Sure. We came over to pick him up for questioning. I left them planted there when we saw he wasn't in, and came on over here by myself to square it up with you while we were waiting. How did you happen to hit on that cement floor?"

I told him about the freak synchronization. "The renting agent showed up taller at the kitchen window in proportion to Thorwald, than he had been a moment before when both were at the living room windows together. It was no secret that they were putting in cement floors, topped by a cork composition, and raising them considerable. But it took on new meaning. Since the top floor one has been finished for some time, it had to be the fifth. Here's the way I have it lined up, just in theory. She's been in ill health for years, and he's been out of work, and he got sick of that and of her both. Met this other—"

"She'll be here later today, they're bringing her down under arrest."

"He probably insured her for all he could get, and then started to poison her slowly, trying not to leave any trace. I imagine—and remember, this is pure conjecture—she caught him at it that night the light was on all night. Caught on in some way, or caught him in the act. He lost his head, and did the very thing he had wanted all along to avoid doing. Killed her by violence—strangulation or a blow. The rest had to be hastily improvised. He got a better break than he deserved at that. He thought of the apartment upstairs, went up and looked around. They'd just finished laying the floor, the cement hadn't hardened yet, and the materials were still around. He gouged a trough out of it just wide enough to take her body, put her in, mixed fresh cement and recemented over her, possibly raising the general level of the flooring an inch or two so that she'd be safely covered. A permanent, odorless coffin. Next day the workmen came back, laid down the cork surfacing on top of it without noticing anything, I suppose he'd used one of their own trowels to smooth it. Then he sent his accessory upstate fast, near where his wife had been several summers before, but to a different farmhouse where she wouldn't be recognized, along with the trunk keys. Sent the trunk up after her, and dropped himself an already used post card into his mailbox, with the year-date blurred. In a week or two she would have probably committed 'suicide' up there as Mrs. Anna Thorwald. Despondency due to ill health. Written him a farewell note and left her clothes beside some body of deep water. It was risky, but they might have succeeded in collecting the insurance at that."

By nine Boyne and the rest had gone. I was still sitting there in the chair, too keyed up to sleep. Sam came in and said: "Here's Doc Preston."

He showed up rubbing his hands, in that way he has. "Guess we can take that cast off your leg now. You must be tired of sitting there all day doing nothing."

MARY ROBERTS RINEHART

(1876–1958)

Mary Roberts Rinehart's early life, though painful, could hardly have been better devised to produce the sort of writer she turned out to be. When she was nine, her father killed himself after failing as a salesman. Her mother took boarders into their Pittsburgh home to make ends meet.

Young Rinehart began writing for her school paper and entering stories in *Pittsburgh Press* contests. She earned a nursing degree, worked on the hospital wards that dealt with the blue-collar and bar-fight traffic, married a doctor, bore three sons, and did not return to writing until she was thirty. Within three years, her second book, *The Man in Lower Ten*, became the first detective novel to become a national best-seller in the United States. In the wake of this phenomenal success, she accompanied her husband to Europe, where he studied his specialty. She applied her writing skills to articles about politics and medicine, became a war correspondent for the *Saturday Evening Post*, used her nursing credentials to avoid the military ban on reporters at the front, and won herself a second national reputation.

Home again after the war, she wrote ten more best-sellers, numerous other books, articles and short stories for the big-circulation "slicks," and two smash-hit plays. In addition, she found time to take part in the woman-suffrage movement and to spread public awareness of breast cancer.

Rinehart changed the course of American detective fiction by infusing into the puzzle the personal details that produce in readers a strong identification with the heroine, thereby causing them to share her fear, bafflement, and final triumph.

Despite its brevity, "The Lipstick" provides a look at the usual characteristics of Rinehart's stories. The narrator is a self-reliant young woman whose eye for domestic detail (the lipstick) leads to the solution of the crime. Rinehart uses a bit of romance, a touch of humor, about as much development of minor characters as was typical of the genre in her day, and an adversarial relationship between the heroine and the police. This short form doesn't sustain a device that Rinehart popularized in her novels—maintaining suspense by keeping the plucky heroine in constant jeopardy. Critics called this the "Had I But Known" tactic, and scoffed at it. But it worked.

1942

The Lipstick

■

I walked home after the coroner's inquest. Mother had gone on in the car, looking rather sick, as she had ever since Elinor's death. Not that she had particularly cared for Elinor. She has a pattern of life which divides people into conformers and nonconformers. The conformers pay their bills the first of the month, go to church, never by any chance get into anything but the society columns of the newspapers, and regard marriage as the *sine qua non* of every female over twenty.

My cousin Elinor Hammond had flouted all this. She had gone gaily through life, as if she wakened each morning wondering what would be the most fun that day; stretching her long lovely body between her silk sheets—how Mother resented those sheets—and calling to poor tired old Fred in his dressing room.

"Let's have some people in for cocktails, Fred."

"Anything you say, darling."

It was always like that. Anything Elinor said was all right with Fred. He worshiped her. As I walked home that day I was remembering his face at the inquest. He had looked dazed.

"You know of no reason why your—why Mrs. Hammond should take her own life?"

"None whatever."

"There was nothing in her state of health to cause her anxiety?"

"Nothing. She had always seemed to be in perfect health."

"She was consulting Dr. Barclay."

"She was tired. She was doing too much," he said unhappily.

Yet there it was. Elinor had either fallen or jumped from that tenth-floor window of Dr. Barclay's waiting room, and the coroner plainly believed she had jumped. The doctor had not seen her at all that day. Only the nurse.

"There was no one else in the reception room," she testified. "The doctor was busy with a patient. Mrs. Hammond sat down and took off her hat. Then she picked up a magazine. I went back to my office to copy some records. I didn't see her again until . . ."

The nurse was a pretty little thing. She looked pale.

"Tell us what happened next," said the coroner gently.

"I heard the other patient leave about five minutes later. She went out from the consulting room. There's a door there into the hall. When the doctor buzzed for the next case I went in to get Mrs. Hammond.

She wasn't there. I saw her hat, but her bag was gone. Then—then I heard people shouting in the street, and I looked out the window."

"What would you say was her mental condition that morning, Miss Comings?" the coroner asked. "Was she depressed?"

"I thought she seemed very cheerful," the nurse said.

"The window was open beside her?"

"Yes. I couldn't believe it until I . . . ."

The coroner excused her then. It was clear that she had told all she knew.

When Dr. Barclay was called, I was surprised. I had expected an elderly man, but he was only in the late thirties and good-looking. Knowing Elinor, I wondered. Except for Fred, who had no looks whatever, she had had a passion for handsome men.

Beside me, I heard Mother give a ladylike snort. "So that's it!" she said. "She had as much need for a psychiatrist as I have for a third leg."

But the doctor added little to what we already knew. He had not seen Elinor at all that morning. When he rang the buzzer and nobody came, he had gone into the reception room. Miss Comings was leaning out the window. All at once she began to scream. Fortunately, a Mrs. Thompson arrived at that time and took charge of her. The doctor had gone down to the street, but the ambulance had already arrived.

He was frank enough up to that time. Queried about the reason for Elinor's consulting him, he tightened. "I have many patients like Mrs. Hammond," he said. "Women who live on their nerves. Mrs. Hammond had been doing that for years."

"That is all? She mentioned no particular trouble?"

He smiled faintly. "We all have troubles," he said. "Some we imagine; some we magnify; some are real. But I would say that Mrs. Hammond was an unusually normal person. I had recommended that she go away for a rest. I believe she meant to do so."

His voice was clipped and professional. If Elinor had been attracted to him, it had been apparently a one-sided affair.

"You did not gather that she contemplated suicide?"

"No. Not at any time."

That is all they got out of him. He evaded them on anything Elinor had imagined or magnified. His relations with his patients, he said, were confidential. If he knew anything of value he would tell it, but he did not.

Mother nudged me as he finished. "Probably in love with her. He's had a shock. That's certain."

He sat down near us, and I watched him. I saw him come to attention when the next witness was called. It was the Mrs. Thompson who had looked after the nurse, a large motherly-looking woman.

She stated at once that she was not a patient. "I clean the doctor's apartment once a week," she said. "That day I needed a little money in advance, so I went to see him."

She had not entered the office at once. She had looked in and seen Elinor, so she had waited in the hall. She had seen the last patient, a woman, leave by the consulting-room door and go down in the elevator. A minute or so later she heard the nurse scream.

"She was leaning out the window yelling her head off. Then the doctor ran in and I got her on a couch. She said somebody had fallen out, but she didn't say who it was."

Asked how long she had been in the hall, she thought about a quarter of an hour. She was certain no other patients had entered during that time. She would have seen them if they had.

"You found something belonging to Mrs. Hammond in the office, didn't you?"

"Yes, sir. I found her bag."

The bag, it seemed, had been behind the radiator in front of the window.

So that was that. Elinor, having put her hat on the table, had dropped her bag behind the radiator before she jumped. Somehow, it didn't make sense to me.

The verdict was suicide while of unsound mind. The window had been examined, but there was the radiator in front of it, and the general opinion seemed to be that a fall would have to be ruled out. Nobody mentioned murder. In the face of Mrs. Thompson's testimony, it looked impossible.

Fred listened to the verdict with blank eyes. His sister Margaret, sitting beside him dressed in mourning, rose. And Dr. Barclay stared straight ahead of him as though he did not hear it. Then he got up and went out, and while I put Mother in the car I saw him driving away, still with that queer fixed look on his face.

I was in a fine state of fury as I walked home. I had always liked Elinor, even when she had snatched Fred from under my nose, as Mother rather inelegantly said. As a matter of cold fact, Fred Hammond never saw me after he met her. He had worshiped her from the start, and his white stunned face at the inquest only added to the mystery.

The fools! I thought. As though Elinor would ever have jumped out of that window, even if she had been in trouble. She had never cared what people thought. I remembered almost the last time I had seen her. Somebody had given a suppressed-desire party, and Elinor had gone with a huge red *A* on the front of her white-satin dress.

Mother nearly had a fit when she saw it. "I trust, Elinor," she said, "that your scarlet letter does not mean what it appears to mean."

Elinor had laughed "What do you think, Aunt Emma? Would you swear that never in your life—"

"That will do, Elinor," Mother said.

Elinor had been very gay that night, and she had enjoyed the little run-in with Mother. Perhaps that was one of the reasons I had liked her. She could cope with Mother. She wasn't an only daughter, living at home on an allowance which was threatened every now and then. And she had brought laughter and gaiety into my small world.

Mother was having tea when I got home. She sat stiffly behind the tea tray and inspected me. "I can't see why you worry about this, Louise. What's done is done. After all, she led Fred a miserable life."

"She made him happy, and now she's dead," I said. "Also, I don't believe she threw herself out that window."

"Then she fell."

"I don't believe that, either."

"Nonsense! What do you believe?"

But I had had enough. I went upstairs to my room. My mind was running in circles. Somebody had killed Elinor and had got away with it. Yet who could have hated her enough for that? A jealous wife? That was possible.

I could see the Hammond place from my window, and the thought of Fred sitting there alone was more than I could bear. Not that I had ever been in love with him, in spite of Mother's hopes. I dressed and went down to dinner, but I couldn't eat. Luckily it was Mother's bridge night, and after she and her three cronies were settled at the table I slipped out through the kitchen.

Annie, the cook, was making sandwiches and cutting cake. I told her to say I had gone to bed if I was asked for, and went out.

Fred's house was only two blocks away, set in its own grounds like ours, and as I entered the driveway I saw a man standing there looking at the place. I must have surprised him, for he turned around and looked at me. It was Dr. Barclay.

He didn't recognize me. He touched his hat and went out to the street, and a moment later I heard his car start. But if he had been in the house Fred did not mention it. I rang, and he opened the door. He seemed relieved when he saw me. "Thought you were the damned police again," he said. "Come in. I've sent the servants to bed."

We went into the library. It looked as if it hadn't been dusted for a month. Elinor's house had always looked that way: full of people and cigarette smoke and used highball glasses. But at least it had looked alive. Now—well, now it didn't. So it was a surprise to see her bag lying on the table. Fred saw me looking at it. "Police returned it today," he said.

"May I look inside it, Fred?"

"Go to it," he said dully. "There's no note there, if that's what you're thinking."

I opened the bag. It was crammed as usual: compact, rouge, coin purse, a zipper compartment with some bills in it, a memorandum book, a handkerchief smeared with lipstick, a tiny perfume vial, and some samples of dress material with a card pinned to them: *Match slippers to these.*

Fred was watching me, his eyes red and sunken. "I told you. Nothing."

I searched the bag again, but I could not find the one thing which should have been there. I closed the bag and put it back on the table.

Fred was staring at a photograph of Elinor in a silver frame. "All this police stuff," he said. "Why can't they just let her rest? She was beautiful, wasn't she, Lou?"

"She was indeed," I said.

"People said things. Margaret thought she was foolish and extravagant." He glanced at the desk, piled high with what looked like unopened bills. "Maybe she was, but what the hell did I care?"

He seemed to expect some comment, so I said, "You didn't have to buy her, Fred. You had her. She was devoted to you."

He gave me a faint smile, like a frightened small boy who has been reassured. "She was, Lou," he said. "I wasn't only her husband. I was her father too. She told me everything. Why she had to go to that damned doctor—"

"Didn't you know she was going, Fred?"

"Not until I found a bill from him," he said grimly. "I told her I could prescribe a rest for her, instead of her sitting for hours with that young puppy. But she only laughed."

He talked on, as if he were glad of an audience. He had made her happy. She went her own way sometimes, but she always came back to him. He considered the coroner's verdict an outrage. "She fell. She was always reckless about heights." And he had made no plans, except that Margaret was coming to stay until he closed the place. And as if the mere mention of her had summoned her, at that minute Margaret walked in.

I had never liked Margaret Hammond. She was a tall angular woman, older than Fred, and she merely nodded to me.

"I decided to come tonight," she said. "I don't like your being alone. And tomorrow I want to inventory the house. I'd like to have Father's portrait, Fred."

He winced at that. There had been a long quarrel about old Joe Hammond's portrait ever since Fred's marriage. Not that Elinor had cared about it, but because Margaret had wanted it she had held on to it. I looked at Margaret. Perhaps she was the nearest to a real enemy Elinor had ever had. She had hated the marriage; had resented Elinor's easy-going extravagant life. Even now, she could not help looking at the desk, piled with bills.

"I'd better straighten that for you, Fred," she said. "We'll have to find out how you stand."

"I know how I stand." He got up and they confronted each other, Fred with his back to the desk, as if even then he were trying to protect Elinor from Margaret's prying eyes.

Fred's sister shrugged and let it go.

It was warm that night. I walked slowly home. I had gone nearly half the way when I realized I was being followed. I stopped and turned. But it was only a girl. She spoke my name. "You're Miss Baring, aren't you?"

"Yes. You scared me half to death."

"I'm sorry. I saw you at the inquest today, and a reporter told me your name. Were you a friend of Mrs. Hammond's?"

"She was my cousin. Why?"

The girl seemed to make a decision. "Because I think she was pushed out that window," she said. "I'm in an office across the street, and I was looking out. I didn't know who she was, of course."

"Do you mean you saw it happen?"

"No. But I saw her at the window hardly a minute before it happened, and she was using a lipstick. When I looked out again she was— she was on the pavement." The girl shivered. "I don't think a woman would use a lipstick just before she did a thing like that, do you?"

"No," I said. "You're sure it was Mrs. Hammond you saw?"

"Yes. She had on a green dress, and I had noticed her hair. She didn't have a hat on. I—well, I went back tonight to see if the lipstick was on the pavement. I couldn't find it. But I'm pretty sure she still had it when she fell."

That was what I had not told Fred—that Elinor's gold lipstick was missing from her bag. "We might go and look again," I said. "Do you mind?"

The girl didn't mind, but she would not tell me her name. "Just call me Smith," she said.

I never saw her again, and unless she reads this she will probably never know that she took the first step that solved the case. Because we found the lipstick in the gutter. A dozen cars must have run over it. It was crushed flat, but Elinor's monogram was perfectly readable.

Miss Smith saw it and gasped. "So I was right," she said. The next minute she had hailed a bus and got on it.

It was late when I got to Dr. Barclay's office the next morning. The reception room was empty, so I went to the window and looked down. I tried to think that I was going to jump, and whether I would use a lipstick or not if I were.

The nurse came in. I gave her my name, and after a short wait she took me to the consulting room.

The doctor got up when he saw me, and I merely put Elinor's lipstick on the desk in front of him and sat down.

"I don't understand," he said.

"Mrs. Hammond was at the window in your reception room using that lipstick only a minute before she fell."

"I suppose you mean it fell with her."

"I mean that she never killed herself. Do you think a woman would rouge her mouth just before she meant to do—what we're supposed to think she did?"

He smiled wryly. "My dear girl, if you saw as much of human nature as I do, that wouldn't surprise you."

"So Elinor Hammond jumped out your window with a lipstick in her hand, and you watch the Hammond house last night and then make a bolt for it when I appear! If that makes sense—"

That shocked him. He hadn't recognized me before. "So it was you in the driveway. Well, I suppose I'd better tell you and trust you to keep it to yourself. I hadn't liked the way Mr. Hammond looked at the inquest. I was afraid he might—well, put a bullet in his head."

"You couldn't stop it standing in the driveway," I said skeptically.

He laughed at that. Then he sobered. "I see," he said. "Well, Miss Baring, whatever happened to Mrs. Hammond, I assure you I didn't do it. As for being outside the house, I've told you the truth. I was wondering how to get in when you came along. His sister had called me up. She was worried."

"I wouldn't rely on what Margaret Hammond says. She hated Elinor."

I got up and retrieved the lipstick. He got up too and surveyed me unsmilingly.

"You're a very young and attractive woman, Miss Baring. Why not let this drop? After all, you can't bring her back."

"I know she never killed herself," I said stubbornly, and went out.

I was less surprised than I might have been to find Margaret in the reception room when I reached it. She was standing close to the open window from which Elinor had fallen, and for a minute I thought she was going to jump herself.

"Margaret!" I said sharply.

She looked terrified when she saw me. "Oh, it's you, Louise," she said. "You frightened me." She sat down abruptly. "She must have slipped, Lou. It would be easy. Try it yourself."

But I shook my head. I had no intention of leaning out that window, not with Margaret behind me. She said she had come to pay Fred's bill for Elinor, and I let it go at that. Nevertheless, I felt shivery as I went down in the elevator.

I had trouble starting my car, which is how I happened to see her when she came out of the building. She looked over the pavement and in the gutter. So she either knew Elinor's lipstick had fallen with her or she had missed it out of the bag.

She didn't see me. She hailed a taxi and got into it. To this day, I don't know why I followed her.

I did follow her, however. The taxi went on into the residential part of town. On a thinly settled street it stopped and Margaret got out. She did not see me or my car. She was looking at a frame house with a narrow front porch, and as I watched, she went up and rang the bell.

She was inside the house for almost an hour. I began to feel idiotic. There were so many possible reasons for her being there; reasons which had nothing to do with Elinor. But when she finally came out I sat up in amazement.

The woman seeing her off on the porch was the Mrs. Thompson of the inquest.

I stooped to fix my shoe as the taxi passed me, but I don't believe Margaret even saw the car. Nor did Mrs. Thompson. She sat down on the porch and was still there when I went up the steps.

She looked surprised rather than apprehensive. "I hope you're not selling anything," she said, not unpleasantly.

"I'm not selling anything," I said. "May I talk to you?"

"What about?" She was suspicious now.

"It's about a murder," I said. "There's such a thing as being accessory after the fact, and I think you know something you didn't tell at the Hammond inquest."

Her florid color faded. "It wasn't a murder," she said. "The verdict—"

"I know all about that. Nevertheless, I think it was a murder. What was Miss Hammond doing here if it wasn't?"

Mrs. Thompson looked startled, but she recovered quickly. "I never saw her before," she said. "She came to thank me for my testimony, because it showed the poor thing did it herself."

"And to pay you for it, I suppose?"

She flushed angrily. "Nobody paid me anything. And now you'd better go. If you think anybody can bribe me to lie, you're wrong. That's all."

She went in and slammed the door, and I drove back to town, puzzled over the whole business. Was she telling the truth, or had there been something she had not told at the inquest? Certainly I believed that the doctor had known more than he had told.

I was late for lunch that day, and Mother was indignant. "I can't imagine why, with nothing to do, you are always late for meals," she said.

"I've had plenty to do, Mother," I said. "I've been working on Elinor's murder."

She gave a ladylike squeal. "Murder? Who would do such a thing?"

"Well, Margaret for one. She always loathed her."

"Women in Margaret's position in life do not commit crimes," Mother said pontifically. "Really, I don't know what has happened to you, Louise. The idea of suspecting your friends—"

"She's no friend of mine. Elinor was."

"So you'll stir up all sorts of scandal. Murder indeed! I warn you, Louise, if you keep on with this idiotic idea you'll find yourself spread all over the newspapers. And I'll stop your allowance."

With this dire threat she departed, and I spent the afternoon wondering what Dr. Barclay and the Thompson woman knew or suspected, and in getting a wave at Elinor's hairdresser's.

The girl who set my hair told me something I hadn't known. "Here I was, waiting for her," she said. "She was always prompt. Of course she never came, and—"

"You mean you expected her here, the day it happened?"

"That's right," she agreed. "She had an appointment for four o'clock. When I got the paper on my way home I simply couldn't believe it. She'd always been so gay. Of course the last few weeks she hadn't been quite the same, but—"

"How long since you noticed a change in her?" I asked.

"Well, let me see. About Easter, I think. I remember I liked a new hat she had, and she gave it to me then and there! She said a funny thing, too. She said sometimes new hats were dangerous!"

I may have looked better when I left the shop, but my mind was doing pinwheels. Why were new hats dangerous? And why had Elinor changed since Easter?

Fred had dinner with us that evening. At last, he sat at the table and pushed his food around with a fork. Margaret hadn't come. He said she was in bed with a headache, and he spent most of the time talking about Elinor.

It was ghastly, of course. Even Mother looked unhappy. "I wish you'd eat something, Fred," she said. "Try to forget the whole thing. You made her very happy. Always remember that."

I asked him if anything had upset Elinor since Easter. He stared at me.

"I don't remember anything, Lou. Except that she started going to that damned psychiatrist then."

"Why did she go to him, Fred?" Mother inquired. "If she had any inhibitions I never noticed them."

If there was a barb in this, he wasn't aware of it. "You saw him," he said. "He is a good-looking devil. Maybe she liked to look at him. It would be a change from looking at me."

He went home soon after that. In spite of his previous protests, I thought he had resented the doctor's good looks and Elinor's visits to him. And I wondered if he was trying to build up a defense against her in his own mind; to remember her as less than perfect in order to ease his tragic sense of loss.

I slept badly, so I was late for breakfast the next morning. Mother had finished the paper, and I took it.

Tucked away on a back page was an item reporting that Mrs. Thompson had been shot the night before!

I read and reread it. She was not dead, but her condition was critical. All the police had been able to learn from the family was that she had been sitting alone on the front porch when it happened. Nobody had even heard the shot. She had been found by her husband when he came home from a lodge meeting at eleven o'clock. She was unconscious, and the hospital reported her as being still too low to make a statement.

So she had known something, poor thing. Something that made her dangerous. And again I remembered Margaret going up the steps of the little house on Charles Street; Margaret searching for Elinor's lipstick in the street. Margaret, who had hated Elinor and who was now in possession of Fred, of old Joe Hammond's portrait, of Elinor's silk sheets, and—I suddenly remembered—of Fred's automatic, which had lain in his desk drawer for years.

I think it was the automatic which finally decided me.

Anyhow, I went to our local precinct stationhouse that afternoon and told a man behind a high desk that I wanted to see the person in charge. "He's busy," the man said, eying me indifferently.

"All right," I said. "If he's too busy to look into a murder, then I'll go downtown to Headquarters."

"Who's been murdered?"

"I'll tell *him* that."

There was an officer passing, and the man called him. "Young lady here's got a murder on her mind," he said. "Might see if the captain's busy."

The captain was not busy, but he wasn't interested either. When I told him it was about Elinor Hammond, he said he understood the case was closed, and anyhow, it hadn't happened in his district. As Mrs. Thompson was not in his district either, and as he plainly thought I was either out of my mind or looking for publicity, I finally gave up.

The man behind the desk grinned at me as I went out. "Want us to call for the corpse?" he inquired.

"I wouldn't ask you to call for a dead dog," I told him bitterly.

But there was a result, after all. I drove around the rest of the afternoon trying to decide what to do. When I got home I found Mother in the hall.

"There's a policeman here to see you," she hissed. "What have you done?"

I said, "I haven't done anything. It's about Elinor. I want to see this man alone, Mother."

"I think you're crazy," she said furiously. "It's all over. She got into trouble and killed herself. She was always headed for trouble. The first thing you know you'll be arrested yourself."

She followed me into the living room, and before I could speak to the detective there she told him I had been acting strangely for days and she was going to call a doctor and put me to bed.

"Suppose we let her talk for herself," he said. "Now, Miss Baring, what's all this about a murder?"

So I told him: about Elinor and the lipstick; about her appointment at the hairdresser's for shortly after the time she was lying dead on the pavement; about my conviction that Mrs. Thompson knew something she hadn't told.

"I gather you think Mrs. Hammond didn't kill herself. Is that it?"

"Does it look like it?" I demanded.

"Then who did it?"

"I think it was her sister-in-law."

Mother almost had a fit at that. She got up saying that I was hysterical.

But the detective did not move. "Let her alone," he said gruffly. "What about this sister-in-law?"

"I found her in Dr. Barclay's office yesterday," I said. "She insisted that Elinor had fallen out the window. Maybe it sounds silly, but she knew about the lipstick. She tried to find it in the street. I think she was in the office the day Elinor was killed. I think the Thompson woman knew it. And I think Margaret Hammond shot her."

"Shot her?" he said sharply. "Is that the woman out on Charles Street?"

"Yes."

He eyed me steadily. "Why do you think Miss Hammond shot her?"

"Because she went there yesterday morning to talk to her. I followed her."

Mother started again. She couldn't understand my behavior. Margaret had been in bed last night with a headache. It would be easy to verify that. The servants . . .

The detective waited patiently and then got up. "I have a little advice for you, Miss Baring," he said. "Leave this to us. If you're right and there's been a murder and a try at another one, that's our job."

It was Mother who went to bed that afternoon, while I waited at the telephone. And when the detective finally called me, the news left me exactly where I had been before. Mrs. Thompson had recovered consciousness and made a statement. She did not know who shot her or why, but she insisted that Margaret had visited her merely to thank her for her testimony, which had shown definitely that Elinor had either fallen or jumped out the window. She had neither been offered nor given any money.

There was more to it, however. It appeared that Mrs. Thompson had been worried since the inquest and had telephoned Margaret to ask her if what bothered her was important. As a matter of fact, someone *had* entered the doctor's office while she was in the hall.

"But it was natural enough," the detective said. "It was the one individual nobody ever really notices. The postman."

"The postman?" I said weakly.

"Exactly. I've talked to him. He saw Mrs. Hammond in the office that morning. He remembers her. She had her hat off, and she was reading a magazine."

"Did he see Mrs. Thompson?"

"He didn't notice her, but she saw him."

"So he shot her last night!"

The detective laughed. "He took his family to the movies last night. And remember this, Miss Baring: that shot may have been an accident. Plenty of people carry guns now who never did before."

It was all very cheerio. Elinor had committed suicide, and Mrs. Thompson had been shot by someone who was practicing for Hitler. Only I just didn't believe it. I believed it even less after I had a visit from Dr. Barclay that night.

Mother was still in bed refusing to see me, and I was listening to the radio when the maid showed him in.

"I'm sorry to butt in like this," he said. "I won't take much of your time."

"Then it's not a professional call?"

He looked surprised. "Certainly not. Why?"

"Because my mother thinks I'm losing my mind," I said rather wildly. "Elinor Hammond is dead, so let her lie. Mrs. Thompson is shot, but why worry? Remember the papers! Remember the family name! No scandal, please!"

"You're in bad shape, aren't you? How about going to bed? I'll talk to you later."

"So I'm to go to bed!" I said nastily. "That would be nice and easy, wouldn't it? Somebody is getting away with murder. Maybe two murders. And everybody tries to hush me up. Even the police!"

That jolted him. "You've been to the police?"

"Why not? Why shouldn't the police be told? Just because you don't want it known that someone was pushed out of your office window—"

He was angry, but he tried to control himself. "See here," he said. "You're dealing with things you don't understand. Why can't you stay out of this case?"

"There wasn't any case until I made one," I said furiously. "Why is everybody warning me off? How do I know you didn't do it yourself? You could have. Either you or the postman. And he was at the movies!"

"The postman!" he said, staring. "What do you mean, the postman?"

I suppose it was his astonished face which made me laugh. I laughed and laughed. I couldn't stop. Then I was crying too. I couldn't stop that either. Without warning he slapped my face.

It jerked my head back, but it stopped me. "That's the girl," he said. "You'd have had the neighbors in in another minute. You'd better go up to bed, and I'll send you some sleeping stuff from the drugstore."

369

"I wouldn't take anything you sent me on a bet."

He ignored that. "Believe it or not," he said, "I didn't come here to attack you! I came to ask you not to go out alone at night until I tell you that you may. I mean what I'm saying," he added. "Don't go out of this house alone at night, Miss Baring—any night."

"Don't be ridiculous!" I said, still raging. "Why shouldn't I go out at night?"

"Because it may be dangerous," he said shortly. "I particularly want you to keep away from the Hammond house."

He banged the front door when he went out, and I spent the next half hour hating him like poison. I was still angry when the phone rang. It was Margaret!

"I suppose we have you to thank for the police coming here to-night," she said. "Why can't you leave us alone? We're in trouble enough, without you making things worse."

"All right," I said recklessly. "Now I'll ask you one. Why did you visit Mrs. Thompson yesterday morning? And who shot her last night?"

She gasped and hung up the receiver.

It was a half hour later when the druggist's boy brought the sleeping tablets. I took them to the kitchen and dropped them in the coal range, while Annie watched me with amazement. She was fixing Mother's hot milk, I remember, and she told me that Clara, the Hammonds' cook, had been over.

"She says things are queer over there," she reported. "Somebody started the furnace last night, and the house was so hot this morning you couldn't live in it."

I didn't pay much attention. I was still shaken. Then I saw Annie look up, and Fred was standing on the kitchen porch.

"May I come in?" he asked. "I was taking a walk and I saw the light."

He looked better, I thought. He said Margaret was in bed, and the house was lonely. Then he asked if Annie would make him a cup of coffee.

"I don't sleep much, anyhow," he said. "It's hard to get adjusted. And the house is hot. I've been getting rid of a lot of stuff. Burning it."

So that explained the furnace.

I walked out with him when he left and watched him as he started home. Then I turned up the driveway again. I was near the house when it happened. I remember the shrubbery rustling, but I never heard the shot. Something hit me on the head. I fell, and after that there was a complete blackout until I heard Mother's voice. I was in my own bed with a bandage around my head and an ache in it that made me dizzy.

"The idea of her going out when you told her not to!" Mother was saying.

"I did my best," said a masculine voice. "But you have a very stubborn daughter."

It was Dr. Barclay. He was standing beside the bed when I opened my eyes. I remember saying, "You slapped me."

"And a lot of good it did," he retorted. "Now look where you are!"

I could see him better by that time. he looked very queer. One of his eyes was almost shut, and his collar was a wilted mess. I stared at him. "What happened?" I asked. "You've been in a fight."

"More or less."

"And what's this thing on my head?"

"That is what you get for disobeying orders."

I began to remember then—the scuffling in the bushes, and something knocking me down. He reached over and took my pulse.

"You've got a very pretty bullet graze on the side of your head," he said. "Also, I've had to shave off quite a bit of your hair." I suppose I wailed at that, for he shifted from my pulse to my hand. "Don't worry about that. It was very pretty hair, but it will grow again. At least, thank God, you're here!"

"Who did it? Who shot at me?"

"The postman, of course," he said, and to my fury went out of the room.

I slept after that. I suppose he had given me something. Anyhow, it was the next morning before I heard the rest of the story. Mother had fallen for Dr. Barclay completely, and she wouldn't let him see me until my best silk blanket cover was on the bed. Even then in a hand mirror I looked dreadful, with my head bandaged and my skin yellowish-gray. The doctor didn't seem to mind, however. He came in, big and smiling, with his right eye completely closed, and told me I looked like the wrath of heaven.

"You're not looking your best yourself," I said.

"Oh, that!" he observed, touching his eye gingerly. "Your mother put a silver knife smeared with butter on it last night. Quite a person, Mother."

He said I was to excuse his appearance, because he had been busy all night with the police. He'd go and clean up.

"You're not moving out of this room until I know what's been going on," I stormed. "I'm running a fever right now, out of pure excitement."

He put a big hand on my forehead. "No fever," he said. "Just your detective mind running in circles. All right. Where do I start?"

"With the postman."

So then he told me. Along in the spring, Elinor had come to him with a queer story. She said she was being followed. It made her nervous. In fact, she was frightened. It seemed that the man who was watching her wore a postman's uniform. She would be having lunch at a restaurant—perhaps with what she called a man friend—and he would be outside a window. He would turn up in all sorts of places. It sounded fantastic, but she swore it was true.

Some faint ray of intelligence came to me. "Do you mean it was this man Mrs. Thompson saw going into your office?"

"She's already identified him. The real letter carrier had been there earlier. He had seen Mrs. Hammond reading a magazine. But he had gone before the Thompson woman arrived. The one she saw was the one who—killed Elinor."

I knew before he told me. I felt sick. "It was Fred, wasn't it?"

"It was Fred Hammond. Yes." Dr. Barclay reached over and took my hand. "Tough luck, my dear. I was worried about it. I tried to get her to go away, but she wouldn't do it. And then she wore a dress at a party with a scarlet *A* on it, and I suppose that finished him."

"It's crazy!" I gasped. "He adored her."

"He had an obsession about her. He loved her, yes. But he was afraid he might lose her. And he was wildly jealous."

"But if he really loved her—"

"The line between love and hate is pretty fine. And it's just possible too that he felt she was never really his until—well, until no one else could have her."

"So he killed her!"

"He killed her," Dr. Barclay said slowly. "He knew that nobody notices the postman, so he walked into my office and—"

"But he was insane," I said. "You can't send him to the chair."

"Nobody will send him to the chair." The doctor hesitated. "I was too late last night. I caught him just as he fired at you, but he put up a real battle. He got loose somehow, and shot himself."

He went on quietly. There was no question of Fred's guilt, he said. Mrs. Thompson had identified his photograph as that of the postman she had seen going into the office and coming out shortly before she heard the nurse screaming. The bullet with which she had been shot had come from Fred's gun. And Margaret—poor Margaret—had been suspicious of his sanity for a long time.

"She came to see me yesterday after she learned the Thompson woman had been shot. She wanted her brother committed to an institution, but she got hysterical when I mentioned the police. I suppose there wasn't much of a case, anyhow. With Mrs. Thompson apparently dying and the uniform gone—"

"Gone? Gone how?"

"He'd burned it in the furnace. We found some charred buttons last night."

"Why did he try to kill Mrs. Thompson?" I asked. "What did she know?"

"She remembered seeing a postman going in and out of my office. She even described him. And Margaret found the uniform in the attic. She knew then.

"She collapsed. She couldn't face Fred. She locked herself in her room, trying to think what to do. But she had told Fred she was going to see Mrs. Thompson that day, and she thinks perhaps he knew she had found the uniform. She doesn't know, nor do I. All we do know is that he left this house that night, got out his car and tried to kill the only witness against him. Except you, of course."

"Except me!" I said.

"Except you," the doctor repeated dryly. "I tried to warn you, you may remember!"

"But why me? He had always liked me. Why would he try to kill me?"

"Because you wouldn't leave things alone. Because you were a danger from the minute you insisted Elinor had been murdered. And because you asked Margaret on the phone why she had visited Mrs. Thompson, and who had shot her."

"You think he was listening in?"

"I know he was listening in. He wasn't afraid of his sister. She would have died to protect him, and he knew it. But here you were, a child with a stick of dynamite, and you come out with a thing like that! That was when Margaret sent me to warn you."

"I'm sorry. I've been a fool all along."

The doctor's good eye twinkled. "I wouldn't go so far as that," he said. "That stubbornness of yours really broke the case. Not that I like stubborn women."

I had difficulty in getting him back to the night before. But he finally admitted that he had been watching the Hammond house all evening, and that when Fred came to our kitchen door he had been just outside. Fred had seemed quiet, drinking his coffee. Then I had walked out to the street with him.

It had looked all right at first. Fred had started down the street toward home, and he followed behind the hedge. But he lost him, and he knew he was on his way back. Fred had his revolver lifted to shoot me when he grabbed him.

Suddenly I was crying. It was all horrible: Elinor at the window, and Fred behind her; Mrs. Thompson resting after a hard day's work, and Fred shooting her. And I myself—

Dr. Barclay got out a grimy handkerchief and dried my eyes. "Stop it," he said. "It's all over now, and you're a plucky young woman, Louise Baring. Don't spoil the record." He rose abruptly. "I'm giving up your case. There'll be someone in to dress that head of yours."

"Why can't you do it?"

"I'm not that sort of doctor."

I looked up at him. He was haggard with strain. He was dirty, he needed a shave, and that eye of his was getting blacker by the minute. But he was big and strong and sane. A woman would be safe with him, I thought. Although she could never tell him her dreams.

"I don't see why you can't look after me," I said. "If I'm to look bald I'd prefer you to see it. After all, you did it."

He grinned. Then to my surprise he leaned down and kissed me lightly on the cheek. "I've wanted to do that ever since you slammed that lipstick down in front of me," he said. "And now will you please stop being a detective and concentrate on growing some hair on the side of your head? Because I'm going to be around for a considerable time."

When I looked up Mother was in the doorway, beaming.

ROBERT LESLIE BELLEM

(1902–1968)

||||||||||||||||||||||||||||||||||||||||| ■ ||||||||||||||||||||||||||||||||||||||||||

In some 3,000 short stories written for the pulp magazines during the 1930s, 1940s, and 1950s, Robert Leslie Bellem demonstrated an ability to conform to the hard-boiled formula and to transcend it at the same time. It is fair enough to describe this prolific maverick with a string of clichés: he possessed an ear for dialogue, an eye for the ladies, a sixth sense for humor. In short, he kept a finger on the pulse of popular fiction. But he did more than that, too.

Critics marvel at Bellem's ability to stand out from the crowd of pulp writers even while remaining an enthusiastic member of the group. He embraced every hard-boiled convention of language, character, and milieu. No slouch at slang, he loved lurid language, wisecracking, and tough talk; but there is always the sense that he was playing with words intentionally rather than working in a limited idiom.

His characters, too, fulfill the stereotypes of the pulps: the femme fatale, the starlet, and, of course, the gumshoe himself. But again, there is a playfulness that endows the characterizations with a "camp" quality.

If his characters are sometimes intentional exaggerations of stereotypes, his choice of milieu is suited to this, particularly in his Dan Turner, Hollywood Detective, stories. With its glitz and glamour contrasting with seediness, with its posturing and poses, and with its false promises, Tinseltown is the perfect backdrop for pulp characters unusually aware of the roles that they are playing on the stage of American life.

Turner is not Bellem's only series character—the prolific author used several others—but the Hollywood Detective is certainly his most memorable. The offbeat exuberance of the Turner stories, with their swift pace and fast talk, kept readers eager for more for almost two decades. From the character's first appearance in *Spicy Detective* in 1934 to his central role in the magazine created and named for him eight years later, *Dan Turner, Hollywood Detective*, this sleuth has been first and foremost an entertainer—who was created, managed, and directed by a true artist of pulp fiction.

1943

Homicide Highball

■

I tossed another coin on the counter and the bleached blonde handed me three more baseballs. I hefted one of them, prepared to heave it; but before I could let fly, the yellow-haired gal dropped dead with a crushed skull. Five minutes later I was collared for the killing.

Putting it that way, it sounds about as impersonal as a telegram condensed to fifty words for economy's sake. It didn't seem so impersonal to me at the time, though. My neck was in a lonely spot and I mighty well realized it. If ever a guy had been draped with a murder frame, I was that guy.

The whole thing started the previous afternoon when Roy Cromwell, ace director for Paravox Pix, ankled into my agency office with an embarrassed look on his handsome mush. He was a stalwart ape in the loudest set of tweeds this side of an air raid alarm, and his fame for making hit films was exceeded only by his rep as a Romeo in private life.

Crossing my threshold, he flashed me a sheepish grin. "Hiya, Philo. How's the best private eye in Hollywood?"

"The name is Dan Turner," I said. "Mister to you."

He reddened. "Still sore, eh?"

"I never forget a raw deal."

"I didn't mean it to be as raw as it turned out," he protested mildly. "Why pack a grudge?"

"I've got every reason to pack a grudge. You had a girl in a Sunset Strip dice club one night a month ago. The joint was raided. You begged me to take the doll off your hands and pretend I was her escort. Like a dope, I agreed."

He said: "I appreciated the favor. Honest I did."

"Sure," I sneered. "Only it developed that she was engaged to Bernie Ballantyne, production mogul for Paravox; in other words, your boss. That's why you palmed her off on me. If Bernie found out you were entertaining his sweetie, he might get even by dropping your option, so you picked me for a fall guy."

"But, Dan, listen—"

I waved him quiet. "So what happened? Bernie made *me* the target of his jealousy; barred me off the lot. I used to get all of the Paravox snooping business; picked up some fat fees. But now, thanks to you, I can't even go through the gates."

"That's where you're wrong," Cromwell said placatingly. "Ballantyne wants to bury the hatchet."

"Yeah. In my dandruff."

"No. He's got a job for you."

I gave him the surly focus. "Quit ribbing."

"A thousand dollars is no rib." He took a check from his wallet, threw it on my desk. It was for a grand, made out to me, and signed with Bernie Ballantyne's scrawled autograph. "That's only the retainer. You'll get more later."

My ire began to fade. "He must crave somebody cooled for this kind of geetus."

All the color leaked out of Cromwell's pan; left it a floury mask. His glimmers bulged. "Wh-what makes you think a thing like th-that?" he choked. Then he recovered some of his poise. "For a minute I thought you were serious. Shall we go on out to the studio? Bernie's waiting."

I said: "Okay," and we hauled bunions. Leaving the building, I wondered why my casual remark had put the director in such a dither. For an instant he'd acted like a bozo with something nasty on his conscience.

His Packard speedster was parked down at the curb, but I preferred my own jalopy for convenience. I trailed him until a traffic semaphore separated us halfway to Culver City. Cromwell beat the red light by a whisker, pulled ahead; and when I finally got a green signal I'd lost him. I remembered this later, although it didn't seem to matter at the time. I didn't need anyone to guide me to Bernie Ballantyne's private sanctum.

The Paravox production bigwig had a layout of offices in the main executive building, just inside the mammoth wrought iron entrance gates. An assortment of secretaries passed me through the various anterooms until I came to the last one, a sort of Gothic waiting chamber architecturally designed to awe you before you entered the holy of holies. I wasn't very impressed, though. I was too interested in a brunette honey who had just stepped out of Ballantyne's room.

I recognized her and said: "Greetings, Toots."

She drew a sharp breath as she tabbed me. She was a fragile little dish, delicate as a Spring breeze in a modish confection of white silk jersey. Her wavy hair was blue-black to match her peepers, and she had a complexion three shades richer than the cream off the top of the bottle. But there was a tremulous quiver to her ripe pomegranate lips, and her mascara was smudged as if she had recently leaked a trace of brine.

This needled my curiosity. Since she was emerging from Bernie Ballantyne's office you'd naturally think he was responsible for her turning on the weeps; which seemed queer in view of the fact that she was his fiancée, Vala DuValle.

She didn't look happy at meeting me. "Mr. T-Turner!"

"Skip the formality and call me Danny-boy. You know, the unfortunate jerk that took you off Roy Cromwell's hands the night a certain dice drop got knocked over. Or have you forgotten how I stuck my neck out for an alleged pal and wound up on the wrong end of a hotfoot?"

She drifted toward me in an aura of expensive fragrance. "Please!" she whispered. "Don't link my n-name with Roy's. Bernie might hear you."

"Would that be such a disaster, hon?"

"You know it would. For Roy, and maybe for m-me, too."

I said: "Then you shouldn't play with fire. Cromwell's dynamite for a jane who's engaged to somebody else."

Her piquant puss got pink. "Roy and I are just good friends, nothing more. You've got to believe that."

"Sure. But does Bernie believe it?"

"He doesn't know anything about it. And he mustn't. He won't either . . . unless somebody carries tales to him. You w-wouldn't do an ugly thing like that, would you, Mr. Turner?"

"Not unless I thought it would pay me dividends," I said. I was only kidding, of course; but the joke seemed to backfire. A dismayed expression crossed her angelic map and she turned, pelted out of the room before I could explain or apologize. I heard her sobbing as she scrammed, and the sound made me feel like the lowest heel in Hollywood.

Well, nuts. I could hunt her up later and make amends, I decided. Meanwhile Ballantyne was waiting for me. I barged to his door, ankled in, hung the squint on him as he sat behind his ornate desk. "You wanted me, Bernie?"

He was a quarrelsome little sourpuss with fretful glims and a thin, petulant kisser surrounded by permanent sneer lines. Not yet thirty, he was one of the most important powers in the flickering tintypes; and like a lot of undersized runts, he used that power the way you'd swing a baseball bat. In fact, he had been a shortstop on several bush league ball teams before he came into the picture industry.

"Sit down," he piped in his high, reedy voice.

I said: "No, thanks," and set fire to a gasper, blew a blob of fumes his way; deliberately stayed on my dogs. This gave me two advantages. It showed him he couldn't boss me around, and it allowed my six-feet-plus to tower over him, stressing his lack of dimensions. You could see he didn't like it.

He held his temper, though. "Climb off your horse, Hawkshaw. So I had you barred from the lot. So I made a mistake. So I'm sorry. Can I help it if I've got a jealous nature?"

"You should learn to call your shots," I said.

He shrugged. "I love Vala so much it gets me down if I think she's interested in another man. If anybody tried to take her away from me, I believe I'd kill him." Then he grinned wryly. "Forget I said that. It doesn't include you."

"Much obliged."

"She explained how you just happened to meet her casually at a party and took her to that dice club the night of the raid. No hard feelings?"

"None at all," I said. If the DuValle cupcake had blown down Ballantyne's suspicions with such an outright lie, it was okay by me. I added: "I just passed her. She looked upset."

"She is upset. That's why I'm hiring you. I want you to find out what's troubling her; why she's drawn large sums of money out of her bank account lately for no plausible reason. I want to be told if she's in some kind of jam."

I said: "A blackmail jam, for instance?"

He twitched. "What gives you that idea?"

"When people act worried and draw big dough from the bank, it usually spells shakedown," I answered. "Any cheap flatfoot could tell you that. Do you know of anything in her past that somebody could use as a basis for extortion?"

"No. She's all right. She's been that way ever since she became our top Paravox star; and there was never any hint of scandal in her private life before that, to my knowledge." His manicured fingernails drummed the polished desk. "I'll admit the blackmail angle occurred to me, though. I even asked her about it point-blank, a moment ago."

"So that's why she looked so woeful," I said. "Did she spill anything?"

"Nothing. She denied she was in trouble of any kind. I don't believe her, of course. I think she's being bled, and I want to know why. More important, I want the blackmailer's name. I'll fix him!"

"Suppose it's a dame instead of a guy?"

A mean glitter came into Ballantyne's shoebutton peepers. "A dame? They make coffins for dames too, don't they?"

I remembered an offhand crack I'd made to Roy Cromwell in my own office about his boss craving somebody cooled. Cromwell had nearly thrown a wing-ding until he saw I wasn't serious. But now, twice in the same dialogue, Bernie Ballantyne was yodeling a murder threat.

CHAPTER II

Under Arrest

My assignment was to keep a constant tail on Vala DuValle during the next few days; check her movements, her contacts. As it happened, she was currently working in a farce comedy opus being produced by Ballantyne and directed by Roy Cromwell; so the next morning I went on a location jaunt with the unit—and ankled into a homicide frame up to my neck.

Outdoor action scenes were to be shot on the amusement pier down at Venice, a once-popular seashore resort that had recently become practically a ghost town since its beach got quarantined by the health authorities because of sewage pollution in the surf. Deserted by vacation tourists, it made an ideal spot for a movie; there was no gawking public to infest the premises, no autograph maniacs to annoy the cast.

Paravox had rented the whole amusement pier; roped it off for camera purposes. Chattering extras thronged the midway, played the sucker games, squealed on the merry-go-rounds and the giant sky-ride that stretched its dizzy dipsy-doodle tracks on slanted trestles over the water. The DuValle quail, playing the heroine, was supposed to meet the leading man for the first time on this sky-ride; according to the screwy scenario she was to fall in love with him while descending an incline at seventy miles an hour. Personally I thought the story smelled, but then I'm just a private snoop, not a critic.

And I didn't seem to be getting very far with my snooping. Cromwell insisted on eleventen rehearsals of the preliminary crowd sequences, in which Vala DuValle didn't even appear. Bored, she retired to her makeshift dressing room in the Fun House; and naturally I couldn't follow her there.

So I did the next best thing; killed time by mingling with a bunch of extras and bit players prowling the pier. There was one concession game that drew my attention: a counter across the narrow open front of a rectangular cubicle. On platforms toward the back wall of this joint, dummy milk bottles were arranged in pyramids, the idea being to knock them down by hurling baseballs at them.

Of course the owner of the caper had leased it to Paravox for the day, the same as all the other concessionaires had done. And the reason the game interested me was because I recognized the contract actress behind the counter, the bleached blonde cutie who was taking the real owner's place. This yellow-haired wren's name was Maizie Murdock and I'd been on many a party with her in the old days.

I leaned an elbow on the counter. "Having fun, babe?"

"Well, dip me in peanut butter if it isn't Dapper Dan, the wolf in sleuth's clothing!" she gave me a welcoming smile. "How are you? Where've you been keeping yourself?"

I said: "Hither and yon. I'm fine. And you?"

"Okay, but lonesome now that you've scratched me from your address book."

I started to tell her I had censorship trouble but never got the words out, because just then somebody laid a hand on my arm. I turned; saw it was Roy Cromwell. "Anything I can do for you?" I asked him.

He said: "Sorry, Sherlock. This is supposed to be the final rehearsal, not a gabfest." Then he seemed to realize he'd sounded like a director throwing his weight around, and he made an apologetic mouth. "Er, I mean—"

"Okay, bub, okay," I waved him off. "I'll powder." I looked at the blonde Murdock filly. "See you soon, hon."

Cromwell registered embarrassment on his handsome pan. "Hey, wait. I've got an idea. As long as you're here among the extras, suppose you toss some baseballs at these bottles. It'll give me some action to focus my cameras on. Can do?"

"Can do," I said. Cromwell faded off behind me and I picked up a ball, hurled it, scored a clean miss. I tried again, twice; did a little better. Then, play-acting, I planked a coin on the counter and Maizie Murdock gave me three more baseballs. I hefted one of them—

Something whammed past my ear like a dirty grey streak. The blur of motion made me duck; and then the Murdock doll let out a stricken bleat that was cut off in the middle as if someone had chopped it with an axe. In fact, I heard a chunking sound; like a blunt hatchet hitting a ripe cocoanut.

I pinned the flabbergasted focus on Maizie just in time to pipe a baseball caroming off her conk, bouncing high in the air. Where it had bashed her, a sudden open fracture appeared. Her blue peepers went glassy and she started to sag.

I yelped: "What the—!" and vaulted the counter; caught her as she toppled. I was too late to do her any good, though. Long before I had lowered her to the floor she had joined up with her ancestors.

She'd been bumped.

For an instant the huge cast and technical crew didn't seem to savvy what had happened. Then chaos spilled over and the panic was on. Three people came sailing at me from the crush: Cromwell, Bernie Ballantyne, and Vala DuValle. I'd known Cromwell was in the crowd, of course; but where Bernie and Vala came from was a mystery to me. One minute they weren't in sight and the following minute they were climbing my back like monkeys picking bananas.

The Ballantyne runt was the worst offender. He kept dragging at my shoulders and yowling: "Call the cops! Get me some law! Help me with this murderer!"

I hunched myself, gave him a flip that sent him flying over into a far corner. This seemed to be the DuValle brunette's cue to dig her fingernails at my glims. She flurried at me, clawing and screeching like a demented banshee. "You beast!" she caterwauled. "You loathesome, slimy beast—!"

I snarled: "Quiet, kiddo," and whapped her a stinger across the chops, hard enough to send her staggering. "Lay off me. I'm not fooling."

Roy Cromwell copped a gander at my palm print on Vala's map and gave a perfect demonstration of a guy blowing his top. "Why, blast your soul!" he roared. Then he grabbed a baseball from the counter and pitched it at my favorite features.

If I hadn't dropped flat on my puss, it would have been just too bad. The throw was an absolute strike; smoked past where my noggin had been an instant before. Had it hit me it would have rendered me defunct. Instead, it crashed against the rear wall of the concession hard enough to split the woodwork in the same way Maizie Murdock's skull had been split by a previous toss. I couldn't help tabbing the similarity.

Rage boiled up inside me. I rolled over, scrambled upright, snaked out my .32 automatic from the shoulder holster where I always carry it for emergencies. I thumbed the safety, curled my finger around the trigger, and got set to blast. "Now, then, chum," I rasped at the director. "One more move out of you and your form will need vulcanizing."

He froze. The DuValle cupcake crouched near him whimpering. Bernie Ballantyne seemed to shrink in his corner, fear scrawled on his rodent profile. "The cops!" he kept mumbling softly. "Isn't anybody going to call the cops?"

"Yeah," I lipped at him. "I am. But first I want to know why you freaks jumped me."

"Because you killed that g-girl," he piped in his reedy falsetto. He stole a furtive glance at the Murdock wren's remainders. "You f-fractured her skull with a baseball!"

I said: "You lie in your teeth, small fry. I hadn't made my throw when she got bopped. Ask Cromwell." I turned to the director. "Tell him, Roy."

Cromwell kept his glims glued on my gat. "Don't expect any help from me, Turner. I saw what happened."

"Meaning what?"

"You threw the ball at her."

I felt my gullet tightening. "So you're trying to frame me, too. Why? Is it for personal reasons, or just because you think it's wise to string along with your boss?"

"I don't need any excuse for telling the truth," he said sullenly. "I saw you heft the ball and draw it back—"

"But I didn't heave it. Did, I, sister?" I asked Vala.

She ran trembling fingers through her blue-black coiffure. "I didn't see you. I didn't know anything about it until I came out of my dressing room and Bernie told me what you'd done. I'd believe him in preference to you, though."

"You would," I sneered. "You know what side your cake's buttered on." Then I tried being reasonable. "Look, all of you. If I croaked this cookie, what was my motive?"

Cromwell said: "Maybe because she was a nuisance."

"Nuisance?" I stared at him.

"I heard her asking you why you scratched her name off your address book. Maybe she'd been your sweetie and you ditched her. Maybe you thought she'd make trouble; the scorned-woman angle. I don't know. That's for the law to decide."

"You want me pinched, huh?"

He lifted a shoulder. "For my money, you saw a chance to get away with murder and you tried it. The girl was a perfect target and you had a baseball in your hand—"

"And why did I have a baseball?" I bleeped. "I'll tell you! You asked me to throw at the bottles." I moved a step toward him. "It was a fishy request; I can see that now."

He turned pallid around the fringes. "Are you accusing me of trying to frame you?"

I said: "It's a thought."

The impact of this idea hit him all of a sudden. "But why would I frame you unless I—?"

"Yeah, exactly. Unless you were the killer yourself. Remember the ball you just slammed at me? It was a perfect strike over the heart of the plate. It splintered the boards of the back wall. A guy who can heave the horsehide that hard could also crack a cupcake's cranium the same way."

Bernie Ballantyne thrust his beak into the conversation. "If you think you can pin your crime on Roy, think again. I was near him at the time. He threw nothing at Miss Murdock. Every bit player and extra in the crowd will testify to it."

"Yeah, if you tell them to," I growled.

He bridled. "You mean I'd use my position to force anyone to perjure—?"

"Damned right you would. And not necessarily for Cromwell's sake, either. Maybe for your own. I seem to recall you used to be a bush league ball player in your early days. A shortstop, I believe."

"What's that got to do with it?"

"Accuracy and throwing power," I fired back at him. "The ability to chuck a baseball and bean somebody. Or am I wrong in remembering how you made two bumpery threats when I talked to you in your office yesterday?"

I figured this ought to set him back on his heels; expected to see him do some squirming. He didn't though. His attention didn't seem to be on me at all. Instead, he was staring past me as if glomming a hinge at something very soothing to the optics. Then, suddenly, he barked: "Arrest this man, officer! He's the one you want. He's the murderer."

I whirled; but I was a split second too slow. A pair of harness bulls from the Venice police force had sneaked up behind me with their roscoes unlimbered; evidently some wise apple in the cast or technical crew had put in a bleat for them while my back was turned. Now they thrust their rods into my ribs and told me I was under arrest, and would I drop my gat before they shoved a load of lead through my liver?

CHAPTER III

One for Dave

There's something about a copper's .38 Positive that spells authority. Two .38's are twice as nasty. Moreover, I didn't have any drag in Venice. Hollywood is my territory, and my private detective badge is no good outside the city limits. I was a cooked goose and I knew it.

"Sure, boys," I said. "Sure I'll drop my gat." I let it fall and held out my mitts for the nippers.

One of the bulls holstered his heater, reached into his handcuff sheath for a pair of bracelets. This reduced the odds, but not too much. I was still in an ugly jackpot.

I yelled: *"Look out! Ballantyne's going to shoot!"*

The second cop had quick reflexes. He pivoted toward Bernie, ready for fireworks. When he realized the undersized producer didn't have a gun, he wheeled back to me, cursing at the top of his adenoids. That was when I kicked his .38 out of his clutch. The weapon went skittering.

He dived after it, which was a serious error on his part. I tripped him as he plunged; sent him skidding on his profile. He collected a nostril full of splinters and loudly called on heaven to witness that he'd been stabbed.

Meanwhile I swung a hell-roaring haymaker at his partner's prow. The punch connected, which made two brass buttoned heroes down on the deck. I tensed my thews and sinews, uncoiled myself, and cleared the counter in one fell swoop. Now I was on the midway of the amusement pier, hemmed in by extras and grips and a miscellaneous movie mob.

Dames squalled and guys tried to hang the grab on me. I lowered my noggin, bucked the line, rammed three carpenters and an electrician floundering on their backs. Directly opposite the baseball target concession there was a high, circular tower thrusting its spire upward like an overgrown totem pole. It even looked like a totem pole, its exterior decorated by a big spiral serpent of papier mâché and plaster of paris.

The head and face of this giant dragon formed the tower's exit at pier-floor level, its vast mouth open and framed by red-painted fangs. The serpentine body coiled upward around the tall structure, with its massive tail forming a sort of spire at the distant top. Away up there you could lamp a sort of platform all guarded by wooden railings.

Down on the pier, alongside the dragon's exit mouth, there was an entrance flanked by a ticket booth. A sign above the little booth said:

VIEW THE SHORE-LINE
FROM THE HIGHEST
SPOT IN VENICE
10¢
Escalator (Moving Stairway)
Now Running
SLIDE DOWN
THE BIGGEST
THRILL ON THE
WEST COAST 10¢

A wild hunch sneaked up my back. I plunged toward the tower entrance, catapulted past the ticket wicket, gained the escalator. Behind me a roscoe sneezed: *Ka-Chow!* and a red hot hornet buzzed past my ear. That would be the cops having a spot of target practice at my expense. I bent low, blipped onto the moving stairs, felt myself being lifted—but not fast enough to suit me. I started running upward.

The first leg of the escalator ended on a little landing. You stepped off, walked onto the next flight which ascended in the reverse direction; a zig-zag effect. This was repeated twice more; then you were on the very top platform, away to hell and gone up in the air, with nothing but a wooden guard rail between you and a sheer drop to the ocean on one side or the pier on the other. The view was terrific.

I wasn't very interested in it, though; at least not the water. In fact, the breaking waves could have been made of Vat 69 and I wouldn't have liked them from that high up. To dive into the drink from such a height would make toothpicks of every bone in your skeleton.

The thought gave me goose pimples big enough to hang pictures on. I turned, stared down at the pier and the crowds milling around the escalator entrance. I could look straight into the baseball concession across the midway; piped Maizie Murdock's crumpled remnants and Bernie Ballantyne holding Vala DuValle in his embrace, trying to soothe her. Cromwell stood to one side, peering toward the base of the tower straight under me.

The people down there were chattering, pointing; but I didn't lamp any trace of the two cops. I thought I knew why. Above the clattery racket of the machinery that worked the moving stairway I heard thumping footfalls getting closer. Those bulls were on their way up to nab me. Both of them.

I breathed a relieved sigh as I doped this out. It meant a break for my side, because the dizzy numbskulls had neglected to post a guard at the lower exit—the mouth of the stucco dragon. My whole future hinged on that omission.

To my right, up on the top platform, there was a maw-like orifice resembling the entrance to a dark tunnel. The tunnel itself slanted downward at a steep pitch, curving spirally, lined with smooth wooden corduroy strips that were polished to a gloss from friction. This tunnel was the interior of the serpentine dragon that wound itself around the tower from spire to foundation. It was a giant slide, the kind where you sit on a chunk of carpet, give yourself a push, and go circling downward at a thundering clip.

I selected a rug sample from the pile at the slide entrance. I adjusted it, settled myself on it and cast off with my fingers crossed. Whammo! My dizzy descent was something I'll keep dreaming about from now on.

Around and around, down and down I went, with gravity pulling me and centrifugal force slamming me sidewise against the chute's hardwood-strip walls. All the breath leaked out of my bellows, and I felt my optics popping like two grapes being squeezed.

The inventor of that maniac contraption had saved an extra thrill for the last third of the journey. Here the spiral pitch increased its rate of drop; you hit a slight hump and then felt the whole tunnel floor going out from under your hip pockets. Blam! I landed in an awkward sprawl, and now I was circling toward the base at ninety miles a minute. A horrible idea gnawed at me. Suppose one of the wooden corduroy strips came loose and skewered me. "Nix!" I moaned. "Not that!"

And then my wild ride ended. I was at pier level, and I shot out of the dragon's mouth like a shell from a cannon. My glims were full of tears and my elbows full of abrasion blisters from friction contact. I landed ker-thump on a mattress placed strategically for the purpose. It felt as if somebody had stuffed it with discarded horseshoes.

I staggered to my pins. Nobody tabbed me. Everyone was hanging the focus on the tower entrance nearby, where those flatfeet had gone up the escalator after me. I spun on my heel and started to run.

My jalopy was parked on the street that ended at the landward front of the pier. I reached it, piled in, kicked the starter a savage wallop. Somebody spotted me as my cylinders came to life. "There he is—!"

I snarled: "You mean there he goes," and stoked my boiler with ethyl. Three minutes later I was careening through Venice under forced draft.

I ditched my bucket in Ocean Park because I knew there would be a radio bleat out for me in short order. I didn't want a lot of prowl cars on the sniff for me, looking for a vee-eight coupe and its contents. A public bus was my best bet; and as luck would have it, a big Pacific Electric red job was just getting ready to pull out. I boarded it, slipped the driver my fare, and sat down in a rear seat, bushed.

The ride back to town gave me time to get my mental cogwheels functioning. Busting loose from those Venice bluecoats had been a screwball move, maybe; but I craved freedom in copious quantities. It was the only way I could hope to haul myself out of this mess I was in; pin Maizie Murdock's murder where it belonged. Of course I was on the lam now; and by powdering I had made myself look guilty. Even so, I was better off than if I'd been languishing in a seashore bastille. You can't do any detecting in a cell.

Moreover, had I meekly submitted to the bulls, they'd have closed the case and thrown away the key. With all that false testimony against me, I wouldn't have had the chance of a hailstone in the hot place.

As it was, I dropped off the bus in Hollywood around noon, cocked and primed for action. There were several angles I wanted to investigate, and first on the list was the deceased Murdock quail's background; her recent activities. Whenever there's a homicide, there's also a motive. Find that motive and you can commence narrowing down your field of suspects.

To start with, though, I needed a spare roscoe; mine had been confiscated on the amusement pier and I feel practically naked if my armpit rig is empty. Besides, my nerves were frazzled around the fringes and the only thing that would mend them in a hurry was a good stiff prescription of Scotch broth. There was an extra rod in my stash, plus a cellarette full of Vat 69. So I decided to go home—provided the coast was clear.

I took a taxi, had it ferry me twice around the block until I was satisfied no local coppers were lurking about the apartment entrance. Then I sneaked in through the basement garage and took the automatic elevator up to my floor; unlocked the door of my igloo and ankled over the threshold. Whereupon a familiar voice said: "Welcome home, wise guy."

It was my friend Dave Donaldson of the homicide squad, and he had me covered with his cannon.

I whirled, hung the stupefied glimpse on his beefy features.

He leered complacently. "I figured you'd show up here so I staked out and made myself comfortable."

"That's breaking and entering," I said.

"Not when I've got a John Doe warrant it isn't. This is an official visit, bud. Can you guess why?"

I said wearily: "Yeah. You're collaborating with those Venice numbskulls. I'm pinched."

He made admiring noises with his mouth. "You sure do catch on quick, don't you? Let's take a little journey down to headquarters. Maybe I'll even let you get in touch with some shyster before I send you back to the beach."

"Damn the beach," I said. "Also the sons who're trying to fasten a frame on my elbows."

"Ah. So it's a frame. It always is." He waggled his rodney reprovingly. "I wish killers would sing a different tune once in a while, just to break the monotony. I get tired of that one. It stinks."

"So it stinks." I dredged a gasper from a crumpled pack on the table, set fire to it. "So I'm not a killer. Have a jolt of skee while I tell you the score."

"I'll take the skee but I won't believe anything you warble. And don't try to slip a mickey in my glass or I'll bend this gat around your ears."

I put an injured expression on my mush as I poured him the snort and handed it to him. I downed a double dollop myself and said: "You know I wouldn't feed you a mickey. I wish I'd thought of it, though. It's a swell idea."

"About the kill," he prompted me. "Why'd you do it?"

"I didn't."

"Who did?"

"I don't know—yet."

"Whale feathers," he said. "I got a full report over the teletype. Fifty-'leven extras say you had the baseball in your fist just before the blonde bim got bopped. Roy Cromwell says it. So does Bernie Ballantyne. What more do you want?"

"Another drink," I said, and had it. "And a chance to prove they're cock-eyed liars."

"About you having the ball?"

I shook my head. "No. That part's true enough."

"Then what *are* they lying about?"

"Me throwing it at Maizie. I didn't."

"Well, who did?" he persisted.

"You already asked me. I told you I don't know—yet."

He looked bland. "You could guess, couldn't you?"

"Sure, but what good would it do me? Quit being clever. You know you're just needling me, trying to make me say something damaging. You're not as coy as you think you are." An inch of dew remained in the bottle. I killed it.

"A fine thing," Dave sounded aggrieved. "You didn't even offer to share it with me." His tone hardened. "If you're so innocent you must have somebody in mind as a candidate. Come on, name him."

"Okay, I'll name two. Cromwell and Ballantyne."

He chuckled sourly. "That's what I thought you'd say."

"Meaning what?"

"They accuse you, so you accuse them. Boy, are you corny!"

I got sore. "Look, I've good reasons for pointing the finger their way. Want to listen?"

"I suppose it won't cost me anything. Speak your piece."

"Well, Cromwell jobbed me into tossing those first few baseballs. And he stood directly behind me when the murder pill zipped past my ear to bash the blonde chick."

Dave rubbed his chin bristles. "All right. By a long stretch of the imagination we'll say he had opportunity, although everybody around him claims he didn't throw anything. Skipping lightly over that, what would be his motive? What did he have against Maizie Murdock to make him want to kill her?"

"I don't know—yet."

"Get a new phrase. That one's tiresome," he said. "Now let's consider your case against Ballantyne."

I shrugged. "The same setup. He was behind me when the death ball was heaved."

"Any motive?"

"Possibly. He's engaged to his star, Vala DuValle. He thinks she's being blackmailed. He hired me to look into it. He hinted he'd like to croak the blackmailer."

"Aha. And maybe Maizie Murdock—"

I nodded. "Could be. Suppose he found out Maizie was bleeding the DuValle cutie? Suppose he carried out his croakery hint? It adds up."

"But why did he then try to pin the job on you?"

I had the answer ready. "Jealousy. I was with Vala DuValle one night in a dice joint that got raided."

"What were you doing? Trying to beat his time?"

"Hell, no. And later he got over his peeve, or pretended to. But he may have been laying for me, waiting for a chance to sink the harpoon in me."

Dave stood up, yawned. "Finished, Sherlock?"

"I've told you all I know, yes."

"Then let's go to the gow. You're still under arrest. Frankly I don't believe a word you've told me."

I goggled at him. "You mean you intend to hand me to those brainless wonders in Venice? Me, your best friend?"

"Yeh." He lowered his voice confidentially. "I even pinched my own grandmother one time for robbing a blind man. All my family are heels, including me. Stick out your fins for the nippers and be quick about it."

I reached in my pocket for a coffin nail. At the same instant, my front door opened a crack and a roscoe stuttered: *Ka-Pow!* behind me. The blast was bad enough but the slug's nearness was worse. It scorched a blister on my left ear as it went by; and then Dave Donaldson clapped a hand to his noggin, lurched drunkenly and fell down. Gore commenced leaking from his furrowed scalp.

CHAPTER IV

The Night of the Raid

I let out a strangled oath, swung around, hurled my heft at the door. It was closed again by the time I reached it. And it wouldn't open when I tugged at the knob. Somebody had jammed it from outside.

An acrid stench of burned gunpowder hung in the air, stung my smeller. I whirled and went racing buckety-blip to the kitchenette, where my stash had a second exit into a short elbow corridor. This portal worked okay. I lunged out to the short hall; pelted for the main one. Nobody was in sight when I got there, though; nobody, that is, except some nosy neighbors poking their beaks out to see what the shooting was about.

"Hey!" I rasped. "Did any of you see—?"

It developed that nobody had tabbed anything. I sailed down the main staircase: no dice. I drew a blank with the automatic elevator, too. But there was still a rear stairway I hadn't covered; and there was no use trying to, now. The gunsel had long since had time to scram out of the building—and out of the entire neighborhood if he had a fast enough jalopy.

Panting fire and brimstone, I returned to my front door and found out what had jammed it. Some sharp disciple had wedged a .32 Colt between the knob and the doorcase in such a way that when you tried to open up from inside, you merely made the wedge tighter.

It was no trick to dislodge the roscoe. It had the same burned cordite odor I'd noticed in my wigwam an instant ago, meaning this was the heater that had drilled Dave Donaldson. I gave vent to a frantic bleat as I realized it now had my fingerprints on it from plucking it away from the knob. And the short hairs prickled at the nape of my neck when I tumbled to another fact that was a lot worse.

The rod was my own: the one those harness bulls had forced me to drop on the amusement pier!

I moaned: "For the love of—!" and shoved my portal open so hard it almost came off its hinges. Once inside, I kicked it shut again to keep out the busybodies. Then I hunkered down alongside Donaldson's sprawled tonnage; forced myself to look at his colorless puss. He and I had been through plenty together, month after month for more than ten years without a break. Now he was defunct . . . and I'd probably be accused of creaming him.

He proved this by mumbling: "Hello. Headquarters. Put out the net for that rat Turner. I was about to handcuff him when he shoved his fist in his pocket and shot me. Hello. Operator. You cut me off. Say, doctor, have you got an aspirin on you? A pound of hamburger, please, and here's the ration stamp. Yeah. Turner shot me, Chief. Delirious? Me? Well, you'd be delirious too if your hospital bed was as hard as mine. Feels like I was sleeping on the floor—" He opened his groggy glimmers, took a swivel and bellowed: "By gosh, I *am* on the floor!"

Realizing he was alive made me feel as good as a guy having an abscessed tooth pulled. The relief was terrific but the aftermath hurt like the devil. That slug from the doorway had merely creased his cranium, maced him silly; but now he was conscious again and thought I was the bozo who'd nicked him.

To make it lousier, he tried to flounder up on his haunches. I restrained him. "Easy, Dave. Easy," I said. Then I realized I was prodding him with the .32 in my duke.

He lamped it and sagged back. "Oh. Going to finish your job, hunh?" His shoulders twitched. "Okay. I'm ready."

I snarled: "Don't be a dope, you dope. I didn't plug you. It came from the doorway."

"Hurry up and pull your trigger," he ignored what I was saying. "And don't miss. Because in another minute I'm going to be strong enough to tangle with you. That's a warning."

"I tell you I—"

He came off the floor slowly, an inch at a time. Mayhem glittered in his glims and there was violence in his knotted mitts. "Gonna beat your brains out," he announced distinctly. He swung a roundhouse haymaker, missed and folded like a punctured balloon. He was snoring before he hit the rug.

I hurdled him, picked up my phone, dialed headquarters. The desk sergeant who came on the line didn't suspect anything when I said: "Lieutenant Donaldson speaking. Look. I've just collared Dan Turner. You can cancel the pickup order we had out for him; I'm bringing him in personally."

"Okay, lieutenant. I'll notify Venice, too."

"Right," I said. Then I hung up and got out of there. Fast.

For a little while I knew I'd be safe. Canceling that pickup order had been a stroke of sheer genius on my part. Now the radio prowl cars would quit hunting me; I could move around without being forced to duck every time I piped a blue uniform and a set of brass buttons. This wouldn't last long, though. Pretty soon Dave Donaldson would wake up again, phone his minions what had really happened. Then the heat would be on.

I blipped downstairs, barged outdoors, whistled a Yellow over to the curb and piled in. "Hollywood *Times*, brother. Don't spare the horses. I'm in a yank."

Presently we came to the newspaper building and I hotfooted up to the file room. The attendant was a guy I knew. "Hi, Larry," I said.

A flabbergasted look came into his optics. "Hawkshaw! Do you know the cops are—?"

"Yeah, you're telling me," I said bitterly. "I'm hotter than the inside of a stove. Let's understand each other. If you figure to stool on me, I'm leaving. If you feel like helping me, I'll be grateful. Take your pick."

"Why, I'll help you, of course; if I can. Stooling is out of my line."

"Thanks. How's for slipping me your envelope of clippings on a certain Sunset Strip dice joint raid about a month ago? You remember the place I mean."

He said yes he remembered, and scuttled to a file; extracted a thick manila folder. "Here's what you want. Your own picture's in it, incidentally."

I knew that as well as he did. The press photogs had made a Roman holiday of the raid, having been tipped in advance that it was going to be pulled. They'd snapped a slew of pix which were smeared all over the following day's front pages. One shot showed Vala DuValle clinging to my arm and looking hysterical, with a caption under it: PARAVOX STAR WITH FAMOUS SHAMUS. This photo was the one that had subsequently given Bernie Ballantyne an attack of the jealous jitters.

I spread the clippings on a desk; began studying them. The silliest picture was of the phony Grand Duke Mike Voronoff, restaurant proprietor and general moocher, trying to sneak through an exit on his hands and knees. There was another of Roy Cromwell haughtily informing a county cop that he'd come stag to the joint—a lie he got away with for the simple reason that he had palmed the DuValle brunette off on me a moment before. And then there was a medium long shot of the whole place, showing almost everybody who'd been there when the law busted in.

This was the snap I particularly wanted to gander. I glued the gaze on it, hunting people I knew. One yellow-haired cookie caught my attention.

She was Maizie Murdock.

393

I took a closer hinge to make sure. There was no mistaking her bleached tresses and gamine pan. She was with a pasty-faced jerk I'd never seen before; a guy who didn't seem to amount to anything unless they gave medals for a Victory Garden of pimples on the chin. I puckered my kisser, whistled softly.

Larry, the newspaper file clerk, ankled over. "Something?" he said.

"Maybe," I told him. "I'd like a phone and some privacy if you can manage it."

He led me to a secluded desk. "Help yourself." He left me there.

I fished a number from my mental note-book; dialed it. The bozo I called was Pedro Criqui, a French Spaniard who'd been in more hot water than used tea-leaves. Most recent on the list of his misfortunes was the fact that he'd been the proprietor of that raided dice drop.

"Pedro?" I said.

"I'll see if he's-a een. Holda wire, *oui?*"

"Stew that stall. This is Dan Turner."

"Oh. That's-a deeference. How you are, you sonagun? You een troubles, hah? Ees een the papers, on radio, you bumpa *mamselle.* You beeg chomp, Sherlock. You wanna keel somebody, ees crazy to pull eet in poblic. Fooey!"

I said patiently: "Fooey on you too, bub. I didn't bump her. Listen. I need some information."

"Whatsa cookeeng? I don't got information. Whats you're wanna knoweeng, hah?"

"How often Roy Cromwell brought Vala DuValle to your joint."

"Lotsa times, two-three, maybe six. Alla time he's-a shoots the snake-eyes. He's can't make point weeth lead pencil. Theesa DuValle pigeon she's like hees company, plenty, you betcha. Boy oh boy."

"Did Cromwell ever take her to one of your private dining rooms?' I said casually.

His tone got distant. "Now waiteeng a meenute, palsy-walsy. Theesa DuValle chicken, she's-a nice *mamselle.*"

"About the private room," I said.

"Theesa Cromwell ees being a rat. Me, I don't know nothing about nothing. Whats you theenking I am, a squealer?"

I grinned. "Thanks. So he did take her to a private dining room."

"You sonagun. I deedn't telling you thees."

"No. You just let it slip, is all."

He cursed me fervently in four languages. "Two minutes they go in private room. She's-a no like the idea, you unnastand me? Maybeso she's-a like theesa Cromwell's company, but not so moch as that. He's telling her they have *petit dejeuner à deux.* Catch what I'm meaning? Dinner for two, cozy by theirselfs. She's go een, look around, she's-a saying nix brother, ees bad for reputation."

I said: "I get it. She didn't mind going out with him, playing the night spots; but when it came to a nest behind closed doors it was no dice. Right?"

"Ees damned right. Whatsa matter, you no unnastand English? Hah?"

"Okay," I soothed him. "So Vala was strictly on the up and up with Cromwell. What night did this private room episode happen?"

He said the night of the raid, and started cursing the cops that knocked him over. "Ees costing me all I ever win from guys like—"

"Remind me to send you a towel to cry in," I said, and hung up on his dolorous moans. Now I had something I could sink my bridgework into. The DuValle cupcake and Roy Cromwell had come downstairs from a private room the night of the raid. Their visit to the second floor had been brief, true enough, *but they had come downstairs.*

And anybody gandering them as they descended might have made gossip of it.

And Maizie Murdock had been in the joint that night.

And later Vala DuValle had apparently been blackmailed.

And Bernie Ballantyne had threatened to kill the blackmailer.

And Maizie Murdock got croaked.

And Bernie had been on the scene of the murder.

And he had tried to frame me for it.

I said softly: "Turner, you're a genius. You'll be a marvelous detective some day if you live long enough." Then I torched a gasper and left the newspaper building. I wasn't very happy, though. I was afraid I might not live as long as a guy should if he hopes to be a marvelous detective.

CHAPTER V

A Foul Ball

Another taxi wafted me across town to the cheap apartment wikiup where the late lamented Murdock quail had lived. It was along toward dusk when I rousted out the manager, a slatternly old hag with henna-red hair that had grey streaks showing through. If she'd paid more than fifty cents a pint for the gin on her breath, she'd been robbed.

"Something, dearie?" she asked me.

I gave her a swift squint at my badge, not long enough to let her know it was only a private op's biscuit. "Official business," I said. "Homicide headquarters."

From within the harridan's flat a sniveling voice full of adenoids whined: "What is it, maw?"

"So you're from headquarters," the dame stared at me. "Just another cop, junior," she called to the voice inside. "Shut your mouth or I'll kick it shut." Then, to me: "Junior's my son. Sometimes I wish I'd drowned him."

"Tell him we're tired of cops," the voice sniveled spitefully. "Tell him to dust, maw."

I said: "I'd like to ask you some questions, lady."

"Questions!" she grumbled. "Questions, questions, always it's questions." A burp boiled up from around her insteps. "Oops, sorry. Something I et, no doubt."

The adenoids got vocal again. "What's he want, maw?"

"Quiet, bum. He wants to know about Maizie, of course." She looked at me. "Don't you?"

"Yeah. Isn't this where Miss Murdock lived?"

"Hey, maw, tell him to blow. You ought to paste him, maw. It would learn him something."

She pitched her voice to a shrill, infuriated screech. "Sock cops, is it? You keep running off at the face and I'll take you apart with a club." Then, with no change of expression on her unlovely puss, she lowered her tone to normal. "Just like his old man. A creep."

"About Miss Murdock," I said.

"How many times have I go to go over it?" she made an indignant mouth. "Ask those other dicks that's already been here. For goodness' sakes, ain't you flatfeet got nothing better to do but pester a body crazy?"

"Heave him out, maw," the adenoids said.

She screamed: "Will you button that lip of yours?"

"Look," I said reasonably. "Can I help it if headquarters assigns me to check up on those other detectives? I'm sorry to put you to so much trouble, but—"

The dame sighed. "Okay." She scratched herself. "I'll tell it again. Maizie Murdock lived here until yesterday."

"You mean she moved?"

"I mean I changed the lock on her door and dragged her trunk to the cellar and held it on account she was six weeks behind in her rent. Don't ask me where she spent last night. I don't know and I don't care."

My gullet felt tight all of a sudden. "What?"

"Hey, maw," the adenoids whined. "The paper just come. I got it off the back step. You wanna hear something?"

She ignored him. "Sure, dearie," she told me. "Maizie hadn't had no movie work in a long time. She was broke. She kept saying she had a job coming up with Paravox, a bit part on a one picture contract. She kept saying she'd have the rent money pretty soon now, when she got her first pay. I got tired waiting, though. I ain't running no charity hall, am I? So last night I locked her out."

I felt as if a mule had kicked me in the short ribs. Maizie Murdock had been broke for six weeks. Her Paravox job, the one that resulted in her decease, had been the first she'd had in a couple of months. This information knocked all my theories into a cocked hat.

She couldn't have been the character who was blackmailing Vala DuValle!

No matter how you figured it, the answer came up that way. If Maizie had been the shakedown artist, she would have had cash enough to pay her rent; save herself from being locked out of her apartment. Since she didn't have the dough, it stood to reason that she hadn't been putting the bite on the brunette DuValle cupcake.

Therefore there was no motive for Bernie Ballantyne to have bumped her!

Of course he might have mistakenly thought Maizie was doing the blackmailing. I couldn't quite see how he could jump at such a haywire conclusion, however, in view of the circumstances. All told, it began to look as if Bernie was in the clear and I would have to hunt around for a fresh suspect.

I considered the director, Roy Cromwell, who could fling a baseball hard enough to splinter woodwork—or a she-male skull. He'd been in a position to heave a lethal pellet at the Murdock filly; but for what motive?

"Listen," I said to the apartment house hag. "Did Maizie ever have a gentleman friend named Cromwell, a tall, handsome guy dressed in loud tweeds?"

"She didn't have no gentlemen friends, dearie."

"You mean they weren't gentlemen?"

"I mean she didn't play that way. Not here, anyhow. She never had no men calling on her. I run a decent house for respectable people and she kept her nose clean. Otherwise I wouldn't have let my junior take her out once in a while. Poor boy, he's all busted up about what happened to her. He liked her. She was the only girl ever looked twice at him."

I said: "But he didn't like her well enough to keep you from putting her out of her apartment when she couldn't pay her rent, hunh?"

"Junior don't interfere with how I run my business. He better not, the little bum. I'd take a broomstick to him."

I was up against a blank wall again. If Cromwell hadn't been on social terms with Maizie, he wouldn't have had any reason for cooling her off. This seemed to erase him from my list of possible suspects, along with Bernie Ballantyne.

From inside the manager's flat, adenoids bleated again. "It says in the paper, maw—"

"Shut up, junior. How do you know what it says in the paper? You can't read."

"I can too read. Listen, maw, it says that private dick got picked up in his own apartment right here in Hollywood; the one that killed Maizie. You know; Turner is his name. A bull by the name of Donaldson nabbed him, but this Turner guy shot him, the paper says, and made a getaway. His picture is in the paper—I mean Turner's picture. Wanna see it, maw?"

"No," the dame said.

Neither did I. The heat was on me again, I realized. Donaldson must have recovered from his swoon, phoned headquarters, and started the dragnet rolling. It was time for me to make myself scarce. I started to say goodbye to the frowsy jane; but all of a sudden my luck ran out.

Junior came to the doorway with his newspaper. "Lookit, maw. Here's the guy's picture I was telling you." He cast an absent-minded hinge at me, twitched and did a double-take. "*Maw!* That's him! That's Turner talking to you, maw!"

I should have whirled and lammed while the lamming was good, but I couldn't. My gams seemed paralyzed. I was hanging the stupefied focus on junior's pimply mush, while recognition slammed through me.

He was the pasty-faced jerk who had been Maizie Murdock's escort in that dice joint, the night of the raid!

The next couple of minutes were pretty blurry. I finally got my brogans unlimbered and made a wild dive for the exit. Maw and junior blammed after me, bellowing like a pair of halfwits. They almost caught up with me as I gained the front door; or at least junior did. This cost him three front teeth.

He went down, squalling. His old lady stopped to inspect the damage to his kisser and I high-tailed out of there with my back pockets dipping sand and my right duke aching where I'd hung a haymaker on the little jerk.

My taxi was still waiting at the curb where I'd left it. The meter registered $3.25, which was felonious, but I was in no condition to argue. I told the hacker to pull the pin and get going. He did.

He also cast a knowing leer at me over his shoulder and said: "I been listenin' to the radio."

"That's nice. Symphony or swing?"

"Newscast. They put out a swell description of you, pal."

"So it's that way," I said.

"Don't get jumpy, Mr. Turner," he grinned at me in the rear-view mirror. "I don't like cops, neither."

"Meaning you don't intend to blow the whistle?"

"Not me," he said virtuously. "That's for heels. Besides, I guess maybe you're the kind that would treat a guy right if the guy leveled with you."

"You're talking about dough, of course," I said.

He blipped past an amber light. "What else is there to talk about at a time like this?"

I said: "You're a man after my own heart. You'd probably be after my kidneys and liver, too, if they were valuable enough." I fished two tens out of my wallet, handed them up to him. "How much loyalty will that buy?"

"I've maimed people for less. You wanna go somewhere in particular or just ride around?"

"I want to go somewhere in particular but I don't know exactly where. First let's find a phone."

He pulled in before a cheap groggery, scouted the territory, and reported no coppers in sight. "There's a booth at the end of the bar, chum. I'll wait."

I barged into the gin-mill, located the telephone, dropped a jitney and dialed Pedro Criqui again. "Pedro?"

"I'll see if he's-a een. Holda wire, *oui?*"

"Let's not repeat that routine. This is Turner."

"*Sacre nom de Dieu*, whatsa your always calleeng me op, hah? Ees bad enough you bumpa *mamselle* in Venice, but when you shooteeng policemans ees too moch. Goodbye, please."

"Now wait a minute," I said. "I didn't shoot Lieutenant Donaldson any more than I creamed Maizie Murdock. I'm in a jam and I need help."

"I'm sayeeng!"

"Listen. The night of the raid, this Murdock doll was there in your drop. Maybe you remember her."

"Maybe I'm do, maybe I'm don't. Who ees caring?"

"She had a kid with her; a yuck with pimples on a face only his mother could love, which she doesn't. Know the jerk I mean? Pasty complexion, skinny, talks with adenoids?"

"Ees sound like Joe Wilson."

This checked with the monicker on the apartment house hag's mailbox: Wilson. "That's the one," I said.

"He's-a no good. A foul ball."

"A regular patron of yours?"

Pedro laughed sourly. "Whatsa you think, hah? I got no time for cheap nickels and dimes guys. Thees Wilson keed, I don't letting him in my place unless he's-a got two tens to rub together. He come once, twice, ees all. He's-a breeng blonde tomato weeth heem, he's-a shoot craps, he losing his shirt and go home."

"Never up in the bucks, eh?"

"Not while my place ees open. Since I am being raided I don't knowing how much dough he's-a got. Hell weeth heem."

"Have you heard if he's been going against any of the floating crap games around town since you got closed?"

"I hearing nothing. You so smart, you finding out for yourself, hah? *Au revoir, adios* and do me a favor, hang op." He cut me off like a bill collector.

Dark had settled when I went back out to my cabby. I handed him another ten-spot. "How's for finding me a couple of games?" I said.

"Dames?" he gave me an admiring look. "You can think of romance in a spot like yours?"

"Not dames. Games. Floating ones. Dice."

"Oh, that. Yeah, sure." He ferried me to a shoddy hotel off Vine Street and talked to a bellhop. Then he told me: "Room 212. Go right up. Want I should join you and hold your winnings?"

"No, thanks." I went upstairs and had a brief conference in Room 212 with a furtive guy. Five minutes later I was down in my cab again. The hacker remarked that I must have thrown an awful jolt of snake-eyes to get through so quick. I said: "I certainly did. Find me another game."

He found me one and I had another conference. Presently I returned to the taxi. "Any luck?" the cabby asked me.

"Not the kind I hoped for," I said. "I've been checking on a dice player with adenoids."

"How can anybody play dice with his adenoids?" the hacker sounded indignant.

I said: "That's the point. He hasn't been." Which was true, according to what I had just learned. Joe Wilson, an inveterate crap shooter, had been hanging around the games for the past few weeks without rattling the bones at all. He was suffering the financial shorts.

This kicked another theory in the teeth. I'd thought perhaps the Wilson jerk was blackmailing Vala DuValle, on the basis of having tabbed her with Roy Cromwell coming downstairs from a private room that night in Pedro Criqui's drop. In turn, Bernie Ballantyne might have erroneously figured Maizie Murdock as the extortionist and made the grave mistake of cooling her.

But the pasty-faced Wilson punk was broke. Therefore he wasn't reaping any shakedown lettuce. He was as clean as Maizie had been—and I was up a stump again.

Riding along in the taxi's tonneau, I flared a match; lit up a gasper. Bye and bye my cabby said: "You done yourself a dirty trick that time, pal."

"How come I did?"

"A cop car went by just as you had that match up to your map. I think you been spotted." He looked in his mirror. "I know damn' well you been spotted. They're turnin' around with the red light on. Here they come."

I sneaked a swivel through the rear glass. He was right. You could pipe that crimson spotlight stabbing the dimout, and a siren started to growl.

They had me on the hook at last.

CHAPTER VI

The Gambler

My hacker romped on his throttle. "Wanna race?"

"Will it do any good?" I said.

"Hang onto your upper plate and we'll see," he advised me. And then he started doing some of the fanciest driving this side of the Indianapolis Speedway. We took the next corner on squealing skins, whammed north, careened to the left at the following intersection, and went rocketing westward like a comet with turpentine on its tail. The speedometer needle crept around to the notch above sixty, hung there a while, and began climbing. Night wind screeched around our flapping fenders and the rear treads commenced to smoke.

The prowl car stayed with us.

"What time is it?" the cabby asked me.

I braced myself, tried to hang the focus on my strap watch. "Not quite nine o'clock. Does it matter?"

"Yah," he said, narrowly missing a pedestrian on a crosswalk. The pedestrian emitted an anguished wail, jumped like a kangaroo, and disappeared down an open manhole. "Yah. There's a street the water wagon always flushes around this time o'night. For another ten bucks I could maybe have a idea."

"The ten's yours," I said. "I don't think you'll ever live to spend it, though."

He offered me odds of two to one, sent the cab catapulting around another corner and gripped his wheel hard. Dead ahead I lamped a block where the asphalt was black and shiny from a recent wetting. We barreled onto this slippery stretch and made a sudden left turn into a narrow alley. Don't ask me how we pulled a bull's-eye; for the life of me I don't know. I bounced on the back seat like a pea in a dry pod; felt the cab's rear end slewing slaunchwise. Hitting the mouth of that alley was like a palsied man threading a darning needle with a hunk of two-inch rope; it just couldn't be done.

We did it.

The prowl chariot blammed into the wet block and tried to make the same maneuver. Goggling backward, I saw it skid out of control and spin like a pinwheel. It made three complete revolutions, while the cops inside it screamed their tonsils to tatters. Then there was a thundering crash, and a geyser of water fountained upward from a busted fireplug.

My cabby slackened speed as we emerged from the far end of the alley. "Them bulls probably needed a bath, anyhow," he remarked. "Now where you wanna go, bud?"

"To a hospital," I said weakly. "For a nervous breakdown."

He made clucking noises. "Doctors won't do no good for what ails you, Hawkshaw. What you need is a snifter." He passed me a depleted pint. It was rotgut rye, but I drained it and it tasted like nectar. Presently my grey matter started functioning again. I was almost back to normal.

I started counting on my fingers adding up what I knew concerning the things that had happened since Maizie Murdock's murder. Both Roy Cromwell and the little Ballantyne blister had attempted to frame me; and yet, as the score stood now, neither of them looked guilty of the actual kill.

Okay. Could it have been some unknown character in the mob of extras and technical crew? Some guy who'd had a personal beef against Maizie and saw a chance to knock her off? If so, I was sunk. Hunted by the law, how could I hope to ferret information regarding the hundred and fifty or more guys and wrens who had been on that amusement pier?

And besides, the cops weren't the only ones gunning for me. There was that anonymous citizen who had fired a shot through the doorway of my stash, missing me and nicking Dave Donaldson. Until now, I'd almost forgotten this incident in the excitement of ensuing events. In fact, I'd paid very little attention to the matter from the outset—largely because of the spot it put me in.

True, the shot had given me a chance to make a getaway from Dave. But it had also made him think I was the trigger guy; and this had deepened my jackpot to such an extent that I hadn't attempted to rationalize it. In fact, for a while I'd thought maybe the bullet had actually been meant for Dave, fired by a misguided friend trying to do me a favor.

Now, though, I realized it could be viewed from a different angle. Suppose I had been the intended target of that slug? Suppose the gunsel's aim had been bad, so that he missed me and hit Donaldson instead?

This new line of reasoning led me to something else. *Suppose the baseball that conked Maizie Murdock had likewise been meant for me?* It certainly had come close enough to my noggin. Maizie could have been just an innocent bystander, bashed by accident; the same as Dave Donaldson, later, was also accidentally nicked. In his case it was a .32 pill; in Maizie's, a baseball. That was the only difference. Everything else meshed into an identical pattern.

And the .32 pill had come from my own roscoe, the one I had dropped on the Venice amusement pier.

So now I was back on the same old merry-go-round. Cromwell could have picked up my gat. Or Bernie Ballantyne. Either of them could have pitched the lethal baseball at the Murdock cupcake, too, hitting her instead of me. Which one of them was the guy that thirsted to render me into a corpse?

Cromwell didn't seem logical; he had no reason to hate my clockworks as far as I knew. In fact, he was in my debt for the favor I'd done him, the night I took Vala DuValle off his hands in that night club raid.

The DuValle chick didn't fit the picture, either. I'd never done anything to earn her enmity; and besides, she was too fragile and dainty to heave a ball hard enough to burst a skull. She didn't have the muscles.

But Bernie Ballantyne—

"What the—!" I said harshly.

The hacker looked back at me. "You feeling bad, friend?"

"Plenty bad. I just thought of a guy who believed I was making a play for his sweetie. He pretended to get over it, later; but maybe he still packed a secret grudge."

"You dicks must have a lot of fun doping things out."

"This one isn't funny," I rasped. "The guy tried to bean me with a baseball. He missed, and it croaked a she-male. Whereupon he framed me for the kill."

"You're sure of that?"

I said: "Reasonably sure. I know a way to check it."

"How?"

I gave him Vala DuValle's address this side of Beverly. "If I can make this bozo's sweetie talk, I may be able to cinch the thing. She can tell me if he was still sore at me."

"Suppose she don't wanna talk, though? No jane likes to put her boy friend in the grease."

"She'll talk," I blew on my mitts. "She'll talk or I'll bat the bicuspids out of her."

It wasn't late enough at night for a flunky to give me such a frigid gander. I had thumbed the DuValle quail's doorbell and waited easily three minutes before I thumbed it again. Now this liveried butler opened up and squinted at me as if I'd been something you'd find under a rock.

"Miss DuValle?" he said to my polite query. "Sorry, my good man."

"You're sorry for what?"

"Really, it's nine-thirty—"

I said: "Yeah, Pacific War Time. I asked for Miss DuValle."

"She has retired."

"Then trot her out of retirement. I want her."

He drew himself up, haughtily. "See here."

"When you say that to me, say see here, *sir*." I grabbed him by his boiled dickey. "How long has it been since you got poked on the trumpet?"

"Why . . . er . . . never." Then he added: "Sir."

I said: "You've missed an experience," and educated him with my knuckles. He fell down, moaning that his nose was broken. Oddly enough, he was right.

Leaping lightly over his reclining form, I ankled toward an ornate marble staircase and chased myself up to the second floor at a brisk trot. The crash of the butler's fall and his piteous moans had preceded me, however, serving as a sort of storm warning. When I reached Vala DuValle's room, she was already at the door.

"Remember me, Toots?" I said.

"Mr. T-Turner . . . !"

"The same, and pardon my warty exterior for barging in this way. It's impolite but necessary."

"You beast!" she said.

I tried to look hurt. "That's no way to talk. In the first place, it's inhospitable, and in the second place, they don't write that sort of dialogue any more. Too mid-Victorian."

"Get out," she put her teeth together and talked through them. "Get out before I call the police."

"I'll call them myself when the time comes," I said. "Right now I crave information."

"Not from me. I don't associate with killers."

I debated whether to deal her a smack on the puss or try a little strategy first. I tossed a mental coin and strategy won. "I'm not a killer, hon," I made my voice humble.

She peeled back her pomegranate lips. "Liar."

"I'm leveling, honest I am. Give me a chance and I'll prove it. I'm trying to save my neck."

"Why should I care about your neck?"

"Maybe you shouldn't, but it's the only one I've got, and it fits all my collars." I unlimbered my nicest smile, meanwhile fishing for an angle. As my hacker had remarked, no jane likes to put her boy friend in the grease; therefore I might not get very far if I came right out and asked this brunette doll about Bernie Ballantyne still being sore at me. If I told her I suspected Bernie himself of being the guilty guy, she would congeal like frozen parsnips.

The thing to do was to sneak up on her, do some verbal sparring until she dropped her guard. Then maybe I'd find out if Bernie hated me so much he would pitch a baseball at me and bean somebody else by mistake. I might learn if he was the one who had picked up my roscoe on the amusement pier, later trying to plug me with it but nicking Donaldson instead.

But what was the best approach? All of a sudden a hunch nipped me. "Look, babe. You know that trouble you've been having?"

"Wh-what trouble?"

"The thing Ballantyne asked you about and made you weep," I said. "The same thing he hired me to investigate. Don't hold out on me. I'm hep to the setup."

"You're t-talking riddles."

"Yeah. It's a riddle when a cute little frail like you gets worried and draws a lot of dough out of her bank account for no logical reason. It's a shakedown riddle."

She sucked in a ragged breath; turned four shades of pale; backed toward her dressing table. "You unspeakable rat!" A cut glass perfume bottle was on the dresser. She picked it up, hurled it at me.

She tossed it with all her heft, which was nothing to boast about. It wabbled through the air almost lazily. I didn't even bother to duck; I just fielded it instead, caught it with a casual left duke. "This stuff is expensive," I reproached her. "It shouldn't be wasted on private snoops." I put it back where she got it.

Her angelic pan contorted darkly. Then she flurried into me, kicking and scratching and panting.

I said: "So you want to fight," and pinioned her. Every time she broke loose I grabbed her arms again. Presently she subsided, whimpering. I let her go; apologized for the bruises and contusions on her elbows and upper arms. "I guess I just don't know my own strength," I said, but I was thinking of something else—and still planning my battle strategy.

"Get out," she whispered.

"Not yet, kitten. I've got to know about that blackmailing."

"As if you didn't!"

I cocked an eyebrow. "Sure, I know you're being bled. Bernie knows it, too."

"You . . . t-told him?"

"He told me," I said. "He hired me to look into it."

Her short laugh had an uneven quality, like cloth being ripped. "What irony!"

"You mean him hiring me when he was jealous of me?"

"You know what I mean."

I said: "Maybe I'm extra stupid tonight. Skip it. About the shakedown geetus you've been paying. What was it based on?"

"Keep it up," she grunted. "Keep right on playing dumb."

"Was it somebody that piped you coming down from upstairs in Pedro Criqui's joint with Roy Cromwell?"

She gave me a sullen, silent stare.

I said: "Did this party threaten to squeal to Bernie Ballantyne, which would have scuttled your engagement? Was that why you paid hush money?"

Her map was a defiant mask. She didn't answer me.

"Look," I said. "I've had a chinfest with Pedro Criqui. He's told me the whole story."

"What story?"

"About how you refused to stay in that room with a wolf like Cromwell. You know, hon, in many respects you're a naïve dope."

She looked baffled. "I don't understand."

"It's very simple," I said. "Somebody put the nibble on you by threatening to tell Bernie you were seen coming from a tryst with your director. But why did you pay this shakedown when you were innocent?"

She fell into the trap; admitted she was being bled. "I had to pay. I was innocent, yes; but who'd believe me?"

"Pedro Criqui would have been happy to clear you. You could have got him to explain how you didn't stay upstairs more than a couple of minutes."

Puzzlement came into her widened glimmers. "That's queer advice, coming from you."

"Not at all. I was hired to help you, remember? And I'm trying to do my job—meanwhile helping myself at the same time. I want to get you out of your blackmail jam and myself out of the homicide jackpot."

"But—but I th-thought you—"

"Never mind what you thought," I said gently. "The point is, we want to finger the blackmailer. Right?"

"Y-yes."

"I think I know him," I said. Which was a lie.

She stiffened. "Wh-who?"

"I've done a lot of checking," I told her. "I've eliminated all the possible shakedown suspects except one."

"Wh-who?" she repeated tautly.

I said: "Roy Cromwell himself."

"No! That's not—why, that's insane!"

"On the contrary, it makes sense."

She stared at me. "Roy wouldn't do a thing like that. He—he makes as much money as I do. He's the highest paid director on the Paravox lot. Why should he—?"

"Look," I said. "He makes big geetus but he gambles it away. Pedro Criqui told me how rotten Cromwell's dice luck has been. I figure the guy lost so much lettuce he got desperate. He decided to use you for a soft touch. He squired you around, jockeyed you into a sour spot and then shoved the needle in you."

This was just a lot of sheep-dip as far as I was concerned. I didn't mean a word of it, actually; but it sounded plausible, and I was trying to gain the jane's confidence.

She fell for it, too. "The filthy, rotten heel!"

"Yeah. And to make it worse, he shoved you off on me when the joint was raided. That got Bernie Ballantyne sore at me. I guess he still is, hunh?"

"Well, a-a little," she admitted. "Although he got over it, pretty much."

I said: "The hell he did. He even tried to frame me for the Murdock filly's murder."

"Oh-h-h, no! I mean he really thinks you k-killed her. He's sincere about it."

"Maybe you're right," I shrugged. "It doesn't matter much." I turned toward the door. "I'll beat the rap, one way or another. In fact, I'm going out to do that very thing right away. Be seeing you, Babe."

"Wait," she said. She came close to me, stood on tiptoe and put her hands on my shoulders. She kissed me. It was a sisterly kiss. "That's for setting me straight on a lot of things," she whispered shyly.

I ankled down to my taxi with my yap still tingling from the warm contact of her lips.

CHAPTER VII

The Force of Gravity

At the nearest public phone I made three calls. First I dialed Roy Cromwell's stash, asked a sleepy servant if the director was home. The answer was yes, so I hung up. I didn't want to gab with the guy; I just craved to make sure he was on deck for the blowoff.

Next I rang Bernie Ballantyne, got him on the line. "Bernie? Dan Turner talking."

"You murderous louse! How dare you call me?"

"Keep your shirt on, small fry," I said. "I thought maybe you'd like to know I've solved a mystery for you."

"What mystery?"

"The one you paid me to ferret out. I know who's been blackmailing Vala DuValle."

"You—wh-what?"

I said: "Yeah. Roy Cromwell. He needed a wad of scratch for his gambling debts, so he lured her into a compromising situation. She was strictly innocent, understand; but it looked bad on the surface. Then he put the bite on her."

Again I was delivering a load of hogwash, maliciously, with a deliberate purpose. The quarrelsome little Paravox mogul stewed and sizzled audibly at the other end of the wire. "Do you actually mean to tell me—?"

"I've got the goods on him," I lied. "And I know something else, too. I know who picked up my gat on the Venice pier. Chew on that a while." I rang off.

Then, finally, I dialed police headquarters and asked for homicide.

"Is Lieutenant Donaldson there or did he go home to sulk over his skinned scalp?"

"He's here with a bandage that makes him look like a Hindu. Whoever you are, I wouldn't advise you to talk to him unless it's pretty important," the desk sergeant said. "He's meaner than six sick skunks."

"Put him on. This is plenty important." I waited. "Hi, Dave. Guess who."

He tabbed my voice; blew his top. *"You!* Well, I'm a son—"

"Hold it. I've cracked that Venice kill and I need you. But quick. There's a pinch to be pulled."

"Yeh. With you as the party of the first part." He softened his tone and I heard him mumbling to somebody.

I said: "Never mind trying to trace this call. It's a public phone and I could be long gone before you sent a squad car after me—if I wanted to play that way. I don't, though."

"Says you."

"All right, be tough. You'll sing a different tune when you meet me at Roy Cromwell's igloo and I hand you Maizie Murdock's murderer."

Dave repressed a strangled bellow. "Say that again!"

"I want you to meet me pronto at Roy Cromwell's wikiup. The killer will be there."

"Meaning yourself, huh?"

"No," I said patiently. "Meaning the character who pitched a baseball at my conk in an attempt to knock me off, but missed me and chilled the Murdock gazelle instead. The same one who fired a slug at me in my apartment dump, missed me again and nicked a notch in your noggin."

"When did you dream that up?"

"A while ago. Good-bye now. I'm on my way to Cromwell's. Be seeing you there." I disconnected and barged back to my cab.

The hacker said: "You look happy. What's brewin'?"

"An explosion," I told him. "Know how you make gunpowder?"

"No. I buy mine ready-made."

I said: "You pour in all the ingredients and stir them. If you stir long enough—"

"Oh-oh. You been stirrin' the ingredients, hunh?"

I nodded; gave him the Cromwell bozo's address. "Let's ramble. The kettle is starting to boil."

Cromwell's rambling Spanish hacienda was pasted against the side of a hill north of Hollywood Boulevard, just off one of the canyon drives.

We parked a block away and I hoofed the rest of the distance; reached the director's driveway just as a sedan slid to a halt at the curb. Dave Donaldson erupted from the sedan with a bandage around his cranium and two plainclothes minions flanking him.

The plainclothes minions had their roscoes out. Dave spotted me in the shadows. "There he is! Grab him! I didn't think he'd have nerve enough to show up. Freeze, Hawkshaw. This time we take no chances with you."

"You don't have to," I said softly, and allowed the flatties to fan me for my rod. When they took it, I added: "Be careful how you handle that heater, chums. It's the one that creased your superior officer."

Dave snatched it. "So this is what you shot me with."

"No."

"Well, then, whose gat is it?"

"Mine."

"Aha. So you confess."

I said: "It's the one those Venice coppers made me drop down on the amusement pier when they tried to collar me. Later the actual killer glommed it, brought it back to Hollywood and blasted from my doorway."

"Still sticking to that malarkey, eh?"

"Sure, because it's the truth. Are you going to stand jawing at me all night or can we go indoors for the payoff?"

Dave lifted a lip. "This *is* the payoff. Handcuff him, men."

They nippered me, and this time I stood still for it. It was the third time I'd been taken in custody that day and I was much too weary to argue. I merely said: "Don't blame me when the case blows up in your kisser. The next kill will be your fault. Think it over."

"What next kill?" Donaldson demanded suspiciously.

"Right here in Cromwell's shanty. I sicced Bernie Ballantyne onto him a while ago, by phone. Judging by the lights in the igloo and that chariot parked across the street, Cromwell's got a visitor this instant."

Dave cleared his throat and spat. "Listen, wisenheimer. If you're pulling a swift one—"

"Use your own judgment," I said indifferently. "I've done my part. It's your picnic now."

He hesitated; seemed to realize I was leveling. "Come along with me," he growled. "But the bracelets stay on you." He turned to his under-lings. "You guys wait here."

"But, lieutenant—"

He snarled: "Quiet," and tugged me toward the director's portal. "Shall I ring?" he whispered to me.

"No. Try the knob."

He did. "It's locked."

"I've got master keys in my pocket. Fish them out and get to work with them. I can't with these manacles."

He frisked me for the keys, found one that operated the doorlatch. "Now what?"

"Inside, fast. And no noise." I took the lead, moving silently. We came to an inside door that stood slightly ajar. Dim light glowed around it and low voices sounded in the room.

Roy Cromwell was panting: "All right. I admit I was the blackmailer. I needed cash. Desperately. I—"

You could have maced me senseless with an ostrich feather as I heard the guy's confession. My phoney accusations against him had turned out to be straight goods; he really *was* the extortionist! I'd fired a blind shot in the dark and scored the screwiest bull's-eye of my crazy career.

Another voice husked hysterically: "You scum. You pulled an unspeakable trick like that and caused me to commit murder. But you're going to pay."

"No—please—don't point that g-gun at me—"

This was my cue for action. I slugged the door wide open so hard it nearly came loose from its moorings; went leaping across the threshold with Dave Donaldson roaring in my wake. I yodeled: *"Drop it, Vala Du-Valle."*

The diminutive brunette cupcake had been aiming a tiny heater at Roy Cromwell, who cowered in a far corner like a weasel in a trap. But now she swung around, hung the glassy focus on me, tabbed Donaldson's cannon making faces at her.

"Oh-h-h . . ." she whimpered faintly, and let her roscoe clatter on the floor. "You . . . you . . ."

"Yeah," I said regretfully, remembering the kiss she'd slipped me not long ago. "Me, hon. Just in time to keep you from another croaking; and to hear you confess the Maizie Murdock bump. I'm sorry, baby. I mean that."

Her map was like a mask made of putty. "How . . . did you . . . how did you . . . suspect . . . ?"

"Your arms," I said. "They gave you away."

Donaldson yipped: "Hey, wait a minute. What's this about her arms? They look okay to me. Only they aren't hefty enough to uncork a baseball pitch that could brain a jane."

"I know it," I said.

"Then how—"

I stared moodily at Vala. "You thought I was the blackmailer, didn't you, kitten?"

"Y-yes."

"I'd made a crack in Bernie Ballantyne's ante-room; something about carrying tales to him if it paid me enough dividends. Since you were already being shaken down, that made you think I was the mug who was putting the bite on you."

"Y-yes," her voice was dull, lifeless.

I said: "You decided to croak me. You tried to with that baseball, but cooled Maizie Murdock by mistake. When everybody called me guilty you let it ride, thereby keeping your own skirts clean while still putting me in a coffin. Correct?"

"Y-yes." She didn't seem to know any other word.

"Then I escaped," I said. "You picked up my automatic; tried to blast me with it, later, at my apartment drop. Again your aim was lousy. You nicked Lieutenant Donaldson."

"Y-yes," she sounded like a victrola with a busted record.

I said: "Well, that's about all of it. Except your arms."

"Wh-what about them?"

"I called on you, hoping to get the deadwood on Bernie Ballantyne. At that time I had him tabbed as the guilty guy. But suddenly I noticed the bruises and scrapes on your elbows. I tumbled to the truth."

"How?" she whispered.

"I've got the same brand of bruises myself," I told her. "And I remembered where I'd collected them. The rest was easy. I spoke of Roy Cromwell being the blackmailer, figuring you would try to cream him the same as you'd tried to bump me. Which you did; and we caught you."

She blinked at me foggily. "The bruises . . . ?"

"From the giant slide," I said. "Whamming down the spiral tunnel was where you got your arms hurt. Just before the murder, you rode the escalator to the observation tower on top of that amusement pier contraption.

"The view platform looked directly down on the baseball concession. You threw a ball at me from up there and gravity gave it murderspeed."

"Y-yes," she was back at that again.

I said: "As soon as you pitched the pill, you slid down through the spiral dragon. This landed you on the pier in plenty of time to establish an apparent alibi. You said you had just come out of your dressing room. Nobody doubted you."

From behind me, a new voice spoke: high, piping, reedy. It belonged to Bernie Ballantyne, who'd arrived to hear the payoff. Now he took Vala in his arms.

"I'll hire the best lawyers in the world to defend you, darling," he said. Then he glared at Cromwell. "You're fired, you chiseling rat. If you ever work in Hollywood again, it'll be over my dead body."

He was a good prophet. The DuValle cutie got off with a life sentence and Roy Cromwell got blackballed out of the galloping snapshots.

And Dave Donaldson actually paid dough out of his own pocket to have my jalopy brought back to me from where I'd ditched it in Ocean Park.

WILLIAM FAULKNER

(1897–1962)

|||||||||||||||||||||||||||||||||||||||||||||||| ■ ||||||||||||||||||||||||||||||||||||||||||||||

When William Faulkner, a Nobel laureate in literature, turned his hand to writing "An Error in Chemistry," it was in response to the First Short-Story Contest, held by *Ellery Queen's Mystery Magazine* in 1946. Faulkner wrote his story with the prize money in mind. The pool of contestants was particularly talented. Faulkner tied with six others for second prize.

That Faulkner went on to write five more stories, collected in the anthology *Knight's Gambit,* and a novel, *Intruder in the Dust,* featuring series character Uncle Gavin Stevens proves that the detective form has long attracted first-rate writers. In the introduction to "An Error in Chemistry" in *Ellery Queen's Mystery Magazine,* Queen compares Faulkner's strong moral sense with that of Melville Davisson Post. Whether or not Faulkner was acquainted with Post's work is uncertain, but Queen is on the mark in pointing out the similarities between the two.

Born William Falkner (he was to change the spelling of his name as a young man) in New Albany, Mississippi, he was the great-grandson of a colorful character, William Clark Falkner, who was a lawyer, planter, railroad builder, novelist, poet, playwright, and travel writer. Faulkner himself studied for two years at the University of Mississippi, served in World War I in both the Canadian Flying Corps and the British Royal Air Force, worked at a number of jobs including postmaster, and launched his literary career in 1924 with *The Marble Faun,* a book of poetry. He then began his long list of unforgettable novels about the corruption and decadence of southern values and southern families.

"An Error in Chemistry" offers a fascinating look at what a writer of Faulkner's caliber can do with a form that—when Faulkner tried his hand at it—was still dominated by the depiction of ratiocination. There is little doubt that Faulkner had learned from earlier writers of detective fiction. For example, his use of Uncle Gavin Stevens as a foil for the sheriff's thinking brings to mind Dr. John H. Watson and Sherlock Holmes. The story begins with a puzzle, focuses on it throughout, and uses a clue that any reader can see to provide the solution. But it is a superlative story because of its Faulknerian qualities—the dark and twisted pride motivating the criminal, the pathos, the authentic sound of the dialogue, the local color, and the provincial stage on which Faulkner plays out his little drama.

From its thought-provoking title to the biblical references at its close, "An Error in Chemistry" demonstrates that a tale of detection can rise to the level of true tragedy featuring, as Faulkner puts it, "that triumvirate of murderer, victim, and bereaved." In Faulkner's hands, murder is not merely the occasion to determine whodunit; violent death gives substance to the victim.

1946

An Error in Chemistry

It was Joel Flint himself who telephoned the sheriff that he had killed his wife. And when the sheriff and his deputy reached the scene, drove the twenty-odd miles into the remote back-country region where old Wesley Pritchel lived, Joel Flint himself met them at the door and asked them in. He was the foreigner, the outlander, the Yankee who had come into our county two years ago as the operator of a pitch—a lighted booth where a roulette wheel spun against a bank of nickel-plated pistols and razors and watches and harmonicas, in a traveling street carnival—and who when the carnival departed had remained, and two months later was married to Pritchel's only living child: the dim-witted spinster of almost forty who until then had shared her irascible and violent-tempered father's almost hermit-existence on the good though small farm which he owned.

But even after the marriage, old Pritchel still seemed to draw the line against his son-in-law. He built a new small house for them two miles from his own, where the daughter was presently raising chickens for the market. According to rumor old Pritchel, who hardly ever went anywhere anyway, had never once entered the new house, so that he saw even this last remaining child only once a week. This would be when she and her husband would drive each Sunday in the second-hand truck in which the son-in-law marketed the chickens, to take Sunday dinner with old Pritchel in the old house where Pritchel now did his own cooking and housework. In fact, the neighbors said the only reason he allowed the son-in-law to enter his house even then was so that his daughter could prepare him a decent hot meal once a week.

So for the next two years, occasionally in Jefferson, the county seat, but more frequently in the little cross-roads hamlet near his home, the son-in-law would be seen and heard too. He was a man in the middle forties, neither short nor tall nor thin nor stout (in fact, he and his father-in-law could easily have cast that same shadow which later for a short time they did), with a cold, contemptuous intelligent face and a voice lazy with anecdotes of the teeming outland which his listeners had never seen—a dweller among the cities, though never from his own accounting long resident in any one of them, who within the first three months of his residence among them had impressed upon the people whose way of life he had assumed, one definite personal habit by which he presently became known throughout the whole county, even by men

415

who had never seen him. This was a harsh and contemptuous deroga-
tion, sometimes without even provocation or reason or opportunity, of
our local southern custom of drinking whiskey by mixing sugar and
water with it. He called it effeminacy, a pap for children, himself drinking even our harsh, violent, illicit and unaged homemade corn whiskey
without even a sip of water to follow it.

Then on this last Sunday morning he telephoned the sheriff that he
had killed his wife and met the officers at his father-in-law's door and
said: "I have already carried her into the house. So you won't need to
waste breath telling me I shouldn't have touched her until you got
here."

"I reckon it was all right to take her up out of the dirt," the sheriff
said. "It was an accident, I believe you said."

"Then you believe wrong," Flint said. "I said I killed her."

And that was all.

The sheriff brought him to Jefferson and locked him in a cell in the
jail. And that evening after supper the sheriff came through the side
door into the study where Uncle Gavin was supervising me in the drawing of a brief. Uncle Gavin was only county, not District, attorney. But
he and the sheriff, who had been sheriff off and on even longer than
Uncle Gavin had been county attorney, had been friends all that while.
I mean friends in the sense that two men who play chess together are
friends, even though sometimes their aims are diametrically opposed. I
heard them discuss it once.

"I'm interested in truth," the sheriff said.

"So am I," Uncle Gavin said. "It's so rare. But I am more interested
in justice and human beings."

"Ain't truth and justice the same thing?" the sheriff said.

"Since when?" Uncle Gavin said. "In my time I have seen truth that
was anything under the sun but just, and I have seen justice using tools
and instruments I wouldn't want to touch with a ten-foot fence rail."

The sheriff told us about the killing, standing, looming above the
table-lamp—a big man with little hard eyes, talking down at Uncle
Gavin's wild shock of prematurely white hair and his quick thin face,
while Uncle Gavin sat on the back of his neck practically, his legs
crossed on the desk, chewing the bit of his corncob pipe and spinning
and unspinning around his finger his watch chain weighted with the
Phi Beta Kappa key he got at Harvard.

"Why?" Uncle Gavin said.

"I asked him that, myself," the sheriff said. "He said, 'Why do men
ever kill their wives? Call it for the insurance.'"

"That's wrong," Uncle Gavin said. "It's women who murder their spouses for immediate personal gain—insurance policies, or at what they believe is the instigation or promise of another man. Men murder their wives from hatred or rage or despair, or to keep them from talking since not even bribery not even simple absence can bridle a woman's tongue."

"Correct," the sheriff said. He blinked his little eyes at Uncle Gavin. "It's like he *wanted* to be locked up in jail. Not like he was submitting to arrest because he had killed his wife, but like he had killed her so that he would be locked up, arrested. Guarded."

"Why?" Uncle Gavin said.

"Correct too," the sheriff said. "When a man deliberately locks doors behind himself, it's because he is afraid. And a man who would voluntarily have himself locked up on suspicion of murder . . ." He batted his hard little eyes at Uncle Gavin for a good ten seconds while Uncle Gavin looked just as hard back at him. "Because he wasn't afraid. Not then nor at any time. Now and then you meet a man that aint ever been afraid, not even of himself. He's one."

"If that's what he wanted you to do," Uncle Gavin said, "why did you do it?"

"You think I should have waited a while?"

They looked at one another a while. Uncle Gavin wasn't spinning the watch chain now. "All right," he said. "Old Man Pritchel—"

"I was coming to that," the sheriff said. "Nothing."

"Nothing?" Uncle Gavin said. "You didn't even see him?" And the sheriff told that too—how as he and the deputy and Flint stood on the gallery, they suddenly saw the old man looking out at them through a window—a face rigid, furious, glaring at them through the glass for a second and then withdrawn, vanished, leaving an impression of furious exultation and raging triumph, and something else. . . .

"Fear?" the sheriff said. "No. I tell you, he wasn't afraid—Oh," he said. "You mean Pritchel." This time he looked at Uncle Gavin so long that at last Uncle Gavin said,

"All right. Go on." And the sheriff told that too: how they entered the house, the hall, and he stopped and knocked at the locked door of the room where they had seen the face and he even called old Pritchel's name and still got no answer. And how they went on and found Mrs. Flint on a bed in the back room with the shotgun wound in her neck, and Flint's battered truck drawn up beside the back steps as if they had just got out of it.

"There were three dead squirrels in the truck," the sheriff said. "I'd say they had been shot since daylight"—and the blood on the steps, and on the ground between the steps and the truck, as if she had been shot from inside the truck, and the gun itself, still containing the spent shell, standing just inside the hall door as a man would put it down when he entered the house. And how the sheriff went back up the hall and knocked again at the locked door—

"Locked where?" Uncle Gavin said.

"On the inside," the sheriff said—and shouted against the door's blank surface that he would break the door in if Mr. Pritchel didn't answer and open it, and how this time the harsh furious old voice answered, shouting:

"Get out of my house! Take that murderer and get out of my house."

"You will have to make a statement," the sheriff answered.

"I'll make my statement when the time comes for it!" the old man shouted. "Get out of my house, all of you!" And how he (the sheriff) sent the deputy in the car to fetch the nearest neighbor, and he and Flint waited until the deputy came back with a man and his wife. Then they brought Flint on to town and locked him up and the sheriff telephoned back to old Pritchel's house and the neighbor answered and told him how the old man was still locked in the room, refusing to come out or even to answer save to order them all (several other neighbors had arrived by now, word of the tragedy having spread) to leave. But some of them would stay in the house, no matter what the seemingly crazed old man said or did, and the funeral would be tomorrow.

"And that's all?" Uncle Gavin said.

"That's all," the sheriff said. "Because it's too late now."

"For instance?" Uncle Gavin said.

"The wrong one is dead."

"That happens," Uncle Gavin said.

"For instance?"

"That clay-pit business."

"What clay-pit business?" Because the whole county knew about old Pritchel's clay-pit. It was a formation of malleable clay right in the middle of his farm, of which people in the adjacent countryside made quite serviceable through crude pottery—those times they could manage to dig that much of it before Mr. Pritchel saw them and drove them off. For generations, Indian and even aboriginal relics—flint arrow-heads, axes and dishes and skulls and thigh-bones and pipes—had been excavated from it by random boys, and a few years ago a party of archaeologists from the State University had dug into it until Old Man Pritchel got there, this time with a shotgun. But everybody knew this; this was not what the sheriff was telling, and now Uncle Gavin was sitting erect in the chair and his feet were on the floor now.

"I hadn't heard about this," Uncle Gavin said.

"It's common knowledge out there," the sheriff said. "In fact, you might call it the local outdoor sport. It began about six weeks ago. They are three northern men. They're trying to buy the whole farm from old Pritchel to get the pit and manufacture some kind of road material out of the clay, I understand. The folks out there are still watching them trying to buy it. Apparently the northerners are the only folks in the country that don't know yet old Pritchel aint got any notion of selling even the clay to them, let alone the farm."

"They've made him an offer, of course."

"Probably a good one. It runs all the way from two hundred and fifty dollars to two hundred and fifty thousand, depending on who's telling it. Them northerners just don't know how to handle him. If they would just set in and convince him that everybody in the county is hoping he won't sell it to them, they could probably buy it before supper tonight." He stared at Uncle Gavin, batting his eyes again. "So the wrong one is dead, you see. If it was that clay-pit, he's no nearer to it than he was yesterday. He's worse off than he was yesterday. Then there wasn't anything between him and his pa-in-law's money but whatever private wishes and hopes and feelings that dim-witted girl might have had. Now there's a penitentiary wall, and likely a rope. It don't make sense. If he was afraid of a possible witness, he not only destroyed the witness before there was anything to be witnessed but also before there was any witness to be destroyed. He set up a sign-board saying 'Watch me and mark me,' not just to this county and this state but to all folks everywhere who believe the Book where it says *Thou Shalt Not Kill*—and then went and got himself locked up in the very place created to punish him for this crime and restrain him from the next one. Something went wrong."

"I hope so," Uncle Gavin said.

"You hope so?"

"Yes. That something went wrong in what has already happened, rather than what has already happened is not finished yet."

"How not finished yet?" the sheriff said. "How can he finish whatever it is he aims to finish? Aint he already locked up in jail, with the only man in the county who might make bond to free him being the father of the woman he as good as confessed he murdered?"

"It looks that way," Uncle Gavin said. "Was there an insurance policy?"

"I don't know," the sheriff said. "I'll find that out tomorrow. But that aint what I want to know. I want to know why he *wanted* to be locked up in jail. Because I tell you he wasn't afraid, then nor at any other time. You already guessed who it was out there that was afraid."

But we were not to learn that answer yet. And there was an insurance policy. But by the time we learned about that, something else had happened which sent everything else temporarily out of mind. At daylight the next morning, when the jailer went and looked into Flint's cell, it was empty. He had not broken out. He had walked out, out of the cell, out of the jail, out of the town and apparently out of the country— no trace, no sign, no man who had seen him or seen anyone who might have been him. It was not yet sunup when I let the sheriff in at the side study door; Uncle Gavin was already sitting up in bed when we reached his bedroom.

"Old Man Pritchel!" Uncle Gavin said. "Only we are already too late."

"What's the matter with you?" the sheriff said. "I told you last night he was already too late the second he pulled that wrong trigger. Besides, just to be in position to ease your mind, I've already telephoned out there. Been a dozen folks in the house all night, sitting up with the—with Mrs. Flint, and old Pritchel's still locked in his room and all right too. They heard him bumping and blundering around in there just before daylight, and so somebody knocked on the door and kept on knocking and calling him until he finally opened the door wide enough to give them all a good cussing and order them again to get out of his house and stay out. Then he locked the door again. Old fellow's been hit pretty hard, I reckon. He must have seen it when it happened, and at his age, and having already druv the whole human race away from his house except that half-wit girl, until at last even she up and left him, even at any cost. I reckon it aint any wonder she married even a man like Flint. What is it the Book says? 'Who lives by the sword, so shall he die'?—the sword in old Pritchel's case being whatever it was he decided he preferred in place of human beings, while he was still young and hale and strong and didn't need them. But to keep your mind easy, I sent Bryan Ewell out there thirty minutes ago and told him not to let that locked door—or old Pritchel himself, if he comes out of it—out of his sight until I told him to, and I sent Ben Berry and some others out to Flint's house and told Ben to telephone me. And I'll call you when I hear anything. Which won't be anything, because that fellow's gone. He got caught yesterday because he made a mistake, and the fellow that can walk out of that jail like he did aint going to make two mistakes within five hundred miles of Jefferson or Mississippi either."

"Mistake?" Uncle Gavin said. "He just told us this morning why he wanted to be put in jail."

"And why was that?"

"So he could escape from it."

"And why get out again, when he was already out and could have stayed out by just running instead of telephoning me he had committed a murder?"

"I don't know," Uncle Gavin said. "Are you sure Old Man Pritchel—"

"Didn't I just tell you folks saw and talked to him through that half-opened door this morning? And Bryan Ewell probably sitting in a chair tilted against that door right this minute—or he better be. I'll telephone you if I hear anything. But I've already told you that too—that it won't be nothing."

He telephoned an hour later. He had just talked to the deputy who had searched Flint's house, reporting only that Flint had been there sometime in the night—the back door open, an oil lamp shattered on the floor where Flint had apparently knocked it while fumbling in the dark, since the deputy found, behind a big, open, hurriedly ransacked trunk, a twisted spill of paper which Flint had obviously used to light his search of the trunk—a scrap of paper torn from a billboard—

"A what?" Uncle Gavin said.

"That's what I said," the sheriff said. "And Ben says, 'All right, then send somebody else out here, if my reading aint good enough to suit you. It was a scrap of paper which was evidently tore from the corner of a billboard because it says on the scrap in English that even I can read—' and I says, 'Tell me exactly what it is you're holding in your hand.' And he did. It's a page, from a magazine or a small paper named *Billboard* or maybe *The Billboard*. There's some more printing on it but Ben can't read it because he lost his spectacles back in the woods while he was surrounding the house to catch Flint doing whatever it was he expected to catch him doing—cooking breakfast, maybe. Do you know what it is?"

"Yes," Uncle Gavin said.

"Do you know what it means, what it was doing there?"

"Yes," Uncle Gavin said. "But why?"

"Well, I can't tell you. And he never will. Because he's gone, Gavin. Oh, we'll catch him—somebody will, I mean, someday, somewhere. But it won't be here, and it won't be for this. It's like that poor, harmless, half-witted girl wasn't important enough for even that justice you claim you prefer above truth, to avenge her."

And that did seem to be all of it. Mrs. Flint was buried that afternoon. The old man was still locked in his room during the funeral, and even after they departed with the coffin for the churchyard, leaving in the house only the deputy in his tilted chair outside the locked door, and two neighbor women who remained to cook a hot meal for old

Pritchel, finally prevailing on him to open the door long enough to take the tray from them. And he thanked them for it, clumsily and gruffly, thanking them for their kindness during all the last twenty-four hours. One of the women was moved enough to offer to return tomorrow and cook another meal for him, whereupon his old-time acerbity and choler returned and the kind-hearted woman was even regretting that she had made the offer at all when the harsh, cracked old voice from inside the half-closed door added: "I don't need no help. I ain't had no darter nohow in two years," and the door slammed in their faces and the bolt shot home.

Then the two women left, and there was only the deputy sitting in his tilted chair beside the door. He was back in town the next morning, telling how the old man had snatched the door suddenly open and kicked the chair out from beneath the dozing deputy before he could move and ordered him off the place with violent curses, and how as he (the deputy) peered at the house from around the corner of the barn a short time later, the shotgun blared from the kitchen window and the charge of squirrel shot slammed into the stable wall not a yard above his head. The sheriff telephoned that to Uncle Gavin too:

"So he's out there alone again. And since that's what he seems to want, it's all right with me. Sure I feel sorry for him. I feel sorry for anybody that has to live with a disposition like his. Old and alone, to have all this happen to him. It's like being snatched up by a tornado and whirled and slung and then slammed right back down where you started from, without even the benefit and pleasure of having taken a trip. What was it I said yesterday about living by the sword?"

"I don't remember," Uncle Gavin said. "You said a lot yesterday."

"And a lot of it was right. I said it was finished yesterday. And it is. That fellow will trip himself again someday, but it won't be here."

Only it was more than that. It was as if Flint had never been here at all—no mark, no scar to show that he had ever been in the jail cell. The meagre group of people who pitied but did not mourn, departing, separating, from the raw grave of the woman who had had little enough hold on our lives at best, whom a few of us had known without ever having seen her and some of us had seen without ever knowing her. . . . The childless old man whom most of us had never seen at all, once more alone in the house where, as he said himself, there had been no child anyway in two years. . . .

"As though none of it had ever happened," Uncle Gavin said. "As if Flint had not only never been in that cell but had never existed at all. That triumvirate of murderer, victim, and bereaved—not three flesh-and-blood people but just an illusion, a shadow-play on a sheet—not only neither men nor women nor young nor old but just three labels which cast two shadows for the simple and only reason that it requires a minimum of two in order to postulate the verities of injustice and grief. That's it. They have never cast but two shadows, even though they did bear three labels, names. It was as though only by dying did that poor woman ever gain enough substance and reality even to cast a shadow."

"But somebody killed her," I said.

"Yes," Uncle Gavin said. "Somebody killed her."

That was at noon. About five that afternoon I answered the telephone. It was the sheriff. "Is your uncle there?" he said. "Tell him to wait. I'm coming right over." He had a stranger with him—a city man, in neat city clothes.

"This is Mr. Workman," the sheriff said. "The adjustor. There was an insurance policy. For five hundred, taken out seventeen months ago. Hardly enough to murder anybody for."

"If it ever was a murder," the adjustor said. His voice was cold too, cold yet at the same time at a sort of seething boil. "That policy will be paid at once, without question or any further investigation. And I'll tell you something else you people here don't seem to know yet. That old man is crazy. It was not the man Flint who should have been brought to town and locked up."

Only it was the sheriff who told that too: how yesterday afternoon the insurance company's Memphis office had received a telegram, signed with Old Man Pritchel's name, notifying them of the insured's death, and the adjustor arrived at Old Man Pritchel's house about two o'clock this afternoon and within thirty minutes had extracted from Old Man Pritchel himself the truth about his daughter's death: the facts of it which the physical evidence—the truck and the three dead squirrels and the blood on the steps and on the ground—supported. This was that while the daughter was cooking dinner, Pritchel and Flint had driven the truck down to Pritchel's woods lot to shoot squirrels for supper—"And that's correct," the sheriff said. "I asked. They did that every Sunday morning. Pritchel wouldn't let anybody but Flint shoot his squirrels, and he wouldn't even let Flint shoot them unless he was along"—and they shot the three squirrels and Flint drove the truck back to the house and up beside the back steps and the woman came out to take the squirrels and Flint opened the door and picked up the gun to get out of the truck and stumbled, caught his heel on the edge of the running-board and flinging up the hand carrying the gun to break his fall, so that the muzzle of the gun was pointing right at his wife's head when it went off. And Old Man Pritchel not only denied having sent the wire, he violently and profanely repudiated any and all implication or suggestion that he even knew the policy existed at all. He denied to the very last that the shooting had been any part of an accident. He tried to revoke his own testimony as to what had happened when the daughter came out to get the dead squirrels and the gun went off, repudiating his own story when he realized that he had cleared his son-in-law of murder, snatching the paper from the adjustor's hand, which he apparently believed was the policy itself, and attempting to tear it up and destroy it before the adjustor could stop him.

"Why?" Uncle Gavin said.

"Why not?" the sheriff said. "We had let Flint get away; Mr. Pritchel knew he was loose somewhere in the world. Do you reckon he aimed to let the man that killed his daughter get paid for it?"

"Maybe," Uncle Gavin said. "But I don't think so. I don't think he is worried about that at all. I think Mr. Pritchel knows that Joel Flint is not going to collect that policy or any other prize. Maybe he knew a little country jail like ours wasn't going to hold a wide-travelled ex-carnival man, and he expected Flint to come back out there and this time he was ready for him. And I think that as soon as people stop worrying him, he will send you word to come out there, and he will tell you so."

"Hah," the adjustor said. "Then they must have stopped worrying him. Listen to this. When I got there this afternoon, there were three men in the parlor with him. They had a certified check. It was a big check. They were buying his farm from him—lock, stock and barrel—and I didn't know land in this country was worth that much either, incidentally. He had the deed all drawn and signed, but when I told them who I was, they agreed to wait until I could get back to town here and tell somebody—the sheriff, probably. And I left, and that old lunatic was still standing in the door, shaking that deed at me and croaking: 'Tell the sheriff, damn you! Get a lawyer, too! Get that lawyer Stevens. I hear tell he claims to be pretty slick!'"

"We thank you," the sheriff said. He spoke and moved with that deliberate, slightly florid, old-fashioned courtesy which only big men can wear, except that his was constant; this was the first time I ever saw him quit anyone shortly, even when he would see them again tomorrow. He didn't even look at the adjustor again. "My car's outside," he told Uncle Gavin.

So just before sunset we drove up to the neat picket fence enclosing Old Man Pritchel's neat, bare little yard and neat, tight little house, in front of which stood the big, dust-covered car with its city license plates and Flint's battered truck with a strange Negro youth at the wheel—

strange because Old Man Pritchel had never had a servant of any sort save his daughter.

"He's leaving too," Uncle Gavin said.

"That's his right," the sheriff said. We mounted the steps. But before we reached the door, Old Man Pritchel was already shouting for us to come in—the harsh, cracked old man's voice shouting at us from beyond the hall, beyond the door to the dining room where a tremendous old-fashioned telescope bag, strapped and bulging, sat on a chair and the three northerners in dusty khaki stood watching the door and Old Man Pritchel himself sat at the table. And I saw for the first time (Uncle Gavin told me he had seen him only twice) the uncombed thatch of white hair, a fierce tangle of eyebrows above steel-framed spectacles, a jut of untrimmed mustache and a scrabble of beard stained with chewing tobacco to the color of dirty cotton.

"Come in," he said. "That lawyer Stevens, heh?"

"Yes, Mr. Pritchel," the sheriff said.

"Hehm," the old man barked. "Well, Hub," he said. "Can I sell my land, or can't I?"

"Of course, Mr. Pritchel," the sheriff said. "We hadn't heard you aimed to."

"Heh," the old man said. "Maybe this changed my mind." The check and the folded deed both lay on the table in front of him. He pushed the check toward the sheriff. He didn't look at Uncle Gavin again; he just said: "You, too." Uncle Gavin and the sheriff moved to the table and stood looking down at the check. Neither of them touched it. I could see their faces. There was nothing in them. "Well?" Mr. Pritchel said.

"It's a good price," the sheriff said.

This time the old man said "Hah!" short and harsh. He unfolded the deed and spun it to face, not the sheriff but Uncle Gavin. "Well?" he said. "You, lawyer?"

"It's all right, Mr. Pritchel," Uncle Gavin said. The old man sat back, both hands on the table before him, his head tilted back as he looked up at the sheriff.

"Well?" he said. "Fish, or cut bait."

"It's your land," the sheriff said. "What you do with it is no man's business else."

"Hah," Mr. Pritchel said. He didn't move. "All right, gentlemen." He didn't move at all: one of the strangers came forward and took up the deed. "I'll be out of the house in thirty minutes. You can take possession then, or you will find the key under the mat tomorrow morning." I don't believe he even looked after them as they went out, though

I couldn't be sure because of the glare on his spectacles. Then I knew that he was looking at the sheriff, had been looking at him for a minute or more, and then I saw that he was trembling, jerking and shaking as the old tremble, although his hands on the table were as motionless as two lumps of the clay would have been.

"So you let him get away," he said.

"That's right," the sheriff said. "But you wait, Mr. Pritchel. We'll catch him."

"When?" the old man said. "Two years? Five years? Ten years? I am seventy-four years old: buried my wife and four children. Where will I be in ten years?"

"Here, I hope," the sheriff said.

"Here?" the old man said. "Didn't you just hear me tell that fellow he could have this house in thirty minutes? I own a automobile truck now; I got money to spend now, and something to spend it for."

"Spend it for what?" the sheriff said. "That check? Even this boy here would have to start early and run late to get shut of that much money in ten years."

"Spend it running down the man that killed my Ellie!" He rose suddenly, thrusting his chair back. He staggered, but when the sheriff stepped quickly toward him, he flung his arm out and seemed actually to strike the sheriff back a pace. "Let be," he said, panting. Then he said, harsh and loud in his cracked shaking voice: "Get out of here! Get out of my house all of you!" But the sheriff didn't move, nor did we, and after a moment the old man stopped trembling. But he was still holding to the table edge. But his voice was quiet. "Hand me my whiskey. On the sideboard. And three glasses." The sheriff fetched them— an old-fashioned cut-glass decanter and three heavy tumblers—and set them before him. And when he spoke this time, his voice was almost gentle and I knew what the woman had felt that evening when she offered to come back tomorrow and cook another meal for him: "You'll have to excuse me. I'm tired. I've had a heap of trouble lately, and I reckon I'm wore out. Maybe a change is what I need."

"But not tonight, Mr. Pritchel," the sheriff said.

And then again, as when the woman had offered to come back and cook, he ruined it. "Maybe I won't start tonight," he said. "And then maybe again I will. But you folks want to get on back to town, so we'll just drink to goodbye and better days." He unstoppered the decanter and poured whiskey into the three tumblers and set the decanter down and looked about the table. "You, boy," he said, "hand me the water bucket. It's on the back gallery shelf." Then, as I turned and started toward the door, I saw him reach and take up the sugar bowl and plunge the spoon into the sugar and then I stopped too. And I remember Uncle Gavin's and the sheriff's faces and I could not believe my eyes either as he put the spoonful of sugar into the raw whiskey and started to stir it. Because I had not only watched Uncle Gavin, and the sheriff when he would come to play chess with Uncle Gavin, but Uncle Gavin's father too who was my grandfather, and my own father before he died, and all the other men who would come to Grandfather's house who drank cold toddies as we call them, and even I knew that to make a cold toddy you do not put the sugar into the whiskey because sugar will not dissolve in raw whiskey but only lies in a little intact swirl like sand at the bottom of the glass; that you first put the water into the glass and dissolve the sugar into the water, in a ritual almost; then you add the whiskey, and that anyone like Old Man Pritchel who must have been watching men make cold toddies for nearly seventy years and had been making and drinking them himself for at least fifty-three, would know this too. And I remember how the man we had thought was Old Man Pritchel realized too late what he was doing and jerked his head up just as Uncle Gavin sprang toward him, and swung his arm back and hurled the glass at Uncle Gavin's head, and the thud of the flung glass against the wall and the dark splash it made and the crash of the table as it went over and the raw stink of the spilled whiskey from the decanter and Uncle Gavin shouting at the sheriff: "Grab him, Hub! Grab him!"

Then we were all three on him. I remember the savage strength and speed of the body which was no old man's body; I saw him duck beneath the sheriff's arm and the entire wig came off; I seemed to see his whole face wrenching itself furiously free from beneath the makeup which bore the painted wrinkles and the false eyebrows. When the sheriff snatched the beard and mustache off, the flesh seemed to come with it, springing quick and pink and then crimson, as though in that last desperate cast he had had to beard, disguise, not his face so much as the very blood which he had spilled.

It took us only thirty minutes to find old Mr. Pritchel's body. It was under the feed room in the stable, in a shallow and hurried trench, scarcely covered from sight. His hair had not only been dyed, it had been trimmed, the eyebrows trimmed and dyed too, and the mustache and beard shaved off. He was wearing the identical garments which Flint had worn to the jail and he had been struck at least one crushing blow on the face, apparently with the flat of the same axe which had split his skull from behind, so that his features were almost unrecognizable and, after another two or three weeks underground, would perhaps have been even unidentifiable as those of the old man. And pillowed carefully beneath the head was a big ledger almost six inches thick and weighing almost twenty pounds and filled with the carefully pasted clippings which covered twenty years and more. It was the record and tale of the gift, the talent, which at the last he had misapplied and betrayed and which had then turned and destroyed him. It was all there: inception, course, peak, and then decline—the handbills, the theatre programs, the news clippings, and even one actual ten-foot poster:

SIGNOR CANOVA
Master of Illusion
He Disappears While You Watch Him
Management Offers One Thousand Dollars
in Cash to Any Man or Woman or
Child Who . . .

Last of all was the final clipping, from our Memphis-printed daily paper, under the Jefferson date line, which was news and not press-agentry. This was the account of that last gamble in which he had cast his gift and his life against money, wealth, and lost—the clipped fragment of news-sheet which recorded the end not of one life but of three, though even here two of them cast but one shadow: not only that of the harmless dim-witted woman but of Joel Flint and Signor Canova too, with scattered among them and marking the date of that death too, the cautiously worded advertisements in *Variety* and *Billboard*, using the new changed name and no takers probably, since Signor Canova the Great was already dead then and already serving his purgatory in this circus for six months and that circus for eight—bandsman, ringman, Bornean wild man, down to the last stage where he touched bottom: the travelling from country town to country town with a roulette wheel wired against imitation watches and pistols which would not shoot, until one day instinct perhaps showed him one more chance to use the gift again.

"And lost this time for good," the sheriff said. We were in the study again. Beyond the open side door fireflies winked and drifted across the summer night and the crickets and tree-frogs cheeped and whirred. "It was that insurance policy. If that adjustor hadn't come to town and sent us back out there in time to watch him try to dissolve sugar in raw whiskey, he would have collected that check and taken that truck and got clean away. Instead, he sends for the adjustor, then he practically dares you and me to come out there and see past that wig and paint—"

"You said something the other day about his destroying his witness too soon," Uncle Gavin said. "She wasn't his witness. The witness he destroyed was the one we were supposed to find under that feed room."

"Witness to what?" the sheriff said. "To the fact that Joel Flint no longer existed?"

"Partly. But mostly to the first crime, the old one: the one in which Signor Canova died. He intended for that witness to be found. That's why he didn't bury it, hide it better and deeper. As soon as somebody found it, he would be at once and forever not only rich but free, free not only of Signor Canova who had betrayed him by dying eight years ago, but of Joel Flint too. Even if we had found it before he had a chance to leave, what would he have said?"

"He ought to have battered the face a little more," the sheriff said.

"I doubt it," Uncle Gavin said. "What would he have said?"

"All right," the sheriff said. "What?"

"'Yes, I killed him. He murdered my daughter.' And what would you have said, being, as you are, the Law?"

"Nothing," the sheriff said after a time.

"Nothing," Uncle Gavin said. A dog was barking somewhere, not a big dog, and then a screech-owl flew into the mulberry tree in the back yard and began to cry, plaintive and tremulous, and all the little furred creatures would be moving now—the field mice, the possums and rabbits and foxes and the legless vertebrates—creeping or scurrying about the dark land which beneath the rainless summer stars was just dark: not desolate. "That's one reason he did it," Uncle Gavin said.

"One reason?" the sheriff said. "What's the other?"

"The other is the real one. It had nothing to do with the money; he probably could not have helped obeying it if he had wanted to. That gift he had. His first regret right now is probably not that he was caught, but that he was caught too soon, before the body was found and he had the chance to identify it as his own; before Signor Canova had had time to toss his gleaming tophat vanishing behind him and bow to the amazed and stormlike staccato of adulant palms and turn and stride once or twice and then himself vanish from the pacing spotlight—gone, to be seen no more. Think what he did: he convicted himself of murder when he could very likely have escaped by flight; he acquitted himself of it after he was already free again. Then he dared you and me to come out there and actually be his witnesses and guarantors in the consummation of the very act which he knew we had been trying to prevent. What else could the possession of such a gift as his have engendered, and the successful practising of it have increased, but a supreme contempt for mankind? You told me yourself that he had never been afraid in his life."

"Yes," the sheriff said. "The Book itself says somewhere, *Know thyself*. Ain't there another book somewhere that says, *Man, fear thyself, thine arrogance and vanity and pride?* You ought to know; you claim to be a book man. Didn't you tell me that's what that luck-charm on your watch chain means? What book is that in?"

"It's in all of them," Uncle Gavin said. "The good ones, I mean. It's said in a lot of different ways, but it's there."

CLAYTON RAWSON

(1906–1971)

||||||||||||||||||||||||||||||||||||||||||||| ■ |||||||||||||||||||||||||||||||||||||||||||||

The mystery writer is often described as an entertainer who possesses a bag of tricks. Inside the bag are devices designed to deceive: sleights of hand, least likely suspects, and apparently impossible situations like locked rooms. Any writer can play with these tricks in a workaday manner; any hack can pull the wool over readers' eyes. But Clayton Rawson proved that the mystery writer who has actual experience as a working magician can trick readers even while urging them to keep their eyes wide open. In so doing, Rawson demonstrated that he could work magic on the page as well as on the stage.

Under the stage and pen name The Great Merlini, Rawson earned the admiration of the best magicians, mystery writers, and mystery editors in the business. Born in Elyria, Ohio, he graduated from Ohio State University and then studied at the Chicago Art Institute before beginning his multiple careers as performing magician, inventor of magic tricks, writer on the subject of magic, and editor and author of detective novels and short stories.

An inventor of some fifty original magic tricks, he is known among magicians for perfecting the gimmick that enables the performance of the famous "floating-lady trick" in one's own backyard. Rawson used his experience to turn out practical volumes on magic, including *How to Entertain Children with Magic You Can Do* and *The Golden Book of Magic*. He also wrote a column for *Hugard's Magic Monthly*.

Rawson's best-known magazine work, however, was in the detective field. After serving as both associate editor of *True Detective Magazine* and editor of *Master Detective Magazine* during the 1940s, he became a director of the Unicorn Mystery Book Club and then editor of the Inner Sanctum Mysteries series at Simon and Schuster. In the mid-1940s, his Great Merlini stories began to appear in *Ellery Queen's Mystery Magazine*, where they were first published without solutions so that readers could compete to solve them. Rawson eventually became the managing editor of that magazine.

In four novels and a dozen short stories featuring The Great Merlini, the magician-sleuth uses his expertise to see through the misleading clues that dumbfound the police. Not only are the solutions discovered through the magician's skills, but the clues themselves are laid out with a professional awareness of how to deceive the reader, as "From Another World" ably demonstrates.

1948

From Another World

■

It was undoubtedly one of the world's strangest rooms. The old-fashioned rolltop desk, the battered typewriter, and the steel filing cabinet indicated that it was an office. There was even a calendar memo pad, a pen and pencil set, and an overflowing ashtray on the desk, but any resemblance to any other office stopped right there.

The desk top also held a pair of handcuffs, half a dozen billiard balls, a shiny nickel-plated revolver, one celluloid egg, several decks of playing cards, a bright green silk handkerchief, and a stack of unopened mail. In one corner of the room stood a large, galvanized-iron milk can with a strait jacket lying on its top. A feathered devil mask from the upper Congo leered down from the wall and the entire opposite wall was papered with a Ringling Bros. and Barnum & Bailey twenty-four sheet poster.

A loose-jointed dummy figure of a small boy with popeyes and violently red hair lay on the filing cabinet together with a skull and a fishbowl filled with paper flowers. And in the cabinet's bottom drawer, which was partly open and lined with paper, there was one half-eaten carrot and a twinkly-nosed, live white rabbit.

A pile of magazines, topped by a French journal, *l'Illusioniste*, was stacked precariously on a chair, and a large bookcase tried vainly to hold an even larger flood of books that overflowed and formed dusty stalagmites growing up from the floor—books whose authors would have been startled at the company they kept. Shaw's *Saint Joan* was sandwiched between Rowan's *Story of the Secret Service* and the *Memoirs of Robert Houdin*. Arthur Machen, Dr. Hans Gross, William Blake, Sir James Jeans, Rebecca West, Robert Louis Stevenson, and Ernest Hemingway were bounded on either side by Devol's *Forty Years a Gambler on the Mississippi* and Reginald Scot's *Discoverie of Witchcraft*.

The merchandise in the shop beyond the office had a similar surrealist quality, but the inscription on the glass of the outer door, although equally strange, did manage to supply an explanation. It read: *Miracles For Sale*—THE MAGIC SHOP, A. Merlini, Prop.

And that gentleman, naturally, was just as unusual as his place of business. For one thing, he hadn't put a foot in it, to my knowledge, in at least a week. When he finally did reappear, I found him at the desk sleepily and somewhat glumly eying the unopened mail.

He greeted me as though he hadn't seen another human being in at least a month, and the swivel chair creaked as he settled back in it, put his long legs up on the desk, and yawned. Then he indicated the card bearing his business slogan—NOTHING IS IMPOSSIBLE—which was tacked on the wall.

"I may have to take that sign down," he said lazily. "I've just met a theatrical producer, a scene designer, and a playwright all of whom are quite impossible. They came in here a week before opening night and asked me to supply several small items mentioned in the script. In one scene a character said 'Begone!' and the stage directions read: 'The genie and his six dancing girl slaves vanish instantly.' Later an elephant, complete with howdah and princess, disappeared the same way. I had to figure out how to manage all that and cook up a few assorted miracles for the big scene in heaven, too. Then I spent thirty-six hours in bed. And I'm still half asleep." He grinned wryly and added, "Ross, if you want anything that is not a stock item, you can whistle for it."

"I don't want a miracle," I said. "Just an interview. What do you know about ESP and PK?"

"Too much," he said. "You're doing another magazine article?"

"Yes. And I've spent the last week with a queer assortment of characters, too—half a dozen psychologists, some professional gamblers, a nuclear physicist, the secretary of the Psychical Research Society, and a neurologist. I've got an appointment in half an hour with a millionaire, and after that I want to hear what you think of it."

"You interviewed Dr. Rhine at Duke University, of course?"

I nodded. "Sure. He started it all. He says he's proved conclusively that there really are such things as telepathy, mind reading, clairvoyance, X-ray vision, and probably crystal gazing as well. He wraps it all up in one package and calls it ESP—meaning extrasensory perception."

"That," Merlini said, "is not the half of it. His psychokinesis, or PK for short, is positively miraculous—and frightening." The magician pulled several issues of the *Journal of Parapsychology* from the stack of magazines and upset the whole pile. "If the conclusions Rhine has published here are correct—if there really is a tangible mental force that can not only reach out and influence the movements of dice but exert its mysterious control over other physical objects as well—then he has completely upset the apple cart of modern psychology and punctured a whole library of general scientific theory as well."

"He's already upset me," I said. "I tried to use PK in a crap game Saturday night. I lost sixty-eight bucks."

My skepticism didn't disturb Merlini. He went right on, gloomier than ever. "If Rhine is right, his ESP and PK have reopened the Pandora's box in which science thought it had forever sealed voodoo and witchcraft and enough other practices of primitive magic to make your hair stand on end. And *you're* growling about losing a few dollars—"

Behind me a hearty, familiar voice said, "I haven't got anything to worry about except a homicidal maniac who has killed three people in the last two days and left absolutely no clues. But can I come in?"

Inspector Homer Gavigan of the New York City Police Department stood in the doorway, his blue eyes twinkling frostily.

Merlini, liking the Cassandra role he was playing, said, "Sure. I've been waiting for you. But don't think that PK won't give you a splitting headache, too. All a murderer would have to do to commit the perfect crime—and a locked room one at that—would be to exert his psychokinetic mental force from a distance against the gun trigger." He pointed at the revolver on the desk. "Like this—"

Gavigan and I both saw the trigger, with no finger on it, move.

Bang!

The gun's report was like a thunderclap in the small room. I knew well enough that it was only a stage prop and the cartridge a blank, but I jumped a foot. So did Gavigan.

"Look, dammit!" the inspector exploded, "how did you—"

The Great Merlini grinned. He was fully awake now and enjoying himself hugely. "No," he said, "that wasn't PK, luckily. Just ordinary run-of-the-mill conjuring. The Rising Cards and the Talking Skull are both sometimes operated the same way. You can have the secret at the usual catalogue price of—"

Like most policemen Gavigan had a healthy respect for firearms and he was still jumpy. "I don't want to buy either of them," he growled. "Do we have a date for dinner—or don't we? I'm starved."

"We do," Merlini said, pulling his long, lean self up out of the chair and reaching for his coat. "Can you join us, Ross?"

I shook my head. "Not this time. I've got a date just now with Andrew Drake."

In the elevator Merlini gave me an odd look and asked, "Andrew Drake? What has he got to do with ESP and PK?"

"What doesn't he have something to do with?" I replied. "Six months ago it was the Drake Plan to Outlaw War; he tried to take over the U.N. single-handed. Two months ago he announced he was setting up a $15-million research foundation to find a cancer cure in six months. 'Polish it off like we did the atom bomb,' he says. 'Put in enough money, and you can accomplish anything.' Now he's head over heels in ESP with some Yoga mixed in. 'Unleash the power of the human mind and solve all our problems.' Just like that."

"So that's what he's up to," Merlini said as we came out on to Forty-second Street, a block from Times Square, to face a bitterly cold January wind. "I wondered."

Then, as he followed Gavigan into the official car that waited and left me shivering on the curb, he threw a last cryptic sentence over his shoulder.

"'When Drake mentions Rosa Rhys," he said, "you might warn him that he's heading for trouble."

Merlini didn't know how right he was. If any of us had had any clair-voyant ability at all, I wouldn't have taken a cab up to Drake's; all three of us would have gone—in Gavigan's car and with the siren going full blast.

As it was, I stepped out all alone in front of the big Ninety-eighth Street house just off Riverside Drive. It was a sixty-year-old mansion built in the tortured style that had been the height of architectural fash-ion in the 1880's but was now a smoke-blackened monstrosity as coldly depressing as the weather.

I nearly froze both ears just getting across the pavement and up the steps, where I found a doctor with his finger glued—or frozen per-haps—to the bell push. A doctor? No, it wasn't ESP; a copy of the *AMA Journal* stuck out of his overcoat pocket, and his left hand carried the customary small black case. But he didn't have the medical man's usual clinical detachment. This doctor was jumpy as hell.

When I asked, "Anything wrong?" his head jerked around, and his pale blue eyes gave me a startled look. He was a thin, well-dressed man in his early forties.

"Yes," he said crisply. "I'm afraid so." He jabbed a long forefinger at the bell again just as the door opened.

At first I didn't recognize the girl who looked out at us. When I had seen her by daylight earlier in the week, I had tagged her as in the brainy-but-a-bit-plain category, a judgment I revised somewhat now, considering what the Charles hair-do and Hattie Carnegie dress did for her.

"Oh, hello, doctor," she said. "Come in."

The doctor began talking even before he crossed the threshold. "Your father, Elinor—is he still in the study?"

"Yes, I think so. But what—"

She stopped because he was already gone, running down the hall toward a door at its end. He rattled the doorknob, then rapped loudly.

"Mr. Drake! Let me in!"

The girl looked puzzled, then frightened. Her dark eyes met mine for an instant, and then her high heels clicked on the polished floor as she too ran down the hall. I didn't wait to be invited. I followed.

The doctor's knuckles rapped again on the door. "Miss Rhys!" he called. "It's Dr. Garrett. Unlock the door!"

There was no answer.

Garrett tried the doorknob once more, then threw his shoulder against the door. It didn't move.

"Elinor, do you have a key? We must get in there—quickly!"

She said, "No. Father has the only keys. Why don't they answer? What's wrong?"

"I don't know," Garrett said. "Your father phoned me just now. He was in pain. He said, *'Hurry! I need you. I'm'*"—the doctor hesitated, watching the girl; then he finished *"'—dying.'* After that—no answer." Garrett turned to me. "You've got more weight than I have. Think you can break this door in?"

I looked at it. The door seemed solid enough, but it was an old house and the wood around the screws that held the lock might give. "I don't know," I said. "I'll try."

Elinor Drake moved to one side and the doctor stepped behind me. I threw myself against the door twice and the second time felt it move a bit. Then I hit it hard. Just as the door gave way I heard the tearing sound of paper.

But before I could discover what caused that, my attention was held by more urgent matters. I found myself staring at a green-shaded desk lamp, the room's only source of light, at the overturned phone on the desk top, and at the sprawled shape that lay on the floor in front of the desk. A coppery highlight glinted on a letter opener near the man's feet. Its blade was discolored with a dark wet stain.

Dr. Garrett said, "Elinor, you stay out," as he moved past me to the body and bent over it. One of his hands lifted Andrew Drake's right eyelid, the other felt his wrist.

I have never heard a ghost speak but the sound that came then was exactly what I would expect—a low, quivering moan shot with pain. I jerked around and saw a glimmer of white move in the darkness on my left.

Behind me, Elinor's whisper, a tense thread of sound, said, "Lights," as she clicked the switch by the door. The glow from the ceiling fixture overhead banished both the darkness and the specter—but what remained was almost as unlikely. A chair lay overturned on the carpet, next to a small table that stood in the center of the room. In a second chair, slumped forward with her head resting on the tabletop, was the body of a woman.

She was young, dark-haired, rather good-looking, and had an excellent figure. This latter fact was instantly apparent because—and I had to look twice before I could believe what I saw—she wore a brief, skin-tight, one-piece bathing suit. Nothing else.

Elinor's eyes were still on the sprawled shape on the floor. "Father. He's—dead?"

Garrett nodded slowly and stood up.

I heard the quick intake of her breath but she made no other sound. Then Garrett strode quickly across to the woman at the table.

"Unconscious," he said after a moment. "Apparently a blow on the head—but she's beginning to come out of it." He looked again at the knife on the floor. "We'll have to call the police."

I hardly heard him. I was wondering why the room was so bare. The hall outside and the living room that opened off it were furnished with the stiff, formal ostentation of the overly rich. But Drake's study, by contrast, was as sparsely furnished as a cell in a Trappist monastery. Except for the desk, the small table, the two chairs, and a three-leaf folding screen that stood in one corner, it contained no other furniture. There were no pictures on the walls, no papers, and although there were shelves for them, no books. There wasn't even a blotter or pen on the desk top. Nothing but the phone, desk lamp and, strangely enough, a roll of gummed paper tape.

But I only glanced at these things briefly. It was the large casement window in the wall behind the desk that held my attention—a dark rectangle beyond which, like a scattered handful of bright jewels, were the lights of New Jersey and, above them, frosty pinpoints of stars shining coldly in a black sky.

The odd thing was that the window's center line, where its two halves joined, was criss-crossed by two-foot strips of brown paper tape pasted to the glass. The window was, quite literally, sealed shut. It was then that I remembered the sound of tearing paper as the lock had given way and the door had come open.

I turned. Elinor still stood there—motionless. And on the inside of the door and on the jamb were more of the paper strips. Four were torn in half, two others had been pulled loose from the wall and hung curled from the door's edge.

At that moment a brisk, energetic voice came from the hall. "How come you leave the front door standing wide open on the coldest day in—"

Elinor turned to face a broad-shouldered young man with wavy hair, hand-painted tie, and a completely self-assured manner. She said, "Paul!" then took one stumbling step and was in his arms.

He blinked at her. "Hey! What's wrong?" Then he saw what lay on the floor by the desk. His self-confidence sagged.

Dr. Garrett moved to the door. "Kendrick," he said, "take Elinor out of here. I'll—"

"No!" It was Elinor's voice. She straightened up, turned suddenly and started into the room.

But Paul caught her. "Where are you going?"

She tried to pull away from him. "I'm going to phone the police." Her eyes followed the trail of bloodstains that led from the body across the beige carpet to the overturned chair and the woman at the table. "She—killed him."

That was when I started for the phone myself. But I hadn't taken more than two steps when the woman in the bathing suit let out a hair-raising shriek.

She was gripping the table with both hands, her eyes fixed on Drake's body with the rigid unblinking stare of a figure carved from stone. Then, suddenly, her body trembled all over, and she opened her mouth again—but Garrett got there first.

He slapped her on the side of the face—hard.

It stopped the scream, but the horror still filled her round dark eyes and she still stared at the body as though it were some demon straight from hell.

"Hysteria," Garrett said. Then seeing me start again toward the phone, "Get an ambulance, too." And when he spoke to Paul Kendrick this time, it was an order. "And get Elinor out of here—quickly!"

Elinor Drake was looking at the girl in the bathing suit with wide, puzzled eyes. "She—she killed him. Why?"

Paul nodded. He turned Elinor around gently but swiftly and led her out.

The cops usually find too many fingerprints on a phone, none of them any good because they are superimposed on each other. But I handled the receiver carefully just the same, picking it up by one end. When headquarters answered, I gave the operator the facts fast, then asked him to locate Inspector Gavigan and have him call me back. I gave Drake's number.

As I talked I watched Dr. Garrett open his black case and take out a hypodermic syringe. He started to apply it to the woman's arm just as I hung up.

"What's that, doc?" I asked.

"Sedative. Otherwise she'll be screaming again in a minute."

The girl didn't seem to feel the needle as it went in.

Then, noticing two bright spots of color on the table, I went across to examine them closely and felt more than ever as though I had stepped straight into a surrealist painting. I was looking at two rounded conical shapes each about two inches in length. Both were striped like candy canes, one in maroon against a white background, the other in thinner brilliant red stripes against an opalescent amber.

"Did Drake," I asked, "collect seashells, too?"

"No." Garrett scowled in a worried way at the shells. "But I once did. These are mollusks, but not from the sea. *Cochlostyla*, a tree snail. Habitat: the Philippines." He turned his scowl from the shells to me. "By the way, just who are you?"

"The name is Ross Harte." I added that I had had an appointment to interview Drake for a magazine article and then asked, "Why is this room sealed as it is? Why is this girl dressed only in—"

Apparently, like many medical men, Garrett took a dim view of reporters. "I'll make my statement," he said a bit stiffly, "to the police."

They arrived a moment later. Two uniformed prowl-car cops first, then the precinct boys and after that, at intervals, the homicide squad, an ambulance intern, a fingerprint man and photographer, the medical examiner, an assistant D.A. and later, because a millionaire rates more attention than the victim of a Harlem stabbing, the D.A. himself, and an assistant chief inspector even looked in for a few minutes.

Of the earlier arrivals the only familiar face was that of the homicide squad's Lieutenant Doran—a hard-boiled, coldly efficient, no-nonsense cop who had so little use for reporters that I suspected he had once been bitten by one.

At Dr. Garrett's suggestion, which the intern seconded, the girl in the bathing suit was taken, under guard, to the nearest hospital. Then Garrett and I were put on ice, also under guard, in the living room. Another detective ushered Paul Kendrick into the room a moment later.

He scowled at Dr. Garrett. "We all thought Rosa Rhys was bad medicine. But I never expected anything like this. Why would *she* want to kill him? It doesn't make sense."

"Self-defense?" I suggested. "Could he have made a pass at her and—"

Kendrick shook his head emphatically. "Not that gal. She was making a fast play for the old man—and his money. A pass would have been just what she wanted." He turned to Garrett. "What were they doing in there—more ESP experiments?"

The doctor laid his overcoat neatly over the back of an ornate Spanish chair. His voice sounded tired and defeated. "No. They had gone beyond that. I told him that she was a fraud, but you know how Drake was—always so absolutely confident that he couldn't be wrong about anything. He said he'd put her through a test that would convince all of us."

"Of what?" I asked. "What was it she claimed she could do?"

The detective at the door moved forward. "My orders," he said, "are that you're not to talk about what happened until after the lieutenant has taken your statements. Make it easy for me, will you?"

That made it difficult for us. Any other conversational subject just then seemed pointless. We sat there silent and uncomfortable. But somehow the nervous tension that had been in our voices was still there—a foreboding, ghostly presence waiting with us for what was to happen next.

A half hour later, although it seemed many times that long, Garrett was taken out for questioning, then Kendrick. And later I got the nod. I saw Elinor Drake, a small, lonely figure in the big hall, moving slowly up the wide stairs. Doran and the police stenographer who waited for me in the stately dining room with its heavy crystal chandelier looked out of place. But the lieutenant didn't feel ill at ease; his questions were as coldly efficient as a surgeon's knife.

I tried to insert a query of my own now and then, but soon gave that up. Doran ignored all such attempts as completely as if they didn't exist. Then, just as he dismissed me, the phone rang. Doran answered, listened, scowled and then held the receiver out to me. "For you," he said.

I heard Merlini's voice. "My ESP isn't working so well today, Ross. Drake is dead. I get that much. But just what happened up there, anyway?"

"ESP my eye," I told him. "If you were a mind reader you'd have been up here long ago. It's a sealed room—in spades. The sealed room to end all sealed rooms."

I saw Doran start forward as if to object. "Merlini," I said quickly, "is Inspector Gavigan still with you?" I lifted the receiver from my ear and let Doran hear the "Yes" that came back.

Merlini's voice went on. "Did you say sealed room? The flash from headquarters didn't mention that. They said an arrest had already been made. It sounded like a routine case."

"Headquarters," I replied, "has no imagination. Or else Doran has been keeping things from them. It isn't even a routine sealed room. Listen. A woman comes to Drake's house on the coldest January day since 1812 dressed only in a bathing suit. She goes with him into his study. They seal the window and door on the inside with gummed paper tape. Then she stabs him with a paper knife. Before he dies, he knocks her out, then manages to get to the phone and send out an SOS.

"She's obviously crazy; she has to be to commit murder under those circumstances. But Drake wasn't crazy. A bit eccentric maybe, but not nuts. So why would he lock himself in so carefully with a homicidal maniac? If headquarters thinks that's routine I'll—" Then I interrupted myself. There was too much silence on the other end of the wire. "Merlini! Are you still there?"

"Yes," his voice said slowly, "I'm still here. Headquarters was much too brief. They didn't tell us her name. But I know it now."

Then, abruptly, I felt as if I had stepped off into some fourth-dimensional hole in space and had dropped on to some other nightmare planet.

Merlini's voice, completely serious, was saying, "Ross, did the police find a silver denarius from the time of the Caesars in that room? Or a freshly picked rose, a string of Buddhist prayer beads, perhaps a bit of damp seaweed?"

I didn't say anything. I couldn't.

After a moment, Merlini added, "So—they did. What was it?"

"Shells," I said dazedly, still quite unconvinced that any conversation could sound like this. "Philippine tree snail shells. Why, in the name of—"

Merlini cut in hastily. "Tell Doran that Gavigan and I will be there in ten minutes. Sit tight and keep your eyes open."

"Merlini!" I objected frantically; "if you hang up without—"

"The shells explain the bathing suit, Ross, and make it clear why the room was sealed. But they also introduce an element that Gavigan and Doran and the D.A. and the commissioner are not going to like at all. I don't like it myself. It's even more frightening as a murder method than PK."

He hesitated a moment, then let me have both barrels.

"Those shells suggest that Drake's death might have been caused by even stranger forces—evil and evanescent ones—from another world!"

My acquaintance with a police inspector cut no ice with Doran; he ordered me right back into the living room.

I heard a siren announce the arrival of Gavigan's car shortly after, but it was a long hour later before Doran came in and said, "The inspector wants to see all of you—in the study."

As I moved with the others out into the hall I saw Merlini waiting for me.

"It's about time," I growled at him. "Another ten minutes and you'd have found me DOA, too—from suspense."

"Sorry you had to cool your heels," he said, "but Gavigan is being difficult. As predicted, he doesn't like the earful Doran has been giving him. Neither do I." The dryly ironic good humor that was almost always in his voice was absent. He was unusually sober.

"Don't build it up," I said. "I've had all the mystery I can stand. Just give me answers. First, why did you tell me to warn Drake about Rosa Rhys?"

"I didn't expect murder, if that's what you're thinking," he replied. "Drake was elaborating on some of Rhine's original experiments aimed at discovering whether ESP operates more efficiently when the subject is in a trance state. Rosa is a medium."

"Oh, so that's it. She and Drake were holding a séance?"

Merlini nodded. "Yes. The Psychical Research Society is extremely interested in ESP and PK. It's given them a new lease on life. And I knew they had recommended Rosa, whom they had previously investigated, to Drake."

"And what about the Roman coins, roses, Buddhist prayer beads— and snail shells? Why the bathing suit and how does that explain why the room was sealed?"

But Doran, holding the study door open, interrupted before he could reply.

"Hurry it up!" he ordered.

Going into that room now was like walking on to a brightly lighted stage. A powerful electric bulb of almost floodlight brilliance had been inserted in the ceiling fixture and its harsh white glare made the room more barren and cell-like than ever. Even Inspector Gavigan seemed to have taken on a menacing air. Perhaps it was the black mask of shadow that his hat brim threw down across the upper part of his face; or it may have been the carefully intent way he watched us as we came in.

Doran did the introductions. "Miss Drake, Miss Potter, Paul Kendrick, Dr. Walter Garrett."

I looked at the middle-aged woman whose gayly frilled, altogether feminine hat contrasted oddly with her angular figure, her prim determined mouth, and the chilly glance of complete disapproval with which she regarded Gavigan.

"How," I whispered to Merlini, "did Isabelle Potter, the secretary of the Psychical Research Society, get here?"

"She came with Rosa," he answered. "The police found her upstairs reading a copy of Tyrrell's *Study of Apparitions*." Merlini smiled faintly. "She and Doran don't get along."

"They wouldn't," I said. "They talk different languages. When I interviewed her, I got a travelogue on the other world—complete with lantern slides."

Inspector Gavigan wasted no time. "Miss Drake," he began, "I understand the medical foundation for cancer research your father thought of endowing was originally your idea."

The girl glanced once at the stains on the carpet, then kept her dark eyes steadily on Gavigan. "Yes," she said slowly, "it was."

"Are you interested in psychical research?"

Elinor frowned. "No."

"Did you object when your father began holding séances with Miss Rhys?"

She shook her head. "That would only have made him more determined."

Gavigan turned to Kendrick. "Did you?"

"Me?" Paul lifted his brows. "I didn't know him well enough for that. Don't think he liked me much, anyway. But why a man like Drake would waste his time—"

"And you, doctor?"

"Did I object?" Garrett seemed surprised. "Naturally. No one but a neurotic middle-aged woman would take a séance seriously."

Miss Potter resented that one. "Dr. Garrett," she said icily, "Sir Oliver Lodge was not a neurotic woman, nor Sir William Crookes, nor Professor Zoëllner, nor—"

"But they were all senile," Garrett replied just as icily. "And as for ESP, no neurologist of any standing admits any such possibility. They leave such things to you and your society, Miss Potter—and to the Sunday supplements."

She gave the doctor a look that would have split an atom, and Gavigan, seeing the danger of a chain reaction if this sort of dialogue were allowed to continue, broke in quickly.

"Miss Potter. You introduced Miss Rhys to Mr. Drake and he was conducting ESP experiments with her. Is that correct?"

Miss Potter's voice was still dangerously radioactive. "It is. And their results were most gratifying and important. Of course, neither you nor Dr. Garrett would understand—"

"And then," Garrett cut in, "they both led him on into an investigation of Miss Rhys's psychic specialty—apports." He pronounced the last word with extreme distaste.

Inspector Gavigan scowled, glanced at Merlini, and the latter promptly produced a definition. "An apport," he said, "from the French *apporter*, to bring, is any physical object supernormally brought into a séance room—from nowhere usually or from some impossible distance. Miss Rhys on previous occasions, according to the Psychical Society's *Journal*, has apported such objects as Roman coins, roses, beads, and seaweed."

"She is the greatest apport medium," Miss Potter declared somewhat belligerently, "since Charles Bailey."

"Then she's good," Merlini said. "Bailey was an apport medium whom Conan Doyle considered bona fide. He produced birds, Oriental plants, small animals, and on one occasion a young shark eighteen inches long which he claimed his spirit guide had whisked instantly via the astral plane from the Indian Ocean and projected, still damp and very much alive, into the séance room."

"So," I said, "that's why this room was sealed. To make absolutely certain that no one could open the door or window in the dark and help Rosa by introducing—"

"Of course," Garrett added. "Obviously there could be no apports if adequate precautions were taken. Drake also moved a lot of his things out of the study and inventoried every object that remained. He also suggested, since I was so skeptical, that I be the one to make certain that Miss Rhys carried nothing into the room on her person. I gave her a most complete physical examination—in a bedroom upstairs. Then she put on one of Miss Drake's bathing suits."

"Did you come down to the study with her and Drake?" Gavigan asked.

The doctor frowned. "No. I had objected to Miss Potter's presence at the séance and Miss Rhys countered by objecting to mine."

"She was quite right," Miss Potter said. "The presence of an unbeliever like yourself would prevent even the strongest psychic forces from making themselves manifest."

"I have no doubt of that," Garrett replied stiffly. "It's the usual excuse, as I told Drake. He tried to get her to let me attend but she refused flatly. So I went back to my office down the street. Drake's phone call came a half hour or so later."

"And yet"—Gavigan eyed the two brightly colored shells on the table—"in spite of all your precautions she produced two of these."

Garrett nodded. "Yes, I know. But the answer is fairly obvious now. She hid them somewhere in the hall outside on her arrival and then secretly picked them up again on her way in here."

Elinor frowned. "I'm afraid not, doctor. Father thought of that and asked me to go down with them to the study. He held one of her hands and I held the other."

Gavigan scowled. Miss Potter beamed.

"Did you go in with them?" Merlini asked.

She shook her head. "No. Only as far as the door. They went in and I heard it lock behind them. I stood there for a moment or two and heard Father begin pasting the tape on the door. Then I went back to my room to dress. I was expecting Paul."

Inspector Gavigan turned to Miss Potter. "You remained upstairs?"

"Yes," she replied in a tone that dared him to deny it. "I did."

Gavigan looked at Elinor. "Paul said a moment ago that your father didn't like him. Why not?"

"Paul exaggerates," the girl said quickly. "Father didn't dislike him. He was just—well, a bit difficult where my men friends were concerned."

"He thought they were all after his money," Kendrick added. "But at the rate he was endowing medical foundations and psychic societies—"

Miss Potter objected. "Mr. Drake did *not* endow the Psychical Society."

"But he was seriously considering it," Garrett said. "Miss Rhys—and Miss Potter—were selling him on the theory that illness is only a mental state due to a psychic imbalance, whatever that is."

"They won't sell me on that," Elinor said, and then turned suddenly on Miss Potter, her voice trembling. "If it weren't for you and your idiotic foolishness Father wouldn't have been—killed." Then to Gavigan, "We've told all this before, to the lieutenant. Is it quite necessary—"

The inspector glanced at Merlini, then said, "I think that will be all for now. Okay, Doran, take them back. But none of them are to leave yet."

When they had gone, he turned to Merlini. "Well, I asked the questions you wanted me to, but I still think it was a waste of time. Rosa Rhys killed Drake. Anything else is impossible."

"What about Kendrick's cabdriver?" Merlini asked. "Have your men located him yet?"

Gavigan's scowl, practically standard operating procedure by now, grew darker. "Yes. Kendrick's definitely out. He entered the cab on the other side of town at just about the time Drake was sealing this room and he was apparently still in it, crossing Central Park, at the time Drake was killed."

"So," I commented, "he's the only one with an alibi."

Gavigan lifted his eyebrows. "The only one? Except for Rosa Rhys they *all* have alibis. The sealed room takes care of that."

"Yes," Merlini said quietly, "but the people with alibis also have motives while the one person who could have killed Drake has none."

"She did it," the inspector answered. "So she's got a motive, and we'll find it."

"I wish I were as confident of that as you are," Merlini said. "Under the circumstances you'll be able to get a conviction without showing motive, but if you don't find one, it will always bother you."

"Maybe," Gavigan admitted, "but that won't be as bad as trying to believe what she says happened in this room."

That was news to me. "You've talked to Rosa?" I asked.

"One of the boys did," Gavigan said sourly. "At the hospital. She's already preparing an insanity defense."

"But why," Merlini asked, "is she still hysterical with fright? Could it be that she's scared because she really believes her story—because something like that really did happen in here?"

"Look," I said impatiently, "is it top secret or will somebody tell me what she says happened?"

Gavigan glowered at Merlini. "Are you going to stand there and tell me that you think Rosa Rhys actually believes—"

It was my question that Merlini answered. He walked to the table in the center of the room. "She says that after Drake sealed the window and door, the lights were turned off and she and Drake sat opposite each other at this table. His back was toward the desk, hers toward that screen in the corner. Drake held her hands. They waited. Finally she felt the psychic forces gathering around her—and then, out of nowhere, the two shells dropped onto the table one after the other. Drake got up, turned on the desk light, and came back to the table. A moment later it happened."

The magician paused for a moment, regarding the bare, empty room with a frown. "Drake," he continued, "was examining the shells, quite excited and pleased about their appearance when suddenly, Rosa says, she heard a movement behind her. She saw Drake look up and then stare incredulously over her shoulder." Merlini spread his hands. "And that's all she remembers. Something hit her. When she came to, she found herself staring at the blood on the floor and at Drake's body."

Gavigan was apparently remembering Merlini's demonstration with the gun in his office. "If you," he warned acidly, "so much as try to hint that one of the people outside this room projected some mental force that knocked Rosa out and then caused the knife to stab Drake—"

"You know," Merlini said, "I half expected Miss Potter would suggest that. But her theory is even more disturbing." He looked at me. "She says that the benign spirits which Rosa usually evoked were overcome by some malign and evil entity whose astral substance materialized momentarily, killed Drake, then returned to the other world from which it came."

"She's a mental case, too," Gavigan said disgustedly. "They have to be crazy if they expect anyone to believe any such—"

"That," Merlini said quietly, "may be another reason Rosa is scared to death. Perhaps she believes it but knows you won't. In her shoes, I'd be scared, too." He frowned. "The difficulty is the knife."

Gavigan blinked. "The knife? What's difficult about that?"

"If I killed Drake," Merlini replied, "and wanted appearances to suggest that psychic forces were responsible, you wouldn't have found a weapon in this room that made it look as if I were guilty. I would have done a little de-apporting and made it disappear. As it is now, even if the knife was propelled supernaturally, Rosa takes the rap."

"And how," Gavigan demanded, "would you make the knife disappear if you were dressed, as she was, in practically nothing?" Then, with sudden suspicion, he added, "Are you suggesting that there's a way she could have done that—and that you think she's not guilty because she didn't?"

Merlini lifted one of the shells from the table and placed it in the center of his left palm. His right hand covered it for a brief moment, then moved away. The shell was no longer there; it had vanished as silently and as easily as a ghost. Merlini turned both hands palms outward; both were unmistakably empty.

"Yes," he said, "she could have made the knife disappear, if she had wanted to. The same way she produced the two shells." He made a reaching gesture with his right hand and the missing shell reappeared suddenly at his fingertips.

Gavigan looked annoyed and relieved at the same time. "So," he said, "you do know how she got those shells in here. I want to hear it. Right now."

But Gavigan had to wait.

At that moment a torpedo hit the water-tight circumstantial case against Rosa Rhys and detonated with a roar.

Doran, who had answered the phone a moment before, was swearing profusely. He was staring at the receiver he held as though it were a live cobra he had picked up by mistake.

"It—it's Doc Hess," he said in a dazed tone. "He just started the autopsy and thought we'd like to know that the point of the murder knife struck a rib and broke off. He just dug out a triangular pointed piece of—steel."

For several seconds after that there wasn't a sound. Then Merlini spoke.

"Gentlemen of the jury. Exhibit A, the paper knife with which my esteemed opponent, the district attorney, claims Rosa Rhys stabbed Andrew Drake, is a copper alloy—and its point, as you can see, is quite intact. The defense rests."

Doran swore again. "Drake's inventory lists that letter opener but that's all. There is no other knife in this room. I'm positive of that."

Gavigan jabbed a thick forefinger at me. "Ross, Dr. Garrett was in here before the police arrived. And Miss Drake and Kendrick."

I shook my head. "Sorry. There was no knife near the door and neither Elinor nor Paul came more than a foot into the room. Dr. Garrett examined Drake and Rosa, but I was watching him, and I'll testify that unless he's as expert at sleight of hand as Merlini, he didn't pick up a thing."

Doran was not convinced. "Look, buddy. Unless Doc Hess has gone crazy too, there was a knife and it's not here now. So somebody took it out." He turned to the detective who stood at the door. "Tom," he said, "have the boys frisk all those people. Get a policewoman for Miss Drake and Potter and search the bedroom where they've been waiting. The living room, too."

Then I had a brainstorm. "You know," I said, "if Elinor is covering up for someone—if three people came in here for the séance instead of two as she says—the third could have killed Drake and then gone out, with the knife. And the paper tape could have been—" I stopped.

"—pasted on the door *after* the murderer left?" Merlini finished. "By Rosa? That would mean she framed herself."

"Besides," Gavigan growled, "the boys fumed all those paper strips. There are fingerprints all over them. All Drake's."

Merlini said, "Doran, I suggest that you phone the hospital and have Rosa searched, too."

The lieutenant blinked. "But she was practically naked. How in blazes could she carry a knife out of here unnoticed?"

Gavigan faced Merlini, scowling. "What did you mean when you said a moment ago that she could have got rid of the knife the same way she produced those shells?"

"If it was a clasp knife," Merlini explained, "she could have used the same method other apport mediums have employed to conceal small objects under test conditions."

"But dammit!" Doran exploded. "The only place Garrett didn't look was in her stomach!"

Merlini grinned. "I know. That was his error. Rosa is a regurgitating medium, like Helen Duncan, in whose stomach the English investigator, Harry Price, found a hidden ghost—a balled-up length of cheese-cloth fastened with a safety pin which showed up when he X-rayed her. X-rays of Rosa seem indicated, too. And search her hospital room and the ambulance that took her over."

"Okay, Doran," Gavigan ordered. "Do it."

I saw an objection. "Now *you've* got Rosa framing herself, too," I said. "If she swallowed the murder knife, why should she put blood on the letter opener? That makes no sense at all."

"None of this does," Gavigan complained.

"I know," Merlini answered. "One knife was bad. Two are much worse. And although X-rays of Rosa before the séance would have shown shells, I predict they won't show a knife. If they do, then Rosa needs a psychiatric examination as well."

"Don't worry," Gavigan said gloomily. "She'll get one. Her attorney will see to that. And they'll prove she's crazier than a bedbug without half trying. But if that knife isn't in her—" His voice died.

"Then you'll never convict her," Merlini finished.

"If that happens," the inspector said ominously, "you're going to have to explain where that knife came from, how it really disappeared, and where it is now."

Merlini's view was even gloomier. "It'll be much worse than that. We'll also have an appearing and vanishing murderer to explain: some-one who entered a sealed room, killed Drake, put blood on the paper knife to incriminate Rosa, then vanished just as neatly as any of Miss Potter's ghosts—into thin air."

And Merlini's prediction came true.

The X-ray plates didn't show the slightest trace of a knife. And it wasn't in Rosa's hospital room or in the ambulance. Nor on Garrett, Paul, Elinor Drake, Isabelle Potter, nor, as Doran discovered, on myself. The Drake house was a mess by the time the boys got through taking it apart—but no knife with a broken point was found anywhere. And it was shown beyond doubt that there were no trapdoors or sliding panels in the study; the door and window were the only exits.

Inspector Gavigan glowered every time the phone rang. The com-missioner had already phoned twice and without mincing words ex-pressed his dissatisfaction with the way things were going.

And Merlini, stretched out in Drake's chair, his heels up on the desk top, his eyes closed, seemed to have gone into a trance.

"Blast it!" Gavigan said. "Rosa Rhys got that knife out of here some-how. She had to! Merlini, are you going to admit that she knows a trick or two you don't?"

The magician didn't answer for a moment. Then he opened one eye. "No," he said slowly, "not just yet." He took his feet off the desk and sat up straight. "You know," he said, "if we don't accept the theory of the murderer from beyond, then Ross must be right after all. Elinor Drake's statement to the contrary, there must have been a third person in this room when that séance began."

"Okay," Gavigan said, "we'll forget Miss Drake's testimony for the moment. At least that gets him into the room. Then what?"

"I don't know," Merlini said. He took the roll of gummed paper tape from the desk, tore off a two-foot length, crossed the room and pasted it across the door and jamb, sealing us in. "Suppose I'm the killer," he said. "I knock Rosa out first, then stab Drake—"

He paused.

Gavigan was not enthusiastic. "You put the murder knife in your pocket, not noticing that the point is broken. You put blood on the paper knife to incriminate Rosa. And then—" He waited. "Well, go on."

"Then," Merlini said, "I get out of here." He scowled at the sealed door and at the window. "I've escaped from handcuffs, strait jackets, milk cans filled with water, packing cases that have been nailed shut. I know the methods Houdini used to break out of safes and jail cells. But I feel like he did when a shrewd old turnkey shut him in a cell in Scotland one time and the lock—a type he'd overcome many times before—failed to budge. No matter how he tried or what he did, the bolt wouldn't move. He was sweating blood because he knew that if he failed, his laboriously built-up reputation as the escape king would be blown to bits. And then—" Merlini blinked. "And then—" This time he came to a full stop, staring at the door.

Suddenly he blinked. "Shades of Hermann, Kellar, Thurston—and Houdini! So that's it!"

Grinning broadly, he turned to Gavigan. "We will now pass a miracle and chase all the ghosts back into their tombs. If you'll get those people in here—"

"You know how the vanishing man vanished?" I asked.

"Yes. It's someone who has been just as canny as that Scotch jailer, and I know who."

Gavigan said, "It's about time." Then he walked across the room and pulled the door open, tearing the paper strip in half as he did so.

Merlini, watching him, grinned again. "The method by which magicians let their audiences fool themselves—the simplest and yet most effective principle of deception in the whole book—and it nearly took me in!"

Elinor Drake's eyes still avoided the stains on the floor. Paul, beside her, puffed nervously on a cigarette, and Dr. Garrett looked drawn and tired. But not the irrepressible Potter. She seemed fresh as a daisy.

"This room," she said to no one in particular, "will become more famous in psychic annals than the home of the Fox sisters at Lilydale."

Quickly, before she could elaborate on that, Merlini cut in. "Miss Potter doesn't believe that Rosa Rhys killed Drake. Neither do I. But the psychic force she says is responsible didn't emanate from another world. It was conjured up out of nothing by someone who was—who had to be—here in this room when Drake died. Someone whom Drake himself asked to be here."

He moved into the center of the room as he spoke and faced them.

"Drake would never have convinced anyone that Rosa could do what she claimed without a witness. So he gave someone a key—someone who came into this room *before* Drake and Rosa and Elinor came downstairs."

The four people watched him without moving—almost, I thought, without breathing.

"That person hid behind that screen and then, after Rosa produced the apports, knocked her out, killed Drake, and left Rosa to face the music."

"All we have to do," Merlini went on, "is show who it was that Drake selected as a witness." He pointed a lean forefinger at Isabelle Potter. "If Drake discovered how Rosa produced the shells and realized she was a fraud, you might have killed him to prevent an exposure and save face for yourself and the society; and you might have then framed Rosa in revenge for having deceived you. But Drake would never have chosen you. Your testimony wouldn't have convinced any of the others. No. Drake would have picked one of the skeptics—someone he was certain could never be accused of assisting the medium."

He faced Elinor. "You said that you accompanied Rosa and your father to the study door and saw them go in alone. We haven't asked Miss Rhys yet, but I think she'll confirm it. You couldn't expect to lie about that and make it stick as long as Rosa could and would contradict you."

I saw Doran move forward silently, closing in.

"And Paul Kendrick," Merlini went on, "is the only one of you who has an alibi that does not depend on the sealed room. That leaves the most skeptical one of the three—the man whose testimony would by far carry the greatest weight.

"It leaves you, Dr. Garrett. The man who is so certain that there are no ghosts is the man who conjured one up!"

Merlini played the scene down; he knew that the content of what he said was dramatic enough. But Garrett's voice was even calmer. He shook his head slowly.

"I am afraid that I can't agree. You have no reason to assume that it must be one of us and no one else. But I would like to hear how you think I or anyone else could have walked out of this room leaving it sealed as it was found."

"That," Merlini said, "is the simplest answer of all. You walked out, but you didn't leave the room sealed. You see, *it was not found that way!*"

I felt as if I were suddenly floating in space.

"But look—" I began.

Merlini ignored me. "The vanishing murderer was a trick. But magic is not, as most people believe, only a matter of gimmicks and trapdoors and mirrors. Its real secret lies deeper than a mere deception of the senses; the magician uses a far more important, more basic weapon— the psychological deception of the mind. *Don't believe everything you see* is excellent advice; but there's a better rule: don't believe everything you *think*."

"Are you trying to tell me," I said incredulously, "that this room wasn't sealed at all? That I just thought it was?"

Merlini kept watching Garrett. "Yes. It's as simple as that. And there was no visual deception at all. It was, like PK, entirely mental. You saw things exactly as they were, but you didn't realize that the visual appearance could be interpreted two ways. Let me ask you a question. When you break into a room the door of which has been sealed with paper tape on the inside, do you find yourself still in a sealed room?"

"No," I said, "of course not. The paper has been torn."

"And if you break into a room that had been sealed but from which someone has *already gone out*, tearing the seals—what then?"

"The paper," I said, "is still torn. The appearance is—"

"—*exactly the same!*" Merlini finished.

He let that soak in a moment, then continued. "When you saw the taped window, and then the torn paper on the door, you made a false assumption—you jumped naturally, but much too quickly, to a wrong conclusion. We all did. We assumed that it was you who had torn the paper when you broke in. Actually, it was Dr. Garrett who tore the paper—when he went out!"

Garrett's voice was a shade less steady now. "You forget that Andrew Drake phoned me—"

Merlini shook his head. "I'm afraid we only have your own statement for that. You overturned the phone and placed Drake's body near it. Then you walked out, returned to your office where you got rid of the knife—probably a surgical instrument which you couldn't leave behind because it might have been traced to you."

Doran, hearing this, whispered a rapid order to the detective stationed at the door.

"Then," Merlini continued, "you came back immediately to ring the front-door bell. You said Drake had called you, partly because it was good misdirection; it made it appear that you were elsewhere when he died. But equally important, it gave you the excuse you needed to break in and find the body without delay—*before Rosa Rhys should regain consciousness and see that the room was no longer sealed!*"

I hated to do it. Merlini was so pleased with the neat way he was tying up all the loose ends. But I had to.

"Merlini," I said. "I'm afraid there is one little thing you don't know. When I smashed the door open, I heard the paper tape tear!"

I have seldom seen the Great Merlini surprised, but that did it. He couldn't have looked more astonished if lightning had struck him.

"You—you *what?*"

Elinor Drake said, "I heard it, too."

Garrett added, "And I."

It stopped Merlini cold for a moment, but only a moment.

"Then that's more misdirection. It has to be." He hesitated, then suddenly looked at Doran. "Lieutenant, get the doctor's overcoat, will you?"

Garrett spoke to the inspector. "This is nonsense. What possible reason could I have for—"

"Your motive was a curious one, doctor," Merlini said. "One that few murderers—"

Merlini stopped as he took the overcoat Doran brought in and removed from its pocket the copy of the *AMA Journal* I had noticed there earlier. He started to open it, then lifted an eyebrow at something he saw on the contents listing.

"I see," he said, and then read: *"A Survey of the Uses of Radioactive Traces in Cancer Research* by Walter M. Garrett, M.D. So that's your special interest?" The magician turned to Elinor Drake. "Who was to head the $15-million foundation for cancer research, Miss Drake?"

The girl didn't need to reply. The answer was in her eyes as she stared at Garrett.

Merlini went on. "You were hidden behind the screen in the corner, doctor. And Rosa Rhys, in spite of all the precautions, successfully produced the apports. You saw the effect that had on Drake, knew Rosa had won, and that Drake was thoroughly hooked. And the thought of seeing all that money wasted on psychical research when it could be put to so much better use in really important medical research made you boil. Any medical man would hate to see that happen, and most of the rest of us, too.

"But we don't all have the coldly rational, scientific attitude you do, and we wouldn't all have realized so quickly that there was one very simple but drastic way to prevent it—murder. You are much too rational. You believe that one man's life is less important than the good his death might bring, and you believed that sufficiently to act upon it. The knife was there, all too handy, in your little black case. And so—Drake died. Am I right, doctor?"

Doran didn't like this as a motive. "He's still a killer," he objected. "And he tried to frame Rosa, didn't he?"

Merlini said, "Do you want to answer that, doctor?"

Garrett hesitated, then glanced at the magazine Merlini still held. His voice was tired. "You are also much too rational." He turned to Doran. "Rosa Rhys was a cheap fraud who capitalized on superstition. The world would be a much better place without such people."

"And what about your getting that job as the head of the medical foundation?" Doran was still unconvinced. "I don't suppose that had anything to do with your reasons for killing Drake?"

The doctor made no answer. And I couldn't tell if it was because Doran was right or because he knew that Doran would not believe him.

He turned to Merlini instead. "The fact still remains that the cancer foundation has been made possible. The only difference is that now two men rather than one pay with their lives."

"A completely rational attitude," Merlini said, "does have its advantages if it allows you to contemplate your own death with so little emotion."

Gavigan wasn't as cynical about Garrett's motives as Doran, but his police training objected. "He took the law into his own hands. If everyone did that, we'd all have to go armed for self-protection. Merlini, why did Ross think he heard paper tearing when he opened that door?"

"He did hear it," Merlini said. Then he turned to me. "Dr. Garrett stood behind you and Miss Drake when you broke in the door, didn't he?"

I nodded. "Yes."

Merlini opened the medical journal and riffled through it. Half a dozen loose pages, their serrated edges showing where they had been torn in half, fluttered to the floor.

Merlini said, "You would have made an excellent magician, doctor. Your deception was not visual, it was auditory."

"That," Gavigan said, "tears it."

Later I had one further question to ask Merlini.

"You didn't explain how Houdini got out of that Scottish jail, nor how it helped you solve the enigma of the unsealed door."

Merlini lifted an empty hand, plucked a lighted cigarette from thin air and puffed at it, grinning.

"Houdini made the same false assumption. When he leaned exhaustedly against the cell door, completely baffled by his failure to overcome the lock, the door suddenly swung open and he fell into the corridor. The old Scot, you see, hadn't locked it at all!"

T. S. STRIBLING

(1881–1965)

|||||||||||||||||||||||||||||||||||||||||||||| ■ ||||||||||||||||||||||||||||||||||||||||||||||

Although some of the work of southern author T(homas) S(igismund) Stribling might be called local-color writing, the mainstream novels of this Pulitzer Prize winner are given substance by the author's stance against racism and his talent for satire. Stribling was the product of Clifton, Tennessee, a small town where he lived for much of his life, and later another small town, Florence, Alabama. Typical of well-educated Southerners of his era, he became a teacher and a lawyer, and still found time to write. In his writing, he experimented with various forms, from a trilogy about life in the South to adventure stories set in exotic climes, such as Venezuela. Despite his 1933 Pulitzer for *The Store*, today he is best remembered for the detective stories in which he introduced the psychological sleuth Dr. Henry Poggioli.

Stribling's stories of detection focus on the workings of the human mind as explained by Poggioli, an Ohio State University professor who specializes in psychology and criminology. The professor's solutions of crimes depend less on interpreting physical clues and more on understanding human behavior.

Stribling published the first series of Poggioli stories in the pulp magazine *Adventure* in 1925 and 1926. Like Sir Arthur Conan Doyle, who became so weary of Sherlock Holmes that he killed him off, only to bring him back again, Stribling tired of his character and used Poggioli's spectacular death as the climax of the "final" tale. But Stribling bowed to popular demand, revived the character, and began a second series in 1929 that took him through the early 1930s. A third, and final, series featured the professor's activities from the end of World War II until 1957.

"A Daylight Adventure" is a good example of Stribling's important contribution to the detective form. In it, psychology is at the center of the ratiocination with which the sleuth solves crimes. Stribling's contribution was broader than that, however. He develops the mildly adversarial relationship between the sleuth and the narrator. And the sardonic wit that Stribling uses to illuminate rural southern society makes him an early exemplar of the detective novelist as regional writer and humorist.

1950

A Daylight Adventure

■

The following notes concerning Mrs. Cordy Cancy were not made at the time of her alleged murder of her husband, James Cancy. Worse than that, they were not taken even at the time of her trial, but seven or eight months later at the perfectly hopeless date when Sheriff Matheny of Lanesburg, Tennessee, was in the act of removing his prisoner from the county jail to the state penitentiary in Nashville.

Such a lapse of time naturally gave neither Professor Henry Poggioli nor the writer opportunity to develop those clues, fingerprints, bullet wounds, and psychological analyses which usually enliven the story of any crime.

Our misfortune was that we motored into Lanesburg only a few minutes before Sheriff Matheny was due to motor out of the village with his prisoner. And even then we knew nothing whatever of the affair. We simply had stopped for lunch at the Monarch café in Courthouse Square, and we had to wait a few minutes to get stools at the counter. Finally, two men vacated their places. As Poggioli sat down, he found a copy of an old local newspaper stuck between the paper-napkin case and a ketchup bottle. He unfolded it and began reading. As he became absorbed almost at once in its contents, I was sure he had found a murder story, because that is about all the professor ever reads.

I myself take no interest in murders. I have always personally considered them deplorable rather than entertaining. The fact that I make my living writing accounts of Professor Poggioli's criminological investigations, I consider simply as an occupational hazard and hardship.

The square outside of our café was crowded with people and filled with movement and noise. In the midst of this general racket I heard the voice of some revivalist preacher booming out through a loudspeaker, asking the Lord to save Sister Cordy Cancy from a sinner's doom, and then he added the rather unconventional phrase that Sister Cordy was not the "right" sinner but was an innocent woman, or nearly so.

That of course was faintly puzzling—why a minister should broadcast such a remark about one of his penitents. Usually the Tennessee hill preacher makes his converts out to be very bad persons indeed, and strongly in need of grace, which I suppose most of us really are. Now to hear one woman mentioned in a prayer as "nearly innocent" was a sharp break from the usual.

I suppose Poggioli also caught the name subconsciously, for he looked up suddenly and asked me if the name "Cancy" had been called. I told him yes, and repeated what I had just heard over the megaphone.

The criminologist made some sort of silent calculation, then said, "Evidently Mrs. Cancy has had her baby and the sheriff is starting with her to the penitentiary in Nashville."

I inquired into the matter. Poggioli tapped his paper. "Just been reading a stenographic account of the woman's trial which took place here in Lanesburg a little over seven months ago. She was sentenced to life imprisonment, but she was pregnant at the time, so the judge ruled that she should remain here in Lanesburg jail until the baby was born and then be transferred to the state penitentiary in Nashville. So I suppose by this noise that the baby has arrived and the mother is on her way to prison."

Just as my companion explained this the preacher's voice boomed out, "Oh, Lord, do something to save Sister Cordy! Sheriff Matheny's fixin' to start with her to Nashville. Work a miracle, Oh, Lord, and convince him she is innocent. You kain't desert her, Lord, when she put all her faith an' trust in You. She done a small crime as You well know, but done it with a pyure heart and for Yore sake. So come down in Yore power an' stop the sheriff and save an innocent woman from an unjust sentence. Amen." Then in an aside which was still audible over the megaphone, "Sheriff Matheny, give us five minutes more. He's bound to send Sister Cordy aid in the next five minutes."

Now I myself am a Tennessean, and I knew how natural it was for a hill-country revivalist to want some special favor from the Lord, and to want it at once; but I had never before heard one ask the rescue of a prisoner on her way to Nashville. I turned to Poggioli and said, "The minister admits the woman has committed some smaller crime. What was that?"

"Forgery," he replied. "She forged her husband's will in favor of herself, then applied the proceeds to build a new roof on the Leatherwood church. That's part of the court record."

"And what's the other crime—the one she claims to be innocent of?"

"The murder of her husband, Jim Cancy. She not only claims to be innocent, she really is. The testimony in the trial proved that beyond a doubt."

I was shocked. "Then why did the judge condemn . . ."

The criminologist drew down his lips. "Because the proof of her innocence is psychological. Naturally, that lay beyond the comprehension of the jury, and the judge too, as far as that goes."

I stared at my companion. "Can you prove her innocence, now, at this late date?"

"Certainly, if this paper has printed the court reporter's notes correctly, and I'm sure it has."

"Why, this is the most amazing thing I ever heard of—hitting in like this!"

"What do you mean 'hitting in like this'?"

"Good heavens, don't you see? Just as the sheriff is starting off with an innocent woman, just as the preacher is asking the Lord to send down some power to save her, here you come along at exactly the right moment. You know she is innocent and can prove it!"

Poggioli gave the dry smile of a scientific man. "Oh, I see. You think my coming here is providential."

"Certainly. What else is there to think?"

"I regret to disillusion you, but it is not. It couldn't be. It is nothing more than an extraordinary coincidence—and I can prove that, too." With this my friend returned to his paper.

This left me frankly in a nervous state. It seemed to me we ought to do something for the woman outside. I looked at the man sitting next to us at the counter. He nodded his head sidewise at Poggioli. "He don't live around here, does he?"

I said he didn't.

"If he don't live here, how does he know what's happened in these parts?"

"You heard him say he read it in the paper."

"He didn't do no such thing. I watched him. He didn't read that paper a tall, he jest turned through it, like I would a picture book."

I told him that was Poggioli's way of reading. It is called sight-reading—just a look and he knew it.

The hill man shook his head, "Naw, Mister, I know better'n that. I've watched hunderds of men read that paper sence it's laid thar on the counter, and the fassest one tuk a hour an' twelve minutes to git through."

I nodded. I was not interested, so I said, "I daresay that's true."

"Of course hit's so," he drawled truculently, "ever'thing I say is so."

"I'm not doubting your word," I placated, "it is you who are doubting mine. You see I know my friend's ability at sight-reading."

This silenced him for a few moments, then he said shrewdly, "Looky here, if he gits what he knows out'n that paper, how come him to say Cordy Cancy is innocent when the paper says she's guilty?"

"Because the judgment in the paper doesn't agree with the evidence it presents. My friend has gone over the evidence and has judged for himself that the woman is guilty of forgery but innocent of murder."

This gave the hill man pause. A certain expression came into his leathery face. "He's a detectif, ain't he?"

"Well, not exactly. He used to be a teacher in the Ohio State University, and he taught detectives how to detect."

"Mm—mm. Who hard [hired] him to come hyar?"

"Nobody," I said, "he just dropped in by chance."

"Chanst, huh? You expeck me to b'leve that?"

"Yes, I must say I do."

"Well, jest look at it from my stan'point—him comin' hyar the very minnit the preacher is prayin' fer he'p and the shurrf startin' with her to the penitentiary—a great detectif like him jest drap in by chanst. Do you expeck me to b'leve that?"

All this was delivered with the greatest heat and my seat-mate seemed to hold me personally responsible for the situation.

"Well, what do you believe?" I asked in an amiable tone which gave him permission to believe anything he wanted to and no hard feelings.

"Why, jess what I said. I b'leve he wuz hard."

His suspicion of Poggioli, who would never accept a penny for his criminological researches, amused me. "Well, that's your privilege, but if it would strengthen your faith in me I will say that to the best of my knowledge and belief Professor Henry Poggioli's arrival in Lanesburg, Tennessee, on the eve of Mrs. Cordy Cancy's committal to the Nashville penitentiary, was a coincidence, a whole coincidence, and nothing but a coincidence, so help me, John Doe."

I had hoped to lighten my companion's dour mood, but he arose gloomily from his stool.

"I hope the Lord forgives you fer mawkin' His holy words."

"They are not the Lord's holy words," I reminded him, "they're the sheriff's words when he swears in a witness."

"Anyway, you tuk His name in vain when you said 'em."

"Didn't mention His name, sir. I said 'John Doe.'"

"Anyway, Brother," he continued in his menacing drawl, "you shore spoke with lightness. The Bible warns you against speakin' with lightness—you kain't git aroun' that." With this he took himself out of the café, scraping his feet in the doorway as a symbol of shaking my dust from his shoes.

As I watched the saturnine fellow go, Poggioli turned from his paper.

"Poses quite a riddle, doesn't he?"

"Not for me," I said. "I was born here in the hills."

"You understand him?"

"I think so."

"You didn't observe any more precise and concrete contradiction about him?"

I tried to think of some simple contradiction in the man, something plain. I knew when Poggioli pointed it out it would be very obvious, but nothing came to my mind. I asked him what he saw.

"Two quite contradictory reactions: he was disturbed about my being a detective and about your near profanity."

"I am afraid I don't quite see what you mean."

"I'll make it simpler. He evidently was a deacon in some church."

"Why do you say that?"

"Because he reproved the 'lightness' of your language. The scriptures instruct deacons to reprove the faults of the brethren, and lightness of language is one of them. So he was probably a deacon."

"All right, say he was. What does that contradict?"

"His disturbance over my being a detective. Deacons are supposed to ally themselves with law and order."

I laughed. "You don't know your Tennessee hill deacons. That contradiction in them is historical. Their ancestors came here before the Revolution to worship God as they pleased and escape the excise tax. They have been for the Lord and against the law ever since."

At this point another man hurried from the square into the Monarch café. I noted the hurry because under ordinary circumstances hill men never hurry, not even in the rain. He glanced up and down the counter, immediately came to my companion, and lifted a hand. "Excuse me, Brother, but you're not a preacher?"

"No, I'm not," said my companion.

"Then you are the detective that was sent. Will you come with me?"

"Just what do you mean by 'sent'?" asked the criminologist.

"Why the Lord sent you," explained the man hurriedly but earnestly. "Brother Johnson was jest prayin' to the Lord to send somebody to prove Sister Cordy Cancy innocent and keep her from going to the pen. Jim Phipps heard you-all talkin' an' hurried out an' told us there was a detectif in here. So He's bound to have sent ye."

Poggioli reflected. "I am sure I can prove the woman innocent—from the evidence printed in this paper. But what good will that do, when the trial is over and the woman already sentenced?"

"Brother," said the countryman, "if the Lord started this work, don't you reckon He can go on an' finish it?"

"Look here, Poggioli," I put in, "we're here for some reason or other."

"Yes, by pure chance, by accident," snapped the psychologist. "Our presence has no more relation to this woman than . . ."

He was looking for a simile when I interrupted, "If you know she is innocent don't you think it your duty to—"

The psychologist stopped me with his hand and his expression. "I believe I do owe a duty . . . yes . . . yes, I owe a duty. I'll go do what I can."

The man who came for him was most grateful; so were all the people in the café, for they had overheard the conversation. Everybody was delighted except me. I didn't like Poggioli's tone, or the expression on his face. I wondered what he really was going to do.

Well, by the time we got out of the restaurant everybody in the square seemed to know who we were. There was a great commotion. The preacher's prayer for help had been answered instantly. It was a miracle.

The sound-truck which had been booming stood in front of the county jail on the south side of the square. Beside the truck was the sheriff's car with the woman prisoner handcuffed in the back seat. Near the car stood another woman holding a young baby in her arms. This infant, I gathered, was the prisoner's child, and would be left behind in the Lanesburg jail while its mother went on to the penitentiary in Nashville. The crowd naturally was in sympathy with the woman and expected us immediately to deliver her from her troubles. I heard one of the men say as we pushed forward, "That heavy man's the detective and that slim 'un's his stooge; he writes down what the big 'un does."

Frankly, I was moved by the situation, and I was most uneasy about the outcome. I asked Poggioli just what he meant to do.

He glanced at me as we walked. "Cure them of an illusion."

"Just what do you mean—cure them of an . . ."

He nodded at the crowd around us. "I will prove to these people the woman is innocent, but at the same time show that my proof can be of no benefit to the prisoner. This ought to convince the crowd that providence had nothing to do with the matter, and it ought to make them, as a group, a little more rationalistic and matter-of-fact. That is what I consider it my duty to do."

His whole plan appeared cruel to me. I said, "Well, thank goodness, you won't be able to do that in five minutes, and the sheriff gave them only that much more time before he starts out."

My hope to avoid Poggioli's demonstration was quashed almost at once. I saw the sheriff, a little man, climb out of his car, walk across to the sound-truck, and take the microphone from the minister. Then I heard the sheriff's voice boom out.

"Ladies and gentlemen, I understand there really is help on the way for Mrs. Cancy. Whether it is miraculous help or jest human help, I don't know. But anyway I'm extendin' Mrs. Cancy's time to prove her innocence one more hour before we start to Nashville."

A roar of approval arose at this. The minister in the truck then took over the loudspeaker, "Brothers and Sisters," he began in his more solemn drawl, "they ain't one ounce of doubt in my soul as to who sent this good man. I'll introduce him to you. He is Dr. Henry Poggioli the great detective some of you have read about in the magazines. The Lord has miraculously sent Dr. Poggioli to clear Sister Cordy Cancy from her troubles. And now I'll introduce Sister Cordy to Dr. Poggioli. Doctor, Sister Cordy don't claim complete innocence, but she's a mighty good woman. She did, however, forge her husban's will by takin' a carbon paper and some of his old love letters and tracin' out a will, letter by letter. She sees now that was wrong, but she was workin' for the glory of the Lord when she done it."

Shouts of approval here—"Glory be!" "Save her, Lord!" and so forth. The divine continued, "Jim Cancy, her husban', was a mawker and a scoffer. He wouldn't contribute a cent to the Lord's cause nor bend his knee in prayer. So Sister Cordy forged his will for religious ends. Now I guess the Lord knew Jim was goin' to git killed. But Sister Cordy didn't have a thing in the world to do with that. He jest got killed. And you all know what she done with his money—put a new roof on the Leatherwood churchhouse. Save her, Oh, Lord, from the penitentiary!" (Another uproar of hope and sympathy here.) "And Brothers and Sisters, look how she acted in the trial, when suspicion fell on her for Jim's murder. She didn't spend one cent o' that money for a lawyer. She said it wasn't hers to spend, it was the Lord's and He would save her. She said she didn't need no lawyer on earth when she had one in Heaven. She said He would send her aid. And now, praise His name, He has sent it here at this eleventh hour." Again he was interrupted by shouts and applause. When a semi-silence was restored, he said, "Dr. Poggioli, you can now prove Sister Cordy innocent of her husband's murder and set her free."

In the renewed uproar the minister solemnly handed the microphone down to Poggioli on the ground. I have seldom been more nervous about any event in Poggioli's eventful career. I didn't suppose he would be in any actual danger from the irate hill people when they found out what he was trying to do, but on the other hand a mob can be formed in the South in about three minutes. And they are likely to do anything—ride a man out of town on a rail, tar and feather him, give him a switching, depending on how annoyed they are. Poggioli never lived in the South, he had no idea what he was tampering with.

He began, "Ladies and gentlemen, I have little to say. I have just read the report of Mrs. Cancy's trial in your county paper. From it I have drawn absolute proof of her innocence of her husband's murder, but unfortunately that proof can be of no benefit to her."

Cries of "Why won't it?" "What's the matter with it?" "What makes you talk like that?"

"Because, my friends, of a legal technicality. If I could produce new evidence the trial judge could reopen her case and acquit Mrs. Cancy.

But a reinterpretation of old evidence is not a legal ground for a rehearing. All I can do now is to demonstrate to you from the evidence printed in your county paper that Mrs. Cancy is innocent of murder, but still she must go on with the Sheriff to the penitentiary in Nashville."

Despair filled the square; there arose outcries, pleas, oaths. The revivalist quashed this. He caught up his microphone and thundered, "Oh, ye of little faith, don't you see Sister Cordy's salvation is at hand? Do you think the Lord would send a detectif here when it wouldn't do no good? I'm as shore of victory as I'm standin' here. Brother Poggioli, go on talkin' with a good heart!"

The irony of the situation stabbed me: for Poggioli to intend a purely materialistic solution to the situation, and the minister who had besought his aid to hope for a miracle. It really was ironic. Fortunately, no one knew of this inner conflict except me or there would have been a swift outbreak of public indignation. The scientist began his proof:

"Ladies and gentlemen, your minister has recalled to your memory how Mrs. Cordy Cancy forged her husband's will by tracing each letter of it with a carbon paper from a package of her husband's old love letters. But he did not mention the fact that after she did this—after she had underscored and overscored these letters and made them the plainest and most conclusive proof of her forgery—she still kept those love letters! She did not destroy them. She put them in a trunk whose key was lost, and kept them in the family living room. Now every man, woman, and I might almost say child, sees clearly what this proves!"

Of course in this he was wrong. He overestimated the intelligence of his audience. Those nearer to him, who could make themselves heard, yelled for him to go on and explain.

"Further explanation is unnecessary," assured the psychologist. "If she felt sufficiently sentimental about her husband to preserve his love letters, obviously she did not mean to murder him. Moreover, she must have realized her marked-over letters would constitute absolute proof of the minor crime of forgery. She must have known that if her husband were murdered, her home would be searched and the tell-tale letters would be found. Therefore, she not only did not murder her husband herself but she had no suspicion that he would be murdered. Those letters in her unlocked trunk make it impossible that she should be either the principal or an accessory to his assassination."

A breath of astonishment went over the crowd at the simplicity of Poggioli's deduction. Everyone felt that he should have thought of that for himself.

Poggioli made a motion for quiet and indicated that his proof was not concluded. Quiet returned and the psychologist continued.

"Your minister tells us, and I also read it in the evidence printed in your county paper, that Mrs. Cancy did not hire an attorney to defend her in her trial. She used the entire money to place a new roof on the old Leatherwood church, and she told the court the reason she did this was because God would defend her."

Here shouts arose. "He did! He's doin' it now! He's sent you here to save her!"

Poggioli held up a hand and shook his head grimly. This was the point of his whole appearance in the square—the materialistic point by which he hoped to rid these hill people of too great a reliance on providential happenings and place them on the more scientific basis of self-help. He intoned slowly:

"I regret to say, ladies and gentlemen, that my appearance here is pure accident. Why? Because I have come too late. If a supernal power had sent me here to save an innocent woman—and she is an innocent woman—if a supernal power had sent me, it would certainly have sent me in time. But I am not in time. The trial is over. All the proof is in. We cannot possibly ask a new trial on the ground of a reinterpretation of old proof, which is what I am giving you. That is no ground for a new trial. So this innocent woman who is on her way to the penitentiary must go on and serve out her unjust term. My appearance here today, therefore, can be of no service to anyone and can be attributed to nothing but pure chance."

At this pitiful negation an uproar arose in the square. Men surged toward the sheriff, yelling for him to turn the woman free or they would do it for him. Cooler heads held back the insurgents and voices shouted out:

"Dr. Poggioli, who did do the murder? You know ever'thing—who done it!"

The criminologist wagged a negative hand. "I have no idea."

"The devil!" cried a thick-set fellow. "Go ahead an' reason out who killed Jim Cancy—jest like you reasoned out his wife was innocent!"

"I can't do that. It's impossible. I haven't studied the evidence of the murder, merely the evidence that proves non-murder—a completely different thing."

"Go ahead! Go ahead!" yelled half a dozen voices. "The Lord has he'ped you so fur—He'll stan by you!"

It was amusing, in a grim fashion, for the crowd to twist the very materialistic point Poggioli was making into a logical basis for a spiritualistic interpretation. However, I do not think Poggioli was amused. He held up his hands.

"Friends, how could I know anything about this when I stopped over for lunch in this village only one hour ago?"

A dried-up old farmer, whose face had about the color and texture of one of his own corn shucks, called out, "Somebody shot Jim, didn't they Dr. Poggioli?"

"Oh, yes, somebody shot him."

"Well, have you got any idyah of the kind of man who shot Jim Cancy?"

"Oh, certainly. I have a fairly clear idea of the kind of man who murdered Cancy."

"I allowed you had, Brother, I allowed you had," nodded the old fellow with satisfaction. "The Lord put it into my heart to ast you exactly that question." The old fellow turned to the officer, "Shurrf Matheny, has he got time to tell what kind of a fellow murdered Jim before you start with Sister Cordy to the pen?"

The officer held up his hand. "I am extendin' Sister Cordy's startin' time two more hours—so we can find out who murdered her husban' instid of her."

"O.K.," called a woman's voice, "go ahead and tell us the kind of skunk that done that!"

"Well, Madam, I would say it was a man who shot Jim Cancy."

"Oh, yes, we all know that," shouted several listeners. "Women don't shoot nobody, they pisen 'em . . . as a rule." "Go on, tell us somp'm else."

"Well, let me see," pondered Poggioli aloud. "Let us begin back with the forgery itself. Mrs. Cancy did this. She admits it. But she did not originate the idea, because that is a highly criminal idea and she does not have a highly criminal psychology. She has, in fact, a very religious and dutiful psychology. I also know that if she had been bright enough to think of tracing the will from her old love letters, she would have realized how dangerous they were to keep in her unlocked trunk and would have destroyed them immediately. Therefore, I know somebody suggested to her how she could forge the will."

More angry shouts interrupted here, as if the crowd were reaching for the real criminal. Some voices tried to hush the others so the psychologist could proceed. Eventually Poggioli went on.

"All right, Mrs. Cancy did not originate the idea of forgery. Then she was used as a tool. But she is not a hard, resolute woman. Just look at her there in the sheriff's car and you can see that. She is a soft, yielding woman and would not carry any plan through to its bitter end.

But in her trial she did carry a plan through to its bitter end, and this end, odd to say, was to put a new roof on the Leatherwood church. Ladies and gentlemen, a new roof on Leatherwood church was the basic motive for Cancy's murder. It is fantastic, but it is the truth. Mrs. Cancy refused to hire a lawyer when she came to trial. Why? To save the money to put a roof on Leatherwood church. So the person who persuaded her to commit the forgery must also have persuaded her to withhold the money for the church roof, and that God would come down and set her free from the charge of murder."

At this the enthusiasm of the crowd knew no bounds. They flung up their hats, they yelled, they cried out that now the Lord had come to help Sister Cordy just like He had promised. The sheriff arose in his car and shouted that he extended Sister Cordy's leaving time for the rest of the day. He yelled that they were hot on the trail of the man who done it and he would remain in town to make the arrest.

I could see Poggioli was unnerved. It would take a cleverer psychologist than I am to explain why he should be. Of course, his demonstration was going awry. He was not getting where he had intended to go. He lifted up his hands and begged the crowd.

"My friends, please remember this. I do not know the man. I have no idea who he is. I can only give you his type."

"All right," shouted many voices, "go on and give us his type, so Sheriff Matheny can arrest him!"

The criminologist collected himself. "As to his type: I ate lunch in the Monarch café a little while ago and was reading an account of Mrs. Cancy's trial in your county paper. As I read, a gentleman beside me said that he had been watching strangers read the story of that trial for months, as it lay there on the lunch counter. It is possible such a man might have some connection with the murder; or he may have been morbidly curious about crime in general—"

Shouts of satisfaction here—"Go ahead, now you're gittin' somewhere!"

Poggioli stopped them. "Wait! Wait! I by no means incriminate this gentleman. I am trying to show you the various hypotheses which a criminologist must apply to every clue or piece of evidence."

"All right, Doctor, if he didn't kill Jim Cancy, who did?"

Poggioli mopped his face. "That I do not know, nor do I know anything whatever about the man in the café. I am simply trying to give you a possible psychological description of the murderer. Now, this man at my table also reprimanded my friend here for what he considered to be an infraction of a religious formality. In fact, he became quite angry about it. That would link up with the fact that Jim Cancy was reported to be a free-thinker. A free-thinker would have irritated such a man very deeply. If Cancy had jibed at this man's faith, the fellow would have felt that any punishment he could inflict on the mocker would be justified, even unto death. Also, he could have persuaded himself that any money he might receive from Cancy's death should be devoted to the welfare of the church—as for example, to put a new roof on the Leatherwood church. Following these plans, he could have easily influenced Mrs. Cancy to forge Cancy's will, with the understanding that the money would go to the church. Then he could have waylaid and shot Cancy, and made the will collectible. This would have accomplished two things; gratify his private revenge and make a contribution to the church. . . . The murderer could be of that type or he could be of a completely different type which I shall now try to analyze. . . ."

How many more types Poggioli would have described nobody knew, for at this juncture the sheriff discovered that his prisoner had fainted. This created a tremendous commotion. For a hill woman to faint was almost as unparalleled as for a horse to faint. Sheriff Matheny arose in his car and hallooed that he would carry no sick woman to the Nashville pen, and that Mrs. Cancy should remain here with her baby until she was completely recovered, even if it took a week. After making this announcement, the officer climbed out of his car and disappeared in the throng.

Everybody was gratified. They came pouring around Poggioli to congratulate him on his speech. A fat man elbowed up, seized Poggioli by the arm, motioned at me, too, and shouted at us to come to dinner in his hotel. Poggioli said we had just eaten at the Monarch café.

"Then you-all are bound to be hungry. Come on, my wife sent me over here to bring ye. She feeds all the revivalists and their singers who come to preach in the square."

The criminologist repeated that we were not hungry, but the fat man came close to him and said in what was meant for an undertone:

"Don't make no diff'runce whether you are hungry or not—my wife wants you to come inside while you and your buddy are alive!"

"Alive!" said my friend.

"Shore, alive. Do you think Deacon Sam Hawley will let any man stand up in the public square and accuse him of waylayin' Jim Cancy, and then not kill the man who does the accusin'?"

My friend was shocked. "Why, I never heard of Deacon Sam Hawley!"

"He's the man you et by, and he knows you. Come on, both of you!"

"But I was simply describing a type—"

"Brother, when you go to a city you find men in types—all dentists look alike, all bankers look alike, all lawyers look alike, and so on; but out here in these Tennessee hills we ain't got but one man to a type. And when you describe a man's type, you've described the man. Come on in to my hotel before you git shot. We're trying to make Lanesburg a summer resort and we don't want it to git a bad name for murderin' tourists."

We could see how a hotel owner would feel that way and we too were anxious to help preserve Lanesburg's reputation for peace and friendliness. We followed our host rather nervously to his hotel across the square and sat down to another lunch.

There was a big crowd in the hotel and they were all talking about the strange way the Lord had brought about the conviction of Deacon Sam Hawley, and rescued a comparatively innocent woman from an unjust sentence. Poggioli pointed out once or twice that the woman was not out of danger yet, but all the diners around us were quite sure that she soon would be.

The whole incident seemed about to end on a kind of unresolved anticlimax. The diners finally finished their meal and started out of the hotel. We asked some of the men if they thought it would be safe for us to go to our car. They said they didn't know, we would have to try it and see. Poggioli and I waited until quite a number of men and women were going out of the hotel and joined them. We were just well out on the sidewalk when a brisk gunfire broke out from behind the office of the *Lane County Weekly Herald*, which was just across the street from the hotel. It was not entirely unexpected. Besides, that sort of thing seemed to happen often enough in Lanesburg to create a pattern for public action. Everybody jumped behind everybody else, and holding that formation made for the nearest doors and alleys. At this point Sheriff Matheny began his counterattack. It was from a butcher's shop close to the hotel. How he knew what point to pick out, I don't know; whether or not he was using us for bait, I still don't know.

At any rate, the sheriff's fourth or fifth shot ended the battle. Our assailant, quite naturally, turned out to be Deacon Sam Hawley. He was dead when the crowd identified him. In the skirmish the sheriff was shot in the arm, and everybody agreed that now he would not be able to take Mrs. Cancy to the penitentiary for a good three months to come. She was reprieved at least for that long.

As we got into our car and drove out of Lanesburg, the crowd was circulating a petition to the Governor to pardon Mrs. Cordelia Cancy of the minor crime of forgery. The petition set forth Mrs. Cancy's charity, her purity of heart, her generosity in using the proceeds of her crime for the church, and a number of her other neighborly virtues. The village lawyer put in a note that a wife cannot forge her husband's signature. He argued that if she cannot steal from him, then she cannot forge his name, which is a form of theft. She simply signs his name for him, she does not forge it.

The petition was signed by two hundred and forty-three registered Democratic voters. The Governor of Tennessee is a Democrat.

At this point we drove out of Lanesburg . . .

WILLIAM CAMPBELL GAULT

(b. 1910)

||||||||||||||||||||||||||||||||||||||||||||| ■ |||||||||||||||||||||||||||||||||||||||||||||

William Campbell Gault epitomized the professional practitioner of the detective and suspense genre through the middle years of the twentieth century. Gault started young, winning a $50 prize for a short story when he was sixteen and making the slim living typical of the business by the time he was nineteen. He was a product of the hard-working middle class, augmenting his writing income by cutting leather in a shoe factory, helping his mother manage a hotel, and, after army service during World War II, working for Douglas Aircraft and the U.S. Postal Service.

Typical of the times and the trade, Gault was versatile and prolific. In the decade and a half during which the magazine fiction market flowered, he sold more than 300 short stories to the sport, science-fiction, and mystery pulps. When television killed the magazine market in the early 1950s, he turned to writing novels for the paperback original and hardcover markets. In 1952, three of his novels were published, and one *(Don't Cry for Me)* won an Edgar award from the Mystery Writers of America.

Gault's work moved forward from the hard-boiled private-eye fiction of the period. His books had a moral purpose. They challenged racial, class, and ethnic stereotypes and won for him the Lifetime Achievement Award of the Private Eye Writers of America.

Gault's most memorable contribution to the advancement of the genre was his development of Brock Callahan, the series character of his later books, as a fully developed personality with a biography that explains his character and his motives and gives these books a special depth. His most significant achievement was his championing of the disadvantaged and his unusual (for his day) respect for females. Gault also pursued a serious career as a writer of sports fiction for the juvenile market. As such, he was concerned with fair play, and he became adept at portraying relationships between males of all ages, especially boys and teenagers.

In "See No Evil," Gault has a young man puzzle out the truth behind a crime while struggling to exonerate his kid brother. This story is an important example of a pulp writer dealing with issues of race and setting the stage for later genre writers who would use their tales to deal with social issues.

1950

See No Evil

■

At breakfast, there was the story again, in the papers. I looked over at my brother, and saw his eyes on me. Big, brown eyes, Manuel's got, and a quick smile, and his brain is quick, too.

"Where were you last night, Manny?" I said.

"Out. Riding the heap around."

The heap is a '36 V8 with a cut-down solid top and two pots. With a Turbo head and Johannsen ignition. Too much car for any punk, but he'd built it. It had cost him many a skinned knuckle, and I couldn't say much about that.

"Around Pico, were you riding?" I asked him.

"Some. What's bothering you, Pete?"

"Kids bother me," I said. "Kids that got a grudge on the world. Kids that ride hot rods around, looking for trouble. In Pico, last night, seven of them beat up a guy; beat up one guy. They held his wife, while she watched. His sister had her baby with her and she ran away, but she fell in running away, and the baby's condition is critical. The man has a broken jaw and he lost three teeth and his back has been cut in seven places. It's all here in the paper, Manny."

"So? You don't have to read it, do you? You could read the sport page. Who's asking you to read it?"

"The kids were dark with brown eyes. Mexican kids, maybe."

"Maybe they're mad at the world, Pete. Maybe they figure they're not getting the break the *gringos* get."

"And that's the way to get a break, beating up strangers with tire irons?"

"I don't know, Pete. What's it to me?"

"I don't know. But this I know. If I thought you were one of them, I'd kill you where you sit."

"Would you? Who's mad now, Pete? What kind of talk is that?"

Mama had gone next door, to Sanchez's to borrow some eggs. Now she said, "That's what I'd like to know. What kind of talk is that, Peter Montello? Why don't you lay off Manuel? He's a good boy."

"He'd better stay a good boy," I said. "Where does he get his spending money?"

"There's ways of making a buck," Manny said. "I don't have to punch a time clock to make a buck."

"You had a black eye last week. Get that making a buck?"

"Maybe."

Mama said, "Peter, it's time for work. Never mind about it, Peter."

"Who's the man around here?" I asked her. "Me or him?"

"What does it matter who's the man?" Mama answered. "I'm the boss. Here's your lunch, Peter."

I stood up and picked up my lunch. I looked at my brother. "You remember what I said."

"Which part?"

"And don't get flip." I got out before he gave me an answer to that.

Ah, he's all right. What kind of a break did he get, Papa dying when he was in seventh grade? High school, Manny had, but how could I send him farther, wrestling freight for Arnold's Cartage? He's a bright kid, and should have gone to college.

But hot rods. Hot rod hoodlums now, running around like maniacs, insulting people, beating them. Wolf packs, some of the papers called them, and the sheriff was adding more deputies.

It was a hot, heavy day and I wore a pair of gloves to rags. Handling sole leather, and it cuts you all to hell.

Gina was sitting on her front porch when I went by on the way home, and I came up. She gave me a glass of lemonade.

"When we're married," she said, "I'll have a glass of it ready for you every night when you come home from work. I'll have a pitcher of it."

"When we're married—that's good," I said.

Her eyes are too soft for this world. She bruises too easy. "Why do you talk like that?" she asked me.

"When are we going to get married? What's wrong with a fact? What have you got against a fact?"

"What have you got against the world lately? Grouchy, grouchy, grouchy all the time. Tell me why should I love a grouch?"

"I don't know," I said. "I don't know."

"Oh, but I do, Peter," she said, and her soft hand stroked my cheek. "Oh, we won't fight. You've had a bad day."

"And Manny," I said.

"Now what?"

"These hoodlums, these hot rod hoodlums. Manny's got a hot rod."

"So?"

"And he had a black eye the other day."

She shook her head and looked at me with the soft eyes, like Manny's. "You're always hunting trouble, like those hoodlums. You don't know Manny's one, but you've got to think he is. Why do you always want to think bad?"

"I don't know. He's so—smart."

473

"You should be proud he is, not resentful. He's never given you any trouble."

Her brother Christy came up on the porch and poured himself a glass of lemonade. "Hi, Pete, how's the feet?"

Short and broad and perfect teeth. Was a fullback at Fullerton High, but no college made an offer.

I asked him, "Were you with Manny last night?"

"That's a good question," he said. "I forget. Ask Manny."

I reached over to grab him by the shirt, but Gina was quicker, and between us. "Peter, for heaven's sakes!" she said. "You're like a wild man."

Christy was looking at me, and his eyes were shiny and his mouth working. Both his fists were clenched.

I could have crushed him with one hand. I went past them and down the steps. I went home, and got in the shower Manny had put in the back yard.

Lots of things around here Manny had fixed up. He was handy with tools. And with tire irons?

Manuel. Manuel, my baby brother. When he was three, I was twelve, and watching him all the time, because I wanted to. Smart, always smart and quick and smiling.

About eight, Gina came over. She said, "You forgot your lunch bucket." She had it in her hand.

"I'm sorry, Gina," I said. "I feel better now."

"I thought you would. Let's go to the park. There's a concert tonight."

We sat on the grass, where it's free. Ortiz had a big voice, and you could sit in Palos Verdes and hear him. A poor man's singer, he must be; you can hear him in the cheap seats. What a voice, what a man.

I held Gina's hand and forgot about her brother. I almost forgot about Manny. Where had he been at suppertime?

Next morning, there were no new troubles in the paper. But the sheriff said there was a possibility the increase in housebreaking might be tied up with these hoodlum gangs. The city police were inclined to agree.

Manny was reading the sport page.

"Why weren't you here for supper?" I asked him.

"Wasn't hungry."

"Look at me when I talk to you."

He put the paper down.

"Did you call Ma that you wouldn't be here for supper?"

He nodded. "She knew about it."

She came from the kitchen with more pancakes. "Now what?"

"Nothing."

"Punching the clock, that's what's the matter with him," Manny said. "If you don't like it, why don't you quit, Pete?"

"And how would you two eat, then?"

"We'd find a way. We don't want to be a burden, Pete." He was grinning at me, that smart grin.

"Be quiet, both of you," Mama said. "I don't want another word out of you two this morning."

Another hot day. Loading refrigerators. The guys you get to work with these days, you might as well be alone. At noon, I sat near the north door, in the shade, with my lunch and the paper.

The voice was Shultz's. Big, round guy with a round head. Thinks he's the original Atlas.

"It's these damned Spanish-Americans, they like to be called. Most of these punks got Mex names, you notice? Manuel, or Leon, or—"

"Or Shultz," I called over.

"That's one of them," he told his buddies. "If I had my way—"

I was up and walking over there now. "What would you do, cabbage-head?" I asked him quietly.

"I'd shoot every one of those punks," he told me. "Beating up innocent people, scaring women into hysterics."

"You've got a big mouth, Shultz," I told him. "If you worked like you talked, we'd all be laid off."

He stood up, his face red. He rubbed his big hands on his cotton pants, looking me over. "Fight?" he said. "You want to fight, Mex?"

I nodded, and he came in.

He came in with a right hand I should have ducked, but didn't. It hit next to the ear and put me down. I saw his foot coming for my jaw as I scrambled on the concrete, and I twisted clear of it.

I was on my feet when he closed again. I put a fine left deep into his belly, and heard him grunt. His head crashed my mouth, and the blood spurted.

I caught him on the nose with a wild left, and he paused for maybe a second. My right caught his left eye.

He started one from the floor, and I beat him to it. It was a button shot, and I hit him twice more while he was falling.

His buddies were still sitting there. One of them said, "Don't get us wrong, Pete. We didn't ask him to sit with us. Sit down, Pete."

"It's cooler over here," I said.

It had been all right while it lasted, but it didn't do any good now. My hands trembled and I couldn't eat my lunch, and I was sick of myself. Hating wasn't any good; fighting wasn't any good. Why was I like this?

Gina was on the porch again. Mrs. Sanchez was there too, but not Christy.

Gina looked at my swollen lip, and her big eyes asked questions.

"Got caught by a packing case," I said. "Lucky it didn't tear my head off."

Mrs. Sanchez rocked in her rocker, saying nothing.

"Peter, poor Peter," Gina said.

"I'm all right," I said. "I'm no poorer than the rest in this block."

Mrs. Sanchez sighed, and said nothing.

"It must be hot in that warehouse," Gina said. "Should I make some lemonade?"

"Not today, not with this lip," I said. "I'll see you later."

"Tonight?"

"Sure. I suppose."

What was there in it? I could sit on her porch the rest of my life. Five years I'd been going with her and not a dime nearer to the priest. What was there in it? Pa hadn't left anything and Manny wasn't good for anything. I had Mama to take care of.

Manny was home for supper that evening. We didn't have any words for each other.

"Some home," Mama said. "Brothers not talking to each other."

Manny grinned. "He'll grow up some day, Ma. He was always the baby."

I looked at him and said nothing.

"Forget to duck?" he asked me.

Mama said, "It was a packing case. Peter is not street brawler, Manuel."

"Oh," Manny said, that smart way.

I asked him, "Don't you believe it?"

"Sure. If you say it. You wouldn't lie, Pete."

Red, things got, and I could feel his steady brown eyes on me. But I remembered Shultz, and how I'd felt after that.

"And if I did fight," I said, "I wouldn't use a tire iron. And I wouldn't need a gang."

Manny said quietly, "What the hell do I care what you'd do? You think you're some kind of an example?"

His eyes were burning; I'd never seen him this way before. He was breathing heavy; you could see his chest going in and out.

"Manuel—" Mama said warningly.

"Well, tell him to lay off of me, then! Picking, picking, picking all the time! I—" He got up and went out of the dining room.

The front door slammed.

Mama was shaking her head. "Peter, Peter, Peter—what is it? He's just a boy."

"He's old enough to work. I was working at his age."

She looked at the tablecloth. She was crying.

"Ma," I said, "I'm—oh, I don't know what I am. I'm sorry, Ma."

She nodded. "I know, I know—Peter, it's not good to hate. It's not good, being suspicious. Is it because of Gina? Because you've waited so long? You think I've been happy about that? Peter—"

"What's the good of talking?" I asked her. "It's a rat race, Ma." I got up, too, and went out.

It was cooler now. I could see Gina, in her kitchen, helping her mother with the dishes. I went over to Fourteenth Street, to Barney's.

I only had two bucks on me, but my credit was good. I drank a lot of whiskey, and it didn't do any good at all. I wasn't happy now, or mad—just sour, dead, empty.

The lights were out at Sanchez's. There was a light on in our house, though, and a prowl car in front. I hurried up the walk.

There was a cop there. Ma was sitting in the big chair, and crying. Manny was sitting on the davenport, looking mad.

The cop had a book in his hand, a bank book. He turned as I came in. He sniffed, and looked at me suspiciously.

"What's the matter?" I said. Sick, I was now, and mad.

"You the brother?"

"That's right. What's the matter?"

"Found this little book in a home that was robbed tonight. It's a bankbook showing a total deposit of eleven hundred dollars, made out to your brother."

"Eleven hundred dollars?" I stared at Manny. "You—"

"It's mine, but I lost it, Pete. I lost it over two weeks ago."

"Eleven hundred dollars," I said, and took a step his way.

"Peter—" Mama said. Her voice was deep and she glared at me. "This is the time, Peter. Now, I'll know if you're a brother."

Manuel, Manuel . . . I fought the whiskey and the hate in me. What a baby he'd been. What a smart, quick, smiling baby. I took a deep breath and faced away from him. I faced the cop.

"He says he lost it. Two weeks ago, he says."

"And reported the loss?"

"The very next day," Manny said. "You could check that at the bank. You want to see the new one they gave me?"

The cop shook his head. "You've got a '36 Ford, a convertible with a cut-down, solid top?"

"Every other rod in town's a '36 with solid top. That's the best model to cut down."

"Maybe. I think you ought to come down anyway. Just a few questions, you know, like where you were tonight."

Well, a test. I turned around and said, "I'll go along, Manny. Don't let him scare you."

"I'm not scared, I'm mad," Manny said. "I'm so mad I'm not scared to admit where I was tonight, though you won't like it, Pete. I was at Gilmore Stadium, driving the Art Willis Special. I won the feature in it. There must have been a couple thousand watching me."

"You, in a race car?" I said. "Manny, baby, you're just a—"

"Pete, I won. I win a lot of races. You should read the sports pages, Pete, not the front pages; you'd learn an awful lot."

Now I saw, and took a deep breath. "And the eleven hundred?"

"Was for you. A truck for you, I was saving for. So you could be in business for yourself, and wouldn't have to punch the clock. Ma knew I was driving, but we were scared to tell you, the way you've been."

"Sounds very fine," the cop said, "but I'm afraid it would sound better if the lieutenant heard it."

"Beat it," I said. "Go someplace and blow your whistle. You're not taking my brother anywhere."

"Peter—" Mama said.

The phone rang.

"That would be for me," the cop said, and went over to pick up the phone.

"Right," he said, and "Oh—I see. Admitted it? Let's see, that would be next door. Makes sense, all right. Sure, I'll run over and talk to his folks."

He hung up, and faced us. He didn't look comfortable. "A—a Christy Sanchez admitted finding that bankbook, and admitted being a member of the gang that robbed that house. Said he left it behind on purpose. Had some kind of grudge against your brother." He looked at me. "That would be you."

I didn't say anything.

He shook his head. "I don't know what's the matter with these kids."

"Christy hasn't a father," I said. "When you're ready to go down with the Sanchezes, I'd like to go along, officer."

"All right. I'll drop back." He went out.

"Manny," I said. "Oh, Manny, baby."

"It's all right, Pete," he said. "You work hard, and it's been rough. But for gosh sakes, don't—ah, [1]Pete."

But I couldn't help it. I was crying. And Pete was crying and Ma too. It was wonderful.

---

[1]The first person narrator, "Pete," is suddenly referred to in the third person. This error is retained from an earlier printing of the story.

ANTHONY BOUCHER

(1911–1968)

||||||||||||||||||||||||||||||||||||||||||||| ■ |||||||||||||||||||||||||||||||||||||||||||||

It may be said that in detective fiction, Anthony Boucher is an exception to the old rule "Them that can, do; them that can't, teach." As the most influential critic of popular literature of his time, Boucher taught readers of the *New York Times Book Review*, the *New York Herald Tribune Book Review*, and the *San Francisco Chronicle* what it takes to make a good detective novel. He also wrote seven of them himself.

The son of two physicians, Boucher was born in California as William Anthony Parker White. He graduated Phi Beta Kappa from the University of Southern California, where he spent much of his free time acting, directing, and writing drama. After earning a Master of Arts degree from the University of California, Berkeley, he began an unsuccessful career as a playwright. After he failed to sell two plays, he began writing detective novels, using the Anthony Boucher pen name because he still regarded himself as a playwright. As Boucher, he created the red-haired private eye Fergus O'Breen and Lieutenant A. Jackson of the Los Angeles Police Department's homicide division as series characters. He used another pen name, H. H. Holmes, for his two novels featuring Sister Ursula, a devout nun and clever sleuth who aids in the cases of LAPD homicide lieutenant Terence Marshall. He also penned radio scripts and wrote and edited science fiction.

In terms of plotting, character development, and social comment, Boucher's mystery writing was not exceptional for the time. Plots tend to center on puzzles, and solutions depend on deductions drawn from plenty of well-placed clues. Boucher's fiction is most notable for the wit and literary allusions that enrich his books and short stories.

While Boucher's fiction was well received, critics agree that his major contribution was his literary criticism. It is impossible to overestimate the importance of Boucher's serious reviewing in the *New York Times* of a genre previously disdained as mere entertainment or trashy fiction. His excellent taste and judgment as a critic were reinforced by his editing of texts and anthologies in the field. He won the Mystery Writers of America's Edgar award three times for his critical work. That organization's annual convention was eventually named for him: the "Bouchercon" now attracts more than a thousand mystery fans, writers, editors, collectors, and hangers-on each year. Its international importance is underlined by the fact that the twenty-sixth Bouchercon, in 1995, was the second to be held in England.

"Crime Must Have a Stop" features Nick Noble, one of Boucher's best-developed characters. Noble is an alcoholic former cop who solves crimes while drinking cheap wine and making allusions to Sherlock Holmes, Shakespeare, and Christopher Marlowe in a Mexican-style bar in Los Angeles.

1951
_____

Crime Must Have a Stop

■

The third set of flashbulbs exploded and the actress relaxed and pulled down her skirt. Lieutenant MacDonald continued to stare somewhat foolishly at the silver trophy in his hands.

"Well?" the actress grinned. "How does it feel to be the recipient of the Real Detective Award for the Real Detective of the Year?"

"Thirstifying," said MacDonald honestly.

The actress nodded. "Well spoken, my fine ferreting friend. I always feel a spot of alcohol is indicated after cheesecake myself. Where are we going?"

MacDonald still contemplated the trophy. It had been exciting, very exciting, to be chosen by the top fact-crime radio program for its annual award; but he'd been feeling uneasy ever since the announcement. Despite the extraordinary record of solved cases that had made him the bright young star of the Los Angeles Police Department, he felt like an impostor.

"Mind a ride downtown?" he asked. "We're going to deliver this trophy to the man it really belongs to."

The actress raised her unplucked brows as they turned east on Sunset. "I've worked in Hollywood for three years," she said, "and I've never known whether Sunset Boulevard ran beyond Gower. They tell me there's a city called Los Angeles down this way. That where we're going?"

"Uh huh. And you're going to meet the damnedest man in that city of the damned . . ." And MacDonald began the story.

He began with his own first case—the case that started with his finding a dead priest and ended with his shooting one of his fellow lieutenants. He explained where he had found the solution of that case, and where he had found the solution for which he had just been awarded the trophy.

"You weren't giving awards back in the early thirties," he said. "But there was a man in the department then who topped anybody you've honored. He had a mind . . . it's hard to describe: a mind of mathematical precision, with a screwball offbeat quality—a mind that could see the shape of things, grasp the inherent pattern—"

"Like a good director," the actress put in.

"Something," MacDonald admitted."Then there came that political scandal—maybe you've heard echoes—and the big shake-up. There was a captain who knew what wires to pull, and there was a lieutenant who took the rap. The lieutenant was our boy. He had a wife then and she needed an operation. The pay checks stopped coming and she didn't get it . . ."

The actress's lively face grew grave as she followed the relentless story of the disintegration of greatness: the brilliant young detective, stripped at once of career and wife, slipping, skidding, until there was nothing left but the comfort of cheap sherry and the occasional quickening of the mind when it was confronted with a problem . . .

MacDonald pulled up in front of the Chula Negra. He peered in, caught sight of Mamá Gonzales' third daughter Rosario, and beckoned her to the door. "You got any marches on your juke box?" he asked, handing her a nickel.

So it was to the strains of the Mexican national hymn that the Real Detective Award trophy entered the little Mexican restaurant. Lieutenant MacDonald bore it proudly aloft and the actress followed him, confused and vaguely delighted.

Mexicanos al grito de guerra . . .

MacDonald halted in front of the fourth booth on the left, with the certainty of finding its sharp-nosed white-skinned inhabitant. He placed the trophy on the table, flourished his hand and proclaimed, "To the Real Detective of the Year!"

The actress placed one foot on the bench and lifted her skirt over her knee. "That makes it an official award," she grinned.

. . . al sonoro rugir del cañón boompty boomp!

Nick Noble's pale blue eyes surveyed the symbolic silver figure of Justice Triumphant Over Wrongdoing. "If it was only a cup . . ." he sighed, and downed his water glass of sherry.

That was the start of an evening memorable in many ways. It was MacDonald's first non-professional visit to the Chula Negra; and he was amazed to realize that Nick Noble could drop cryptic comments on the theater of twenty years ago which fascinated the actress as much as his comments on crime had stimulated the lieutenant. He was further amazed to realize the warmth and vitality of the girl beside him, whom he had at first regarded solely as the inevitable wench demanded by cameramen.

They fitted together somehow, her bubbling eagerness and Noble's weary terseness. They belonged together because they were the same thing underneath, the same piercing through of conventional acceptance, straight to reality. MacDonald was growing more and more aware of the girl, more and more aware of the peculiarity of a man's being single in his thirties, when the episode began which was to make the evening completely memorable.

It started unspectacularly enough, with a voice calling, "Hi, Don!"

The voice was high-pitched, but firmly male—a tenor with baritone quality. The man was slight but firmly built, dressed in the standard mismatched uniform of middle-bracket Hollywood, and MacDonald was certain he'd never seen him before. But even as the man seized his hand, as the actress looked up curiously and Nick Noble finished his latest sherry, MacDonald began thinking back. Far back, obviously. Anyone who called him Don dated from college days at USC. Now he was Mac or Lieutenant or Loot. A faint but ghastly picture flitted across his mind, of something called an Apolliad, an evening of students' creative contributions to the higher literature. There must be some reason why he was thinking of that—there must, in fact, have been some reason why he had attended it . . .

"Steve Harnett!" he cried. "You old son of a—" He broke off, glancing sideways at the actress.

"I've heard the word," she said dryly. "I just didn't think men ever greeted each other that way outside of bad plays and Rotary Club meetings."

"It's grand to see you, Don," Harnett was saying. "I kept reading about you in the papers and saying I've got to look you up and then . . . well, you know how it is."

"Don't I," MacDonald confessed. "I read about you too. I'll go you one better: I even listen to *Pursuit*, just to see how far away from real murder you can get."

"Oh! Do you write *Pursuit?*" Only half of the girl's breathlessness was good technique.

"I should've warned you." MacDonald looked rueful. "She's a radio actress."

"And therefore should know by now that a writer's introduction to the producer is the kiss of death. Still you might as well introduce us."

"Sure . . . Good Lord! Do you realize that in all the hullabaloo of those publicity photographs I never did catch your name?"

"Lynn Dvorak," said Nick Noble quietly.

"Don't tell me that's a deduction!"

"Asked her. While you were greeting your friend."

MacDonald grinned. "If all your rabbits-out-of-sherry-bottles were as simple as that—"

"They are," said Noble. "To me." His washed-out blue eyes glazed over oddly as he contemplated the actress and the radio writer.

Someone presumably introduced Tristan to Iseult and Paolo to Francesca. No one introduced Petrarch to Laura, so no one wrote a tragedy on the subject culminating in murder. Someone introduced Harvey Hawley Crippen to Ethel LeNeve and someone introduced Judd Gray to Ruth Snyder.

And Lieutenant Donald MacDonald, Homicide, LAPD, said, "Lynn Dvorak, may I present Steve Harnett?"

So for once, MacDonald was later to reflect, Nick Noble had been in on a murder even before it happened. It was in October, that first and fatal interview, and throughout that winter the lieutenant kept running into Steve and Lynn, at the Philharmonic, at Musso and Frank's, at the Biltmore Theater, until he began thinking of them as SteveandLynn in one word, and automatically looking for one if he saw the other.

"I started something," he would muse ruefully as he had a drink with them after a concert. It was not only that they were physically in love (even to the hand-holding-in-public stage, which was embarrassing in a man of Steve's thirty-six years); but they obviously fitted together so well in so many non-physical respects. Their ears heard the same music; their mouths laughed the same laughter.

But with Steve at least there was something under the laughter, something that caused moments when the successful writer, the man happily in love, gave way for an instant to a small boy, terrified of some incalculable but certain retribution.

It was one of those moments that seized Steve as the three of them were drinking after an unusually interesting production of one-acts at the Actors' Lab. He had said nothing for five minutes, and there was supplication in the glance Lynn cast to MacDonald as she gave up her single-handed attempt at brightness and retired to the ladies' room.

MacDonald could think of nothing to do but emit that wordless questioning noise and assume that sympathetic half-smile which had caused the Pengcraft murderer to reveal where he had hidden the other half of the body.

Steve Harnett roused himself from his brooding. "I've got to talk to you, Don," he said abruptly. "It's getting me down. I can't think straight."

"Any time," said MacDonald. "Unless a crime wave takes priority."

"Dinner next Thursday?" Steve said eagerly. "I'm in Brentwood; it's in the phone book. Say around seven for drinks?"

MacDonald made a note and tried to smile reassuringly at Lynn when she came back.

"That couple you introduced here?" Nick Noble asked two nights later, when MacDonald had dropped in with a report on the death-cell confession of a man in whose career Noble had taken a certain decisive interest. "They all right?"

"Sure. I guess so."

"Liked the girl. Alive—like Martha . . . Trouble for her. Sorry . . ."

"Why should there be trouble?" MacDonald asked uneasily.

Nick Noble paused and deliberately brushed away the fly which always perched invisibly on his sharp nose. "Call it . . . the Unspeckled Band," he said.

There were times, MacDonald reflected as he beckoned to Rosario, when Nick Noble's cryptic impulses seemed to spring from pure malice.

The Harnett home was small, comfortable, unpretentious, and therefore probably only mildly fabulous in cost. Steve Harnett, MacDonald had learned from a few questions of other friends in radio, was well in the charge-account-at-the-Brown-Derby class but somewhat short of the swimming pool level. His questions should have prepared him for his first surprise; but there was one question he hadn't thought to ask.

The woman who answered the door was in her early thirties—slender, a trifle pale, and more than a trifle attractive, again in a comfortable, unpretentious, and mildly expensive manner. She held out a hand and said, "Good evening. Lieutenant MacDonald? I'm Harriet—Steve's wife."

Abruptly MacDonald understood the Unspeckled Band—the colorless strip on Steve's third finger, left hand. He was still trying to mask his angry amazement with polite conversation when Steve came in, followed by a plain heavy-set girl with a handful of papers. Here in Brentwood domesticity, MacDonald observed, Steve wore a plain gold wedding ring.

"Glad you could make it, Don. You and Harriet getting yourselves acquainted? This is Pat McVeagh, my secretary—Lieutenant MacDonald." And he was suddenly very busy with ice and gin and vermouth and lemon peel and the careful avoidance of MacDonald's eyes.

The secretary left after one drink, without having opened her mouth for any non-alcoholic purpose. Then, just as MacDonald was trying to get the feel of the Harriet–Steve relationship, the elder Mrs. Harnett slipped in and there were more introductions.

MacDonald could not have told you, an hour after dinner, what he had eaten. He was too concentrated on trying to persuade himself that he was on a social and not a professional visit. He was too surrounded by all too tangible undercurrents.

Mrs. Harnett Sr., he decided, was the most obtrusively unobtrusive little old lady he had ever known. She effaced herself completely—a gray wraith in a corner, coming to life only with an occasional plaintive don't-mind-me. But whatever topic was under discussion—another round of drinks, a proposed weekend at La Jolla, a new limerick of Steve's composition—her quiet reminder of her own self-effacement had the power of a Security Council veto.

There were other undercurrents: a barb from Steve to Harriet about the cooking of the dinner, a barb from Harriet to Steve about his prospects in radio, some obscure reference to the absent secretary . . .

It was with great relief that MacDonald let Steve drag him off to the study as soon as decently possible after dinner. It was a good room, from the outmodedly comfortable chairs to the cases full of erratically and lovingly chosen books, from the battered standard typewriter to the miniature electric icebox, of the type usually employed for baby formula.

Steve Harnett took two cans of beer from the box, punctured them, handed one to his guest, kicked off his shoes, and began to pace around the room.

"Necessary adjunct to work, beer," he muttered. "Always figure it takes me exactly a quart to a script."

"You work on beer and Nick Noble on sherry," MacDonald observed. "And I can't drink on duty. There's no justice in this world." He waited, but Steve kept on pacing. "You never mentioned Harriet," he said expressionlessly. "I suppose I must've read about your marriage in an alumni bulletin, but I'd forgotten."

"We've been married ten years." Steve's voice was more tenor than baritone now.

"Any children?"

"Last fall we were hoping . . . That's when I met you. But in December Harriet had to go to the hospital. Now they say we won't ever."

"So it all started while Harriet was—"

Steve stopped pacing. "Don't think I'm saying that to justify it, Don. I'm not. I can't justify it, not even to myself. But it's happened—hell, it happened that night down at your little Mex joint. *Dead Shepherd, now I find thy saw of might . . .*"

". . . *Who ever loved that loved not at first sight?*" MacDonald finished for him. "I remember, Steve. You always were a sucker for quotations. Lends authority, doesn't it? Takes away your own responsibility for what you're saying."

"Does my radio-trained ear detect what we cliché-experts call a thinly-veiled edge of contempt in your voice, Don?"

"It's no business of mine," MacDonald said optimistically. "But you're getting yourself into one sweet mess. Does Harriet know?"

"I don't think so."

"She's bound to eventually. You haven't been precisely discreet, and there's always a helpful friend . . . Does Lynn know about Harriet?"

"Yes . . ." Steve's eyes rested on the gold band on his left hand.

"In other words, now she does but she didn't at first?"

Steve didn't answer that one. Instead he said, "But, Don, you don't understand. Maybe nobody can until it happens to him. But this . . . this isn't just an affair."

"Are they ever?"

"It isn't just . . . fun in bed. It's being together—being *us*."

"So what did you want me for? Name of a good lawyer?"

Steve drew back suddenly. "But I couldn't divorce Harriet. I love her."

"Let them eat cake," MacDonald snorted, "and have it too!"

"Don't you see, Don? They're both so . . . so right. Both things. The thing with me and Harriet and the thing with me and Lynn. I can't say: this I cleave to, this I discard. It wouldn't be fair to either of them."

"Which the present situation, of course, is."

"Hell, Don, I'm not an adulterer." Steve managed an odd sort of smile. "I'm a bigamist." He added hesitantly, "There's a quotation for that too: *How happy could I be with either, were 'tother fair charmer away* . . ."

MacDonald could not swear why he shivered at that moment, but he had a rough idea. "I still don't see why you wanted to talk to me about it. I did introduce you, but . . ."

"I think it's because I knew you pretty well a long time ago, but you're not a part of my present life. I had to talk to somebody. I can't talk to people who know me and Harriet now. I had to talk it out just to see if . . ."

MacDonald knew very well why he was shivering as he replied, "You know, Steve, I don't think that was the reason . . . underneath."

"And it wasn't, I'm sure," MacDonald said later that night to Nick Noble. "You asked about trouble. Here it is, and your Unspeckled Band can prove as venomous as a swamp adder, if that's what it was. And subconsciously, at least, Steve sees it too: that this is the buildup to a standard, cliché-expert murder situation. Each woman has a motive for killing the other; and if Steve ever gets out of the equipoise of his *Beggars' Opera* how-happy-could-I-be-with-either, he'll have a motive for getting rid of the girl left over. That subconscious fear of murder led him to expose the situation to a Homicide officer."

There was a water glass full of sherry in front of Nick Noble. He took what seemed like a casual swig, and the glass was half full. Then he muttered *"Beggars' Opera?"* and shook his head. "Groucho Marx," he said decisively.

Even after long years of inoculation Lieutenant MacDonald could still occasionally be taken aback in the Chula Negra. "And how did Groucho Marx get into this?"

"Didn't ever see *Animal Crackers?*" Noble murmured regretfully. "Long time ago. 'Way back when . . ."

His voice trailed away. MacDonald understood. 'Way back when Lieutenant Nicholas Noble, the pride of Homicide, took his beautiful wife Martha to the pictures . . .

"But what can I do?" MacDonald insisted. "What can any officer do when he sees a murder building up in front of him—cast and motives complete and nothing to do but wait until it happens?"

For once Nick Noble had not even a cryptic answer.

That was in March. The murder did not come until late April. In the interval MacDonald steered away from any contact with Steve and Lynn; a meeting now could prove too embarrassing. But he heard enough gossip to know that Harriet, if still ignorant, must have no friends and no telephone. And he heard other gossip, too, to the effect that Steve Harnett was cracking up as a radio writer, that his option wouldn't be picked up at the end of this thirteen on *Pursuit*, which with the free-lance market shot to pieces . . .

MacDonald had tried to avoid embarrassment in seeing Steve again. But it was not embarrassment that he felt now in April as he faced Steve Harnett, beside the pink-ruffled bed which held Harriet's curiously arched body. There was no emotion save cold rage in MacDonald's voice as he roared, "So you finally made up your mind!"

Steve had his shoes off and a tumbler of straight whiskey in his hand. He looked up helplessly and said, "You won't believe me, Don. Why should you? But you don't understand . . ."

MacDonald controlled his voice. "Look, Steve. There's only one way to play this. I'm just any cop and you're just any . . . husband of the deceased. All right, we know it's strychnine; even a layman could tell that. Now tell me how."

Steve's vitality and charm had yielded to bewildered chaos. "As I was saying, it must have been the candy. I was working late and Harriet took the candy to bed with her. I worked so late I slept on the couch in the study. This morning Mother . . . found her."

"Nobody heard anything? She must've gone through hell."

"Mother's not well; she usually takes phenobarbital at night. And when a script's going hot, the house could fall down and I wouldn't know it."

"Now this candy . . . ?"

"I was telling you, it just came in the mail and we thought whoever forgot to put in a card would phone about it. It's a kind Harriet likes, so—"

"And you write mystery shows!" MacDonald gasped. "One of the oldest clichés—in fact and fiction—and you let your wife . . . ! I suppose there's independent evidence that the candy actually did come in the mail?"

"Mother was with us when Harriet opened the package. She didn't want any; sweets upset her. And I was drinking beer, so Harriet took them to bed later on. I think the wrapper's still in the waste-basket . . ."

A brand-new machine had replaced the battered standard in Steve's study. MacDonald found a label in the drawer of the desk and inserted it in the typewriter. When he had finished typing, he set it beside the label on the wrapper from the wastebasket. There was no telling the two labels apart.

Steve's mouth opened wide. "But does that prove . . . ?"

"No," MacDonald grunted. "It doesn't. It's a new machine. It hasn't had time to develop obvious idiosyncrasies. Any new typewriter of the same model would have approximately the same result. But it does indicate—"

The phone rang. MacDonald picked it up.

An impersonal voice announced, "I have a call from New York for Mr. Stephen Harnett."

"New York for you," said MacDonald.

"Sponsor trouble," Steve groaned. "Or the network on that last script—I was afraid it was a little too . . . Blast it! I can't handle things like that now. I can't . . ."

"Try," said MacDonald. "Occupy your mind while I see Lynn Dvorak."

Steve had started to reach a shaky hand toward the phone. Now he snatched it back. "Lynn! You can't drag her into this!"

"Can't I? You say you're innocent. OK. Who else has a motive? Go talk to your sponsor."

"Lynn . . ." There was horror in Steve's eyes. "She couldn't have . . ."

"Go on. Telephone. See you later."

Steve laughed harshly. "Life must go on and stuff. *And life's crime's fool . . .*"

Steve Harnett's hand wavered halfway to the telephone. As Mac-Donald left the room he could hear angry squawks coming from the still unanswered receiver.

The lieutenant had never been more wretched on professional business than he was as he drove to the little house in the hills east of Highland, almost in downtown Hollywood.

A baffling case was one thing. That you could sink your teeth into; or if it was too flatly impossible, you could take it to the Chula Negra and watch Nick Noble's eyes glaze over as he probed to the truth. But something so wretchedly obvious as this . . .

He had, inadvertently, started it all. He had, quite advertently, foreseen its inevitable outcome. And here it was.

He remembered Steve Harnett, even back at the University, as flashy, clever, plausible, entertaining—but essentially weak. There'd been something (he couldn't recall the details) about a girl that Mrs. Harnett didn't quite approve of and how she'd managed to break up the relationship. And there'd been that odd episode when Steve was directing a play: the two girls, both beautiful, both good actresses, both avid for the lead—and Steve's sudden pneumonia followed by two weeks' convalescence on the desert while someone else took over the direction and casting . . .

A psychoanalyst, he reflected, could have fun—probably would have, if there was enough money in the defense. And meanwhile the layman could content himself with the old-fashioned verdict that there were certain people who simply didn't have the courage to face up to things.

There was, of course, the remote possibility that Lynn might be the actual sender of the strychnine-laden chocolates. But how much did that direct responsibility matter compared with the ultimate responsibility of what Steve had done to both women? Except, of course, that in that case Lynn would go to the gas chamber and Steve would probably go on writing radio melodramas . . .

There was no answer to his ring. The door was unlocked, so he didn't have to worry about skeleton keys.

He didn't have to worry about Lynn and the gas chamber, either.

She sat in a chair half-facing the door, well lit by the reading lamp which must have been left burning from the night before. Her face grinned at him, in that sardonic welcome which only a strychnine-fed host can provide.

There were smudges of chocolate on the grinning lips, and there was a box of chocolates on the table by the phone.

MacDonald used the phone to call the necessary technicians. Before they arrived he had discovered in the wastebasket the familiar wrapper and the familiar typed label.

"And now," MacDonald demanded in the fourth booth on the left of the Chula Negra, "where the hell are we?"

"Hell," said Nick Noble succinctly and truthfully.

"It made sense before. Steve had made up his mind. He didn't have the heart or the guts to make a clean cut, so he simply removed the one he didn't want. It would've made the same kind of sense if we'd found only Lynn. But both of them . . . that switches the motivation altogether. Now we have to look for somebody who wants *both women* out of Steve Harnett's life. And who has such a motive?" He paused and tried to answer himself. "I've got to look into the secretary. Every so often there's something in this office-wife business. She's a dowdy, homely wench, but she probably doesn't see herself that way."

"Labels," said Nick Noble. "Let's see."

MacDonald placed them before him:

Mrs Stephen Harnett
11749 Verdugo Drive
Los Angeles 24, Calif.

Mrs Lynn Dvorak
6708 Las Aves Road
Hollywood 28, Calif.

Nick Noble leaned back in the booth and a film seemed to obscure his eyes. "Mrs. . . . ?" he said softly.

"Lynn? Divorced. Three years ago. That doesn't enter in. You'll notice the postmark, too. Downtown Hollywood. Steve admitted he'd been in to see the advertising agency; but that doesn't help now. The secretary lives near here—which might be a good reason for not mailing here. And that reminds me: I'm down in this part of town to see her. I'd better—"

"Why?" said Nick Noble.

MacDonald smilingly disregarded the query. "Oh—one odd thing I forgot to tell you about Steve. When that New York call came through he muttered something about life goes on, and added: *Life's crime's fool.* I told you he's a sucker for quotations, but I couldn't spot this one; it bothered me, so I stopped at the library to use a concordance. It's Hotspur's death speech in *Henry IV, Part I*, the same speech Huxley used for a title a while back, only it's properly *Life's* time's *fool.* Interesting subconscious twist, don't you think?"

Nick Noble's lips moved softly, almost inaudibly:

> But thought's the slave of life, and
>   life's time's fool;
> And time, that takes survey of all the
>   world,
> Must have a stop . . .

He broke off, looking almost embarrassed by so long and articulate a speech. "Wife and I," he explained. "Used to read Shakespeare. *Time . . . crime . . . must have a stop.*"

"Lieutenant MacDonald?"

This was a strange new voice, deep, with a slight Central European accent. Bitterly remembering what had begun when last a new voice accosted him in the Chula Negra, MacDonald looked up to see a dapper little man waving a sheet of notepaper at him.

"They tell me at your Headquarters," the little man was saying, "I may possibly find you in this *Lokal;* so I come. Our friend Stephen Harnett gives me this letter for you long since, but I am first now in Los Angeles with the opportunity to present it."

Puzzled, MacDonald began to read:

Dear Don:

This is to introduce Dr Ferdinand Wahrschein, who is (need I say?) a friend of the sponsor's wife and who is conducting a technical investigation into American police methods. I'd deeply appreciate (and so would the sponsor) any help which you can give him.

Sincerely,
STEVE

The lieutenant rose, tossing the letter to Nick Noble. "Delighted to meet you, but you catch me just when I am leaving to interview a witness, and I'd sooner do it alone. But I tell you what: if you really want to know how the local department cracks its toughest nuts, you stay right here with The Master."

And he was gone. Dr. Ferdinand Wahrschein stared speculatively at the pinched white face in the booth, then gingerly seated himself and resignedly began, "*Na also!* Is it your finding that anthropometric method—"

"Sherry?" suggested Nick Noble hospitably.

Miss Patricia McVeagh had a room (adjacent bath—no cooking priv.) in what had once been an old family mansion on Bunker Hill. Lieutenant MacDonald walked from the Chula Negra to Third and Hill and there rode up the funicular Angels' Flight. He was glad he was in plain clothes. The once fashionable Bunker Hill district is now tenanted largely by Mexicans and by Americans of Spanish-Indian descent, many of whom feel they have good reason not to care for uniformed members of the Los Angeles Police Department.

Miss McVeagh opened the door and said, "Lieutenant MacDonald, isn't it? What on earth . . . ?" Her tone meant (a) she hadn't seen to-day's papers, or (b) such an actress was wasting her time as a secretary.

She hadn't grown any more glamorous since the martinis in March; but there was something possibly preferable to glamor in the smile of hospitality which managed to conquer her puzzlement.

MacDonald began abruptly, "I don't need to bother you with the complete fill-in," which is one of the best known ways of causing witnesses to volunteer their own suggestions. "It's just a routine matter of checking certain movements in the Harnett household. I gather you weren't working there today?"

Miss McVeagh smiled. "Is that what Mr. Harnett told you? I suppose I shouldn't . . . Look, Lieutenant; I don't have anything to drink, but how about some Nescafé? I could talk easier with a cup in my hand. Do you mind?"

MacDonald did not mind. He liked people to talk easy. And while he waited for the Nescafé, he decided he liked people who lived in cheap rooms and spent the money they saved on a judicious balance of Bach (Johann Sebastian) and Tatum (Art).

Miss McVeagh came back with two cups and a carbon copy of a letter. "If it's just where do I stand with the Harnett household, this letter ought to clear things up. I mailed it this morning."

MacDonald read:

Dear Mr. Harnett:

I realize that your financial position since "Pursuit" did not pick up the option makes my regular employment out of the question. But I still feel, as I told you that time when I so mistakenly took a second of your martinis, that a good secretary is also a collaborator.

For that reason, I'd like to offer to place my secretarial services on a speculative basis. The exact terms we can work out if you like the idea; but the general notion would be that I'd work on the usual schedule, but be paid anywhere from $0.00 to $?.?? according to your monthly level.

He stopped reading there and said, "You love him that much?"

"Love?" Her mouth opened wide.

"You'd work for nothing just to try to pull him back on his feet?"

"I would. So where does love come in?"

"It would seem," MacDonald observed between swallows of Nescafé, "to indicate at least a certain . . . devotion."

"Sure," she nodded. "Devotion to Pat McVeagh. Look, Lieutenant. Steve Harnett's good. When he does write, he can write like a blue streak. And when he gets himself straightened out, he's going to hit the big time. What's radio? What's five hundred a week . . . said she blithely on Bunker Hill. But it's true: it's the real big time Steve Harnett's headed for, and when he hits it, I want in."

"This not being straightened out," MacDonald ventured. "It's been bad?"

"It's been hell," she said flatly. "I'll tell you: Last week I was typing some letters on the standard out in the patio. He was supposed to be roughing out a plot in the study on his portable. Comes time for me to go home, he has to sign the letters, he hasn't emerged, I take a chance on his wrath and knock on the study door. He doesn't shout. He just whispers 'Come in,' and I come in and there he is. He's been in there eight hours. He hasn't done one blessed word. His hands are shaking and his eyes look like he's going to cry. I give him the letters, he picks up a pen, and it falls out of his fingers. That's how bad it's been, Lieutenant; but I'm still sold on him and I'll take my chances."

Dr. Ferdinand Wahrschein felt a buzzing in his head. He was not sure whether to attribute it to his first experience with California sherry by the water glass, or to the answers he was receiving to his methodically prepared questionnaire. Nine out of ten of those answers would baffle him completely; but the tenth would cast a lightning flash of clarification on a long obscure problem.

Pleasantly bebuzzed, he sat back and listened to Lieutenant MacDonald's résumé of his conversation with Miss McVeagh. "I'm sold on her, Nick," MacDonald ended. "Here: read her letter. I'll swear that's an absolutely honest expression of just what her interest in Steve Harnett is. And if she's out on motive, who's left?"

Nick Noble accepted the letter and handed back another paper in exchange. "Something for you to read too. Came by messenger."

My Dear Mr. Noble:

My son informs me that he has once met you, and that you have had extraordinary success in solving problems perplexing to the regular police.

Though I do not know you, may I beg you to exert your abilities on the problem of the deaths of my son's wife and of his friend? My son is no ordinary man; and his peace of mind, if you can secure it, will be deeply valued by

Your sincere friend,
FLORENCE HARNETT
(Mrs. S. T. Harnett)

"See it now?" said Nick Noble.

MacDonald felt Dr. Wahrschein's beady and eager eyes on him, and sensed vaguely that the honor of the department depended on him. "I can't say . . ." he began.

"Labels," said Nick Noble. "Look at them."

MacDonald looked at the labels. He stared at them. He glared at them. He scrutinized their inscrutability. Then suddenly he seized the other three papers which lay on the table, spread them in a row before him, looked from one to the other, and slowly nodded.

"You see?" said Nick Noble. "Clear pattern. Three main points. 1: Groucho Marx."

MacDonald nodded gravely; he'd remembered that one. Meanwhile Dr. Ferdinand Wahrschein stared at him.

"2," Noble went on: "the cliché."

"Cliché?"

"The chocolates. Everybody knows gimmick. Botkin, Molineux, Anthony Berkeley. Why eat? Unless . . ."

"Of course. And the third point . . ." MacDonald indicated the assorted papers before him and echoed Noble's own statement. "Crime must have a stop."

Dr. Ferdinand Wahrschein giggled and beckoned to Rosario for more sherry. This essay on American police methods should be *aber fabelhaft!*

Steve Harnett filled his glass of straight whiskey. "I'm alone," he said thickly. "Alone. They're gone. Harriet's gone. Lynn's gone too. *How happy* . . . But they're gone." His bare toes wiggled in anguish. "And *Pursuit*'s gone too, come Thursday week. And McVeagh's gone on account of I can't pay her any more. I'm alone . . ."

"Are you?" Mrs. Harnett asked gently. She sat unobtrusively in a corner while her son paced the room.

"I know," Steve muttered. "You're here. You're always here, darling, and you know how much . . . Blast it, there is truth in clichés. A man's best mother is his—"

The phone rang.

"I'll take it, dear." Mrs. Harnett seemed hardly to move, but the phone had not rung three times before she answered it. "Just a minute," she said quietly into the mouthpiece. "I'll see if he's in." She put her hand over the diaphragm as she whispered, "New York."

Steve let out a yell. "They fire me and still they own my soul while the contract runs! But I can't. Not now I can't. Look at my hands. They're quivering like an aspen . . . an aspic . . . an aspen . . ."

He was still judiciously weighing the two words when Mrs. Harnett had finished murmuring apologies and hung up. "I'll stand between you and these things now, dear," she murmured. "I'll—"

But the next ring was on the doorbell, and Lieutenant MacDonald was not having any standing between. He strode in, snatched the glass from Steve, and began talking.

"This thing sticking out of my pocket," he said, "is a warrant. Just so a mystery plot man like you gets all the gimmicks straight, we'll brief it. You couldn't make up your mind, could you? You kept quoting *How happy could I be with either* . . . Only there's another quote that starts like that. It was Groucho Marx who said, *How happy I could be with either of these women* . . . *if only both of them would go away!* And that's the decision you reached. You were going to pieces; and what a nice simple life you could have if only you weren't bothered with *either* Harriet or Lynn. No more problems, no decisions, no impingements . . . just you alone, in your insufficient self-sufficiency . . . !"

Steve said, "If I had that glass back I could think better."

"You don't want things outside yourself, but you can't live without them. You've found that out by now, haven't you? OK, take the glass. And take the proof. There's been too much written about poisoned chocolates. Nobody'd eat an anonymous gift nowadays—especially no one close to a gimmick-conscious man like you. *Unless* they were reassured. 'Stupid of me, darling; I forgot to put in the card.' And who's the only person who, immediately or by phone, could reassure *both* Harriet and Lynn?

"And the best proof. Crime must have a stop. A full stop. The typewriter was almost certainly the one in your study, but that proved nothing. Anybody could've used it—Miss McVeagh, your mother . . . But typing habits are something else. And typists are divided into those who do and do not put a period, a full stop, after abbreviations like *Mr.*

and *Mrs.* I saw a letter of McVeagh's; she wrote *Mr. Harnett*—M, R, period. I saw a note from your mother; she wrote *Mr. Noble*—M, R, period. I saw a note from you; you wrote *Dr Ferdinand Wahrschein*—D, R, no period. And the murder labels were both addressed *Mrs*—M, R, S, *no period.*

"The D. A.'ll want to know where the strychnine came from. I'll make a guess. Your mother's a semi-invalid, I gather. Maybe heart-trouble? Maybe using strychnine? Maybe missing a few tablets lately?"

Lieutenant MacDonald had never seen anyone wring her hands before, but there was no other description for what Mrs. Harnett was doing. "I have noticed," she struggled to say, "twice recently, I've had to have a prescription refilled before I needed to."

Steve gulped and set his glass down. "Hitting it too hard, Don," he choked out. "Minute in the bathroom. Then you can . . ." He gestured at the warrant.

"You must understand, Lieutenant," Mrs. Harnett began as Steve left. "It isn't as if my Stephen were like other men. This isn't an ordinary case. Of course I have to tell the truth when it comes to something like the strychnine, but—"

A dim fear clutched at Lieutenant MacDonald as he callously shoved past the old lady toward bathroom. He threw open the unlatched door. Stephen Harnett stood there by the basin. MacDonald remembered McVeagh's description: *His hands are shaking and his eyes look like he's going to cry.* His trembling fingers were unable to bring the razor blade functionally close to the veins of his wrist. The blade slipped from his hand and clattered into the bowl as he turned and surrendered to the law.

"He'll never have to make another decision of his own," MacDonald said to Nick Noble when he dropped into the Chula Negra after his testimony on the first day of the trial. "From now on it's all up to his lawyers and the State. I think he likes it.

"Of course they've made that nonsensical double plea: *Not guilty* and *Not guilty by reason of insanity.* In other words, I didn't do it but if I did you can't hurt me. It may stick; I think he'll like it better if it doesn't."

"Is he?" Noble wondered into his glass.

"I don't know. What's sane? Like the majority of people? Then no murderer's sane: the majority aren't murderers. But the big trouble is with the people who are *almost* like the majority, the people you can't tell from anybody else till the push comes which they can't take. The people who could be the guy in the next apartment, the gal in the same bed . . . or me. So who's sane? Who's the majority? Maybe the majority is the people who haven't been pushed . . ."

Nick Noble opened his pale blue eyes to their widest. "You're growing up, Mac," he said, and finished his sherry hopefully.

ED McBAIN
(b. 1926)

||||||||||||||||||||||||||||||||||||||||||| ■ |||||||||||||||||||||||||||||||||||||||||||

He was born Salvatore A. Lombino in an impoverished New York City neighborhood, but he has written under the names Ezra Hannon, Richard Marstan, Evan Hunter, and Ed McBain—the last two of which made him famous. McBain studied at both the New York City Art Students League and Cooper Union Art School on scholarships, but even then his love was writing. After service on a destroyer during World War II, he switched to Hunter College to earn a degree in English and membership in Phi Beta Kapa.

McBain worked as a lobster salesman and a substitute teacher, among other jobs, and published scores of short stories and three novels before *The Blackboard Jungle*, written as Evan Hunter, brought him financial success in 1954. Remarkably prolific, he also has written two plays, four film scripts, two television plays, and a number of books for children. But his fame and his reputation rest principally on his Eighty-seventh Precinct series, which began in 1956 with the publication of *Cop Hater*.

These novels—many of which feature Steve Carela, the precinct's chief detective, but often focus on other members of the force—won for McBain the 1986 Grand Master award of the Mystery Writers of America and a reputation among his peers as the preeminent creator of the police-procedural form. His plots focus on the crime and on the exhausting work required of lawmen to catch the criminal. McBain makes his policemen human, with lives outside their duty, and he peoples the streets with minor characters who are interesting because he makes them real.

The Eighty-seventh Precinct works, with their multiple story lines, require the length of the novel form. But a similar atmosphere is depicted in many of McBain's short stories. While it does not use the characters who made the Eighty-seventh Precinct famous, "Small Homicide" is illustrative of McBain's keen knowledge of the details of police work and of the human misery that lies behind so many crimes. It stands as the prime example of a police procedural that induces an overwhelming sensation of pity in the reader.

1953

Small Homicide

■

Her face was small and chubby, the eyes blue and innocently rounded, but seeing nothing. Her body rested on the seat of the wooden bench, one arm twisted awkwardly beneath her.

The candles near the altar flickered and cast their dancing shadows on her face. There was a faded, pink blanket wrapped around her, and against the whiteness of her throat were the purple bruises that told us she'd been strangled.

Her mouth was open, exposing two small teeth and the beginnings of a third.

She was no more than eight months old.

The church was quiet and immense, with early-morning sunlight lighting the stained-glass windows. Dust motes filtered down the long, slanting columns of sunlight, and Father Barron stood tall and darkly somber at the end of the pew, the sun touching his hair like an angel's kiss.

"This is the way you found her, Father?" I asked.

"Yes. Just that way." The priest's eyes were a deep brown against the chalky whiteness of his face. "I didn't touch her."

Pat Travers scratched his jaw and stood up, reaching for the pad in his back pocket. His mouth was set in a tight, angry line. Pat had three children of his own. "What time was this, Father?"

"At about five-thirty. We have six o'clock mass, and I came out to see that the altar was prepared. Our altar boys go to school, you understand, and they usually arrive at the last moment. I generally attend to the altar myself."

"No sexton?" Pat asked.

"Yes, we have a sexton, but he doesn't arrive until about eight every morning. He comes earlier on Sundays."

I nodded while Pat jotted the information in his pad. "How did you happen to see her, Father?"

"I was walking to the back of the church to open the doors. I saw something in the pew, and I . . . well, at first I thought it was just a package someone had forgotten. When I came closer, I saw it was . . . was a baby." He sighed deeply and shook his head.

"The doors were locked, Father?"

"No. No, they're never locked. This is God's house, you know. They were simply closed. I was walking back to open them. I usually open them before the first mass in the morning."

"They were unlocked all night?"

"Yes, of course."

"I see." I looked down at the baby again. "You . . . you wouldn't know who she is, would you, Father?"

Father Barron shook his head again. "I'm afraid not. She may have been baptized here, but infants all look alike, you know. It would be different if I saw her every Sunday. But . . ." He spread his hands wide in a helpless gesture.

Pat nodded, and kept looking at the dead child. "We'll have to send some of the boys to take pictures and prints, Father. I hope you don't mind. And we'll have to chalk up the pew. It shouldn't take too long, and we'll have the body out as soon as possible."

Father Barron looked down at the dead baby. He crossed himself then and said, "God have mercy on her soul."

I was sipping at my hot coffee when the buzzer on my desk sounded. I pushed down the toggle and said, "Levine here."

"Dave, want to come into my office a minute? This is the lieutenant."

"Sure thing," I told him. I put down the cup and said, "Be right back," to Pat, and headed for the Skipper's office.

He was sitting behind his desk with our report in his hands. He glanced up when I came in and said, "Sit down, Dave. Hell of a thing, isn't it?"

"Yes," I said.

"I'm holding it back from the papers, Dave. If this breaks, we'll have every mother in the city telephoning us. You know what that means?"

"You want it fast."

"I want it damned fast. I'm pulling six men from other jobs to help you and Pat. I don't want to go to another precinct for help because the bigger this gets, the better its chances of breaking print are. I want it quiet and small, and I want it fast." He stopped and shook his head, and then muttered, "Goddamn thing."

"We're waiting for the autopsy report now," I said. "As soon as we get it, we may be able to—"

"What did it look like to you?"

"Strangulation. It's there in our report."

The lieutenant glanced at the typewritten sheet in his hands, mumbled, "Uhm," and then said, "While you're waiting, you'd better start checking the Missing Persons calls."

"Pat's doing that now, sir."

"Good, good. You know what to do, Dave. Just get me an answer to it fast."

"We'll do our best, sir."

He leaned back in his leather chair. "A little girl, huh?" He shook his head. "Damn shame. Damn shame." He kept shaking his head and looking at the report, and then he dropped the report on his desk and said, "Here're the boys you've got to work with." He handed me a typewritten list of names. "All good, Dave. Get me results."

"I'll try, sir."

Pat had a list of calls on his desk when I went outside again. I picked it up and glanced through it rapidly. A few older kids were lost, and there had been the usual frantic pleas from frantic mothers who should have watched their kids more carefully in the first place.

"What's this?" I asked. I put my forefinger alongside a call clocked in at eight-fifteen. A Mrs. Wilkes had phoned to say she'd left her baby outside in the carriage, and the carriage was gone.

"They found the kid," Pat said. "Her older daughter had simply taken the kid for a walk. There's nothing there, Dave."

"The Skipper wants action, Pat. The photos come in yet?"

"Over there." He indicated a pile of glossy photographs on his desk. I picked up the stack and thumbed through it. They'd shot the baby from every conceivable angle, and there were two good close-ups of her face. I fanned the pictures out on my desk top and phoned the lab. I recognized Caputo's voice at once.

"Any luck, Cappy?"

"That you, Dave?"

"Yep."

"You mean on the baby?"

"Yeah."

"The boys brought in a whole slew of stuff. A pew collects a lot of prints, Dave."

"Anything we can use?"

"I'm running them through now. If we get anything, I'll let you know."

"Fine. I want the baby's footprints taken and a stat sent to every hospital in the state."

"Okay. It's going to be tough if the baby was born outside, though."

"Maybe we'll be lucky. Put the stat on the machine, will you? And tell them we want immediate replies."

"I'll have it taken care of, Dave."

"Good. Cappy, we're going to need all the help we can get on this one. So . . ."

"I'll do all I can."

"Thanks. Let me know if you get anything."

"I will. So long, Dave. I've got work."

He clicked off, and I leaned back and lighted a cigarette. Pat picked up one of the baby's photos and glumly studied it.

"When they get him, they should cut off his . . ."

"He'll get the chair," I said. "That's for sure."

"I'll pull the switch. Personally. Just ask me. Just ask me and I'll do it."

The baby was stretched out on the long white table when I went down to see Doc Edwards. A sheet covered the corpse, and Doc was busy typing up a report. I looked over his shoulder:

POLICE DEPARTMENT
City of New York

Date: _June 12, 1963_

From: Commanding Officer, _Charles R. Brandon, 77th Pct._

To: Chief Medical Examiner

SUBJECT: DEATH OF _Baby girl (unidentified)_

Please furnish information on items checked below in connection with the death of the above named. Body was found on _June 12,_

_1963_ at _Church of the Holy Mother,_

1220 Benson Avenue, Bronx, New York

Autopsy performed or examination made? _Yes_

By Dr. _James L. Edwards, Fordham Hospital Mortuary_

Date: _June 12, 1963_ Where? _Bronx County_

Cause of death: _Broken neck_

Doc Edwards looked up from the typewriter.

"Not nice, Dave."

"No, not nice at all." I saw that he was ready to type in the *Result of chemical analysis* space. "Anything else on her?"

"Not much. Dried tears on her face. Urine on her abdomen, buttocks, and genitals. Traces of Desitin and petroleum jelly there, too. That's about it."

"Time of death?"

"I'd put it at about three A.M. last night."

"Uh-huh."

"You want a guess?"

"Sure."

"Somebody doesn't like his sleep to be disturbed by a crying kid. That's my guess."

"Nobody likes his sleep disturbed," I said. "What's the Desitin and petroleum jelly for? That normal?"

"Yeah, sure. Lots of mothers use it. Mostly for minor irritations. Urine burn, diaper rash, that sort of thing."

"I see."

"This shouldn't be too tough, Dave. You know who the kid is yet?"

"We're working on that now."

"Well, good luck."

"Thanks."

I turned to go, and Doc Edwards began pecking at the typewriter again, completing the autopsy report on a dead girl.

There was good news waiting for me back at the office. Pat rushed over with a smile on his face and a thick sheet of paper in his hands.

"Here's the ticket," he said.

I took the paper and looked at it. It was the photostat of a birth certificate.

U. S. NAVAL HOSPITAL   St. Albans, N. Y.   Birth Certificate

This certifies that _____Louise Ann Dreiser_____ was born to

_____Alice Dreiser_____ in this hospital at __4:15 P.M.__ on

the __tenth__ day of __November, 1952__

Weight ____7____ lbs. ____6____ ozs.

In witness whereof, the said hospital has caused this certificate to be issued, properly signed and the seal of the hospital hereunto affixed.

Gregory Freeman, Lt(jg) MC USN

Gregory Freeman, LTJG MC USN
Attending Physician

Frederick L. Mann

Frederick L. Mann, CAPTAIN MC
Commanding Officer USN

"Here's how they got it," Pat said, handing me another stat. I looked at it quickly. It was obviously the reverse side of the birth certificate.

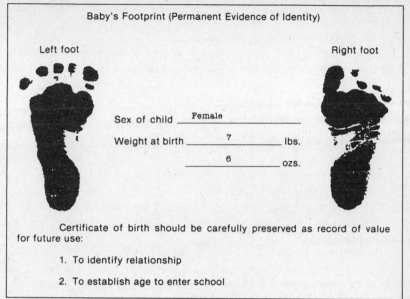

Baby's Footprint (Permanent Evidence of Identity)

Left foot   Right foot

Sex of child _____Female_____

Weight at birth _____7_____ lbs.

_____6_____ ozs.

Certificate of birth should be carefully preserved as record of value for future use:

1. To identify relationship

2. To establish age to enter school

There were several more good reasons why a birth certificate should be kept in the sugar bowl, and then below that:

Official registration at _____148–15 Archer Avenue,_____

Jamaica, L.I., N.Y.

_____

_____

Mother's left thumb   Mother's right thumb

"Alice Dreiser," I said.

"That's the mother. Prints and all. I've already sent a copy down to Cappy to check against the ones they lifted from the pew."

"Fine. Pick one of the boys from the list the Skipper gave us, Pat. Tell him to get whatever he can on Alice Dreiser and her husband. They have to be sailors or relations to get admitted to a naval hospital, don't they?"

"Yeah. You've got to prove dependency."

"Fine. Get the guy's last address, and we'll try to run down the woman, or him, or both. Get whoever you pick to call right away, will you?"

"Right. Why pick anyone? I'll make the call myself."

"No, I want you to check the phone book for any Alice Dreisers. In the meantime, I'll be looking over the baby's garments."

"You'll be down at the lab?"

"Yeah. Phone me, Pat."

"Right."

Caputo had the garments separated and tagged when I got there.

"You're not going to get much out of these," he told me.

"No luck, huh?"

He held out the pink blanket. "Black River Mills. A big trade name. You can probably buy it in any retail shop in the city." He picked up the small pink sweater with the pearl buttons. "Toddlers, Inc., ditto. The socks have no markings at all. The undershirt came from Gilman's here in the city. It's the largest department store in the world, so you can imagine how many of these they sell every day. The cotton pajamas were bought there, too."

"No shoes?"

"No shoes."

"What about the diaper?"

"What about it? It's a plain diaper. No label. You got any kids, Dave?"

"One."

"You ever see a diaper with a label?"

"I don't recall."

"If you did, it wasn't in it long. Diapers take a hell of a beating."

"Maybe this one came from a diaper service."

"Maybe. You can check that."

"Safety pins?"

"Two. No identifying marks. Look like five-and-dime stuff."

"Any prints?"

"Yeah. There are smudged prints on the pins, but there's a good partial thumbprint on one of the pajama snaps."

"Whose?"

"It matches the right thumbprint on the stat you sent down. Mrs. Dreiser's."

"Uh-huh. Did you check her prints against the ones from the pew?"

"Nothing, Dave. None of her, anyway."

"Okay, Cappy. Thanks a lot."

Cappy shrugged. "I get paid," he said. He grinned and waved as I walked out and headed upstairs again. I met Pat in the hallway, coming down to the lab after me.

"What's up?" I asked.

"I called the Naval Hospital. They gave me the last address they had for the guy. His name is Carl Dreiser, lived at 831 East 217th Street, Bronx, when the baby was born."

"How come?"

"He was a yeoman, working downtown on Church Street. Lived with his wife uptown, got an allotment. You know the story."

"Yeah. So?"

"I sent Artie to check at that address. He should be calling in soon now."

"What about the sailor?"

"I called the Church Street office, spoke to the commanding officer, Captain"—he consulted a slip of paper—"Captain Thibot. This Dreiser was working there back in November. He got orders in January, reported aboard the U.S.S. *Hanfield*, DD 981, at the Brooklyn Navy Yard on January fifth of this year."

"Where is he now?"

"That's the problem, Dave."

'What kind of problem?"

"The *Hanfield* was sunk off Pyongyang in March."

"Oh."

"Dreiser is listed as missing in action."

I didn't say anything. I nodded, and waited.

"A telegram was sent to Mrs. Dreiser at the Bronx address. The Navy says the telegram was delivered and signed for by Alice Dreiser."

"Let's wait for Artie to call in," I said.

We ordered more coffee and waited. Pat had checked the phone book, and there'd been no listing for either Carl or Alice Dreiser. He'd had a list typed of every Dreiser in the city, and it ran longer than my arm.

"Why didn't you ask the Navy what his parents' names are?" I said.

"I did. Both parents are dead."

"Who does he list as next of kin?"

"His wife. Alice Dreiser."

"Great."

In a half hour, Artie called in. There was no Alice Dreiser living at the Bronx address. The landlady said she'd lived there until April and had left without giving a forwarding address. Yes, she'd had a baby daughter. I told Artie to keep the place staked out, and then buzzed George Tabin and told him to check the Post Office Department for any forwarding address.

When he buzzed back in twenty minutes, he said, "Nothing, Dave. Nothing at all."

We split the available force of men, and I managed to wangle four more men from the lieutenant. Half of us began checking on the Dreisers listed in the phone directory, and the rest of us began checking the diaper services.

The first diaper place I called on had a manager who needed only a beard to look like Santa Claus. He greeted me affably and offered all his assistance. Unfortunately, they'd never had a customer named Alice Dreiser.

At my fourth stop, I got what looked like a lead.

I spoke directly to the vice-president, and he listened intently.

"Perhaps," he said, "perhaps." He was a big man, with a wide waist, a gold watch chain spraddling it. He leaned over and pushed down on his intercom buzzer.

"Yes, sir?"

"Bring in a list of our customers. Starting with November of 1952."

"Sir?"

"Starting with November of 1952."

"Yes, sir."

We chatted about the diaper business in general until the list came, and then he handed it to me and I began checking off the names. There were a hell of a lot of names on it. For the month of December, I found a listing for Alice Dreiser. The address given was the one we'd checked in the Bronx.

"Here she is," I said. "Can you get her records?"

The vice-president looked at the name. "Certainly, just a moment." He buzzed his secretary again, told her what he wanted, and she brought the yellow file cards in a few minutes later. The cards told me that Alice Dreiser had continued the diaper service through February. She'd been late on her February payment, and had cancelled service in March. She'd had the diapers delivered for the first week in March but had not paid for them. She did not notify the company that she was moving. She had not returned the diapers they'd sent her that first week in March. The company did not know where she was.

"If you find her," the vice-president told me, "I'd like to know. She owes us money."

"I'll keep that in mind," I said.

The reports on the Dreisers were waiting for me back at the precinct. George had found a couple who claimed to be Carl's aunt and uncle. They knew he was married. They gave Alice's maiden name as Grant. They said she lived somewhere on Walton Avenue in the Bronx, or at least *had* lived there when Carl first met her, they hadn't seen either her or Carl for months. Yes, they knew the Dreisers had had a daughter. They'd received an announcement card. They had never seen the baby.

Pat and I looked up the Grants on Walton Avenue, found a listing for Peter Grant, and went there together.

A bald man in his undershirt, his suspenders hanging over his trousers, opened the door.

"What is it?" he asked.

"Police officers," I said. "We'd like to ask a few questions."

"What about? Let me see your badges."

Pat and I flashed our buzzers and the bald man studied them.

"What kind of questions do you want to ask?"

"Are you Peter Grant?"

"Yeah, that's right. What's this all about?"

"May we come in?"

"Sure, come on in." We followed him into the apartment, and he motioned us to chairs in the small living room. "Now, what is it?" he asked.

"Your daughter is Alice Dreiser?"

"Yes," he said.

"Do you know where she lives?"

"No."

"Come on, mister," Pat said. "You know where your daughter lives."

"I don't," Grant snapped, "and I don't give a damn, either."

"Why? What's wrong, mister?"

"Nothing. Nothing's wrong. It's none of your business, anyway."

"Her daughter had her neck broken," I said. "It is our business."

"I don't give a . . ." he started to say. He stopped then and looked straight ahead of him, his brows pulled together into a tight frown. "I'm sorry. I still don't know where she lives."

"Did you know she was married?"

"To that sailor. Yes, I knew."

"And you knew she had a daughter?"

"Don't make me laugh," Grant said.

"What's funny, mister?" Pat said.

"Did I know she had a daughter? Why the hell do you think she married the sailor? Don't make me laugh!"

"When was your daughter married, Mr. Grant?"

"Last September." He saw the look on my face, and added, "Go ahead, you count it. The kid was born in November."

"Have you seen her since the marriage?"

"No."

"Have you ever seen the baby?"

"No."

"Do you have a picture of your daughter?"

"I think so. Is she in trouble? Do you think she did it?"

"We don't know who did it yet."

"Maybe she did," Grant said softly. "She just maybe did. I'll get you the picture."

He came back in a few minutes with a picture of a plain girl wearing a cap and gown. She had light eyes and straight hair, and her face was intently serious.

"She favors her mother," Grant said, "God rest her soul."

"Your wife is dead?"

"Yes. That picture was taken when Alice graduated high school. She graduated in June and married the sailor in September. She's . . . she's only just nineteen now, you know."

"May we have this?"

He hesitated and said, "It's the only one I've got. She . . . she didn't take many pictures. She wasn't a very . . . pretty kid."

"We'll return it."

"All right," he said. His eyes began to blink. "She . . . If she's in trouble, you'll . . . you'll let me know, won't you?"

"We'll let you know."

"Kids . . . kids make mistakes sometimes." He stood up abruptly. "Let me know."

We had copies of the photo made, and then we staked out every church in the neighborhood in which the baby was found. Pat and I covered the Church of the Holy Mother, because we figured the suspect was most likely to come back there.

We didn't talk much. There is something about a church of any denomination that makes a man think rather than talk. Pat and I knocked off at about seven every night, and the night boys took over then. We were back on the job at seven in the morning, every morning.

It was a week before she came in.

She was a thin girl, with the body of a child and a pinched, tired face. She stopped at the font in the rear of the church, dipped her hand in the holy water, and crossed herself. Then she walked to the altar, stopped before an idol of the Virgin Mary, lighted a candle, and knelt before it.

"That's her," I said.

"Let's go," Pat answered.

"Not here. Outside."

Pat's eyes locked with mine for an instant. "Sure," he said.

She knelt before the idol for a long time, and then got to her feet slowly, drying her eyes. She walked up the aisle, stopped at the font, crossed herself, and then walked outside.

We followed her out, catching up with her at the corner. I pulled up on one side of her and Pat on the other.

"Mrs. Dreiser?" I asked.

She stopped walking. "Yes?"

I showed my buzzer. "Police officers," I said. "We'd like to ask some questions."

She stared at my face for a long time. She drew a trembling breath then, and said, "I killed her. I . . . Carl was dead, you see. I . . . I guess that was it. It wasn't right—his getting killed, I mean. And she was crying." She nodded blankly. "Yes, that was it. She just cried all the time, not knowing that I was crying inside. You don't know how I cried inside. Carl . . . he was all I had. I . . . I couldn't stand it anymore. I told her to shut up and when she didn't I . . . I . . . ."

"Come on now, ma'm," I said.

"I brought her to the church." She nodded, remembering it all now. "She was innocent, you know. So I brought her to the church. Did you find her there?"

"Yes, ma'm," I said. "That's where we found her."

She seemed pleased. A small smile covered her mouth and she said, "I'm glad you found her."

She told the story again to the lieutenant. Pat and I checked out and on the way to the subway, I asked him, "Do you still want to pull the switch, Pat?"

He didn't answer.

ROSS MACDONALD

(1915–1983)

||||||||||||||||||||||||||||||||||||||||||||||| ■ |||||||||||||||||||||||||||||||||||||||||||||

Ross Macdonald was the intellectual of American detective fiction, an honors graduate with a doctorate in literature, and a master of the simile. He might also be called the poet of the dysfunctional family, the abandoned child, and the sins of the father bearing fruit in later generations. His peers gave Macdonald almost every honor the genre has to offer—including the Mystery Writers of America's Grand Master award, the Gold Dagger of the British Crime Writers, the Lifetime Achievement Award of the Private Eye Writers of America, and the Popular Culture Association's Award for Excellence.

Macdonald was born as Kenneth Millar, an only child, in Los Gatos, California. The family moved to Vancouver, British Columbia. There the father abandoned his wife and child when the latter was three, and the boy spent his formative years living with various relatives. His first story was published when he was a teenage student in Ontario. The same edition of the magazine published a story by another student, Margaret Sturm. The two were married after his graduation from college.

As Kenneth Millar, Macdonald wrote short fiction and four novels, which gained little attention, before inventing Lew Archer in *The Moving Target* in 1949. Since his wife, Margaret Millar, had already established herself as an author, he published *The Moving Target* under the name John Macdonald. To avoid confusion with the writer John D. MacDonald, he then wrote as John Ross Macdonald and, beginning in 1956, used only the pen name Ross Macdonald.

Macdonald's protagonist, Archer, is a private investigator in the line of Dashiell Hammett's Sam Spade and Raymond Chandler's Philip Marlowe. In him, Spade's hard-edged, cryptic cynicism and Marlowe's moral romanticism are replaced with a sort of sympathetic applied psychology. Archer finds his solutions to crimes less in the physical evidence of bloodstains, hairs, and footprints than in the damaged lives of the victim's family.

In many of Macdonald's books, the violence under investigation is traced back a generation or two to a family abandonment or betrayal. One thinks of Macdonald's own life and remembers that he once said that the fictional sleuth is the author's way of dealing with emotional material too hard to handle otherwise. Whatever the driving force behind his work, it opened the gates to more and better psychological detective fiction.

"Guilt-Edged Blonde," a typical Macdonald story, gives us a crime in a dysfunctional family and a look at the skill with language that made the author famous. The man who meets Archer's plane "wore a stained tan windbreaker, baggy slacks, a hat as squashed and dubious as his face." More typical of Macdonald's style, his eyes were "dark and evasive, moving here and there as if to

512

avoid getting hurt. He had been hurt often and badly, I guessed." Only Chandler could have said it better.

1954

Guilt-Edged Blonde

■

A man was waiting for me at the gate at the edge of the runway. He didn't look like the man I expected to meet. He wore a stained tan windbreaker, baggy slacks, a hat as squashed and dubious as his face. He must have been forty years old, to judge by the gray in his hair and the lines around his eyes. His eyes were dark and evasive, moving here and there as if to avoid getting hurt. He had been hurt often and badly, I guessed.

"You Archer?"

I said I was. I offered him my hand. He didn't know what to do with it. He regarded it suspiciously, as if I was planning to try a Judo hold on him. He kept his hands in the pockets of his windbreaker.

"I'm Harry Nemo." His voice was a grudging whine. It cost him an effort to give his name away. "My brother told me to come and pick you up. You ready to go?"

"As soon as I get my luggage."

I collected my overnight bag at the counter in the empty waiting room. The bag was very heavy for its size. It contained, besides a toothbrush and spare linen, two guns and the ammunition for them. A .38 special for sudden work, and a .32 automatic as a spare.

Harry Nemo took me outside to his car. It was a new seven-passenger custom job, as long and black as death. The windshield and side windows were very thick, and they had the yellowish tinge of bulletproof glass.

"Are you expecting to be shot at?"

"Not me." His smile was dismal. "This is Nick's car."

"Why didn't Nick come himself?"

He looked around the deserted field. The plane I had arrived on was a flashing speck in the sky above the red sun. The only human being in sight was the operator in the control tower. But Nemo leaned towards me in the seat, and spoke in a whisper:

"Nick's a scared pigeon. He's scared to leave the house. Ever since this morning."

"What happened this morning?"

"Didn't he tell you? You talked to him on the phone."

"He didn't say very much. He told me he wanted to hire a body-guard for six days, until his boat sails. He didn't tell me why."

"They're gunning for him, that's why. He went to the beach this morning. He has a private beach along the back of his ranch, and he went down there by himself for his morning dip. Somebody took a shot at him from the top of the bluff. Five or six shots. He was in the water, see, with no gun handy. He told me the slugs were splashing around him like hailstones. He ducked and swam under water out to sea. Lucky for him he's a good swimmer, or he wouldn't of got away. It's no wonder he's scared. It means they caught up with him, see."

"Who are 'they,' or is that a family secret?"

Nemo turned from the wheel to peer into my face. His breath was sour, his look incredulous. "Christ, don't you know who Nick is? Didn't he tell you?"

"He's a lemon-grower, isn't he?"

"He is now."

"What did he used to be?"

The bitter beaten face closed on itself. "I oughtn't to be flapping at the mouth. He can tell you himself if he wants to."

Two hundred horses yanked us away from the curb. I rode with my heavy leather bag on my knees. Nemo drove as if driving was the one thing in life he enjoyed, rapt in silent communion with the engine. It whisked us along the highway, then down a gradual incline between geometrically planted lemon groves. The sunset sea glimmered red at the foot of the slope.

Before we reached it, we turned off the blacktop into a private lane which ran like a straight hair-parting between the dark green trees. Straight for half a mile or more to a low house in a clearing.

The house was flat-roofed, made of concrete and fieldstone, with an attached garage. All of its windows were blinded with heavy draperies. It was surrounded with well-kept shrubbery and lawn, the lawn with a ten-foot wire fence surmounted by barbed wire.

Nemo stopped in front of the closed and padlocked gate, and honked the horn. There was no response. He honked the horn again.

About halfway between the house and the gate, a crawling thing came out of the shrubbery. It was a man, moving very slowly on hands and knees. His head hung down almost to the ground. One side of his head was bright red, as if he had fallen in paint. He left a jagged red trail in the gravel of the driveway.

Harry Nemo said, "Nick!" He scrambled out of the car. "What happened, Nick?"

The crawling man lifted his heavy head and looked at us. Cumbrously, he rose to his feet. He came forward with his legs spraddled and loose, like a huge infant learning to walk. He breathed loudly and horribly, looking at us with a dreadful hopefulness. Then he died on his feet, still walking. I saw the change in his face before it struck the gravel.

Harry Nemo went over the fence like a weary monkey, snagging his slacks on the barbed wire. He knelt beside his brother and turned him over and palmed his chest. He stood up shaking his head.

I had my bag unzipped and my hand on the revolver. I went to the gate. "Open up, Harry."

Harry was saying, "They got him," over and over. He crossed himself several times. "The dirty bastards."

"Open up, " I said.

He found a key ring in the dead man's pocket and opened the padlocked gate. Our dragging footsteps crunched the gravel. I looked down at the specks of gravel in Nicky Nemo's eyes, the bullet hole in the temple.

"Who got him, Harry?"

"I dunno. Fats Jordan, or Artie Castola, or Faronese. It must have been one of them."

"The Purple Gang."

"You called it. Nicky was their treasurer back in the thirties. He was the one that didn't get into the papers. He handled the payoff, see. When the heat went on and the gang got busted up, he had some money in a safe deposit box. He was the only one that got away."

"How much money?"

"Nicky never told me. All I know, he come out here before the war and bought a thousand acres of lemon land. It took them fifteen years to catch up with him. He always knew they were gonna, though. He knew it."

"Artie Castola got off the Rock last spring."

"You're telling me. That's when Nicky bought himself the bulletproof car and put up the fence."

"Are they gunning for you?"

He looked around at the darkening groves and the sky. The sky was streaked with running red, as if the sun had died a violent death.

"I dunno," he answered nervously. "They got no reason to. I'm as clean as soap. I never been in the rackets. Not since I was young, anyway. The wife made me go straight, see?"

I said: "We better get into the house and call the police."

The front door was standing a few inches ajar. I could see at the edge that it was sheathed with quarter-inch steel plate. Harry put my thoughts into words.

"Why in hell would he go outside? He was safe as houses as long as he stayed inside."

"Did he live alone?"

"More or less alone."

"What does that mean?"

He pretended not to hear me, but I got some kind of an answer. Looking through the doorless arch into the living room, I saw a leopardskin coat folded across the back of the chesterfield. There were red-tipped cigarette butts mingled with cigar butts in the ash trays.

"Nicky was married?"

"Not exactly."

"You know the woman?"

"Naw." But he was lying.

Somewhere behind the thick walls of the house, there was a creak of springs, a crashing bump, the broken roar of a cold engine, grinding of tires in gravel. I got to the door in time to see a cerise convertible hurtling down the driveway. The top was down, and a yellow-haired girl was small and intent at the wheel. She swerved around Nick's body and got through the gate somehow, with her tires screaming. I aimed at the right rear tire, and missed. Harry came up behind me. He pushed my gun-arm down before I could fire again. The convertible disappeared in the direction of the highway.

"Let her go," he said.

"Who is she?"

He thought about it, his slow brain clicking almost audibly. "I dunno. Some pig that Nicky picked up some place. Her name is Flossie or Florrie or something. She didn't shoot him, if that's what you're worried about."

"You know her pretty well, do you?"

"The hell I do. I don't mess with Nicky's dames." He tried to work up a rage to go with the strong words, but he didn't have the makings. The best he could produce was petulance: "Listen, mister, why should you hang around? The guy that hired you is dead."

"I haven't been paid, for one thing."

"I'll fix that."

He trotted across the lawn to the body and came back with an alligator billfold. It was thick with money.

"How much?"

"A hundred will do it."

He handed me a hundred-dollar bill. "Now how about you amscray, bud, before the law gets here?"

"I need transportation."

"Take Nicky's car. He won't be using it. You can park it at the airport and leave the key with the agent."

"I can, eh?"

"Sure. I'm telling you you can."

"Aren't you getting a little free with your brother's property?"

"It's my property now, bud." A bright thought struck him, disorganizing his face. "Incidentally, how would you like to get off my land?"

"I'm staying, Harry. I like this place. I always say it's people that make a place."

The gun was still my hand. He looked down at it.

"Get on the telephone, Harry. Call the police."

"Who do you think you are, ordering me around? I took my last order from anybody, see?" He glanced over his shoulder at the dark and shapeless object on the gravel, and spat venomously.

"I'm a citizen, working for Nicky. Not for you."

He changed his tune very suddenly "How much to go to work for me?"

"Depends on the line of work."

He manipulated the alligator wallet. "Here's another hundred. If you got to hang around, keep the lip buttoned down about the dame, eh? Is it a deal?"

I didn't answer, but I took the money. I put it in a separate pocket by itself. Harry telephoned the county sheriff.

He emptied the ash trays before the sheriff's men arrived, and stuffed the leopardskin coat into the woodbox. I sat and watched him.

We spent the next two hours with loud-mouthed deputies. They were angry with the dead man for having the kind of past that attracted bullets. They were angry with Harry for being his brother. They were secretly angry with themselves for being inexperienced and incompetent. They didn't even uncover the leopardskin coat.

Harry Nemo left for the courthouse first. I waited for him to leave, and followed him home, on foot.

Where a leaning palm tree reared its ragged head above the pavements, there was a court lined with jerry-built frame cottages. Harry turned up the walk between them and entered the first cottage. Light flashed on his face from inside. I heard a woman's voice say something to him. Then light and sound were cut off by the closing door.

An old gabled house with boarded-up windows stood opposite the court. I crossed the street and settled down in the shadows of its veranda to watch Harry Nemo's cottage. Three cigarettes later, a tall woman in a dark hat and a light coat came out of the cottage and walked briskly to the corner and out of sight. Two cigarettes after that, she reappeared at the corner on my side of the street, still walking briskly. I noticed that she had a large straw handbag under her arm. Her face was long and stony under the streetlight.

Leaving the street, she marched up the broken sidewalk to the veranda where I was leaning against the shadowed wall. The stairs groaned under her decisive footsteps. I put my hand on the gun in my pocket, and waited. With the rigid assurance of a WAC corporal marching at the head of her platoon, she crossed the veranda to me, a thin high-shouldered silhouette against the light from the corner. Her hand was in her straw bag, and the end of the bag was pointed at my stomach. Her shadowed face was a gleam of eyes, a glint of teeth.

"I wouldn't try it if I were you," she said. "I have a gun here, and the safety is off, and I know how to shoot it, mister."

"Congratulations."

"I'm not joking." Her deep contralto rose a notch. "Rapid fire used to be my specialty. So you better take your hands out of your pockets."

I showed her my hands, empty. Moving very quickly, she relieved my pocket of the weight of my gun, and frisked me for other weapons.

"Who are you, mister?" she said as she stepped back. "You can't be Arturo Castola, you're not old enough."

"Are you a policewoman?"

"I'll ask the questions. What are you doing here?"

"Waiting for a friend."

"You're a liar. You've been watching my house for an hour and a half. I tabbed you through the window."

"So you went and bought yourself a gun?"

"I did. You followed Harry home. I'm Mrs. Nemo, and I want to know why."

"Harry's the friend I'm waiting for."

"You're a double liar. Harry's afraid of you. You're no friend of his."

"That depends on Harry. I'm a detective."

She snorted. "Very likely. Where's your buzzer?"

"I'm a private detective," I said. "I have identification in my wallet."

"Show me. And don't try any tricks."

I produced my photostat. She held it up to the light from the street, and handed it back to me. "So you're a detective. You better do something about your tailing technique. It's obvious."

"I didn't know I was dealing with a cop."

"I was a cop," she said. "Not any more."

"Then give me back my .38. It cost me seventy dollars."

"First tell me, what's your interest in my husband? Who hired you?"

"Nick, your brother-in-law. He called me in Los Angeles today, said he needed a bodyguard for a week. Didn't Harry tell you?"

She didn't answer.

"By the time I got to Nick, he didn't need a bodyguard, or anything. But I thought I'd stick around and see what I could find out about his death. He was a client, after all."

"You should pick your clients more carefully."

"What about picking brothers-in-law?"

She shook her head stiffly. The hair that escaped from under her hat was almost white. "I'm not responsible for Nick or anything about him. Harry is my responsibility. I met him in line of duty and I straightened him out, understand? I tore him loose from Detroit and the rackets, and I brought him out here. I couldn't cut him off from his brother entirely. But he hasn't been in trouble since I married him. Not once."

"Until now."

"Harry isn't in trouble now."

"Not yet. Not officially."

"What do you mean?"

"Give me my gun, and put yours down. I can't talk into iron."

She hesitated, a grim and anxious woman under pressure. I wondered what quirk of fate or psychology had married her to a hood, and decided it must have been love. Only love would send a woman across a dark street to face down an unknown gunman. Mrs. Nemo was horse-faced and aging and not pretty, but she had courage.

She handed me my gun. Its butt was soothing to the palm of my hand. I dropped it into my pocket. A gang of Negro boys at loose ends went by in the street, hooting and whistling purposelessly.

She leaned towards me, almost as tall as I was. Her voice was a low sibilance forced between her teeth:

"Harry had nothing to do with his brother's death. You're crazy if you think so."

"What makes you so sure, Mrs. Nemo?"

"Harry couldn't, that's all. I know Harry, I can read him like a book.

Even if he had the guts, which he hasn't, he wouldn't dare to think of killing Nick. Nick was his older brother, understand, the successful one in the family." Her voice rasped contemptuously. "In spite of everything I could do or say, Harry worshipped Nick right up to the end."

"Those brotherly feelings sometimes cut two ways. And Harry had a lot to gain."

"Not a cent. Nothing."

"He's Nick's heir, isn't he?"

"Not as long as he stays married to me. I wouldn't let him touch a cent of Nick Nemo's filthy money. Is that clear?"

"It's clear to me. But is it clear to Harry?"

"I made it clear to him, many times. Anyway, this is ridiculous. Harry wouldn't lay a finger on that precious brother of his."

"Maybe he didn't do it himself. He could have had it done for him. I know he's covering for somebody."

"Who?"

"A blonde girl left the house after we arrived. She got away in a cherry-colored convertible. Harry recognized her."

"A cherry-colored convertible?"

"Yes. Does that mean something to you?"

"No. Nothing in particular. She must have been one of Nick's girls. He always had girls."

"Why would Harry cover for her?"

"What do you mean, cover for her?"

"She left a leopardskin coat behind. Harry hid it, and paid me not to tell the police."

"Harry did that?"

"Unless I'm having delusions."

"Maybe you are at that. If you think that Harry paid that girl to shoot Nick, or had anything—"

"I know. Don't say it. I'm crazy."

Mrs. Nemo laid a thin hand on my arm. "Anyway, lay off Harry. Please. I have a hard enough time handling him as it is. He's worse than my first husband. The first one was a drunk, believe it or not." She glanced at the lighted cottage across the street, and I saw one half of her bitter smile. "I wonder what makes a woman go for the lame ducks the way I did."

"I wouldn't know, Mrs. Nemo. Okay, I lay off Harry."

But I had no intention of laying off Harry. When she went back to her cottage, I walked around three-quarters of the block and took up a new position in the doorway of a dry-cleaning establishment. This time

I didn't smoke. I didn't even move, except to look at my watch from time to time.

Around eleven o'clock, the lights went out behind the blinds in the Nemo cottage. Shortly before midnight the front door opened and Harry slipped out. He looked up and down the street and began to walk. He passed within six feet of my dark doorway, hustling along in a kind of furtive shuffle.

Working very cautiously, at a distance, I tailed him downtown. He disappeared into the lighted cavern of an all night garage. He came out of the garage a few minutes later, driving a prewar Chevrolet.

My money also talked to the attendant. I drew a prewar Buick which would still do seventy-five. I proved that it would, as soon as I hit the highway. I reached the entrance to Nick Nemo's private lane in time to see Harry's lights approaching the dark ranch house.

I cut my lights and parked at the roadside a hundred yards below the entrance to the lane, and facing it. The Chevrolet reappeared in a few minutes. Harry was still alone in the front seat. I followed it blind as far as the highway before I risked my lights. Then down the highway to the edge of town.

In the middle of the motel and drive-in district he turned off onto a side road and in under a neon sign which spelled out TRAILER COURT across the darkness. The trailers stood along the bank of a dry creek. The Chevrolet stopped in front of one of them, which had a light in the window. Harry got out with a spotted bundle under his arm. He knocked on the door of the trailer.

I U-turned at the next corner and put in more waiting time. The Chevrolet rolled out under the neon sign and turned towards the highway. I let it go.

Leaving my car, I walked along the creek bank to the lighted trailer. The windows were curtained. The cerise convertible was parked on its far side. I tapped on the aluminum door.

"Harry?" a girl's voice said. "Is that you, Harry?"

I muttered something indistinguishable. The door opened, and the yellow-haired girl looked out. She was very young, but her round blue eyes were heavy and sick with hangover, or remorse. She had on a nylon slip, nothing else.

"What is this?"

She tried to shut the door. I held it open.

"Get away from here. Leave me alone. I'll scream."

"All right. Scream."

She opened her mouth. No sound came out. She closed her mouth again. It was small and fleshy and defiant. "Who are you? Law?"

"Close enough. I'm coming in."

"Come in then, damn you. I got nothing to hide."

"I can see that."

I brushed in past her. There were dead Martinis on her breath. The little room was a jumble of feminine clothes, silk and cashmere and tweed and gossamer nylon, some of them flung on the floor, others hung up to dry. The leopardskin coat lay on the bunk bed, staring with innumerable bold eyes. She picked it up and covered her shoulders with it. Unconsciously, her nervous hands began to pick the wood-chips out of the fur. I said:

"Harry did you a favor, didn't he?"

"Maybe he did."

"Have you been doing any favors for Harry?"

"Such as?"

"Such as knocking off his brother."

"You're way off the beam, mister. I was very fond of Uncle Nick."

"Why run out on the killing then?"

"I panicked," she said. "It would happen to any girl. I was asleep when he got it, see, passed out if you want the truth. I heard the gun go off. It woke me up, but it took me quite a while to bring myself to and sober up enough to put my clothes on. By the time I made it to the bedroom window, Harry was back, with some guy." She peered into my face. "Were you the guy?"

I nodded.

"I thought so. I thought you were the law at the time. I saw Nick lying there in the driveway, all bloody, and I put two and two together and got trouble. Bad trouble for me, unless I got out. So I got out. It wasn't nice to do, after what Nick meant to me, but it was the only sensible thing. I got my career to think of."

"What career is that?"

"Modeling. Acting. Uncle Nick was gonna send me to school."

"Unless you talk, you'll finish your education at Corona. Who shot Nick?"

A thin edge of terror entered her voice. "I don't know, I tell you. I was passed out in the bedroom. I didn't see nothing."

"Why did Harry bring you your coat?"

"He didn't want me to get involved. He's my father, after all."

"Harry Nemo is your father?"

"Yes."

"You'll have to do better than that. What's your name?"

"Jeannine. Jeannine Larue."

"Why isn't your name Nemo if Harry is your father? Why do you call him Harry?"

"He's my stepfather, I mean."

"Sure," I said. "And Nick was really your uncle, and you were having a family reunion with him."

"He wasn't any blood relation to me. I always called him uncle, though."

"If Harry's your father, why don't you live with him?"

"I used to. Honest. This is the truth I'm telling you. I had to get out on account of the old lady. The old lady hates my guts. She's a real creep, a square. She can't stand for a girl to have any fun. Just because my old man was a rummy—"

"What's your idea of fun, Jeannine?"

She shook her feathercut hair at me. It exhaled a heavy perfume which was worth its weight in blood. She bared one pearly shoulder and smiled an artificial hustler's smile. "What's yours? Maybe we can get together."

"You mean the way you got together with Nick?"

"You're prettier than him."

"I'm also smarter, I hope. Is Harry really your stepfather?"

"Ask him if you don't believe me. Ask him. He lives in a place on Tule Street—I don't remember the number."

"I know where he lives."

But Harry wasn't at home. I knocked on the door of the frame cottage and got no answer. I turned the knob and found that the door was unlocked. There was a light behind it. The other cottages in the court were dark. It was long past midnight, and the street was deserted. I went into the cottage, preceded by my gun.

A ceiling bulb glared down on sparse and threadbare furniture, a time-eaten rug. Besides the living room, the house contained a cubbyhole of a bedroom and a closet kitchenette. Everything in the poverty-stricken place was pathetically clean. There were moral mottoes on the walls, and one picture. It was a photograph of a tow-headed girl in a teen-age party dress. Jeannine, before she learned that a pretty face and a sleek body could buy her the things she wanted. The things she thought she wanted.

For some reason, I felt sick. I went outside. Somewhere out of sight, an old car-engine muttered. Its muttering grew on the night. Harry Nemo's rented Chevrolet turned the corner under the streetlight. Its front wheels were weaving. One of the wheels climbed the curb in front of the cottage. The Chevrolet came to a halt at a drunken angle.

I crossed the sidewalk and opened the car door. Harry was at the wheel, clinging to it desperately as if he needed it to hold him up. His chest was bloody. His mouth was bright with blood. He spoke through it thickly:

"She got me."

"Who got you, Harry? Jeannine?"

"No. Not her. She was the reason for it, though. We had it coming."

Those were his final words. I caught his body as it fell sideways out of the seat. I laid it out on the sidewalk and left it for the cop on the beat to find.

I drove across town to the trailer court. Jeannine's trailer still had light in it, filtered through the curtains over the windows. I pushed the door open.

The girl was packing a suitcase on the bunk bed. She looked at me over her shoulder, and froze. Her blonde head was cocked like a frightened bird's, hypnotized by my gun.

"Where are you off to, kid?"

"Out of this town. I'm getting out."

"You have some talking to do first."

She straightened up. "I told you all I know. You didn't believe me. What's the matter, didn't you get to see Harry?"

"I saw him. Harry's dead. Your whole family is dying like flies."

She half-turned and sat down limply on the disordered bed. "Dead? You think I did it?"

"I think you know who did. Harry said before he died that you were the reason for it all."

"Me the reason for it?" Her eyes widened in false naiveté, but there was thought behind them, quick and desperate thought. "You mean that Harry got killed on account of me?"

"Harry and Nick both. It was a woman who shot them."

"God," she said. The desperate thought behind her eyes crystallized into knowledge. Which I shared.

The aching silence was broken by a big diesel rolling by on the highway. She said above its roar:

"That crazy old bat. So *she* killed Nick."

"You're talking about your mother. Mrs. Nemo."

"Yeah."

"Did you see her shoot him?"

"No. I was blotto like I told you. But I saw her out there this week, keeping an eye on the house. She's always watched me like a hawk."

"Is that why you were getting out of town? Because you knew she killed Nick?"

"Maybe it was. I don't know. I wouldn't let myself think about it."

Her blue gaze shifted from my face to something behind me. I turned. Mrs. Nemo was in the doorway. She was hugging the straw bag to her thin chest.

Her right hand dove into the bag. I shot her in the right arm. She leaned against the doorframe and held her dangling arm with her left hand. Her face was granite in whose crevices her eyes were like live things caught.

The gun she dropped was a cheap .32 revolver, its nickel plating worn and corroded. I spun the cylinder. One shot had been fired from it.

"This accounts for Harry," I said. "You didn't shoot Nick with this gun, not at that distance."

"No." She was looking down at her dripping hand. "I used my old police gun on Nick Nemo. After I killed him, I threw the gun into the sea. I didn't know I'd have further use for a gun. I bought that little suicide gun tonight."

"To use on Harry?"

"To use on you. I thought you were on to me. I didn't know until you told me that Harry knew about Nick and Jeannine."

"Jeannine is your daughter by your first husband?"

"My only daughter." She said to the girl: "I did it for you, Jeannine. I've seen too much—the awful things that can happen."

The girl didn't answer. I said:

"I can understand why you shot Nick. But why did Harry have to die?"

"Nick paid him," she said. "Nick paid him for Jeannine. I found Harry in a bar an hour ago, and he admitted it. I hope I killed him."

"You killed him, Mrs. Nemo. What brought you here? Was Jeannine the third on your list?"

"No. No. She's my own girl. I came to tell her what I did for her. I wanted her to know."

She looked at the girl on the bed. Her eyes were terrible with pain and love. The girl said in a stunned voice:

"Mother. You're hurt. I'm sorry."

"Let's go, Mrs. Nemo," I said.

REX STOUT

(1886–1975)

|||||||||||||||||||||||||||||||||||||||||||||||| ■ ||||||||||||||||||||||||||||||||||||||||||||||||

Rex Stout's great sleuthing team, Nero Wolfe and Archie Goodwin, is often compared with the Sherlock Holmes and Dr. John H. Watson duo of Sir Arthur Conan Doyle. There are many similarities. Both pairs share digs at addresses so real to their readers that they draw aficionados to their doors. Both masterminds are unmarried and, with rare exceptions, shun women. Both sleuths are eccentric geniuses who solve mysteries in the tradition of Edgar Allan Poe's Chevalier Auguste Dupin, by remarkable powers of reasoning. But the greatest similarity between the teams is that both succeed in becoming so real to their readers that the characters take on lives of their own.

The differences are also obvious. Unlike the lanky Holmes, Wolfe is literally larger than life. His girth and his inclination to reclusiveness and physical inactivity lead him to hire sidekick Archie Goodwin to do his legwork. Goodwin is much more than a passive and admiring narrator. He is the professional collector of data and doer of dangerous deeds, freeing Wolfe to stay home to nurture his orchids (as faithfully as Wilkie Collins's Sergeant Cuff of *The Moonstone* nurtured his roses). More important, Goodwin's telling of the tale is spiced by his irritation and disgruntlement with his employer and friend. This and the gallery of lively characters who populate the tales add considerably to the interest of the puzzle that Stout creates.

Named a Grand Master by the Mystery Writers of America, Stout was a downright excellent writer. He came by that skill as all writers do—by reading. He was born in Indiana but raised in a Kansas farmhouse that had more than a thousand books on its shelves, all of which he says he had read by his eleventh birthday. He was a talented student with a great memory and a love of poetry and politics. Stout was already forty-eight when he published *Fer-de-Lance* in 1934 and gave the world Wolfe and Goodwin. Before this, he founded a school-banking system and published eight mainstream novels. But his forte, fame, and fortune lay in detective fiction.

Stout may have written "Christmas Party" to satisfy the demand of magazine editors for such material for the holiday season. At the same time, however, it gave him a creditable way to have Wolfe break his habits of reclusiveness and leave his brownstone on business and to celebrate, as detective fiction so often does, the power of cerebration and of friendship between men.

1957

Christmas Party

■

"I'm sorry, sir," I said. I tried to sound sorry. "But I told you two days ago, Monday, that I had a date for Friday afternoon, and you said all right. So I'll drive you to Long Island Saturday or Sunday."

Nero Wolfe shook his head. "That won't do. Mr. Thompson's ship docks Friday morning, and he will be at Mr. Hewitt's place only until Saturday noon, when he leaves for New Orleans. As you know, he is the best hybridizer in England, and I am grateful to Mr. Hewitt for inviting me to spend a few hours with him. As I remember, the drive takes about an hour and a half, so we should leave at twelve-thirty."

I decided to count ten, and swiveled my chair, facing my desk, so as to have privacy for it. As usual when we have no important case going, we had been getting on each other's nerves for a week, and I admit I was a little touchy, but his taking it for granted like that was a little too much. When I had finished the count I turned my head, to where he was perched on this throne behind his desk, and darned if he hadn't gone back to his book, making it plain that he regarded it as settled. That was much too much. I swiveled my chair to confront him.

"I really am sorry," I said, not trying to sound sorry, "but I have to keep that date Friday afternoon. It's a Christmas party at the office of Kurt Bottweill—you remember him, we did a job for him a few months ago, the stolen tapestries. You may not remember a member of his staff named Margot Dickey, but I do. I have been seeing her some, and I promised her I'd go to the party. We never have a Christmas office party here. As for going to Long Island, your idea that a car is a death trap if I'm not driving it is unsound. You can take a taxi, or hire a Baxter man, or get Saul Panzer to drive you."

Wolfe had lowered his book. "I hope to get some useful information from Mr. Thompson, and you will take notes."

"Not if I'm not there. Hewitt's secretary knows orchid terms as well as I do. So do you."

I admit those last three words were a bit strong, but he shouldn't have gone back to his book. His lips tightened. "Archie. How many times in the past year have I asked you to drive me somewhere?"

"If you call it asking, maybe eighteen or twenty."

"Not excessive, surely. If my feeling that you alone are to be trusted at the wheel of a car is an aberration, I have it. We will leave for Mr. Hewitt's place Friday at twelve-thirty."

So there we were. I took a breath, but I didn't need to count ten again. If he was to be taught a lesson, and he certainly needed one, luckily I had in my possession a document that would make it good. Reaching to my inside breast pocket, I took out a folded sheet of paper.

"I didn't intend," I told him, "to spring this on you until tomorrow, or maybe even later, but I guess it will have to be now. Just as well, I suppose."

I left my chair, unfolded the paper, and handed it to him. He put his book down to take it, gave it a look, shot a glance at me, looked at the paper again, and let it drop on his desk.

He snorted. "Pfui. What flummery is this?"

"No flummery. As you see, it's a marriage license for Archie Goodwin and Margot Dickey. It cost me two bucks. I could be mushy about it, but I won't. I will only say that if I am hooked at last, it took an expert. She intends to spread the tidings at the Christmas office party, and of course I have to be there. When you announce you have caught a fish it helps to have the fish present in person. Frankly, I would prefer to drive you to Long Island, but it can't be done."

The effect was all I could have asked. He gazed at me through narrowed eyes long enough to count eleven, then picked up the document and gazed at it. He flicked it from him to the edge of the desk as if it were crawling with germs, and focused on me again.

"You are deranged," he said evenly and distinctly. "Sit down."

I nodded. "I suppose," I agreed, remaining upright, "it's a form of madness, but so what if I've got it? Like what Margot was reading to me the other night—some poet, I think it was some Greek—'O love, resistless in thy might, thou triumphest even—'"

"Shut up and sit down!"

"Yes, sir." I didn't move. "But we're not rushing it. We haven't set the date, and there'll be plenty of time to decide on adjustments. You may not want me here any more, but that's up to you. As far as I'm concerned, I would like to stay. My long association with you has had its flaws, but I would hate to end it. The pay is okay, especially if I get a raise the first of the year, which is a week from Monday. I have grown to regard this old brownstone as my home, although you own it and although there are two creaky boards in the floor of my room. I appreciate working for the greatest private detective in the free world, no matter how eccentric he is. I appreciate being able to go up to the plant rooms whenever I feel like it and look at ten thousand orchids, especially the odontoglossums. I fully appreciate—"

"Sit down!"

"I'm too worked up to sit. I fully appreciate Fritz's cooking. I like the billiard table in the basement. I like West Thirty-fifth Street. I like the one-way glass panel in the front door. I like this rug I'm standing on. I like your favorite color, yellow. I have told Margot all this, and more, including the fact that you are allergic to women. We have discussed it, and we think it may be worth trying, say for a month, when we get back from the honeymoon. My room could be our bedroom, and the other room on that floor could be our living room. There are plenty of closets. We could eat with you, as I have been, or we could eat up there, as you prefer. If the trial works out, new furniture or redecorating would be up to us. She will keep her job with Kurt Bottweill, so she wouldn't be here during the day, and since he's an interior decorator we would get things wholesale. Of course we merely suggest this for your consideration. It's your house."

I picked up my marriage license, folded it, and returned it to my pocket.

His eyes had stayed narrow and his lips tight. "I don't believe it," he growled. "What about Miss Rowan?"

"We won't drag Miss Rowan into this," I said stiffly.

"What about the thousands of others you dally with?"

"Not thousands. Not even a thousand. I'll have to look up 'dally.' They'll get theirs, as Margot has got hers. As you see, I'm deranged only up to a point. I realize—"

"Sit down."

"No, sir. I know this will have to be discussed, but right now you're stirred up and it would be better to wait for a day or two, or maybe more. By Saturday the idea of a woman in the house may have you boiling even worse than you are now, or it may have cooled you down to a simmer. If the former, no discussion will be needed. If the latter, you may decide it's worth a try. I hope you do."

I turned and walked out.

In the hall I hesitated. I could have gone up to my room and phoned from there, but in his present state it was quite possible he would listen in from the desk, and the call I wanted to make was personal. So I got my hat and coat from the rack, let myself out, descended the stoop steps, walked to the drugstore on Ninth Avenue, found the booth unoccupied, and dialed a number. In a moment a musical little voice—more a chirp than a voice—was in my ear.

"Kurt Bottweill's studio, good morning."

"This is Archie Goodwin, Cherry. May I speak to Margot?"

"Why, certainly. Just a moment."

It was a fairly long moment. Then another voice. "Archie, darling!"

"Yes, my own. I've got it."

"I knew you could!"

"Sure, I can do anything. Not only that, you said up to a hundred bucks, and I thought I would have to part with twenty at least, but it only took five. And not only that, but it's on me, because I've already had my money's worth of fun out of it, and more. I'll tell you about it when I see you. Shall I send it up by messenger?"

"No, I don't think—I'd better come and get it. Where are you?"

"In a phone booth. I'd just as soon not go back to the office right now because Mr. Wolfe wants to be alone to boil, so how about the Tulip Bar at the Churchill in twenty minutes? I feel like buying you a drink."

"I feel like buying *you* a drink!"

She should, since I was treating her to a marriage license.

II

When, at three o'clock Friday afternoon, I wriggled out of the taxi at the curb in front of the four-story building in the East Sixties, it was snowing. If it kept up, New York might have an off-white Christmas.

During the two days that had passed since I got my money's worth from the marriage license, the atmosphere around Wolfe's place had not been very seasonable. If we had had a case going, frequent and sustained communication would have been unavoidable, but without one there was nothing that absolutely had to be said, and we said it. Our handling of that trying period showed our true natures. At table, for instance, I was polite and reserved, and spoke, when speaking seemed necessary, in low and cultured tones. When Wolfe spoke he either snapped or barked. Neither of us mentioned the state of bliss I was headed for, or the adjustments that would have to be made, or my Friday date with my fiancée, or his trip to Long Island. But he arranged it somehow, for precisely at twelve-thirty on Friday a black limousine drew up in front of the house, and Wolfe, with the brim of his old black hat turned down and the collar of his new gray overcoat turned up for the snow, descended the stoop, stood massively, the mountain of him, on the bottom step until the uniformed chauffeur had opened the door, and crossed the sidewalk and climbed in. I watched it from above, from a window of my room.

I admit I was relieved and felt better. He had unquestionably needed a lesson and I didn't regret giving him one, but if he had passed up a chance for an orchid powwow with the best hybridizer in England I would never have heard the last of it. I went down to the kitchen and ate lunch with Fritz, who was so upset by the atmosphere that he forgot to put the lemon juice in the soufflé. I wanted to console him by telling him that everything would be rosy by Christmas, only three days off, but of course that wouldn't do.

I had a notion to toss a coin to decide whether I would have a look at the new exhibit of dinosaurs at the Natural History Museum or go to the Bottweill party, but I was curious to know how Margot was making out with the license, and also how the other Bottweill personnel were making out with each other. It was surprising that they were still making out at all. Cherry Quon's position in the setup was apparently minor, since she functioned chiefly as a receptionist and phone-answerer, but I had seen her black eyes dart daggers at Margot Dickey, who should have been clear out of her reach. I had gathered that it was Margot who was mainly relied upon to wrangle prospective customers into the corral, that Bottweill himself put them under the spell, and that Alfred Kiernan's part was to make sure that before the spell wore off an order got signed on the dotted line.

Of course that wasn't all. The order had to be filled, and that was handled, under Bottweill's supervision, by Emil Hatch in the workshop. Also funds were required to buy the ingredients, and they were furnished by a specimen named Mrs. Perry Porter Jerome. Margot had told me that Mrs. Jerome would be at the party and would bring her son Leo, whom I had never met. According to Margot, Leo, who had no connection with the Bottweill business or any other business, devoted his time to two important activities: getting enough cash from his mother to keep going as a junior playboy, and stopping the flow of cash to Bottweill, or at least slowing it down.

It was quite a tangle, an interesting exhibit of bipeds alive and kicking, and, deciding it promised more entertainment than the dead dinosaurs, I took a taxi to the East Sixties.

The ground floor of the four-story building, formerly a deluxe double-width residence, was now a beauty shop. The second floor was a real-estate office. The third floor was Kurt Bottweill's workshop, and on top was his studio. From the vestibule I took the do-it-yourself elevator to the top, opened the door, and stepped out into the glossy gold-leaf elegance I had first seen some months back, when Bottweill had hired Wolfe to find out who had swiped some tapestries. On that first visit I had decided that the only big difference between chrome modern and Bottweill gold-leaf modern was the color, and I still thought so. Not even skin deep; just a two-hundred-thousandth of an inch deep. But on the panels and racks and furniture frames it gave the big skylighted studio quite a tone, and the rugs and drapes and pictures, all modern, joined in. It would have been a fine den for a blind millionaire.

"Archie!" a voice called. "Come and help us sample!"

It was Margot Dickey. In a far corner was a gold-leaf bar, some eight feet long, and she was at it on a gold-leaf stool. Cherry Quon and Alfred Kiernan were with her, also on stools, and behind the bar was Santa Claus, pouring from a champagne bottle. It was certainly a modern touch to have Santa Claus tend bar, but there was nothing modern about his costume. He was strictly traditional, cut, color, size, mask, and all, except that the hand grasping the champagne bottle wore a white glove. I assumed, crossing to them over the thick rugs, that that was a touch of Bottweill elegance, and didn't learn until later how wrong I was.

They gave me the season's greetings, and Santa Claus poured a glass of bubbles for me. No gold leaf on the glass. I was glad I had come. To drink champagne with a blonde at one elbow and a brunette at the other gives a man a sense of well-being, and those two were fine specimens—the tall, slender Margot relaxed, all curves, on the stool, and little slant-eyed black-eyed Cherry Quon, who came only up to my collar when standing, sitting with her spine as straight as a plumb line, yet not stiff. I thought Cherry worthy of notice not only as a statuette, though she was highly decorative, but as a possible source of new light on human relations. Margot had told me that her father was half Chinese and half Indian—not American Indian—and her mother was Dutch.

I said that apparently I had come too early, but Alfred Kiernan said no, the others were around and would be in shortly. He added that it was a pleasant surprise to see me, as it was just a little family gathering and he hadn't known others had been invited. Kiernan, whose title was business manager, had not liked a certain step I had taken when I was hunting the tapestries, and he still didn't, but an Irishman at a Christmas party likes everybody. My impression was that he really was pleased, so I was too. Margot said she had invited me, and Kiernan patted her on the arm and said that if she hadn't he would. About my age and fully as handsome, he was the kind who can pat the arm of a queen or a president's wife without making eyebrows go up.

He said we needed another sample and turned to the bartender. "Mr. Claus, we'll try the Veuve Clicquot." To us: "Just like Kurt to provide different brands. No monotony for Kurt." To the bartender: "May I call you by your first name, Santy?"

"Certainly, sir," Santa Claus told him from behind the mask in a thin falsetto that didn't match his size. As he stooped and came up with a bottle a door at the left opened and two men entered. One of them, Emil Hatch, I had met before. When briefing Wolfe on the tapestries and telling us about his staff, Bottweill had called Margot Dickey his contact woman, Cherry Quon his handy girl, and Emil Hatch his pet wizard, and when I met Hatch I found that he both looked the part and acted it. He wasn't much taller than Cherry Quon and skinny, and something had either pushed his left shoulder down or his right shoulder up, making him lop-sided, and he had a sour face, a sour voice, and a sour taste.

When the stranger was named to me as Leo Jerome, that placed him. I was acquainted with his mother, Mrs. Perry Porter Jerome. She was a widow and an angel—that is, Kurt Bottweill's angel. During the investigation she had talked as if the tapestries belonged to her, but that might have only been her manners, of which she had plenty. I could have made guesses about her personal relations with Bottweill, but hadn't bothered. I have enough to do to handle my own personal relations without wasting my brain power on other people's. As for her son Leo, he must have got his physique from his father—tall, bony, big-eared and long-armed. He was probably approaching thirty, below Kiernan but above Margot and Cherry.

When he shoved in between Cherry and me, giving me his back, and Emil Hatch had something to tell Kiernan, sour no doubt, I touched Margot's elbow and she slid off the stool and let herself be steered across to a divan which had been covered with designs by Euclid in six or seven colors. We stood looking down at it.

"Mighty pretty," I said, "but nothing like as pretty as you. If only that license were real! I can get a real one for two dollars. What do you say?"

"*You!*" she said scornfully. "You wouldn't marry Miss Universe if she came on her knees with a billion dollars."

"I dare her to try it. Did it work?"

"Perfect. Simply perfect."

"Then you're ditching me?"

"Yes, Archie darling. But I'll be a sister to you."

"I've got a sister. I want the license back for a souvenir, and anyway I don't want it kicking around. I could be hooked for forgery. You can mail it to me, once my own."

"No, I can't. He tore it up."

"The hell he did. Where are the pieces?"

"Gone. He put them in his wastebasket. Will you come to the wedding?"

"What wastebasket where?"

"The gold one by his desk in his office. Last evening after dinner. Will you come to the wedding?"

"I will not. My heart is bleeding. So will Mr. Wolfe's—and by the way, I'd better get out of here. I'm not going to stand around and sulk."

"You won't have to. He won't know I've told you, and anyway, you wouldn't be expected—Here he comes!"

She darted off to the bar and I headed that way. Through the door on the left appeared Mrs. Perry Porter Jerome, all of her, plump and plushy, with folds of mink trying to keep up as she breezed in. As she approached, those on stools left them and got onto their feet, but that courtesy could have been as much for her companion as for her. She was the angel, but Kurt Bottweill was the boss. He stopped five paces short of the bar, extended his arms as far as they would go, and sang out, "Merry Christmas, all my blessings! Merry merry merry!"

I still hadn't labeled him. My first impression, months ago, had been that he was one of them, but that had been wrong. He was a man all right, but the question was what kind. About average in height, round but not pudgy, maybe forty-two or -three, his fine black hair slicked back so that he looked balder than he was, he was nothing great to look at, but he had something, not only for women but for men too. Wolfe had once invited him to stay for dinner, and they had talked about the scrolls from the Dead Sea. I had seen him twice at baseball games. His label would have to wait.

As I joined them at the bar, where Santa Claus was pouring Mumms Cordon Rouge, Bottweill squinted at me a moment and then grinned. "Goodwin! You here? Good! Edith, your pet sleuth!"

Mrs. Perry Porter Jerome, reaching for a glass, stopped her hand to look at me. "Who asked you?" she demanded, then went on, with no room for a reply, "Cherry, I suppose. Cherry *is* a blessing. Leo, quit tugging at me. Very well, take it. It's warm in here." She let her son pull her coat off, then reached for a glass. By the time Leo got back from depositing the mink on the divan we all had glasses, and when he had his we raised them, and our eyes went to Bottweill.

His eyes flashed around. "There are times," he said, "when love takes over. There are times—"

"Wait a minute," Alfred Kiernan cut in. "You enjoy it too. You don't like this stuff."

"I can stand a sip, Al."

"But you won't enjoy it. Wait." Kiernan put his glass on the bar and marched to the door on the left and on out. In five seconds he was back, with a bottle in his hand, and as he rejoined us and asked Santa Claus for a glass I saw the Pernod label. He pulled the cork, which had been pulled before, filled the glass halfway, and held it out to Bottweill. "There," he said. "That will make it unanimous."

"Thanks, Al." Bottweill took it. "My secret public vice." He raised the glass. "I repeat, there are times when love takes over. (Santa Claus, where is yours? but I suppose you can't drink through that mask.) There are times when all the little demons disappear down their rat-holes, and ugliness itself takes on the shape of beauty; when the darkest corner is touched by light; when the coldest heart feels the glow of warmth; when the trumpet call of good will and good cheer drowns out all the Babel of mean little noises. This is such a time. Merry Christmas! Merry merry merry!"

I was ready to touch glasses, but both the angel and the boss steered theirs to their lips, so I and the others followed suit. I thought Bottweill's eloquence deserved more than a sip, so I took a healthy gulp, and from the corner of my eye I saw that he was doing likewise with the Pernod. As I lowered the glass my eyes went to Mrs. Jerome, as she spoke.

"That was lovely," she declared. "Simply lovely. I must write it down and have it printed. That part about the trumpet call—*Kurt!* What is it? *Kurt!*"

He had dropped the glass and was clutching his throat with both hands. As I moved he turned loose of his throat, thrust his arms out, and let out a yell. I think he yelled *"Merry!"* but I wasn't really listening. Others started for him too, but my reflexes were better trained for emergencies than any of theirs, so I got him first. As I got my arms around him he started choking and gurgling, and a spasm went over him from head to foot that nearly loosened my grip. They were making noises, but no screams, and someone was clawing at my arm. As I was telling them to get back and give me room, he was suddenly a dead weight, and I almost went down with him and might have if Kiernan hadn't grabbed his arm.

I called, "Get a doctor!" and Cherry ran to a table where there was a gold-leaf phone. Kiernan and I let Bottweill down on the rug. He was out, breathing fast and hard, but as I was straightening his head his breathing slowed down and foam showed on his lips. Mrs. Jerome was commanding us, "Do something, do something!"

There was nothing to do and I knew it. While I was holding onto him I had got a whiff of his breath, and now, kneeling, I leaned over to get my nose an inch from his, and I knew that smell, and it takes a big dose to hit that quick and hard. Kiernan was loosening Bottweill's tie and collar. Cherry Quon called to us that she had tried a doctor and couldn't get him and was trying another. Margot was squatting at Bott-weill's feet, taking his shoes off, and I could have told her she might as well let him die with his boots on but didn't. I had two fingers on his wrist and my other hand inside his shirt, and could feel him going.

When I could feel nothing I abandoned the chest and wrist, took his hand, which was a fist, straightened the middle finger, and pressed its nail with my thumbtip until it was white. When I removed my thumb the nail stayed white. Dropping the hand, I yanked a little cluster of fibers from the rug, told Kiernan not to move, placed the fibers against Bottweill's nostrils, fastened my eyes on them, and held my breath for thirty seconds. The fibers didn't move.

I stood up and spoke. "His heart has stopped and he's not breathing. If a doctor came within three minutes and washed out his stomach with chemicals he wouldn't have with him, there might be one chance in a thousand. As it is—"

"Can't you *do* something?" Mrs. Jerome squawked.

"Not for him, no. I'm not an officer of the law, but I'm a licensed detective, and I'm supposed to know how to act in these circumstances, and I'll get it if I don't follow the rules. Of course—"

"*Do something!*" Mrs. Jerome squawked.

Kiernan's voice came from behind me. "He's dead."

I didn't turn to ask what test he had used. "Of course," I told them, "his drink was poisoned. Until the police come no one will touch anything, especially the bottle of Pernod, and no one will leave this room. You will—"

I stopped dead. Then I demanded, "Where is Santa Claus?"

Their heads turned to look at the bar. No bartender. On the chance that it had been too much for him, I pushed between Leo Jerome and Emil Hatch to step to the end of the bar, but he wasn't on the floor either.

I wheeled. "Did anyone see him go?"

They hadn't. Hatch said, "He didn't take the elevator. I'm sure he didn't. He must have—" He started off.

I blocked him. "You stay here. I'll take a look. Kiernan, phone the police. Spring seven-three-one-hundred."

I made for the door on the left and passed through, pulling it shut as I went, and was in Bottweill's office, which I had seen before. It was one-fourth the size of the studio, and much more subdued, but was by no means squalid. I crossed to the far end, saw through the glass panel that Bottweill's private elevator wasn't there, and pressed the button. A clank and a whirr came from inside the shaft, and it was coming. When it was up and had jolted to a stop I opened the door, and there on the floor was Santa Claus, but only the outside of him. He had molted. Jacket, breeches, mask, wig . . . I didn't check to see if it was all there, because I had another errand and not much time for it.

Propping the elevator door open with a chair, I went and circled around Bottweill's big gold-leaf desk to his gold-leaf wastebasket. It was one-third full. Bending, I started to paw, decided that was inefficient, picked it up and dumped it, and began tossing things back in one by one. Some of the items were torn pieces of paper, but none of them came from a marriage license. When I had finished I stayed down a moment, squatting, wondering if I had hurried too much and possibly missed it, and I might have gone through it again if I hadn't heard a faint noise from the studio that sounded like the elevator door opening. I went to the door to the studio and opened it, and as I crossed the sill two uniformed cops were deciding whether to give their first glance to the dead or the living.

III

Three hours later we were seated, more or less in a group, and my old friend and foe, Sergeant Purley Stebbins of Homicide, stood surveying us, his square jaw jutting and his big burly frame erect.

He spoke. "Mr. Kiernan and Mr. Hatch will be taken to the District Attorney's office for further questioning. The rest of you can go for the present, but you will keep yourselves available at the addresses you have given. Before you go I want to ask you again, here together, about the man who was here as Santa Claus. You have all claimed you know nothing about him. Do you still claim that?"

It was twenty minutes to seven. Some two dozen city employees—medical examiner, photographer, fingerprinters, meat-basket bearers, the whole kaboodle—had finished the on-the-scene routine, including private interviews with the eyewitnesses. I had made the highest score, having had sessions with Stebbins, a precinct man, and Inspector Cramer, who had departed around five o'clock to organize the hunt for Santa Claus.

"I'm not objecting," Kiernan told Stebbins, "to going to the District Attorney's office. I'm not objecting to anything. But we've told you all we can, I know I have. It seems to me your job is to find him."

"Do you mean to say," Mrs. Jerome demanded, "that no one knows anything at all about him?"

"So they say," Purley told her. "No one even knew there was going to be a Santa Claus, so they say. He was brought to this room by Bottweill, about a quarter to three, from his office. The idea is that Bottweill himself had arranged for him, and he came up in the private elevator and put on the costume in Bottweill's office. You may as well know there is some corroboration of that. We have found out where the costume came from—Burleson's on Forty-sixth Street. Bottweill phoned them yesterday afternoon and ordered it sent here, marked personal.

Miss Quon admits receiving the package and taking it to Bottweill in his office."

For a cop, you never just state a fact, or report it or declare it or say it. You admit it.

"We are also," Purley admitted, "covering agencies which might have supplied a man to act Santa Claus, but that's a big order. If Bottweill got a man through an agency there's no telling what he got. If it was a man with a record, when he saw trouble coming he beat it. With everybody's attention on Bottweill, he sneaked out, got his clothes, whatever he had taken off, in Bottweill's office, and went down in the elevator he had come up in. He shed the costume on the way down and after he was down, and left it in the elevator. If that was it, if he was just a man Bottweill hired, he wouldn't have had any reason to kill him—and besides, he wouldn't have known that Bottweill's only drink was Pernod, and he wouldn't have known where the poison was."

"Also," Emil Hatch said, surer than ever, "if he was just hired for the job he was a damn fool to sneak out. He might have known he'd be found. So he wasn't just hired. He was someone who knew Bottweill, and knew about the Pernod and the poison, and had some good reason for wanting to kill him. You're wasting your time on the agencies."

Stebbins lifted his heavy broad shoulders and dropped them. "We waste most of our time, Mr. Hatch. Maybe he was too scared to think. I just want you to understand that if we find him and that's how Bottweill got him, it's going to be hard to believe that he put poison in that bottle, but somebody did. I want you to understand that so you'll understand why you are all to be available at the addresses you have given. Don't make any mistake about that."

"Do you mean," Mrs. Jerome demanded, "that we are under suspicion? That I and *my son* are under suspicion?"

Purley opened his mouth and shut it again. With that kind he always had trouble with his impulses. He wanted to say, "You're goddam right you are." He did say, "I mean we're going to find that Santa Claus, and when we do we'll see. If we can't see him for it we'll have to look further, and we'll expect all of you to help us. I'm taking it for granted you'll all want to help. Don't you want to, Mrs. Jerome?"

"I would help if I could, but I know nothing about it. I only know that my very dear friend is dead, and I don't intend to be abused and threatened. What about the poison?"

"You know about it. You have been questioned about it."

"I know I have, but what about it?"

"It must have been apparent from the questions. The medical examiner thinks it was cyanide and expects the autopsy to verify it. Emil Hatch uses potassium cyanide in his work with metals and plating, and there is a large jar of it on a cupboard shelf in the workshop one floor below, and there is a stair from Bottweill's office to the workroom. Anyone who knew that, and who also knew that Bottweill kept a case of Pernod in a cabinet in his office, and an open bottle of it in a drawer of his desk, couldn't have asked for a better setup. Four of you have admitted knowing both of those things. Three of you—Mrs. Jerome, Leo Jerome, and Archie Goodwin—admit they knew about the Pernod but deny they knew about the potassium cyanide. That will—"

"That's not true! She did know about it!"

Mrs. Perry Porter Jerome's hand shot out across her son's knees and slapped Cherry Quon's cheek or mouth or both. Her son grabbed her arm. Alfred Kiernan sprang to his feet, and for a second I thought he was going to sock Mrs. Jerome, and he did too, and possibly would have if Margot Dickey hadn't jerked at his coattail. Cherry put her hand to her face but, except for that, didn't move.

"Sit down," Stebbins told Kiernan. "Take it easy. Miss Quon, you say that Mrs. Jerome knew about the potassium cyanide?"

"Of course she did." Cherry's chirp was pitched lower than normal, but it was still a chirp. "In the workshop one day I heard Mr. Hatch telling her how he used it and how careful he had to be."

"Mr. Hatch? Do you verify—"

"Nonsense," Mrs. Jerome snapped. "What if he did? Perhaps he did. I had forgotten all about it. I told you I won't tolerate this abuse!"

Purley eyed her. "Look here, Mrs. Jerome. When we find that Santa Claus, if it was someone who knew Bottweill and had a motive, that may settle it. If not, it won't help anyone to talk about abuse, and that includes you. So far as I know now, only one of you has told us a lie. You. That's on the record. I'm telling you, and all of you, lies only make it harder for you, but sometimes they make it easier for us. I'll leave it at that for now. Mr. Kiernan and Mr. Hatch, these men"—he aimed a thumb over his shoulder at two dicks standing back of him—"will take you downtown. The rest of you can go, but remember what I said. Goodwin, I want to see you."

He had already seen me, but I wouldn't make a point of it. Kiernan, however, had a point to make, and made it: he had to leave last so he could lock up. It was so arranged. The three women, Leo Jerome, and Stebbins and I took the elevator down, leaving the two dicks with Kiernan and Hatch. Down the sidewalk, as they headed in different directions, I could see no sign of tails taking after them. It was still snowing, a fine prospect for Christmas and the street cleaners. There were two police cars at the curb, and Purley went to one and opened the door and motioned to me to get in.

I objected. "If I'm invited downtown too I'm willing to oblige, but I'm going to eat first. I damn near starved to death there once."

"You're not wanted downtown, not right now. Get in out of the snow."

I did so, and slid across under the wheel to make room for him. He needs room. He joined me and pulled the door shut.

"If we're going to sit here," I suggested, "we might as well be rolling. Don't bother to cross town, just drop me at Thirty-fifth."

He objected. "I don't like to drive and talk. Or listen. What were you doing there today?"

"I've told you. Having fun. Three kinds of champagne. Miss Dickey invited me."

"I'm giving you another chance. You were the only outsider there. Why? You're nothing special to Miss Dickey. She was going to marry Bottweill. Why?"

"Ask her."

"We have asked her. She says there was no particular reason, she knew Bottweill liked you, and they've regarded you as one of them since you found some tapestries for them. She stuttered around about it. What I say, any time I find you anywhere near a murder, I want to know. I'm giving you another chance."

So she hadn't mentioned the marriage license. Good for her. I would rather have eaten all the snow that had fallen since noon than explain that damn license to Sergeant Stebbins or Inspector Cramer. That was why I had gone through the wastebasket. "Thanks for the chance," I told him, "but I can't use it. I've told you everything I saw and heard there today." That put me in a class with Mrs. Jerome, since I had left out my little talk with Margot. "I've told you all I know about those people. Lay off and go find your murderer."

"I know you, Goodwin."

"Yeah, you've even called me Archie. I treasure that memory."

"I know you." His head was turned on his bull neck, and our eyes were meeting. "Do you expect me to believe that guy got out of that room and away without you knowing it?"

"Nuts. I was kneeling on the floor, watching a man die, and they were around us. Anyway, you're just talking to hear yourself. You don't think I was accessory to the murder or to the murderer's escape."

"I didn't say I did. Even if he was wearing gloves—and what for if not to leave no prints?—I don't say he was the murderer. But if you knew who he was and didn't want him involved in it and let him get away, and if you let us wear out our ankles looking for him, what about that?"

"That would be bad. If I asked my advice I would be against it."

"Goddamn it, " he barked, "do you know who he is?"

"No."

"Did you or Wolfe have anything to do with getting him there?"

"No."

"All right, pile out. They'll be wanting you downtown."

"I hope not tonight. I'm tired." I opened the door. "You have my address." I stepped out into the snow, and he started the engine and rolled off.

It should have been a good hour for an empty taxi, but in a Christmas-season snowstorm it took me ten minutes to find one. When it pulled up in front of the old brownstone on West Thirty-fifth Street it was eight minutes to eight.

As usual in my absence, the chain-bolt was on, and I had to ring for Fritz to let me in. I asked him if Wolfe was back, and he said yes, he was at dinner. As I put my hat on the shelf and my coat on a hanger I asked if there was any left for me, and he said plenty, and moved aside for me to precede him down the hall to the door of the dining room. Fritz has fine manners.

Wolfe, in his oversized chair at the end of the table, told me good evening, not snapping or barking. I returned it, got seated at my place, picked up my napkin, and apologized for being late. Fritz came, from the kitchen, with a warm plate, a platter of braised boned ducklings, and a dish of potatoes baked with mushrooms and cheese. I took enough. Wolfe asked if it was still snowing and I said yes. After a good mouthful had been disposed of, I spoke.

"As you know, I approve of your rule not to discuss business during a meal, but I've got something on my chest and it's not business. It's personal."

He grunted. "The death of Mr. Bottweill was reported on the radio at seven o'clock. You were there."

"Yeah. I was there. I was kneeling by him while he died." I replenished my mouth. Damn the radio. I hadn't intended to mention the murder until I had dealt with the main issue from my standpoint. When there was room enough for my tongue to work I went on. "I'll report on that in full if you want it, but I doubt if there's a job in it. Mrs. Perry Porter Jerome is the only suspect with enough jack to pay your fee, and she has already notified Purley Stebbins that she won't be abused. Besides, when they find Santa Claus that may settle it. What I want to report on happened before Bottweill died. That marriage license I showed you is for the birds. Miss Dickey has called it off. I am out two bucks. She told me she had decided to marry Bottweill."

He was sopping a crust in the sauce on his plate. "Indeed," he said.

"Yes, sir. It was a jolt, but I would have recovered, in time. Then ten minutes later Bottweill was dead. Where does that leave me? Sitting around up there through the routine, I considered it. Perhaps I could get her back now, but no thank you. That license has been destroyed. I get another one, another two bucks, and then she tells me she has decided to marry Joe Doakes. I'm going to forget her. I'm going to blot her out."

I resumed on the duckling. Wolfe was busy chewing. When he could he said, "For me, of course, this is satisfactory."

"I know it is. Do you want to hear about Bottweill?"

"After dinner."

"Okay. How did you make out with Thompson?"

But that didn't appeal to him as a dinner topic either. In fact, nothing did. Usually he likes table talk, about anything from refrigerators to Republicans, but apparently the trip to Long Island and back, with all its dangers, had tired him out. It suited me all right, since I had had a noisy afternoon too and could stand a little silence. When we had both done well with the duckling and potatoes and salad and baked pears and cheese and coffee, he pushed back his chair.

"There's a book," he said, "that I want to look at. It's up in your room—*Here and Now*, by Herbert Block. Will you bring it down, please?"

Though it meant climbing two flights with a full stomach, I was glad to oblige, out of appreciation for his calm acceptance of my announcement of my shattered hopes. He could have been very vocal. So I mounted the stairs cheerfully, went to my room, and crossed to the shelves where I keep a few books. There were only a couple of dozen of them, and I knew where each one was, but *Here and Now* wasn't there. Where it should have been was a gap. I looked around, saw a book on the dresser, and stepped to it. It was *Here and Now*, and lying on top of it was a pair of white cotton gloves.

I gawked.

IV

I would like to say that I caught on immediately, the second I spotted them, but I didn't. I had picked them up and looked them over, and put one of them on and taken it off again, before I fully realized that there was only one possible explanation. Having realized it, instantly there was a traffic jam inside my skull, horns blowing, brakes squealing, head-on collisions. To deal with it I went to a chair and sat. It took me maybe a minute to reach my first clear conclusion.

He had taken this method of telling me he was Santa Claus, instead of just telling me, because he wanted me to think it over on my own before we talked it over together.

Why did he want me to think it over on my own? That took a little longer, but with the traffic under control I found my way through to the only acceptable answer. He had decided to give up his trip to see Thompson, and instead to arrange with Bottweill to attend the Christmas party disguised as Santa Claus, because the idea of a woman living in his house—or of the only alternative, my leaving—had made him absolutely desperate, and he had to see for himself. He had to see Margot and me together, and to talk with her if possible. If he found out that the marriage license was a hoax he would have me by the tail; he could tell me he would be delighted to welcome my bride and watch me wriggle out. If he found that I really meant it he would know what he was up against and go on from there. The point was this, that he had shown what he really thought of me. He had shown that rather than lose me he would do something that he wouldn't have done for any fee anybody could name. He would rather have gone without beer for a week than admit it, but now he was a fugitive from justice in a murder case and needed me. So he had to let me know, but he wanted it understood that that aspect of the matter was not to be mentioned. The assumption would be that he had gone to Bottweill's instead of Long Island because he loved to dress up like Santa Claus and tend bar.

A cell in my brain tried to get the right of way for the question, considering this development, how big a raise should I get after New Year's? but I waved it to the curb.

I thought over other aspects. He had worn the gloves so I couldn't recognize his hands. Where did he get them? What time had he got to Bottweill's and who had seen him? Did Fritz know where he was going? How had he got back home? But after a little of that I realized that he hadn't sent me up to my room to ask myself questions he could answer, so I went back to considering whether there was anything else he wanted me to think over alone. Deciding there wasn't, after chewing it thoroughly, I got *Here and Now* and the gloves from the dresser, went to the stairs and descended, and entered the office.

From behind his desk, he glared at me as I crossed over.

"Here it is," I said, and handed him the book. "And much obliged for the gloves." I held them up, one in each hand, dangling them from thumb and fingertip.

"It is no occasion for clowning," he growled.

"It sure isn't." I dropped the gloves on my desk, whirled my chair, and sat. "Where do we start? Do you want to know what happened after you left?"

"The details can wait. First where we stand. Was Mr. Cramer there?"

"Yes. Certainly."

"Did he get anywhere?"

"No. He probably won't until he finds Santa Claus. Until they find Santa Claus they won't dig very hard at the others. The longer it takes to find him the surer they'll be he's it. Three things about him: nobody knows who he was, he beat it, and he wore gloves. A thousand men are looking for him. You were right to wear the gloves, I would have recognized your hands, but where did you get them?"

"At a store on Ninth Avenue. Confound it, I didn't know a man was going to be murdered!"

"I know you didn't. May I ask some questions?"

He scowled. I took it for yes. "When did you phone Bottweill to arrange it?"

"At two-thirty yesterday afternoon. You had gone to the bank."

"Have you any reason to think he told anyone about it?"

"No. He said he wouldn't."

"I know he got the costume, so that's okay. When you left here today at twelve-thirty did you go straight to Bottweill's?"

"No. I left at that hour because you and Fritz expected me to. I stopped to buy the gloves, and met him at Rusterman's, and we had lunch. From there we took a cab to his place, arriving shortly after two o'clock, and took his private elevator up to his office. Immediately upon entering his office, he got a bottle of Pernod from a drawer of his desk, said he always had a little after lunch, and invited me to join him. I declined. He poured a liberal portion in a glass, about two ounces, drank it in two gulps, and returned the bottle to the drawer."

"My God." I whistled. "The cops would like to know *that*."

"No doubt. The costume was there in a box. There is a dressing room at the rear of his office, with a bathroom—"

"I know. I've used it."

"I took the costume there and put it on. He had ordered the largest size, but it was a squeeze and it took a while. I was in there half an hour or more. When I re-entered the office it was empty, but soon Bottweill came, up the stairs from the workshop, and helped me with the mask and wig. They had barely been adjusted when Emil Hatch and Mrs. Jerome and her son appeared, also coming up the stairs from the workshop. I left, going to the studio, and found Miss Quon and Miss Dickey and Mr. Kiernan there."

"And before long I was there. Then no one saw you unmasked. When did you put the gloves on?"

"The last thing. Just before I entered the studio."

"Then you may have left prints. I know, you didn't know there was going to be a murder. You left your clothes in the dressing room? Are you sure you got everything when you left?"

"Yes. I am not a complete ass."

I let that by. "Why didn't you leave the gloves in the elevator with the costume?"

"Because they hadn't come with it, and I thought it better to take them."

"That private elevator is at the rear of the hall downstairs. Did anyone see you leaving it or passing through the hall?"

"No. The hall was empty."

"How did you get home? Taxi?"

"No. Fritz didn't expect me until six or later. I walked to the public library, spent some two hours there, and then took a cab."

I pursed my lips and shook my head to indicate sympathy. That was his longest and hardest tramp since Montenegro. Over a mile. Fighting his way through the blizzard, in terror of the law on his tail. But all the return I got for my look of sympathy was a scowl, so I let loose. I laughed. I put my head back and let it come. I had wanted to ever since I had learned he was Santa Claus, but had been too busy thinking. It was bottled up in me, and I let it out, good. I was about to taper off to a cackle when he exploded.

"Confound it," he bellowed, "marry and be damned!"

That was dangerous. That attitude could easily get us onto the aspect he had sent me up to my room to think over alone, and if we got started on that anything could happen. It called for tact.

"I beg your pardon," I said. "Something caught in my throat. Do you want to describe the situation, or do you want me to?"

"I would like to hear you try," he said grimly.

"Yes, sir. I suspect that the only thing to do is to phone Inspector Cramer right now and invite him to come and have a chat, and when he comes open the bag. That will—"

"No. I will not do that."

"Then, next best, I go to him and spill it there. Of course—"

"No." He meant every word of it.

"Okay, I'll describe it. They'll mark time on the others until they find Santa Claus. They've got to find him. If he left any prints they'll compare them with every file they've got, and sooner or later they'll get to yours. They'll cover all the stores for sales of white cotton gloves to men. They'll trace Bottweill's movements and learn that he lunched with you at Rusterman's, and you left together, and they'll trace you to Bottweill's place. Of course your going there won't prove you were Santa Claus, you might talk your way out of that, and it will account for your prints if they find some, but what about the gloves? They'll trace that sale if you give them time, and with a description of the buyer they'll find Santa Claus. You're sunk."

I had never seen his face blacker.

"If you sit tight till they find him," I argued, "it will be quite a nuisance. Cramer has been itching for years to lock you up, and any judge would commit you as a material witness who had run out. Whereas if you call Cramer now, and I mean now, and invite him to come and have some beer, while it will still be a nuisance, it will be bearable. Of course he'll want to know why you went there and played Santa Claus, but you can tell him anything you please. Tell him you bet me a hundred bucks, or what the hell, make it a grand, that you could be in a room with me for ten minutes and I wouldn't recognize you. I'll be glad to cooperate."

I leaned forward. "Another thing. If you wait till they find you, you won't dare tell them that Bottweill took a drink from that bottle shortly after two o'clock and it didn't hurt him. If you told about that after they dug you up, they could book you for withholding evidence, and they probably would, and make it stick. If you get Cramer here now and tell him he'll appreciate it, though naturally he won't say so. He's probably at his office. Shall I ring him?"

"No. I will not confess that performance to Mr. Cramer. I will not unfold the morning paper to a disclosure of that outlandish masquerade."

"Then you're going to sit and read *Here and Now* until they come with a warrant?"

"No. That would be fatuous." He took in air through his mouth, as far down as it would go, and let it out through his nose. "I'm going to find the murderer and present him to Mr. Cramer. There's nothing else."

"Oh. You are."

"Yes."

"You might have said so and saved my breath, instead of letting me spout."

"I wanted to see if your appraisal of the situation agreed with mine. It does."

"That's fine. Then you also know that we may have two weeks and we may have two minutes. At this very second some expert may be phoning Homicide to say that he has found fingerprints that match on the card of Wolfe, Nero—"

The phone rang, and I jerked around as if someone had stuck a needle in me. Maybe we wouldn't have even two minutes. My hand wasn't trembling as I lifted the receiver, I hope. Wolfe seldom lifts his until I have found out who it is, but that time he did.

"Nero Wolfe's office, Archie Goodwin speaking."

"This is the District Attorney's office, Mr. Goodwin. Regarding the murder of Kurt Bottweill. We would like you to be here at ten o'clock tomorrow morning."

"All right. Sure."

"At ten o'clock sharp, please."

"I'll be there."

We hung up. Wolfe sighed. I sighed.

"Well," I said, "I've already told them six times that I know absolutely nothing about Santa Claus, so they may not ask me again. If they do, it will be interesting to compare my voice when I'm lying with when I'm telling the truth."

He grunted. "Now. I want a complete report of what happened there after I left, but first I want background. In your intimate association with Miss Dickey you must have learned things about those people. What?"

"Not much." I cleared my throat. "I guess I'll have to explain something. My association with Miss Dickey was not intimate." I stopped. It wasn't easy.

"Choose your own adjective. I meant no innuendo."

"It's not a question of adjectives. Miss Dickey is a good dancer, exceptionally good, and for the past couple of months I have been taking her here and there, some six or eight times altogether. Monday evening at the Flamingo Club she asked me to do her a favor. She said Bottweill was giving her a runaround, that he had been going to marry her for a year but kept stalling, and she wanted to do something. She said Cherry Quon was making a play for him, and she didn't intend to let Cherry take the rail. She asked me to get a marriage-license blank and fill it out for her and me and give it to her. She would show it to Bottweill and tell him now or never. It struck me as a good deed with no risk involved, and, as I say, she is a good dancer. Tuesday afternoon I got a blank, no matter how, and that evening, up in my room, I filled it in, including a fancy signature."

Wolfe made a noise.

"That's all," I said, "except that I want to make it clear that I had no intention of showing it to you. I did that on the spur of the moment when you picked up your book. Your memory is as good as mine. Also, to close it up, no doubt you noticed that today just before Bottweill and Mrs. Jerome joined the party Margot and I stepped aside for a little chat. She told me the license did the trick. Her words were, 'Perfect, simply perfect.' She said that last evening, in his office, he tore the license up and put the pieces in his wastebasket. That's okay, the cops didn't find them. I looked before they came, and the pieces weren't there."

His mouth was working, but he didn't open it. He didn't dare. He would have liked to tear into me, to tell me that my insufferable flummery had got him into this awful mess, but if he did so he would be dragging in the aspect he didn't want mentioned. He saw that in time, and saw that I saw it. His mouth worked, but that was all. Finally he spoke.

"Then you are not on intimate terms with Miss Dickey."

"No, sir."

"Even so, she must have spoken of that establishment and those people."

"Some, yes."

"And one of them killed Bottweill. The poison was put in the bottle between two-ten, when I saw him take a drink, and three-thirty when Kiernan went and got the bottle. No one came up in the private elevator during the half-hour or more I was in the dressing room. I was getting into that costume and gave no heed to footsteps or other sounds in the office, but the elevator shaft adjoins the dressing room, and I would have heard it. It is a strong probability that the opportunity was even narrower, that the poison was put in the bottle while I was in the dressing room, since three of them were in the office with Bottweill when I left. It must be assumed that one of those three, or one of the three in the studio, had grasped an earlier opportunity. What about them?"

"Not much. Mostly from Monday evening, when Margot was talking about Bottweill. So it's all hearsay, from her. Mrs. Jerome has put half a million in the business—probably you should divide that by two at least—and thinks she owns him. Or thought. She was jealous of Margot and Cherry. As for Leo, if his mother was dishing out the dough he expected to inherit to a guy who was trying to corner the world's supply of gold leaf, and possibly might also marry him, and if he knew about the jar of poison in the workshop, he might have been tempted. Kiernan, I don't know, but from a remark Margot made and from the way he looked at Cherry this afternoon, I suspect he would like to mix some Irish with her Chinese and Indian and Dutch, and if he thought Bottweill had him stymied he might have been tempted too. So much for hearsay."

"Mr. Hatch?"

"Nothing on him from Margot, but, dealing with him during the tapestry job, I wouldn't have been surprised if he had wiped out the whole bunch on general principles. His heart pumps acid instead of blood. He's a creative artist, he told me so. He practically told me that he was responsible for the success of that enterprise but got no credit. He didn't tell me that he regarded Bottweill as a phony and a four-flusher, but he did. You may remember that I told you he had a perse-cution complex and you told me to stop using other people's jargon."

"That's four of them. Miss Dickey?"

I raised my brows. "I got her a license to marry, not to kill. If she was lying when she said it worked, she's almost as good a liar as she is a dancer. Maybe she is. If it didn't work she might have been tempted too."

"And Miss Quon?"

"She's half Oriental. I'm not up on Orientals, but I understand they slant their eyes to keep you guessing. That's what makes them inscruta-ble. If I had to be poisoned by one of that bunch I would want it to be her. Except for what Margot told me—"

The doorbell rang. That was worse than the phone. If they had hit on Santa Claus's trail and it led to Nero Wolfe, Cramer was much more apt to come than to call. Wolfe and I exchanged glances. Looking at my wristwatch and seeing 10:08, I arose, went to the hall and flipped the switch for the stoop light, and took a look through the one-way glass panel of the front door. I have good eyes, but the figure was muffled in a heavy coat with a hood, so I stepped halfway to the door to make sure. Then I returned to the office and told Wolfe, "Cherry Quon. Alone."

He frowned. "I wanted—" He cut it off. "Very well. Bring her in."

V

As I have said, Cherry was highly decorative, and she went fine with the red leather chair at the end of Wolfe's desk. It would have held three of her. She had let me take her coat in the hall and still had on the neat little woolen number she had worn at the party. It wasn't ex-actly yellow, but there was yellow in it. I would have called it off-gold, and it and the red chair and the tea tint of her smooth little carved face would have made a very nice kodachrome.

She sat on the edge, her spine straight and her hands together in her lap. "I was afraid to telephone," she said, "because you might tell me not to come. So I just came. Will you forgive me?"

Wolfe grunted. No commitment. She smiled at him, a friendly smile, or so I thought. After all, she was half Oriental.

"I must get myself together," she chirped. "I'm nervous because it's so exciting to be here." She turned her head. "There's the globe, and the bookshelves, and the safe, and the couch, and of course Archie Goodwin. And you. You behind your desk in your enormous chair! Oh, I know this place! I have read about you so much—everything there is, I think. It's exciting to be here, actually here in this chair, and see you. Of course I saw you this afternoon, but that wasn't the same thing, you could have been anybody in that silly Santa Claus costume. I wanted to pull your whiskers."

She laughed, a friendly little tinkle like a bell.

I think I looked bewildered. That was my idea, after it had got through my ears to the switchboard inside and been routed. I was too busy handling my face to look at Wolfe, but he was probably even busier, since she was looking straight at him. I moved my eyes to him when he spoke.

"If I understand you, Miss Quon, I'm at a loss. If you think you saw me this afternoon in a Santa Claus costume, you're mistaken."

"Oh, I'm sorry!" she exclaimed. "Then you haven't told them?"

"My dear madam." His voice sharpened. "If you must talk in riddles, talk to Mr. Goodwin. He enjoys them."

"But I *am* sorry, Mr. Wolfe. I should have explained first how I know. This morning at breakfast Kurt told me you had phoned him and arranged to appear at the party as Santa Claus, and this afternoon I asked him if you had come and he said you had and you were putting on the costume. That's how I know. But you haven't told the police? Then it's a good thing I haven't told them either, isn't it?"

"This is interesting," Wolfe said coldly. "What do you expect to accomplish by this fantastic folderol?"

She shook her pretty little head. "You, with so much sense. You must see that it's no use. If I tell them, even if they don't like to believe me they will investigate. I know they can't investigate as well as you can, but surely they will find something."

He shut his eyes, tightened his lips, and leaned back in his chair. I kept mine opened, on her. She weighed about a hundred and two. I could carry her under one arm with my other hand clamped on her mouth. Putting her in the spare room upstairs wouldn't do, since she could open a window and scream, but there was a cubbyhole in the basement, next to Fritz's room, with an old couch in it. Or, as an alternative, I could get a gun from my desk drawer and shoot her. Probably no one knew she had come here.

Wolfe opened his eyes and straightened up. "Very well. It is still fantastic, but I concede that you could create an unpleasant situation by taking that yarn to the police. I don't suppose you came here merely to tell me that you intend to. What do you intend?"

"I think we understand each other," she chirped.

"I understand only that you want something. What?"

"You are so direct," she complained. "So very abrupt, that I must have said something wrong. But I do want something. You see, since the police think it was the man who acted Santa Claus and ran away, they may not get on the right track until it's too late. You wouldn't want that, would you?"

No reply.

"I wouldn't want it," she said, and her hands on her lap curled into little fists. "I wouldn't want whoever killed Kurt to get away, no matter who it was, but you see, I know who killed him. I have told the police, but they won't listen until they find Santa Claus, or if they listen they think I'm just a jealous cat, and besides, I'm an Oriental and their ideas of Orientals are very primitive. I was going to make them listen by telling them who Santa Claus was, but I know how they feel about you from what I've read, and I was afraid they would try to prove it was you who killed Kurt, and of course it could have been you, and you did run away, and they still wouldn't listen to me when I told them who did kill him."

She stopped for breath. Wolfe inquired, "Who did?"

She nodded. "I'll tell you. Margot Dickey and Kurt were having an affair. A few months ago Kurt began on me, and it was hard for me because I—I—" she frowned for a word, and found one. "I had a feeling for him. I had a strong feeling. But you see, I am a virgin, and I wouldn't give in to him. I don't know what I would have done if I hadn't known he was having an affair with Margot, but I did know, and I told him the first man I slept with would be my husband. He said he was willing to give up Margot, but even if he did he couldn't marry me on account of Mrs. Jerome, because she would stop backing him with her money. I don't know what he was to Mrs. Jerome, but I know what she was to him."

Her hands opened and closed again to be fists. "That went on and on, but Kurt had a feeling for me too. Last night late, it was after midnight, he phoned me that he had broken with Margot for good and he wanted to marry me. He wanted to come and see me, but I told him I was in bed and we would see each other in the morning. He said that would be at the studio with other people there, so finally I said I would go to his apartment for breakfast, and I did, this morning. But I am still a virgin, Mr. Wolfe."

He was focused on her with half-closed eyes. "That is your privilege, madam."

"Oh," she said. "Is it a privilege? It was there, at breakfast, that he told me about you, your arranging to be Santa Claus. When I got to the studio I was surprised to see Margot there, and how friendly she was. That was part of her plan, to be friendly and cheerful with everyone. She has told the police that Kurt was going to marry her, that they decided last night to get married next week. Christmas week. I am a Christian."

Wolfe stirred in his chair. "Have we reached the point? Did Miss Dickey kill Mr. Bottweill?"

"Yes. Of course she did."

"Have you told the police that?"

"Yes. I didn't tell them all I have told you, but enough."

"With evidence?"

"No. I have no evidence."

"Then you're vulnerable to an action for slander."

She opened her fists and turned her palms up. "Does that matter? When I know I'm right? When I *know* it? But she was so clever, the way she did it, that there can't be any evidence. Everybody there today knew about the poison, and they all had a chance to put it in the bottle. They can never prove she did it. They can't even prove she is lying when she says Kurt was going to marry her, because he is dead. She acted today the way she would have acted if that had been true. But it has got to be proved somehow. There has got to be evidence to prove it."

"And you want me to get it?"

She let that pass. "What I was thinking, Mr. Wolfe, you are vulnerable too. There will always be the danger that the police will find out who Santa Claus was, and if they find it was you and you didn't tell them—"

"I haven't conceded that," Wolfe snapped.

"Then we'll just say there will always be the danger that I'll tell them what Kurt told me, and you did concede that that would be unpleasant. So it would be better if the evidence proved who killed Kurt and also proved who Santa Claus was. Wouldn't it?"

"Go on."

"So I thought how easy it would be for you to get the evidence. You have men who do things for you, who would do anything for you, and one of them can say that you asked him to go there and be Santa Claus, and he did. Of course it couldn't be Mr. Goodwin, since he was at the party, and it would have to be a man they couldn't prove was somewhere else. He can say that while he was in the dressing room putting on the costume he heard someone in the office and peeked out to see who it was, and he saw Margot Dickey get the bottle from the desk drawer and put something in it and put the bottle back in the drawer, and go out. That must have been when she did it, because Kurt always took a drink of Pernod when he came back from lunch."

Wolfe was rubbing his lip with a fingertip. "I see," he muttered.

She wasn't through. "He can say," she went on, "that he ran away because he was frightened and wanted to tell you about it first. I don't think they would do anything to him if he went to them tomorrow morning and told them all about it, would they? Just like me. I don't think they would do anything to me if I went to them tomorrow morning and told them I had remembered that Kurt told me that you were going to be Santa Claus, and this afternoon he told me you were in the dressing room putting on the costume. That would be the same kind of thing, wouldn't it?"

Her little carved mouth thinned and widened with a smile. "That's what I want," she chirped. "Did I say it so you understand it?"

"You did indeed," Wolfe assured her. "You put it admirably."

"Would it be better, instead of him going to tell them, for you to have Inspector Cramer come here, and you tell him? You could have the man here. You see, I know how you do things, from all I have read."

"That might be better," he allowed. His tone was dry but not hostile. I could see a muscle twitching beneath his right ear, but she couldn't. "I suppose, Miss Quon, it is futile to advance the possibility that one of the others killed him, and if so it would be a pity—"

"Excuse me. I interrupt." The chirp was still a chirp, but it had hard steel in it. "I know she killed him."

"I don't. And even if I bow to your conviction, before I could undertake the stratagem you propose I would have to make sure there are no facts that would scuttle it. It won't take me long. You'll hear from me tomorrow. I'll want—"

She interrupted again. "I can't wait longer than tomorrow morning to tell them what Kurt told me."

"Pfui. You can and will. The moment you disclose that, you no longer have a whip to dangle at me. You will hear from me tomorrow. Now I want to think. Archie?"

I left my chair. She looked up at me and back at Wolfe. For some seconds she sat, considering, inscrutable of course, then stood up.

"It was very exciting to be here," she said, the steel gone, "to see you here. You must forgive me for not phoning. I hope it will be early tomorrow." She turned and headed for the door, and I followed.

After I had helped her on with her hooded coat, and let her out, and watched her picking her way down the seven steps, I shut the door, put the chain-bolt on, returned to the office, and told Wolfe, "It has stopped snowing. Who do you think will be best for it, Saul or Fred or Orrie or Bill?"

"Sit down," he growled. "You see through women. Well?"

"Not that one. I pass. I wouldn't bet a dime on her one way or the other. Would you?"

"No. She is probably a liar and possibly a murderer. Sit down. I must have everything that happened there today after I left. Every word and gesture."

I sat and gave it to him. Including the question period, it took an hour and thirty-five minutes. It was after one o'clock when he pushed his chair back, levered his bulk upright, told me good night, and went up to bed.

VI

At half past two the following afternoon, Saturday, I sat in a room in a building on Leonard Street, the room where I had once swiped an assistant district attorney's lunch. There would be no need for me to repeat the performance, since I had just come back from Ost's restaurant, where I had put away a plateful of pig's knuckles and sauerkraut.

As far as I knew, there had not only been no steps to frame Margot for murder; there had been no steps at all. Since Wolfe is up in the plant rooms every morning from nine to eleven, and since he breakfasts from a tray up in his room, and since I was expected downtown at ten o'clock, I had buzzed him on the house phone a little before nine to ask for instructions and had been told that he had none. Downtown Assistant DA Farrell, after letting me wait in the anteroom for an hour, had spent two hours with me, together with a stenographer and a dick who had been on the scene Friday afternoon, going back and forth and zig-zag, not only over what I had already reported, but also over my previous association with the Bottweill personnel. He only asked me once if I knew anything about Santa Claus, so I only had to lie once, if you don't count my omitting any mention of the marriage license. When he called a recess and told me to come back at two-thirty, on my way to Ost's for the pig's knuckles I phoned Wolfe to tell him I didn't know when I would be home, and again he had no instructions. I said I doubted if Cherry Quon would wait until after New Year's to spill the beans, and he said he did too and hung up.

When I was ushered back into Farrell's office at two-thirty he was alone—no stenographer and no dick. He asked me if I had had a good lunch, and even waited for me to answer, handed me some typewritten sheets, and leaned back in his chair.

"Read it over," he said, "and see if you want to sign it."

His tone seemed to imply that I might not, so I went over it carefully, five full pages. Finding no editorial revisions to object to, I pulled my chair forward to a corner of his desk, put the statement on the desk top, and got my pen from my pocket.

"Wait a minute," Farrell said. "You're not a bad guy even if you are cocky, and why not give you a break? That says specifically that you have reported everything you did there yesterday afternoon."

"Yeah, I've read it. So?"

"So who put your fingerprints on some of the pieces of paper in Bottweill's wastebasket?"

"I'll be damned," I said. "I forgot to put gloves on."

"All right, you're cocky. I already know that." His eyes were pinning me. "You must have gone through that wastebasket, every item, when you went to Bottweill's office ostensibly to look for Santa Claus, and you hadn't just forgotten it. You don't forget things. So you have deliberately left it out. I want to know why, and I want to know what you took from that wastebasket and what you did with it."

I grinned at him. "I am also damned because I thought I knew how thorough they are and apparently I didn't. I wouldn't have supposed they went so far as to dust the contents of a wastebasket when there was nothing to connect them, but I see I was wrong, and I hate to be wrong." I shrugged. "Well, we learn something new every day." I screwed the statement around to position, signed it at the bottom of the last page, slid it across to him, and folded the carbon copy and put it in my pocket.

"I'll write it in if you insist," I told him, "but I doubt if it's worth the trouble. Santa Claus had run, Kiernan was calling the police, and I guess I was a little rattled. I must have looked around for something that might give me a line on Santa Claus, and my eye lit on the wastebasket, and I went through it. I haven't mentioned it because it wasn't very bright, and I like people to think I'm bright, especially cops. There's your why. As for what I took, the answer is nothing. I dumped the wastebasket, put everything back in, and took nothing. Do you want me to write that in?"

"No. I want to discuss it. I know you *are* bright. And you weren't rattled. You don't rattle. I want to know the real reason you went through the wastebasket, what you were after, whether you got it, and what you did with it."

It cost me more than an hour, twenty minutes of which were spent in the office of the District Attorney himself, with Farrell and another assistant present. At one point it looked as if they were going to hold me as a material witness, but that takes a warrant, the Christmas weekend had started, and there was nothing to show that I had monkeyed with anything that could be evidence, so finally they shooed me out, after I had handwritten an insert in my statement. It was too bad keeping such important public servants sitting there while I copied the insert on my carbon, but I like to do things right.

By the time I got home it was ten minutes past four, and of course Wolfe wasn't in the office, since his afternoon session up in the plant rooms is from four to six. There was no note on my desk from him, so apparently there were still no instructions, but there was information on it. My desk ashtray, which is mostly for decoration since I seldom smoke—a gift, not to Wolfe but to me, from a former client—is a jade bowl six inches across. It was there in its place, and in it were stubs from Pharaoh cigarettes.

Saul Panzer smokes Pharaohs, Egyptians. I suppose a few other people do too, but the chance that one of them had been sitting at my desk while I was gone was too slim to bother with. And not only had Saul been there, but Wolfe wanted me to know it, since one of the eight million things he will not tolerate in the office is ashtrays with remains. He will actually walk clear to the bathroom himself to empty one.

So steps were being taken, after all. What steps? Saul, a free lance and the best operative anywhere around, asks and gets sixty bucks a day, and is worth twice that. Wolfe had not called him in for any routine errand, and of course the idea that he had undertaken to sell him on doubling for Santa Claus never entered my head. Framing someone for murder, even a woman who might be guilty, was not in his bag of tricks. I got at the house phone and buzzed the plant rooms, and after a wait had Wolfe's voice in my ear.

"Yes, Fritz?"

"Not Fritz. Me. I'm back. Nothing urgent to report. They found my prints on stuff in the wastebasket, but I escaped without loss of blood. Is it all right for me to empty my ashtray?"

"Yes. Please do so."

"Then what do I do?"

"I'll tell you at six o'clock. Possibly earlier."

He hung up. I went to the safe and looked in the cash drawer to see if Saul had been supplied with generous funds, but the cash was as I had last seen it and there was no entry in the book. I emptied the ashtray. I went to the kitchen, where I found Fritz pouring a mixture into a bowl of pork tenderloin, and said I hoped Saul had enjoyed his lunch, and Fritz said he hadn't stayed for lunch. So steps must have been begun right after I left in the morning. I went back to the office, read over the carbon copy of my statement before filing it, and passed the time by thinking up eight different steps that Saul might have been assigned, but none of them struck me as promising. A little after five the phone rang and I answered. It was Saul. He said he was glad to know I was back home safe, and I said I was too.

"Just a message for Mr. Wolfe," he said. "Tell him everything is set, no snags."

"That's all?"

"Right. I'll be seeing you."

I cradled the receiver, sat a moment to consider whether to go up to the plant rooms or use the house phone, decided the latter would do, and pulled it to me and pushed the button. When Wolfe's voice came it was peevish; he hates to be disturbed up there.

"Yes?"

"Saul called and said to tell you everything is set, no snags. Congratulations. Am I in the way?"

"Oddly enough, no. Have chairs in place for visitors; ten should be enough. Four or five will come shortly after six o'clock; I hope not more. Others will come later."

"Refreshments?"

"Liquids, of course. Nothing else."

"Anything else for me?"

"No."

He was gone. Before going to the front room for chairs, and to the kitchen for supplies, I took time out to ask myself whether I had the slightest notion what kind of charade he was cooking up this time. I hadn't.

VII

It was four. They all arrived between six-fifteen and six-twenty—first Mrs. Perry Porter Jerome and her son Leo, then Cherry Quon, and last Emil Hatch. Mrs. Jerome copped the red leather chair, but I moved her, mink and all, to one of the yellow ones when Cherry came. I was willing to concede that Cherry might be headed for a very different kind of chair, wired for power, but even so I thought she rated that background and Mrs. Jerome didn't. By six-thirty, when I left them to cross the hall to the dining room, not a word had passed among them.

In the dining room Wolfe had just finished a bottle of beer. "Okay," I told him, "it's six-thirty-one. Only four. Kiernan and Margot Dickey haven't shown."

"Satisfactory." He arose. "Have they demanded information?"

"Two of them have, Hatch and Mrs. Jerome. I told them it will come from you, as instructed. That was easy, since I have none."

He headed for the office, and I followed. Though they didn't know, except Cherry, that he had poured champagne for them the day before, introductions weren't necessary because they had all met him during the tapestry hunt. After circling around Cherry in the red leather chair, he stood behind his desk to ask them how they did, then sat.

"I don't thank you for coming," he said, "because you came in your own interest, not mine. I sent—"

"I came," Hatch cut in, sourer than ever, "to find out what you're up to."

"You will," Wolfe assured him. "I sent each of you an identical message, saying that Mr. Goodwin has certain information which he feels he must give the police not later than tonight, but I have persuaded him to let me discuss it with you first. Before I—"

"I didn't know others would be here," Mrs. Jerome blurted, glaring at Cherry.

"Neither did I," Hatch said, glaring at Mrs. Jerome.

Wolfe ignored it. "The message I sent Miss Quon was somewhat different, but that need not concern you. Before I tell you what Mr. Goodwin's information is, I need a few facts from you. For instance, I understand that any of you—including Miss Dickey and Mr. Kiernan, who will probably join us later—could have found an opportunity to put the poison in the bottle. Do any of you challenge that?"

Cherry, Mrs. Jerome, and Leo all spoke at once. Hatch merely looked sour.

Wolfe showed them a palm. "If you please. I point no finger of accusation at any of you. I merely say that none of you, including Miss Dickey and Mr. Kiernan, can prove that you had no opportunity. Can you?"

"Nuts." Leo Jerome was disgusted. "It was that guy playing Santa Claus. Of course it was. I was with Bottweill and my mother all the time, first in the workshop and then in his office. I can prove *that*."

"But Bottweill is dead," Wolfe reminded him, "and your mother is your mother. Did you go up to the office a little before them, or did your mother go up a little before you and Bottweill did? Is there acceptable proof that you didn't? The others have the same problem. Miss Quon?"

There was no danger of Cherry's spoiling it. Wolfe had told me what he had told her on the phone: that he had made a plan which he thought she would find satisfactory, and if she came at a quarter past six she would see it work. She had kept her eyes fixed on him ever since he entered. Now she chirped, "If you mean I can't prove I wasn't in the office alone yesterday, no, I can't."

"Mr. Hatch?"

"I didn't come here to prove anything. I told you what I came for. What information has Goodwin got?"

"We'll get to that. A few more facts first. Mrs. Jerome, when did you learn that Bottweill had decided to marry Miss Quon?"

Leo shouted, "No!" but his mother was too busy staring at Wolfe to hear him. "What?" she croaked. Then she found her voice. "Kurt marry *her*? That little strumpet?"

Cherry didn't move a muscle, her eyes still on Wolfe.

"This is wonderful!" Leo said. "This is marvelous!"

"Not so damn wonderful," Emil Hatch declared. "I get the idea, Wolfe. Goodwin hasn't got any information, and neither have you. Why you wanted to get us together and start us clawing at each other, I don't see that, I don't know why you're interested, but maybe I'll find out if I give you a hand. This crowd has produced as fine a collection of venom as you could find. Maybe we all put poison in the bottle and that's why it was such a big dose. If it's true that Kurt had decided to marry Cherry, and Al Kiernan knew it, that would have done it. Al would have killed a hundred Kurts if it would get him Cherry. If Mrs. Jerome knew it, I would think she would have gone for Cherry instead of Kurt, but maybe she figured there would soon be another one and she might as well settle it for good. As for Leo, I think he rather liked Kurt, but what can you expect? Kurt was milking mamma of the pile Leo hoped to get some day, and I suspect that the pile is not all it's supposed to be. Actually—"

He stopped, and I left my chair. Leo was on his way up, obviously with the intention of plugging the creative artist. I moved to head him off, and at the same instant I gave him a shove and his mother jerked at his coattail. That not only halted him but nearly upset him, and with my other hand I steered him back onto his chair and then stood beside him.

Hatch inquired, "Shall I go on?"

"By all means," Wolfe said.

"Actually, though, Cherry would seem to be the most likely. She has the best brain of the lot and by far the strongest will. But I understand that while she says Kurt was going to marry her, Margot claims that he was going to marry *her*. Of course that complicates it, and anyway Margot would be my second choice. Margot has more than her share of the kind of pride that is only skin deep and therefore can't stand a scratch. If Kurt did decide to marry Cherry and told Margot so, he was even a bigger imbecile than I thought he was. Which brings us to me. I am in a class by myself. I despise all of them. If I had decided to take to poison I would have put it in the champagne as well as the Pernod, and I would have drunk vodka, which I prefer—and by the way, on that table is a bottle with the Korbeloff vodka label. I haven't had a taste of Korbeloff for fifteen years. Is it real?"

"It is. Archie?"

Serving liquid refreshments to a group of invited guests can be a pleasant chore, but it wasn't that time. When I asked Mrs. Jerome to name it she only glowered at me, but by the time I had filled Cherry's order for scotch and soda, and supplied Hatch with a liberal dose of Korbeloff, no dilution, and Leo had said he would take bourbon and water, his mother muttered that she would have that too. As I was pouring the bourbon I wondered where we would go from there. It looked as if the time had come for Wolfe to pass on the information which I felt I must give the police without delay, which made it difficult because I didn't have any. That had been fine for a bait to get them there, but what now? I suppose Wolfe would have held them somehow, but he didn't have to. He had rung for beer, and Fritz had brought it and was putting the tray on his desk when the doorbell rang. I handed Leo his bourbon and water and went to the hall. Out on the stoop, with his big round face nearly touching the glass, was Inspector Cramer of Homicide.

Wolfe had told me enough, before the company came, to give me a general idea of the program, so the sight of Cramer, just Cramer, was a letdown. But as I went down the hall other figures appeared, none of them strangers, and that looked better. In fact it looked fine. I swung the door wide and in they came—Cramer, then Saul Panzer, then Margot Dickey, then Alfred Kiernan, and, bringing up the rear, Sergeant Purley Stebbins. By the time I had the door closed and bolted they had their coats off, including Cramer, and it was also fine to see that he expected to stay a while. Ordinarily, once in, he marches down the hall and into the office without ceremony, but that time he waved the others ahead, including me, and he and Stebbins came last, herding us in. Crossing the sill, I stepped aside for the pleasure of seeing his face when his eyes lit on those already there and the empty chairs waiting.

Undoubtedly he had expected to find Wolfe alone, reading a book. He came in two paces, glared around, fastened the glare on Wolfe, and barked, "What's all this?"

"I was expecting you," Wolfe said politely. "Miss Quon, if you don't mind moving, Mr. Cramer likes that chair. Good evening, Miss Dickey. Mr. Kiernan, Mr. Stebbins. If you will all be seated—"

"Panzer!" Cramer barked. Saul, who had started for a chair in the rear, stopped and turned.

"I'm running this," Cramer declared. "Panzer, you're under arrest and you'll stay with Stebbins and keep your mouth shut. I don't want—"

"No," Wolfe said sharply. "If he's under arrest take him out of here. You are not running this, not in my house. If you have warrants for anyone present, or have taken them by lawful police power, take them and leave these premises. Would you bulldoze me, Mr. Cramer? You should know better."

That was the point, Cramer did know him. There was the stage, all set. There were Mrs. Jerome and Leo and Cherry and Emil Hatch, and the empty chairs, and above all, there was the fact that he had been expected. He wouldn't have taken Wolfe's word for that; he wouldn't have taken Wolfe's word for anything; but whenever he appeared on our stoop *not* expected I always left the chain-bolt on until he had stated his business and I had reported to Wolfe. And if he had been expected there was no telling what Wolfe had ready to spring. So Cramer gave up the bark and merely growled, "I want to talk with you."

"Certainly." Wolfe indicated the red leather chair, which Cherry had vacated. "Be seated."

"Not here. Alone."

Wolfe shook his head. "It would be a waste of time. This way is better and quicker. You know quite well, sir, it was a mistake to barge in here and roar at me that you are running my house. Either go, with whomever you can lawfully take, or sit down while I tell you who killed Kurt Bottweill." Wolfe wiggled a finger. "Your chair."

Cramer's round red face had been redder than normal from the outside cold, and now was redder still. He glanced around, compressed his lips until he didn't have any, and went to the red leather chair and sat.

VIII

Wolfe sent his eyes around as I circled to my desk. Saul had got to a chair in the rear after all, but Stebbins had too and was at his elbow. Margot had passed in front of the Jeromes and Emil Hatch to get to the chair at the end nearest me, and Cherry and Al Kiernan were at the other end, a little back of the others. Hatch had finished his Korbeloff and put the glass on the floor, but Cherry and the Jeromes were hanging on to their tall ones.

Wolfe's eyes came to rest on Cramer and he spoke. "I must confess that I stretched it a little. I can't tell you, at the moment, who killed Bottweill; I have only a supposition; but soon I can, and will. First some facts for you. I assume you know that for the past two months Mr. Goodwin has been seeing something of Miss Dickey. He says she dances well."

"Yeah." Cramer's voice came over sandpaper of the roughest grit. "You can save that for later. I want to know if you sent Panzer to meet—"

Wolfe cut him off. "You will. I'm headed for that. But you may prefer this firsthand. Archie, if you please. What Miss Dickey asked you to do last Monday evening, and what happened."

I cleared my throat. "We were dancing at the Flamingo Club. She said Bottweill had been telling her for a year that he would marry her next week, but next week never came, and she was going to have a showdown with him. She asked me to get a blank marriage license and fill it out for her and me and give it to her, and she would show it to Bottweill and tell him now or never. I got the blank on Tuesday, and filled it in, and Wednesday I gave it to her."

I stopped. Wolfe prompted me. "And yesterday afternoon?"

"She told me that the license trick had worked perfectly. That was about a minute before Bottweill entered the studio. I said in my statement to the District Attorney that she told me Bottweill was going to marry her, but I didn't mention the license. It was immaterial."

"Did she tell you what happened to the license?"

So we were emptying the bag. I nodded. "She said Bottweill had torn it up and put the pieces in the wastebasket by the desk in his office. The night before. Thursday evening."

"And what did you do when you went to the office after Bottweill had died?"

"I dumped the wastebasket and put the stuff back in it, piece by piece. No part of the license was there."

"You made sure of that?"

"Yes."

Wolfe left me and asked Cramer, "Any questions?"

"No. He lied in his statement. I'll attend to that later. What I want—"

Margot Dickey blurted, "Then Cherry took it!" She craned her neck to see across the others. "You took it, you slut!"

"I did not." The steel was in Cherry's chirp again. Her eyes didn't leave Wolfe, and she told him, "I'm not going to wait any longer—"

"Miss Quon!" he snapped. "I'm doing this." He returned to Cramer. "Now another fact. Yesterday I had a luncheon appointment with Mr. Bottweill at Rusterman's restaurant. He had once dined at my table and wished to reciprocate. Shortly before I left to keep the appointment he phoned to ask me to do him a favor. He said he was extremely busy and might be a few minutes late, and he needed a pair of white cotton gloves, medium size, for a man, and would I stop at some shop on the way and get them. It struck me as a peculiar request, but he was a peculiar man. Since Mr. Goodwin had chores to do, and I will not ride in taxicabs if there is any alternative, I had engaged a car at Baxter's, and the chauffeur recommended a shop on Eighth Avenue between Thirty-ninth and Fortieth Streets. We stopped there and I bought the gloves."

Cramer's eyes were such narrow slits that none of the blue-gray showed. He wasn't buying any part of it, which was unjustified, since some of it was true.

Wolfe went on. "At the lunch table I gave the gloves to Mr. Bottweill, and he explained, somewhat vaguely, what he wanted them for. I gathered that he had taken pity on some vagabond he had seen on a park bench, and had hired him to serve refreshments at his office party, costumed as Santa Claus, and he had decided that the only way to make his hands presentable was to have him wear gloves. You shake your head, Mr. Cramer?"

"You're damn right I do. You would have reported that. No reason on earth not to. Go ahead and finish."

"I'll finish this first. I didn't report it because I thought you would find the murderer without it. It was practically certain that the vagabond had merely skeddaddled out of fright, since he couldn't possibly have known of the jar of poison in the workshop, not to mention other considerations. And as you know, I have a strong aversion to involvement in matters where I have no concern or interest. You can of course check this—with the staff at Rusterman's, my presence there with Mr. Bottweill, and with the chauffeur, my conferring with him about the gloves and our stopping at the shop to buy them."

"You're reporting it now."

"I am indeed." Wolfe was unruffled. "Because I understood from Mr. Goodwin that you were extending and intensifying your search for the man who was there as Santa Claus, and with your army and your resources it probably wouldn't take you long when the holiday had ended to learn where the gloves were bought and get a description of the man who bought them. My physique is not unique, but it is—uncommon, and the only question was how long it would take you to get to me, and then I would be under inquisition. Obviously I had to report the episode to you and suffer your rebuke for not reporting it earlier, but I wanted to make it as tolerable as possible. I had one big advantage: I knew that the man who acted as Santa Claus was almost certainly not the murderer, and I decided to use it. I needed first to have a talk with one of those people, and I did so, with Miss Quon, who came here last evening."

"Why Miss Quon?"

Wolfe turned a hand over. "When I have finished you can decide whether such details are important. With her I discussed her associates at that place and their relationships, and I became satisfied that Bottweill had in fact decided to marry her. That was all. You can also decide later whether it is worth while to ask her to corroborate that, and I have no doubt she will."

He was looking at Cherry, of course, for any sign of danger. She had started to blurt it out once, and might again. But, meeting his gaze, she didn't move a muscle.

Wolfe returned to Cramer. "This morning I acted. Mr. Goodwin was absent, at the District Attorney's office, so I called in Mr. Panzer. After spending an hour with me here he went to do some errands. The first one was to learn whether Bottweill's wastebasket had been emptied since his conversation with Miss Dickey in his office Thursday evening. As you know, Mr. Panzer is highly competent. Through Miss Quon he got the name and address of the cleaning woman, found her and talked with her, and was told that the wastebasket had been emptied at about six o'clock Thursday afternoon and not since then. Meanwhile I—"

"Cherry took it—the pieces," Margot said.

Wolfe ignored her. "Meanwhile I was phoning everyone concerned—Mrs. Jerome and her son, Miss Dickey, Miss Quon, Mr. Hatch, and Mr. Kiernan—and inviting them to come here for a conference at six-fifteen. I told them that Mr. Goodwin had information which he intended to give the police, which was not true, and that I thought it best to discuss it first with them."

"I told you so," Hatch muttered.

Wolfe ignored him too. "Mr. Panzer's second errand, or series of errands, was the delivery of some messages. He had written them in longhand, at my dictation here this morning, on plain sheets of paper, and had addressed plain envelopes. They were identical and ran as follows:

When I was there yesterday putting on my costume I saw you through a crack in the door and I saw what you did. Do you want me to tell the cops? Be at Grand Central information booth upper level at 6:30 today. I'll come up to you and say "Saint Nick."

"By god," Cramer said, "you admit it."

Wolfe nodded. "I proclaim it. The messages were signed 'Santa Claus.' Mr. Panzer accompanied the messenger who took them to the persons I have named, and made sure they were delivered. They were not so much shots at random as they may appear. If one of those people had killed Bottweill it was likely that the poison had been put in the bottle while the vagabond was donning the Santa Claus costume; Miss Quon had told me, as no doubt she has told you, that Bottweill invariably took a drink of Pernod when he returned from lunch; and, since the appearance of Santa Claus at the party had been a surprise to all of them, and none of them knew who he was, it was highly probable that the murderer would believe he had been observed and would be irresistibly impelled to meet the writer of the message. So it was a reasonable assumption that one of the shots would reach its target. The question was, which one?"

Wolfe stopped to pour beer. He did pour it, but I suspected that what he really stopped for was to offer an opening for comment or protest. No one had any, not even Cramer. They all just sat and gazed at him. I was thinking that he had neatly skipped one detail: that the message from Santa Claus had not gone to Cherry Quon. She knew too much about him.

Wolfe put the bottle down and turned to go on to Cramer. "There was the possibility, of course, that more than one of them would go to you with the message, but even if you decided, because it had been sent to more than one, that it was some hoax, you would want to know who perpetrated it, and you would send one of them to the rendezvous under surveillance. Any one or more, excepting the murderer, might go to you, or none might; and surely only the murderer would go to the rendezvous without first consulting you. So if one of those six people were guilty, and if it had been possible for Santa Claus to observe him, disclosure seemed next to certain. Saul, you may now report. What happened? You were in the vicinity of the information booth shortly before six-thirty?"

Necks were twisted for a view of Saul Panzer. He nodded. "Yes, sir. At six-twenty. Within three minutes I had recognized three Homicide men scattered around in different spots. I don't know if they recognized me or not. At six twenty-eight I saw Alfred Kiernan walk up near the booth and stand there, about ten feet away from it. I was just about to go and speak to him when I saw Margot Dickey coming up from the Forty-second Street side. She approached to within thirty feet of the booth and stood looking around. Following your instructions in case more than one of them appeared and Miss Dickey was one of them, I went to her and said, 'Saint Nick.' She said, 'Who are you and what do you want?' I said, 'Excuse me, I'll be right back,' and went over to Alfred Kiernan and said to him, 'Saint Nick.' As soon as I said that he raised a hand to his ear, and then here they came, the three I had recognized and two more, and then Inspector Cramer and Sergeant Stebbins. I was afraid Miss Dickey would run, and she did start to, but they had seen me speak to her, and two of them stopped her and had her."

Saul halted because of an interruption. Purley Stebbins, seated next to him, got up and stepped over to Margot Dickey and stood there behind her chair. To me it seemed unnecessary, since I was sitting not much more than arm's length from her and might have been trusted to grab her if she tried to start anything, but Purley is never very considerate of other people's feelings, especially mine.

Saul resumed, "Naturally it was Miss Dickey I was interested in, since they had moved in on a signal from Kiernan. But they had her, so that was okay. They took us to a room back of the parcel room and started in on me, and I followed your instructions. I told them I would answer no questions, would say nothing whatever, except in the presence of Nero Wolfe, because I was acting under your orders. When they saw I meant it they took us out to two police cars and brought us here. Anything else?"

"No," Wolfe told him. "Satisfactory." He turned to Cramer. "I assume Mr. Panzer is correct in concluding that Mr. Kiernan gave your men a signal. So Mr. Kiernan had gone to you with the message?"

"Yes." Cramer had taken a cigar from his pocket and was squeezing it in his hand. He does that sometimes when he would like to squeeze Wolfe's throat instead. "So had three of the others—Mrs. Jerome, her son, and Hatch."

"But Miss Dickey hadn't?"

"No. Neither had Miss Quon."

"Miss Quon was probably reluctant, understandably. She told me last evening that the police's ideas of Orientals are very primitive. As for Miss Dickey, I may say that I am not surprised. For a reason that does not concern you, I am even a little gratified. I have told you that she told Mr. Goodwin that Bottweill had torn up the marriage license and put the pieces in his wastebasket, and they weren't there when Mr. Goodwin looked for them, and the wastebasket hadn't been emptied since early Thursday evening. It was difficult to conceive a reason for anyone to fish around in the wastebasket to remove those pieces, so presumably Miss Dickey lied; and if she lied about the license, the rest of what she told Mr. Goodwin was under suspicion."

Wolfe upturned a palm. "Why would she tell him that Bottweill was going to marry her if it wasn't true? Surely a stupid thing to do, since he would inevitably learn the truth. But it wasn't so stupid if she knew that Bottweill would soon die; indeed it was far from stupid if she had already put the poison in the bottle; it would purge her of motive, or at least help. It was a fair surmise that at their meeting in his office Thursday evening Bottweill had told her, not that he would marry her, but that he had decided to marry Miss Quon, and she decided to kill him and proceeded to do so. And it must be admitted that she would probably never have been exposed but for the complications injected by Santa Claus and my resulting intervention. Have you any comment, Miss Dickey?"

Cramer left his chair, commanding her, "Don't answer! I'm running this now," but she spoke.

"Cherry took those pieces from the wastebasket! She did it! She killed him!" She started up, but Purley had her arm and Cramer told her, moving for her, "She didn't go there to meet a blackmailer, and you did. Look in her bag, Purley. I'll watch her."

IX

Cherry Quon was back in the red leather chair. The others had gone, and she and Wolfe and I were alone. They hadn't put cuffs on Margot Dickey, but Purley had kept hold of her arm as they crossed the threshold, with Cramer right behind. Saul Panzer, no longer in custody, had gone along by request. Mrs. Jerome and Leo had been the first to leave. Kiernan had asked Cherry if he could take her home, but Wolfe had said no, he wanted to speak with her privately, and Kiernan and Hatch had left together, which showed a fine Christmas spirit, since Hatch had made no exceptions when he said he despised all of them.

Cherry was on the edge of the chair, spine straight, hands together in her lap. "You didn't do it the way I said," she chirped, without steel.

"No," Wolfe agreed, "but I did it." He was curt. "You ignored one complication, the possibility that you had killed Bottweill yourself. I didn't, I assure you. I couldn't very well send you one of the notes from Santa Claus, under the circumstances; but if those notes had flushed no prey, if none of them had gone to the rendezvous without first notifying the police, I would have assumed that you were guilty and would have proceeded to expose you. How, I don't know; I let that wait on the event; and now that Miss Dickey has taken the bait and betrayed herself it doesn't matter."

Her eyes had widened. "You really thought I might have killed Kurt?"

"Certainly. A woman capable of trying to blackmail me to manufacture evidence of murder would be capable of anything. And, speaking of evidence, while there can be no certainty about a jury's decision when a personable young woman is on trial for murder, now that Miss Dickey is manifestly guilty you may be sure that Mr. Cramer will dig up all he can get, and there should be enough. That brings me to the point I wanted to speak about. In the quest for evidence you will all be questioned, exhaustively and repeatedly. It will—"

"We wouldn't," Cherry put in, "if you had done it the way I said. That would have been proof."

"I preferred my way." Wolfe, having a point to make, was controlling himself. "It will be an ordeal for you. They will question you at length about your talk with Bottweill yesterday morning at breakfast, wanting to know all that he said about his meeting with Miss Dickey in his office Thursday evening, and under the pressure of inquisition you might inadvertently let something slip regarding what he told you about Santa Claus. If you do they will certainly follow it up. I strongly advise you to avoid making such a slip. Even if they believe you, the identity of Santa Claus is no longer important, since they have the murderer, and if they come to me with such a tale I'll have no great difficulty dealing with it."

He turned a hand over. "And in the end they probably won't believe you. They'll think you invented it for some cunning and obscure purpose—as you say, you are an Oriental—and all you would get for it would be more questions. They might even suspect that you were somehow involved in the murder itself. They are quite capable of unreasonable suspicions. So I suggest these considerations as much on your behalf as on mine. I think you will be wise to forget about Santa Claus."

She was eyeing him, straight and steady. "I like to be wise," she said.

"I'm sure you do, Miss Quon."

"I still think you should have done it my way, but it's done now. Is that all?"

He nodded. "That's all."

She looked at me, and it took a second for me to realize that she was smiling at me. I thought it wouldn't hurt to smile back, and did. She left the chair and came to me, extending a hand, and I arose and took it. She looked up at me.

"I would like to shake hands with Mr. Wolfe, but I know he doesn't like to shake hands. You know, Mr. Goodwin, it must be a very great pleasure to work for a man as clever as Mr. Wolfe. So extremely clever. It has been very exciting to be here. Now I say good-by."

She turned and went.

DOROTHY SALISBURY DAVIS

(b. 1916)

||||||||||||||||||||||||||||||||||||||||||| ■ |||||||||||||||||||||||||||||||||||||||||||

Dorothy Salisbury Davis's character-driven fiction marks her as a crime writer rather than an author of detection-oriented whodunits. Particularly in her short stories, she rarely relies on series sleuths or on puzzling the reader with the facts of the case. More fascinated by psychological motivation than by material motive, even in stories featuring police detectives, she would rather toy with their relationships to the criminals than dog their footsteps as they follow police procedure.

Davis became a Mystery Writers of America Grand Master in 1985. Spanning nearly four decades of the genre's development, her highly respected work is very significant in placing value on the inner lives of her characters and granting dignity to female characters, in particular. In the early part of her career, when many female characters were portrayed as helpless women in jeopardy, Davis was endowing her women with intelligence and stamina rather than mere beauty and pluck.

Born in Chicago, Davis spent her childhood and adolescence on midwestern farms and her adulthood in or near cities. This dual background is used to advantage in her fiction. The rural setting and small-town mentality are often essential to the atmosphere of her short stories, while the city is more likely to provide the large canvas for her longer works. She claims that she left the farm only physically, taking the experience with her into later life. She felt similarly about her Catholic faith. Although she has stated that she turned to mystery writing because she was quite certain that she did not wish to write about herself, her work reveals a woman anchored in everyday, small-town reality who nonetheless has a penchant for puzzling out large philosophical questions about just what it means to be human.

Accidental insights, quiet but traumatic discoveries—these are Davis's forte. Her own life was jarred by her accidental discovery, when she was seventeen, that she was adopted. "The whole room tilted over on its side and then somehow fell back into place again," she recalled. "I put everything back the way I found it. Except me." This is what her fiction does: the order of things is shattered and then put back together, but is never quite the same.

"A Matter of Public Notice" incorporates more police detection than do most of Davis's stories. But even while the author would like us to wonder "Whodunit?" her greater concern is to induce us to question ourselves.

1957

A Matter of Public Notice

■

. . . the victim, Mrs. Mary Philips, was the estranged wife of Clement Philips of this city who is now being sought by the police for questioning . . .

Nancy Fox reread the sentence. It was from the Rockland, Minnesota *Gazette*, reporting the latest of three murders to occur in the city within a month. "Estranged wife" was the phrase that gave her pause. Common newspaper parlance it might be, but for her it held a special meaning: for all its commonplaceness, it most often signals the tragic story of a woman suddenly alone—a story that she, Nancy Fox, could tell. Oh, how very well she could tell it!—being now an estranged wife herself.

How, she wondered, had Mary Philips taken her estrangement from a husband she probably once adored? Did he drink? Gamble? Was he unfaithful? Reason enough—any one of them—for some women. Or was it a cruelty surprised in him that had started the falling away of love, piece by piece, like the petals from a wasting flower?

Had the making of the final decision consumed Mary Philips's every thought for months and had the moment of telling it been too terrible to remember? And did it recur, fragmenting the peace it was supposed to have brought? Did the sudden aloneness leave her with the feeling that part of her was missing, that she might never again be a whole person?

Idle questions, surely, to ask now of Mrs. Philips. Mary Philips, age thirty-nine, occupation beauty operator, was dead—strangled at the rear of her shop with an electric cord at the hands of an unknown assailant. And Clement Philips was being sought by the police—in point of fact, by Captain Edward Allan Fox of the Rockland force, which was why Nancy Fox had read the story so interestedly in the first place.

Clement Philips was sought, found, and dismissed, having been two thousand miles from Rockland at the time of Mary Philips's murder. Several others, picked up after each of the three murders, were also dismissed. It was only natural that these suspects were getting testy, talking about their rights.

The chief of police was getting testy also. His was a long history of political survival in Rockland. Only in recent years had his work appeared worthy of public confidence, and that was due to the addition, since the war, of Captain Fox to the force. Fox knew it. No one knew his own worth better than "The Fox" did. And he knew how many years past retirement the old chief had stretched his tenure.

The chief paced back and forth before Captain Fox's desk, grinding one hand into the other behind his back. "I never thought the day would come when we'd turn up such a maniac in this town! He doesn't belong here, Fox!"

"Ah, but he does—by right of conquest," Fox said with the quiet sort of provocation he knew grated on the old man.

The chief whirled on him. "You never had such a good time in your life, did you?"

Fox sighed. He was accustomed to the bombast, the show of wrath that made his superior seem almost a caricature. He did not have to take it: the last of the chief's whipping boys was the custodian now of the city morgue. "Once or twice before, sir," Fox said, his eyes unwavering before the chief's.

The old man gave ground. He knew who was running the force, and he was not discontented. He had correctly estimated Fox's ambition: what Fox had of power, he had only with the old man's sanction. "In this morning's brief for me and the mayor, you made quite a thing of the fact that all three victims were separated from their husbands. Now I'm not very deep in this psychology business—and the missus and I haven't ever been separated more than the weekend it took to bury her sister—so you're going to have to explain what you meant. Does this separation from their husbands make 'em more—ah—attractive? Is that what you're getting at? More willing?"

Fox could feel a sudden pulse-throb at his temple. It was a lecher's picture the old man had conjured with his words and gestures, and his reference to Fox's own vulnerability—Nancy having left him—stirred him to a fury a weaker man would not have been able to control.

But he managed it, saying, "Only more available—and therefore more susceptible to the advances of their assailant."

The old man pulled at the loose skin of his throat. "It's interesting, Fox, how you got at it from the woman's point of view. The mayor says it makes damn good reading."

"Thank you, sir," Fox said for something that obviously was not intended as a compliment. "Do you remember Thomas Coyne?"

"Thomas Coyne," the chief repeated.

"The carpenter—the friend of Elsie Troy's husband," Fox prompted. Elsie Troy had been the first of the three victims. "We've picked him up again. No better alibi this time than last—this time, his landlady. I think he's too damned smug to have the conscience most men live with, so I've set a little trap for him. I thought maybe you'd like to be there."

"Think you can make a case against him?"

Fox rose and took the reports from where the old man had put them. "Chief," he said then, "there are perhaps a half dozen men in Rockland against whom a case could be made . . . including myself."

The old man's jaw sagged. A lot of other people were also unsure of Ed Fox—of the working mechanism they suspected ran him instead of a heart. "Let's see this Coyne fellow," the chief said. "I don't have much taste for humor at a time like this."

"I was only pointing up, sir, that our killer's mania is not apparent to either friends or victims—until it is too late."

The old man grunted and thrust his bent shoulders as far back as they would go—in subconscious imitation of The Fox's military bearing. On the way to the "Sun Room"—so called because of the brilliance of its lighting—where Thomas Coyne was waiting, the chief paused and asked, "Is it safe to say for sure now that Elsie Troy was the first victim? That we don't have a transient killer with Rockland just one stop on his itinerary?"

There had been several indications of such a possibility.

"I think we may assume that Elsie Troy was the beginning," Fox said. "I think now that her murder was a random business, unpremeditated. She was killed at night—in her bedroom, with the lights on and the window shades up. She was fully dressed, unmolested. It wasn't a setup for murder. It was pure luck that someone didn't see it happening.

"But having walked out of Elsie Troy's house a free man, her assailant got a new sense of power—a thrill he'd never had in his life. And then there began in him what amounted to a craving for murder. How he chooses victims, I don't know. That's why I called attention to the . . . the state of suspension in the marriages of the victims." Fox shrugged. "At least, that's my reconstruction of the pattern."

"You make it sound like you were there," the old man said.

"Yes," Fox said, "I suppose I do." He watched the old man bull his neck and plow down the hall ahead of him, contemplating the bit of sadism in himself—in, he suspected, all policemen. It was their devil, as was avarice the plague of merchants, conceit the foe of actors, complacency the doctor's demon, pride the clergyman's. He believed firmly that man's worst enemy was within himself. His own, Fox thought grimly, had cost him a wife, and beyond that, God Almighty knew what else. There were times since Nancy's going when he felt the very structure of his being tremble. There was no joy without her, only the sometimes bitter pleasure of enduring pain.

Coyne sat in the bright light, as Fox had expected, with the serenity of a religious mendicant. His arms folded, he could wait out eternity by his manner. It was unnatural behavior for any man under police inquisition. Fox was himself very casual. "Well, Tom, it's about time for us to start all over again. You know the chief?"

Coyne made a gesture of recognition. The chief merely glared down at him, his face a wrinkled mask of distaste.

"April twenty-ninth," Fox led. "That was the night you decided finally that you had time to fix Mrs. Troy's back steps."

"Afternoon," Coyne corrected. "I was home at night."

"What do you call the dividing line between afternoon and night?"

"Dark—at night it gets dark . . . sir."

"And you want it understood that you were home *before* dark?"

"I was home before dark," Coyne said calmly.

There had never been reference in the newspaper to the hour of Elsie Troy's death, partly because the medical examiner could put it no closer than between seven and nine. The month being April, darkness fell by seven.

"Suppose you tell the chief just what happened while you were there."

"Nothing happened. I went there on my way home from work. I fixed the steps. Then I called in to her that the job was done. She came out and said, 'That's fine, Tom. I'll pay you next week.' I never did get paid, but I guess that don't matter now."

Told by melancholy rote, Fox thought, having heard even the philosophic ending before. But then, most people repeated themselves under normal circumstances, especially about grievances they never expected to be righted.

"What I can't understand, Tom, is why you decided to fix the steps that day, and not, say, the week before?"

Coyne shrugged. "I just had the time then, I guess."

"She hadn't called you?"

"No, sir," he said with emphasis.

"You say that as though she would not have called you under any circumstances."

Coyne merely shrugged again.

"As a matter of fact, it was the husband—when they were still together—who asked you to repair the steps, wasn't it, Tom?"

"I guess it was."

"And you happened to remember it on the day she was about to be murdered."

"I didn't plan it that way," Coyne said, the words insolent, but his manner still serene. He tilted his chair back.

"It's a funny thing, Chief," Fox said. "Here's a man commissioned to do a job on a friend's house. He doesn't get around to it until the home has broken up. If it was me, I'd have forgotten all about the job under those circumstances—never done it at all."

"So would I," the chief said, "unless I was looking for an excuse to go there."

"Exactly," Fox said, still in a casual voice.

"It wouldn't be on account of you they broke up, would it, Coyne?" the chief suggested.

Coyne seemed to suppress a laugh. It was the first time his effort at control showed. "No, sir."

"Don't you like women?" the chief snapped.

"I'm living with one now," Coyne said.

"Mrs. Tuttle?" said Fox, naming Coyne's landlady.

"What's wrong with that? She's a widow."

Fox did not say what was wrong with it. But Mr. Thomas Coyne was not going to have it both ways: he had alibied himself with Mrs. Tuttle for the hours of all three murders. A paramour was not the most believable of witnesses. But then, from what Fox had seen of Mrs. Tuttle, he would not have called her the most believable of paramours, either.

With deliberate ease Fox then led Coyne through an account of his activities on the nights of the two subsequent murders. By the suspect's telling they brought Coyne nowhere near the scenes.

Finally Fox exchanged glances with the old man. He had had more than enough of Coyne by now and very little confidence that the carpenter had been worth bringing in again. "You can go now, Tom," Fox said, "but don't leave town." He nodded at the uniformed policeman by the door. And then, after a pause, "By the way, Tom, when was the last time you went swimming?"

"Oh, two or three weeks ago."

"Where?"

"Baker's Beach," Coyne said, naming the public park.

Fox nodded, held the door for the chief, and then closed it behind them.

"That guy should go on the radio," the old man said. "He knows all the answers."

"Seems like it," Fox said.

The second victim, Jane Mullins, had been strangled on the beach. But if Tom Coyne, as he said, had gone swimming two or three weeks ago, that would account for the sand found in Coyne's room.

Sand and a stack of newspapers—the only clues to Thomas Coyne's interests . . . and a clue also to the personality of his landlady; Mrs. Tuttle was a very careless housekeeper to leave sand and old newspapers lying around for weeks. She might be as careless with time—even with the truth.

Three strangulations—all of women who lived alone—within a month. It was enough to set the whole of a city the size of Rockland—population 110,000—on edge. As the *Gazette* editorialized: "When murder can match statistics with traffic deaths, it is time to investigate the investigators."

Knowing Ed Fox so well, Nancy wondered if he had not planted that line with the *Gazette;* it had The Fox's bite. It would be like him, if he was not getting all the cooperation he wanted from his superiors.

She looked at the clock and poured herself another cup of coffee. She was due at the radio station at eleven. Her broadcast time was noon: "The Woman's Way."

How cynical she had become about him, and through him about so many things. As much as anything, that cynicism had enabled her to make the break: the realization that she was turning into a bitter woman with a slant on the world that made her see first the propensity for evil in a man, and only incidentally his struggle against it. This philosophy might make Ed a good policeman, but it made her a poor educator. And she considered herself an educator despite his belittlement of her work. A radio commentator was responsible to her audience to teach them a little truth. Why just a little? Ed had always said to that.

She wondered if Ed thought about her at all these days, when she could scarcely think of anything except him. It was as though she bore his heelmark on her soul. A cruel image—oh, she had them. For a month she had lived apart from him, yet the morbid trauma of their life together still hung about her. If she could not banish the memories, she must find psychiatric help. That would greatly amuse Ed—one more useless occupation by his reckoning. Worse than useless, the enemy of justice: his hardest catch could escape the punishment that fit his crime by a psychiatrist's testimony.

Nancy folded the morning paper and rinsed her coffee cup.

Strange, the occupations of the three victims: Mary Philips had operated a beauty parlor, Elsie Troy had run a nursery school. She could hear Ed lecture on that: why have children if you pushed them out of the house in rompers? And poor Jane Mullins had written advertising copy—to Ed, perhaps the most useless nonsense of all. Well, that would give Ed something in common with the murderer—contempt for his victims. Ed always liked to have a little sympathy for the murderer: it made him easier to find. And no man ever suffered such anguish of soul as did Ed Fox at the hour of his man's execution.

There, surely, was the worst moment in all her five years of marriage to him: the night Mort Simmons was executed. Simmons had shot a man and Ed had made the arrest and got the confession. Nancy had known her husband was suffering, and she had ventured to console him with some not very original remarks about his having only done his duty, and that doubts were perfectly natural at such an hour.

"Doubts!" he had screamed at her. "I have no more doubt about his guilt than the devil waiting for him at the gates of hell!"

She had thought a long time about that. Slowly then the realization had come to her that Ed Fox suffered when such a man died because, in the pursuit and capture of him, Ed identified himself with the criminal. And fast upon that realization the thought had taken hold of her that never in their marriage had she been that close to him.

Nancy opened her hand and saw the marks of her nails in the palm. She looked at her nails. They needed polish. A beauty operator, Mary Philips. If Nancy had been in the habit of having her hair done by a professional, she might possibly have known Mrs. Philips. The shop was in the neighborhood where she and Ed had lived, where Ed still lived. . . .

She caught up her purse and brief case and forced her thoughts onto a recipe for which she had no appetite. Ed was not troubled that way in his work. . . .

"Damn it, Fox, give them something! They're riding my back like a cart-load of monkeys." This was the old man's complaint on the third day after Mary Philips's murder. Reporters were coming into Rockland from all over the country. The mayor had turned over the facilities of his own office to them.

So Captain Fox sat down and composed a description of a man who might have been the slayer. He did it aware of his cynicism.

The state police laboratory had been unable to bring out any really pertinent physical evidence in any of the cases. The murderer was a wily one—a maniac or a genius . . . except in the instance of Elsie Troy. Fox could not help but dwell on that random start to so successful a career.

The detective stood over the stenographer while she typed the description—twenty copies on the electric machine. He then dictated a few lines calculated to counteract the description, to placate the rising hysteria of all the lonely women in Rockland. So many lonely women, whether or not they lived alone . . . Did Nancy feel alarmed? he wondered. If she did, she had not called on him for reassurance. But then she would not. There was that streak of stubborn pride in her that made her run like a wounded animal from the hand most willing to help.

"Forty-eight complaints have already been investigated, twenty-one suspects questioned . . ." Give them statistics, Fox thought. Nowadays they mean more to people than words. Maybe figures didn't lie, but they made a convincing camouflage for the truth.

He handed out the release over the chief of police's name, and found himself free once more to do the proper work of a detective, something unrelated to public relations. Suspect Number 22 had been waiting for over an hour in the Sun Room.

It gave Fox a degree of satisfaction to know that he was there— "Deacon" Alvin Rugg. Rugg with two g's. G as in God, he thought. The young man was a religious fanatic—either a fanatic or a charlatan, possibly both, in Fox's mind. And he was The Fox's own special catch, having been flushed out in the policeman's persistent search for something the three women might have had in common besides the shedding of their husbands. All three—Elsie Troy, Jane Mullins, and Mary Philips—were interested in a revivalist sect called "Church of the Morning."

On his way to the Sun Room, Fox changed his mind about tackling the suspect there. Why not treat him as if he were only a witness?—the better to disarm him. He had no police record, young Mr. Rugg, except for a violation of the peace ordinance in a nearby town: the complaint had been filed against his father and himself—their zeal had simply begat too large a crowd.

Fox had the young man brought to the office, and there he offered him the most comfortable chair in the room. Rugg chose a straight one instead. Fox thought he might prove rugged, Rugg.

The lithe youth wore his hair crested around his head a little like a brushed-up halo, for it was almost the color of gold. His eyes were large, blue, and vacuous, though no doubt some would call them deep.

"Church of the Morning," Fox started, trying without much success to keep the cynicism from his voice. "When did you join up?"

"I was called at birth," Alvin replied with a rotish piety.

He was older than he looked, Fox realized, and a sure phony. "How old are you, Rugg?"

"Twenty."

"Let's see your draft registration. This is no newspaper interview."

"Thirty-two," Rugg amended, wistful as a woman.

"What do you do for a living?"

"Odd jobs. I'm a handyman when I'm not doing the Lord's work."

"How do you get these . . . these odd jobs?"

"My father recommends me."

"That would be the Reverend Rugg?"

The young man nodded—there was scarcely the shadow of a beard on his face. Fox was trying to calculate how the women to whom his father recommended him would feel about Alvin of the halo. Fox himself would have had more feeling for a goldfish, but then he was not a lonely woman. He must look up some of them, those still among the living. Fox had gone to the revival tent the night before—he and one-tenth the population of Rockland, almost 12,000 people. It did not seem so extraordinary then that all three victims had chanced to catch the fervor of the Church of the Morning.

"I suppose you talk religion with your employers?"

"That is why I am for hire, Captain."

The arrogance of an angel on its way to hell, Fox thought. "Who was your mother?" he snapped, on the chance that this was the young man's point of vulnerability.

"A Magdalen," Rugg said. "I have never asked further. My father is a holy man."

Fox muttered a vulgarity beneath his breath. He was a believer in orthodoxy, himself. Revivalists were not for him, especially one like Reverend Rugg whom he had heard last night speak of this boy, this golden lad, as sent to him like a pure spirit, a reward—this golden lad . . . of thirty-two.

"The reason I asked you to come in, Alvin," Fox said, forcing amiability upon himself, and quite as though he had not sent two officers to pick Rugg up, "I thought you might be able to help us on these murders. You've heard about them?"

"I . . . I had thought of coming in myself," Rugg said.

"When did that thought occur to you?"

"Well, two or three weeks ago at least—the first time, I mean. You see, I worked for that Mrs. Troy—cleaned her windows, things like that. Her husband was a bitter, vengeful man. He doesn't have the spiritual consolation his wife had."

A nice distinction of the present and past tenses, Fox thought. But what Troy did have was an unbreakable alibi: five witnesses to his continuous presence at a poker table on the night Elsie Troy was slain.

"She told you that about him?" Fox prompted cheerfully.

"Well, not exactly. She wanted to make a donation to the church but she couldn't. He had their bank account tied up . . . she said."

The hesitation before the last two words was marked by Fox. Either the Ruggs had investigated Elsie Troy's finances, he thought, or Alvin was covering up an intimacy he feared the detective suspected or had evidence of.

"But Mrs. Troy ran a nursery school," Fox said blandly. "I don't suppose she took the little ones in out of charity, do you?"

"Her husband had put up the money for the school. He insisted his investment should be paid back to him first."

"I wouldn't call that unreasonable, would you, Alvin? A trifle unchivalrous, perhaps, but not unreasonable?"

A vivid dislike came into the boy's, the man's, eyes. He had suddenly made an enemy of him, Fox thought with grim satisfaction. He would soon provoke the unguarded word. "Didn't you and Mrs. Troy talk about anything besides money?"

"We talked about faith," Rugg said, and then clamped his lips tight.

"Did you also do chores for Mrs. Mullins?"

"No. But she offered once to get me a messenger's job at the advertising company where she worked. Said I could do a lot of good there."

"I'll bet," Fox said. "And how about Mary Philips? What was she going to do for you?" He resisted the temptation to refer to the beauty shop.

"Nothing. She was a very nice woman."

That, Fox thought, was a revelatory answer. It had peace of soul in it. The captain then proceeded to turn the heat on "Deacon" Rugg, and before half an hour was over he got from the golden boy the admission that both Elsie Troy and Jane Mullins had made amatory advances. Seeking more than religion, the self-widowed starvelings! They kicked out husbands and then welcomed any quack in trousers. Lady breadwinners! Fox could feel the explosion of his own anger; it spiced his powers of inquisition.

Alvin Rugg was then given such mental punishment as might have made a less vulnerable sinner threaten suit against the city. But while "The Deacon" lacked airtight alibis for the nights of the 29th of April, the 16th of May, and June 2nd, he had been seen about his father's tent by many people, and he maintained his innocence through sweat and tears, finally sobbing his protestations on his knees.

The extent of The Fox's mercy was to leave Rugg alone to compose himself and find his own way to the street.

"Until tomorrow then, this is Nancy Fox going 'The Woman's Way.'"

Nancy gathered her papers so as not to make a sound the microphone could pick up. The newscaster took over. The next instant Nancy was listening with all the concentration of her being.

". . . a man about forty, quick of movement, near six feet tall, a hundred and sixty pounds, extremely agile; he probably dresses conservatively and speaks softly. One of his victims is thought to have been describing him when she told a friend, 'You never know when he is going to smile or when he isn't—he changes moods so quickly . . .'"

Nancy pressed her lips together and leaned far away from the table. Her breathing was loud enough to carry into the mike. That was her own husband the newscaster was describing—Ed Fox himself right down to the unpredictable smile! Actually, it could be any of a dozen men, she tried to tell herself. Of course. Any of a hundred! What nonsense to put such a description over the air!

She had regained her composure by the time the reporter had finished his newscast. Then she had coffee with him, as she often did. But what a fantastic experience! Fantasy—that was the only word for it. The description had been part of a release from the office of the chief of police, which meant it had had Ed's own approval.

"But now I'm going to tell you what it sounded like to me," the newsman said. "Like somebody—maybe on the inside—deliberately muddying up the tracks. I tell you somebody down there knows more than we're getting in these handouts."

"What a strange idea!" Nancy cried, and gave a deprecating laugh as hollow as the clink of her dime on the counter.

She spent the next couple of hours in the municipal library, trying to learn something about water rights. A bill on the water supply was before the city council. Two years of research would have been more adequate to the subject, she discovered. Once more she had dived into something only to crack her head in the shallows of her own ignorance. Then she drove out to the county fairgrounds to judge the cake contest of the Grange women. She fled the conversational suggestion that the murderer might be scouting there. Some women squealed with a sort of ecstatic terror.

A feeling of deepening urgency pursued her from one chore to the next: there was something she ought to do, something she must return to and attend to. And yet the specific identity of this duty did not reveal itself. Sometimes she seemed on the brink of comprehension . . . but she escaped. Oh, yes, that much of herself she knew: she was fleeing it, not it fleeing her.

With that admission she cornered herself beyond flight. There was a question hanging in the dark reaches of her mind, unasked now even as it was five years ago. Since the night Mort Simmons died in the electric chair, it clung like monstrous fungi at the end of every cavern through which she fled. And by leaving her husband's house she had not escaped it.

Ask it now, she demanded—ask it now!

She drove off the pavement and braked the car to a shrieking halt. "All right!" she cried aloud. "I ask it before God—is Ed Fox capable of . . ." But she could not finish the sentence. She bent her head over the wheel and sobbed, "Eddie, oh, Eddie dear, forgive me . . ."

Without food, without rest, she drove herself until the day was spent, and with it most of her energy. Only her nerves remained taut. She returned just before dark to the apartment she had subleased from a friend. It was in no way her home: she had changed nothing in it, not even the leaf on the calendar. And so the place gave her no message when she entered—neither warning nor welcome.

She left the hall door ajar while she groped her way to the table where the lamp stood, and at the moment of switching on the light she sensed that someone had followed her into the apartment. Before she could fully see him, he caught her into his arms.

"Don't, please don't!" she cried. Her struggling but made him tighten his grip.

"For God's sake, Nancy, it's me!"

"I know!" she said, and leaped away as Ed gave up his grasp of her. She could taste the retch of fear. She whirled and looked at him as if she were measuring the distance between them.

"You knew?" he said incredulously. "You knew that it was me and yet you acted like that?"

She could only stare at him and nod in giddy acknowledgment of the truth.

His hands fell limp to his sides. "My God," he murmured.

A world of revelation opened to her in that mute gesture, in the simple dropping of his hands.

Neither of them moved. She felt the ache that comes with unshed tears gathering in her throat as the bitter taste of fear now ran out. It was a long moment until the tears were loosed and welled into her eyes, a moment in which they measured each other in the other's understanding—or in the other's misunderstanding.

"I thought I might surprise an old love—if I surprised you," he said flatly. "And then when I realized you were afraid, it seemed so crazy—so inconsiderate a thing to do, with a maniac abroad." He stood, self-pilloried and miserable—immobile, lest one move of his start up the fear in her again.

At last she managed the words: "Eddie, I do love you."

Fox raised his arms and held them out to her and she ran to him with utter abandon.

Presently he asked. "How long have you been afraid of me?"

"I think since the night Mort Simmons was executed," she said, and then clinging to him again, "Oh, my dear, my beloved husband."

He nodded and lifted her fingers to his lips. "How did you conceal it? Fear kills love. They say like that." He snapped his fingers.

"I never called it fear," she said, lifting her chin—and that, she thought, that inward courage was what he mistook for pride—"not until . . ." She bit her lip against the confession of the final truth.

"Until the murder of one, two, three women," Fox said evenly, "with whose lives you knew I'd have no sympathy."

"I didn't know that exactly," she said. "I only knew your prejudices."

"Pride and Prejudice," he mused. He pushed her gently an arm's distance from him. "Take another look at my prejudices, Nancy, and see who suffers most by them."

"May I come home now, Eddie?"

"Soon, darling. Very soon." He picked up his hat from where it had fallen in their struggle. "But you must let me tell you when."

He should have known it, really, Fox thought, closing the apartment door behind him. He was so alert to it in others, he should have seen the fear grow in her since the night she caught him naked-souled, suffering the death of Mort Simmons. Suppose that night he had tried to explain what had happened to him? How could he have said that it was not Mort Simmons's guilt he doubted, but his own innocence? How tell her that at the hour of his death, Mort Simmons was in a very special way the victim of Ed Fox?

Fox drove to within a block of Thomas Coyne's boarding house. He parked the car and walked up the street to where the tail he had put on Coyne was sitting, a newspaper before him, in a nondescript Ford. Fox slipped in beside him.

"Coyne's in there," the other detective said. "Been there since he came home from work. Ten minutes ago he went down to the corner for a paper. Came right back."

Fox decided to talk first with Mrs. Tuttle. He approached her by way of the kitchen door, identified himself, and got a cup of warmed-over coffee at the table. A voluble, lusty, good-natured woman, she responded easily to his question—whether she was interested in the Church of the Morning. She shook her head. Fox described "Deacon" Alvin Rugg and his relationship to the murdered women.

Mrs. Tuttle clucked disapproval and admitted she had heard of him, but where she could not remember. To the captain's direct question as to whether she had ever seen the golden boy, she shook her head again. "I tell you, Mr. Fox, I like my men and my whiskey 100 proof, and my religion in a church with a stone foundation."

Fox laughed. "Anybody in the house here interested in the Revival?"

"What you want to know," she said, looking at him sidewide, "is if it was Tom Coyne who told me about him. Isn't that it?"

Fox admitted to the bush he had been beating around. "I'd like to know if Coyne has shown any interest in the sect."

"I don't know for sure. He takes sudden fancies, that one does."

"I understand he has a very deep fancy for you," Fox said bluntly.

Mrs. Tuttle frowned, the good nature fleeing her face. She took his cup and saucer to the sink and clattered it into the dish basin.

"I'm sorry to be clumsy about a delicate matter," Fox said, getting up from the table and following to where he could see her face. Shame or wrath? he wondered. Perhaps both. "It was very necessary to Coyne that he confide that information to the police," he elaborated, in subtle quest of further information.

"Was it?" she said. "Then maybe it was necessary for him to come to me in the first place. Can you tell me that, mister?"

"If you tell me when it was he first came to you—in that sense, I mean," Fox said.

"A couple of nights ago," she said. "Till then it was just . . . well, we were pals, that's all."

Fox examined his own fingernails. "He didn't take very long to tell about it, did he?"

"Now answer my question to you," she said. "Did he come just so he could tell you him and me were—like that?"

Fox ventured to lay his hand on her arm. She pulled away from his touch as though it were fire. Her shame was deep, her affair shallow, he thought. "Just stay in the kitchen," he said. She would have her answer soon enough.

He moved through the hall and alerted the detective on watch at the front. Then he went upstairs. Thomas Coyne was sitting in his room, the newspaper open on the table before him, a pencil in his hand. He had been caught in the obviously pleasurable act of marking an item in the paper, and he gathered himself up on seeing Fox—like a bather surprised in the nude.

It gave an ironic sequence to the pretense on which Fox had come. "I wanted to see your swim trunks," Captain Fox said.

Coyne was still gaping. Slowly he uncoiled himself and then pointed to the dresser drawer.

"You get them," Fox said. "I don't like to invade your privacy." He turned partially away, in fact, to suggest that he was unaware of the newspaper over which he had surprised the man. He waited until Coyne reached the dresser, and then moved toward the table, but even there Fox pointed to the picture on the wall beyond it, and remarked that he remembered its like from his school days. A similar print, he said, had hung in the study hall. On and on he talked, and if Coyne was aware of the detective's quick scrutiny of his marked newspaper, it was less fearful for the man to pretend he had not seen it.

"My wife, Ellen, having left my bed and board, I am no longer responsible. . . ."

Fox had seen it. So, likely, had the husbands of Mary Philips and Jane Mullins and Elsie Troy given public notice sometime or other. The decision he needed to reach instantly was whether he had sufficient evidence to indict Tom Coyne: it was so tempting to let him now pursue the pattern once more—up to its dire culmination.

The detective stood, his arms folded, while Coyne brought the swim trunks. "Here you are, Captain," he said.

"Haven't worn them much," Fox said, not touching them.

"It's early," Coyne said.

"So it is," Fox said, "The fifth of June. Baker's Beach just opened Memorial Day, didn't it?"

There was no serenity in Coyne now. He realized the trap into which he had betrayed himself while under questioning by Fox and the chief of police. So many things he had made seem right—even an affair with Mrs. Tuttle; and now that one little thing, by Fox's prompting, was wrong. He would not have been allowed in the waters of Baker's Beach before the thirtieth of May. In order to account for the sand in his room following the murder of Jane Mullins, he had said he had gone swimming at Baker's Beach two or three weeks before.

Before midnight Coyne confessed to the three homicides, the last two premeditated. He had not intended to kill Elsie Troy. But he had been watching her behavior with young Alvin Rugg, and as her husband's friend he had taken the excuse of fixing her steps to gain her company and reproach her. She had called him "a nasty little man," and where matters had gone from that, he said, he could not clearly remember . . . except that he killed her. He was sure because of the wonderful exhilaration it gave him after he had done it—so wonderful it had to be repeated.

The chief had pride in his eyes, commending Captain Fox for so fine a job. They went upstairs together to see the mayor, and there the chief took major credit as his due. He announced, however, that this would be his last case before retirement, and he put his arm about Captain Fox as the reporters were invited in. Fox asked to be excused.

"Damn it, man, you've got to do the talking," the chief protested.

"Yes, sir, if you say so," Fox said. "But first I want to call my wife."

"By all means," the chief said. "Here, use the mayor's phone."

Nancy answered on the first ring.

"Will you pick me up tonight, my dear, on your way home?" Fox said.

ELLERY QUEEN

|||||||||||||||||||||||||||||||||||||||||||| ■ ||||||||||||||||||||||||||||||||||||||||||||

Frederic Dannay (Daniel Nathan, 1905–1982) and Manfred Bennington Lee (Manfred Lepofsky, 1905–1971) were cousins who together created the highly popular detective Ellery Queen. Both were born in Brooklyn, New York; attended Boys' High School in the borough; and began their careers in Manhattan. Dannay worked as a writer and an art director for an advertising agency, while Lee wrote publicity for film studios.

When they were twenty-three, the two decided to enter a detective-fiction contest. They collaborated on what came to be *The Roman Hat Mystery*, using a very sophisticated young man named Ellery Queen as a mystery writer and amateur sleuth. Inspector Richard Queen of the New York Police Department is also introduced as Ellery's doting father. Dannay and Lee used the Ellery Queen name for themselves as well, so that it is memorable for referring to both character and co-authors. The story originally won the contest, but the prize went to another author when the magazine that held the contest changed hands. Even so, *The Roman Hat Mystery* was published the following year—and the rest is history.

The two also produced a four-book series in the early 1930s under the pen name Barnaby Ross, but Ellery Queen was quickly and hugely popular and occupied most of their time. Queen promptly reappeared in *The French Powder Mystery* and *The Dutch Shoe Mystery*, and in 1931 the two young men quit their jobs to write full time.

By the early 1980s, other writers—including Avram Davidson, Richard Deming, Paul W. Fairman, Edward D. Hoch, Stephen Marlowe, Talmadge Powell, Theodore Sturgeon, and John Holbrook Vance—using plots created by Dannay, had been pulled into the Ellery Queen persona, turning out books under the supervision of the cousins. By the time of Dannay's death, at least 150 million Ellery Queen books had been sold worldwide, and the *Ellery Queen Mystery Magazine* was maintaining some semblance of a market for short fiction. The two helped found the Mystery Writers of America, and their peers gave them four Edgar awards and the Grand Master award.

"The Adventure of Abraham Lincoln's Clue" illustrates the typical Queen technique. It is solidly in the classical tradition, with the plot revolving around a clever puzzle whose solution requires the sleuth to make brilliant deductions from clues that are displayed to the reader, who is challenged to outwit the detective. The mere hint of romantic interest is also typical of both the form and the times.

1965

The Adventure of Abraham Lincoln's Clue

■

The case began on the outskirts of an upstate–New York city with the dreadful name of Eulalia, behind the flaking shutters of a fat and curli-cued house with architectural dandruff, recalling for all the world some blowsy ex–Bloomer Girl from the Gay Nineties of its origin.

The owner, a formerly wealthy man named DiCampo, possessed a grandeur not shared by his property, although it was no less fallen into ruin. His falcon's face, more Florentine than Victorian, was—like the house—ravaged by time and the inclemencies of fortune; but haughtily so, and indeed DiCampo wore his scurfy purple velvet house jacket like the prince he was entitled to call himself, but did not. He was proud, and stubborn, and useless; and he had a lovely daughter named Bianca, who taught at a Eulalia grade school and, through marvels of economy, supported them both.

How Lorenzo San Marco Borghese-Ruffo DiCampo came to this de-cayed estate is no concern of ours. The presence there this day of a man named Harbidger and a man named Tungston, however, is to the point: they had come, Harbidger from Chicago, Tungston from Philadelphia, to buy something each wanted very much, and DiCampo had sum-moned them in order to sell it. The two visitors were collectors, Har-bidger's passion being Lincoln, Tungston's Poe.

The Lincoln collector, an elderly man who looked like a migrant fruit picker, had plucked his fruits well: Harbidger was worth about $40,000,000, every dollar of which was at the beck of his mania for Lin-colniana. Tungston, who was almost as rich, had the aging body of a poet and the eyes of a starving panther, armament that had served him well in the wars of Poeana.

"I must say, Mr. DiCampo," remarked Harbidger, "that your letter surprised me." He paused to savor the wine his host had poured from an ancient and honorable bottle (DiCampo had filled it with California claret before their arrival). "May I ask what has finally induced you to offer the book and document for sale?"

"To quote Lincoln in another context, Mr. Harbidger," said Di-Campo with a shrug of his wasted shoulders, "'the dogmas of the quiet past are inadequate to the stormy present.' In short, a hungry man sells his blood."

"Only if it's of the right type," said old Tungston, unmoved. "You've made that book and document less accessible to collectors and

588

historians, DiCampo, than the gold in Fort Knox. Have you got them here? I'd like to examine them."

"No other hand will ever touch them except by right of ownership," Lorenzo DiCampo replied bitterly. He had taken a miser's glee in his lucky finds, vowing never to part with them; now forced by his need to sell them, he was like a suspicion-caked old prospector who, stumbling at last on pay dirt, draws cryptic maps to keep the world from stealing the secret of its location. "As I informed you gentlemen, I represent the book as bearing the signatures of Poe and Lincoln, and the document as being in Lincoln's hand; I am offering them with the customary proviso that they are returnable if they should prove to be not as represented; and if this does not satisfy you," and the old prince actually rose, "let us terminate our business here and now."

"Sit down, sit down, Mr. DiCampo," Harbidger said.

"No one is questioning your integrity," snapped old Tungston. "It's just that I'm not used to buying sight unseen. If there's a money-back guarantee, we'll do it your way."

Lorenzo DiCampo reseated himself stiffly. "Very well, gentlemen. Then I take it you are both prepared to buy?"

"Oh, yes!" said Harbidger. "What is your price?"

"Oh, no," said DiCampo. "What is your bid?"

The Lincoln collector cleared his throat, which was full of slaver. "If the book and document are as represented, Mr. DiCampo, you might hope to get from a dealer or realize at auction—oh—$50,000. I offer you $55,000."

"$56,000," said Tungston.

"$57,000," said Harbidger.

"$58,000," said Tungston.

"$59,000," said Harbidger.

Tungston showed his fangs. "$60,000," he said.

Harbidger fell silent, and DiCampo waited. He did not expect miracles. To these men, five times $60,000 was of less moment than the undistinguished wine they were smacking their lips over; but they were veterans of many a hard auction-room campaign, and a collector's victory tasted very nearly as sweet for the price as for the prize.

So the impoverished prince was not surprised when the Lincoln collector suddenly said, "Would you be good enough to allow Mr. Tungston and me to talk privately for a moment?"

DiCampo rose and strolled out of the room, to gaze somberly through a cracked window at the jungle growth that had once been his Italian formal gardens.

It was the Poe collector who summoned him back. "Harbidger has convinced me that for the two of us to try to outbid each other would simply run the price up out of all reason. We're going to make you a sporting proposition."

"I've proposed to Mr. Tungston, and he has agreed," nodded Harbidger, "that our bid for the book and document be $65,000. Each of us is prepared to pay that sum, and not a penny more."

"So that is how the screws are turned," said DiCampo, smiling. "But I do not understand. If each of you makes the identical bid, which of you gets the book and document?"

"Ah," grinned the Poe man, "that's where the sporting proposition comes in."

"You see, Mr. DiCampo," said the Lincoln man, "we are going to leave that decision to you."

Even the old prince, who had seen more than his share of the astonishing, was astonished. He looked at the two rich men really for the first time. "I must confess," he murmured, "that your compact is an amusement. Permit me?" He sank into thought while the two collectors sat expectantly. When the old man looked up he was smiling like a fox. "The very thing, gentlemen! From the typewritten copies of the document I sent you, you both know that Lincoln himself left a clue to a theoretical hiding place for the book which he never explained. Some time ago I arrived at a possible solution to the President's little mystery. I propose to hide the book and document in accordance with it."

"You mean whichever of us figures out your interpretation of the Lincoln clue and finds the book and document where you will hide them, Mr. DiCampo, gets both for the agreed price?"

"That is it exactly."

The Lincoln collector looked dubious. "I don't know . . ."

"Oh, come, Harbidger," said Tungston, eyes glittering. "A deal is a deal. We accept, DiCampo! Now what?"

"You gentlemen will of course have to give me a little time. Shall we say three days?"

Ellery let himself into the Queen apartment, tossed his suitcase aside, and set about opening windows. He had been out of town for a week on a case, and Inspector Queen was in Atlantic City attending a police convention.

Breathable air having been restored, Ellery sat down to the week's accumulation of mail. One envelope made him pause. It had come by airmail special delivery, it was postmarked four days earlier, and in the lower left corner, in red, flamed the word URGENT. The printed return address on the flap said: *L.S.M.B-R DiCampo, Post Office Box 69, Southern*

District, Eulalia, N.Y. The initials of the name had been crossed out and "Bianca" written above them.

The enclosure, in a large agitated female hand on inexpensive note-paper, said:

Dear Mr. Queen,
The most important detective book in the world has disappeared. Will you please find it for me?
Phone me on arrival at the Eulalia RR station or airport and I will pick you up.

BIANCA DICAMPO

A yellow envelope then caught his eye. It was a telegram, dated the previous day:

WHY HAVE I NOT HEARD FROM YOU STOP AM IN DESPERATE NEED YOUR SERVICES

BIANCA DICAMPO

He had no sooner finished reading the telegram than the telephone on his desk trilled. It was a long-distance call.

"Mr. Queen?" throbbed a contralto voice. "Thank heaven I've finally got through to you! I've been calling all day—"

"I've been away," said Ellery, "and you would be Miss Bianca Di-Campo of Eulalia. In two words, Miss DiCampo: Why me?"

"In two words, Mr. Queen: Abraham Lincoln."

Ellery was startled. "You plead a persuasive case," he chuckled. "It's true, I'm an incurable Lincoln addict. How did you find out? Well, never mind. Your letter refers to a book, Miss DiCampo. Which book?"

The husky voice told him, and certain other provocative things as well. "So you will come, Mr. Queen?"

"Tonight if I could! Suppose I drive up first thing in the morning. I ought to make Eulalia by noon. Harbidger and Tungston are still around, I take it?"

"Oh, yes. They're staying at a motel downtown."

"Would you ask them to be there?"

The moment he hung up Ellery leaped to his bookshelves. He snatched out his volume of *Murder for Pleasure*, the historical work on detective stories by his good friend Howard Haycraft, and found what he was looking for on page 26:

And . . . young William Dean Howells thought it significant praise to assert of a nominee for President of the United States:

The bent of his mind is mathematical and metaphysical, and he is therefore pleased with the absolute and logical method of

591

Poe's tales and sketches, in which the problem of mystery is given, and wrought out into everyday facts by processes of cunning analysis. It is said that he suffers no year to pass without a perusal of this author.

Abraham Lincoln subsequently confirmed this statement, which appeared in his little known "campaign biography" by Howells in 1860 . . . The instance is chiefly notable, of course, for its revelation of a little suspected affinity between two great Americans . . .

Very early the next morning Ellery gathered some papers from his files, stuffed them into his briefcase, scribbled a note for his father, and ran for his car, Eulalia-bound . . .

He was enchanted by the DiCampo house, which looked like something out of Poe by Charles Addams; and, for other reasons, by Bianca, who turned out to be a genetic product supreme of northern Italy, with titian hair and Mediterranean blue eyes and a figure that needed only some solid steaks to qualify her for Miss Universe competition. Also, she was in deep mourning; so her conquest of the Queen heart was immediate and complete.

"He died of a cerebral hemorrhage, Mr. Queen," Bianca said, dabbing at her absurd little nose. "In the middle of the second night after his session with Mr. Harbidger and Mr. Tungston."

So Lorenzo San Marco Borghese-Ruffo DiCampo was unexpectedly dead, bequeathing the lovely Bianca near-destitution and a mystery.

"The only things of value father really left me are that book and the Lincoln document. The $65,000 they now represent would pay off father's debts and give me a fresh start. But I can't find them, Mr. Queen, and neither can Mr. Harbidger and Mr. Tungston—who'll be here soon, by the way. Father hid the two things, as he told them he would; but where? We've ransacked the place."

"Tell me about the book, Miss DiCampo."

"As I said over the phone, it's called *The Gift: 1845*. The Christmas annual that contained the earliest appearance of Edgar Allan Poe's *The Purloined Letter*."

"Published in Philadelphia by Carey & Hart? Bound in red?" At Bianca's nod Ellery said, "You understand that an ordinary copy of *The Gift: 1845* isn't worth more than $50. What makes your father's copy unique is that double autograph you mentioned."

"That's what he said, Mr. Queen. I wish I had the book here to show you—that beautifully handwritten *Edgar Allan Poe* on the flyleaf, and under Poe's signature the signature *Abraham Lincoln*."

"Poe's own copy, once owned, signed, and read by Lincoln," Ellery said slowly. "Yes, that would be a collector's item for the ages. By the way, Miss DiCampo, what's the story behind the other piece—the Lincoln document?"

Bianca told him what her father had told her.

One morning in the spring of 1865, Abraham Lincoln opened the rosewood door of his bedroom in the southwest corner of the second floor of the White House and stepped out into the red-carpeted hall at the unusually late hour—for him—of 7:00 A.M.; he was more accustomed to beginning his work day at six.

But (as Lorenzo DiCampo had reconstructed events) Mr. Lincoln that morning had lingered in his bedchamber. He had awakened at his usual hour but, instead of leaving immediately on dressing for his office, he had pulled one of the cane chairs over to the round table, with its gas-fed reading lamp, and sat down to reread Poe's *The Purloined Letter* in his copy of the 1845 annual; it was a dreary morning, and the natural light was poor. The President was alone; the folding doors to Mrs. Lincoln's bedroom remained closed.

Impressed as always with Poe's tale, Mr. Lincoln on this occasion was struck by a whimsical thought; and, apparently finding no paper handy, he took an envelope from his pocket, discarded its enclosure, slit the two short edges so that the envelope opened out into a single sheet, and began to write on the blank side.

"Describe it to me, please."

"It's a long envelope, one that must have contained a bulky letter. It is addressed to the White House, but there is no return address, and father was never able to identify the sender from the handwriting. We do know that the letter came through the regular mails, because there are two Lincoln stamps on it, lightly but unmistakably cancelled."

"May I see your father's transcript of what Lincoln wrote out that morning on the inside of the envelope?"

Bianca handed him a typewritten copy and, in spite of himself, Ellery felt goose-flesh rise as he read:

Apr. 14, 1865

Mr. Poe's The Purloined Letter is a work of singular originality. Its simplicity is a master-stroke of cunning, which never fails to arouse my wonder.

Reading the tale over this morning has given me a "notion." Suppose I wished to hide a book, this very book, perhaps? Where best to do so? Well, as Mr. Poe in his tale hid a letter *among letters,* might not a book be hidden *among books?* Why, if this very copy of the tale were to be deposited in a library and on purpose not recorded—would not the Library of Congress make a prime depository!—well might it repose there, undiscovered, for a generation.

593

On the other hand, let us regard Mr. Poe's "notion" turn-about: suppose the book were to be placed, not amongst other books, but *where no book would reasonably be expected?* (I may follow the example of Mr. Poe, and, myself, compose a tale of "ratiocination"!)

The "notion" beguiles me, it is nearly seven o'clock. Later to-day, if the vultures and my appointments leave me a few moments of leisure, I may write further of my imagined hiding-place.

In self-reminder: the hiding-place of the book is in 30d, which

Ellery looked up. "The document ends there?"

"Father said that Mr. Lincoln must have glanced again at his watch, and shamefacedly jumped up to go to his office, leaving the sentence unfinished. Evidently he never found the time to get back to it."

Ellery brooded. Evidently indeed. From the moment when Abraham Lincoln stepped out of his bedroom that Good Friday morning, fingering his thick gold watch on its vest chain, to bid the still-unrelieved night guard his customary courteous "Good morning" and make for his office at the other end of the hall, his day was spoken for. The usual patient push through the clutching crowd of favor-seekers, many of whom had bedded down all night on the hall carpet; sanctuary in his sprawling office, where he read official correspondence; by 8:00 A.M. having breakfast with his family—Mrs. Lincoln chattering away about plans for the evening, 12-year-old Tad of the cleft palate lisping a complaint that "nobody asked me to go," and young Robert Lincoln, just returned from duty, bubbling with stories about his hero Ulysses Grant and the last days of the war; then back to the presidential office to look over the morning newspapers (which Lincoln had once remarked he "never" read, but these were happy days, with good news everywhere), sign two documents, and signal the soldier at the door to admit the morning's first caller, Speaker of the House Schuyler Colfax (who was angling for a Cabinet post and had to be tactfully handled); and so on throughout the day—the historic Cabinet meeting at 11:00 A.M., attended by General Grant himself, that stretched well into the afternoon; a hurried lunch at almost half-past two with Mrs. Lincoln (had this 45-pounds-underweight man eaten his usual midday meal of a biscuit, a glass of milk, and an apple?); more visitors to see in his office (including the unscheduled Mrs. Nancy Bushrod, escaped slave and wife of an escaped slave and mother of three small children, weeping that Tom, a soldier in the Army of the Potomac, was no longer getting his pay: "You are entitled to your husband's pay. Come this time tomorrow," and the tall President escorted her to the door, bowing her out "like I was a natural-born lady"); the late afternoon drive in the barouche to the Navy Yard and back with Mrs. Lincoln; more work, more visitors, into the evening . . . until finally, at five minutes past 8:00 P.M., Abraham Lincoln stepped into the White House formal coach after his wife, waved, and sank back to be driven off to see a play he did not much want to see, *Our American Cousin,* at Ford's Theatre . . .

Ellery mused over that black day in silence. And, like a relative hanging on the specialist's yet undelivered diagnosis, Bianca DiCampo sat watching him with anxiety.

Harbidger and Tungston arrived in a taxi to greet Ellery with the fervor of castaways grasping at a smudge of smoke on the horizon.

"As I understand it, gentlemen," Ellery said when he had calmed them down, "neither of you has been able to solve Mr. DiCampo's interpretation of the Lincoln clue. If I succeed in finding the book and paper where DiCampo hid them, which of you gets them?"

"We intend to split the $65,000 payment to Miss DiCampo," said Harbidger, "and take joint ownership of the two pieces."

"An arrangement," growled old Tungston, "I'm against on principle, in practice, and by plain horse sense."

"So am I," sighed the Lincoln collector, "but what else can we do?"

"Well," and the Poe man regarded Bianca DiCampo with the icy intimacy of the cat that long ago marked the bird as its prey, "Miss DiCampo, who now owns the two pieces, is quite free to renegotiate a sale on her own terms."

"Miss DiCampo," said Miss DiCampo, giving Tungston stare for stare, "considers herself bound by her father's wishes. His terms stand."

"In all likelihood then," said the other millionaire, "one of us will retain the book, the other the document, and we'll exchange them every year, or some such thing." Harbidger sounded unhappy.

"Only practical arrangement under the circumstances," grunted Tungston, and *he* sounded unhappy. "But all this is academic, Queen, unless and until the book and document are found."

Ellery nodded. "The problem, then, is to fathom DiCampo's interpretation of that *30d* in the document. 30d . . . I notice, Miss Di-Campo—or, may I? Bianca?—that your father's typewritten copy of the Lincoln holograph text runs the 3 and 0 and *d* together—no spacing in between. Is that the way it occurs in the longhand?"

"Yes."

"Hmm. Still . . . 30d . . . Could *d* stand for *days* . . . or the British *pence* . . . or *died,* as used in obituaries? Does any of these make sense to you, Bianca?"

"No."

"Did your father have any special interest in, say, pharmacology? chemistry? physics? algebra? electricity? Small *d* is an abbreviation used in all those." But Bianca shook her splendid head. "Banking? Small *d* for *dollars, dividends?*"

"Hardly," the girl said with a sad smile.

"How about theatricals? Was your father ever involved in a play production? Small *d* stands for *door* in playscript stage directions."

"Mr. Queen, I've gone through every darned abbreviation my dictionary lists, and I haven't found one that has a point of contact with any interest of my father's."

Ellery scowled. "At that—I assume the typewritten copy is accurate—the manuscript shows no period after the *d*, making an abbreviation unlikely. 30d . . . let us concentrate on the number. Does the number 30 have any significance for you?"

"Yes, indeed," said Bianca, making all three men sit up. But then they sank back. "In a few years it will represent my age, and that has enormous significance. But only for me, I'm afraid."

"You'll be drawing wolf whistles at twice thirty," quoth Ellery warmly. "However! Could the number have cross-referred to anything in your father's life or habits?"

"None that I can think of, Mr. Queen. And," Bianca said, having grown roses in her cheeks, "thank you."

"I think," said old Tungston testily, "we had better stick to the subject."

"Just the same, Bianca, let me run over some 'thirty' associations as they come to mind. Stop me if one of them hits a nerve. The Thirty Tyrants—was your father interested in classical Athens? Thirty Years War—in Seventeenth Century European history? Thirty all—did he play or follow tennis? Or . . . did he ever live at an address that included the number 30?"

Ellery went on and on, but to each suggestion Bianca DiCampo could only shake her head.

"The lack of spacing, come to think of it, doesn't necessarily mean that Mr. DiCampo chose to view the clue that way," said Ellery thoughtfully. "He might have interpreted it arbitrarily as *3-space-0-d.*"

"Three od?" echoed old Tungston. "What the devil could that mean?"

"Od? Od is the hypothetical force or power claimed by Baron von Reichenbach—in 1850, wasn't it?—to pervade the whole of nature. Manifests itself in magnets, crystals, and such, which according to the excited Baron explained animal magnetism and mesmerism. Was your father by any chance interested in hypnosis, Bianca? Or the occult?"

"Not in the slightest."

"Mr. Queen," exclaimed Harbidger, "are you serious about all this—this semantic sludge?"

"Why, I don't know," said Ellery. "I never know till I stumble over something. Od . . . the word was used with prefixes, too—*biod*, the force of animal life; *elod*, the force of electricity; and so forth. *Three*od . . . or *triod*, the triune force—it's all right, Mr. Harbidger, it's not ignorance on your part, I just coined the word. But it does rather suggest the Trinity, doesn't it? Bianca, did your father tie up to the Church in a personal, scholarly, or any other way? No? That's too bad, really, because Od—capitalized—has been a minced form of the word God since the Sixteenth Century. Or . . . you wouldn't happen to have three Bibles on the premises, would you? Because—"

Ellery stopped with the smashing abruptness of an ordinary force meeting an absolutely immovable object. The girl and the two collectors gawped. Bianca had idly picked up the typewritten copy of the Lincoln document. She was not reading it, she was simply holding it on her knees, but Ellery, sitting opposite her, had shot forward in a crouch, rather like a pointer, and he was regarding the paper in her lap with a glare of pure discovery.

"That's it!" he cried.

"What's it, Mr. Queen?" the girl asked, bewildered.

"Please—the transcript!" He plucked the paper from her. "Of course. Hear this: 'On the other hand, let us regard Mr. Poe's "notion" turn-about.' *Turn-about.* Look at the 30d 'turn-about'—as I just saw it!"

He turned the Lincoln message upside down for their inspection. In that position the 30d became:

POƐ

"*Poe!*" exploded Tungston.

"Yes, crude but recognizable," Ellery said swiftly. "So now we read the Lincoln clue as: 'The hiding-place of the book is in *Poe*'!"

There was a silence.

"In Poe," said Harbidger blankly.

"In Poe?" muttered Tungston. "There are only a couple of trade editions of Poe in DiCampo's library, Harbidger, and we went through those. We looked in every book here."

"He might have meant among the Poe books in the *public* library. Miss DiCampo—"

"Wait." Bianca sped away. But when she came back she was drooping. "It isn't. We have two public libraries in Eulalia, and I know the

597

head librarian in both. I just called them. Father didn't visit either library."

Ellery gnawed a fingernail. "Is there a bust of Poe in the house, Bianca? Or any other Poe-associated object, aside from books?"

"I'm afraid not."

"Queer," he mumbled. "Yet I'm positive your father interpreted 'the hiding-place of the book' as being 'in Poe.' So he'd have hidden it 'in Poe' . . ."

Ellery's mumbling dribbled away into a tormented sort of silence: his eyebrows worked up and down, Groucho Marx–fashion; he pinched the tip of his nose until it was scarlet; he yanked at his unoffending ears; he munched on his lip . . . until, all at once, his face cleared; and he sprang to his feet. "Bianca, may I use your phone?"

The girl could only nod, and Ellery dashed. They heard him telephoning in the entrance hall, although they could not make out the words. He was back in two minutes.

"One thing more," he said briskly, "and we're out of the woods. I suppose your father had a key ring or a key case, Bianca? May I have it, please?"

She fetched a key case. To the two millionaires it seemed the sorriest of objects, a scuffed and dirty tan leatherette case. But Ellery received it from the girl as if it were an artifact of historic importance from a newly discovered IV Dynasty tomb. He unsnapped it with concentrated love; he fingered its contents like a scientist. Finally he decided on a certain key.

"Wait here!" Thus Mr. Queen; and exit, running.

"I can't decide," old Tungston said after a while, "whether that fellow is a genius or an escaped lunatic."

Neither Harbidger nor Bianca replied. Apparently they could not decide, either.

They waited through twenty elongated minutes; at the twenty-first they heard his car, champing. All three were in the front doorway as Ellery strode up the walk.

He was carrying a book with a red cover, and smiling. It was a compassionate smile, but none of them noticed.

"You—" said Bianca, "—found—" said Tungston, "—the book!" shouted Harbidger. "Is the Lincoln holograph in it?"

"It is," said Ellery. "Shall we all go into the house, where we may mourn in decent privacy?"

"Because," Ellery said to Bianca and the two quivering collectors as they sat across a refectory table from him, "I have foul news. Mr. Tungston,

I believe you have never actually seen Mr. DiCampo's book. Will you now look at the Poe signature on the flyleaf?"

The panther claws leaped. There, toward the top of the flyleaf, in faded inkscript, was the signature *Edgar Allan Poe.*

The claws curled, and old Tungston looked up sharply. "DiCampo never mentioned that it's a full autograph—he kept referring to it as 'the Poe signature.' Edgar *Allan* Poe . . . Why, I don't know of a single instance after his West Point days when Poe wrote out his middle name in an autograph! And the earliest he could have signed this 1845 edition is obviously when it was published, which was around the fall of 1844. In 1844 he'd surely have abbreviated the 'Allan,' signing 'Edgar A. Poe,' the way he signed everything! This is a forgery."

"My God," murmured Bianca, clearly intending no impiety; she was as pale as Poe's Lenore. "Is that true, Mr. Queen?"

"I'm afraid it is," Ellery said sadly. "I was suspicious the moment you told me the Poe signature on the flyleaf contained the 'Allan.' And if the Poe signature is a forgery, the book itself can hardly be considered Poe's own copy."

Harbidger was moaning. "And the Lincoln signature underneath the Poe, Mr. Queen! DiCampo never told me it reads *Abraham* Lincoln—the full Christian name. Except on official documents, Lincoln practically always signed his name '*A.* Lincoln.' Don't tell me this Lincoln autograph is a forgery, too?"

Ellery forbore to look at poor Bianca. "I was struck by the 'Abraham' as well, Mr. Harbidger, when Miss DiCampo mentioned it to me, and I came equipped to test it. I have here—" and Ellery tapped the pile of documents he had taken from his briefcase "—facsimiles of Lincoln signatures from the most frequently reproduced of the historic documents he signed. Now I'm going to make a precise tracing of the Lincoln signature on the flyleaf of the book—" he proceeded to do so "—and I shall superimpose the tracing on the various signatures of the authentic Lincoln documents. So."

He worked rapidly. On his third superimposition Ellery looked up. "Yes. See here. The tracing of the purported Lincoln signature from the flyleaf fits in minutest detail over the authentic Lincoln signature on this facsimile of the Emancipation Proclamation. It's a fact of life that's tripped many a forger that *nobody ever writes his name exactly the same way twice.* There are always variations. If two signatures are identical, then, one must be a tracing of the other. So the 'Abraham Lincoln' signed on this flyleaf can be dismissed without further consideration as a forgery also. It's a tracing of the Emancipation Proclamation signature.

"Not only was this book not Poe's own copy; it was never signed—

and therefore probably never owned—by Lincoln. However your father came into possession of the book, Bianca, he was swindled."

It was the measure of Bianca DiCampo's quality that she said quietly, "Poor, poor father," nothing more.

Harbidger was poring over the worn old envelope on whose inside appeared the dearly beloved handscript of the Martyr President. "At least," he muttered, "we have *this*."

"Do we?" asked Ellery. "Turn it over, Mr. Harbidger."

Harbidger looked up, scowling. "No! You're not going to deprive me of this, too!"

"Turn it over," Ellery repeated in the same gentle way. The Lincoln collector obeyed reluctantly. "What do you see?"

"An authentic envelope of the period! With two authentic Lincoln stamps!"

"Exactly. And the United States has never issued postage stamps depicting living Americans; you have to be dead to qualify. The earliest U.S. stamp showing a portrait of Lincoln went on sale April 15, 1866— a year to the day after his death. Then a living Lincoln could scarcely have used this envelope, with these stamps on it, as writing paper. The document is spurious, too. I am so very sorry, Bianca."

Incredibly, Lorenzo DiCampo's daughter managed a smile with her *"Non importa, signor."* He could have wept for her. As for the two collectors, Harbidger was in shock; but old Tungston managed to croak, "Where the devil did DiCampo hide the book, Queen? And how did you know?"

"Oh, that," said Ellery, wishing the two old men would go away so that he might comfort this admirable creature. "I was convinced that DiCampo interpreted what we now know was the forger's, not Lincoln's, clue, as *30d* read upside down; or, crudely, *Poe*. But 'the hiding-place of the book is in Poe' led nowhere.

"So I reconsidered. P, o, e. If those three letters of the alphabet didn't mean Poe, what could they mean? Then I remembered something about the letter you wrote me, Bianca. You'd used one of your father's envelopes, on the flap of which appeared his address: *Post Office Box 69, Southern District, Eulalia, N.Y.* If there was a Southern District in Eulalia, it seemed reasonable to conclude that there were post offices for other points of the compass, too. As, for instance, an Eastern District. Post Office Eastern, P.O. East. P.O.E."

"Poe!" cried Bianca.

"To answer your question, Mr. Tungston: I phoned the main post office, confirmed the existence of a Post Office East, got directions as to how to get there, looked for a postal box key in Mr. DiCampo's key case, found the right one, located the box DiCampo had rented especially for the occasion, unlocked it—and there was the book." He added, hopefully, "And that is that."

"And that *is* that," Bianca said when she returned from seeing the two collectors off. "I'm not going to cry over an empty milk bottle, Mr. Queen. I'll straighten out father's affairs somehow. Right now all I can think of is how glad I am he didn't live to see the signatures and documents declared forgeries publicly, as they would surely have been when they were expertized."

"I think you'll find there's still some milk in the bottle, Bianca."

"I beg your pardon?" said Bianca.

Ellery tapped the pseudo-Lincolnian envelope. "You know, you didn't do a very good job describing this envelope to me. All you said was that there were two cancelled Lincoln stamps on it."

"Well, there are."

"I can see you misspent your childhood. No, little girls don't collect things, do they? Why, if you'll examine these 'two cancelled Lincoln stamps,' you'll see that they're a great deal more than that. In the first place, they're not separate stamps. They're a vertical pair—that is, one stamp is joined to the other at the horizontal edges. Now look at this upper stamp of the pair."

The Mediterranean eyes widened. "It's upside down, isn't it?"

"Yes, it's upside down," said Ellery, "and what's more, while the pair have perforations all around, there are no perforations between them, where they're joined.

"What you have here, young lady—and what our unknown forger didn't realize when he fished around for an authentic White House cover of the period on which to perpetrate the Lincoln forgery—is what stamp collectors might call a double printing error: a pair of 1866 black 15-cent Lincolns imperforate horizontally, with one of the pair printed upside down. No such error of the Lincoln issue has ever been reported. You're the owner, Bianca, of what may well be the rarest item in U.S. philately, and the most valuable."

The world will little note, nor long remember.

But don't try to prove it by Bianca DiCampo.

BILL PRONZINI

(b. 1943)

|||||||||||||||||||||||||||||||||||||||||||||||| ■ ||||||||||||||||||||||||||||||||||||||||||||||||

When the Private Eye Writers of America voted Bill Pronzini their Lifetime Achievement Award in 1987, he was a mere stripling of forty-four—an age when most writers of the form are still learning. But Pronzini had already done just about everything the category offers, and done it remarkably well.

Pronzini, born in Petaluma, California, is the son of a farm laborer. He began writing for the Petaluma newspaper at fourteen, attended a junior college, and began writing short stories for mystery magazines. In 1971, he published *The Snatch*, in which he introduced Nameless, a soft-hearted, middle-aged, overweight, and sloppy private eye endowed with all those problems that beset normal man. Thus began Pronzini's most notable (though certainly not his only) contribution to the detective form.

The Nameless series follows the ordinary-man private-eye formula already established by earlier writers, but with a notable difference. Pronzini has said that he modeled Nameless after himself, having him read and collect pulp magazines, smoke too much, worry about his health, and so on. As a result, the protagonist's believable relationship with his police-detective best friend, his wit, his weakness for puns, and his tendency to make mistakes take the books to a level of realism concerning character that is rarely attained in a genre where plot has long been the name of the game.

In addition to creating Nameless, Pronzini has penned myriad short stories, many written under pseudonyms, and produced literary criticism that has earned him a well-deserved reputation as an expert on popular literature, including Westerns. His personable nature and sense of humor are reflected in his *Gun in Cheek* and *Son of Gun in Cheek* anthologies, which bring together examples of prose so overdone that it becomes hilarious. Pronzini is known as one of the truly great collaborators and is equally at home co-editing anthologies and co-authoring novels and even short stories. Critics agree that some of his best collaborations are the ones written with his wife, Marcia Muller.

Short-short stories, which often depend on an ironic punch line, are notoriously tough to write. "Words Do Not a Book Make" demonstrates Pronzini's craftsmanship—as well as his penchant for puns.

1968

Words Do Not a Book Make

■

I went to the rear window, lifted the shade, and looked out. Then I pulled the shade down in a hurry and spun around to glare at Herbie.

"You fathead!" I yelled.

"What's the matter, boss?"

"The police station is across the street!"

"I know," Herbie said calmly.

"You know. Well, that's nice, isn't it?" I waved my hand at the telephones, the dope sheets, the rolls of flash paper, and the other stuff we had just unpacked. "Won't the cops be ever so happy when they bust in here? No long rides in the wagon. Just down the back stairs, across the street, and into a cell. Think of the time and expense we'll be saving the taxpayers. You fathead!"

"They aren't going to bust in here," Herbie said.

"No, huh?"

Herbie shook his head. "Don't you see? The setup is perfect. It couldn't be any better."

"All I see is a cold cell in that cop house over there."

"Didn't you ever read 'The Purloined Letter?'"

"The which letter?"

"Purloined," Herbie said. "'The Purloined Letter.' By Edgar Allan Poe."

"Yeah?" I said. "Never heard of him. What is he, some handicapper for one of the Eastern tracks?"

"He was a writer," Herbie said. "He died over a hundred years ago."

"What's some croaked writer got to do with this?"

"I'm trying to tell you, boss. He wrote this story called 'The Purloined Letter,' see, and everybody in it is trying to find a letter that was supposed to have been swiped, only nobody can find it. You know why?"

I shrugged. "Why?"

"Because it was under their noses all the time."

"I don't get it."

"Everybody's looking for the letter to be *hidden* some place," Herbie said. "So they never think to look in the only place left—the most obvious place, right in front of them."

"So?"

Herbie sighed. "We got the same type of thing right here. If the cops get wind a new bookie joint has opened up in town, they'll look for it everywhere *except* under their noses. Everywhere except right across the street."

I thought about it. "I don't know," I said. "It sounds crazy."

"Sure," Herbie said. "That's the beauty of it. It's so crazy it's perfect. It can't miss."

"What'd you tell the guy you rented this place from?"

"I said we were manufacturer's representatives for industrial valves. No warehouse stock; just a sales office. I even had some sign painters put a phony name on the windows, front and back."

"This landlord," I said. "Any chance of him coming up here when we ain't expecting him?"

"None, as long as we pay the rent on time. He's not that kind of guy."

"What's downstairs?"

"Insurance company. No bother on that end, either."

I did some more thinking. Herbie might be right, I decided. Why would the cops think of looking out their front door for the new book in town? No reason, none at all.

"Okay," I said, "we stay. But you better be right."

"Don't worry," Herbie said. "I am."

"All the contacts lined up?"

"I took care of everything before I called you, boss. I got eight guys—five bars, a cigar store, a billiards parlor, and a lunchroom. Phone number only, no address."

I nodded. "Put the word out, then. We're in business."

Herbie smiled. "'Of making many books there is no end,'" he said.

"Huh?"

"I read that somewhere once."

"Keep your mind off reading and on the book," I said.

For some reason Herbie thought that was funny.

At nine the next morning, the first contact phoned in his bets. The other seven followed at ten-minute intervals, just the way Herbie had set it up. From the size and number of the bets, I figured this town was going to be a gold mine.

We split up the work, Herbie taking the calls and putting the bets down on the flash paper, and me figuring odds and laying off some of the scratch with the big books in Vegas and L.A. The flash paper is thin stuff, like onionskin, and the reason we use it is that in case of a raid you just touch a match to it and the whole roll goes up in nothing flat. No evidence, no conviction.

So there we were, humming right along, getting ready for the first races at Santa Anita and Golden Gate Fields, when somebody knocked on the door.

Herbie and I looked at each other. Then I looked at my watch, as if the watch could tell me who was knocking on the damn door. It was ten forty-five, one hour and fifteen minutes after we'd opened for business.

"Who can that be?" Herbie said. "The landlord, maybe?"

"I thought you said he wouldn't bother us."

Two of the telephones began ringing at the same time.

I jumped: "Muffle those things!"

Herbie hauled up both receivers, said, "Ring back" into each one, and put them down again.

There was another knock on the door, louder this time.

"We better answer it," Herbie said. "If it's not the landlord, maybe it's the mailman."

"Yeah," I said.

"Anyway, it's nothing to worry about. I mean, cops wouldn't *knock*, would they?"

I relaxed. Sure, if it was the cops they would have come busting in already. They wouldn't stand out there knocking.

I got up and went over to the door and cracked it open. And the first thing I saw was a badge—a big shiny badge pinned to the front of a blue uniform shirt. My eyes moved upward to a neck, a huge red neck, and then on up to a huge, red head with a blue-and-gold cap perched on top of it.

"Hello," the head said.

I saw another blue uniform behind it. "Arrgh!" I said.

"I'm Chief of Police Wiggins," the head said, "and I—"

I slammed the door. "Cops!" I yelled. "The flash paper—Herbie, the flash paper!"

"*Cops?*" he yelled.

The door burst open. My backside was in the way, but not for long. It felt like a bull had hit that door, which in a manner of speaking was just what had happened. I flew into the room, collided with a chair, and fell down on my head.

A booming voice said, "What's going on in—" And then, "Well, I'll be damned!"

"Cops!" Herbie yelled.

"Watch it, Jed!" the booming voice boomed. "Flash paper!"

A blue uniform blurred past me as I struggled to my knees. I saw the uniform brush Herbie aside, saw a hand sweep across the desk. Saw all the paper flutter to the floor, intact.

"Bookies," the blue uniform said, amazed.

"Hoo-haw!" the booming voice said. "Hoo-haw-*haw*!"

"Right across the street," the blue uniform said, still amazed.

I reached up and touched my head. I could feel a lump sprouting there. Then I looked over at Herbie, who was now cowering in the grip of a long arm. "Herbie," I said, "I am going to kill you, Herbie."

"Right across the *street*," the blue uniform said again, shaking his head in wonder.

"Hoo, hoo, hoo!"

So, down the back stairs we went. Across the street we went. Into a cell we went.

Fortunately for Herbie, it wasn't the same cell.

I sat on the hard cot. The lump on my head seemed to be growing. But it was nothing, I told myself, to the lump that would soon grow on Herbie's head.

A little while later the blue uniform came back and took me to the chief's office. He took one look at me and broke off into a fresh series of hoo-hoos and hoo-haws. I sat in a chair and glared at the wall.

The chief wiped his eyes with a handkerchief. "Damnedest thing I ever heard of," he said. "Setting up a bookie joint within spitting distance of the police station."

I ground my teeth.

"It's one for the books, that's what it is," he said, and commenced hoo-hawing again.

I ground my teeth some more.

When his latest spasm ended the chief said, "What could have possessed you, son?"

Instead of answering I asked him, "Can I have a couple of minutes alone with Herbie?"

"What for?" Then he nodded his big red head and grinned and said, "Oh, I get it. His idea, was it?"

"Yeah. His idea."

"Damnedest thing I ever heard of," the chief said again. "It really is one for the—"

"All *right*," I said. "Look, how did you find out, anyway?"

"Well, to tell you the truth, we didn't."

"You . . . didn't?"

"We had no idea what you fellas were doing over there until we busted in."

"Then why were you there?"

"Business license. You got to have one to operate a business in this town."

I didn't get it. "I don't get it," I said.

"Saw some sign painters over there the other day," the chief said, "painting the name of a valve company on the windows."

"So?"

"New company setting up shop in town," the chief said. "Good for the growth of our fair city. But like I said, every business has got to have a license. So I did some checking, on account of it was a slow day, and found out this valve company never applied for one. Technically, they were breaking the law."

Herbie, I thought, I'm going to break your *head*.

"Wasn't a big deal, but still, the law's the law. So I figured to sort of welcome them officially and then bring up the matter of the license afterwards. Keep from ruffling feathers that way."

"You always go calling in person for something like that? Why didn't you use the phone?"

"Probably would have," the chief said. "Except for one thing."

I sighed. "What's that?"

"Well, son," he said with more hoo-haws lurking in his voice, "you were right across the street."

EDWARD D. HOCH

(b. 1930)

||||||||||||||||||||||||||||||||||||||||||||| ■ |||||||||||||||||||||||||||||||||||||||||||||

Edward D. Hoch began writing short stories while a high-school student in Rochester, New York; kept at it as a student at the University of Rochester; persisted in the practice during a stint in the army; and finally—while working for an advertising agency—sold "The Village of the Dead" to *Famous Detective*. The year was 1955, Hoch was twenty-five, and his trouble selling his stories was behind him. Although his stories were selling well, he continued to work in advertising and public relations, not taking the plunge into full-time writing until 1968.

It's ironic that the man who was to become such a prolific author of short stories should begin his career just as the great market for short fiction was in its death throes. *Famous Detective* was one of the last of the scores of pulp magazines that had crowded the drugstore racks and newsstands for generations and had been the primary source of income for literally thousands of American writers. The pulps began to die in the early 1950s as television siphoned away their audience, and the decline of the "slick magazine" market—*Saturday Evening Post*, *Collier's*, and others—soon followed. Despite this, from 1955 to 1957, Hoch published twenty-five more stories. He wrote under a variety of pen names and was one of the many writers of the day who used the Ellery Queen pseudonym.

Hoch is the ultimate "writers' writer." He has written five novels; science-fiction, fantasy, and detective stories; and nonfiction. He is now near the 800-mark in short-story output. He has produced whatever the market is buying, but has made his name in the detective short story. He prefers them, he has said, because he can do one in "a week or two," while a novel requires three months and "I find myself losing interest about halfway through."

"Christmas Is for Cops" comes as close to typifying Hoch's work as is possible for such a versatile writer. It was written for the Christmas-story market, contrasting the good will of the season with the evil of murder. It features Captain Leopold, star performer in one of Hoch's series. It focuses on a single idea, and it follows the tenets of the classic tale of detection, with the clues honestly presented and the crime solved by deduction.

1970

Christmas Is for Cops

■

"Going to the Christmas party, Captain?" Fletcher asked from the doorway. Captain Leopold glanced up from his eternally cluttered desk. Fletcher was now a lieutenant in the newly reorganized Violent Crimes

608

Division, and they did not work together as closely as they once had. "I'll be there," Leopold said. "In fact, I've been invited to speak."

This news brought a grin to Fletcher's face. "Nobody speaks at the Christmas party, Captain. They just drink."

"Well, this year you're going to hear a speech, and I'm going to give it."

"Lots of luck."

"Is your wife helping with the decorations again this year?"

"I suppose she'll be around," Fletcher chuckled. "She doesn't trust me at any Christmas party without her."

The annual Detective Bureau party was, by tradition, a stag affair. But in recent years Carol Fletcher and some of the other wives had come down to Eagles Hall in the afternoon to trim the tree and hang the holly. Somehow these members of the unofficial Decorations Committee usually managed to stay on for the evening's festivities.

The party was the following evening, and Captain Leopold was looking forward to it. But he had one unpleasant task to perform first. That afternoon, feeling he could delay it no longer, he summoned Sergeant Tommy Gibson to his office and closed the door.

Gibson was a tough cop of the old school, a bleak and burly man who'd campaigned actively for the lieutenancy which had finally been given to Fletcher. Leopold had never liked Gibson, but until now he'd managed to overlook the petty graft with which Gibson's name was occasionally linked.

"What seems to be the trouble, Captain?" Gibson asked, taking a seat. "You look unhappy."

"I am unhappy, Gibson. Damned unhappy! While you were working the assault and robbery detail I had no direct command over your activities. But now that I'm in charge of a combined Violent Crimes Division, I feel I should take a greater interest in them." He reached across his desk to pick up a folder. "I have a report here from the District Attorney's office. The report mentions you, Gibson, and makes some very grave charges."

"What kind of charges?" the sergeant's tongue forked out to lick his dry lips.

"That you've been accepting regular payments from a man named Freese."

Gibson went pale. "I don't know what you're talking about."

"Carl Freese, the man who runs the numbers racket in every factory in this city. You know who he is, and you know what he's done. Men who've opposed him, or tried to report his operations to the police, have been beaten and nearly killed. I have a report here of a foreman at Lecko Industries. When some of his men started losing a whole week's pay in the numbers and other gambling controlled by Freese, he went to his supervisor and reported it. That night on the way home his car was forced off the road and he was badly beaten, so badly that he spent three weeks in the hospital. You should be familiar with that case, Gibson, because you investigated it just last summer."

"I guess I remember it."

"Remember your report, too? You wrote it off as a routine robbery attempt, despite the fact that no money was taken from the victim. The victim reported it to the District Attorney's office, and they've been investigating the whole matter of gambling in local industrial plants. I have their report here."

"I investigate a lot of cases, Captain. I try to do the best job I can."

"Nuts!" Leopold was on his feet, angry now. There was nothing that angered him more than a crooked cop. "Look, Gibson, the D.A.'s office has all of Freese's records. They show payments of $100 a week to you. What in hell were you doing for $100 a week, unless you were covering up for them when they beat some poor guy senseless?"

"Those records are wrong," Gibson said. "I didn't get any hundred bucks a week."

"Then how much did you get?"

Leopold towered over him in the chair, and Gibson's burly frame seemed to shrivel. "I think I want a lawyer," he mumbled.

"I'm suspending you from the force without pay, effective at once. Thank God you don't have a wife and family to suffer through this."

Tommy Gibson sat silently for a moment, staring at the floor. Then at last he looked up, seeking Leopold's eyes. "Give me a chance, Captain. I wasn't in this alone."

"What's that supposed to mean?"

"I didn't get the whole hundred by myself. I had to split it with one of the other men—and he's the one who introduced me to Freese in the first place."

"There's someone else involved in this? One of the detectives?"

"Yes."

"Give me his name."

"Not yet." Gibson hesitated. "Because you wouldn't believe it. Let me give you evidence."

"What sort of evidence?"

"He and Freese came to me at my apartment and told me the type of protection they needed. That was the night we agreed on the amount of money to be paid each week. I wasn't taking any chances, Captain, so I dug out an old recording machine I'd bought after the war, and rigged up a hidden microphone behind my sofa. I got down every word they said."

"When was this?" Leopold asked.

"More than a year ago, and I've kept the recording of the conversation ever since. What's it worth to me if I bring it in?"

"I'm not in a position to make deals, Gibson."

"Would the D.A. make one?"

"I could talk to him," Leopold replied cautiously. "Let's hear what you've got first."

Gibson nodded. "I'll take the reel off my machine and bring it in to you tomorrow."

"If you're kidding me, Gibson, or stalling—"

"I'm not, Captain! I swear! I just don't want to take the whole rap myself."

"I'll give you twenty-four hours. Then the suspension goes into effect regardless."

"Thank you, Captain."

"Get the hell out of here now."

"Thank you, Captain," he said again. "And Merry Christmas."

On the day of the Christmas party, activities around the Detective Bureau slacked off very little. It was always pretty much business as usual until around four o'clock, when some of the men started drifting out, exchanging friendly seasonal comments. The party would really commence around five, when the men on the day shift arrived at Eagles Hall, and it continued until well past midnight, enabling the evening men to join in after their tours of duty.

Then there would be a buffet supper, and lots of beer, and even some group singing around the big Christmas tree. Without the family attachments of Fletcher and the other men, Leopold tended to look forward to the party. In many years it was the main event of his otherwise lonely holiday season.

By four o'clock he had heard nothing from Sergeant Tommy Gibson. With growing irritation he called Fletcher into his office. "Gibson's under your command now, isn't he, Fletcher?"

"That's right, Captain."

"What's he working on today?"

Fletcher's face flushed unexpectedly. "Well, Captain, it seems—"

"Where is he?"

"Things were a bit slower than usual, so I told him he could go over to Eagles Hall and help put up the tree for the party."

"What!"

Fletcher shifted his feet uneasily. "I know, Captain. But usually I help Carol and the other wives get it up. Now that I'm a lieutenant I didn't feel I could take the time off, so I sent Gibson in my place."

Leopold sighed and stood up. "All right, Fletcher. Let's get over there right away."

"Why? What's up?"

"I'll tell you on the way."

Eagles Hall was a large reasonably modern building that was rented out for wedding receptions and private parties by a local fraternal group. The Detective Bureau, through its Benevolent Association, had held a Christmas party there for the past five seasons, and its central location had helped make it a popular choice. It was close enough to attract some of the uniformed force as well as the detective squad. All were invited, and most came at some time during the long evening.

Now, before five o'clock, a handful of plainclothesmen from various divisions had already arrived. Leopold waved to Sergeant Riker of the Vice Squad, who was helping Carol Fletcher light her cigarette with a balky lighter. Then he stopped to exchange a few words with Lieutenant Williams, a bony young man who headed up the Narcotics Squad. Williams had made his reputation during a single year on the force, masquerading as a hippie musician to penetrate a group selling drugs to high school students. Leopold liked him, liked his honesty and friendliness.

"I hear you're giving a little speech tonight," Williams said, pouring him a glass of beer.

"Herb Clarke roped me into it," Leopold answered with a chuckle. "I'd better do it early, before you guys get too beered up to listen." He glanced around the big hall, taking in the twenty-foot Christmas tree with its lights and tinsel. Three guy wires held it firmly in place next to an old upright piano. "See Tommy Gibson around?"

Williams stood on tiptoe to see over the heads of some newly arrived uniformed men. "I think he's helping Carol finish up the decorations."

"Thanks." Leopold took his beer and drifted over to the far end of the room. Carol had put down her cigarette long enough to tug at one of the wires holding the tree in place. Leopold helped her tighten it and then stepped back. She was a charming, intelligent woman, and this was not the first time he'd envied Fletcher. As wife and mother she'd given him a fine home life.

"I'm surprised to see you here so early, Captain."

He helped her secure another of the wires and said, "I'm always on time to help charming wives with Christmas trees."

"And thank you for Sergeant Gibson too! He was a great help with the tree."

"I'll bet. Where is he now?"

"He took the hammer and things into the kitchen. I think he's pouring beer now." She produced another cigarette and searched her purse. Finally she asked, "Do you have a light?"

He lit it for her. "You smoke too much."

"Nervous energy. Do you like our tree?"

"Fine. Just like Christmas."

"Do you know, somewhere in Chesterton there's mention of a tree that devours birds nesting in its branches, and when spring comes the tree grows feathers instead of leaves!"

"You read too much, Carol."

She smiled up at him. "The nights are lonely being a detective's wife." The smile was just a bit forced. She didn't always approve of her husband's work.

He left her by the tree and went in search of Gibson. The burly sergeant was in the kitchen, filling pitchers of beer. He looked up, surprised, as Leopold entered. "Hello, Captain."

"I thought we had an appointment for today."

"I didn't forget. Fletcher wanted me over here."

"Where's the evidence you mentioned?"

"What?"

Leopold was growing impatient. "Come on, damn it!"

Tommy Gibson glanced out at the growing crowd. "I've got it, but I had to hide it. He's here."

"Who? The man who's in this with you?"

"Yes. I'm afraid Freese might have tipped him off about the D.A.'s investigation."

Leopold had never seen this side of Gibson—a lonely, trapped man who was actually afraid. Or else was an awfully good actor. "I've given you your twenty-four hours, Gibson. Either produce this recording you've got or—"

"Captain!" a voice interrupted. "We're ready for your speech."

Leopold turned to see Sergeant Turner of Missing Persons, standing in the doorway. "I'll be right there, Jim." Turner seemed to linger just a bit too long before he turned and walked away. Leopold looked back at Gibson. "That him?"

"I can't talk now, Captain."

"Where'd you hide it?"

"Over by the tree. It's safe."

"Stick around till after my talk. Then we'll get to the bottom of this thing."

Leopold left him pouring another pitcher of beer and walked out through the crowd. With the end of the afternoon shifts the place had filled rapidly. There were perhaps sixty members of the force present already, about evenly divided between detectives and uniformed patrolmen. Several shook his hand or patted him on the back as he made his way to the dais next to the tree.

Herb Clarke, president of the Detective Bureau Benevolent Association, was already on the platform, holding up his hands for silence. He shook Leopold's hand and then turned to his audience. "Gather around now, men. The beer'll still be there in five minutes. You all know we're not much for speeches at these Christmas parties, but I thought it might be well this year to hear a few words from a man we all know and admire. Leopold has been in the Detective Bureau for as long as most of us can remember—" The laughter caused him to add quickly, "Though of course he's still a young man. But this year, in addition to his duties as Captain of Homicide, he's taken on a whole new set of responsibilities. He's now head of the entire Violent Crimes Division of the Bureau, a position that places him in more direct contact with us all. I'm going to ask him to say just a few words, and then we'll have some caroling around the piano."

Leopold stepped over to the microphone, adjusting it upward from the position Herb Clarke had used. Then he looked out at the sea of familiar faces. Carol Fletcher and the other wives hovered in the rear, out of the way, while their husbands and the others crowded around. Fletcher himself stood with Sergeant Riker, an old friend, and Leopold noticed that Lieutenant Williams had moved over near Tommy Gibson. He couldn't see Jim Turner at the moment.

"Men, I'm going to make this worth listening to for all that. You hear a lot at this time of the year about Christmas being the season for kids, but I want to add something to that. Christmas is for kids, sure— but Christmas is for cops, too. Know what I mean by that? I'll tell you. Christmas is perhaps the one time of the year when the cop on the beat, or the detective on assignment, has a chance to undo some of the ill will generated during the other eleven months. This has been a bad year for cops around the country—most years are bad ones, it seems. We take a hell of a lot of abuse, some deserved, but most of it not. And this is the season to maybe right some of those wrongs. Don't be afraid to get out on a corner with the Salvation Army to ring a few bells, or help some lady through a puddle of slush. Most of all, don't be afraid to smile and talk to young people."

He paused and glanced down at Tommy Gibson. "There have always been some bad cops, and I guess there always will be. That just means the rest of us have to work a lot harder. Maybe we can just pretend the whole year is Christmas, and go about righting those wrongs. Anyway, I've talked so long already I've grown a bit thirsty. Let's get back to the beer and the singing, and make it good and loud!"

Leopold jumped off the platform and shook more hands. He'd meant to speak longer, to give them something a bit meatier to chew on, but far at the back of the crowd some of the younger cops were already growing restless. And, after all, they'd come here to enjoy themselves, not to listen to a lecture. He couldn't really blame them.

Herb Clarke was gathering everyone around the piano for songs, but Leopold noticed that Tommy Gibson had suddenly disappeared. The Captain threaded his way through the crowd, searching the familiar faces for the man he wanted. "Great talk, Captain," Fletcher said, coming up by his side.

"Did he tell you any more?"

"Only that he had to hide the tape near the Christmas tree. He said the other guy was here."

"Who do you make it, Captain?"

Leopold bit his lower lip. "I make it that Tommy Gibson is one smart cookie. I think he's playing for time, maybe waiting for Freese to get him off the hook somehow."

"You don't think there's another crooked cop in the Detective Bureau?"

"I don't know, Fletcher. I guess I don't want to think so."

The door to the Men's Room sprang open with a suddenness that surprised them both. Sergeant Riker, his usually placid face full of alarm, stood motioning to them. Leopold quickly covered the ground to his side. "What is it, Riker?"

"In there! My God, Captain—in there! It's Gibson!"

"What?"

"Tommy Gibson. He's been stabbed. I think he's dead."

Leopold pushed past him, into the tiled Men's Room with its scrubbed look and disinfectant odor. Tommy Gibson was there, all right, crumpled between two of the wash basins, his eyes glazed and open. A long pair of scissors protruded from his chest.

"Lock all the outside doors, Fletcher," Leopold barked. "Don't let anyone leave."

"Is he dead, Captain?"

"As dead as he'll ever be. What a mess!"

"You think one of our men did it?"

"Who else? Call in and report it, and get the squad on duty over here. Everyone else is a suspect." He stood up from examining the body and turned to Riker. "Now tell me everything you know, Sergeant."

Riker was a Vice Squad detective, a middle-aged man with a placid disposition and a friendly manner. There were those who said he could even make a street-walker like him while he was arresting her. Just now he looked sick and pale. "I walked in and there he was, Captain. My God! I couldn't believe my eyes at first. I thought he was faking, playing some sort of a trick."

"Notice anyone leaving before you went in?"

"No, nobody."

"But he's only been dead a few minutes. That makes you a suspect, Sergeant."

Riker's pale complexion seemed to shade into green at Leopold's words. "You can't think I killed him! He was a friend of mine! Why in hell would I kill Tommy Gibson?"

"We'll see," Leopold said, motioning him out of the Men's Room. The other detectives and officers were clustered around, trying to see. There was a low somber hum of conversation. "All right, everyone!" the Captain ordered. "Keep down at the other end of the room, away from the tree! That's right, move away from it."

"Captain!" It was little Herb Clarke, pushing his way through. "Captain, what's happened?"

"Someone killed Tommy Gibson."

"Tommy!"

"One of us. That's why nobody leaves here."

"You can't be serious, Captain. Murder at the police Christmas party—the newspapers will crucify us."

"Probably," Leopold pushed past him. "Nobody enters the Men's Room," he bellowed. "Fletcher, Williams—come with me." They were the only two lieutenants present, and he had to trust them. Fletcher he'd trust with his life. He only hoped he could rely on Williams too.

"I can't believe it," the bony young Narcotics lieutenant said. "Why would anyone kill Tommy?"

Leopold cleared his throat. "I'll tell you why, though you may not want to believe it. Gibson was implicated in the District Attorney's investigation of Carl Freese's gambling empire. He had a tape recording of a conversation between Freese, himself, and another detective, apparently concerning bribery. The other detective had a dandy motive for killing him."

"Did he say who it was?" Williams asked.

"No. Only that it was someone who got here fairly early today. Who was here before Fletcher and I arrived?"

Williams creased his brow in thought. "Riker was here, and Jim Turner. And a few uniformed men."

"No, just detectives."

"Well, I guess Riker and Tuner were the only ones. And Herb Clarke, of course. He was here all day with the ladies, arranging for the food and the beer."

"Those three," Leopold mused. "And you, of course."

Lieutenant Williams grinned. "Yeah, and me."

Leopold turned toward the big Christmas tree. "Gibson told me he hid the tape recording near the tree. Start looking, and don't miss anything. It might even be in the branches."

The investigating officers were arriving now, and Leopold turned his attention to them. There was something decidedly bizarre in the entire situation, a fact which was emphasized as the doctor and morgue attendants and police photographers exchanged muted greetings with the milling party guests. One of the young investigating detectives who'd known Tommy Gibson turned pale at the sight of the body and had to go outside.

When the photographers had finished, one of the morgue men started to lift the body. He paused and called to Leopold. "Captain, here's something. A cigarette lighter on the floor under him."

Leopold bent close to examine it without disturbing possible prints. "Initials. C. F."

Lieutenant Williams had come in behind him, standing at the door of the Men's Room. "Carl Freese?" he suggested.

Leopold used a handkerchief to pick it up carefully by the corners. "Are we supposed to believe that Freese entered this place in the midst of sixty cops and killed Gibson without anybody seeing him?"

"There's a window in the wall over there."

Leopold walked to the frosted pane and examined it. "Locked from the inside. Gibson might have been stabbed from outside, but he couldn't have locked the window and gotten across this room without leaving a trail of blood."

Fletcher had come in while they were talking. "No dice on that, Captain. My wife just identified the scissors as a pair she was using earlier with the decorations. It's an inside job, all right."

Leopold showed the lighter. "C. F. Could be Carl Freese."

Fletcher frowned and licked his lips. "Yeah." He turned away.

"Nothing," Williams reported.

"Nothing *in* the tree? It could be a fairly small reel."

"Nothing."

Leopold sighed and motioned Fletcher and Williams to one side. He didn't want the others to hear. "Look, I think Gibson was probably lying, too. But he's dead, and that very fact indicates he might have been telling the truth. I have to figure all the angles. Now that you two have searched the tree I want you to go into the kitchen, close the door, and search each other. Carefully."

"But—" Williams began. "All right, Captain."

"Then line everybody up and do a search of them. You know what you're looking for—a reel of recording tape."

"What about the wives, Captain?"

"Get a matron down for them. I'm sorry to have to do it, but if that tape is here we have to find it."

He walked to the center of the hall and stood looking at the tree. Lights and tinsel, holiday wreaths and sprigs of mistletoe. All the trappings. He tried to imagine Tommy Gibson helping to decorate the place, helping with the tree. Where would he have hidden the tape?

Herb Clarke came over and said, "They're searching everybody."

"Yes. I'm sorry to spoil the party this way, but I guess it was spoiled for Gibson already."

"Captain, do you have to go on with this? Isn't one dishonest man in the Bureau enough?"

"One is too many, Herb. But the man we're looking for is more than a dishonest cop now. He's a murderer."

Fletcher came over to them. "We've searched all the detectives, Captain. They're clean. We're working on the uniformed men now."

Leopold grunted unhappily. He was sure they'd find nothing. "Suppose," he said slowly. "Suppose Gibson unreeled the tape. Suppose he strung it on the tree like tinsel."

"You see any brown tinsel hanging anywhere, Captain? See any tinsel of any color long enough to be a taped message?"

"No, I don't," Leopold said.

Two of the sergeants, Riker and Turner, came over to join them. "Could he have done it to himself?" Turner asked. "The word is you were going to link him with the Freese investigation."

"Stabbing yourself in the chest with a pair of scissors isn't exactly common as a suicide method," Leopold pointed out. "Besides, it would be out of character for a man like Gibson."

One of the investigating officers came over with the lighter. "Only smudges on it, Captain. Nothing we could identify."

"Thanks." Leopold took it, turning it over between his fingers.

C. F. Carl Freese.

He flicked the lever a couple of times but it didn't light. Finally, on the fourth try, a flame appeared. "All right," he said quietly. Now he knew.

"Captain—" Fletcher began.

"Damn it, Fletcher, it's your wife's lighter and you know it! C. F. Not Carl Freese but Carol Fletcher!"

"Captain, I—" Fletcher stopped.

Leopold felt suddenly very tired. The colored lights of the tree seemed to blur, and he wished he was far away, in a land where all cops were honest and everyone died of old age.

Sergeant Riker moved in. "Captain, are you trying to say that Fletcher's *wife* stabbed Tommy Gibson?"

"Of course not, Riker. That would have been quite a trick for her to follow him into the Men's Room unnoticed. Besides, I had to give her a match at one point this evening, because she didn't have this lighter."

"Then who?"

"When I first arrived, you were helping Carol Fletcher with a balky lighter. Yes, you, Riker! You dropped it into your pocket, unthinking, and that's why she didn't have it later. It fell out while you were struggling with Gibson. While you were killing him, Riker."

Riker muttered a single obscenity and his hand went for the service revolver on his belt. Leopold had expected it. He moved in fast and threw two quick punches, one to the stomach and one to the jaw. Riker went down and it was over.

Carol Fletcher heard what had happened and she came over to Leopold. "Thanks for recovering my lighter," she said. "I hope you didn't suspect me."

He shook his head, eyeing Fletcher. "Of course not. But I sure as hell wish your husband had told me it was yours."

"I had to find out what it was doing there," Fletcher mumbled. "God, it's not every day your wife's lighter, that you gave her two Christmases ago, turns up as a clue in a murder."

Leopold handed it back to her. "Maybe this'll teach you to stop smoking."

"You knew it was Riker anyway?"

"I was pretty sure. With sixty men drinking beer all around here, no murderer could take a chance of walking out of that Men's Room unseen. His best bet was to pretend finding the body, which is just what he did. Besides that, of the four detectives on the scene early, Riker's Vice Squad position was the most logical for Freese's bribery."

"Was there a tape recording?" Fletcher asked.

Leopold was staring at the Christmas tree. "I think Gibson was telling the truth on that one. Except that *he* never called it a tape. I did that. I jumped to a conclusion. He simply told me it was an old machine, purchased after the war. In those early days tape recorders weren't the only kind. For a while wire recorders were almost as popular."

"Wire!"

Leopold nodded and started toward the Christmas tree. "We know that Gibson helped you put up the tree, Carol. I'm betting that one of those wires holding it in place is none other than the recorded conversation of Carl Freese, Tommy Gibson, and Sergeant Riker."

LINDA BARNES
(b. 1949)

||||||||||||||||||||||||||||||||||||||||||||| ■ |||||||||||||||||||||||||||||||||||||||||||||||

Before Detroit native and longtime Boston resident Linda Barnes created her semi-tough female private eye Carlotta Carlyle, she worked as a theater instructor and director in Massachusetts high schools and wrote two one-act plays and four whodunits featuring the actor-sleuth Michael Spraggue. While her first four mysteries were successful, it was the 6-foot-1, red-haired, taxi-driving Carlyle who really put Barnes on the map.

The Spraggue books were written in the British tradition of the dilettante sleuth who has the money, and thus the free time, to help a group of friends who are being threatened or done in at a statistically improbable rate. Spraggue, while identified with Boston, also travels to the California wine country in *Bitter Finish* and to New Orleans in *Cities of the Dead,* thereby indulging his creator's passions for wine and Cajun cooking, respectively. Perhaps his most memorable Boston appearance entails running down a killer during the Boston Marathon. Like the other Spraggue books, the action and solutions to the crimes depend more on the situation than on character.

Carlyle's first appearance, in the short story "Lucky Penny," shows Barnes utilizing her theater background in order to portray character through internal monologues and wisecracking dialogue. It also sets the stage, complete with Boston backdrop, for the six novels to date in which Carlyle plays the lead among a cast of characters that includes her erstwhile colleague and would-be lover, Lieutenant Mooney, and Gloria, the wheelchair-bound late-night taxi dispatcher.

Like her colleagues in crime Kinsey Millhone and V. I. Warshawski, Carlyle pursues personal relationships along with her cases, and even when she doesn't know her clients and villains at the start of an adventure, she often becomes intimately acquainted with them—sometimes physically—before the solution is reached. Says Barnes, "I am *not* Carlotta even if we do share some characteristics. We both play blues guitar when we need to think. She plays better than I do. But then I have much better taste in men!"

1985

Lucky Penny

■

Lieutenant Mooney made me dish it all out for the record. He's a good cop, if such an animal exists. We used to work the same shift before I decided—wrongly—that there was room for a lady P.I. in this town.

Who knows? With this case under my belt, maybe business'll take a 180-degree spin, and I can quit driving a hack.

See, I've already written the official report for Mooney and the cops, but the kind of stuff they wanted: date, place, and time, cold as ice and submitted in triplicate, doesn't even start to tell the tale. So I'm doing it over again, my way.

Don't worry, Mooney. I'm not gonna file this one.

The Thayler case was still splattered across the front page of the *Boston Globe*. I'd soaked it up with my midnight coffee and was puzzling it out—my cab on automatic pilot, my mind on crime—when the mad tea party began.

"Take your next right, sister. Then pull over, and douse the lights. Quick!"

I heard the bastard all right, but it must have taken me thirty seconds or so to react. Something hard rapped on the cab's dividing shield. I didn't bother turning around. I hate staring down gun barrels.

I said, "Jimmy Cagney, right? No, your voice is too high. Let me guess, don't tell me—"

"Shut up!"

"*Kill* the lights, *turn off* the lights, okay. But *douse* the lights? You've been tuning in too many old gangster flicks."

"I hate a mouthy broad," the guy snarled. I kid you not.

"*Broad*," I said. "Christ! *Broad?* You trying to grow hair on your balls?"

"Look, I mean it, lady!"

"*Lady's* better. Now you wanna vacate my cab and go rob a phone booth?" My heart was beating like a tin drum, but I didn't let my voice shake, and all the time I was gabbing at him, I kept trying to catch his face in the mirror. He must have been crouching way back on the passenger side. I couldn't see a damn thing.

"I want all your dough," he said.

Who can you trust? This guy was a spiffy dresser: charcoal-gray three-piece suit and rep tie, no less. And picked up in front of the swank Copley Plaza. I looked like I needed the bucks more than he did, and I'm no charity case. A woman can make good tips driving a hack in Boston. Oh, she's gotta take precautions, all right. When you can't smell a disaster fare from thirty feet, it's time to quit. I pride myself on my judgment. I'm careful. I always know where the police checkpoints are, so I can roll my cab past and flash the old lights if a guy starts acting up. This dude fooled me cold.

I was ripped. Not only had I been conned, I had a considerable wad to give away. It was near the end of my shift, and like I said, I do all right. I've got a lot of regulars. Once you see me, you don't forget me—or my cab.

It's gorgeous. Part of my inheritance. A '59 Chevy, shiny as new, kept on blocks in a heated garage by the proverbial dotty old lady. It's the pits of the design world. Glossy blue with those giant chromium fins. Restrained decor; just the phone number and a few gilt curlicues on the door. I was afraid all my old pals at the police department would pull me over for minor traffic violations if I went whole hog and painted "Carlotta's Cab" in ornate script on the hood. Some do it anyway.

So where the hell were all the cops now? Where are they when you need 'em?

He told me to shove the cash through that little hole they leave for the passenger to pass the fare forward. I told him he had it backwards. He didn't laugh. I shoved bills.

"Now the change," the guy said. Can you imagine the nerve?

I must have cast my eyes up to heaven. I do that a lot these days.

"I mean it." He rapped the plastic shield with the shiny barrel of his gun. I checked it out this time. Funny how big a little .22 looks when it's pointed just right.

I fished in my pockets for change, emptied them.

"Is that all?"

"You want the gold cap on my left front molar?" I said.

"Turn around," the guy barked. "Keep both hands on the steering wheel. High."

I heard jingling, then a quick intake of breath.

"Okay," the crook said, sounding happy as a clam, "I'm gonna take my leave—"

"Good. Don't call this cab again."

"Listen!" The gun tapped. "You cool it here for ten minutes. And I mean frozen. Don't twitch. Don't blow your nose. Then take off."

"Gee, thanks."

"Thank *you*," he said politely. The door slammed.

At times like that, you just feel ridiculous. You *know* the guy isn't going to hang around, waiting to see whether you're big on insubordination. *But*, he might. And who wants to tangle with a .22 slug? I rate pretty high in insubordination. That's why I messed up as a cop. I figured I'd give him two minutes to get lost. Meantime I listened.

Not much traffic goes by those little streets on Beacon Hill at one o'clock on a Wednesday morn. Too residential. So I could hear the guy's footsteps tap along the pavement. About ten steps back, he stopped.

Was he the one in a million who'd wait to see if I turned around? I heard a funny kind of whooshing noise. Not loud enough to make me jump, and anything much louder than the ticking of my watch would have put me through the roof. Then the footsteps patted on, straight back and out of hearing.

One minute more. The only saving grace of the situation was the location: District One. That's Mooney's district. Nice guy to talk to.

I took a deep breath, hoping it would have an encore, and pivoted quickly, keeping my head low. Makes you feel stupid when you do that and there's no one around.

I got out and strolled to the corner, stuck my head around a building kind of cautiously. Nothing, of course.

I backtracked. Ten steps, then whoosh. Along the sidewalk stood one of those new "Keep Beacon Hill Beautiful" trash cans, the kind with the swinging lid. I gave it a shove as I passed. I could just as easily have kicked it; I was in that kind of funk.

Whoosh, it said, just as pretty as could be.

Breaking into one of those trash cans is probably tougher than busting into your local bank vault. Since I didn't even have a dime left to fiddle the screws on the lid, I was forced to deface city property. I got the damn thing open and dumped the contents on somebody's front lawn, smack in the middle of a circle of light from one of those snooty Beacon Hill gas streetlamps.

Halfway through the whiskey bottles, wadded napkins, and beer cans, I made my discovery. I was doing a thorough search. If you're going to stink like garbage anyway, why leave anything untouched, right? So I was opening all the brown bags—you know, the good old brown lunch-and-bottle bags—looking for a clue. My most valuable find so far had been the moldy rind of a bologna sandwich. Then I hit it big: one neatly creased bag stuffed full of cash.

To say I was stunned is to entirely underestimate how I felt as I crouched there, knee-deep in garbage, my jaw hanging wide. I don't know what I'd expected to find. Maybe the guy's gloves. Or his hat, if he'd wanted to get rid of it fast in order to melt back into anonymity. I pawed through the rest of the debris. My change was gone.

I was so befuddled I left the trash right on the front lawn. There's probably still a warrant out for my arrest.

District One Headquarters is off the beaten path, over on New Sudbury Street. I would have called first, if I'd had a dime.

One of the few things I'd enjoyed about being a cop was gabbing with Mooney. I like driving a cab better, but, face it, most of my fares aren't scintillating conversationalists. The Red Sox and the weather usually covers it. Talking to Mooney was so much fun, I wouldn't even consider dating him. Lots of guys are good at sex, but conversation—now there's an art form.

Mooney, all six-foot-four, 240 linebacker pounds of him, gave me the glad eye when I waltzed in. He hasn't given up trying. Keeps telling me he talks even better in bed.

"Nice hat," was all he said, his big fingers pecking at the typewriter keys.

I took it off and shook out my hair. I wear an old slouch cap when I drive to keep people from saying the inevitable. One jerk even misquoted Yeats at me: "Only God, my dear, could love you for yourself alone and not your long red hair." Since I'm seated when I drive, he missed the chance to ask me how the weather is up here. I'm six-one in my stocking feet and skinny enough to make every inch count twice. I've got a wide forehead, green eyes, and a pointy chin. If you want to be nice about my nose, you say it's got character.

Thirty's still hovering in my future. It's part of Mooney's past.

I told him I had a robbery to report and his dark eyes steered me to a chair. He leaned back and took a puff of one of his low-tar cigarettes. He can't quite give 'em up, but he feels guilty as hell about 'em.

When I got to the part about the bag in the trash, Mooney lost his sense of humor. He crushed a half-smoked butt in a crowded ashtray.

"Know why you never made it as a cop?" he said.

"Didn't brown-nose enough."

"You got no sense of proportion! Always going after crackpot stuff!"

"Christ, Mooney, aren't you interested? Some guy heists a cab, at gunpoint, then tosses the money. Aren't you the least bit *intrigued?*"

"I'm a cop, Ms. Carlyle. I've got to be more than intrigued. I've got murders, bank robberies, assaults—"

"Well, excuse me. I'm just a poor citizen reporting a crime. Trying to help—"

"Want to help, Carlotta? Go away." He stared at the sheet of paper in the typewriter and lit another cigarette. "Or dig me up something on the Thayler case."

"You working that sucker?"

"Wish to hell I wasn't."

I could see his point. It's tough enough trying to solve any murder, but when your victim is *the* Jennifer (Mrs. Justin) Thayler, wife of the famed Harvard Law prof, and the society reporters are breathing down your neck along with the usual crime-beat scribblers, you got a special kind of problem.

"So who did it?" I asked.

Mooney put his size twelves up on the desk. "Colonel Mustard in the library with the candlestick! How the hell do I know? Some scumbag housebreaker. The lady of the house interrupted his haul. Probably didn't mean to hit her that hard. He must have freaked when he saw all the blood, 'cause he left some of the ritziest stereo equipment this side of heaven, plus enough silverware to blind your average hophead. He snatched most of old man Thayler's goddam idiot artworks, collections, collectibles—whatever the hell you call 'em—which ought to set him up for the next few hundred years, if he's smart enough to get rid of them."

"Alarm system?"

"Yeah, they had one. Looks like Mrs. Thayler forgot to turn it on. According to the maid, she had a habit of forgetting just about anything after a martini or three."

"Think the maid's in on it?"

"Christ, Carlotta. There you go again. No witnesses. No fingerprints. Servants asleep. Husband asleep. We've got word out to all the fences here and in New York that we want this guy. The pawnbrokers know the stuff's hot. We're checking out known art thieves and shady museums—"

"Well, don't let me keep you from your serious business," I said, getting up to go. "I'll give you the collar when I find out who robbed my cab."

"Sure," he said. His fingers started playing with the typewriter again.

"Wanna bet on it?" Betting's an old custom with Mooney and me.

"I'm not gonna take the few piddling bucks you earn with that ridiculous car."

"Right you are, boy. I'm gonna take the money the city pays you to be unimaginative! Fifty bucks I nail him within the week."

Mooney hates to be called "boy." He hates to be called "unimaginative." I hate to hear my car called "ridiculous." We shook hands on the deal. Hard.

Chinatown's about the only chunk of Boston that's alive after midnight. I headed over to Yee Hong's for a bowl of wonton soup.

The service was the usual low-key, slow-motion routine. I used a newspaper as a shield; if you're really involved in the *Wall Street Journal*, the casual male may think twice before deciding he's the answer to your prayers. But I didn't read a single stock quote. I tugged at strands of my hair, a bad habit of mine. Why would somebody rob me and then toss the money away?

Solution Number One: He didn't. The trash bin was some mob

drop, and the money I'd found in the trash had absolutely nothing to do with the money filched from my cab. Except that it was the same amount—and that was too big a coincidence for me to swallow.

Two: The cash I'd found was counterfeit and this was a clever way of getting it into circulation. Nah. Too baroque entirely. How the hell would the guy know I was the pawing-through-the-trash type?

Three: It was a training session. Some fool had used me to perfect his robbery technique. Couldn't he learn from TV like the rest of the crooks?

Four: It was a frat hazing. Robbing a hack at gunpoint isn't exactly in the same league as swallowing goldfish.

I closed my eyes.

My face came to a fortunate halt about an inch above a bowl of steaming broth. That's when I decided to pack it in and head for home. Wonton soup is lousy for the complexion.

I checked out the log I keep in the Chevy, totaled my fares: $4.82 missing, all in change. A very reasonable robbery.

By the time I got home, the sleepiness had passed. You know how it is: one moment you're yawning, the next your eyes won't close. Usually happens when my head hits the pillow; this time I didn't even make it that far. What woke me up was the idea that my robber hadn't meant to steal a thing. Maybe he'd left me something instead. You know, something hot, cleverly concealed. Something he could pick up in a few weeks, after things cooled off.

I went over that backseat with a vengeance, but I didn't find anything besides old Kleenex and bent paperclips. My brainstorm wasn't too clever after all. I mean, if the guy wanted to use my cab as a hiding place, why advertise by pulling a five-and-dime robbery?

I sat in the driver's seat, tugged my hair, and stewed. What did I have to go on? The memory of a nervous thief who talked like a B movie and stole only change. Maybe a mad toll-booth collector.

I live in a Cambridge dump. In any other city, I couldn't sell the damned thing if I wanted to. Here, I turn real estate agents away daily. The key to my home's value is the fact that I can hoof it to Harvard Square in five minutes. It's a seller's market for tarpaper shacks within walking distance of the Square. Under a hundred thou only if the plumbing's outside.

It took me a while to get in the door. I've got about five locks on it. Neighborhood's popular with thieves as well as gentry. I'm neither. I inherited the house from my weird Aunt Bea, all paid for. I consider the property taxes my rent, and the rent's getting steeper all the time.

I slammed my log down on the dining room table. I've got rooms galore in that old house, rent a couple of them to Harvard students. I've got my own office on the second floor, but I do most of my work at the dining room table. I like the view of the refrigerator.

I started over from square one. I called Gloria. She's the late-night dispatcher for the Independent Taxi Owners Association. I've never seen her, but her voice is as smooth as mink oil and I'll bet we get a lot of calls from guys who just want to hear her say she'll pick 'em up in five minutes.

"Gloria, it's Carlotta."

"Hi, babe. You been pretty popular today."

"Was I popular at one-thirty-five this morning?"

"Huh?"

"I picked up a fare in front of the Copley Plaza at one-thirty-five. Did you hand that one out to all comers or did you give it to me solo?"

"Just a sec." I could hear her charming the pants off some caller in the background. Then she got back to me.

"I just gave him to you, babe. He asked for the lady in the '59 Chevy. Not a lot of those on the road."

"Thanks, Gloria."

"Trouble?" she asked.

"Is mah middle name," I twanged. We both laughed and I hung up before she got a chance to cross-examine me.

So. The robber wanted my cab. I wished I'd concentrated on his face instead of his snazzy clothes. Maybe it was somebody I knew, some jokester in mid-prank. I killed that idea; I don't know anybody who'd pull a stunt like that, at gunpoint and all. I don't want to know anybody like that.

Why rob my cab, then toss the dough?

I pondered sudden religious conversion. Discarded it. Maybe my robber was some perpetual screwup who'd ditched the cash by mistake.

Or . . . maybe he got exactly what he wanted. Maybe he desperately desired my change.

Why?

Because my change was special, valuable beyond its $4.82 replacement cost.

So how would somebody know my change was valuable?

Because he'd given it to me himself, earlier in the day.

"Not bad," I said out loud. "Not bad." It was the kind of reasoning they'd bounced me off the police force for, what my so-called superiors termed the "fevered product of an overimaginative mind." I leapt at it because it was the only explanation I could think of. I do like life to make some sort of sense.

I pored over my log. I keep pretty good notes: where I pick up a fare, where I drop him, whether he's a hailer or a radio call.

First, I ruled out all the women. That made the task slightly less impossible: sixteen suspects down from thirty-five. Then I yanked my hair and stared at the blank white porcelain of the refrigerator door. Got up and made myself a sandwich: ham, Swiss cheese, salami, lettuce and tomato, on rye. Ate it. Stared at the porcelain some more until the suspects started coming into focus.

Five of the guys were just plain fat and one was decidedly on the hefty side; I'd felt like telling them all to walk. Might do them some good, might bring on a heart attack. I crossed them all out. Making a thin person look plump is hard enough; it's damn near impossible to make a fatty look thin.

Then I considered my regulars: Jonah Ashley, a tiny blond southern gent; muscle-bound "just-call-me-Harold" at Longfellow Place; Dr. Homewood getting his daily ferry from Beth Israel to MGH; Marvin of the gay bars; and Professor Dickerman, Harvard's answer to Berkeley's sixties radicals.

I crossed them all off. I could see Dickerman holding up the First Filthy Capitalist Bank, or disobeying civilly at Seabrook, even blowing up an oil company or two. But my mind boggled at the thought of the great liberal Dickerman robbing some poor cabbie. It would be like Robin Hood joining the sheriff of Nottingham on some particularly rotten peasant swindle. Then they'd both rape Maid Marian and go off pals together.

Dickerman *was* a lousy tipper. That ought to be a crime.

So what did I have? Eleven out of sixteen guys cleared without leaving my chair. Me and Sherlock Holmes, the famous armchair detectives.

I'm stubborn; that was one of my good cop traits. I stared at that log till my eyes bugged out. I remembered two of the five pretty easily; they were handsome and I'm far from blind. The first had one of those elegant bony faces and far-apart eyes. He was taller than my bandit. I'd ceased eyeballing him when I noticed the ring on his left hand; I never fuss with the married kind. The other one was built, a weight lifter. Not an Arnold Schwarzenegger extremist, but built. I think I'd have noticed that bod on my bandit. Like I said, I'm not blind.

That left three.

Okay. I closed my eyes. Who had I picked up at the Hyatt on Memorial Drive? Yeah, that was the salesman guy, the one who looked so uncomfortable that I'd figured he'd been hoping to ask his cabbie for a few pointers concerning the best skirt-chasing areas in our fair city. Too low a voice. Too broad in the beam.

The log said I'd picked up a hailer at Kenmore Square when I'd let out the salesman. Ah, yes, a talker. The weather, mostly. Don't you think it's dangerous for you to be driving a cab? Yeah, I remembered him, all right: a fatherly type, clasping a briefcase, heading to the financial district. Too old.

Down to one. I was exhausted but not the least bit sleepy. All I had to do was remember who I'd picked up on Beacon near Charles. A hailer. Before five o'clock, which was fine by me because I wanted to be long gone before rush hour gridlocked the city. I'd gotten onto Storrow and taken him along the river into Newton Center. Dropped him off at the Bay Bank Middlesex, right before closing time. It was coming back. Little nervous guy. Pegged him as an accountant when I'd let him out at the bank. Measly, undernourished soul. Skinny as a rail, stooped, with pits left from teenage acne.

Shit. I let my head sink down onto the dining room table when I realized what I'd done. I'd ruled them all out, every one. So much for my brilliant deductive powers.

I retired to my bedroom, disgusted. Not only had I lost $4.82 in assorted alloy metals, I was going to lose fifty dollars to Mooney. I stared at myself in the mirror, but what I was really seeing was the round hole at the end of a .22, held in a neat, gloved hand.

Somehow, the gloves made me feel better. I'd remembered another detail about my piggy-bank robber. I consulted the mirror and kept the recall going. A hat. The guy wore a hat. Not like my cap, but like a hat out of a forties gangster flick. I had one of those: I'm a sucker for hats. I plunked it on my head, jamming my hair up underneath—and I drew in my breath sharply.

A shoulder-padded jacket, a slim build, a low slouched hat. Gloves. Boots with enough heel to click as he walked away. Voice? High. Breathy, almost whispered. Not unpleasant. Accentless. No Boston *r*.

I had a man's jacket and a couple of ties in my closet. Don't ask. They may have dated from as far back as my ex-husband, but not necessarily so. I slipped into the jacket, knotted the tie, tilted the hat down over one eye.

I'd have trouble pulling it off. I'm skinny, but my build is decidedly female. Still, I wondered—enough to traipse back downstairs, pull a chicken leg out of the fridge, go back to the log, and review the feminine possibilities. Good thing I did.

Everything clicked. One lady fit the bill exactly: mannish walk and clothes, tall for a woman. And I was in luck. While I'd picked her up in Harvard Square, I'd dropped her at a real address, a house in Brookline: 782 Mason Terrace, at the tope of Corey Hill.

JoJo's garage opens at seven. That gave me a big two hours to sleep.

I took my beloved car in for some repair work it really didn't need yet and sweet-talked JoJo into giving me a loaner. I needed a hack, but not mine. Only trouble with that Chevy is it's too damn conspicuous.

I figured I'd lose way more than fifty bucks staking out Mason Terrace. I also figured it would be worth it to see old Mooney's face.

She was regular as clockwork, a dream to tail. Eight-thirty-seven every morning, she got a ride to the Square with a next-door neighbor. Took a cab home at five-fifteen. A working woman. Well, she couldn't make much of a living from robbing hacks and dumping the loot in the garbage.

I was damn curious by now. I knew as soon as I looked her over that she was the one, but she seemed so blah, so *normal*. She must have been five-seven or -eight, but the way she stooped, she didn't look tall. Her hair was long and brown with a lot of blond in it, the kind of hair that would have been terrific loose and wild, like a horse's mane. She tied it back with a scarf. A brown scarf. She wore suits. Brown suits. She had a tiny nose, brown eyes under pale eyebrows, a sharp chin. I never saw her smile. Maybe what she needed was a shrink, not a session with Mooney. Maybe she'd done it for the excitement. God knows, if I had her routine, her job, I'd probably be dressing up like King Kong and assaulting skyscrapers.

See, I followed her to work. It wasn't even tricky. She trudged the same path, went in the same entrance to Harvard Yard, probably walked the same number of steps every morning. Her name was Marcia Heidegger and she was a secretary in the admissions office of the college of fine arts.

I got friendly with one of her coworkers.

There was this guy typing away like mad at a desk in her office. I could just see him from the side window. He had grad student written all over his face. Longish wispy hair. Gold-rimmed glasses. Serious. Given to deep sighs and bright velour V necks. Probably writing his thesis on "Courtly Love and the Theories of Chrétien de Troyes."

I latched onto him at Bailey's the day after I'd tracked Lady Heidegger to her Harvard lair.

Too bad Roger was so short. Most short guys find it hard to believe that I'm really trying to pick them up. They look for ulterior motives. Not the Napoleon type of short guy; he assumes I've been waiting years for a chance to dance with a guy who doesn't have to bend to stare down my cleavage. But Roger was no Napoleon. So I had to engineer things a little.

I got into line ahead of him and ordered, after long deliberation, a

BLT on toast. While the guy made it up and shoved it on a plate with three measly potato chips and a sliver of pickle you could barely see, I searched through my wallet, opened my change purse, counted out silver, got to $1.60 on the last five pennies. The counterman sang out, "That'll be a buck eighty-five." I pawed through my pockets, found a nickel, two pennies. The line was growing restive. I concentrated on looking like a damsel in need of a knight, a tough task for a woman over six feet.

Roger (I didn't know he was Roger then) smiled ruefully and passed over a quarter. I was effusive in my thanks. I sat at a table for two, and when he'd gotten his tray (ham-and-cheese and a strawberry ice cream soda), I motioned him into my extra chair.

He was a sweetie. Sitting down, he forgot the difference in our height, and decided I might be someone he could talk to. I encouraged him. I hung shamelessly on his every word. A Harvard man, imagine that. We got around slowly, ever so slowly, to his work at the admissions office. He wanted to duck it and talk about more important issues, but I persisted. I'd been thinking about getting a job at Harvard, possibly in admissions. What kind of people did he work with? Were they congenial? What was the atmosphere like? Was it a big office? How many people? Men? Women? Any soulmates? Readers? Or just, you know, office people?

According to him, every soul he worked with was brain dead. I interrupted a stream of complaint with "Gee, I know somebody who works for Harvard. I wonder if you know her."

"It's a big place," he said, hoping to avoid the whole endless business.

"I met her at a party. Always meant to look her up." I searched through my bag, found a scrap of paper and pretended to read Marcia Heidegger's name off it.

"Marcia? Geez, I work with Marcia. Same office."

"Do you think she likes her work? I mean I got some strange vibes from her," I said. I actually said "strange vibes" and he didn't laugh his head off. People in the Square say things like that and other people take them seriously.

His face got conspiratorial, of all things, and he leaned closer to me.

"You want it, I bet you could get Marcia's job."

"You mean it?" What a compliment—a place for me among the brain dead.

"She's gonna get fired if she doesn't snap out of it."

"Snap out of what?"

"It was bad enough working with her when she first came over.

She's one of those crazy neat people, can't stand to see papers lying on a desktop, you know? She almost threw out the first chapter of my thesis!"

I made a suitably horrified noise and he went on.

"Well, you know, about Marcia, it's kind of tragic. She doesn't talk about it."

But he was dying to.

"Yes?" I said, as if he needed egging on.

He lowered his voice. "She used to work for Justin Thayler over at the law school, that guy in the news, whose wife got killed. You know, her work hasn't been worth shit since it happened. She's always on the phone, talking real soft, hanging up if anybody comes in the room. I mean, you'd think she was in love with the guy or something, the way she. . . ."

I don't remember what I said. For all I know, I may have volunteered to type his thesis. But I got rid of him somehow and then I scooted around the corner of Church Street and found a pay phone and dialed Mooney.

"Don't tell me," he said. "Somebody mugged you, but they only took your trading stamps."

"I have just one question for you, Moon."

"I accept. A June wedding, but I'll have to break it to Mother gently."

"Tell me what kind of junk Justin Thayler collected."

I could hear him breathing into the phone.

"Just tell me," I said, "for curiosity's sake."

"You onto something, Carlotta?"

"I'm curious, Mooney. And you're not the only source of information in the world."

"Thayler collected Roman stuff. Antiques. And I mean old. Artifacts, statues—"

"Coins?"

"Whole mess of them."

"Thanks."

"Carlotta—"

I never did find out what he was about to say because I hung up. Rude, I know. But I had things to do. And it was better Mooney shouldn't know what they were, because they came under the heading of illegal activities.

When I knocked at the front door of the Mason Terrace house at 10:00 A.M. the next day, I was dressed in dark slacks, a white blouse, and my old police department hat. I looked very much like the guy who reads your gas meter. I've never heard of anyone being arrested for impersonating the gasman. I've never heard of anyone really giving the gasman a second look. He fades into the background and that's exactly what I wanted to do.

I knew Marcia Heidegger wouldn't be home for hours. Old reliable had left for the Square at her usual time, precise to the minute. But I wasn't 100 percent sure Marcia lived alone. Hence the gasman. I could knock on the door and check it out.

Those Brookline neighborhoods kill me. Act sneaky and the neighbors call the cops in twenty seconds, but walk right up to the front door, knock, talk to yourself while you're sticking a shim in the crack of the door, let yourself in, and nobody does a thing. Boldness is all.

The place wasn't bad. Three rooms, kitchen and bath, light and airy. Marcia was incredibly organized, obsessively neat, which meant I had to keep track of where everything was and put it back just so. There was no clutter in the woman's life. The smell of coffee and toast lingered, but if she'd eaten breakfast, she'd already washed, dried, and put away the dishes. The morning paper had been read and tossed in the trash. The mail was sorted in one of those plastic accordion files. I mean, she folded her underwear like origami.

Now coins are hard to look for. They're small; you can hide 'em anywhere. So this search took me one hell of a long time. Nine out of ten women hide things that are dear to them in the bedroom. They keep their finest jewelry closest to the bed, sometimes in the nightstand, sometimes right under the mattress. That's where I started.

Marcia had a jewelry box on top of her dresser. I felt like hiding it for her. She had some nice stuff and a burglar could have made quite a haul with no effort.

The next favorite place for women to stash valuables is the kitchen. I sifted through her flour. I removed every Kellogg's Rice Krispy from the giant economy-sized box—and returned it. I went through her place like no burglar ever will. When I say thorough, I mean thorough.

I found four odd things. A neatly squared pile of clippings from the *Globe* and the *Herald*, all the articles about the Thayler killing. A manila envelope containing five different safe-deposit-box keys. A Tupperware container full of superstitious junk, good luck charms mostly, the kind of stuff I'd never have associated with a straight-arrow like Marcia: rabbits' feet galore, a little leather bag on a string that looked like some kind of voodoo charm, a pendant in the shape of a cross surmounted by a hook, and, I swear to God, a pack of worn tarot cards. Oh, yes, and a .22 automatic, looking a lot less threatening stuck in an ice cube tray. I took the bullets; the unloaded gun threatened a defenseless box of Breyers' mint chocolate-chip ice cream.

I left everything else just the way I'd found it and went home. And tugged my hair. And stewed. And brooded. And ate half the stuff in the refrigerator, I kid you not.

At about one in the morning, it all made blinding, crystal-clear sense.

The next afternoon, at five-fifteen, I made sure I was the cabbie who picked up Marcia Heidegger in Harvard Square. Now cabstands have the most rigid protocol since Queen Victoria; you do not grab a fare out of turn or your fellow cabbies are definitely not amused. There was nothing for it but bribing the ranks. This bet with Mooney was costing me plenty.

I got her. She swung open the door and gave the Mason Terrace number. I grunted, kept my face turned front, and took off.

Some people really watch where you're going in a cab, scared to death you'll take them a block out of their way and squeeze them for an extra nickel. Others just lean back and dream. She was a dreamer, thank God. I was almost at District One Headquarters before she woke up.

"Excuse me," she said, polite as ever, "that's Mason Terrace in *Brookline*."

"Take the next right, pull over, and douse your lights," I said in a low Bogart voice. My imitation was not that good, but it got the point across. Her eyes widened and she made an instinctive grab for the door handle.

"Don't try it, lady," I Bogied on. "You think I'm dumb enough to take you in alone? There's a cop car behind us, just waiting for you to make a move."

Her hand froze. She was a sap for movie dialogue.

"Where's the cop?" was all she said on the way up to Mooney's office.

"What cop?"

"The one following us."

"You have touching faith in our law-enforcement system," I said.

She tried a bolt, I kid you not. I've had experience with runners a lot trickier than Marcia. I grabbed her in approved cop hold number three and marched her into Mooney's office.

He actually stopped typing and raised an eyebrow, an expression of great shock for Mooney.

"Citizen's arrest," I said.

"Charges?"

"Petty theft. Commission of a felony using a firearm." I rattled off a few more charges, using the numbers I remembered from cop school.

"This woman is crazy," Marcia Heidegger said with all the dignity she could muster.

"Search her," I said. "Get a matron in here. I want my four dollars and eighty-two cents back."

Mooney looked like he agreed with Marcia's opinion of my mental state. He said, "Wait up, Carlotta. You'd have to be able to identify that four dollars and eighty-two cents as yours. Can you do that? Quarters are quarters. Dimes are dimes."

"One of the coins she took was quite unusual," I said. "I'm sure I'd be able to identify it."

"Do you have any objection to displaying the change in your purse?" Mooney said to Marcia. He got me mad the way he said it, like he was humoring an idiot.

"Of course not," old Marcia said, cool as a frozen daiquiri.

"That's because she's stashed it somewhere else, Mooney," I said patiently. "She used to keep it in her purse, see. But then she goofed. She handed it over to a cabbie in her change. She should have just let it go, but she panicked because it was worth a pile and she was just babysitting it for someone else. So when she got it back, she hid it somewhere. Like in her shoe. Didn't you ever carry your lucky penny in your shoe?"

"No," Mooney said. "Now, Miss—"

"Heidegger," I said clearly. "Marcia Heidegger. She used to work at Harvard Law School." I wanted to see if Mooney picked up on it, but he didn't. He went on: "This can be taken care of with a minimum of fuss. If you'll agree to be searched by—"

"I want to see my lawyer," she said.

"For four dollars and eighty-two cents?" he said. "It'll cost you more than that to get your lawyer up here."

"Do I get my phone call or not?"

Mooney shrugged wearily and wrote up the charge sheet. Called a cop to take her to the phone.

He got Jo Ann, which was good. Under cover of our old-friend-long-time-no-see greetings, I whispered in her ear.

"You'll find it fifty well spent," I said to Mooney when we were alone.

Jo Ann came back, shoving Marcia slightly ahead of her. She plunked her prisoner down in one of Mooney's hard wooden chairs and turned to me, grinning from ear to ear.

"Got it?" I said. "Good for you."

"What's going on?" Mooney said.

"She got real clumsy on the way to the pay phone," Jo Ann said. "Practically fell on the floor. Got up with her right hand clenched tight. When we got to the phone, I offered to drop her dime for her. She wanted to do it herself. I insisted and she got clumsy again. Somehow this coin got kicked clear across the floor."

She held it up. The coin could have been a dime, except the color was off: warm, rosy gold instead of dead silver. How I missed it the first time around I'll never know.

"What the hell is that?" Mooney said.

"What kind of coins were in Justin Thayler's collection?" I asked. "Roman?"

Marcia jumped out of the chair, snapped her bag open, and drew out her little .22. I kid you not. She was closest to Mooney and she just stepped up to him and rested it above his left ear. He swallowed, didn't say a word. I never realized how prominent his Adam's apple was. Jo Ann froze, hand on her holster.

Good old reliable, methodical Marcia. Why, I said to myself, *why* pick today of all days to trot your gun out of the freezer? Did you read bad luck in your tarot cards? Then I had a truly rotten thought. What if she had two guns? What if the disarmed .22 was still staring down the mint chocolate-chip ice cream?

"Give it back," Marcia said. She held out one hand, made an impatient waving motion.

"Hey, you don't need it, Marcia," I said. "You've got plenty more. In all those safe deposit boxes."

"I'm going to count to five—" she began.

"Were you in on the murder from day one? You know, from the planning stages?" I asked. I kept my voice low, but it echoed off the walls of Mooney's tiny office. The hum of everyday activity kept going in the main room. Nobody noticed the little gun in the well-dressed lady's hand. "Or did you just do your beau a favor and hide the loot after he iced his wife? In order to back up his burglary tale? I mean, if Justin Thayler really wanted to marry you, there is such a thing as divorce. Or was old Jennifer the one with the bucks?"

"I want that coin," she said softly. "Then I want the two of you"— she motioned to Jo Ann and me—"to sit down facing that wall. If you yell, or do anything before I'm out of the building, I'll shoot this gentleman. He's coming with me."

"Come on, Marcia," I said, "put it down. I mean, look at you. A week ago you just wanted Thayler's coin back. You didn't want to rob my cab, right? You just didn't know how else to get your good luck charm back with no questions asked. You didn't do it for money, right? You did it for love. You were so straight you threw away the cash. Now here you are with a gun pointed at a cop—"

"Shut up!"

I took a deep breath and said, "You haven't got the style, Marcia. Your gun's not even loaded."

Mooney didn't relax a hair. Sometimes I think the guy hasn't ever believed a word I've said to him. But Marcia got shook. She pulled the barrel away from Mooney's skull and peered at it with a puzzled frown. Jo Ann and I both tackled her before she got a chance to pull the trigger. I twisted the gun out of her hand. I was almost afraid to look inside. Mooney stared at me and I felt my mouth go dry and a trickle of sweat worm its way down my back.

I looked.

No bullets. My heart stopped fibrillating, and Mooney actually cracked a smile in my direction.

So that's all. I sure hope Mooney will spread the word around that I helped him nail Thayler. And I think he will; he's a fair kind of guy. Maybe it'll get me a case or two. Driving a cab is hard on the backside, you know?

SUE GRAFTON

(b. 1940)

||||||||||||||||||||||||||||||||||||||||||||||| ■ ||||||||||||||||||||||||||||||||||||||||||||||

In the evolution of American detective fiction, the rise of the well-wrought, believable female private eye may be the most important trend of the past twenty years. There can be no doubt about Sue Grafton's contribution to this development as the creator of Kinsey Millhone, a self-confident, independent, smart divorcée in her thirties whose outlook on life, Grafton says, is patterned after her own. After all, Grafton admits to having turned to mystery writing as a means of getting her aggressions out on the page at a particularly difficult time in her life.

Millhone's clients—Californians who work for a living—and their problems are also realistic. In her novels, memorably titled after successive letters of the alphabet, Grafton's sleuth deals with issues that have directly affected the author's own life. For instance, in *D Is for Deadbeat* Grafton deals with alcoholism, a problem that she knew firsthand as the daughter of two alcoholics. Grafton says that her family was "classically dysfunctional," but it was also a household that revered the written word. Grafton's father was C. F. Grafton, a lawyer who wrote the classic courtroom novel *Beyond a Reasonable Doubt*.

It has been said that Grafton's work takes that of Ross Macdonald into another dimension. As did Macdonald, Grafton lives in Santa Barbara, California. And in homage to Macdonald, Grafton has Kinsey Millhone, like Lew Archer, reside in the fictional Santa Teresa.

Grafton notes that "The Parker Shotgun" grew out of reading that a long-defunct firearms company had made only two copies of a particular model, of which one had been lost. "I know nothing at all about guns, but here was a chance to make the murder weapon also the motive," Grafton says. The story displays another of the strengths that make her work notable: the minor characters have personalities of their own—something difficult to accomplish in short fiction. And while the reader is more likely to remember the grimness of this dysfunctional family than the detection involved, the doer of the fatal deed is nicely concealed until the end.

1986

The Parker Shotgun

■

The Christmas holidays had come and gone, and the new year was under way. January, in California, is as good as it gets—cool, clear, and green, with a sky the color of wisteria and a surf that thunders like a volley of gunfire in a distant field. My name is Kinsey Millhone. I'm a private investigator, licensed, bonded, insured; white, female, age thirty-two, unmarried, and physically fit. That Monday morning, I was sitting in my office with my feet up, wondering what life would bring, when a woman walked in and tossed a photograph on my desk. My introduction to the Parker shotgun began with a graphic view of its apparent effect when fired at a formerly nice-looking man at close range. His face was still largely intact, but he had no use now for a pocket comb. With effort, I kept my expression neutral as I glanced up at her.

"Somebody killed my husband."

"I can see that," I said.

She snatched the picture back and stared at it as though she might have missed some telling detail. Her face suffused with pink, and she blinked back tears. "Jesus. Rudd was killed five months ago, and the cops have done shit. I'm so sick of getting the runaround I could scream."

She sat down abruptly and pressed a hand to her mouth, trying to compose herself. She was in her late twenties, with a gaudy prettiness. Her hair was an odd shade of brown, like cherry Coke, worn shoulder length and straight. Her eyes were large, a lush mink brown; her mouth was full. Her complexion was all warm tones, tanned, and clear. She didn't seem to be wearing makeup, but she was still as vivid as a magazine illustration, a good four-color run on slick paper. She was seven months pregnant by the look of her; not voluminous yet, but rotund. When she was calmer, she identified herself as Lisa Osterling.

"That's a crime lab photo. How'd you come by it?" I said when the preliminaries were disposed of.

She fumbled in her handbag for a tissue and blew her nose. "I have my little ways," she said morosely. "Actually I know the photographer and I stole a print. I'm going to have it blown up and hung on the wall just so I won't forget. The police are hoping I'll drop the whole thing, but I got news for *them*." Her mouth was starting to tremble again, and a tear splashed onto her skirt as though my ceiling had a leak.

"What's the story?" I said. "The cops in this town are usually pretty good." I got up and filled a paper cup with water from my Sparklett's dispenser, passing it over to her.

She murmured a thank-you and drank it down, staring into the bottom of the cup as she spoke. "Rudd was a cocaine dealer until a month or so before he died. They haven't said as much, but I know they've written him off as some kind of small-time punk. What do they care? They'd like to think he was killed in a drug deal—a double cross or something like that. He wasn't, though. He'd given it all up because of this."

She glanced down at the swell of her belly. She was wearing a Kelly green T-shirt with an arrow down the front. The word "Oops!" was written across her breasts in machine embroidery.

"What's your theory?" I asked. Already I was leaning toward the official police version of events. Drug dealing isn't synonymous with longevity. There's too much money involved and too many amateurs getting into the act. This was Santa Teresa—ninety-five miles north of the big time in L.A., but there are still standards to maintain. A shotgun blast is the underworld equivalent of a bad annual review.

"I don't have a theory. I just don't like theirs. I want you to look into it so I can clear Rudd's name before the baby comes."

I shrugged. "I'll do what I can, but I can't guarantee the results. How are you going to feel if the cops are right?"

She stood up, giving me a flat look. "I don't know why Rudd died, but it had nothing to do with drugs," she said. She opened her handbag and extracted a roll of bills the size of a wad of socks. "What do you charge?"

"Thirty bucks an hour plus expenses."

She peeled off several hundred-dollar bills and laid them on the desk.

I got out a contract.

My second encounter with the Parker shotgun came in the form of a dealer's appraisal slip that I discovered when I was nosing through Rudd Osterling's private possessions an hour later at the house. The address she'd given me was on the Bluffs, a residential area on the west side of town, overlooking the Pacific. It should have been an elegant neighborhood, but the ocean generated too much fog and too much corrosive salt air. The houses were small and had a temporary feel to them, as though the occupants intended to move on when the month was up. No one seemed to get around to painting the trim, and the yards looked like they were kept by people who spent all day at the beach. I followed her in my car, reviewing the information she'd given me as I urged my ancient VW up Capilla Hill and took a right on Presipio.

The late Rudd Osterling had been in Santa Teresa since the sixties, when he migrated to the West Coast in search of sunshine, good surf, good dope, and casual sex. Lisa told me he'd lived in vans and communes, working variously as a roofer, tree trimmer, bean picker, fry cook, and forklift operator—never with any noticeable ambition or success. He'd started dealing cocaine two years earlier, apparently netting more money than he was accustomed to. Then he'd met and married Lisa, and she'd been determined to see him clean up his act. According to her, he'd retired from the drug trade and was just in the process of setting himself up in a landscape maintenance business when someone blew the top of his head off.

I pulled into the driveway behind her, glancing at the frame and stucco bungalow with its patchy grass and dilapidated fence. It looked like one of those households where there's always something under construction, probably without permits and not up to code. In this case, a foundation had been laid for an addition to the garage, but the weeds were already growing up through cracks in the concrete. A wooden outbuilding had been dismantled, the old lumber tossed in an unsightly pile. Closer to the house, there were stacks of cheap pecan wood paneling, sun-bleached in places and warped along one edge. It was all hapless and depressing, but she scarcely looked at it.

I followed her into the house.

"We were just getting the house fixed up when he died," she remarked.

"When did you buy the place?" I was manufacturing small talk, trying to cover my distaste at the sight of the old linoleum counter, where a line of ants stretched from a crust of toast and jelly all the way out the back door.

"We didn't really. This was my mother's. She and my stepdad moved back to the Midwest last year."

"What about Rudd? Did he have any family out here?"

"They're all in Connecticut, I think, real la-di-dah. His parents are dead, and his sisters wouldn't even come out to the funeral."

"Did he have a lot of friends?"

"All cocaine dealers have friends."

"Enemies?"

"Not that I ever heard about."

"Who was his supplier?"

"I don't know that."

"No disputes? Suits pending? Quarrels with the neighbors? Family arguments about the inheritance?"

She gave me a no on all four counts.

I had told her I wanted to go through his personal belongings, so she showed me into the tiny back bedroom, where he'd set up a card table and some cardboard file boxes. A real entrepreneur. I began to search while she leaned against the doorframe, watching.

I said, "Tell me about what was going on the week he died?" I was sorting through canceled checks in a Nike shoe box. Most were written to the neighborhood supermarket, utilities, telephone company.

She moved to the desk chair and sat down. "I can't tell you much because I was at work. I do alterations and repairs at a dry cleaner's up at Presipio Mall. Rudd would stop in now and then when he was out running around. He'd picked up a few jobs already, but he really wasn't doing the gardening full time. He was trying to get all his old business squared away. Some kid owed him money. I remember that."

"He sold cocaine on *credit?*"

She shrugged. "Maybe it was grass or pills. Somehow the kid owed him a bundle. That's all I know."

"I don't suppose he kept any records."

"Un-uhn. It was all in his head. He was too paranoid to put anything down in black and white."

The file boxes were jammed with old letters, tax returns, receipts. It all looked like junk to me.

"What about the day he was killed? Were you at work then?"

She shook her head. "It was a Saturday. I was off work, but I'd gone to the market. I was out maybe an hour and a half, and when I got home, police cars were parked in front, and the paramedics were here. Neighbors were standing out on the street." She stopped talking, and I was left to imagine the rest.

"Had he been expecting anyone?"

"If he was, he never said anything to me. He was in the garage, doing I don't know what. Chauncey, next door, heard the shotgun go off, but by the time he got here to investigate, whoever did it was gone."

I got up and moved toward the hallway. "Is this the bedroom down here?"

"Right. I haven't gotten rid of his stuff yet. I guess I'll have to eventually. I'm going to use his office for the nursery."

I moved into the master bedroom and went through his hanging clothes. "Did the police find anything?"

"They didn't look. Well, one guy came through and poked around some. About five minutes' worth."

I began to check through the drawers she indicated were his. Nothing remarkable came to light. On top of the chest was one of those brass and walnut caddies, where Rudd apparently kept his watch, keys, loose change. Almost idly, I picked it up. Under it there was a folded slip of paper. It was a partially completed appraisal form from a gun shop out in Colgate, a township to the north of us. "What's a Parker?" I said when I'd glanced at it. She peered over the slip.

"Oh. That's probably the appraisal on the shotgun he got."

"The one he was killed with?"

"Well, I don't know. They never found the weapon, but the homicide detective said they couldn't run it through ballistics, anyway—or whatever it is they do."

"Why'd he have it appraised in the first place?"

"He was taking it in trade for a big drug debt, and he needed to know if it was worth it."

"Was this the kid you mentioned before or someone else?"

"The same one, I think. At first, Rudd intended to turn around and sell the gun, but then he found out it was a collector's item so he decided to keep it. The gun dealer called a couple of times after Rudd died, but it was gone by then."

"And you told the cops all this stuff?"

"Sure. They couldn't have cared less."

I doubted that, but I tucked the slip in my pocket anyway. I'd check it out and then talk to Dolan in Homicide.

The gun shop was located on a narrow side street in Colgate, just off the main thoroughfare. Colgate looks like it's made up of hardware stores, U-Haul rentals, and plant nurseries; places that seem to have half their merchandise outside, surrounded by chain-link fence. The gun shop had been set up in someone's front parlor in a dinky white frame house. There were some glass counters filled with gun paraphernalia, but no guns in sight.

The man who came out of the back room was in his fifties, with a narrow face and graying hair, gray eyes made luminous by rimless glasses. He wore a dress shirt with the sleeves rolled up and a long gray apron tied around his waist. He had perfect teeth, but when he talked I could see the rim of pink where his upper plate was fit, and it spoiled the effect. Still, I had to give him credit for a certain level of good looks, maybe a seven on a scale of ten. Not bad for a man his age. "Yes, ma'am," he said. He had a trace of an accent, Virginia, I thought.

"Are you Avery Lamb?"

"That's right. What can I help you with?"

"I'm not sure. I'm wondering what you can tell me about this appraisal you did." I handed him the slip.

He glanced down and then looked up at me. "Where did you get this?"

"Rudd Osterling's widow," I said.

"She told me she didn't have the gun."

"That's right."

His manner was a combination of confusion and wariness. "What's your connection to the matter?"

I took out a business card and gave it to him. "She hired me to look into Rudd's death. I thought the shotgun might be relevant since he was killed with one."

He shook his head. "I don't know what's going on. This is the second time it's disappeared."

"Meaning what?"

"Some woman brought it in to have it appraised back in June. I made an offer on it then, but before we could work out a deal, she claimed the gun was stolen."

"I take it you had some doubts about that."

"Sure I did. I don't think she ever filed a police report, and I suspect she knew damn well who took it but didn't intend to pursue it. Next thing I knew, this Osterling fellow brought the same gun in. It had a beavertail fore-end and an English grip. There was no mistaking it."

"Wasn't that a bit of a coincidence? His bringing the gun in to you?"

"Not really. I'm one of the few master gunsmiths in this area. All he had to do was ask around the same way she did."

"Did you tell her the gun had showed up?"

He shrugged with his mouth and a lift of his brows. "Before I could talk to her, he was dead and the Parker was gone again."

I checked the date on the slip. "That was in August?"

"That's right, and I haven't seen the gun since."

"Did he tell you how he acquired it?"

"Said he took it in trade. I told him this other woman showed up with it first, but he didn't seem to care about that."

"How much was the Parker worth?"

He hesitated, weighing his words. "I offered him six thousand."

"But what's its value out in the marketplace?"

"Depends on what people are willing to pay."

I tried to control the little surge of impatience he had sparked. I could tell he'd jumped into his crafty negotiator's mode, unwilling to tip his hand in case the gun showed up and he could nick it off cheap. "Look," I said, "I'm asking you in confidence. This won't go any further unless it becomes a police matter, and then neither one of us will have a choice. Right now, the gun's missing anyway, so what difference does it make?"

He didn't seem entirely convinced, but he got my point. He cleared his throat with obvious embarrassment. "Ninety-six."

I stared at him. "Thousand dollars?"

He nodded.

"Jesus. That's a lot for a gun, isn't it?"

His voice dropped. "Ms. Millhone, that gun is priceless. It's an A-1 Special 28-gauge with a two-barrel set. There were only two of them made."

"But why so much?"

"For one thing, the Parker's a beautifully crafted shotgun. There are different grades, of course, but this one was exceptional. Fine wood. Some of the most incredible scroll-work you'll ever see. Parker had an Italian working for him back then who'd spend sometimes five thousand hours on the engraving alone. The company went out of business around 1942, so there aren't any more to be had."

"You said there were two. Where's the other one, or would you know?"

"Only what I've heard. A dealer in Ohio bought the one at auction a couple years back for ninety-six. I understand some fella down in Texas has it now, part of a collection of Parkers. The gun Rudd Osterling brought in has been missing for years. I don't think he knew what he had on his hands."

"And you didn't tell him."

Lamb shifted his gaze. "I told him enough," he said carefully. "I can't help it if the man didn't do his homework."

"How'd you know it was the missing Parker?"

"The serial number matched, and so did everything else. It wasn't a fake, either. I examined the gun under heavy magnification, checking for fill-in welds and traces of markings that might have been overstamped. After I checked it out, I showed it to a buddy of mine, a big gun buff, and he recognized it, too."

"Who else knew about it besides you and this friend?"

"Whoever Rudd Osterling got it from, I guess."

"I'll want the woman's name and address if you've still got it. Maybe she knows how the gun fell into Rudd's hands."

Again he hesitated for a moment, and then he shrugged. "I don't see why not." He made a note on a piece of scratch paper and pushed it across the counter to me. "I'd like to know if the gun shows up," he said.

"Sure, as long as Mrs. Osterling doesn't object."

I didn't have any questions for the moment. I moved toward the door, then glanced back at him. "How could Rudd have sold the gun if it was stolen property? Wouldn't he have needed a bill of sale for it? Some proof of ownership?"

Avery Lamb's face was devoid of expression. "Not necessarily. If an avid collector got hold of that gun, it would sink out of sight, and that's the last you'd ever see of it. He'd keep it in his basement and never show it to a soul. It'd be enough if he knew he had it. You don't need a bill of sale for that."

I sat out in my car and made some notes while the information was fresh. Then I checked the address Lamb had given me, and I could feel the adrenaline stir. It was right back in Rudd's neighborhood.

The woman's name was Jackie Barnett. The address was two streets over from the Osterling house and just about parallel; a big corner lot planted with avocado trees and bracketed with palms. The house itself was yellow stucco with flaking brown shutters and a yard that needed mowing. The mailbox read "Squires," but the house number seemed to match. There was a basketball hoop nailed up above the two-car garage and a dismantled motorcycle in the driveway.

I parked my car and got out. As I approached the house, I saw an old man in a wheelchair planted in the side yard like a lawn ornament. He was parchment pale, with baby-fine white hair and rheumy eyes. The left half of his face had been disconnected by a stroke, and his left arm and hand rested uselessly in his lap. I caught sight of a woman peering through the window, apparently drawn by the sound of my car door slamming shut. I crossed the yard, moving toward the front porch. She opened the door before I had a chance to knock.

"You must be Kinsey Millhone. I just got off the phone with Avery. He said you'd be stopping by."

"That was quick. I didn't realize he'd be calling ahead. Saves me an explanation. I take it you're Jackie Barnett."

"That's right. Come in if you like. I just have to check on him," she said, indicating the man in the yard.

"Your father?"

She shot me a look. "Husband," she said. I watched her cross the grass toward the old man, grateful for a chance to recover from my gaffe. I could see now that she was older than she'd first appeared. She must have been in her fifties—at that stage where women wear too much makeup and dye their hair too bold a shade of blond. She was buxom, clearly overweight, but lush. In a seventeenth-century painting, she'd have been depicted supine, her plump naked body draped in sheer white. Standing over her, something with a goat's rear end would be poised for assault. Both would look coy but excited at the prospects.

The old man was beyond the pleasures of the flesh, yet the noises he made—garbled and indistinguishable because of the stroke—had the same intimate quality as sounds uttered in the throes of passion, a disquieting effect.

I looked away from him, thinking of Avery Lamb instead. He hadn't actually told me the woman was a stranger to him, but he'd certainly implied as much. I wondered now what their relationship consisted of.

Jackie spoke to the old man briefly, adjusting his lap robe. Then she came back and we went inside.

"Is your name Barnett or Squires?" I asked.

"Technically it's Squires, but I still use Barnett for the most part," she said. She seemed angry, and I thought at first the rage was directed at me. She caught my look. "I'm sorry," she said, "but I've about had it with him. Have you ever dealt with a stroke victim?"

"I understand it's difficult."

"It's impossible! I know I sound hard-hearted, but he was always short-tempered and now he's frustrated on top of that. Self-centered, demanding. Nothing suits him. Nothing. I put him out in the yard sometimes just so I won't have to fool with him. Have a seat, hon."

I sat. "How long has he been sick?"

"He had the first stroke in June. He's been in and out of the hospital ever since."

"What's the story on the gun you took out to Avery's shop?"

"Oh, that's right. He said you were looking into some fellow's death. He lived right here on the Bluffs, too, didn't he?"

"Over on Whitmore."

"That was terrible. I read about it in the papers, but I never did hear the end of it. What went on?"

"I wasn't given the details," I said briefly. "Actually, I'm trying to track down a shotgun that belonged to him. Avery Lamb says it was the same gun you brought in."

She had automatically proceeded to get out two cups and saucers, so her answer was delayed until she'd poured coffee for us both. She passed a cup over to me, and then she sat down, stirring milk into hers. She glanced at me self-consciously. "I just took that gun to spite *him*," she said with a nod toward the yard. "I've been married to Bill for six years and miserable for every one of them. It was my own damn fault. I'd been divorced for ages and I was doing fine, but somehow when I hit fifty, I got in a panic. Afraid of growing old alone, I guess. I ran into Bill, and he looked like a catch. He was retired, but he had loads of money, or so he said. He promised me the moon. Said we'd travel. Said he'd buy me clothes and a car and I don't know what all. Turns out he's a penny-pinching miser with a mean mouth and a quick fist. At least he can't do that anymore." She paused to shake her head, staring down at her coffee cup.

"The gun was his?"

"Well, yes, it was. He has a collection of shotguns. I swear he took better care of them than he did of me. I just despise guns. I was always after him to get rid of them. Makes me nervous to have them in the house. Anyway, when he got sick, it turned out he had insurance, but it only paid eighty percent. I was afraid his whole life savings would go up in smoke. I figured he'd go on for years, using up all the money, and then I'd be stuck with his debts when he died. So I just picked up one of the guns and took it out to that gun place to sell. I was going to buy me some clothes."

"What made you change your mind?"

"Well, I didn't think it'd be worth but eight or nine hundred dollars. Then Avery said he'd give me six thousand for it, so I had to guess it was worth at least twice that. I got nervous and thought I better put it back."

"How soon after that did the gun disappear?"

"Oh, gee, I don't know. I didn't pay much attention until Bill got out of the hospital the second time. He's the one who noticed it was gone," she said. "Of course, he raised pluperfect hell. You should have seen him. He had a conniption fit for two days, and then he had another stroke and had to be hospitalized all over again. Served him right if you ask me. At least I had Labor Day weekend to myself. I needed it."

"Do you have any idea who might have taken the gun?"

She gave me a long, candid look. Her eyes were very blue and couldn't have appeared more guileless. "Not the faintest."

I let her practice her wide-eyed stare for a moment, and then I laid out a little bait just to see what she'd do. "God, that's too bad," I said. "I'm assuming you reported it to the police."

I could see her debate briefly before she replied. Yes or no. Check one. "Well, of course," she said.

She was one of those liars who blush from lack of practice.

I kept my tone of voice mild. "What about the insurance? Did you put in a claim?"

She looked at me blankly, and I had the feeling I'd taken her by surprise on that one. She said, "You know, it never even occurred to me. But of course he probably would have it insured, wouldn't he?"

"Sure, if the gun's worth that much. What company is he with?"

"I don't remember offhand. I'd have to look it up."

"I'd do that if I were you," I said. "You can file a claim, and then all you have to do is give the agent the case number."

"Case number?"

"The police will give you that from their report."

She stirred restlessly, glancing at her watch. "Oh, lordy, I'm going to have to give him his medicine. Was there anything else you wanted to ask while you were here?" Now that she'd told me a fib or two, she was anxious to get rid of me so she could assess the situation. Avery Lamb had told me she'd never reported it to the cops. I wondered if she'd call him up now to compare notes.

"Could I take a quick look at his collection?" I said, getting up.

"I suppose that'd be all right. It's in here," she said. She moved toward a small paneled den, and I followed, stepping around a suitcase near the door.

A rack of six guns was enclosed in a glass-fronted cabinet. All of them were beautifully engraved, with fine wood stocks, and I wondered how a priceless Parker could really be distinguished. Both the cabinet and the rack were locked, and there were no empty slots. "Did he keep the Parker in here?"

She shook her head. "The Parker had its own case." She hauled out a handsome wood case from behind the couch and opened it for me, demonstrating its emptiness as though she might be setting up a magic trick. Actually, there was a set of barrels in the box, but nothing else.

I glanced around. There was a shotgun propped in one corner, and I picked it up, checking the manufacturer's imprint on the frame. L. C. Smith. Too bad. For a moment I'd thought it might be the missing Parker. I'm always hoping for the obvious. I set the Smith back in the corner with regret.

"Well, I guess that'll do," I said. "Thanks for the coffee."

"No trouble. I wish I could be more help." She started easing me toward the door.

I held out my hand. "Nice meeting you," I said. "Thanks again for your time."

She gave my hand a perfunctory shake. "That's all right. Sorry I'm in such a rush, but you know how it is when you have someone sick."

Next thing I knew, the door was closing at my back and I was heading toward my car, wondering what she was up to.

I'd just reached the driveway when a white Corvette came roaring down the street and rumbled into the drive. The kid at the wheel flipped the ignition key and cantilevered himself up onto the seat top. "Hi. You know if my mom's here?"

"Who, Jackie? Sure," I said, taking a flyer. "You must be Doug."

He looked puzzled. "No, Eric. Do I know you?"

I shook my head. "I'm just a friend passing through."

He hopped out of the Corvette. I moved on toward my car, keeping an eye on him as he headed toward the house. He looked about seventeen, blond, blue-eyed, with good cheekbones, a moody, sensual mouth, lean surfer's body. I pictured him in a few years, hanging out in resort hotels, picking up women three times his age. He'd do well. So would they.

Jackie had apparently heard him pull in, and she came out onto the porch, intercepting him with a quick look at me. She put her arm through his, and the two moved into the house. I looked over at the old man. He was making noises again, plucking aimlessly at his bad hand with his good one. I felt a mental jolt, like an interior tremor shifting the ground under me. I was beginning to get it.

I drove the two blocks to Lisa Osterling's. She was in the backyard, stretched out on a chaise in a sunsuit that made her belly look like a watermelon in a laundry bag. Her face and arms were rosy, and her tanned legs glistened with tanning oil. As I crossed the grass, she raised a hand to her eyes, shading her face from the winter sunlight so she could look at me. "I didn't expect to see you back so soon."

"I have a question," I said, "and then I need to use your phone. Did Rudd know a kid named Eric Barnett?"

"I'm not sure. What's he look like?"

I gave her a quick rundown, including a description of the white Corvette. I could see the recognition in her face as she sat up.

"Oh, him. Sure. He was over here two or three times a week. I just never knew his name. Rudd said he lived around here somewhere and stopped by to borrow tools so he could work on his motorcycle. Is he the one who owed Rudd the money?"

"Well, I don't know how we're going to prove it, but I suspect he was."

"You think he killed him?"

"I can't answer that yet, but I'm working on it. Is the phone in here?" I was moving toward the kitchen. She struggled to her feet and followed me into the house. There was a wall phone near the back door. I tucked the receiver against my shoulder, pulling the appraisal slip out of my pocket. I dialed Avery Lamb's gun shop. The phone rang twice.

Somebody picked up on the other end. "Gun shop."

"Mr. Lamb?"

"This is Orville Lamb. Did you want me or my brother, Avery?"

"Avery, actually. I have a quick question for him."

"Well, he left a short while ago, and I'm not sure when he'll be back. Is it something I can help you with?"

"Maybe so," I said. "If you had a priceless shotgun—say, an Ithaca or a Parker, one of the classics—would you shoot a gun like that?"

"You could," he said dubiously, "but it wouldn't be a good idea, especially if it was in mint condition to begin with. You wouldn't want to take a chance on lowering the value. Now if it'd been in use previously, I don't guess it would matter much, but still I wouldn't advise it—just speaking for myself. Is this a gun of yours?"

But I'd hung up. Lisa was right behind me, her expression anxious. "I've got to go in a minute," I said, "but here's what I think went on. Eric Barnett's stepfather has a collection of fine shotguns, one of which turns out to be very, very valuable. The old man was hospitalized, and Eric's mother decided to hock one of the guns in order to do a little something for herself before he'd blown every asset he had on his medical bills. She had no idea the gun she chose was worth so much, but the gun dealer recognized it as the find of a lifetime. I don't know whether he told her that or not, but when she realized it was more valuable than she thought, she lost her nerve and put it back."

"Was that the same gun Rudd took in trade?"

"Exactly. My guess is that she mentioned it to her son, who saw a chance to square his drug debt. He offered Rudd the shotgun in trade, and Rudd decided he'd better get the gun appraised, so he took it out to the same place. The gun dealer recognized it when he brought it in."

She stared at me. "Rudd was killed over the gun itself, wasn't he?" she said.

"I think so, yes. It might have been an accident. Maybe there was a struggle and the gun went off."

She closed her eyes and nodded. "Okay. Oh, wow. That feels better. I can live with that." Her eyes came open, and she smiled painfully. "Now what?"

"I have one more hunch to check out, and then I think we'll know what's what."

She reached over and squeezed my arm. "Thanks."

"Yeah, well, it's not over yet, but we're getting there."

When I got back to Jackie Barnett's, the white Corvette was still in the driveway, but the old man in the wheelchair had apparently been moved into the house. I knocked, and after an interval, Eric opened the door, his expression altering only slightly when he saw me.

I said, "Hello again. Can I talk to your mom?"

"Well, not really. She's gone right now."

"Did she and Avery go off together?"

"Who?"

I smiled briefly. "You can drop the bullshit, Eric. I saw the suitcase in the hall when I was here the first time. Are they gone for good or just for a quick jaunt?"

"They said they'd be back by the end of the week," he mumbled. It was clear he looked a lot slicker than he really was. I almost felt bad that he was so far outclassed.

"Do you mind if I talk to your stepfather?"

He flushed. "She doesn't want him upset."

"I won't upset him."

He shifted uneasily, trying to decide what to do with me.

I thought I'd help him out. "Could I just make a suggestion here? According to the California penal code, grand theft is committed when the real or personal property taken is of a value exceeding two hundred dollars. Now that includes domestic fowl, avocados, olives, citrus, nuts, and artichokes. Also shotguns, and it's punishable by imprisonment in the county jail or state prison for not more than one year. I don't think you'd care for it."

He stepped away from the door and let me in.

The old man was huddled in his wheelchair in the den. The rheumy eyes came up to meet mine, but there was no recognition in them. Or maybe there was recognition but no interest. I hunkered beside his wheelchair. "Is your hearing okay?"

He began to pluck aimlessly at his pant leg with his good hand, looking away from me. I've seen dogs with the same expression when they've done pottie on the rug and know you've got a roll of newspaper tucked behind your back.

"Want me to tell you what I think happened?" I didn't really need to wait. He couldn't answer in any mode that I could interpret. "I think when you came home from the hospital the first time and found out the gun was gone, the shit hit the fan. You must have figured out that Eric took it. He'd probably taken other things if he'd been doing cocaine for long. You probably hounded him until you found out what he'd done with it, and then you went over to Rudd's to get it. Maybe you took the L. C. Smith with you the first time, or maybe you came back for it when he refused to return the Parker. In either case, you blew his head off and then came back across the yards. And then you had another stroke."

I became aware of Eric in the doorway behind me. I glanced back at him. "You want to talk about this stuff?" I asked.

"Did he kill Rudd?"

"I think so," I said. I stared at the old man.

His face had taken on a canny stubbornness, and what was I going to do? I'd have to talk to Lieutenant Dolan about the situation, but the cops would probably never find any real proof, and even if they did, what could they do to him? He'd be lucky if he lived out the year.

"Rudd was a nice guy," Eric said.

"God, Eric. You *all* must have guessed what happened," I said snappishly.

He had the good grace to color up at that, and then he left the room. I stood up. To save myself, I couldn't work up any righteous anger at the pitiful remainder of a human being hunched in front of me. I crossed to the gun cabinet.

The Parker shotgun was in the rack, three slots down, looking like the other classic shotguns in the case. The old man would die, and Jackie would inherit it from his estate. Then she'd marry Avery and they'd all have what they wanted. I stood there for a moment, and then I started looking through the desk drawers until I found the keys. I unlocked the cabinet and then unlocked the rack. I substituted the L. C. Smith for the Parker and then locked the whole business up again. The old man was whimpering, but he never looked at me, and Eric was nowhere in sight when I left.

The last I saw of the Parker shotgun, Lisa Osterling was holding it somewhat awkwardly across her bulky midriff. I'd talk to Lieutenant Dolan all right, but I wasn't going to tell him everything. Sometimes justice is served in other ways.

TONY HILLERMAN

(b. 1925)

|||||||||||||||||||||||||||||||||||||||||||||||| ■ ||||||||||||||||||||||||||||||||||||||||||||||||

Tony Hillerman's procedurals featuring the Navajo Tribal Police officers Joe Leaphorn and Jim Chee represent all the strengths of the American regional mystery novel. Not only does Hillerman open a vista of the southwestern landscape, with which he is intimately acquainted, but his work offers an understanding of Native American culture.

Hillerman was born in the dust-bowl village of Sacred Heart, Oklahoma, where he enjoyed a supportive family life and attended a boarding school for Potawatomie Indian girls. By growing up with Potawatomie and Seminole friends and neighbors, he learned, he says, that "racial difference exists only in the bigot's imagination but that cultural differences are fascinating."

Hillerman's youthful hopes of becoming a chemical engineer were already dimmed by bad grades in math and chemistry courses when he was drafted to fight in World War II. In the infantry, he twice attained the rank of private first class and won the Silver Star and the Bronze Star with cluster. He also suffered a wound that left him with only one good eye and a need for a job outside a chemistry lab.

While he was home from Europe on a convalescent furlough, two crucial incidents occurred. A reporter who had read his letters to his family told him that he should be a writer. And while driving a truck to the Navajo Reservation, he witnessed a curing ceremony that later became the center of *The Blessing Way*, his first novel introducing Leaphorn.

Before he wrote that novel, Hillerman studied journalism at the University of Oklahoma, persuaded Marie Unzne. to marry him, and spent seventeen years as a journalist and another five years as a journalism professor at the University of New Mexico. After writing his second novel, which features a political reporter as its sleuth, Hillerman returned to Leaphorn, sending him to the nearby Zuñi Reservation to help find a Navajo boy suspected of murder. This book, *The Dance Hall of the Dead*, won the "best novel" Edgar award from the Mystery Writers of America.

The series of novels that followed feature either Leaphorn or Jim Chee, a younger, more traditional Navajo police officer. In the most recent five books, the two work in uneasy tandem, solving crimes through their knowledge of the culture of their people. Hillerman's books have won awards from the Navajos, the Center for the American Indian, the American Anthropological Association, and the Department of the Interior. His colleagues in the Mystery Writers of America named him a Grand Master.

With its background of witchcraft and atmosphere of an impending desert storm, "Chee's Witch" demonstrates how Hillerman makes tribal culture and the desert landscape germane to his plots. In his tale, the unraveling of a contemporary crime is impossible without an intimate knowledge of timeless ritual.

1986

Chee's Witch

■

Snow is so important to the Eskimos they have nine nouns to describe its variations. Corporal Jimmy Chee of the Navajo Tribal Police had heard that as an anthropology student at the University of New Mexico. He remembered it now because he was thinking of all the words you need in Navajo to account for the many forms of witchcraft. The word Old Woman Tso had used was "anti'l," which is the ultimate sort, the absolute worst. And so, in fact, was the deed which seemed to have been done. Murder, apparently. Mutilation, certainly, if Old Woman Tso had her facts right. And then, if one believed all the mythology of witchery told among the fifty clans who comprised The People, there must also be cannibalism, incest, even necrophilia.

On the radio in Chee's pickup truck, the voice of the young Navajo reading a Gallup used-car commercial was replaced by Willie Nelson singing of trouble and a worried mind. The ballad fit Chee's mood. He was tired. He was thirsty. He was sticky with sweat. He was worried. His pickup jolted along the ruts in a windless heat, leaving a white fog of dust to mark its winding passage across the Rainbow Plateau. The truck was gray with it. So was Jimmy Chee. Since sunrise he had covered maybe two hundred miles of half-graded gravel and unmarked wagon tracks of the Arizona–Utah–New Mexico border country. Routine at first—a check into a witch story at the Tsossie hogan north of Teec Nos Pos to stop trouble before it started. Routine and logical. A bitter winter, a sand storm spring, a summer of rainless, desiccating heat. Hopes dying, things going wrong, anger growing, and then the witch gossip. The logical. A bitter winter, a sand storm spring, a summer awry. The trouble at the summer hogan of the Tsossies was a sick child and a water well that had turned alkaline—nothing unexpected. But you didn't expect such a specific witch. The skinwalker, the Tsossies agreed, was the City Navajo, the man who had come to live in one of the government houses at Kayenta. Why the City Navajo? Because everybody knew he was a witch. Where had they heard that, the first time? The People who came to the trading post at Mexican Water said it. And so Chee had driven westward over Tohache Wash, past Red

Mesa and Rabbit Ears to Mexican Water. He had spent hours on the shady porch giving those who came to buy, and to fill their water barrels, and to visit, a chance to know who he was until finally they might risk talking about witchcraft to a stranger. They were Mud Clan, and Many Goats People, and Standing Rock Clan—foreign to Chee's own Slow Talking People—but finally some of them talked a little.

A witch was at work on the Rainbow Plateau. Adeline Etcitty's mare had foaled a two-headed colt. Hosteen Musket had seen the witch. He'd seen a man walk into a grove of cottonwoods, but when he got there an owl flew away. Rudolph Bisti's boys lost three rams while driving their flocks up into the Chuska high pastures, and when they found the bodies, the huge tracks of a werewolf were all around them. The daughter of Rosemary Nashibitti had seen a big dog bothering her horses and had shot at it with her .22 and the dog had turned into a man wearing a wolfskin and had fled, half running, half flying. The old man they called Afraid of His Horses had heard the sound of the witch on the roof of his winter hogan, and saw the dirt falling through the smoke hole as the skinwalker tried to throw in his corpse powder. The next morning the old man had followed the tracks of the Navajo Wolf for a mile, hoping to kill him. But the tracks had faded away. There was nothing very unusual in the stories, except their number and the recurring hints that the City Navajo was the witch. But then came what Chee hadn't expected. The witch had killed a man.

The police dispatcher at Window Rock had been interrupting Willie Nelson with an occasional blurted message. Now she spoke directly to Chee. He acknowledged. She asked his location.

"About fifteen miles south of Dennehotso," Chee said. "Homeward bound for Tuba City. Dirty, thirsty, hungry, and tired."

"I have a message."

"Tuba City," Chee repeated, "which I hope to reach in about two hours, just in time to avoid running up a lot of overtime for which I never get paid."

"The message is FBI Agent Wells needs to contact you. Can you make a meeting at Kayenta Holiday Inn at eight P.M.?"

"What's it about?" Chee asked. The dispatcher's name was Virgie Endecheenie, and she had a very pretty voice and the first time Chee had met her at the Window Rock headquarters of the Navajo Tribal Police he had been instantly smitten. Unfortunately, Virgie was a born-into Salt Cedar Clan, which was the clan of Chee's father, which put an instant end to that. Even thinking about it would violate the complex incest taboo of the Navajos.

"Nothing on what it's about," Virgie said, her voice strictly business.

"It just says confirm meeting time and place with Chee or obtain alternate time."

"Any first name on Wells?" Chee asked. The only FBI Wells he knew was Jake Wells. He hoped it wouldn't be Jake.

"Negative on the first name," Virgie said.

"All right," Chee said. "I'll be there."

The road tilted downward now into the vast barrens of erosion which the Navajos call Beautiful Valley. Far to the west, the edge of the sun dipped behind a cloud—one of the line of thunderheads forming in the evening heat over the San Francisco Peaks and the Cococino Rim. The Hopis had been holding their Niman Kachina dances, calling the clouds to come and bless them.

Chee reached Kayenta just a little late. It was early twilight and the clouds had risen black against the sunset. The breeze brought the faint smells that rising humidity carries across desert country—the perfume of sage, creosote brush, and dust. The desk clerk said that Wells was in room 284 and the first name was Jake. Chee no longer cared. Jake Wells was abrasive but he was also smart. He had the best record in the special FBI Academy class Chee had attended, a quick, tough intelligence. Chee could tolerate the man's personality for a while to learn what Wells could make of his witchcraft puzzle.

"It's unlocked," Wells said. "Come on in." He was propped against the padded headboard of the bed, shirt off, shoes on, glass in hand. He glanced at Chee and then back at the television set. He was as tall as Chee remembered, and the eyes were just as blue. He waved the glass at Chee without looking away from the set. "Mix yourself one," he said, nodding toward a bottle beside the sink in the dressing alcove.

"How you doing, Jake?" Chee asked.

Now the blue eyes reexamined Chee. The question in them abruptly went away. "Yeah," Wells said. "You were the one at the Academy." He eased himself on his left elbow and extended a hand. "Jake Wells," he said.

Chee shook the hand. "Chee," he said.

Wells shifted his weight again and handed Chee his glass. "Pour me a little more while you're at it," he said, "and turn down the sound."

Chee turned down the sound.

"About thirty percent booze," Wells demonstrated the proportion with his hands. "This is your district then. You're in charge around Kayenta? Window Rock said I should talk to you. They said you were out chasing around in the desert today. What are you working on?"

"Nothing much," Chee said. He ran a glass of water, drinking it thirstily. His face in the mirror was dirty—the lines around mouth and eyes whitish with dust. The sticker on the glass reminded guests that the laws of the Navajo Tribal Council prohibited possession of alcoholic beverages on the reservation. He refilled his own glass with water and mixed Wells's drink. "As a matter of fact, I'm working on a witchcraft case."

"Witchcraft?" Wells laughed. "Really?" He took the drink from Chee and examined it. "How does it work? Spells and like that?"

"Not exactly," Chee said. "It depends. A few years ago a little girl got sick down near Burnt Water. Her dad killed three people with a shotgun. He said they blew corpse powder on his daughter and made her sick."

Wells was watching him. "The kind of crime where you have the insanity plea."

"Sometimes," Chee said. "Whatever you have, witch talk makes you nervous. It happens more when you have a bad year like this. You hear it and you try to find out what's starting it before things get worse."

"So you're not really expecting to find a witch?"

"Usually not," Chee said.

"Usually?"

"Judge for yourself," Chee said. "I'll tell you what I've picked up today. You tell me what to make of it. Have time?"

Wells shrugged. "What I really want to talk about is a guy named Simon Begay." He looked quizzically at Chee. "You heard the name?"

"Yes," Chee said.

"Well, shit," Wells said. "You shouldn't have. What do you know about him?"

"Showed up maybe three months ago. Moved into one of those U.S. Public Health Service houses over by the Kayenta clinic. Stranger. Keeps to himself. From off the reservation somewhere. I figured you federals put him here to keep him out of sight."

Wells frowned. "How long you known about him?"

"Quite a while," Chee said. He'd known about Begay within a week after his arrival.

"He's a witness," Wells said. "They broke a car-theft operation in Los Angeles. Big deal. National connections. One of those where they have hired hands picking up expensive models and they drive 'em right on the ship and off-load in South America. This Begay is one of the hired hands. Nobody much. Criminal record going all the way back to juvenile, but all nickel-and-dime stuff. I gather he saw some things that help tie some big boys into the crime, so Justice made a deal with him."

"And they hide him out here until the trial?"

Something apparently showed in the tone of the question. "If you want to hide an apple, you drop it in with the other apples," Wells said. "What better place?"

Chee had been looking at Wells's shoes, which were glossy with polish. Now he examined his own boots, which were not. But he was thinking of Justice Department stupidity. The appearance of any new human in a country as empty as the Navajo Reservation provoked instant interest. If the stranger was a Navajo, there were instant questions. What was his clan? Who was his mother? What was his father's clan? Who were his relatives? The City Navajo had no answers to any of these crucial questions. He was (as Chee had been repeatedly told) unfriendly. It was quickly guessed that he was a "relocation Navajo," born to one of those hundreds of Navajo families which the federal government had tried to reestablish forty years ago in Chicago, Los Angeles, and other urban centers. He was a stranger. In a year of witches, he would certainly be suspected. Chee sat looking at his boots, wondering if that was the only basis for the charge that City Navajo was a skinwalker. Or had someone seen something? Had someone seen the murder?

"The thing about apples is they don't gossip," Chee said.

"You hear gossip about Begay?" Wells was sitting up now, his feet on the floor.

"Sure," Chee said. "I hear he's a witch."

Wells produced a pro-forma chuckle. "Tell me about it," he said.

Chee knew exactly how he wanted to tell it. Wells would have to wait awhile before he came to the part about Begay. "The Eskimos have nine nouns for snow," Chee began. He told Wells about the variety of witchcraft on the reservations and its environs: about frenzy witchcraft, used for sexual conquests, of witchery distortions, of curing ceremonials, of the exotic two-heart witchcraft of the Hope Fog Clan, of the Zuñi Sorcery Fraternity, of the Navajo "chindi," which is more like a ghost than a witch, and finally of the Navajo Wolf, the anti'l witchcraft, the werewolves who pervert every taboo of the Navajo Way and use corpse powder to kill their victims.

Wells rattled the ice in his glass and glanced at his watch.

"To get to the part about your Begay," Chee said, "about two months ago we started picking up witch gossip. Nothing much, and you expect it during a drought. Lately it got to be more than usual." He described some of the tales and how uneasiness and dread had spread across the plateau. He described what he had learned today, the Tsossies' naming City Navajo as the witch, his trip to Mexican Water, of learning there that the witch had killed a man.

"They said it happened in the spring—couple of months ago. They told me the ones who knew about it were the Tso outfit." The talk of murder, Chee noticed, had revived Wells's interest. "I went up there," he continued, "and found the old woman who runs the outfit. Emma Tso. She told me her son-in-law had been out looking for some sheep, and smelled something, and found the body under some chamiso brush in a dry wash. A witch had killed him."

"How—"

Chee cut off the question. "I asked her how he knew it was a witch killing. She said the hands were stretched out like this." Chee extended his hands, palms up. "They were flayed. The skin was cut off the palms and fingers."

Wells raised his eyebrows.

"That's what the witch uses to make corpse powder," Chee explained. "They take the skin that has the whorls and ridges of the individual personality—the skin from the palms and the finger pads, and the soles of the feet. They take that, and the skin from the glans of the penis, and the small bones where the neck joins the skull, and they dry it, and pulverize it, and use it as poison."

"You're going to get to Begay any minute now," Wells said. "That right?"

"We got to him," Chee said. "He's the one they think is the witch. He's the City Navajo."

"I thought you were going to say that," Wells said. He rubbed the back of his hand across one blue eye. "City Navajo. Is it that obvious?"

"Yes," Chee said. "And then he's a stranger. People suspect strangers."

"Were they coming around him? Accusing him? Any threats? Anything like that, you think?"

"It wouldn't work that way—not unless somebody had someone in their family killed. The way you deal with a witch is hire a singer and hold a special kind of curing ceremony. That turns the witchcraft around and kills the witch."

Wells made an impatient gesture. "Whatever," he said. "I think something has made this Begay spooky." He stared into his glass, communing with the bourbon. "I don't know."

"Something unusual about the way he's acting?"

"Hell of it is I don't know how he usually acts. This wasn't my case. The agent who worked him retired or some damn thing, so I got stuck with being the delivery man." He shifted his eyes from glass to Chee. "But if it was me, and I was holed up here waiting, and the guy came along who was going to take me home again, then I'd be glad to see him. Happy to have it over with. All that."

"He wasn't?"

Wells shook his head. "Seemed edgy. Maybe that's natural, though. He's going to make trouble for some hard people."

"I'd be nervous," Chee said.

"I guess it doesn't matter much anyway," Wells said. "He's small potatoes. The guy who's handling it now in the U.S. Attorney's Office said it must have been a toss-up whether to fool with him at all. He said the assistant who handled it decided to hide him out just to be on the safe side."

"Begay doesn't know much?"

"I guess not. That, and they've got better witnesses."

"So why worry?"

Wells laughed. "I bring this sucker back and they put him on the witness stand and he answers all the questions with I don't know and it makes the USDA look like a horse's ass. When a U.S. Attorney looks like that, he finds an FBI agent to blame it on." He yawned. "Therefore," he said through the yawn, "I want to ask you what you think. This is your territory. You are the officer in charge. Is it your opinion that someone got to my witness?"

Chee let the question hang. He spent a fraction of a second reaching the answer, which was they could have if they wanted to try. Then he thought about the real reason Wells had kept him working late without a meal or a shower. Two sentences in Wells's report. One would note that the possibility the witness had been approached had been checked with local Navajo Police. The next would report whatever Chee said next. Wells would have followed Federal Rule One—Protect Your Ass.

Chee shrugged. "You want to hear the rest of my witchcraft business?"

Wells put his drink on the lamp table and untied his shoe. "Does it bear on this?"

"Who knows? Anyway there's not much left. I'll let you decide. The point is we had already picked up this corpse Emma Tso's son-in-law found. Somebody had reported it weeks ago. It had been collected, and taken in for an autopsy. The word we got on the body was Navajo male in his thirties probably. No identification on him."

"How was this bird killed?"

"No sign of foul play," Chee said. "By the time the body was brought in, decay and the scavengers hadn't left a lot. Mostly bone and gristle, I guess. This was a long time after Emma Tso's son-in-law saw him."

"So why do they think Begay killed him?" Wells removed his second shoe and headed for the bathroom.

Chee picked up the telephone and dialed the Kayenta clinic. He got the night supervisor and waited while the supervisor dug out the file. Wells came out of the bathroom with his toothbrush. Chee covered the mouthpiece. "I'm having them read me the autopsy report," Chee explained. Wilson began brushing his teeth at the sink in the dressing alcove. The voice of the night supervisor droned into Chee's ear.

"That all?" Chee asked. "Nothing added on? No identity yet? Still no cause?"

"That's him," the voice said.

"How about shoes?" Chee asked. "He have shoes on?"

"Just a sec," the voice said. "Yep. Size ten D. And a hat, and . . ."

"No mention of the neck or skull, right? I didn't miss that? No bones missing?"

Silence. "Nothing about neck or skull bones."

"Ah," Chee said. "Fine. I thank you." He felt great. He felt wonderful. Finally things had clicked into place. The witch was exorcised. "Jake," he said. "Let me tell you a little more about my witch case."

Wells was rinsing his mouth. He spit out the water and looked at Chee, amused. "I didn't think of this before," Wells said, "but you really don't have a witch problem. If you leave that corpse a death by natural causes, there's no case to work. If you decide it's a homicide, you don't have jurisdiction anyway. Homicide on an Indian reservation, FBI has jurisdiction." Wells grinned. "We'll come in and find your witch for you."

Chee looked at his boots, which were still dusty. His appetite had left him, as it usually did an hour or so after he missed a meal. He still hungered for a bath. He picked up his hat and pushed himself to his feet.

"I'll go home now," he said. "The only thing you don't know about the witch case is what I just got from the autopsy report. The corpse had his shoes on and no bones were missing from the base of the skull."

Chee opened the door and stood in it, looking back. Wells was taking his pajamas out of his suitcase. "So what advice do you have for me? What can you tell me about my witch case?"

"To tell the absolute truth, Chee, I'm not into witches," Wells said. "Haven't been since I was a boy."

"But we don't really have a witch case now," Chee said. He spoke earnestly. "The shoes were still on, so the skin wasn't taken from the soles of his feet. No bones missing from the neck. You need those to make corpse powder."

Wells was pulling his undershirt over his head. Chee hurried.

"What we have now is another little puzzle," Chee said. "If you're not collecting stuff for corpse powder, why cut the skin off this guy's hands?"

"I'm going to take a shower," Wells said. "Got to get my Begay back to L.A. tomorrow."

Outside the temperature had dropped. The air moved softly from the west, carrying the smell of rain. Over the Utah border, over the Cococino Rim, over the Rainbow Plateau, lightning flickered and glowed. The storm had formed. The storm was moving. The sky was black with it. Chee stood in the darkness, listening to the mutter of thunder, inhaling the perfume, exulting in it.

He climbed into the truck and started it. How had they set it up, and why? Perhaps the FBI agent who knew Begay had been ready to retire. Perhaps an accident had been arranged. Getting rid of the assistant prosecutor who knew the witness would have been even simpler— a matter of hiring him away from the government job. That left no one who knew this minor witness was not Simon Begay. And who was he? Probably they had other Navajos from the Los Angeles community stealing cars for them. Perhaps that's what had suggested the scheme. To most white men all Navajos looked pretty much alike, just as in his first years at college all Chee had seen in white men was pink skin, freckles, and light-colored eyes. And what would the imposter say? Chee grinned. He'd say whatever was necessary to cast doubt on the prosecution, to cast the fatal "reasonable doubt," to make—as Wells had put it—the U.S. District Attorney look like a horse's ass.

Chee drove into the rain twenty miles west of Kayenta. Huge, cold drops drummed on the pickup roof and turned the highway into a ribbon of water. Tomorrow the backcountry roads would be impassable. As soon as they dried and the washouts had been repaired, he'd go back to the Tsossie hogan, and the Tso place, and to all the other places from which the word would quickly spread. He'd tell the people that the witch was in custody of the FBI and was gone forever from the Rainbow Plateau.

MARCIA MULLER

(b. 1944)

|||||||||||||||||||||||||||||||||||||||||||||| ■ |||||||||||||||||||||||||||||||||||||||||||||

Marcia Muller has won her way into the record books of detective fiction as the creator of the first well-known, fully licensed, totally believable, hard-boiled female private investigator. While Muller has used two other women sleuths, both amateurs, Sharon McCone remains her best-known creation.

Muller was born in Detroit and studied English and journalism at the University of Michigan before moving to California, where she worked on the staff of *Sunset* magazine, as an interviewer in San Francisco for the University of Michigan's Institute of Social Research, and as a partner in Invisible Ink, a consulting service for writers.

Although Maxine O'Callaghan introduced a female private eye, Delilah West, in a 1974 short story, Muller's first McCone mystery, *Edwin of the Iron Shoes,* published in 1977, is credited with establishing conventions for such characters that are still observed today. Muller provided her sleuth with a family of characters that includes professional associates at the All Souls Legal Cooperative in San Francisco. She also endowed her with a sense of humor, a mission to see justice prevail, and a concern for the powerless. Many of McCone's cases arise from problems faced by people whom she knows personally, and they take place in notably realistic settings, generally in California. The verbal skills—in particular, the interviewing expertise—that McCone employs are very significant to solving her cases, making verbal acuity another strength emulated by later writers.

Muller's two other series characters are Elena Oliverez, curator at the Museum of Mexican Arts in Santa Barbara, and Joanna Stark, who heads an art security firm. The books in which these characters appear often focus on secrets of the past that affect the present.

In addition to producing fiction, Muller is an accomplished critic and anthologist, having collaborated on a dozen books, including three detective novels written with her husband, Bill Pronzini. In *Double,* for instance, the story is told in alternating chapters from the points of view of Muller's McCone and Pronzini's detective, Nameless.

"Benny's Space" provides an excellent illustration of Muller's technique: McCone's confident personality emerges; the problem she confronts is contemporary; the sociology of the neighborhood is genuine; the dialogue rings true; and, despite the brevity the form requires, Muller's quick sketches bring even the secondary characters so fully to life that the reader is truly moved by their circumstances.

1991
_____

Benny's Space

■

Amorfina Angeles was terrified, and I could fully empathize with her. Merely living in the neighborhood would have terrified me—all the more so had I been harassed by members of one of its many street gangs.

Hers was a rundown side street in the extreme southeast of San Francisco, only blocks from the drug- and crime-infested Sunnydale public housing projects. There were bars over the windows and grilles on the doors of the small stucco houses; dead and vandalized cars stood at the broken curbs; in the weed-choked yard next door, a mangy guard dog of indeterminate breed paced and snarled. Fear was written on this street as plainly as the graffiti on the walls and fences. Fear and hopelessness and a dull resignation to a life that none of its residents would willingly have opted to lead.

I watched Mrs. Angeles as she crossed her tiny living room to the front window, pulled the edge of the curtain aside a fraction, and peered out at the street. She was no more than five feet tall, with rounded shoulders, sallow skin, and graying black hair that curled in short, unruly ringlets. Her shapeless flower-printed dress did little to conceal a body made soft and fleshy by bad food and too much childbearing. Although she was only forty, she moved like a much older woman.

Her attorney and my colleague, Jack Stuart of All Souls Legal Cooperative, had given me a brief history of his client when he'd asked me to undertake an investigation on her behalf. She was a Filipina who had emigrated to the states with her husband in search of their own piece of the good life that was reputed to be had here. But as with many of their countrymen and -women, things hadn't worked out as the Angeleses had envisioned: first Amorfina's husband had gone into the import-export business with a friend from Manila; the friend absconded two years later with Joe Angeles's life savings. Then, a year after that, Joe was killed in a freak accident at a construction site where he was working. Amorfina and their six children were left with no means of support, and in the years since Joe's death their circumstances had gradually been reduced to this two-bedroom rental cottage in one of the worst areas of the city.

Mrs. Angeles, Jack told me, had done the best she could for her family, keeping them off the welfare rolls with a daytime job at a Mission district sewing factory and nighttime work doing alterations. As they grew older, the children helped with part-time jobs. Now there were only two left at home: sixteen-year-old Alex and fourteen-year-old Isabel. It was typical of their mother, Jack said, that in the current crisis she was more concerned for them than for herself.

She turned from the window now, her face taut with fear, deep lines bracketing her full lips. I asked, "Is someone out there?"

She shook her head and walked wearily to the worn recliner opposite me. I occupied the place of honor on a red brocade sofa encased in the same plastic that doubtless had protected it long ago upon delivery from the store. "I never see anybody," she said. "Not till it's too late."

"Mrs. Angeles, Jack Stuart told me about your problem, but I'd like to hear it in your own words—from the beginning, if you would."

She nodded, smoothing her bright dress over her plump thighs. "It goes back a long time, to when Benny Crespo was . . . they called him the Prince of Omega Street, you know."

Hearing the name of her street spoken made me aware of its ironic appropriateness: the last letter of the Greek alphabet is symbolic of endings, and for most of the people living here, Omega Street was the end of a steady decline into poverty.

Mrs. Angeles went on, "Benny Crespo was Filipino. His gang controlled the drugs here. A lot of people looked up to him; he had power, and that don't happen much with our people. Once I caught Alex and one of my older boys calling him a hero. I let them have it pretty good, you bet, and there wasn't any more of *that* kind of talk around this house. I got no use for the gangs—Filipino or otherwise."

"What was the name of Benny Crespo's gang?"

"The *Kabalyeros*. That's Tagalog for Knights."

"Okay—what happened to Benny?"

"The house next door, the one with the dog—that was where Benny lived. He always parked his fancy Corvette out front, and people knew better than to mess with it. Late one night he was getting out of the car and somebody shot him. A drug burn, they say. After that the *Kabalyeros* decided to make the parking space a shrine to Benny. They roped it off, put flowers there every week. On All Saints Day and the other fiestas, it was something to see."

"And that brings us to last March thirteenth," I said.

Mrs. Angeles bit her lower lip and smoothed her dress again.

When she didn't speak, I prompted her. "You'd just come home from work."

"Yeah. It was late, dark. Isabel wasn't here, and I got worried. I kept looking out the window, like a mother does."

"And you saw . . . ?"

"The guy who moved into the house next door after Benny got shot, Reg Dawson. He was black, one of a gang called the Victors. They say he moved into that house to show the *Kabalyeros* that the Victors were taking over their turf. Anyway, he drives up and stops a little way down the block. Waits there, revving his engine. People start showing up; the word's been put out that something's gonna go down. And when there's a big crowd, Reg Dawson guns his car and drives right into Benny's space, over the rope and the flowers.

"Well, that started one hell of a fight—Victors and *Kabalyeros* and folks from the neighborhood. And while it's going on, Reg Dawson just stands there in Benny's space acting macho. That's when it happened, what I saw."

"And what was that?"

She hesitated, wet her lips. "The leader of the *Kabalyeros*, Tommy Dragón—the Dragon, they call him—was over by the fence in front of Reg Dawson's house, where you couldn't see him unless you were really looking. I was, 'cause I was trying to see if Isabel was anyplace out there. And I saw Tommy Dragón point this gun at Reg Dawson and shoot him dead."

"What did you do then?"

"Ran and hid in the bathroom. That's where I was when the cops came to the door. Somebody'd told them I was in the window when it all went down and then ran away when Reg got shot. Well, what was I supposed to do? I got no use for the *Kabalyeros* or the Victors, so I told the truth. And now here I am in this mess."

Mrs. Angeles had been slated to be the chief prosecution witness at Tommy Dragón's trial this week. But a month ago the threats had started: anonymous letters and phone calls warning her against testifying. As the trial date approached, this had escalated into blatant intimidation: a fire was set in her trash can; someone shot out her kitchen window; a dead dog turned up on her doorstep. The previous Friday, Isabel had been accosted on her way home from the bus stop by two masked men with guns. And that had finally made Mrs. Angeles capitulate; in court yesterday, she'd refused to take the stand against Dragón.

The state needed her testimony; there were no other witnesses, Dragón insisted on his innocence, and the murder gun had not been found. The judge had tried to reason with Mrs. Angeles, then cited her for contempt—reluctantly, he said. "The court is aware that there have been threats made against you and your family," he told her, "but it is unable to guarantee your protection." Then he gave her forty-eight hours to reconsider her decision.

As it turned out, Mrs. Angeles had a champion in her employer. The owner of the sewing factory was unwilling to allow one of his long-term workers to go to jail or to risk her own and her family's safety. He brought her to All Souls, where he held a membership in our legal-services plan, and this morning Jack Stuart had asked me to do something for her.

What? I'd asked. What could I do that the SFPD couldn't to stop vicious harassment by a street gang?

Well, he said, get proof against whoever was threatening her so they could be arrested and she'd feel free to testify.

Sure, Jack, I said. And exactly why *hadn't* the police been able to do anything about the situation?

His answer was not surprising: lack of funds. Intimidation of prosecution witnesses in cases relating to gang violence was becoming more and more prevalent and open in San Francisco, but the city did not have the resources to protect them. An old story nowadays—not enough money to go around.

Mrs. Angeles was watching my face, her eyes tentative. As I looked back at her, her gaze began to waver. She'd experienced too much disappointment in her life to expect much in the way of help from me.

I said, "Yes, you certainly are in a mess. Let's see if we can get you out of it."

We talked for a while longer, and I soon realized that Amor—as she asked me to call her—held the misconception that there was some way I could get the contempt citation dropped. I asked her if she'd known beforehand that a balky witness could be sent to jail. She shook her head. A person had a right to change her mind, didn't she? When I set her straight on that, she seemed to lose interest in the conversation; it was difficult to get her to focus long enough to compile a list of people I should talk with. I settled for enough names to keep me occupied for the rest of the afternoon.

I was ready to leave when angry voices came from the front steps. A young man and woman entered. They stopped speaking when they saw the room was occupied, but their faces remained set in lines of contention. Amor hastened to introduce them as her son and daughter, Alex and Isabel. To them she explained that I was a detective "helping with the trouble with the judge."

Alex, a stocky youth with a tracery of moustache on his upper lip, seemed disinterested. He shrugged out of his high school letter jacket and vanished through a door to the rear of the house. Isabel studied me with frank curiosity. She was a slender beauty, with black hair that fell in soft curls to her shoulders; her features had a delicacy lacking in those of her mother and brother. Unfortunately, bright blue eyeshadow and garish orange lipstick detracted from her natural good looks, and she wore an imitation leather outfit in a particularly gaudy shade of purple. However, she was polite and well-spoken as she questioned me about what I could do to help her mother. Then, after a comment to Amor about an assignment that was due the next day, she left through the door her brother had used.

I turned to Amor, who was fingering the leaves of a philodendron plant that stood on a stand near the front window. Her posture was stiff, and when I spoke to her she didn't meet my eyes. Now I was aware of a tension in her that hadn't been there before her children returned home. Anxiety, because of the danger her witnessing the shooting had placed them in? Or something else? It might have had to do with the quarrel they'd been having, but weren't arguments between siblings fairly common? They certainly had been in my childhood home in San Diego.

I told Amor I'd be back to check on her in a couple of hours. Then, after a few precautionary and probably unnecessary reminders about locking doors and staying clear of windows, I went out into the chill November afternoon.

The first name on my list was Madeline Dawson, the slain gang leader's widow. I glanced at the house next door and saw with some relief that the guard dog no longer paced in its yard. When I pushed through the gate in the chain link fence, the creature's whereabouts quickly became apparent: a bellowing emanated from the small, shabby cottage. I went up a broken walk bordered by weeds, climbed the sagging front steps, and pressed the bell. A woman's voice yelled for the dog to shut up, then a door slammed somewhere within, muffling the barking. Footsteps approached, and the woman called, "Yes, who is it?"

"My name's Sharon McCone, from All Souls Legal Cooperative. I'm investigating the threats your neighbor, Mrs. Angeles, has been receiving."

A couple of locks turned and the door opened on its chain. The face that peered out at me was very thin and pale, with wisps of red hair straggling over the high forehead; the Dawson marriage had been an interracial one, then. The woman stared at me for a moment before she asked, "What threats?"

"You don't know that Mrs. Angeles and her children have been threatened because she's to testify against the man who shot your husband?"

She shook her head and stepped back, shivering slightly—whether from the cold outside or the memory of the murder, I couldn't tell. "I . . . don't get out much these days."

"May I come in, talk with you about the shooting?"

She shrugged, unhooked the chain, and opened the door. "I don't know what good it will do. Amor's a damned fool for saying she'd testify in the first place."

"Aren't you glad she did? The man killed your husband."

She shrugged again and motioned me into a living room the same size as that in the Angeles house. All resemblance stopped there, however. Dirty glasses and dishes, full ashtrays, piles of newspapers and magazines covered every surface; dust balls the size of rats lurked under the shabby Danish modern furniture. Madeline Dawson picked up a heap of tabloids from the couch and dumped it on the floor, then indicated I should sit there and took a hassock for herself.

I said, "You *are* glad that Mrs. Angeles was willing to testify, aren't you?"

"Not particularly."

"You don't care if your husband's killer is convicted or not?"

"Reg was asking to be killed. Not that I wouldn't mind seeing the Dragon get the gas chamber—he may not have killed Reg, but he killed plenty of other people—"

"What did you say?" I spoke sharply, and Madeline Dawson blinked in surprise. It made me pay closer attention to her eyes; they were glassy, their pupils dilated. The woman, I realized, was high.

"I said the Dragon killed plenty of other people."

"No, about him not killing Reg."

"Did I say that?"

"Yes."

"I can't imagine why. I mean, Amor must know. She was up there in the window watching for sweet Isabel like always."

"You don't sound as if you like Isabel Angeles."

"I'm not fond of flips in general. Look at the way they're taking over this area. Daly City's turning into another Manila. All they do is buy, buy, buy—houses, cars, stuff by the truckload. You know, there's a joke that the first three words their babies learn are 'Mama, Papa, and Serramonte.'" Serramonte was a large shopping mall south of San Francisco.

The roots of the resentment she voiced were clear to me. One of our largest immigrant groups today, the Filipinos are highly westernized and by and large better educated and more affluent than other recently arrived Asians—or many of their neighbors, black or white. Isabel Angeles, for all her bright, cheap clothing and excessive makeup, had behind her a tradition of industriousness and upward mobility that might help her to secure a better place in the world than Madeline Dawson could aspire to.

I wasn't going to allow Madeline's biases to interfere with my line of questioning. I said, "About Dragón not having shot your husband—"

"Hey, who knows? Or cares? The bastard's dead, and good riddance."

"Why good riddance?"

"The man was a pig. A pusher who cheated and gouged people—people like me who need the stuff to get through. You think I was always like this, lady? No way. I was a nice Irish Catholic girl from the Avenues when Reg got his hands on me. Turned me on to coke and a lot of other things when I was only thirteen. Liked his pussy young, Reg did. But then I got old—I'm all of nineteen now—and I needed more and more stuff just to keep going, and all of a sudden Reg didn't even *see* me anymore. Yeah, the man was a pig, and I'm glad he's dead."

"But you don't think Dragón killed him."

She sighed in exasperation. "I don't know what I think. It's just that I always supposed that when Reg got it it would be for something more personal than driving his car into a stupid shrine in a parking space. You know what I mean? But what does it matter who killed him, anyway?"

"It matters to Tommy Dragón, for one."

She dismissed the accused man's life with a flick of her hand. "Like I said, the Dragon's a killer. He might as well die for Reg's murder as for any of the others. In a way it'd be the one good thing Reg did for the world."

Perhaps in a certain primitive sense she was right, but her offhandedness made me uncomfortable. I changed the subject. "About the threats to Mrs. Angeles—which of the *Kabalyeros* would be behind them?"

"All of them. The guys in the gangs, they work together."

But I knew enough about the structure of street gangs—my degree in sociology from UC Berkeley hadn't been totally worthless—to be reasonably sure that wasn't so. There is usually one dominant personality, supported by two or three lieutenants; take away these leaders, and the followers become ineffectual, purposeless. If I could turn up enough evidence against the leaders of the *Kabalyeros* to have them arrested, the harassment would stop.

I asked, "Who took over the *Kabalyeros* after Dragón went to jail?"

"Hector Bulis."

It was a name that didn't appear on my list; Amor had claimed not to know who was the current head of the Filipino gang. "Where can I find him?"

"There's a fast-food joint over on Geneva, near the Cow Palace. Fat Robbie's. That's where the *Kabalyeros* hang out."

The second person I'd intended to talk with was the young man who had reportedly taken over the leadership of the Victors after Dawson's death, Jimmy Willis. Willis could generally be found at a bowling alley, also on Geneva Avenue near the Cow Palace. I thanked Madeline for taking the time to talk with me and headed for the Daly City line.

The first of the two establishments that I spotted was Fat Robbie's, a cinderblock-and-glass relic of the early sixties whose specialties appeared to be burgers and chicken-in-a-basket. I turned into a parking lot that was half-full of mostly shabby cars and left my MG beside one of the defunct drive-in speaker poles.

The interior of the restaurant took me back to my high school days: orange leatherette booths beside the plate glass windows; a long Formica counter with stools; laminated color pictures of disgusting-looking food on the wall above the pass-through counter from the kitchen. Instead of a jukebox there was a bank of video games along one wall. Three Filipino youths in jeans and denim jackets gathered around one called "Invader!" The *Kabalyeros*, I assumed.

I crossed to the counter with only a cursory glance at the trio, sat, and ordered coffee from a young waitress who looked to be Eurasian. The *Kabalyeros* didn't conceal their interest in me; they stared openly, and after a moment one of them said something that sounded like "tick-tick," and they all laughed nastily. Some sort of Tagalog obscenity, I supposed. I ignored them, sipping the dishwater-weak coffee, and after a bit they went back to their game.

I took out the paperback that I keep in my bag for protective coloration and pretended to read, listening to the few snatches of conversation that drifted over from the three. I caught the names of two: Sal and Hector—the latter presumably Bulis, the gang's leader. When I glanced covertly at him, I saw he was tallish and thin, with long hair caught back in a ponytail; his features were razor-sharp and slightly skewed, creating the impression of a perpetual sneer. The trio kept their voices low, and although I strained to hear, I could make out nothing of what they were saying. After about five minutes Hector turned away from the video machine. With a final glance at me he motioned to his companions, and they all left the restaurant.

I waited until they'd driven away in an old green Pontiac before I called the waitress over and showed her my identification. "The three men who just left," I said. "Is the tall one Hector Bulis?"

Her lips formed a little "O" as she stared at the ID. Finally she nodded.

"May I talk with you about them?"

She glanced toward the pass-through to the kitchen. "My boss, he don't like me talking with the customers when I'm supposed to be working."

"Take a break. Just five minutes."

Now she looked nervously around the restaurant. "I shouldn't—".

I slipped a twenty-dollar bill from my wallet and showed it to her. "Just five minutes."

She still seemed edgy, but fear lost out to greed. "Okay, but I don't want anybody to see me talking to you. Go back to the restroom—it's through that door by the video games. I'll meet you there as soon as I can."

I got up and found the ladies room. It was tiny, dimly lit, with a badly cracked mirror. The walls were covered with a mass of graffiti; some of it looked as if it had been painted over and had later worked its way back into view through the fading layers of enamel. The air in there was redolent of grease, cheap perfume, and stale cigarette and marijuana smoke. I leaned against the sink as I waited.

The young Eurasian woman appeared a few minutes later. "Bastard gave me a hard time," she said. "Tried to tell me I'd already taken my break."

"What's your name?"

"Anna Smith."

"Anna, the three men who just left—do they come in here often?"

"Uh-huh."

"Keep pretty much to themselves, don't they?"

"It's more like other people stay away from them." She hesitated. "They're from one of the gangs; you don't mess with them. That's why I wanted to talk with you back here."

"Have you ever heard them say anything about Tommy Dragón?"

"The Dragon? Sure. He's in jail; they say he was framed."

Of course they would claim that. "What about a Mrs. Angeles— Amorfina Angeles?"

". . . Not that one, no."

"What about trying to intimidate someone? Setting fires, going after someone with a gun?"

"Uh-uh. That's gang business; they keep it pretty close. But it wouldn't surprise me. Filipinos—I'm part Filipina myself, my mom met my dad when he was stationed at Subic Bay—they've got this saying, *kumukuló ang dugó*. It means 'the blood is boiling.' They can get pretty damn mad, 'specially the men. So stuff like what you said—sure they do it."

"Do you work on Fridays?"

"Yeah, two to ten."

"Did you see any of the *Kabalyeros* in here last Friday around six?" That was the time when Isabel had been accosted.

Anna Smith scrunched up her face in concentration. "Last Friday . . . oh, yeah, sure. That was when they had the big meeting, all of them."

"*All* of them?"

"Uh-huh. Started around five thirty, went on a couple of hours. My boss, he was worried something heavy was gonna go down, but the way it turned out, all he did was sell a lot of food."

"What was this meeting about?"

"Had to do with the Dragon, who was gonna be character witnesses at the trial, what they'd say."

The image of the three I'd seen earlier—or any of their ilk—as character witnesses was somewhat ludicrous, but I supposed in Tommy Dragón's position you took what you could get. "Are you sure they were all there?"

"Uh-huh."

"And no one at the meeting said anything about trying to keep Mrs. Angeles from testifying?"

"No. That lawyer the Dragon's got, he was there too."

Now that was odd. Why had Dragón's public defender chosen to meet with his witnesses in a public place? I could think of one good reason: he was afraid of them, didn't want them in his office. But what if the *Kabalyeros* had set the time and place—as an alibi for when Isabel was to be assaulted?

"I better get back to work," Anna Smith said. "Before the boss comes looking for me."

I gave her the twenty dollars. "Thanks for your time."

"Sure." Halfway out the door she paused, frowning. "I hope I didn't get any of the *Kabalyeros* in trouble."

"You didn't."

"Good. I kind of like them. I mean, they push dope and all, but these days, who doesn't?"

These days, who doesn't? I thought. *Good Lord. . . .*

The Starlight Lanes was an old-fashioned bowling alley girded by a rough cliff face and an auto dismantler's yard. The parking lot was crowded, so I left the MG around back by the garbage cans. Inside, the lanes were brightly lit and noisy with the sound of crashing pins, rumbling balls, shouts, and groans. I paused by the front counter and asked where I might find Jimmy Willis. The woman behind it directed me to a lane at the far end.

Bowling alleys—or lanes, as the new upscale bowler prefers to call them—are familiar territory to me. Up until a few years ago my favorite uncle Jim was a top player on the pro tour. The Starlight Lanes reminded me of the ones where Jim used to practice in San Diego—from the racks full of tired-looking rental shoes to the greasy-spoon coffeeshop smells to the molded plastic chairs and cigarette-burned scorekeeping consoles. I walked along, soaking up the ambience—some people would say the lack of it—until I came to lane 32 and spotted an agile young black man bowling alone. Jimmy Willis was a left-hander, and his ball hooked back with deadly precision. I waited in the spectator area, admiring his accuracy and graceful form. His concentration was so great that he didn't notice me until he'd finished the last frame and retrieved his ball.

"You're quite a bowler," I said. "What's your average?"

He gave me a long look before he replied. "Two hundred."

"Almost good enough to turn pro."

"That's what I'm looking to do."

Odd, for the head of a street gang that dealt in drugs and death. "You ever hear of Jim McCone?" I asked.

"Sure. Damned good in his day."

"He's my uncle."

"No kidding." Willis studied me again, now as if looking for a resemblance.

Rapport established, I showed him my ID and explained that I wanted to talk about Reg Dawson's murder. He frowned, hesitated, then nodded. "Okay, since you're Jim McCone's niece, but you'll have to buy me a beer."

"Deal."

Willis toweled off his ball, stowed it and his shoes in their bag, and led me to a typical smoke-filled, murkily lighted bowling alley bar. He took one of the booths while I fetched us a pair of Buds.

As I slid into the booth I said, "What can you tell me about the murder?"

"The way I see it, Dawson was asking for it."

So he and Dawson's wife were of a mind about that. "I can understand what you mean, but it seems strange, coming from you. I hear you were his friend, that you took over the Victors after his death."

"You heard wrong on both counts. Yeah, I was in the Victors, and when Dawson bought it, they tried to get me to take over. But by then I'd figured out—never mind how, doesn't matter—that I wanted out of that life. Ain't nothing in it but what happened to Benny Crespo and Dawson—or what's gonna happen to the Dragon. So I decided to put my hand to something with a future." He patted the bowling bag that sat on the banquette beside him. "Got a job here now—not much, but my bowling's free and I'm on my way."

"Good for you. What about Dragón—do you think he's guilty?"

Willis hesitated, looking thoughtful. "Why you ask?"

"Just wondering."

". . . Well, to tell you the truth, I never did believe the Dragon shot Reg."

"Who did, then?"

He shrugged.

I asked him if he'd heard about the *Kabalyeros* trying to intimidate the chief prosecution witness. When he nodded, I said, "They also threatened the life of her daughter last Friday."

He laughed mirthlessly. "Wish I could of seen that. Kind of surprises me, though. That lawyer of Dragón's, he found out what the *Kabalyeros* were up to, read them the riot act. Said they'd put Dragón in the gas chamber for sure. So they called it off."

"When was this?"

"Week, ten days ago."

Long before Isabel had been accosted. Before the dead dog and shooting incidents, too. "Are you sure?"

"It's what I hear. You know, in a way I'm surprised that they'd go after Mrs. Angeles at all."

"Why?"

"The Filipinos have this macho tradition. 'Specially when it comes to their women. They don't like them messed with, 'specially by non-Filipinos. So how come they'd turn around and mess with one of their own?"

"Well, her testimony *would* jeopardize the life of one of their fellow gang members. It's an extreme situation."

"Can't argue with that."

Jimmy Willis and I talked a bit more, but he couldn't—or wouldn't—offer any further information. I bought him a second beer, then went out to where I'd left my car.

And came face-to-face with Hector Bulis and the man called Sal.

Sal grabbed me by the arm, twisted it behind me, and forced me up against the latticework fence surrounding the garbage cans. The stench from them filled my nostrils; Sal's breath rivaled it in foulness. I struggled, but he got hold of my other arm and pinned me tighter. I looked around, saw no one, nothing but the cliff face and the high board fence of the auto dismantler's yard. Bulis approached, flicking open a switchblade, his twisty face intense. I stiffened, went very still, eyes on the knife.

Bulis placed the tip of the knife against my jawbone, then traced a line across my cheek. "Don't want to hurt you, bitch," he said. "You do what I say, I won't have to mess you up."

The Tagalog phrase that Anna Smith had translated for me—*kumukuló ang dugó*—flashed through my mind. *The blood is boiling.* I sensed Bulis's was—and dangerously high.

I wet my dry lips, tried to keep my voice from shaking as I said, "What do you want me to do?"

"We hear you're asking around about Dawson's murder, trying to prove the Dragon did it."

"That's not—"

"We want you to quit. Go back to your own part of town and leave our business alone."

"Whoever told you that is lying. I'm only trying to help the Angeles family."

"They wouldn't lie." He moved the knife's tip to the hollow at the base of my throat. I felt it pierce my skin—a mere pinprick, but frightening enough.

When I could speak, I did so slowly, phrasing my words carefully. "What I hear is that Dragón is innocent. And that the *Kabalyeros* aren't behind the harassment of the Angeleses—at least not for a week or ten days."

Bulis exchanged a look with his companion—quick, unreadable.

"Someone's trying to frame you." I added, "Just like they did Dragón."

Bulis continued to hold the knife to my throat, his hand firm. His gaze wavered, however, as if he was considering what I'd said. After a moment he asked, "All right—who?"

"I'm not sure, but I think I can find out."

He thought a bit longer, then let his arm drop and snapped the knife shut. "I'll give you till this time tomorrow," he said. Then he stuffed the knife into his pocket, motioned for Sal to let go of me, and the two quickly walked away.

I sagged against the latticework fence, feeling my throat where the knife had pricked it. It had bled a little, but the flow already was clotting. My knees were weak and my breath came fast, but I was too caught up in the possibilities to panic. There were plenty of them—and the most likely was the most unpleasant.

Kumukuló ang dugó. The blood is boiling. . . .

Two hours later I was back at the Angeles house on Omega Street. When Amor admitted me, the tension I'd felt in her earlier had drained. Her body sagged, as if the extra weight she carried had finally proved to be too much for her frail bones; the skin of her face looked flaccid, like melting putty; her eyes were sunken and vague. After she shut the door and motioned for me to sit, she sank into the recliner, expelling a sigh. The house was quiet—too quiet.

"I have a question for you," I said. "What does 'tick-tick' mean in Tagalog?"

Her eyes flickered with dull interest. *"Tiktík."* She corrected my pronunciation. "It's a word for detective."

Ever since Hector Bulis and Sal had accosted me I'd suspected as much.

"Where did you hear that?" Amor asked.

"One of the *Kabalyeros* said it when I went to Fat Robbie's earlier. Someone had told them I was a detective, probably described me. Whoever it was said I was trying to prove Tommy Dragón killed Reg Dawson."

"Why would—"

"More to the point, *who* would? At the time, only four people knew that I'm a detective."

She wet her lips, but remained silent.

"Amor, the night of the shooting, you were standing in your front window, watching for Isabel."

"Yes."

"Do you do that often?"

". . . Yes."

"Because Isabel is often late coming home. Because you're afraid she may have gotten into trouble."

"A mother worries—"

"Especially when she's given good cause. Isabel is running out of control, isn't she?"

"No, she—"

"Amor, when I spoke with Madeline Dawson, she said you were standing in the window watching for 'sweet Isabel, like always.' She didn't say 'sweet' in a pleasant way. Later, Jimmy Willis implied that your daughter is not . . . exactly a vulnerable young girl."

Amor's eyes sparked. "The Dawson woman is jealous."

"Of course she is. There's something else: when I asked the waitress at Fat Robbie's if she'd ever overheard the *Kabalyeros* discussing you, she said, 'No, not that one.' It didn't register at the time, but when I talked to her again a little while ago, she told me Isabel is the member of your family they discuss. They say she's wild, runs around with the men in the gangs. You know that, so does Alex. And so does Madeline Dawson. She just told me the first man Isabel became involved with was her husband."

Amor seemed to shrivel. She gripped the arms of the chair, white-knuckled.

"It's true, isn't it?" I asked more gently.

She lowered her eyes, nodding. When she spoke her voice was ragged. "I don't know what to do with her anymore. Ever since that Reg Dawson got to her, she's been different, not my girl at all."

"Is she on drugs?"

"Alex says no, but I'm not so sure."

I let it go; it didn't really matter. "When she came home earlier," I said, "Isabel seemed very interested in me. She asked questions, looked me over carefully enough to be able to describe me to the *Kabalyeros*. She was afraid of what I might find out. For instance, that she wasn't accosted by any men with guns last Friday."

"She was!"

"No, Amor. That was just a story, to make it look as if your life—and your children's—were in danger if you testified. In spite of what you said early on, you haven't wanted to testify against Tommy Dragón from the very beginning.

"When the *Kabalyeros* began harassing you a month ago, you saw that as the perfect excuse not to take the stand. But you didn't foresee that Dragón's lawyer would convince the gang to stop the harassment. When that happened, you and Isabel, and probably Alex, too, manufactured incidents—the shot-out window, the dead dog on the doorstep, the men with the guns—to make it look as if the harassment was still going on."

"Why would I? They're going to put me in jail."

"But at the time you didn't know they could do that—or that your employer would hire me. My investigating poses yet another danger to you and your family."

"This is . . . why would I do all that?"

"Because basically you're an honest woman, a good woman. You didn't want to testify because you knew Dragón didn't shoot Dawson. It's my guess you gave the police his name because it was the first one that came to mind."

"I had no reason to—"

"You had the best reason in the world: a mother's desire to protect her child."

She was silent, sunken eyes registering despair and defeat.

I kept on, even though I hated to inflict further pain on her. "The day he died, Dawson had let the word out that he was going to desecrate Benny's space. The person who shot him knew there would be fighting and confusion, counted on that as a cover. The killer hated Dawson—"

"Lots of people did."

"But only one person you'd want to protect so badly that you'd accuse an innocent man."

"Leave my mother alone. She's suffered enough on account of what I did."

I turned. Alex had come into the room so quietly I hadn't noticed. Now he moved midway between Amor and me, a Saturday night special clutched in his right hand.

The missing murder weapon.

I tensed, but one look at his face told me he didn't intend to use it. Instead he raised his arm and extended the gun, grip first.

"Take this," he said. "I never should of bought it. Never should of used it. I hated Dawson on account of what he did to my sister. But killing him wasn't worth what we've all gone through since."

I glanced at Amor; tears were trickling down her face.

Alex said, "Mama, don't cry. I'm not worth it."

When she spoke, it was to me. "What will happen to him?"

"Nothing like what might have happened to Dragón; Alex is a juvenile. You, however—"

"I don't care about myself, only my children."

Maybe that was the trouble. She was the archetypal selfless mother: living only for her children, sheltering them from the consequences of their actions—and in the end doing them irreparable harm.

There were times when I felt thankful that I had no children. And there were times when I was thankful that Jack Stuart was a very good criminal lawyer. This was a time when I was thankful on both counts. I went to the phone, called Jack, and asked him to come over here. At least I could leave the Angeles family in good legal hands.

After he arrived, I went out into the gathering dusk. An old yellow VW was pulling out of Benny's space. I walked down there and stood on the curb. Nothing remained of the shrine to Benny Crespo. Nothing remained to show that blood had boiled and been shed here. It was merely a stretch of cracked asphalt, splotched with oil drippings, littered with the detritus of urban life. I stared at it for close to a minute, then turned away from the bleak landscape of Omega Street.

CREDITS

NAME INDEX

||||||||||||||||||||||||||||||||||||||||| ■ |||||||||||||||||||||||||||||||||||||||||||

Numbers in boldface type refer to pages on which stories appear.

Barnes, Linda, 9, **621**
Barzun, Jacques, 3, 5, 6, 7
Bellem, Robert Leslie, 8, 9, **375**
Boucher, Anthony, **480**
Bramah, Ernest, 184

Carr, John Dickson, **310**
Chandler, Raymond, 5, 7, 8, 162, **295**, 512, 513
Christie, Agatha, 4, 93
Collins, Wilkie, 310, 526
Cook, George Cram, 142
Coxe, George Harmon, 8

Daly, Carroll John, **162**
Dannay, Frederic (Daniel Nathan). *See* Queen, Ellery
Davidson, Avram, 587
Davis, Dorothy Salisbury, **570**
Demming, Richard, 587
Dickson, Carter. *See* Carr, John Dickson
Doyle, Adrian Conan, 310
Doyle, Arthur Conan, 4, 49, 93, 456, 526

Eberhart, A. C., 239
Eberhart, Mignon G., 9, **239**
Edison, Thomas, 124

Fairman, Paul W., 587
Falkner, William Clark, 414
Faulkner, William, 9, **414**
Fitzgerald, F. Scott, 5, 295
Futrelle, Jacques, 5, 8, **49**

Gardner, Erle Stanley, 49, **261**
Gault, William Campbell, **471**
Glaspell, Susan, 5, 9, **142**
Grafton, C. F., 639
Grafton, Sue, 9, **639**
Green, Anna Katharine, 7, 9, **93**

Hammett, Dashiell, 5, 7, 162, 295, 512
Harte, Bret, 5, 9, **40**
Hillerman, Marie Unzner, 655
Hillerman, Tony, 8, 9, **655**
Hoch, Edward D., 587, **608**
Holmes, H. H. *See* Boucher, Anthony
Hunter, Evan. *See* McBain, Ed

Irish, William. *See* Woolrich, Cornell

Kendrick, Baynard, 184
Knox, Ronald, 4, 7, 8

Lee, Manfred Bennington (Manfred Lepofsky). *See* Queen, Ellery
Loos, Mary, 217

MacDonald, John D., 512
Macdonald, Ross, **512**, 639
Marlowe, Stephen, 587
McBain, Ed, 7, 8, 9, **499**
Millar, Kenneth. *See* Macdonald, Ross
Millar, Margaret Sturm, 512
Muller, Marcia, 602, **665**

O'Callaghan, Maxine, 665
O'Neill, Eugene, 142

Penzler, Otto, 81
Poe, Edgar Allan, 3, 4, 6, 8, **10**, 49, 526
Post, Melville Davisson, 9, **81**, 414
Powell, Talmadge, 587
Pronzini, Bill, **602**, 665

Queen, Ellery, 414, **587**, 608

Rawson, Clayton, 9, **431**
Reeve, Arthur B., 8, 9, **124**
Rinehart, Mary Roberts, 9, 239, **356**

685

Sale, Richard, 8, **217**
Stagg, Clinton H., 9, **184**
Steinbrunner, Chris, 81
Stewart, Jimmy, 326
Stout, Rex, 8, 49, **526**
Stribling, T. S., **456**
Sturgeon, Theodore, 587
Symons, Julian, 6

Taylor, Wendell Hertig, 7

Vance, John Holbrook, 587
Van Dine, S. S., 5
Vidocq, Eugène François, 49

Woolrich, Cornell, **326**